Charter of Social Rights of the Council of Europe

Studies in Employment and Social Policy

In the series Studies in Employment and Social Policy this book *Charter of Social Rights of the Council of Europe* is the thirty-third title.

The titles published in this series are listed at the end of this volume.

Studies in Employment and Social Policy

Charter of Social Rights of the Council of Europe

Andrzej Marian Świątkowski

KLUWER LAW
INTERNATIONAL

Published by:
Kluwer Law International
P.O. Box 316, 2400 AH Alphen aan den Rijn, The Netherlands
sales@kluwerlaw.com
http://www.kluwerlaw.com

Sold and Distributed in North, Central and South America by:
Aspen Publishers, Inc.
7201 McKinney Circle, Frederick, MD 21704, USA

Sold and Distributed in all other countries by:
Extenza-Turpin Distribution Services
Stratton Business Park, Pegasus Drive, Biggleswade,
Bedfordshire, SG18 8QB, United Kingdom

Printed on acid-free paper.

ISBN 978-90-411-2608-5

Printed in The Netherlands.

TABLE OF CONTENTS

INTRODUCTION

The European Social Charter of the Council of Europe is recognized by lawyers specializing in international and comparative labour law and social security as well as by specialists in international social policies to define the following treaties and international agreements enacted between 1961 and 1996[1]:

- European Social Charter of 18 October 1961;
- Additional Protocol to the European Social Charter of 5 May 1988;
- Amending Protocol to the European Social Charter of 21 October 1991;
- Additional Protocol to the European Social Charter providing for a system of collective complaints, of 9 November 1995;
- Revised European Social Charter of 3 May 1996.

The Charter is an international treaty in which social rights are regulated by labour and social security laws. These rights are regarded as human rights[2] and guarantee protection for the European continent. The European Social Charter is a regional document passed after World War II by the Congress of Europe, organized by the International Committee of Movements for European Unity. The concept for the Charter of Human Rights, the Court of Justice and the European Assembly was also presented in the Congress at the Hague in May 1948. The statute for the establishment of the Council of Europe was ratified in London on 5 May 1949. This newly established international organization brought forth the concept of the European Union (EU), where membership was allocated to countries located on the European continent. Members accept the fundamental regulations of the Human Rights Charter and agree to abide by its laws, guaranteeing all persons basic human rights and liberties under each member's jurisdiction. The goal of the Council of

---

1. Published in: *European Social Charter. Collected Texts* (4th edition) Council of Europe Publishing, Strasbourg 2003. Polish version of these documents was published in: Podstawowe dokumenty Rady Europy z dziedziny polityki społecznej, wybór i opracowanie R.A.Henczel, J.Maciejewska, Wydawnictwo Naukowe Scholar, Warszawa 1997.
2. *See* R. Allen QC, R.Crasnow, *Employment Law and Human Rights,* Oxford University Press, Oxford 2002, *passim*; *Labour Rights as Human Rights,* ed. Ph. Alston, Oxford University Press, Oxford 2005.

Europe is to ensure unity amongst its member countries, to implement common ideas and rules and to enhance social and economic development.

The Council of Europe prepares international documentation aimed at protecting human rights. It consists of permanent and interim committees whose role is to establish and protect human rights, which can be divided into the following categories: political and civil rights, and economic, social and cultural rights. These distinctions were created by the Council of Europe in its first international treaty, the Convention for the Protection of Human Rights and Fundamental Freedoms (also known as the European Convention on Human Rights) passed on 4 November 1950.[3]

The architects of the Convention emphasized the need for political democracy and legal institutions in post-war Europe. The Convention identified human rights as their civil equivalents.[4] At this stage, the Council of Europe did not find it necessary to protect economic, social and cultural rights. This situation derived from the highly varying economic development of Western European countries. Central and Eastern European economies, exposed to various political influences, were faltering after World War II. In 1950, the Council of Europe recognized the possibility of expanding human rights to include economic, social and cultural rights under appropriate circumstances.[5]

Paradoxically, the division of Europe contributed to the protection of economic, social and cultural rights. The Western European democracies viewed political and civil rights as highly important while the Central and Eastern European socialist countries emphasized the economic, social and cultural aspect of human rights which were consistent with the socialist ideology prevalent in these countries. The various approaches to human rights, added to the regional composition of the countries, resulted in the enactment of two international treaties by the Council of Europe:

The European Convention on the Protection of Human Rights and Fundamental Liberties ensures the protection of political and civil rights, and some social rights, such as: the right to work (Article 4), prohibiting compulsory or coercive labour (Article 4, s. 2), and the freedom to establish and join trade unions to protect workers' interests (Article 11, s. 1).

The European Social Charter of 1961, along with the three already mentioned Protocols (add footnote reference) and the Revised European Social Charter of 1996 are treaties guaranteeing the following social rights:

- Regulation of rights through domestic labour laws: the right to work (Article 1), the right to just conditions of work (Article 2), the right to safe and healthy working

3. D. Gomien, D. Harris, L. Zwaak, *Law and Practice of the European Convention on Human Rights and the European Social Charter*, Council of Europe Publishing, Strasbourg 1999, *passim*. Compare with Polish works J.Sozański, Prawa zasadnicze a prawa człowieka we wspólnotowym systemie prawnym (Fundamental Rights and Human Rights in a Common System of Law), Warszawa-Poznań 2003.
4. Parliamentary Assembly of the Council of Europe, Doc. 4213, p. 6.
5. *Ibid.*; Compare A.Delpérée, Les droits sociaux et la Charte Sociale Européenne, Revue de Droits de l'Homme, 1968, vol. 1, No. 4, 577; A. Michalska, Europejska Karta Społeczna, Ruch Prawniczy, Ekonomiczny i Socjologiczny (European Social Charter, the Legal, Economic and Social Movement), 1978, z. 4, p. 77.

conditions (Article 3), the right to fair remuneration (Article 4), the right of children and young persons to protection (Article 7), the right of employed women on maternity to protection (Article 8), the right to vocational guidance (Article 9), the right to vocational training (Article 10), the right to equal opportunities and equal treatment in matters of employment and occupation without gender discrimination (Article 20), the right to protection in cases of termination of employment (Article 24), the right of workers to protection of their claims in the event of insolvency of their employer (Article 25), the right to dignity at work (Article 26), and the right of workers with family responsibilities to equal treatment and equal opportunity (Article 27);

- Regulation of rights through collective labour laws: the right of workers and employers to organize (Article 5), the right to bargain collectively (Article 6), the right of workers to information and consultation (Article 21), the right of workers to take part in the determination and improvement of the working conditions and working environment (Article 22), the right of workers to be informed and consulted in collective redundancy procedures (Article 29), and the right of workers' representatives to protection and the availability of appropriate facilities (Article 28);
- Regulation of rights through social security laws: the right to the protection of health (Article 11), the right to social security (Article 12), the right to social and medical assistance (Article 13), the right to benefit from social welfare services (Article 14), the right of disabled persons to independence, social integration and to participation in the life of the community (Article 15), the right of families to social, legal and economic protection (Article 16), the right of elderly persons to protection (Article 23), the right to protection against poverty and social exclusion (Article 30), and the right to housing (Article 31).

The Social Charter protects the social rights of citizens of other Council of Europe Member States, including the right of nationals to engage in gainful occupation on the territories of other countries (Article 18), as well as the right of migrant workers and their families to protection and assistance (Article 19).

These international documents, protecting human rights in Europe, are guaranteed by global treaties, such as the UN Universal Declaration of Human Rights of 10 December 1948[6], the International Covenant on Civil and Political Rights of 16 December 1966[7], and the International Covenant on Economic, Social and Cultural Rights of 16 December 1966[8]. The United Nations (UN) reflects the European methods of protecting human rights.

---

6. Prawa człowieka. Dokumenty (Human Rights. Documents), ed. Z. Kędzia, Ossolineum, Wrocław 1989, pp. 24 and following.
7. The Covenant came into force on 23 March 1976; Poland ratified the Covenant on 3 March 1977 r., Dz.U. No. 38, pos. 167.
8. Poland ratified the Covenant on 3 March 1977, Dz.U. Nr 38, pos. 169.

Social rights are regarded by the human rights doctrine as 'second generational' rights.[9] This term, however, does not mean that social rights are lower on the scale of human rights. Separating human rights into three generational categories carries historical relevance. The first generation of human rights included civil and political rights. The second generation of human rights included social rights, influenced by the socialist ideology of the predecessors of trade unions at the turn of the 20th Century.[10] The third generation of human rights emphasizes social groups such as workers, members of particular communities, ethnic minorities, immigrants and families, rather than individual persons. Third generational rights are protected by international treaties, guaranteeing, for example, the right of workers to participate in decision-making as a collective group and the right of citizens to take part in a cultural lifestyle. The social rights of groups were considered as a third generation category of human rights in the 1980s.[11]

This breakdown of human rights into categories generations is generally accepted. Sometimes a generation will adopt a right belonging to another generation, e.g., the right of workers to establish and join trade unions is included as a second generation right despite being legislated along with political and civil rights. The law provides the right to association, which has political connotations. However, it benefits individuals as well as social groups such as workers, self-employed individuals and farmers. Undoubtedly, its origin lies in economy, as people associate with trade unions to protect their own economic, social and employment interests as well as to safeguard their own rights. Although the separation of human rights into two primary categories (as opposed to international treaties declared by the Organization of United Nations) – political and social rights – is clear and justified by international treaties, it is not purely a separatist concept.[12]

It is also important to acknowledge the social rights that attend the development and promotion of political rights that are fundamental to democracy and liberty.[13] The EU has noted the importance of these issues and has included a catalogue of social rights in its Constitution project for Europe.[14] For legal practitioners specializing in

---

9. *Social Rights as Human Rights: A European Challenge,* eds. K. Drzewiecki, C. Krause, A. Rosas, Institute of Human Rights, Åbo Akademii University 1994, pp. 156 and following.
10. *See* B. Weston, 'Human Rights', *Human Rights Quarterly,* vol. 6, 1984, pp. 257 and following.
11. *See* S. Marks, 'Emerging Human Rights: A New Generation for the 1980s', *Rutgers Law Review,* vol.33, 1981, pp. 435 and following; P. Alston, 'A Third Generation of Solidarity Rights: Progressive Development or Obfuscation of International Human Rights Law?' *Netherlands International Law Review,* vol. 29, 1982, pp. 307 and following; *Ibid.*, 'Labour Rights as Human Rights: The Not So Happy State of the Art', in *Labour Rights as Human Rights, op. cit.*, pp. 1 and following.
12. A. Michalska, Prawa człowieka w systemie norm międzynarodowych (Human Rights in a System of International Standards), PWN, Warszawa-Poznań 1982, pp. 125–126.
13. M. Abram, 'Human Rights and the UN: Past as Prologue', *Harvard Human Rights Journal,* vol. 4, 1991, pp. 69 and following; I. Hare, 'Social Rights as Fundamental Human Rights' in *Social and Labour Rights in a Global Context. International and Comparative Perspectives,* ed. B. Hepple, Cambridge University Press, Cambridge 2002, pp. 153 and following.
14. W. Sanetra, Prawo pracy w świetle projektu Konstytucji dla Europy (Labour Law in Perspective of the Constitutional Project for Europe), Przegląd Sądowy, 2004, No. 9, p. 3 and following; J. Sozański,

European social rights, the definition of these laws has become a point of discussion.[15] On the one hand, governmental compliance with social rights can be seen as a form of protection of civil and political rights for individuals and social groups. On the other hand, the level of such protection is dependent on the economic development of a specific country. Therefore, despite the interdependency of political and social rights, the division of human rights is based on the differing level of execution of the regulations by the varying Member States belonging either to the UN or to the Council of Europe. While political rights must be afforded immediate protection, social rights, such as the right to social welfare services (Article 14 of the Revised European Social Charter – RESC) or the right of a family to economical, legal and social protection (Article 16 RESC), due to the costs involved in implementation can be implemented in a more gradual manner.[16] Many social rights regulated by the Charter are progressive. The European Social Rights Charter expects its Member States, for example, to act towards the elimination of diseases (Article 11 – the right to the protection of health RESC), the integration of disabled persons into the life of the community (Article 15 – RESC), and the integration of the elderly, ensuring them a place in the community as rightful citizens for as long as it is necessary (Article 23 – RESC). However, the protection of human rights and the speed with which they are protected is subject to whether they are categorized as political or social. All Member States are expected to take immediate action to guarantee the political rights of all individuals. Furthermore, international treaties also place similar duties on Member States to guarantee human rights for all individuals as well as social groups regardless of whether they are political or social rights:[17]

– A duty not to violate such rights. For example, a duty not to violate workers' rights to freedom of association for the protection of their economic and social interests

Specyfika sądowej i pozasądowej ochrony praw człowieka w Unii Europejskiej a Karta Praw Podstawowych jako część druga Konstytucji dla Europy (Judicial and Non-Judicial Protection of Human Rights in the European Union – Basic Rights Charter as Part II for the European Constitution), Przegląd Sądowy 2005, No. 1, pp. 154 and following.

15. K. D. Ewing, *The EU Charter of Fundamental Rights: Waste of Time or Wasted Opportunity?* The Institute of Employment Rights, London 2002; L. Betten, 'The EU Charter on Fundamental Rights: a Trojan Horse or a Mouse?', *International Journal of Comparative Labour Law and Industrial Relations*, 2001, vol. 17, Issue 2, pp. 151 and following.
16. M. Bossuyt, 'La distinction juridique entre les droits civils et politiques et les droits économiques, sociaux et culturels', *Human Rights Law Journal,* vol. 8, 1975, p. 790; o. Kahn-Freund, 'The European Social Charter' in *European Law and the Individual,* ed. F.G. Jacobs, Nort-Holland Publishing Company 1976, pp. 181 and following; K. Fuchs, 'The European Social Charter: Its Role in Present day Europe and Its Reform' in *Social Rights as Human Rights . . . op. cit.*, pp. 156 and following; P. Laroque, La Charte Sociale Européenne, Droit Social 1979, pp. 100 and following; H. Wiebringhaus, 'Le droit a la sécurité sociale et la Charte sociale europénne' in *Le droit social a l'aube du XXIe siècle,* Payot, Lausanne 1989, pp. 355 and following; R. Brillat, 'The European Social Charter' in *International Human Rights Monitoring Mechanisms. Essays in honour of Jakob Th. Möller,* M.Nijfoff Publishers, The Hague/Boston/London 2001, pp. 601 and following.
17. I. Hare, *Social Rights . . . op. cit.,* p. 159 and following.

(Article 5, right to organize - Social Charter) in national or international organizations;
- A duty to provide the entitled individuals protection against any rights violation, e.g., a duty to protect workers' representatives and provide them with appropriate facilities (Article 28);
- A duty to protect groups and individuals whose rights have been violated. This is also seen in Article 24, which protects workers in cases of unjust termination of employment, guaranteeing them a due process.

Along with the Convention for the Protection of Human Rights and Fundamental Freedoms, the European Social Rights Charter is a fundamental international treaty for the protection of human rights. Both treaties complement each other and are similar in their legal structure.[18] Substantively, these treaties include provisions protecting civil and political rights (European Convention), and social and economical rights (Social Charter). Procedurally, provisions are made for supervisory bodies to monitor human rights compliance within the Member States. The European Court of Human Rights supervises compliance with political rights, and the Committee for Social Rights of the Council of Europe is in charge of monitoring social rights.

This monograph focuses on an array of rights, as well as the legal supervisory mechanisms to monitor compliance of the rights through the standards established by European Committee of Social Rights. The tremendous volume of resources dealing with the European Social Rights Charter published in Poland is either used as a source[19] or as a guideline.[20] Further analysis deals with: legal institutions called upon by the Charter[21] and some of the functions of the Committee of Social Rights,[22] as well as with the selected categories of social rights and standards of their protection established by the Committee.[23] The monograph dedicated to the analysis of the

18. O. De Schutter, L'interdépendance des droits et l'interaction des systèmes de protection: les scénarios du systeme européen de protection des droits fondamentaux, Droit en Quart Monde, Bruxelles, No. 28-29, 2000, pp. 3 and following.
19. Podstawowe dokumenty Rady Europy . . . (Primary Documents of the Council of Europe), *op. cit.*
20. Przewodnik po Europejskiej Karcie Społecznej (Guide to the European Social Charter), Wydawnictwo Prawnicze LexisNexis, Warszawa 2002.
21. A. Świątkowski, Karty Społeczne Rady Europy (Social Charters of the Council of Europe), Państwo i Prawo (State and the Law) 2003, No.. 8, pp. 36 and following; *Idem*, European Social Charter: the right to strike, Managerial Law, 2005, vol.47, No.6, p. 284 ff.
22. A. Świątkowski, *Quasi* judakcyjna funkcja Komitetu Praw Społecznych Rady Europy (The Quasi-judicial Function of the Committee of Social Rights of the Council of Europe), Państwo i Prawo (State and the Law), 2004, No. 9, p. 46 i nast.; *Idem,* Funcjones causijurisdiccionales del Comité de Derechos Sociales del Consejo Europeo, Revista de Derecho Laboral y Seguridad Social, 2005, No. 7, p. 533.
23. A. Świątkowski, Scope rationae personae of Article 5 of the European Social Charter (the Right to Organize) and its application in Poland, Archivum Iuridicum Cracoviaense, vol. XXXV-XXXVI, 2002-2003, pp. 83 and following; Idem, Standardy europejskie w zakresie zbiorowego prawa pracy (European Standards in Collective Labour Law), Państwo i Społeczeństwo (State and Society), 2003, No. 4, pp. 203 and following; *Idem,* European fundamental social rights and the legal, social and

European Social Rights Charter of the Council of Europe deals with the complex physical, legal and procedural issues of protecting social rights.

economic position of young workers and adolescents in European industrial relations during the period of globalization, Tilburg Foreign Law Review 2005, vol.13, No2, p. 141 ff.; Idem, Control Administrativo del Derecho de Trabajo (Desde la perspective de la Carta Social Europea), Revista de Derecho Laboral y Seguridad Social, Agosto 2004, No. 16, pp. 1120 ff; Idem, Rola i znaczenie europejskich standardów zabezpieczenia społecznego dla polskiego ustawodawstwa na XXI wiek (The Role and the Meaning of Social Security Standards for Polish Legislature in the 21st Century), Polityka Społeczna (Social Policy), 2004, No. 11-12; Idem, Administracyjna kontrola prawa pracy (Administrative Control of Labour Law), Monitor Prawa Pracy (Labour Law Monitor), 2004, No. 11; Idem, Dorobek Rady Europy w zakresie kształtowania i ochrony praw społecznych. W kierunku powszechnej ratyfikacji Zrewidowanej Europejskiej Karty Społecznej (European Social Charter Towards Common Application of the Revised Charter), ed. A.M. Świątkowski, Wydawnictwo C.H.Beck, Warszawa 2005; Idem, Prawo socjalne Rady Europy (Social Law of the Council of Europe), Cracow 2006; G. Uścińska, Europejskie standardy zabezpieczenia społecznego a współczesne rozwiązania polskie (European Social Security Standards and Current Polish Solutions), IPiSS, Warszawa 2005, pp. 322 and following.

Part I The Structure of the European Social Charter and Protocols

CHAPTER 1 THE EUROPEAN SOCIAL CHARTER OF 1961

The European Social Charter was ratified by 18 Member States of the Council of Europe on 18 October 1961, in Turin during the centenary of Italy's unification. On this day, 13 countries signed the Charter.[1] Appropriately, under Article 35, Section 2, the Charter came into being 30 days after its ratification by competent authorities of five Member States on 26 February 1965.[2] The Member States who ratified and signed the Charter were[3] (signing date, ratification date respectively):

- Austria (22 July 1963/ 29 October 1969);
- Belgium (18 October 1961/ 16 October 1990);
- Croatia (8 March 1999/ 26 February 2003);
- Cyprus (22 May 1967/ 7 March 1968);
- Czech Republic (27 May 1992/[4] 3 November 1999);
- Denmark (18 October 1961/ 3 March 1965);
- Finland (9 February 1990/ 29 April 1991);
- France (18 October 1961/ 9 March 1973);
- Greece (18 October 1961/ 6 June 1984);
- Spain (27 April 1978/ 6 May 1980);
- The Netherlands (18 October 1961/ 22 April 1980);
- Ireland (18 October 1961/ 7 October 1964);
- Iceland (15 January 1976/ 15 January 1976);
- Liechtenstein (9 October 1991);[5]

1. Belgium, Denmark, Greece, the Netherlands, Ireland, Luxembourg, Germany, Norway, Sweden, Turkey, Great Britain, and Italy.
2. After ratification by: Ireland (7 October 1964); Germany (27 January 1965); Norway (26 October 1962); Sweden (17 December 1962); and Great Britain (11 July 1962).
3. *European Social Charter Collected Texts* (4th Edition), Council of Europe, Publishing, Strasbourg 2004, pp.77 and the following.
4. Ratified as Czechoslovakia.
5. Liechtenstein did not ratify the European Social Charter. It did not ratify the Additional Protocol, or the Revised European Social Charter of 1996.

- The former Yugoslavian Republic of Macedonia (5 May 1998);[6]
- Malta (26 May 1988/ 4 October 1988);
- Germany (18 October 1961/ 27 January 1965);
- Norway (18 October 1961/ 26 October 1962);
- Poland (26 November 1991/ 25 June 1997);
- Portugal (1 June 1982/ 30 September 1991);
- Romania (4 October 1994);[7]
- Slovakia (27 May 1992/[8] 22 June 1998);
- Slovenia (11 October 1997);[9]
- Switzerland (6 May 1976);[10]
- Sweden (18 October 1961/ 17 December 1962);
- Turkey (18 November 1961/ 24 November 1989);
- Ukraine (2 May 1996);[11]
- Hungary (13 December 1991/ 8 July 1999);
- Great Britain (18 October 1961/ 11 July 1962);
- Italy (18 October 1961/ 22 May 1965).

The drafting of the European Social Charter commenced a year after the European Convention of Human Rights had been passed. In 1951, the Consultative Assembly of the Council of Europe passed the resolution addressed to the Committee of Ministers in which Member States were advised to accept a unanimous approach to social policies. In a 1953 memorandum addressed to the Committee of Ministers, it was explicitly stated that the common goals and rules to be brought about were to become the cornerstones of such policy.

The basic task for the Council of Europe in respect to the protection of social rights is defined by these goals and rules. An international document formulating common goals of social policies and rules of their execution for Member States was to be given a legal structure in the European Social Charter, and the Charter was meant to be a signpost for the Council of Europe, helpful in the process of technical development and strengthening the relations between Member States.

The goal of the Council of Europe, according to Article 1(a) of its statute, is to form a cohesive union among the Member States by the realization of common ideas

6. Macedonia did not ratify the European Social Charter, but it signed the Additional Protocols of 1988 and 1991 (5 May 1998).
7. Romania did not ratify the European Social Charter. It signed (14 May 1997) and ratified (7 May 1999) the Revised European Social Charter.
8. As Czechoslovakia.
9. Slovenia did not ratify the European Social Charter. It signed (11 October 1997) and ratified (7 May 1990) the Revised European Social Charter.
10. Switzerland did not ratify the European Social Charter. It did not sign or ratify any Protocols nor did it sign or ratify the Revised European Social Charter.
11. Ukraine did not ratify the European Social Charter. It signed (7 May 1999) the Revised European Social Charter and deposited the instrument of ratification of the RESC (21 December 2006). The RESC enters in force for Ukraine on 1 February 2007.

and rules, based on the concept of a uniform European cultural heritage and to ensure economic and social development.

The Consultative Assembly of the Council of Europe unanimously accepted this proposition. Doubts about the proposition arose during debates in the Committee of Ministers, a political body comprised of ministers of foreign affairs of the Member States of the Council of Europe. There were two major reservations about the proposition. One concerned the formal character of the proposition. The ministers were concerned that the abovementioned proposal would not be original in its structure nor follow the international regional treaty model that the European Social Charter was meant to represent. It would rather mimic the standards introduced by the UN and their agenda, primarily by the International Labour Organization.

Another reservation dealt with the regulation and protective mechanisms for social rights in an international treaty. There were also concerns whether general and declarative statements, commonly used in international documents, would create enough of a legal foundation of execution for common protection of the abovementioned entitlements. Eventually, it was noted that the standards of protection of social rights would be constructed in order to function in Western European democracies and would be of little significance or irrelevant in other European countries.

The third type of argument involved political reservations based on insecurities that the European Social Charter, proposed as an international treaty, would fulfil a function that contradicts Article 1(a) of the Statute of the Council of Europe. It was feared that the Charter would create political divisions on the European continent caused by the Yalta Treaty and would not be capable of destroying 'the Iron Curtain', as declared in Winston Churchill's 1946 speech in Fulton, Missouri.

The Committee of Ministers of the Council of Europe unanimously agreed during its session on 20 May 1954 to direct and authorize the Social Committee to prepare a draft of a European Social Rights Charter. The international treaty would deal with all social policy goals for Member States, as well as provide a guideline for the Council of Europe in matters of social policies within the European continent. The Committee of Ministers applauded this momentous decision.

This international treaty draft was to supplement the Convention for the Protection of Human Rights and Fundamental Freedoms.[12] The Social Committee to the Committee of Ministers of the Council of Europe did not create in full within the European Social Charter a legal equivalent to the Convention for the Protection of Human Rights and Fundamental Freedoms. It did not allocate legal power to all Charter provisions, although it had the option to do so in the drafting process. Instead, it distinguished two categories of rights: those that obligate the Member States and those that can be utilized by their own decisions.

Despite its earlier reservations in the drafting of the Social Charter, the determination of the Council of Europe, the Consultative Assembly and the Committee

12. *See Special Message of the Committee of Ministers of the Council of Europe to the Consultative Assembly of the Council of Europe the Programme of Work of the Council of Europe*, European Consultative Assembly, 6th Session (1954), Document No. 238, paragraphs 38–39.

of Ministers simultaneously undertook individual approaches to the Charter, which were later compiled as one. This took place almost immediately after the draft of the Charter was accepted by the Consultative Assembly[13] of the Council of Europe. The Committee of Ministers treated seriously the propositions of the Consultative Assembly to commence the draft of this international treaty without any further delay. To ensure the quick commencement of the Social Charter project, the Consultative Assembly called upon its own social and economic experts to commission the draft.

After the rejection of both projects, one developed by a body dealing with social matters[14] in 1955 and the other developed by an economical body a year later, the Consultative Assembly in October of 1956[15] introduced the original version of the Charter to the Committee of Ministers. This version was termed 'the original', as it was never voted on during the sittings of the Consultative Assembly, as there was a fear of it being rejected.[16] The Social Committee for the Committee of Ministers prepared its own version of the Charter in February 1958.[17] It advanced a legal and political compromise between Member States' representatives who wanted to give the draft of the international document a political character. The representatives of the remaining countries had differing ideas regarding the definition and roles of democratic legal principles in particular Member States and in the processes of protecting legal elements of human rights (social rights) that were to be guaranteed by the European Social Charter.

As a result of this compromise, the draft of the European Social Charter consisted of two parts. In the first part, Member States (defined as parties to the Charter) defined the standards of social policy as a priority and listed them in 19 points outlining rights and regulations. The first 15 points enumerate specific rights:

1. The right to work;
2. The right to just conditions of work;
3. The right to safe and healthy working conditions;
4. The right to fair remuneration;
5. The right to freedom of association in national or international organizations for the protection of economic and social interests;
6. The right to bargain collectively;
7. The right of children and young persons to special protection against physical and moral dangers;
8. The right of employed women to protection in cases of maternity and other appropriate cases;

13. From 1973 named the Parliamentary Assembly.
14. European Consultative Assembly, 7th Session, Document No. 403 (1955).
15. European Consultative Assembly, 8th Session, Document No. 488 (1956).
16. European Consultative Assembly, 8th Session, Document No. 536 (1956).
17. European Consultative Assembly, 11th Session, Document No. 927 (1959).

9. The right to appropriate facilities for vocational guidance with a view to help people choose occupations in line with their personal capabilities and interests;
10. The right to vocational training;
11. The right to benefit from any measures enabling the highest possible standard of health;
12. The right to social security;
13. The right of those without adequate resources to social and medical assistance;
14. The right to benefit from social welfare services.

The Charter also allocates rights to people of selected categories: the disabled, regardless of the reason for or the type of their disability, the right to vocational training, rehabilitation, vocational and social resettlement (point 15); the family, as a fundamental unit of society, the right to social, legal and economic protection (point 16); mothers and children, irrespective of marital status and family relations, the right to social, legal and economic protection (point 17); foreign nationals, citizens of any one of the parties to the Council of Europe, the right to engage in any gainful occupation in the territory of any other Member State, equal to the citizens of the latter, subject to restrictions based on cogent economic of social reasons (point 18); migrant workers, who are nationals of a party to the Charter, and their families the right to protection and assistance in the territory of any other party (point 19).

In Part II of the draft of the 'old' European Social Charter of 1961, 19 social rights were codified that obligated all Member States of the Council of Europe. The Social Charter draft was then presented to gain an opinion of the Tripartite Commission, consisting of governmental representatives, as well as social stakeholders: employers and employees (trade unions). This Commission was introduced and structured according to the model of the Conference of the International Labour Organization, and commenced its sittings in December 1958 in the chambers of the Council of Europe.

The role of the Tripartite Commission was to compile and analyse proposed changes of possible European Social Charter projects, subject to the international scale of social rights protection. Mainly due to the initiative of trade union delegates, the right to strike and the obligation for Member States to retain the highest possible and stable level of employment was introduced by the Tripartite Commission into the European Charter draft. It was also suggested that the regulations in Part II be divided into two categories: generally binding and binding based on the decisions of Member States. A majority of the regulations in Part II were thus heavily edited.[18]

In 1959, the Consultative Assembly presented to the Committee of Ministers a final proposition for the European Social Charter, based on changes to the existing draft. The Social Committee to the Committee of Ministers accepted the proposition, including its alterations, from the Consultative Assembly. It accepted the division of the Charter into two categories: one was strict and general for all members, whilst the second obligated Member States to decisions made by their own authorities. Accepting

18. European Consultative Assembly, 11th Session, Document No. 1035 (1959).

the abovementioned proposition as a whole, the Social Committee to the Committee of Ministers confirmed the two categories of the Charter as a legal structure.

The Consultative Assembly prescribed seven compulsory regulations instead of the six mandatory regulations in Part II. Member States were allowed to choose a minimum of five of these seven regulations. The Social Committee to the Committee of Ministers did not accept the proposition made by the Consultative Assembly that Member States had to ratify the remainder of the regulations mentioned in Part II within five years of the original ratification.

Under the final version of the European Social Charter, Article 20(1) encourages Member States to achieve goals declared within Part I (a) with the help of particular sources, as well as to ratify at least five of the ten following regulations of Part II: Article 1, 5, 6, 12, 13, 16, 19(b). In addition, Member States are encouraged to ratify at least five of the seven regulations mentioned under Article 20 § 2(b). Member States are also obliged to accept ten of 19 ratified articles or 45 of 72 paragraphs listed in Part II in accordance with Article 20 § 1(c).

The established standards of protecting social rights by the European Social Charter were designed to allow the ratification of some numbered paragraphs within the 19 stated Articles. For example, Poland did not ratify Article 2 § 2, Article 4 § 1, Article 6 § 3, Article 7 § 1, 3, 5, Article 10 § 3, 4, Article 13 § 1, 4, Article 14 § 2, Article 18 § 1, 2, 3, but did ratify paragraphs belonging to other numbered articles.

A Member State must inform the Secretary-General of the Council of Europe which regulations of the Charter it would follow (Article 20 § 2). Member States can choose to abide by all the regulations if they so desire and, in fact, Belgium and Spain did do so. All Member States who are signatories to the international treaty have the right to inform the Secretary-General of the Council of Europe at any time that they wish to accept additional regulations. The additional obligations are regarded as an integral part of the original ratification (Article 20 § 3).

Member States may also provide explanations for their choice of regulations which they chose to follow. For example, France[19] informed the Secretary-General they could not accept the obligations implemented by Article 2 § 4, dealing with the obligatory standards of reducing work hours or guaranteeing additional paid leave for those employed in jobs that are hazardous and dangerous to health, as French social policies focus instead on eliminating threats and improving the working conditions for those employed in jobs that are hazardous and dangerous to health.

The French also refused to ratify Article 12 § 4(a), which provides for the equal treatment of insured nationals, regardless of their citizenship within the Council of Europe. This was due to the fact that, because of demographic reasons, only babies born in French territory were entitled to social security benefits. Aware of the criticism of Article L 519 of the French Code of Social Security by the international forum dealing with maternity entitlements, French authorities made it clear that they have undertaken steps to change this regulation. However, they have also stipulated that accommodating

19. European Social Charter. Collected texts, *op. cit.*, pp. 102–103.

the standards of the national social security system to that of Article 1 § 4(a) of the European Social Charter would require time. This position, represented by the French declaration, is a signal for the possibility of accepting the obligations by a particular nation in meeting standards of Article 12 § 4(a). Refusing to ratify Article 13 § 2, the regulation that forces Member States to guarantee those benefiting from social and medical entitlements the full scope of their political and social rights, was legally argued by the Bill of 1884 that deprived those benefiting from social assistance voting rights in local elections.

France was the only Member State of the Council of Europe to explain its decision for not accepting a number of the regulations in the European Social Charter under its jurisdiction. France signed the Revised European Social Charter on 3 May 1996, and later ratified it on 7 May 1999. It ratified the Charter in full, meaning it accepted the obligations of regulations to which it was previously hesitant in the areas of labour law and international standards of protection.

Member States who signed the Social Charter and, influenced by France's actions, also signed and ratified the Revised European Social Charter are listed alphabetically. Bracketed is the signing date, followed by the date of ratification, if applicable. They are:

- Austria (7 May 1999);
- Belgium (3 May 1996);
- Cyprus (3 May 1996/ 27 September 2000);
- Czech Republic (4 November 2000);
- Denmark (3 March 1996);
- Finland (3 May 1996/ 21 June 2002);
- Great Britain (7 November 1997);
- Greece (3 March 1996);
- Iceland (4 November 1998);
- Ireland (4 November 2000/ 4 November 2000);
- Italy (3 May 1996/ 5 July 1999);
- Luxembourg (11 February 1998);
- Malta (signed and ratified RESC 27 July 2005);
- Norway (7 May 2001/ 7 May 2001);
- Netherlands (ratified ESC 3 May, 2006);
- Poland (signed RESC 25 October 2005);
- Portugal (3 May 1996/ 30 May 2002);
- Slovakia (18 November 1999);
- Slovenia (11 October 1997/ 7 May 1999);
- Spain (23 October 2000);
- Sweden (3 March 1996/ 29 May 1998);
- Ukraine (7 May 1999/ 21 December 2006).

Countries that ratified or signed the Revised European Social Charter without ratifying the earlier international treaty (the European Social Charter) are listed in Chapter 3 Part I of this book.

The European Social Charter was criticized by experts for not effectively protecting social rights nor clearly establishing the standards of social rights protection. It also came under criticism for not introducing enough obligations for Member States or for failing to place pressure on Member States to abide by all regulations stipulated by Part II. It also failed to allocate entitlements for individuals whose rights have not been met.[20]

More than 50 years have past since the enactment of the European Social Charter. The Charter is a legal compromise between the Social Committee of the Committee of Ministers, the Consultative Assembly and the Tripartite Commission. Even though it was described as an 'imperfect document'[21] because it preserves existing social rights protection but does not create new ones, the Charter provided a basis for unanimous social policies in Europe, promoted the protection of labour rights and underlined the need to form a uniform and general social protection mechanism. It built the cornerstones for a European social model, encompassing the deep political division of the European continent. Legal experts regarded the Charter as an international treaty supplementing the European Convention on Human Rights, a document that lifted social rights to the importance as political and civil rights. The European Social Charter began to be treated as a *pendant* of the Convention for the Protection of Human Rights and Fundamental Freedoms.[22]

Legal experts in the field of international public law and human rights regard the Charter as an important international treaty. For the first time in history, international social rights were accorded identical attention as civil and political rights on the international platform. The European Social Charter is the first international document to value social rights.

Legal practitioners dealing with the protection of national labour and social security laws regard the European Social Charter with greater reserve. Its scope guarantees protection of chosen legal categories. The Charter protects the following categories of rights:

- The right to work (Article 1);
- The right to just conditions of work (Article 2);
- The right to safe and healthy working conditions (Article 3);
- The right to freedom of association (Article 5);
- The right to bargain collectively (Article 6);
- The right to vocational guidance (Article 9);
- The right to vocational training (Article 10);

20. F. Tennfijord, *The European Social Charter – An Instrument of Social Collaboration in Europe*, 1962 Eur. Y. B., p. 71 and following; H. Wiebringhaus, *La Charte Sociale Européenne*, 9 Annuaire Francais de Droit International (1963), p. 710 and following; G. Jannssen-Pevtschin, 'Les engagements des parties contractantes et la mise en oeuvre de la Charte sociale européenne', *1966 Revue de l'Institut de Sociologie,* p. 9 and following; D. Pugsley, The European Social Charter, 39 Y. B. A. A. (1969), p. 97 and following; D. Harris, J. Darcy, *op. cit.,* p. 1 and following.
21. D. Harris, J. Darcy, *op. cit.,* p. 7.
22. G. Cohen-Jonathan, 'Droits de l'Homme et pluralité des systèmes européens de protection internationale', *Human Rights Journal,* vol. 5, 1972, p. 638.

- The right to health protection (Article 11);
- The right to social security (Article 12);
- The right to social and medical assistance (Article 13);
- The right to benefit from social welfare services (Article 14).

It guarantees general protection for all citizens of Member States who have ratified the Charter as well as those lawfully residing on such territories. The scope of this protection is not dependent on the decisions undertaken by the individual countries bound by the Charter.

The aforementioned selection of regulations that are regarded as obligatory for individual Member States, such as Article 20, could cause difficulties in the process of appropriating Charter regulations for citizens of other Member States that are party to the treaty. For this reason, nations who have not ratified certain regulations are obligated to guarantee foreigners (defined as citizens and those legally residing on territories of other Member States that are party to the international treaty) the right to Charter provisions.

The Charter guarantees the protection of rights according to social categories: child and young female workers, the disabled, families, mothers and children, citizens of other Member States, and migrant workers and their families. The scope of such protection varies in accordance with the categories it protects.

- Children and female employees before or after childbirth have the right to protection (Article 7 and 8).
- The disabled are guaranteed independence, social integration and participation in community life (Article 15).
- Families have the right to social, legal and economic protection (Article 16).
- The right to economic and social protection is granted to mothers and children (Article 17).
- Citizens of other Member States that are party to the international treaty (Charter) have guaranteed rights to engage in gainful occupation on territories of other Member States (Article 18).
- Migrant workers and their families have the right to protection and assistance (Article 19).

The rights protected by the European Social Charter in 1961 were supported by the following documents: the Additional Protocol to the European Social Charter in 1988, which broadened the scope of protection rights with the creation of four further regulations:

- The right to equal opportunity and equal treatment in matters of employment and occupation without gender discrimination (Article 1);
- The right to information and consultation (Article 2);
- the right to take part in the determination and improvement of working conditions and working environment (Article 3);
- The right of the elderly to social protection (Article 4).

The Revised European Social Charter expanded the following eight rights:

- The right to protection in cases of employment termination (Article 24);
- The workers' right to protection of their claims in the event of insolvency of their employer (Article 25);
- The right to dignity at work (Article 26);
- The right of workers with family responsibilities to equal opportunity and equal treatment (Article 27);
- The right of workers' representatives to protection and appropriate facilities (Article 28);
- The right of workers to be informed and consulted in collective redundancy procedures (Article 29);
- The right to protection against poverty and social exclusion (Article 30);
- The right to housing (Article 31).

Apart from the introduction of the first two parts of the European Social Charter, the treaty consists of Parts III and IV, as well as the Appendix.

Part IV (Articles 21–23) deals with reporting obligations. It also requires the provision of copies of reports to social stakeholders. Employer and employee organizations have a similar obligation to provide the Secretary-General to the Council of Europe with reports. The Charter obligates Member States to file two types of reports: one type to provide documents specified by the rules ratified by a given country (Article 21), and another type dealing with national labour, social security laws and other treaties regarding regulations by Charter rules that were not ratified by a Member State (Article 22). Reports dealing with ratified regulations are regularly filed every two years. These reports deal with Part II. Reports concerning provisions that were not accepted during the time of its ratification should be filed accordingly in a period defined by the Committee of Ministers. Copies of such reports should be given by Member States to national employee and employer organizations that are associated with their international counterparts and are invited to partake in Subcommittee of the Governmental Social Committee sittings.

Part V provides for the monitoring of compliance on the part of the Member States with their chosen regulations of the Charter. This compliance is monitored by the Committee of Experts (Article 24). Originally, this committee was called the Committee of Independent Experts. This name emphasized the lack of dependency between members of the Committee and the Member States. From 1988, the Committee adopted a new name: the European Committee of Social Rights. The supervisory system is referred to in Chapter 1, Part III of this book. We shall refer to the terminology used in the initial version of the Charter.

The Committee of Ministers nominates members to the Committee of Experts. The Committee of Experts is comprised of individuals held in great esteem and regard in international social matters. The Committee of Experts consists of no more than seven members.[23] Members of the Committee are appointed for six year terms, but may be re-appointed. Two first-time members, have tenure for four years.

The International Labour Organization takes part in the deliberations of the Committee, where it also enjoys advisory status (Article 26).

The European Social Charter stated that the reports of Member States dealing with the Charter's regulations and conclusions of the Committee of Experts (since 1988, the Committee of Social Rights) should be submitted to the Committee of Experts after the conclusion of a supervisory cycle for analysis This committee is made up of Member States who are signatories to the Charter. Each country has one representative. Observers invited to take part in the sessions of the Committee as advisors may be representatives of no more than two employers and trade union organizations. The Committee has the right to seek opinions from no more than two international organizations outside the Committee, to whom the Council of Europe gives consultative status. Organizations may give advice on issues pertinent to their causes, such as social welfare or a family's economic and social protection. The reports of the Member States and the conclusions of the Committee of Experts are then submitted for examination to a Subcommittee of the Governmental Social Committee of the Council of Europe (Article 27).

The Subcommittee of the Governmental Social Committee, whose role has since been taken over by the Governmental Committee, is a political organ. Reports and conclusions were presented by the Committee of Independent Experts. The Governmental Committee analysed compliance with the responsibilities undertaken by Member States of Part II. The results were then transferred to the Secretary-General by the Committee of Experts, who, in turn, presented the findings to the Advisory Assembly. The Advisory Assembly transferred any remarks about the results to the Committee of Ministers (Article 28). Based on the report of the Subcommittee of the Governmental Social Committee, and after hearing the Advisory Assembly, the Committee of Ministers by a majority of 2:3 Member State votes made the decision to

23. The members of the Committee of Experts were: B. Bull (Norway, 1966-1990), Sir Otto Kahn-Freund (Britain, 1966-1972), Ph. Laroque (France, 1966-1976), H. Armbruster (Germany, 1966-1972 and 1973-1976), S. Busuttil (Malta, 1966-1972), R. Greary (Ireland, 1966-1972), C. Arena (Italy, 1966-1967), F. Parrillo (Italy, 1967-1970), R. Strasser (Italy, 1970-1973), G. Kojanec (Italy, 1972-1996), A. Loizou (Cyprus, 1972-1984), Troclet (Belgium, 1972-1978), B. Zanetti (Switzerland, 1972-1984), F. Fabricius (Germany, 1976-1994), A. Morgan (Britain, 1976-1980), W. de Gaay Fortman (Netherlands, 1978-1990), W. James (Britain, 1980-1982), T. Ohlinger (Austria, 1984-1990), J. Vida Soria (Spain, 1984-1996), D. Harris (Britain, 1990-1996), S. Billum (Sweden, 1990-1996), T. Jaspers (Netherlands, 1990-1996), S. Grévisse (France, 1988-2000), M. Jomoulle (Belgium, 1996-2002); K. Grillberger (Austria, 1994-2004), L. Samuel (Cyprus, 2005) In March 2005 Mr. G. Quinn resigned from the Committee. Currently in the Committee of Social Rights are: P. Koncar (Slovenia - president), A. Światkowski (Poland - First Vicepresident), T. Akillioglu (Turkey - Second Vice-president), J.-M. Belorgey (General Rapporteur), N. Aliprantis (Greece), T. Akillioglu (Turkey), C. Kolonai-Lehocky (Hungary), A. Bruto da Costa (Portugal), S. Evju (Norway), R. Birk (Germany), L. Francois (Belgium), Beatrix Karl (Austria), Lauri Leppik (Estonia), E. Spatafora (Italy). In November 2006, mandates of J-M. Belorgay, C. Kolonai-Lehocky and A. Świątkowski were renewed. New Committee members C. O'Cinneide (Ireland) and M.Schlachter (Germany) were elected.

aim its essential recommendations to Member States that are party to the Charter (Article 29).

Part VI provides for ways by which Member States can retract their commitments or levels of commitments to the obligations they accepted under the charter. This part also regulates the interdependency between the Charter, international agreements and domestic laws. Also discussed are ways to include the Charter in a country's domestic law. The territorial domain of the Charter was thus defined. Procedures regarding the setting of signatures, ratification, the incorporation of the Charter into being, amendments, and giving it notice are specified.

In exceptional circumstances, such as war or other threats to public security endangering the life of the nation, Member States have the right to take measures to repeal regulations ratified by the Charter in accordance with specific situations. They cannot be in conflict with other obligations of Member States resulting from international agreements. Member States who utilize the right to repeal regulations are obligated to inform the Secretary-General of the Council of Europe within a reasonable time frame of their undertaken actions and decisions. The Secretary-General must also be informed about the time frame during which the repeal will take place, as well as of the date from which Member States will recommence their obligations arising from the ratified Charter regulations. The Secretary-General will in turn inform other Member States and parties to the Charter of the repealed regulation undertaken by the given Member State, as well as inform the Director to the International Labour Office (Article 30).

Member States generally do not have the right to impose restrictions on rules and regulations set by Parts I and II. They can only impose such restrictions to the Charter, according to national law, where it is necessary to do so in a democratic society in order to protect laws and values, public security, national safety, public health, or good customs. The Charter unanimously dictates that allowing restrictions on rules and obligations specified by this international treaty cannot be used for any unforeseeable reasons (Article 31).

The Charter sets minimum standards for the protection of social rights. For this reason, the regulations within the Charter cannot obstruct national laws, bilateral or multilateral treaties, conventions or agreements, in accordance with those entitled to broader protection (Article 32).

The Member States are responsible for conforming their practices and regulations with the Charter. In some countries, regulations of working conditions and the employment of youth, as well as the organization of vocational training for workers determined by social stakeholders. In Member States where work and holiday hours are regulated by trade agreements, the authorities can declare that they will comply with Article 2 § 1, 2, 3, 4 and 5, when the abovementioned regulations are applicable to the majority of workers by such agreements (Article 33 (1)). This rule can be applied in the process of implementing standards regulated under Article 7 § 4, 6 and 7 and regulations which can reduce working time of young workers, providing them with just remuneration or appropriate benefits, as well as annual paid leave (at least three weeks). Article 10 obligates Member States to allow all, including the disabled, access to technical and vocational training and apprenticeships.

Article 3 deals with the 'majority principle'. Bodies supervising the obligations of Member States to the Charter consider the standards to be met when parties to the Charter ensure that obligations under Article 33 § 1 (Article 2 § 1, 2, 3, 4 and 5; Article 7 § 1, 2, 3 and 4) are met for the majority of the interested workers. The Committee of Independent Experts claims that the abovementioned rule is met when the national regulations and the practice of the application protect at least 80 per cent of those covered by the law.

The European Social Charter governs the metropolitan territory of every party. Each Member State defines the territorial scope of the Charter application by filing a statement addressed to the Secretary-General to the Council of Europe. This statement, filed during the signing or ratification of the Charter, defines a specific territory to be regarded as a metropolitan territory, for the purposes of application of the Charter regulations. Each Member State can also file a statement bringing the whole Charter or some of its regulations into force on non-metropolitan territories or their parts, which are governed by its state. The Secretary-General is obliged to inform other Member States and the Director of the International Labour Office once he receives such a notification (Article 34).

In accordance with the abovementioned regulation, the following statements were filed: Denmark excluded Faroe Island and Greenland from the territorial application of the Charter, and Germany submitted an application to the Charter regarding the area of Berlin after it had been incorporated into Western Germany. According to Dutch authorities, the terms 'metropolitan' and 'non-metropolitan', used by the Charter to determine its geographical scope, have currently lost their meanings and have been replaced by the terms 'European' and 'non-European'. On non-European territories, the Dutch authorities declared the following binding regulations in the Dutch Antilles: Article 1, 5, 6 (with the exception of civil servants) and Article 16. As a result of attaining partial autonomy by Aruba, an earlier part of the Dutch Antilles, the Netherlands decided to apply the Charter separately to three bodies: the Netherlands (a monarchy within Europe), the Dutch Antilles, and Aruba. Norway filed a declaration to withhold Charter application on Svalbard (Spitsbergen) and Jan Mayen Territories. Great Britain declared the application of the Charter on the Isle of Man according to the identical ratifying conditions applied in the rest of Great Britain.

Each Member State has the right to propose amendments to the Charter by addressing the Secretary-General of the Council of Europe. Amendments are also passed on to other Member States. A Committee of Ministers then decides whether to accept or reject such amendments. These amendments, analysed by the Committee, are then passed on to the Consultative Assembly for an opinion. Amendments accepted by the Committee of Ministers enter into effect on the 30th day from the date the Secretary-General has been informed of their acceptance. The Secretary-General officially informs all Member States, as well as the Director of the International Labour Office, of the amendment entering into effect (Article 36).

The whole Charter can be denounced by each Member State after the passage of five years from the date on which it comes into effect with respect to each country or during the following two-year period. The denunciation period is six months. An application of denunciation is made to the Secretary-General, who has the responsibility to inform the other Member States, parties to the treaty, and the Director of the International Labour Office accordingly.

The denunciation of the Charter does not affect the obligations of the remaining signatories if their number is not less than five. Each country, in accordance with the abovementioned principles, may denounce any part of the accepted regulations of Part II, as long as the number of Charter regulations obligating a given country is not less than 10 (in the case of enumerated Articles) or 45 (in the case of enumerated paragraphs). A further important condition to consider in the case of denunciation of certain parts of the Charter is acceptance within the framework of the abovementioned minimum number of Articles and paragraphs. This includes five of the seven obligations named under Article 20(1)(b), regulating Member States (Article 1, 5, 6, 12, 13, 16, 19).

These principles, associated with the denunciation of either the whole Charter or some of its regulations, are applicable to all non-metropolitan territories in which the Charter has taken on the strength of the separate pronouncement of authorities of the appropriate state. (Article 37)

An integral part of the Charter is its Appendix. In it are defined certain legal terms and regulations which are used within the Charter, such as: 'foreigner'; 'work freely entered upon' (Article 1 § 2); 'period of notice for termination' (Article 4 § 4); 'deductions from wages' (Article 4 § 5); 'right to strike' (Article 6 § 4), 'young persons shall not be employed in night work' (Article 7 § 8); 'the retention of benefits arising out of social security' (Article 12 § 4); 'European Convention on Social and Medical Assistance' (Article 13 § 4); 'family' (Article 16); 'family of a migrant worker' (Article 19 § 6); 'numbered paragraphs' (Article 20 § 1); 'war' (Article 30); and 'scope of control' (Part III). These definitions are discussed in Part II, in chapters that discuss the protection of social regulations of the Charter, as well as in Part III, in chapters that discuss the supervisory mechanisms that monitor Member States and whether they abide by regulations.

CHAPTER 2 ADDITIONAL PROTOCOLS

The Additional Protocol of 1988, Amending Protocol of 1991, and Additional Protocol of 1995 are the most recent additions to the Charter.

2.1. The Additional Protocol of 1988

The Additional Protocol of 1988 was prepared for Member States to sign on 5 May 1988.[1] It came into being on 4 September 1992, on the 30th day from the date that the third ratifying document was tendered. It was signed or signed and ratified by the following Member States, in alphabetical order (date of signing/ date of ratification): Austria (4 December 1990); Belgium (20 May 1992/ 23 June 2003); Croatia (8 March 1999/ 26 February 2003); Cyprus (5 May 1998); Czech Republic (27 May 1992/ 17 November 1999); Finland (9 February 1990/ 29 April 1991); France (22 June 1989); Germany (5 May 1988); Greece (5 May 1988/ 18 June 1998); Iceland (5 May 1988); Italy (5 May 1988/ 16 May 1994); Latvia (29 May 1997); Luxembourg (5 May 1988); Macedonia (5 May 1998); the Netherlands (14 June 1990/ 5 August 1992), Norway (10 December 1993/ 10 December 1993); Slovakia (27 May 1992/ 22 June 1988); Slovenia (11 October 1997); Spain (5 May 1988/ 24 January 2000); Turkey (5 May 1998). Some Member States signed the Additional Protocol in 1988 but did not ratify it, ratifying and signing instead the Revised European Social Charter.[2] Other Member States signed or signed and ratified, as one international treaty, the Revised European Social Charter.[3] They did not sign either the European Social Charter or any of the abovementioned Protocols to this Charter.

The Additional Protocol of 1988 included three additional regulations to the list of protected social rights. The concept of increasing this catalogue of social rights was presented in the Declaration on Human Rights passed by Council of Europe Member States on 27 April 1978.[4] Carrying out this declaration, the Committee of Ministers

1. R. Aguilera Izuierdo, *El protocolo addicional a la Carta Social Europea, Actalidad laboral*. Las Rozas, Madrid, No.31, 2000, p. 61 and following.
2. Austria, France, Iceland, Luxembourg, Slovenia.
3. Albania, Andorra, Armenia, Bulgaria, Georgia, Lithuania, Moldova, Russia.
4. *Explanatory Report to the 1988 Protocol, European Social Charter*. Collected texts, *op. cit.*, p. 127.

initiated a number of consultations with other Council of Europe Committees as well as other stakeholders, including The European Trade Union Confederation (ETUC) and Union of Industries of the European Committee (UNICE), giving power to the Committee for Social Affairs to increase the scope of social rights protection in the European Convention on Human Rights and in the European Social Charter. The Committee for Social Affairs prepared materials for the Committee of Ministers and sat during six sessions in March, July, and October of 1983 and again in June, July, and October 1984, discussing and accepting the propositions to pass the Additional Protocol to the European Social Charter. The above proposition was tendered to the Committee of Ministers. This committee decided during its 387th sitting in November/December 1984 to undertake consultations with stakeholders regarding the Additional Protocol project. The opinions of ETUC and UNICE were passed onto the Committee of Social Affairs with a recommendation to be discussed during the next Additional Protocol draft. The amended project was presented to the Parliamentary Assembly, which, in opinion No. 131 in 1987, inserted a couple of its own changes to the Protocol, dealing with the new protection of social rights, the ratifying process and its range of application.

During Session 81 on 26 November 1987, the Committee of Ministers passed the Additional Protocol. The Protocol is a separate international document dealing mainly with the increase in the range of ways of applying the European Social Charter and is structured in the same manner as the Charter in four parts. It adds four additional social rights set by the European Social Charter and incorporates them into the international protection of human rights. It has four parts: The first consists of declarations, which repeat the same arguments found in the introduction to Part I. It declares a concentration on social policy as a goal and the creation of favourable conditions for the efficient execution of the following workers rights: equal opportunity and equal treatment in matters of employment and occupation without gender discrimination; the right to information and consultation; and the right to take part in the determination and improvement of working conditions and working environment (Articles 1-3). Article 4 ensures the right of the elderly to social protection.

Part II of the Protocol compiles all rights mentioned above, expanding the category of social rights. These are: equal opportunity and equal treatment in matters of employment and occupation without gender discrimination (Article 1); the right to information and consultation (Article 2); the right to take part in the determination and improvement of working conditions and working environment (Article 3); and the right of the elderly to social protection (Article 4).

Part III of the Protocol consists of one regulation (Article 5), about the ratification conditions. Member States that are going to ratify the Protocol should consider Part I of the Protocol as a declaration of goals they are to accomplish by using all adequate and appropriate means and should accept the regulations under at least one of the Articles of Part II of the Protocol. The four Articles of Part II consist of 11 paragraphs.

The essential condition of the ratification is reporting to the Secretary-General that one out of four Articles have been met in full. Unlike the ratification procedure of the Charter, where each paragraph is considered a separate regulation, the Protocol allows only Articles to be ratified, as the paragraphs are not regarded as separate regulations.

Parts IV and V of the Protocol were constructed according to the pertinent regulations of the Charter. An Appendix was added to the protocol which determines the scope of subjects protected by the Protocol. It allows the exclusion of the ensured from the right to equal opportunity and equal treatment in matters of employment and occupation without gender discrimination. The Protocol leaves it to the discretion of Member States to define a workers' representative body entitled to participate in the determination and improvement of working conditions and the working environment. It excludes religious communities from the right to information and consultation and the right to take part in the determination and improvement of working conditions and the working environment, even though they may be regarded as 'enterprises' according to the Appendix to the Protocol.

2.2. Amending Protocol of 1991

The Amending Protocol of 1991 is an international document aimed at reinforcing the significance of the European Social Charter and the Additional Protocol to the identical stature of the European Convention on Human Rights. Unlike the Convention, which protects human rights in the category of political and civil rights,[5] the Charter employs its supervisory mechanism to monitor compliance with the protection of human rights. These are classified as social rights and both the provision and the enforcement of these rights may suffer from ineffectiveness. During an informal meeting on 5 November 1990 in Rome, ministers of Member States remarked on the need for giving the Charter, and particularly its controlling mechanism, a 'fresh impetus'. The Committee of Ministers was called upon to conduct a detailed analysis of the Charter, taking into account its role, content and functioning.[6] Thus, the Committee for Improving the Efficiency of the European Social Charter was established during the 449th session of the Committee in November/October 1990. The Committee was named *Charte-Rel,* and had an *ad hoc* status. It consisted of experts designated by Member States. Each party delegated one expert to the Committee. Representatives of the Parliamentary Assembly, ILO, ETUC, UNICE, members of the Committee of Social Rights, the Governmental Committee, and other committees to the Council of Europe participated in the sittings of the *Charte-Rel* Committee, but they had voting rights.

During its first sitting in February 1991 the *Charte-Rel* prepared drafts for the Amending Protocol and the Additional Protocol aimed at increasing the efficiency of the supervisory mechanisms over the reports by Member States of their compliance

5. It was considered to broaden the scope of the social protection guaranteed by the European Convention on Human Rights to social and economical rights. The concept, however, was abandoned as these rights were regarded to be of an impersonal character for which legal instruments of the Convention cannot guarantee execution. *See* F. Jacobs, *The Extension of the European Convention on Human Rights to Include Economic, Social and Cultural Rights*, 3 Human Rights Review (1978), p. 1878 and following.
6. Explanatory report to the 1991 Amending Protocol, European Social Charter. Collected texts, *op. cit.*, p. 139.

with the Charter's regulations. The Additional Protocol dealt with collective complaints as well as changes in the reporting procedure.

The project of the Amending Protocol was accepted during the third sitting in September 1991 and presented to the Committee of Ministers. The abovementioned Protocol was passed by the Committee of Ministers during its sitting on 16 October 1991, with a ceremonial signing held in Turin on 21 October 1991, to commemorate the 30th anniversary of the ratification of the European Social Charter.

The *Charte-Rel* Committee focused on two main issues in its Amending Protocol. First, it provided that the efficiency of the supervision of compliance with the Charter should be increased by giving the Committee of Ministers the right to address recommendations to the Member States who were believed to have violated social rights protected by the Charter. Second, it emphasized the need for resources for effective supervision of compliance with the Charter.

The *Charte-Rel* Committee recommended that the various authorities of the Committee of Social Rights, the Governmental Committee and the Parliamentary Assembly should be changed, that the supervisory process should be reduced, that stakeholders should be invited to take part in the process of adjusting national labour law and social protection systems to the standards set by the Charter, and that actions towards propagating the Charter in Member States should be undertaken.

First, the *Charte-Rel* Committee regulated the relationship between the Committee of Social Rights and the Governmental Committee. The former was comprised of outstanding individuals, independent of Member States. The latter consisted of high-ranking civil servants, mostly employed by Labour and Social Affairs Ministries, who were responsible for the preparation of the reports reviewed by the Committee of Social Rights. The Governmental Committee drafted, modified, and even rejected substantial opinions of the reports made by the Committee of Social Rights. The *Charte-Rel* Committee recommended that the two committees should be combined for making decisions about the reports sent by Member States. It stated that the role of the Governmental Committee should be limited to analysis of the reports previously examined by the Committee of Social Rights, which focused on social and economic policies. It also held that the Governmental Committee should take domestic conditions into consideration and present the most problematic violations of social rights to the Committee of Ministers. The *Charte-Rel* Committee wanted to change the image of the Governmental Committee from a political body *per se* into an advisory body to the Committee of Ministers.

The membership of the Committee of Social Rights was increased to nine members with a maximum tenure of two six-year terms. The Committee of Social Rights was responsible for examining the conformity of domestic legislation, executive regulations and practices with the provisions of the Charter. The Committee was authorized to directly contact the Member States to obtain additional information or explanations. Members of the Committee were given the right to arrange meetings with representatives of Member States, either at their own initiative or through representatives of Member States. Motions and rulings are to be published and delivered to the Governmental

Committee, the Parliamentary Assembly, and stakeholders entitled to obtain copies of national reports under Article 32 § 1.

The Parliamentary Assembly no longer played a role in supervising compliance with the Charter. The Governmental Committee was now responsible for preparing decisions for the Committee of Ministers on the basis of rulings of the Committee of Social Rights. In particular, the Governmental Committee would choose which recommendations should be addressed to a given Member State after taking into account social and economic policies, rulings of the Committee of Social Rights and reports sent by Member States. The Government Committee reports prepared for the Committee of Ministers are public. The Committee of Ministers, after analysing reports produced by the Committee of Social Rights and the Governmental Committee, can adopt, by a 2/3 majority of votes, resolutions concerning the whole supervisory cycle of Member State reports, as well as individual recommendations for a given Member State. Reports of the Committee of Social Rights and the Governmental Committee involve a plenary discussion.

The Amending Protocol of 1991 changed the administrative structure of the Council of Europe. In the period leading up to the Amending Protocol of 1991, all issues connected with substantial supervision of compliance with the European Social Charter were handled by the Department of Human Rights, a body responsible for dealing with the protection of human rights. Until 1989, the Department of Human Rights only handled the protection of political and civil rights. Organizational changes to increase the efficiency of monitoring processes of social rights coincided with extensive political changes in Europe, introducing free market economies to former communist countries. These countries began to be increasingly interested in social and economic rights as they experienced serious difficulties with controlling aggressively growing capitalism on their own[7] and began looking for models on which to base themselves. Notwithstanding the fact that the European Social Charter or the Committee of Social Rights did not provide such models for social rights, the standards set under the Charter as well as rulings of the Committee of Social Rights were able to give the authorities enough information to determine whether their domestic labour policy and social protection regulations were in conformity with the standards accepted by the Council of Europe.

The European Social Charter, together with the Protocols, inspired European Communities to pass the Charter of Fundamental Social Rights for Workers. This document was intended for states that were not part of highly developed countries where there was a need to regulate social rights of workers according to the Protocols to the European Social Charter. Heads of states and prime ministers of 11 European Community Member States[8] assembled in Strasburg on 9 December 1989 to declare the necessity of supporting living and working conditions within the EU in order to equalize standards of social and workers' rights. The Community Charter of

7. D. Harris, J. Darcy, *op. cit.*, pp. 13–14.
8. Without Great Britain.

Fundamental Social Rights for Workers[9] declared the requirement to abide by the following rights: the right to move freely within the whole EU, excluding restrictions arising from public order, the right to public health and security; the right to engage in all types of employment and activity and equal treatment in employment procedures, working conditions and social protection in the host country within the EU; the right to appropriate remuneration; access to free public employment services; the right to weekly rest and to annual paid leave; the right to legally determined working conditions; the right to collective agreements as well as work placement agreements; the right to appropriate social protection; the right to social welfare given on appropriate terms; the right to freely associate in labour organizations and trade unions to protect social and economic interests; the right to join or not join these organizations without the threat to personal or professional consequences; the right to carry out collective negotiations and enter into collective agreements; the right to collective actions in cases of conflicts of interests, including the right to strike; the right to vocational training during the entire professional period; the right to be equally treated regardless of sex, in particular where employment, remuneration, working conditions, social protection, education, vocational training and professional development are concerned; the right to take advantages from measures making it possible for both women and men to combine professional and family duties; and the right to information, consultation and participation at work, especially in cases of:

– Technological changes having a significant impact for workers in terms of working conditions and organization of work.
– Restructuring or merging of firms influencing workers employment.
– Collective redundancy.

The Community Charter of Fundamental Social Rights for Workers declares the common right to health and safety protection at work. It sets the minimum age for a young person to start a professional life, ensuring training, with the exception of excluding some light work, at 15 years of age. It grants the employed young person the right to just remuneration. It orders the introduction of restricting work time for persons less than 18 years of age. It disallows evasion of the abovementioned regulation by giving a young person extra hours and employing such staff at night time. It also gives young people the right to enrol for initial vocational training in order to adjust to the requirements of future professional life.

The Community Charter also states that the elderly are entitled, as soon as they retire, to benefits ensuring a decent standard of living. Retired age demographics who are not entitled to pension benefits and who do not have other resources to support themselves should be guaranteed the right to adequate benefits as well as the right to social and medical assistance according to their needs. It states that all disabled people

9. English text published as an Appendix in vol. 39, *Bulletin of Comparative Labour Relations*, The Council of Europe and the Social Challenges of the 21st Century, ed. R. Blanpain, Kluwer International, The Hague/London/Boston 2001, pp. 343 and following.

regardless of the cause and type of disability should have the right to access extra resources that will aid them in the process of work and social integration. Depending on the level of disability, the abovementioned resources should take into account vocational training, ergonomics, accessibility to facilities, the ability to be mobile, access to transport and appropriate housing standards.

2.3. Additional Protocol of 1995 — Establishing a System Considering Collective Complaints

When the Amending Protocol to the European Social Charter was finalized, the *Charte-Rel* Committee undertook a draft of the Additional Protocol considering collective complaints.[10] The inspiration for this Protocol came from the Parliamentary Assembly recommendation No. 838 of 1978. The intention of this recommendation was to construct a system of collective complaints that would, on the one hand, increase the effectiveness of the European Committee of Social Rights supervision of reports on compliance with the Charter by Member States, while, on the other hand, allow for greater participation by stakeholders in the supervision process of adjusting national labour law and social protection regulations to the standards set by the European Social Charter.

During the second sitting, on 22–24 May 1991, a working group was appointed to draft the Additional Protocol for collective complaints. A short while after the gatherings on 3–4 July 1994, the working group presented the draft of the Additional Protocol to the *Charte-Rel* Committee. The determination of procedural matters related to the collective complaints were left to the Committee of Independent Experts (currently the Committee of Social Rights). The Committee of Experts gave its opinion on the draft prepared by the working group. Stakeholders (ETUC, UNICE) also presented their viewpoint. On the basis of the gathered opinions, the *Charte-Rel* Committee, during the third sitting from 3-–6 September 1991, prepared the finalized version of the Additional Protocol draft. It was then presented to the Committee of Ministers on 21 October 1991 in Turin, where the 30th anniversary ceremony of signing the European Social Charter took place. The Committee of Ministers passed a resolution with the goals expected from the Protocol. It repeated views expounded by the Parliamentary Assembly resolution No. 839 of 1978 concerning the increasing effectiveness of the European Social Charter regulations and maximization of stakeholder participation in the process of supervising Member State obligations.

According to the Committee of Ministers, social dialogue would have been improved by establishing rules of recognition in cases of collective complaints against Member States not abiding regulations of the Charter, filed by international employee and employer organizations.

---

10. Explanatory report to the 1995 Protocol, European Social Charter. Collected texts, *op. cit.*, p. 149 and following.

The *Charte-Rel* Committee completed works on the Additional Protocol draft during the fifth sitting, which took place between 18–20 May 1992, and presented the final version of the Protocol draft to the Committee of Ministers. The finalization of discussions was preceded by two *Charte-Rel* Committee work sittings on 3–6 February 1992 and 30–31 March 1992. After consultations with the Committee of Independent Experts and the Parliamentary Assembly, the Committee of Ministers passed the Additional Protocol on 22 June 1995 and presented it for signature to the Member States on 9 November 1995.

The Additional Protocol took effect on 1 July 1998, on the first day of the month after a monthly period since the day when five Member States[11] filed ratification documents. All countries wanting to join the Protocol in the future will be bound by its regulations from the first day of the month after a monthly period of the ratification date when appropriate documents are filed or the Protocol is adopted or ratified. All parties to the Protocol can denounce giving a 12-month notice period starting on–the day when the Secretary-General is given a denouncement notification. The Secretary-General is obligated to inform all Member States about the following: Signing of the Protocol, filing ratification documents, adopting or approving the Protocol, the date when the Protocol takes effect and any other action connected with the Additional Protocol.

Signatories of the Additional Protocol of 1995 are the following states (the signing date followed by the ratifying date of the Protocol): Belgium (14 May 1996/ 23 June 2003); Croatia (8 March 1999/ 26 February 2003); Cyprus (9 November 1995/ 6 August 1996); Czech Republic (26 February 2002), Denmark (9 November 1995); Finland (9 November 1995/ 17 July 1998); France (9 November 1995/ 7 May 1999); Greece (18 June 1998/ 18 June 1998); the Netherlands (3 May 2006); Ireland (4 November 2000/ 4 November 2000); Italy (9 November 1995/ 3 November 1997), Norway (20 March 1997/ 20 March 1997); Portugal (9 November 1995/ 20 March 1998), Slovakia (18 November 1999), Slovenia (1 October 1997), Sweden (9 September 1995/ 29 May 1998).

Bulgaria and Slovenia became parties to the Additional Protocol of 1995 by declaration of abiding by regulations under Article D Part IV of the Revised European Social Charter. This regulation emphasizes that the provisions of the Additional Protocol to the European Social Charter concerning a system of collective complaints are imperative to the regulations of the Revised European Social Charter for countries who ratified both documents. Countries not bound by the Additional Protocol to the European Social Charter concerning a system of collective complaints may notify the Secretary-General of the Council of Europe to take over control of regulations under the Revised European Social Charter, according to the Additional Protocol of 1995 during applying, adopting or ratifying the Revised European Social Charter, or in any other moment.

11. Cyprus, Italy, Norway, Portugal, Sweden.

Bulgaria declared the abovementioned notification on 21 September 1998 and then addressed it to the Secretary-General on 7 June 2000. Slovenia signed the Additional Protocol of 1995 (11 October 1997) and then signed (11 October 1997) and ratified (7 May 1999) the Revised European Social Charter.

The structure of the Additional Protocol of 1995 is not complicated. The Protocol consists of the Preamble and 16 provisions. The document is not divided into parts. The Protocol determines that subjects are entitled to register collective complaints against Member States. It defines a body of the Council of Europe authorized to recognize these complaints. It also describes fundamental rules of conduct in cases of collective complaints. Chapter III Part III of this book gives the details on the abovementioned issues.

The right to register such complaints was granted to some international employee and employer organizations, to other non-governmental organizations of advisable character to the Council of Europe and to representative national organizations of stakeholders appointed by Member States. Currently, only Finland has agreed to allow national employee and employer organizations to register collective complaints to the Committee of Social Rights.

Each collective complaint is analysed by the Committee of Social Rights who, at the initial stage, debates on the legitimacy of the complaint and then, after hearing the interested sides, makes a ruling stating either violation of Charter regulations by the charged state or the conformity between Charter provisions and state conduct, in which case the complaint is dismissed. A ruling of the Committee of Social Rights gives the basis for the Committee of Ministers to pass an adequate resolution. Member States against whom a collective complaint was registered are obligated to deliver a report to the Secretary-General on means undertaken in order to bring the resolution passed by the Committee of Ministers into life.

The Additional Protocol of 1995 created a legal mechanism that has enabled the Committee of Social Rights to supervise effectively Member States following the standards set by the European Social Charter in 1961 and the Revised European Social Charter in 1996. One of the Council of Europe's bodies is an institution independent of Member States that recognizes collective disputes and is formed with the highest class of professionals. The Governmental Committee, a political body consisting of Member States, does not evaluate rulings made by the Committee of Social Rights.

During the drafting of the Additional Protocol, representatives of Member States partaking in the Committee of Ministers as well as in committees and working groups invited by the Committee of Ministers to aid in the drafting of the protocol. They were split about the Governmental Committee's approach to collective complaints. Those who supported the Governmental Committee were of the view that the Committee should have the right to evaluate the rulings in a report, legal in its status, prepared for the Committee of Ministers. The opinion of those against was that the above proposition would remove the ability for the Council of Europe to supervise Member States' behaviour accordingly to the standards of the Charter. As a compromise, the Council of Europe was allowed to take part in collective complaints procedures if the Committee of Social Rights made a decision differing with the interpretation of Charter regulations that formed a legal basis for the complaint. A necessary condition for the Governmental Committee to take part in collective complaints procedures on the basis of a report prepared by the Committee of Social Rights, is to lodge a proposal by the charged Member State and for the Committee of Ministers to pass the bill by a 2/3 majority, allowing the report made by the Committee of Social Rights to be deduced by the Governmental Committee (Article 9 § 2 of the Additional Protocol).

CHAPTER 3 REVISED EUROPEAN SOCIAL CHARTER OF 1996

The last international document prepared by the *Charte-Rel* Committee is the Revised European Social Charter. The idea for passing a second Social Rights Charter of the Council of Europe was declared during an informal ministerial conference dealing with human rights protection on 5 November 1996 in Rome.

One of the topics discussed was the European Social Charter and its meaning in the process of human rights protection. The remarks made under Part 2 in the chapter mentioned below, deal with the giving of a 'fresh impetus' to the European Social Charter of 1961 in Rome and are still valid to the historical component of developing the Revised European Social Charter. The political process, which aimed to guarantee fuller and more effective human rights protection, proceeded on a double-track. On one hand, it is the method used to amend and alter the European Social Charter of 1961 through the Protocols, referred to in Parts 1-3 of the chapter mentioned below. On the other hand, through the passing of the Revised European Social Charter, both Charters (the 'old' from 1961 and the 'new' from 1996) are not in competition with each other even though they both address human rights protection.

The Revised Social Charter is an international treaty that modified and took over the former legal regulations of the European Social Charter and the earlier three Protocols protecting social rights. The original 19 regulations of Part II of the European Social Charter, utilized in the amended demands for social rights protection and completed by four supplementary regulations by the Additional Protocol of 1988, were enriched by a further eight regulations.

The Revised European Social Charter does not replace the European Social Charter. Those Member States that initially ratified the European Social Charter either with or without the Additional Protocols and further ratified the Revised European Social Charter automatically ceased producing reports that address the obeying of European Social Charter regulations.

Member States are no longer bound by the earlier European Social Charter, albeit considering the vast differences in the standards of social rights protection between the 'old' and 'new' Charter, the discontinuation of abiding the 'old' Charter regulations is not influential on the level of such social rights. Member States that ratified the

European Social Charter, signing the Revised European Social Charter but not ratifying it,[1] are bound by the 'old' Charter. Article B in Part III of the Revised European Social Charter of 1996 regulates the relationship between itself and the European Social Charter of 1961 and the Additional Protocols of 1988. The regulation in question disallows any Member State, party to the European Social Charter of 1961 or to the Additional Protocol of 1988, to ratify, accept or approve the Revised European Social Charter without considering itself to be bound by at least the provisions comparable to the provisions of the European Social Charter, to which it was bound up until this point (Article B(1)).

The aim of the above provision is to secure the continuation of fulfilling obligations accepted by the Member States, which by being parties to the European Social Charter ratified the Revised European Social Charter. Article B(1) of the Revised European Social Charter determines by its legal power that Member States who were obligated by provisions stipulated by European Social Charter provisions are substituted by the necessity to abide appropriate Revised European Social Charter provisions. The above legally binding mechanism is exclusively appropriated to the first 23 Revised European Social Charter provisions.

The provisions of Articles 24-31 consist of norms that became regulated for the first time in the Revised European Social Charter. In practice, the ratified provisions of Part I and II of the European Social Charter by Member States will be *ex lege* replaced by the appropriate provisions found within these Parts of the Revised European Social Charter.

Because neither the European Social Charter nor the Additional Protocol have any provisions which are equivalent to the norms codified in Articles 24-31 of the Revised European Social Charter, the automatic conversion of provisions can encompass exclusively the declarations entailed in Part I as well as some of the norms entailed in Part II of both Charters and therefore all provisions, excluding Articles 24-31 introduced to the Revised European Social Charter.

Article B(2) of the Revised European Social Charter ceases to apply obligations to Member States of any provisions of this Charter from the responsibility of abiding obligations resulting from the corresponding European Social Charter or the Additional Protocol provisions. The exemption from the abovementioned duty is enforced from the day of entry into similar duties regulated by the Revised European Social Charter provisions. The goal of this provision is to guarantee that a ratifying Member State of the Revised European Social Charter does not take advantage of the above provision to exempt itself from earlier obligations passed by the European Social Charter provisions. Article B(2) of the Revised European Social Charter addresses Member States that have fulfilled only the minimal requirements stipulated by Article 20 of the European Social Charter (i.e., those that have only ratified the minimum amount of provisions, adhering to the compulsory as well as the chosen obligations) and want to free themselves from some of their obligations under the charter. This refers to those

1. Austria, Belgium, Czech Republic, Denmark, Great Britain, Greece, Ireland, Luxembourg, Slovakia, Spain.

provisions of the Revised European Social Charter that are equivalent to the provisions of the European Social Charter and the Additional Protocol of 1988.

A Member State may relieve itself from the obligations imposed on it by the previous ratification of the old Charter on the day that the ratification of the new Charter is presented to the Secretary-General of the Council of Europe. From a legal standpoint, declaring to change the chosen provisions by a Member State who has ratified the Charter may be regarded as a sufficiently clear intention to denounce the application of provisions to which a given country has no intention of applying from the day it accepts itself to be bound to the 'new' Charter. Regardless, the abovementioned provision of Article 37 § 2 of the European Social Charter introduces the obligation to produce a clear statement stipulating the acceptance or the denouncement of a given provision or paragraph of Part II by a Member State.

The Appendix to Article B § 2 of the Revised European Social Charter indicates the equivalent provisions of this Charter, which are the supplementing provisions to the European Social Charter. The rule is to supplement the 'old' provision of the Charter with provisions with the same numbering as the 'new' Charter. In relation to the above Appendix to Article B § 2 of the Revised European Social Charter, provisions that were determined to be equivalent to the European Social Charter were kept. Article 3 § 2 of the Revised European Social Charter are equivalent to Article 3 § 1 and 3 of the European Social Charter. Article 3 § 3 of the Revised European Social Charter is equivalent to 3 § 2 and 3 of the European Social Charter. Article 10 § 5 of the Revised European Social Charter is equivalent to Article 10 § 4 of the European Social Charter. Article 17 § 1 of the Revised European Social Charter is equivalent to Article 17 of the European Social Charter. With the exception of a couple of countries which gained legal entity within international relations, such as Armenia, Azerbajdzhan, Estonia, Georgia, Lithuania, Moldova, and Russia, the majority of the remaining Member States firstly signed and/or ratified the European Social Charter, then signed and/or ratified the Revised European Social Charter. The abovementioned countries signed and/or ratified only the Revised European Social Charter (bracketed firstly is the signing date; secondly the ratification date): Armenia (18 January 2001/ 21 January 2004); Azerbajdzhan (18 October 2001/ 2 September 2004); Bosnia and Herzegovina (11 May 2004); Estonia (4 May 1998/ 11 September 2000); Georgia (30 June 2000/ 22 August 2005); Lithuania (8 September 1997/ 29 June 2001); Moldova (3 November 1998/ 8 November 2001); Russia (14 September 2000); and Serbia[2] (22 March 2005). Albania signed neither the European Social Charter nor any of the three Additional Protocols. It did, however, directly sign and ratify the Revised European Social Charter (21 September 1998/ 14 November 2002).

The exception among the 'new' Member States of the Council of Europe was the former Yugoslav Republic of Macedonia, which signed the European Social Charter of 1961 on 5 May 1998 and ratified it on 31 March 2005. Ukraine first signed but did not ratify the European Social Charter on the 2 May 1996, and then signed the Revised

2. At the time, it was one State called 'Serbia and Montenegro'. As a result of the split between Serbia and Montenegro, Montenegro had to resume the procedure to re-join the Council of Europe.

European Social Charter (7 May 1999). Among the countries taking advantage of their legal entity in international relations before 1990, only Bulgaria, towards the end of the 1990s, signed and ratified the European Social Charter (21September 1998/ 7 June 2000).

The Revised European Social Charter was signed and/or ratified by the following countries (alphabetical order, firstly is the signing date; secondly the ratification date): Albania (21 September1998/ 14 November 2002); Andorra (4 November 2000); Armenia (18 October 2001); Austria (7 May 1999); Azerbajdzhan (18 October 2001); Belgium (3 May 1996); Bulgaria (21 September 1998/ 7 June 2000); Cyprus (3 May 1996/ 27 September 2000); Czech Republic (4 November 2000); Denmark (3 May 1996); Great Britain (7 November 1997); Greece (3 March 1996); Iceland (4 November 1998); Luxembourg (11 February 1998); San Marino (18 October 2001); Slovakia (18 November 1999); Slovenia (11 October 1997/ 7 May 1999); Spain (23 October 2000); Sweden (3 May 1996/ 29 May 1998); and Ukraine (7 May 1999).

All 46 Council of Europe Member States have signed the Charter. Forty states have signed the Revised Charter and only six states have signed the 'old' 1961 Charter. Thirty-eight of the Council of Europe's Member States have ratified the Charter. Twenty-two Member States are bound by the Revised Charter, while only 16 are bound by the 1961 Charter.

Some European countries that are Member States of the Council of Europe did not ratify any of the Charters. They signed only either the European Social Charter (Liechtenstein, 9 October 1991) or the Revised European Social Charter (San Marino, 18 October 2001).[3]

3. The detailed table on the signatures and ratifications of the 1961 European Social Charter, the Protocols and the Revised European Social Charter prepared by the Documentation Center of the European Social Charter headed by Mrs. Brigitte Napiwocki in Strasbourg reads as follows:

Signatures and ratifications of the European Social Charter,
its Protocols and the European Social Charter (revised)
Situation at 21 December 2006
Member States
European Social Charter
1961

ETS 035

Signature Ratification
Additional Protocol
1988
ETS 128
Signature Ratification
Amending Protocol
1991
ETS 142
Signature Ratification **Collective Complaints Protocol**
1995
ETS 158
Signature Ratification **Revised European Social Charter**

1996
ETS 163
Signature Ratification
Albania (2) (2) (3) (3) (2) (2) (2) — 21/9/98 14/11/02
Andorra (2) (2) (3) (3) (2) (2) (2) — 4/11/00 12/11/04
Armenia (2) (2) (3) (3) (2) (2) (2) — 18/10/01 21/1/04
Austria 22/7/63 29/10/69 4/12/90 — 7/5/92 13/7/95 7/5/99 — 7/5/99 —
Azerbaïjan (2) (2) (3) (3) (2) (2) (2) — 18/10/01 2/9/04
Belgium 18/10/61 16/10/90 20/5/92 23/6/03 22/10/91 21/9/00 14/5/96 23/6/03 3/5/96 2/3/04
Bosnia and Herzegovina (1) — (1) — (1) — (1) — 11/5/04 —
Bulgaria (2) (2) (3) (3) (2) (2) (4) (4) 21/9/98 7/6/00
Croatia 8/3/99 26/2/03 8/3/99 26/2/03 8/3/99 26/2/03 8/3/99 26/2/03 — —
Cyprus 22/5/67 7/3/68 5/5/88 (3) 21/10/91 1/6/93 9/11/95 6/8/96 3/5/96 27/9/00
Czech Republic 27/5/92* 3/11/99 27/5/92* 17/11/99 27/5/92* 17/11/99 26/2/02 — 4/11/00 —
Denmark 18/10/61 3/3/65 27/8/96 27/8/96 — *** 9/11/95 — 3/5/96 —
Estonia (2) (2) (3) (3) (2) (2) (2) — 4/5/98 11/9/00
Finland 9/2/90 29/4/91 9/2/90 29/4/91 16/3/92 18/8/94 9/11/95 17/7/98 3/5/96 21/6/02
France 18/10/61 9/3/73 22/6/89 (3) 21/10/91 24/5/95 9/11/95 7/5/99 3/5/96 7/5/99
Georgia (2) (2) (3) (3) (2) (2) (2) — 30/6/00 22/8/05
Germany 18/10/61 27/1/65 5/5/88 — — *** — — — —
Greece 18/10/61 6/6/84 5/5/88 18/6/98 29/11/91 12/9/96 18/6/98 18/6/98 3/5/96 —
Hungary 13/12/91 8/7/99 7/10/04 1/6/05 13/12/91 4/2/04 7/10/04 — 7/10/04 —
Iceland 15/1/76 15/1/76 5/5/88 — 12/12/01 21/2/02 — — 4/11/98 —
Ireland 18/10/61 7/10/64 (3) (3) 14/5/97 14/5/97 4/11/00 4/11/00 4/11/00 4/11/00
Italy 18/10/61 22/10/65 5/5/88 26/5/94 21/10/91 27/1/95 9/11/95 3/11/97 3/5/96 5/7/99
Latvia 29/5/97 31/1/02 29/5/97 — 29/5/97 9/12/03 — — — —
Liechtenstein 9/10/91 — — — — — — — — —
Lithuania (2) (2) (3) (3) (2) (2) (2) — 8/9/97 29/6/01
Luxembourg 18/10/61 10/10/91 5/5/88 — 21/10/91 *** — — 11/2/98 —
Malta 26/5/88 4/10/88 (3) (3) 21/10/91 16/2/94 (2) — 27/7/05 27/7/05
Moldova (2) (2) (3) (3) (2) (2) (2) — 3/11/98 8/11/01
Monaco (1) (1) (1) (1) 5/10/04 —
Netherlands 18/10/61 22/4/80 14/6/90 5/8/92 21/10/91 1/6/93 23/1/04 3/5/06 23/1/04 3/5/06
Norway 18/10/61 26/10/62 10/12/93 10/12/93 21/10/91 21/10/91 20/3/97 20/3/97 7/5/01 7/5/01
Poland 26/11/91 25/6/97 (1) — 18/4/97 25/6/97 (1) — 25/10/05 —
Portugal 1/6/82 30/9/91 (3) (3) 24/2/92 8/3/93 9/11/95 20/3/98 3/5/96 30/5/02
Romania 4/10/94 (2) (3) (3) (2) (2) (2) — 14/5/97 7/5/99
Russia (1) — (1) — (1) — (1) — 14/9/00 —
San Marino (1) — (1) — (1) — (1) — 18/10/01 —
Serbia (1) — (1) — (1) — (1) — 22/3/05** —
Slovak Republic 27/5/92* 22/6/98 27/5/92* 22/6/98 27/5/92* 22/6/98 18/11/99 — 18/11/99 —
Slovenia 11/10/97 (2) 11/10/97 (3) 11/10/97 (2) 11/10/97 (4) 11/10/97 7/5/99
Spain 27/4/78 6/5/80 5/5/88 24/1/00 21/10/91 24/1/00 — — 23/10/00 —
Sweden 18/10/61 17/12/62 5/5/88 5/5/89 21/10/91 18/3/92 9/11/95 29/5/98 3/5/96 29/5/98
Switzerland 6/5/76 — — — — — — — — —
'The former Yugoslav Republic of Macedonia' 5/5/98 31/3/05 5/5/98 — 5/5/98 31/3/05 — — — —
Turkey 18/10/61 24/11/89 5/5/98 — 6/10/04 *** — — 6/10/04 —
Ukraine 2/5/96 (2) (3) (3) (2) (2) (2) — 7/5/99 21/12/06
United Kingdom 18/10/61 11/7/62 — — 21/10/91 *** — — 7/11/97 —
* Date of signature by the Czech and Slovak Federal Republic.
** Date of signature by the state union of Serbia and Montenegro.
*** State whose ratification is necessary for the entry into force of the protocol.

Changes introduced to the first 23 provisions of Part II of the Revised European Social Charter dealing with the legal regulations accepted by the European Social Charter are as follows:[4]

- An increase of the right to annual holiday pay from two to four weeks (Article 2 § 3);
- An obligation by first row Member States to eliminate risk in dangerous or unhealthy occupations, and when such risk is not able to be eliminated or reduced, to reduce the working hours or provide additional paid leave for workers engaged in such occupations (Article 2 § 4);
- An obligation for employers to ensure workers are informed by writing, as soon as it is possible, and not later than two months from commencing their employment, of the essential aspects of the contract or employment relationship (Article 2 § 6);
- An obligation that workers performing night work should benefit from measures which take into account the special nature of their work (Article 2 § 7);
- An obligation by Member States to formulate, implement and periodically review policy on matters of occupational safety and work hygiene, occupational health and working environment (Article 3 § 1);
- An obligation to promote the progressive development of occupational health services with preventative and advisory functions and a right to access such facilities for all workers (Article 3 § 4);
- A broadening of the scope of competency of stakeholders who under the European Social Charter take advantage of engaging in positions dealing with the improvement of safety and hygiene at work (Article 3 § 3) to include all categories regulated by Article 3 of the Revised European Social Charter;
- A minimum age requirement of 18 for admission of employment into occupations regarded as dangerous or unhealthy (Article 7 § 2);
- A change in the age level of young persons from 16 to 18 years of age, limiting their working hours in accordance with their needs of development and with their need for vocational training (Article 7 § 4);
- An increase in the annual paid leave of employees under the age of 18 from three to four weeks (Article 7 § 7);
- An increase in maternity leave from 12 to 14 weeks (Article 8 § 1);
- A broadening of the scope of protecting pregnant workers, including a revision making it unlawful to give a woman notice of dismissal during the period of time she notifies her employer that she is pregnant (Article 8 § 2);

---

(1) State having signed the European Social Charter (revised).
(2) State having ratified the European Social Charter (revised).
(3) State having accepted the rights (or certain of the rights) guaranteed by the Protocol by ratifying the European Social Charter (revised).
(4) State having accepted the collective complaints procedure by a declaration made in application of Article D para. 2 of Part IV of the European Social Charter (revised).

4. Explanatory note to the Revised European Social Charter, European Social Charter. Collected texts, *op. cit.*, pp. 159 and following.

- An obligation to regulate employment for pregnant women, women who have recently given birth, or who are nursing their infants during night hours (Article 8 § 4);
- A prohibition of employing pregnant women, women who have recently given birth and women who are nursing their infants in underground mining and all other work considered to be dangerous or unhealthy or arduous in nature and to take appropriate measures to protect the employment rights of these women (Article 8 § 5);
- An order to provide or promote as necessary special measures for the retraining and reintegration of the long-term unemployed in order to allow them the possibility of re-entering the working environment (Article 10 § 4);
- An obligation to prevent epidemic, endemic and other diseases, as well as accidents (Article 11 § 3);
- A change to the accepted minimum standards of social security placed on given countries. In place of the Convention No. 102 MOP dealing with the minimum social security norms, which were a point of reference for the supervisory process monitoring national reports dealing with how countries observe Article 12 § 2, was the introduction of the European Code of Social Security exemplar. The standards of this Code surpass those found in Convention No. 102 MOP expectations (Article 12 § 2);
- Expansion of the scope of the application of Article 15. The European Social Charter introduced legal guarantees that were to enable both mentally and physically disabled persons access to vocational training, rehabilitation and reintegration into the working and social environments. This provision, bestowed by the tone of the Revised European Social Charter, guarantees disabled persons regardless of their age, character or reason for their disability, the ability to utilize their rights for independent functioning, social integration and participation in community life;
- Social, legal and economic protection for single-parent families (Appendix to Article 16);
- Expansion of the scope of utilization of social and economic rights.

The above provision encompasses children and young persons. The European Social Charter grants this right to mothers and their children. The legal scope has been further developed. It guarantees children and young persons the right to health care, assistance, essential development and schooling. They are protected from negligence, violence and exploitation. It includes prescribed temporary or constant protection and special assistance for children and young persons of Member States who lack family support. They also have a right to free primary and secondary education with obligations put in place to encourage them to systematically utilize the above rights (Article 17).

A change in the circumstances required to establish the circle of family members of a migrant worker who can benefit from re-settling assistance in the host country in which the migrant worker is employed. The above rights are granted to a migrant worker and family members according to the definition under Appendix to Article 19 of the Revised European Social Charter, which include the spouse of the migrant worker (according to the European Social Charter only the wife of a migrant worker is granted such rights) and unmarried children of the migrant worker who are still minors. The Appendix to Article 19 § 6 of the European Social Charter stipulates the age limit of minors to be 21 in order to receive the above rights. In the Appendix to Article 19 § 6 of the Revised European Social Charter, no general age limit has been introduced. Determining such matters has been left to each individual Member State. It was decided that the above rights are allocated to children who are considered to be minors according to the laws and regulations operating in each Member State (Appendix to Article 19 § 6).

An addition of two extra paragraphs (11 and 12) to Article 19 that stipulate that each Member State has the responsibility and obligation to promote and facilitate migrant workers and members of their families with the teaching of the national language of the host state (§ 11) and to promote and facilitate the teaching of the migrant worker's mother tongue to his/her children (§ 12).

The new provisions introduced to the Revised European Social Charter (Articles 24–31) guarantee the protection of the following rights:

- The right of workers to protection of their employment durability (Article 24), in which the provision forbids employers to terminate employment without valid reasons and gives the right to those workers who have had their employment terminated without a valid reason to adequate compensation;
- The right of workers to protect their pecuniary claims in cases of insolvency of their employer (Article 25). Satisfying such claims, employees contracts or employment relationships should be done by guaranteeing institutions or such mechanism, which for example, can give precedence to workers in such implementation proceedings;
- The right of workers to dignity at work (Article 26) and protection from harassment, sexual harassment and mobs;
- The right of workers with family responsibilities to equal opportunities and equal treatment (Article 27). The above provision has obligated Member States to undertake the appropriate measures to enable such workers to enter and remain in employment and to re-enter employment after absence due to family responsibilities. Member States are also to take into account workers' needs in terms of conditions of employment and social security, to develop and promote child care services, to allow for the availability of parental leave and to ensure that family responsibilities shall not constitute a valid reason for termination of employment;
- The right of workers' representatives to protection in the undertaking of facilities to be accorded to them (Article 28);
- The right of workers and/or their representatives to information and consultation in collective redundancy procedures (Article 29);
- The right to protection against poverty and social exclusion (Article 30), which entails taking measures within the framework of an overall and coordinated approach to promote the effective access of persons or their families who live or risk living in a situation of poverty or social exclusion and the right to employment, housing, training, education, culture, social and medical assistance;

- The right to housing (Article 31). In order to abide by this provision, Member States have been obliged to take measures designed to promote access to housing of an adequate standard, to prevent and reduce homelessness, and to make the price of housing accessible to those without adequate resources.

The Revised European Social Charter is made up of six parts and an appendix. The first three parts of the Revised European Social Charter were structured according to the standards implemented in the construction of the European Social Charter. However, unlike the 'old' Charter, Part III of the Revised European Social Charter expanded its demands on Member States to increase their catalogue of strict social rights protection. Two new provisions (Article 7 and 20) were added to the existing seven and strictly binding provisions regulating the European Social Charter, of which those Member States interested in ratifying the Revised European Social Charter must choose to ratify at least six (Article A(1)(b)). As already mentioned, in fulfilling the chosen provisions according to Article A(1)(b) of the Revised European Social Charter, Member States are to consider themselves bound to those articles or numbered paragraphs of Part II that have been selected on the condition that the overall amount of articles or numbered provisions binding is not less than 16 articles or 63 paragraphs (Article A(1)(c)).

Among the Member States of the Council of Europe that have ratified the European Social Charter, only Greece and Turkey chose not to be bound by Article 5 and 6 of this Charter.

Parts III, IV, V and VI of the Revised European Social Charter, lettered A to O, resolve the following matters: supervision of the implementation of the undertakings contained in the Charter (Article C); collective complaints (Article D); non-discrimination for reasons specified within the Charter (Article E); exceptions for a Member State not to abide by the provisions of the Charter (Article F); the introduction of restrictions in the realization of rules and provisions specified in Part I as well as their effective implementation as specified by Part II (Article G); relations between the Charter and domestic law or international arrangements (Article H); means by which a Member State can fulfil its obligations specified in the Charter (Article J); signature, ratification and entry into force of the Charter (Article K); territorial application of the Charter (Article L); principles involved in denouncing the provisions regulated by the Charter (Article M); the legal status of the Appendix to the Charter (Article N); and notification procedure (Article O).

Until the Revised European Social Charter is universally ratified in Europe, two Charters remain in effect.[5] Compliance with the legal obligations set out by both Charters is monitored equally by the Committee of Social Rights. The decisions of the Committee are politically reviewed by the Governmental Committee. Their opinion is forwarded to the Committee of Ministers for resolution. The period between 1 July 1999 (the day of the Revised European Social Charter coming into force) and the day of

5. *See* A. Świątkowski, *Social Charter of the Council of Europe*, *op. cit.*

the Charter's ratification by the Member States who are associated with the European Social Charter is a transitional period.

The goal of the Council of Europe was to establish a uniform mechanism for the protection of social rights to which all of its Member States would adhere. This aspiration found its answer in the Revised European Social Charter. Member States voluntarily adopt the standards of the Revised European Social Charter. This Charter has been implemented with supervising structures identical to those introduced by the European Social Charter neither to discourage nor to induce Member States from firstly signing and then ratifying the Revised European Social Charter.

It is worth pointing out that the Committee of Social Rights carries out its substantive supervision over reports of countries. It is therefore obvious that during its decision-making by the Committee, the standards established by the Revised European Social Charter are also utilized in the supervisory process of abiding by the European Social Charter to the greatest degree possible. Despite the fact that the designers of the Revised European Social Charter tried to uphold neutrality in matters associated with the decision-making process of Member States in selecting which out of the two international treaties protecting social rights they would like to follow, the Council of Europe nonetheless has established substantive supervision over Member States abiding by the detailed provisions of the Charters where possible. This is a model guaranteeing a higher level of social rights protection. The Revised European Social Charter establishes these standards.

Article D of the Revised European Social Charter deals with collective complaints. It addresses those Member States that have ratified the Additional Protocol of 1995 and have adhered to the provisions set by the Revised European Social Charter. The power of Article D of the Revised European Social Charter obligates Member States to be subject to the supervisory standards established by the Revised European Social Charter according to the procedure outlined in the Additional Protocol.

Article D(1) of the Revised European Social Charter does not allow the above Member States to withdraw from the obligations set by the Additional Protocol of 1995 dealing with procedures of collective complaints simply because they have ratified the Revised European Social Charter. If, by ratifying the Revised European Social Charter, a Member State becomes bound to a higher level of social rights protection, a collective complaint made against this Member State for not complying with the obligations set up by the 'new' Charter should be diagnosed by the Additional Protocol of 1995 binding the Member State in matters dealing with collective complaints.

Those Member States that have ratified the Revised European Social Charter but are not bound by the provisions of the Additional Protocol of 1995 can give notice to the Secretary-General of the Council of Europe that it considers itself bound to the Additional Protocol of 1995 (Article D § 2) when filing its ratification documents or at any time thereafter. This provision intends to simplify the procedure for Member States that are connected to the European Social Charter, have ratified the Revised European Social Charter, and find reconnaissance in the provisions of the Additional Protocol of 1995. Accepting the obligations of the Additional Protocol is not done by separate mechanisms. A further ratification is usually not dealt with by a legislative body or president, but rather through notification by the authorized government.

Article E of the Revised European Social Charter prohibits discrimination based on grounds such as: race, colour, sex, language, religion, political or other opinion, national extraction or social origin, health, association with a national minority, and has in its parameters the protection of all social rights guaranteed by the Charter. It is modelled on Article 14 of the European Convention on Human Rights. The rulings of the Committee of Social Rights, presented in Part II of this book, illustrate the scope of social rights that protect against discrimination.

A temporary exemption from the fulfilment of obligations under the Revised European Social Charter may be granted only in wartime or during other public emergencies. Any derogation must be strictly related to the circumstances for which the exemption is requested. The Member State must be in unanimity with other obligations set up by international law. Any Member State seeking the right of derogation must inform the Secretary-General of the Council of Europe of its reasons for making such a request within a reasonable timeframe. The Secretary-General should also be informed about the planned period of derogation and the day from which the provisions of the Charter, once they have been accepted, will again be fully executed.

Article G § 1 of the Revised European Social Charter stipulates that no Member State has the right to restrict the effective realization of principles and laws outlined within the Charter. This Article, however, does introduce an exception to the rule. It states that laws accepted and abided by in a democratic society can introduce restrictions in the utilization of social rights guaranteed by the Charter when such laws are essential for the protection of rights and freedoms of others or essential for the protection of public order, national security, public health or good customs. Part II of this book looks at the decree of the Committee of Social Rights and how the above provision is interpreted. Article G § 2 determines boundaries by which Member States can utilize the above exception in the provision. The permitted restrictions to the rights and obligations set forth by this Charter shall not be applied for any purpose other than for which they have been prescribed (Article G § 2).

The Revised European Social Charter also sets minimal standards for social rights protection. The provisions of this Charter do not prejudice the provisions of domestic law or bilateral and multilateral international treaties, conventions or agreements, which guarantee an effective right protection (Article H).

Introducing the provisions of the Charter and its coming into force by Member States may be done so in a way chosen by the given Member State. Following in the footsteps of the undertakings in Article 7 of the Additional Protocol of 1988, Article I of the Revised European Social Charter states that the implementation of the Charter may take place due to domestic laws (laws or regulations) or by normative agreements (agreements with workers' organizations) with stakeholders. Implementation may also take place by combining the already mentioned alternative methods regulating such provisions as work rights and social security. Article I of the Revised European Social Charter allows for Member States the freedom to choose methods other than the abovementioned implementation stated by the Charter. It is important for the chosen methods in implementing the Charter to be effective.[6]

In the case of some of the provisions (Article 2 § 1-5 and 7, Article 7 § 4, 6, and 7, Article 10 § 1-3 and 5 as well as Article 21 and 22), compliance with the undertakings from these provisions by Member States shall be regarded as effective if the provisions of this Charter are applied to the great majority (80 per cent) of the workers concerned (Article I § 2).

Amendments to all six Parts of the Revised European Social Charter are shaped according to the procedure stipulated by Article 36 of the European Social Charter. Despite the fact that this last provision was never implemented due to its restrictive character, Article J of the Revised European Social Charter repeats the latter mechanism, so as not to inhibit the legal ability of either Member States or Council of Europe bodies to amend the Charter. Even though the procedure to amending both the Charters is the same, Article J of the Revised European Social Charter stipulates that amendments made to Part I and II of this Charter can be introduced solely for the broadening of rights guaranteed by the Charter.

The concept of 'amendments' does not only hide the possibility of changing the obligating provisions of Part I and II, but it also the suggests new protections of social rights. There are, however, no restrictions to introducing amendments to the remaining parts of the Charter. Member States that are party to the Charter and the Governmental Committee are able to propose amendments to the Revised European Social Charter. All proposals should be addressed to the Secretary-General of the Council of Europe. The Secretary-General passes on each proposal to each Member State that is a signatory to the Charter. Each proposal for an amendment is considered by the Governmental Committee, and when it is accepted it is then passed on to the Committee of Ministers. This procedure is not appropriated when proposals are made by the Governmental Committee.

The right to amend proposals considered by the Committee of Ministers to the Revised European Social Charter is given to all Member States, including those who have not ratified either the Revised European Social Charter or the European Social Charter, or have signed or ratified one of the mentioned international treaties. The Committee of Ministers has developed the principles for the participation of these countries in amendments made to the Revised European Social Charter.[7]

Decisions made by the Committee are preceded by consultations with the Parliamentary Assembly. After confirming the final text of the amendment, the Committee of Ministers presents it to Member States, party to the Revised European Social Charter, by way of acceptance. Each amendment to Part I and II comes into force into the country, party to the Charter who decides to accept it on the first day of the following month, a month after the day on which a third Member State, party to the Charter, informs the Secretary-General that it accepts the amendment. With

6. Explanatory note to the Revised European Social Charter, European Social Charter. Collected texts, *op. cit.*, p. 179.
7. *Ibid.*, p. 180.

reference to the fourth Member State and following states, amendments come into force on the first day of the following month, after one month has passed from the day on which a country that is a signatory to the Charter informs the Secretary-General of its acceptance.

Amendments to Part III, IV, V, and VI come into force on the first day of the following month, after one month has passed, in which all the countries party to the Charter, inform the Secretary-General of their acceptance.

Part VI of this Charter includes decisions based on earlier decisions made in other international treaties accepted by the Committee of Ministers. The Revised European Social Charter is open to be signed by all Member States of the Council of Europe. Like all other international treaties, it is subject to ratification, acceptance or approval. Ratification documents are filed with the Secretary-General of the Council of Europe. As already mentioned, the Charter came into force on 1 July 1999 after the first three Member States filed ratifying documents. It is not possible to indicate the first three Member States, as documents by five Member States were all filed on the same day, being 7 May 1999 (in alphabetical order): France, Italy, Norway, Romania and Slovenia. In reference to the subsequent countries which consented at a later date, the Charter came into force on the first day of the month following the expiration of one month passing after the day ratifying documents were filed, or when it was accepted or approved (Article K).

Similar to the European Social Charter, the Additional Protocol and their Amendments, the Revised European Social Charter also has a provision of territorial application (Article L). This provision states that the Charter shall apply to the metropolitan territory of each party. The provision authorizes each signatory to the Charter to declare by notification to the Secretary-General of the Council of Europe that the Charter shall extend to non-metropolitan territories. This declaration should be made during the same time as the signing or the filing of the ratifying documents for the Charter. The declarations of a country ratifying the Charter should specify the non-metropolitan territories for whose international relations it is responsible for or assumes international responsibility for, which will be bound by the Charter.

The Charter will be in force on the specified territories as declared, from the first day of the month following the period of one month after the date the Secretary-General of the Council of Europe accepts the notification. It is also possible to notify the Secretary-General of the Council of Europe of accepting any article or paragraph in respect of a non-metropolitan territory which it has not already accepted in respect of the specified territory, as binding. The provisions, which are accepted later, are regarded as the integral element of the initial declaration concerning a given non-metropolitan territory. They come into legal force from the first day of the month following the period of one month after the date the Secretary-General has accepted the notification (Article L).

No Member States that ratified the Revised European Social Charter have filed a declaration concerning non-metropolitan territories to be bound by the Charter,[8] even

8. *Ibid.*, pp. 116 and the following.

though some of these countries filed similar declarations during the ratification of the European Social Charter.

Article M regulates Denunciating Procedures of the Revised European Social Charter. This provision allows that each Member State and parties to the Charter can denounce the Charter no earlier than five years from the date the Charter came into force after being ratified by the given country. It is also possible to denounce the Charter at the end of any subsequent period of two years. In each case, an essential condition in the denouncing procedure is to give the Secretary-General of the Council of Europe six months notice. The Secretary-General informs all other parties accordingly about the denunciation of the Member State, party to the Charter. Each party that has ratified the Charter may denounce any article or paragraph of Part II, provided that the number of articles or paragraphs by which it is bound is 16 or 63 respectively. These must include at least six out of nine obligating provisions: Articles 1, 5, 6, 7, 12, 13, 19 and 20. Any Member State has the right to denounce the Charter or any of its articles or paragraphs of Part II, with respect to any territory to which the Charter is applicable, by virtue made in accordance wit Article L § 2.

The actions undertaken by Member States including the signing of the Charter, filing ratifying documents, accepting or approving the Charter, entering the Charter into force, declarations and amendments concerning the Charter, denunciations or amendment made to the Charter, or any other act dealing with the Charter, are made by the Secretary-General and notified to all Member States and to the Director-General of the International Labour Office. (Article O).

The Revised European Social Charter has an Appendix, in which some significant provisions are clarified.

CHAPTER 4 SUMMARY

The European Social Charters are unique international documents. These treaties uphold social rights to: Employment and work, education, health, housing, legal and social protection, social security and the ability of citizens and lawful residents of Member States to move about freely.

Other international treaties that are currently enforced in Europe regulate the issues and the detailed sections that are raised within the Charters in a complex fashion. Social protection is regulated by four treaties: The European Convention on Social Protection, the Protocol to this Convention, the European Code for Social Security, both the 'old' European Code for Social Security of 16 April 1964 and the 'new' Revised European Code for Social Security, the European Temporary Agreement concerning systems of social security in case of old age, disability and for those remaining and systems of social security, excluding the above. The scope of social and medical assistance is outlined in the European Convention on Social and Medical Assistance. Migrant workers' right are guaranteed under the European Convention on the Legal Status of Migrant Workers.[1] In the introduction to the Convention for the Protection of Human Rights and Fundamental Freedoms in 1950 is a guarantee to the right of association, regarded as particular entitlements in the category of social and civic rights.

Treaties and declarations concerning social rights include universal treaties of the UN, such as the Universal Declaration of Human Rights of 1948, the International Covenant on Economic, Social and Cultural Rights of 1966, international conventions passed intending to eliminate all forms of racial discrimination (1966); eliminate all forms of discrimination against women (1979); guarantee protection for children (1989); migrant workers and their families (1990) and numerous conventions on the UN agenda specializing in matters of employment protection and social protection, such as the International Labour Organization. The mentioned directives of the EU

1. The abovementioned international treaties were published in the following collection: *Podstawowe dokumenty Rady Europey z dziedziny polityki spolecznej, (Primary Sources of the Council of Europe in the Field of Social Politics)*, Wydawnictwo Naukowe Scholar (Publisher), Warszawa 1997, p. 83 and the following.

guarantee a uniform standard of some social rights in Member States of the EU. The European Social Rights Charters are therefore not the only international documents that legally declare and ensure protection on an international scale. The standards of social rights protection set in the abovementioned documents are interconnected.[2] The position of the Committee of Social Rights that evaluates the level of conformity of domestic labour law and social security to the demands set in the Charters conforms to the standards implemented by the EU directives and the ILO conventions.[3]

Among other international treaties that bind countries associated within the Council of Europe mentioned at the beginning of this Chapter, the European Social Charter can be characterized as complex and synthetic in terms of its legal regulations. The Charter is distinguished from other international documents by a special mode of supervision by Member States over the abiding of social rights guaranteed by this international treaty. It may be discussed whether social rights are efficiently protected. The European Social Charter is unique among the other binding treaties ratified by member countries of the Council of Europe. It contains a special apparatus for monitoring compliance with its social rights regulations. The European Convention on Social Rights Protection of 1950 protects political and civil rights. Under this Convention, the protection is afforded by a system of individual complaints filed with the European Tribunal of Human Rights.[4]

Under the Charter, individuals cannot appeal to an international tribunal if a domestic court did not rule on the social rights violation. This is a major flaw of the Charter.

Obviously, if the complaint system would contain some sort of mechanism for individuals and not just collective bodies, to file complaints with an international tribunal the social rights protection would be more efficiently achieved. However, redrafting the system to allow for such type of litigation would have required extensive changes to the existing systems due to the complex, dual protection (administrative supervision of the Committee of Social Rights[5] as well as quasi-judicial functions of this committee), afforded to social rights under the European Social Charter.

---

2. Prof. P. O'Higgins, *The Interaction of the ILO, the Council of Europe and European Union Labour Standards* (in:) Social and Labour Rights.... *Op. cit.*, p. 55 and following.
3. The above occurrence caused by two circumstances: the globalization of legal regulations in matters of labour laws, social security laws (*see* Lord Wederburn, *Common Law, Labour Law, Global Law (in:) Social and Labour Rights ... op. cit.*, p. 19 and following) as well as economic requirements that even out the standards of labour law protection – 'social dumping factor' (*see* E. Vogel-Polsky, 'What Future is there for a Social Europe Following the Strasbourg Summit?' *International Labour Journal*, vol. 19, 1990, p. 72).
4. Amongst social rights protected under the European Social Charter and the Revised European Social Charter only the right of employers to associate within trade unions is additionally protected by The European Convention on Social Rights Protection. *See* D. J. Harris, M. O'Boyle, C.Waribric, *Law of the European Convention on Human Rights*, Butterworth, London, Dublin, Edinburgh 1995, p. 424 and following; C. Ovey, R. White, Jacobs and White, *The European Convention on Human Rights*, 3rd ed., Oxford University Press, Oxford 2002, p. 294 and following.
5. A. Świątkowski, *Control Administrativo del Derecho de Trabajo* (Desde la perspective de la Carta Social Europea, Revista de Derecho Laboral y Seguridad Social, Agosto 2004 (16), pp. 1120 and following.

The European system of social rights protection has fostered interest among human rights organizations in South America. In 2004, an Inter-American Charter of Social Rights was drafted. This Charter was modelled on the Revised European Social Charter. This is worth mentioning because human rights are protected by a number of treaties and international documents such as the American Declaration of Human Rights and Duties (1948), the American Countries Organization Charter (1948), the American Convention on Human Rights (1969) and the Additional Protocol to the American Convention on Human Rights concerning Social, Economic and Cultural Rights (1988), also known as *Protocol of San Salvador.*[6]

6. International Human Rights, *op. cit.,* pp. 120 and following.

Part II Social Rights

CHAPTER 5 INTRODUCTION: CATEGORIES OF SOCIAL RIGHTS AND METHODS OF THEIR PROTECTION

Construction of social rights protection evolved in stages. The scope and the methods of social rights protection developed along the way. From the methodological point of view, it is important to present this process properly. Social rights guaranteed under the Charter apply to all individuals in their everyday lives. Depending on the criteria, they can be divided into a few categories. Looking at the various protected spheres, the following elements are: employment and work, social security, health, education, housing, and legal and social protection, as well as protection against discrimination and freedom of movement. Monographs looking at labour law in the context of social rights and their legal protection, social security, and social policy suggest a division based on the branch of law justifying protection. National labour law and social protection regulations, as well as social policies of Member States, parties to the Charter, are systematically analysed by experts of the Committee of Social Rights to the Council of Europe. For this reason, the most important part of the monograph concerning the legal protection of human rights was divided into chapters, explaining the social rights being protected under individual and collective labour law, as well as by widely seen rights of social protection.

Charters are international treaties subject to the interpretation formulated in the Vienna Convention of 1969 concerning the law of treaties. A theoretical interpretation of international treaties can be regarded part of their characteristics. The European Tribunal of Human Rights emphasized this in its ruling in *Wemhoff v. F.R.G.* 27.6.1968.[1] The Tribunal ordered an interpretation of Article 5 of the European Convention for the Protection of Human Rights, as well as Article 1 of the Protocol No. 1, two documents which guarantee the protection of freedom and personal security rights according to the requirements of the Convention, to enable the realization of the international treaty's intention to embrace basic legal and civil liberties. The Tribunal was against an interpretation of the European Convention for the Protection of Human

1. European Court of Human Rights (Series A), No.1, pp. 24–25.

Rights which would greatly limit the obligations taken on by Member States, which are bound by the provisions of this international treaty.[2] In the first decision made by the European Committee of Social Rights regarding a complaint filed by the International Commission of Jurists against Portugal (Complaint No. 1/1998), for violating Article 7 § 1 – a provision forbidding the employment of children under the age of 15 – the Committee emphasized that international treaties which are accepted as a form of protecting human rights should guarantee these rights not only theoretically but practically.[3] It ruled that Portuguese had not effectively introduced Article 7 § 1 into force, as 60 per cent of children who declared employment in agriculture were under the age of 15.[4] The Committee underlined that the effective adaptation of domestic labour laws to the standards set by the Charter cannot be reduced to orders and prohibitions. The complaint made against Portugal regarded the prohibition of employing children under the age of 15 years; thus, the Committee pointed to the role of labour inspections, which are meant to prevent such employment. The complaint heightened the necessity for dynamic interpretations of the Charter provisions.[5] The problem lies in the fact that Article 7 § 1 does not order the Committee (like some of the provisions in this treaty) to assess the level of change taking place in the employment of children and young persons. During the legal proceedings, evidence was presented showing Portugal employing children under the age of 15 in the following fields: agriculture 66 per cent, industry 7.1 per cent, and construction 2.7 per cent. Regardless of the percentages of employed children under the age of 15, what was of concern during these proceedings was Portugal's inability to abide by the provision forbidding the employment of children under this age. Portugal is guilty of not fulfilling obligations concerning effective governmental labour inspections that should ensure that private employers are obeying provisions forbidding the employment of children. The Committee of Social Rights deemed legitimate the accusation made against Portugal, since despite formal provisions, Portugal still permitted the illegal employment of children under the age of 15 years. The case of Portugal shows that a Member State may be regarded as acting against the provisions set by the Charter when the State does not adapt its domestic laws to the standards of the Charter and fails to enforce such provisions. Research conducted into whether a Member State's laws and practices are abiding by the standards imposed by the Charter is a characteristic supervisory mechanism over States who have voluntarily accepted the obligations set by the Charter. Pursuant to the terms of Article 7 § 1, the Member States are expected to organize governmental labour inspections in such a way as to eradicate the possibility of employing children under the age of 15 years. The experience of the International Labour Organization show that this is possible, with the proper political determination

---

2. D.J. Harris , M. O'Boyle, C. Warbrick, *op. cit.* p. 55 ff.
3. Complaint No.1/1998: International Commission of Jurists against Portugal. Documents, Human Rights Social Charter monographs – No.9, Council of Europe Publishing, Strasbourg 2000, s. 159.
4. *Ibid.*, pp. 154-155, p. 160.
5. Dissenting opinion of Mr. Alfredo Bruto Da Costa, Complaint No.1/1998, *op. cit.,* pp. 163–164.

and clear regulations that empower labour inspectors to force employers to abide by prohibitions and orders developed by State authorities.[6]

Depending on the types of obligations set forth by the Charter, the Committee of Social Rights expects expressed behaviour from Member States in adopting rules and applied practices set by Charter requirements; undertaking actions which deliver specified social assistance; and organizing social assistance accordingly with the demands set by the Charter. Member States are obligated, amongst other things, to organize the following services:

- A service which will assist all persons, including the disabled, to solve problems associated with occupational choice (Article 9 RESC);
- Technical and vocational training, as well as apprenticeships (Article 10 § 1 and 2 RESC);
- Social welfare services (Article 14 § 1 RESC);
- Guidance, education and vocational training for the disabled (Article 15 § 1 RESC).

The Committee of Social Rights assesses whether Member States have fulfilled their aforesaid obligations. Because some provisions require the fulfilment of the above obligations dependant upon specified needs (e.g. Article 9 and 10 RESC), the Committee researches whether a given situation in a Member State needs an organization of appropriate services; the Committee also assesses whether a Member State has fulfilled its obligations under the Charter. It may be the case that the Committee judges the situation differently from the Member State. Whether there is a need for particular services – such as, for example, employment guidance and/ or vocational training – the decision is made independently by a given Member State. The Committee of Social Rights assesses the reports filed by the Member States, as well as analyses the complaints made against a country where Charter obligations are allegedly not being met. The Committee makes decisions accordingly, as to whether the behaviour of a Member State complies with the standards set in the Charter. The Committee of Social Rights does not have the ability to take into consideration the economic situation or the financial capabilities of a Member State, which has undertaken to provide social services, as set out by the Charter. There is no provision in the Charter which takes into consideration the adequacy of a Member State's financial wealth when fulfilling set obligations under the Charter. No provision in the Charter excuses a Member State for not fulfilling the obligations it has undertaken voluntarily.

This point is illustrated by the following example of a committee decision. Article 3 § 3 of the Revised European Social Charter obligates Member States to provide enforcement and supervision regarding regulations requiring by hygienic and safe conditions for workers. The above provision requires the organization of governmental inspections to assess whether security and hygiene regulations are being met. In practical terms, this requires places of employment to be examined by

6. W. Von Richthofen, Labour Inspection. A Guide to the Profession, ILO, Geneva 2002, pp. 215, 221.

labour inspectors. During the 12th supervisory cycle regarding whether obligations set by the Charter were being met by Member States, the Committee declared a 10 cent decrease in inspections being properly carried out in places of employment in Austria. Due to organizational reasons, Cyprus also had a decrease in governmental work inspections. The largest decrease in work inspections was in Germany (from 710,000 in 1987 to 558,000 in 1990).[7] There was also a reduction in the number of plants being controlled by work inspectors (from 313,000 in 1987 to 250,000 in 1990). Already in the previous 11th supervisory cycle, the Committee had declared that the reason for the decrease in active governmental work inspections in Germany was the simultaneous increase in governmental inspections concerning environmental protection in eastern states of the Federal Republic of Germany.[8] The Committee of Social Rights ruled that new priorities of governmental labour inspections in Germany could not hinder the actions of German authorities obligated to monitor workplace security and hygiene obligations. The Committee required the FRG to produce in reports indicating actions undertaken in meeting the requirements specified in Article 3 § 3. The above three cases (Austria, Cyprus and Germany) illustrate the proposition that Member States must meet the obligations created by the Charter, regardless of the costs[9] or other tasks commissioned by Member States to be carried out by governmental labour inspection bodies.

Other types of obligations set by the Charter provisions commit Member States to undertake systematic actions. During the first supervisory cycle dealing with whether obligations of the European Social Charter were being met by Member States, such provisions were mentioned and were classified into the 'dynamic norms' category.[10] 'In the opinion of the Committee of Independent Experts, some Charter provisions are dynamic in their character: they place obligations to accept given behaviours in certain timeframes in order to gain desirable results'.[11] Member States that have obligated themselves to abide by the abovementioned provisions have the responsibility to inform the Committee of any changes which may take place during periods between supervisory cycles. The Committee of Independent Experts clearly expressed that such reports that are presented in statistical format, i.e., including only statistical information without reference to previous requirements of the supervisory cycle, cannot be regarded as fulfilling the required obligations accepted voluntarily by Member States when ratifying the so-called 'dynamic' provisions. The responsibility of the given Member States is to execute a presentation of the changes that have taken place between supervisory cycles, so that the Committee can assess whether progress has been made in adapting domestic laws concerned with the protection of social rights, with those of the changing standards accepted by the Charter. The Committee

7. Conclusions XII-2 1989-1990, Council of Europe Press, Strasbourg 1993, pp. 72–74.
8. Conclusions XI-2, Council of Europe Press, Strasbourg 1995, p. 63.
9. D. Harris, J. Darcy, *op. cit.*, pp. 26–27.
10. Conclusions 1969-70, Council of Europe Press, Strasbourg 1995, p. 9.
11. *Ibid.*

stipulated as examples, the following provisions of the European Social Charter, which are 'dynamic' in their character:

- Article 1 § 1, ordering Member States to achieve and maintain the most stable and highest level of employment with an aim to reach full employment;
- Article 2 § 1, obligating Member States to progressively reduce the working week to the extent that the increase in productivity and other relevant factors permit;
- Article 12 § 3, ordering Member States to raise progressively the system of social security;
- Article 18 § 2, ordering Member States to simplify existing formalities and to reduce or abolish administrative costs and other charges payable by foreign workers or their employers;
- Article 18 § 3, ordering Member States to liberate (individually or collectively) regulations governing the employment of foreign workers.

The European Social Charter and the Revised European Social Charter are international treaties, which seek to raise the level of social rights protection in Europe. The 'old' Charter, regarded as being dynamic in character, has been supplanted by the Revised European Social Charter, as well as having resolutions added by the 'new' Charter. Giving the provisions dynamic attributes are the unidentifiable standards, which are general in their clauses. These are provisions which obligate Member States to recognize workers' rights to 'decent' remuneration (Article 4 § 1); 'adequate' social and medical assistance (Article 13 § 1); 'required' advice and personal help (Article 13 § 3); and 'adequate' compensation or other 'adequate' relief when employment is terminated without a valid reason by the employer (Article 24(b)). These examples, which contain unclear terms, form a legal basis for the Committee of Social Rights to establish social rights protection standards. The difference between the level of protection in the provisions of the 'old' and 'new' Charters means that the Committee may impose the standards established by the 'new' Charter upon Member States who are under the obligations of a less rigorous 'old' Charter.

When determining the standards of social rights protection, the Committee of Social Rights assesses the reports of Member States and takes advantage of the experiences of various international institutions, under the authority of other international regulations, to supervise whether the Member States are abiding by the obligations. It was not without reason that Part I of this monograph referred to international conditions by which supervisory institutions monitoring Member States of the Council of Europe function. The Committee of Social Rights, for example, takes note of the experiences of the European Tribunal of Human Rights in matters of protecting workers' freedom of association with trade unions. The European Tribunal of Human Rights uses the experience of the Committee of Social Rights regarding matters of social rights protection. The Tribunal considered complaints made by workers who lost their employment for not joining a trade union, whilst the employer, according to the normative understanding (collective work agreement) made with a trade union, was obligated to employ only workers who were members of the given trade union.

The so-called 'closed shop' institution was a subject in the decisions handed down by the European Tribunal of Human Rights in the matters of *Young, James and Webster v United Kingdom,*[12] *Sigurdur A Sigurjónsson v Iceland,*[13] as well as *Sibson v United Kingdom.*[14] The provision of Article 11(1) of the European Convention on the Protection of Human Rights does not forbid Member States from tolerating collective bargaining agreements and other normative agreements which limit workers' rights – especially those that limit the right to work for people who do not belong to trade unions, particularly trade unions negotiating for the side of the employer or its organizations. In the decision of *Young, James and Webster,* the European Tribunal on Human Rights placed an obligation on Member States to guarantee legal protection for individuals against being taken advantage of by trade unions and their dominating position within the labour market.

The so-called negative aspect of the freedom to associate was analysed by the Tribunal in a matter not dealing with employees, but rather with those who run their own businesses (e.g., taxi drivers). The complainant raised the issue that Iceland issued licences allowing individuals to drive taxis by way of paid work, on the condition that drivers join a given workers' association (*Frami*) for taxi drivers. In the decision handed down in the matter of *Sigurjónsson*, the European Court of Justice took the view of the Committee of Independent Experts, which asserted that the negative right to associate is protected by Article 5, even if this right was not explicitly stated in the provision. The Committee of Independent Experts criticized the practice of the 'closed shop' in some European countries (Finland, Great Britain, Iceland, Sweden), claiming it to be inconsistent with the concept of freedom of association.[15] The ILO Committee on Freedom of Association claims membership in a trade union as a condition of employment is against convention No. 87 concerning freedom of association.

The negative law of membership in an organization representing work interests is also applicable to employers. In the decision of the *Gustafsson v Sweden,*[16] the European Tribunal for Human Rights stated that an employer does not have an obligation to join an employers' organization for bargaining purposes regarding work conditions and workers' wages, or to hold collective agreements with trade unions. The specificity of the Nordic model concerning work relations is based upon social dialogue with stakeholders. The Nordic model also negotiates work and wage conditions in collective labour agreements through trade unions and employer organizations.[17] In a decision handed down on 31 March 2003, collective complaint No. 12/2002,

---

12. Decision from 13 August 1981, Series A. No. 44; (1981) 4 EHRR 38.
13. Decision from 30 June 1993, Series A No.264-A; (1993) 16 EHRR 462.
14. Decision from 20 April 1993, Series A No.258-A (1994) 17 EHRR 193.
15. M. A. Nowicki, *Europejska Konwencja Praw Człowieka. Wybór Orzecznictwa*, Publisher C. H. Beck, Warszawa 1998, pp. 365-366 (translation: 'European Convention on Human Rights. Selecting Rulings').
16. Decided on 25 April 1996, (1996) 22 EHRR 409.
17. N. Bruun, B. Flodgren, M. Halvorsen, H. Hydén, R. Nielsen, The Nordic Labour Relations Model. Labour Law and Trade Unions in the Nordic Countries – Today and Tomorrow, Dartmouth, Aldershot, Brookfield USA, Hong Kong, Singapore, Sydney 1992, pp. 43 and following.

Confederation of Swedish Enterprise v Sweden, the Committee of Social Rights ruled the 'closed shop' clause is in contradiction with the individual rights (of both employees and employers) not to join organizations, which are formed to represent occupational, economic and social interests of employees and employers. Less defined are international conditional standards protecting other social rights guaranteed by the Charter. The abovementioned comments concerning protecting the rights to membership or disassociation with organizations representing employer and employee interests, suggest an interdependency between international organizations setting the standards of such protection and with the Member States abiding those standards. The Committee of Social Rights daily carries out supervisory processes monitoring Member States, even those who are not part of the European Union, to see whether the standards set by the European Union directives are being followed.

The Committee of Social Rights, however, does not automatically employ international standards when supervising Member States. Interpreting certain provisions whilst supervising Member States, it takes into consideration economic and social factors. The Committee proceeds according to classic Aristotelian principles, which criticize the identical treatment of all subjects functioning within a given society. Currently, countries are joining the Council of Europe, having decided to abide by the international treaties chosen for them by their governments. Accepting Article 4 § 1 or Article 23 § 1(a) as a measuring stick in the supervisory process (provisions which allocate workers the right to decent remuneration, and allocate adequate resources for elderly persons to enable them to lead a decent life and be active in public, social and cultural life) – provisions which deduce automatic equality ignoring the varying standards of living amongst Member States – means the Committee of Social Rights would be forced to establish uniform standards of wages and welfare benefits across Europe. This is not possible due to the vast range of living standards amongst workers and their families. A similar issue is evident when applying standards of protection to cases where employment is terminated without a valid reason by an employer (Article 24(b) RESC), as well as in cases involving the right of workers to the protection of their claims in the event of insolvency of their employer (Article 25 RESC). The Committee of Social Rights interprets the implied terms within the provisions, allocating them a definition according to the particular specificity of a given Member State and its labour market, when considering the appropriate standard of work protection. Conducting itself in this way, it does not lose sight of the necessity of establishing objective measures. When examining whether Member States are abiding by the provisions in the Charter, the most important rule is to satisfy the needs of workers and their families, measured objectively by the 'just' and 'adequate' indicator of remuneration, established under Article 4 § 1 RESC, in comparison to the average paid remuneration in a given country. Examining the level of damages paid out in cases of illegal termination of a work agreement by an employer (Article 24(b) RESC), debating Member States' fulfilment of the obligation to satisfy wage claims filed due to the insolvency of employers (Article 25 RESC), the Committee of Social Rights looked at the period of time required to calculate the level of compensation or guaranteed remuneration. In such cases, using indicators that are objective and applicable to all Member

State does not lead to the application of mechanized rules of equality, due to the individual nature of cases (labour law and social security regulations) existing within Member States.

Some provisions leave a margin of liberty for Member States that are obligated by them. Interpreting those provisions that order particular undertakings such as: promoting voluntary negotiations between stakeholders (Article 6 § 2 RESC), ensuring the right to vocational guidance (Article 9 RESC), vocational training (Article 10 § 1 RESC), or training for adults when it is 'necessary and proper' or when such necessities eventuate (Article 10 § 3 RESC), then the Committee of Social Rights depends upon the assessment of particular state authorities. It is these assessments which are the deciding factor regarding the necessity to fulfil obligations set by the abovementioned provisions. This is because the Committee does not construct frameworks of rights protection appropriate to each country. It rather only assesses the frameworks provided by Member States and either considers them as sufficient, unnecessary, unsuitable or insufficient. Accepting such criteria during the supervisory process, which monitors whether obligations are being followed, and where the Charter allows room for liberal assessment by Member States, does not inhibit the responsibility of the Committee to assess social political goals, especially when a given Member State is stalling in its acceptance of undertaking obligations, which will support voluntary negotiations and access to guidance and vocational training. The Committee carries out observations concerning collective bargaining situations, access to and usage of employment agencies and vocational training. It is under an obligation to determine whether the Member States are assessing correctly the existence or the lack of legal mechanisms supporting social dialogue, the level of satisfactory vocational guidance services, and the level of development of vocational training.

By employing 'dynamic' methods made available by the provisions of the Charter, the Committee of Social Rights utilizes the accomplishments of the other abovementioned international organizations, within the confines of the standards of social rights protection, as well as institutions ensuring the protection of human rights established by the Council of Europe, whose two categories (political and civic as well as social and economic) are included in international treaties. Where provisions of the Charter allow, the Committee seeks that Member States take advantage of the margin of liberty granted in the social rights protection process. In its supervisory and quasi-judicial role, the Committee also formally ensures human rights protection according to domestic laws codified within a given country, to its practices and applications. The above approach to the issues at hand, while obeying social rights, illustrates arguments dedicated to protecting rights, which are regulated by individual and collective work rights provisions, as well as by a widely interpreted scope of social security rights.

CHAPTER 6 REGULATION OF SOCIAL RIGHTS THROUGH INDIVIDUAL LABOUR LAW REGULATIONS

6.1. The Right to Work (Article 1)

Article 1, ensuring the right to work, belongs to the category of strict obligatory Charter provisions. Despite the popular definition of 'the right to work', this provision does not force Member States to provide those seeking employment or wanting employment, with work. Those Member States that have obligated themselves to abide by this provision are required to fulfil the demands set in three paragraphs of Article 1. Article 1, setting the principles of the right to work, regulates most importantly the legal measures which can implement the above principles. Implementing the above principles are designed for:

- Full employment (§ 1);
- The ability to freely enter employment (§ 2);
- Free employment services (§ 3);
- And vocational guidance, training and rehabilitation (§ 4).

6.1.1. Full Employment (Article 1 § 1)

Countries that have ratified this provision are obligated to accept and maintain the highest and most stable level of employment possible, with a view to the attainment of full employment. Article 1 is considered by legal practitioners to be part of the category of 'dynamic' provisions. Ratifying this provision means those Member States that obligated themselves to attain a level of full employment are bound to present information regarding the level of unemployment. The Committee of Social Rights first assesses the level of unemployment, then during the following supervisory cycles, it ascertains whether unemployment levels have increased or decreased compared to the levels given at previous supervisory cycles. Member States that have ratified Article 1 § 1 are not permitted to simply present reports with statistical information concerning labour market issues. To a certain degree, with the exception of the first report, which forms an assessment basis for the following reports dealing with whether obligations to the provision are being followed, the following reports are statistical in their nature. The reports present a level of unemployment in following supervisory cycles. Comparing each scale of unemployment to the next, directly following each other in supervisory cycles, the Committee of Social Rights may attribute the provision with a dynamic character. However, it was within the first supervisory cycle that the Committee placed an obligation on Member States to present changes that have occurred on the labour market, and to compare those changes with the national report given during the previous supervisory council.[1] The reports submitted by Member States should be prepared according to the form accepted by the Committee of Ministers during its 689th sitting on 24 November 1999 and modified during its 737th sitting on 17 January 2001.[2]

Member States are obligated to answer questions posed by the Committee of Social Rights. In assessing the actions undertaken by Member States to achieve the goals of reaching full employment, questions are asked regarding the realization of social political issues in order to achieve and maintain full employment, or at least to reduce the level of unemployment. Member States have the responsibility to present social programmes initiated and offered that are conducted with the view of stabilizing the level of employment. Those programmes undertaken and continued during the period of a supervisory cycle should be presented on a tendency basis of employment policies occurring in the last five years, particularly taking into consideration active (employment programmes, research into occupation, education) and passive (unemployment benefits) techniques counteracting unemployment. The Committee of Social Rights turns to Member States to incorporate active techniques to fight against unemployment, addressing those social groups particularly at risk of losing their jobs, or those social categories which have great difficulties in attaining a first job or are trying to re-enter the workforce: young people aged 15–24 years, women, older persons, those seeking employment for more than one year, the disabled, immigrants, and ethnic minority members. In order to conduct comparisons of the labour markets between Member States, statistical information as well as definitions must be presented in the national reports in written format.[3] These national reports should include the number of persons who are encompassed by these programmes, as well as an introductory assessment concerning the effectiveness of these programmes. The presentation of these programmes should also include details which illustrate the trends accordingly to the national, regional and local labour markets, within all trade sectors,[4] so that the Committee of Social Rights may assess the details concerning the number of people in active occupation, employed (in full-time employment based on a work agreement

1. Conclusions I, p. 9.
2. Form for the reports submitted in pursuance of the European Social Charter, European Social Charter. Collected texts, *op. cit.*, p. 241 and following.
3. Conclusions XIV-1, vol. 1, pp. 34–35.
4. In the case of Cyprus, the Committee in its second supervisory cycle was interested in the scale of hidden employment in the agricultural sector. Conclusions II, p. 179.

irrespective of a time frame, based on temporary work agreements, or in part-time employment), or operating their own businesses. The unemployment numbers should be presented with the same number of details, including periods of unemployment and its distribution, as well as the amount and types of positions vacant. All answers relating to the abovementioned questions should enable the Committee of Social Rights to formulate an opinion regarding the social political stance undertaken by a given Member State during a supervisory cycle. In particular, the subject of the Committee's assessment is the action taken by Member States, which should be forming cohesive employment measures. These actions should be well planned, and systematically and consistently carried out.

In the case of Denmark, for example, the Committee was unable to judge whether Denmark was in compliance with the provisions stipulated under Article 1 § 1, even though the information presented in the second report indicated an unusual reduction in an already low unemployment level. This was due to a lack of information presented in the report, which would enable the Committee to conclude that the Denmark was implementing previously planned employment measures.[5] Similar views were held during the same supervisory cycle concerning Great Britain's report. This country did not present the Committee with sufficient information to enable it to form an opinion in matters concerning employment policies in Northern Ireland and short-term goals relating to social measures of fighting against unemployment. The Committee was able to hand down a decision indicating its negative position towards Great Britain's stance and declared that it was unable to decide whether the country fulfilled its obligations according to Article 1 § 1. The Committee strives to find whether Member States have drawn up short-term, mid-term and long-term plans counteracting unemployment. It pays close attention to structural or economic types of unemployment,[6] the standard of unemployment within regions of particular countries,[7] necessary undertakings in reducing the scale of unemployment amongst women and young persons between the ages of 20–29 years of age,[8] and amongst older persons. It considers that particular measures should be taken in order to improve employment chances for women, young and older persons, as their loss of employment is at a higher risk.[9] It also pays close attention to measures undertaken by Member States to even out the regional disproportions of unemployment levels.[10] In principle, the Committee does not limit itself to the information concerning the reduction of unemployment presented to it by Member States.[11] It views that reducing the scale of unemployment alone is not a sufficient factor in attaining the goal of full

5. Conclusions II, 1971, Council of Europe Press, Strasbourg 1995, p. 3.
6. Conclusions IV 1975, Council of Europe Press, Strasbourg 1995, p. 5 (Sweden).
7. In the case of Great Britain – North England, Scotland, North Ireland, Conclusions IV, *op. cit.,* p. 5.
8. Austria, Conclusions IV, *op. cit.,* p. 3.
9. Conclusions IV, *op. cit.,* p. XIV.
10. Denmark, Conclusions IV, *op. cit.*, p. 4.
11. In its 4th supervisory cycle, the Committee decided based on the information provided by Cyprus, without any additional information, that the country did not fulfil its obligations under Article 1 § 2 of the Charter, Conclusions IV, *op. cit.*, p. 3.

employment, as 5 per cent of those in the active age group who are able and willing to work remain without jobs.[12]

This does not indicate however, that the Committee simply looks to unemployment percentage rates. As mentioned earlier, Article 1 § 1 is a 'dynamic' norm. First of all, the Committee looks to actions taken by Member States in reducing the level of unemployment. If Member States can indicate in their report to the Committee that measures are planned and are being implemented to rectify the issue of a sudden rise in unemployment during a supervisory cycle, the Committee will not automatically rule negatively, claiming obligations were not met under Article 1 § 2.[13] If the level of unemployment is retained at the same level for a period of time longer than one year, the Committee will view this as a dangerous levitation, meaning the constant number of unemployed increases the risk of marginalization leading to a negative occurrence of social exclusion. The Committee, in its general report concluding the first part of the 14th supervisory cycle, stated that in the reporting period (1995-1996), there were 22–23 million unemployed persons within Member States. Unemployment had different levels of intensity in different Member States. It increased in Germany and France and decreased in Denmark, Finland, the Netherlands, and Great Britain. There was a significant difference in unemployment rates, starting from 2–6 per cent in Austria, Iceland, Norway, and reaching over 20 per cent in Cyprus and Malta and 22 per cent in Spain. Progress in fighting against long-term unemployment has been achieved, even though in some states (Belgium, Greece, Ireland, Italy, Portugal, and Spain), over half of the unemployed remain without job for longer than a year.[14] The unemployment rate remains high amongst women (Cyprus, Finland, and Greece)[15] and migrant workers (Austria).[16] Within the following decade, the situation has not improved much. In fact, Austria saw a 17.6 per cent increase in the unemployment rate of migrant workers.

In accordance with stable practices, the Committee of Social Rights withheld from indicating to Member States following supervisory cycles which means should be undertaken in order to reach the goals of achieving full employment, meaning also fulfilling obligations in accordance with Article 1 § 1. The Committee is of the opinion that making any sort of suggestions concerning methods to be incorporated to achieve unemployment reduction and to reach a standard of full employment, would be an imposition on the sovereignty of a given Member State. During the drafting of the European Social Charter in 1956, propositions were made to edit Article § 1, in which there would be guidelines for the Member States regarding measures to be undertaken in order to reach the goals of provisions obligations. These measures were supposed to encompass the establishing of employment policies, the preparation of a separate national budget for employment matters, passing long-term employment programmes and counteracting unemployment, and planning public sector work.[17] For the

12. Introduction of the Committee to the third supervisory cycle. Conclusions III, p. 3.
13. *Ibid.*
14. Conclusions, XIV, vol.1, p. 33.
15. *Ibid.*, pp. 147, 203, 346.
16. *Ibid.*, p. 65.
17. D. Harris, J. Darcy, *op. cit.*, p. 42, footnote 41.

abovementioned reason, these measures were never implemented during the crafting, for fear of interfering with the internal matters of Member States. In an introduction of a report drawn up during the first supervisory cycle, the Committee stated that all policies of economic growth which tend to keep the unemployment rate at a stable level, will be considered a violation of the abovementioned regulation of the Charter.[18] This opinion was also repeated in the XIV supervisory cycle report. The Committee concluded that coexistence of a high economic growth index and a significant and stable unemployment rate in periods of mid- and long-term economic growth is a phenomenon that cannot be accepted legally under Article 1 § 1.[19] According to the Committee, the analysed regulation of Article 1 § 1 obliges Member States to thoughtfully conduct themselves by not imposing on them the goal of a 0 per cent unemployment rate. Supervising Member States to abide this regulation, the Committee analyses social programmes and grants funds for this purpose as well as for accomplished results.

6.1.2. Freedom of Work (Article 1 § 2)

The Charter has introduced a provision which ensures effective protection of workers' rights to earn a living in an occupation freely entered upon. During its first supervisory cycle the Committee of Social Rights became convinced that Article 1 § 2 is strictly associated with the prohibition of forced employment, as well as with removing any form of employment discrimination.[20] This view of the Committee was upheld during the second and third supervisory cycles.[21]

6.1.2.1 Prohibition of Forced Labour

In the 1st supervisory cycle, the Committee already had doubts when reviewing the reports presented by Member States of the International Labour Organization (ILO), as to whether British, Danish, Norwegian and Swedish provisions regarding the employment of seamen – allowing for the utilization of forced measures to be undertaken against members of crews who refused to carry out certain tasks or refused to return to their ships – were contradictory to the principle of freedom of work. In the second supervisory cycle the Committee came to the conclusion that provisions contradicting the principle of freedom of work were also applicable in Iceland and the Federal Republic of Germany. In the third supervisory cycle the Committee generalized its previous views and presented a definition of forced labour. Forced labour is defined as labour conducted by a worker who has been forced to undertake it against his free will, carrying it out without first voluntarily signing an agreement. Forced labour is also found when work has been voluntarily accepted, but has continued against the will of

18. Conclusions I, *op. cit.*, p. 14.
19. Addendum to Conclusions XV-2 (Slovakia), European Social Charter, Council of Europe Publishing, Strasbourg 2001, p. 133.
20. Conclusions I, *op. cit.*, p. 15.
21. Conclusions II, *op. cit.*, pp. 4–5; Conclusions III, p. 5.

the worker who is unable, in legal terms, to terminate it.[22] Accepting the above basis for the definition of forced labour, the Committee analysed further such instances included in the presented reports of Member States. It used national reports presented according to the guidelines, in which a question was formulated concerning any forms of forced or compulsory labour as defined by No. 29 ILO of 10 June 1930.[23] The Committee used the definition of forced or compulsory labour as defined by Article 2(1) of the above convention. For the purpose of this convention the term 'forced or compulsory labour' was defined as any work or services expected from a given individual under threat or from an individual who has not accepted the work voluntarily (Article 2(1)). The Convention No. 29 ILO excludes from the scope of forced and compulsory labour:

- Any form of work or services expected according to national regulations concerning compulsory military service, of a pure military character;
- Any form of work or services encroaching into the normal scope of civic responsibilities in an independent country;
- Any form of work or services, obligating those under court order, carried out under the supervision or control of public authorities, and not for the favour of physical persons, companies or associations;
- Any form of work or services required in instances of necessity, meaning in case of war, disasters or threats of a disaster such as: fire, floods, famine, earthquakes, sudden epidemics and cattle diseases, plagues of animals, insects or harmful vegetation parasites or any other such circumstances which may endanger or create a possibility of endangering the lives or normal living conditions for all or certain parts of the population;
- Minor rural work, i.e., work carried out directly for the interest of a local community by its members, work, which may be considered, due to its character as normal civic responsibility resting on the members of the local community, on the condition that the community or its representatives will have the right to comment on the work's purpose.

Accepting the standards of the protection of work rights set by the convention No. 29 ILO, the Committee of Social Rights analysed the following instances in reports presented by the Member States and regarded them as contravening obligations set by Article 1 § 2:

- Cases of forced slave labour;[24]

22. Conclusions III, p. 5.
23. Conventions and recommendations ... *op. cit.,* pp. 112 and the following.
24. No reports presented by Member States have given any indication regarding such labour existing in Europe. In the opinion of D. Harris and J. Darcy, *op. cit.,* 44, case 57 – there was a case exposing slave labour in reports prepared by Dutch authorities, which discussed such a situation in the Dutch Antilles. The Committee's analysis of reports during the conclusion of the tenth supervisory cycle did not conclude that slave labour was present. Conclusions X-1, p. 36.

- The possibility of penalty sanctions for people who remain without resources needed for living;[25]
- Allocating unemployment benefits on the condition employment is actively being sought;[26]
- Penalty sanctions for members of crews of merchant ships or fishing vessels in cases where work discipline is violated for:
- a) The infringement of work responsibilities, which threaten the safety of the vessel but do not threaten the life or the health of the persons found on the vessel;[27]
- b) Abandonment of a work post or refusing to carry out a work task;[28]
- c) Refusal to report to work,[29] particularly due to strike action,[30] or the refusal of employees taking part in legal strike action to assume basic services;[31]
- Placing penalty sanctions on government employees who abandon work posts in an attempt to disorganize the functioning of government offices;[32]
- The responsibility of the employees to gain the approval of a director of an administrative or regional employment body to terminate a work agreement;[33]
- Establishing an inability to resign from duty for professional soldiers before reaching the national retirement age[34] or before completing national service requirements;[35]
- Prolonging compulsory military service for those who refuse it. For example, persons who refuse to serve the compulsory 12 months military service in Greece are under the obligation to undertake alternative employment of 30 months advised by governmental administration.[36] In the decision handed down in the matter of *Quaker Council for European Affairs v Greece*,[37] the Committee of Social Rights declared that the alternative form of employment specified for a period significantly longer than the military service is a violation of the provision of Article 2 § 1. The decision of the Committee was adopted by the Resolution of the Committee of Ministers on 6 March 2002, claiming Greece was in breach of Article 2 § 1, which prohibits forced labour.[38] The Committee claims increasing twofold the period of

25. Conclusions XIII-1, pp. 45–46 (Denmark).
26. Conclusions XIV-1, p. 293 (Germany).
27. Conclusions XIII-4, p. 330; Conclusions XIV01, p. 104; Conclusions XV-1, s.71–72 (Belgium), p. 237 (France), pp. 294–295 (Greece).
28. Conclusions XV-1, p. 356 (Italy). Also includes aviation employees Conclusions XIV-1, pp. 467, 650 (Portugal), Conclusions XIII-3, pp. 74–75 (Spain).
29. Conclusions XIII-3, p. 238; Conclusions XIV-1, p. 762; Conclusions XV-1, s. 592 (Turkey).
30. Conclusions XV-1, p. 626 (Great Britain).
31. Conclusions XIV-1, p. ; Conclusions XV-1, p. 356 (Italy).
32. Conclusions XIV-1, pp. 649–650 (Portugal).
33. Conclusions X1, p. 37; XIII-3, p. 71; Addendum to Conclusions XV-1, s.83 (The Netherlands).
34. Conclusions XIV-1, p. 409 (Ireland).
35. Conclusions XIII-3, p. 64, Case of Greece, allowing for soldiers to resign from professional military service upon the completion of specialist courses after 25 years.
36. Conclusions XVII-1, p. 239.
37. Complaint No. 8/2000.
38. ResChS (2003) 3 *See* European Social Charter. Collected texts, *op. cit.*, p. 499.

the alternative employment to that of the compulsory military service is against the right to freely choose one's employment pursuant to Article 2 § 1;[39]
– Prohibiting private entrepreneurs from being able to employ prisoners without prior consent from interested employees. Prisoners' labour should be regulated by the state. Governmental employers may employ prisoners. Private employers may employ prisoners, after receiving consent, on the same grounds as employing other workers.[40]

The Committee of Social Rights analyses cases in which states have invoked the provisions allowing for the temporary exclusion from the provision of freedom to choose employment. This primarily occurs in circumstances of threat, where legislating statutes allow authorities to introduce the obligation to work, as well as the prohibition of protest actions, specifically, the organization of strikes.[41] The Committee's stance concerning the conformity or nonconformity of such provisions with Article 1 § 2 is dependent upon the reasons for the exclusion from the provision in question. In the case of Cyprus, the Committee came to the conclusion that the constructions which guarantee the freedom to work are too general. However, procedural guarantees – such as the ability to appeal against legislation which repeals freedom of work, placing an obligation on citizens to carry out work in particular instances – are not sufficient, as they do not guarantee protection for citizens against administrative orders to undertake employment. The definition incorporated in the Constitution of Cyprus, which prohibited obligations on citizens to undertake employment with the exception of circumstances related to the endangering of life and health of the citizens, was termed as too general, and seen as a possible opening for the suspension the right to freedom of work. The crucial element is the definition of 'endangerment', which would justify the temporary suspension of obligations to abide by the freedom to choose employment provision. Assessing the case of Finland, which defined its terms in greater detail than Cyprus, referring to extraordinary circumstances which would allow for the temporary suspension of Article 1 § 2, the Committee concluded that the existing Finnish provisions on extraordinary circumstances were deemed to be in accordance with Article 1 § 2. These provisions were seen to be detailed enough in their definition of circumstances regarded as extraordinary: war, life threatening disaster, as well as a great threat to the lives and the economy of the country. The seriousness of the above-mentioned threats, although the last appears to be lacking in precision, are all meant to prevent the state from controlling the circumstances of the suspension of the Article. The Committee of Social Rights was convinced by these arguments; however, it did obligate Finland to present detailed information regarding the last type of extraordinary circumstance needed to suspend the Article, and it also recommended that every such instance be reported to the Council of Europe.[42]

39. Conclusions XVII-1, p. 239 (Greece).
40. Digest of the case law of the ECSR, European Social Charter, Strasbourg 2004, p. 10.
41. Case of Cyprus. Conclusions XIII-3, pp. 59–60.
42. Conclusions XIV-1, pp. 209–210.

6.1.2.2. Eliminating Forms of Discrimination in Employment

The Charter accepts the concept of protection against discrimination in the field of employing or carrying out employment, according to Convention No. 111 ILO, implemented on 4 June 1958.[43] According to Article 2 of the convention in question, Member States are obliged to establish and undertake policies dealing with support for equal chances and treatment in the field of employing or carrying out employment in an attempt to eliminate any form of discrimination. Discrimination was defined by the abovementioned convention as distinction or exclusion based on race, skin colour, sex, religion, political views, or national or social origin that thwarts or impedes upon equal opportunity or treatment in the field of employing or carrying out employment (Article 1(1)(a)). A Member State that allows for discrimination in the field of employing or carrying out employment does not guarantee sufficient protection of workers' rights to undertake freely chosen employment to support a standard of living. In the preamble to the European Social Charter of 1961, the law was passed to utilize social rights protected by the Charter without any discrimination on the basis of race, skin colour, sex, religion, political views, or national or social origin. Not fulfilling the principles of equal treatment and equal opportunity in the field of employing is regarded as a contravention of the obligations set under Article 1 § 2. The Committee of Social Rights anal national reports paid particular attention to legal and practical regulations, which lead to discrimination against people who were applying for employment as well as workers, according to differentiating criteria that is legally prohibited. Amongst the abovementioned prohibited circumstances differentiating workers, the Committee paid close attention to gender and a worker's family situation as well as those of work candidates. Based on Article 1 § 2, the Committee ensured the protection of workers' rights, particularly those employed in private and public sectors. For example, the Committee declared a violation of freedom of employment rights in Ireland, where married women had been prevented from taking positions in civil service,[44] and in Great Britain, where men had been disallowed from working as midwives.[45] However, the Committee did accept restrictions in the employment of women, including a total ban of women employed in hard physical labour, as well as in combat positions within the military service.[46] It emphasized the need for regulations protecting against discrimination within the workplace based on gender, in both the private and public sectors.[47] The Committee imposed the obligation on Member States to undertake efforts to efficiently execute regulations of equal treatment and regulations forbidding discrimination within the workplace. It did not indicate a method for the abovementioned propositions to be carried out; however, the Committee required Member States to undertake all possible measures in order to ensure equal opportunity

43. Conventions and suggestions ... *op. cit.*, pp. 552 and following.
44. Conclusions I, p. 166.
45. Conclusions VIII, p. 33, Conclusions IX-1, p. 24.
46. Conclusions II, p. 4 (Sweden).
47. Conclusions XIII-5, p. 254.

in the workplace and equal treatment of men and women workers.[48] According to the Committee, Article 1 § 2 did not create a sufficient legal basis to commence litigation against employers not abiding by regulations regarding equal treatment of men and women within the workplace, or prohibiting discrimination against workers according to gender. The Committee did, however, empower national authorities to analyse collective agreements and other normative agreements in order to determine whether they consist of any clauses discriminating against workers according to prohibited criteria, especially gender.[49]

The Committee of Social Rights prioritized the regulation of discrimination against workers based on gender. It took great effort to analyse issues concerning equal treatment of women's access to employment, their relations within the workplace and their right to partake in vocational training.[50] After discovering significant disproportions in the utility of vocational training options, the Committee appealed for the equalization of the access to vocational training by women, which was considered to be a necessary precondition to equal treatment of men and women in accessing employment and within the workplace. In order for this to be achieved, the Committee paid heed to the idea of preferential treatment of women within the workplace.[51] Utilizing the principles of *acqui communitaire,* the Committee found preferential treatment of women within the workplace to be allowable, but not obligatory under Article 1 § 2.[52] The Committee did not change its conservative approach to the abovementioned issue, even though the supervisory process indicated no changes were being implemented. For example, the Committee permitted the Greek police force to limit the number of women allowed into police school academies to 20 per cent, and to higher-ranked officers' academies to15 per cent.[53] The Committee was, however, interested in the practical aspects as well as the processes involved in the protection of rights of workers based on gender, taking into consideration a balance of evidential material concerning discrimination,[54] the amount of compensation for victims of discrimination,[55] and matters concerning harassment and sexual harassment of workers.[56]

Besides being concerned with issues of discrimination within the workforce based on gender, the Committee also was concerned with issue of discrimination based on trade union membership or the lack thereof.[57] Ultimately, considering the content of the Appendix to the Charter, which in part relates to Article 1 § 2, the Committee came to the conclusion that the above provision cannot be regarded as a norm permitting or forbidding the introduction of union security clauses, forcing workers to join certain

48. Conclusions VIII, p. 29 (Austria).
49. Conclusions XIII-3, pp. 71–72 (the Netherlands).
50. Conclusions XIV–1, p. 148 (Cyprus).
51. Conclusions XIII-5, p. 254.
52. D. Harris, J. Darcy, *op. cit.,* p. 50.
53. Conclusions XIV-1, p. 293.
54. Conclusions XIII-1, p. 49 (Iceland).
55. Conclusions XIV-1, p. 68 (Austria).
56. Conclusions XIII-3, p. 61 (France).
57. Conclusions XIII-1, p. 57, Conclusions XIII-3, p. 77 (Great Britain).

union organizations. The Charter thus creates an obligation to treat all workers equally regardless of trade union membership, and specifically prohibits discrimination against workers who are members of a trade union or are active in it, requiring national practices in these matters to be carried out in accordance with Article 5.[58]

The Committee of Social Rights was concerned with the protection of social rights in matters of discrimination based on religious and political premises in Northern Ireland,[59] religious premises in Greece,[60] Denmark and Norway,[61] as well as political premises in Germany.[62] Accepting the right of state to exclude a religious faction from equal treatment in relation to religious beliefs, carries the same connotations as discrimination based on denomination approved by the law; the Committee therefore decided that the abovementioned exclusions are not applicable to the state as an employer. In the last case, the Committee recognized the authority of the Federal Republic of Germany to be loyal to the provisions of its own constitution, which requires a condition of neutrality when it comes to matters of denomination of civil servants, with respect to applicants seeking physical jobs in the following governmental employment sectors: drivers, postmen, and municipal park landscape employees.

The Charter assures general protection against discrimination based on illegal criteria, which differentiates workers as well as those seeking employment. It is applicable to those employed in the private or public sector, to individuals in small-scale work places,[63] and to those who are self-employed.[64] The addressees of the Charter are the Member States, which are responsible for eliminating various obstacles in attaining employment for those who are regarded as part of a minority, separated due to illegal criteria, within the employment process.

6.1.3. To Establish and Maintain the Function of General Access to Free Employment Services (Article 1 § 3)

Member States that ratified Article 1 § 3 are obligated to establish or maintain free employment services for all workers. This provision is not drawn up clearly. The grammatical format of this provision may lead to a false proposal or to a necessity to establish or to maintain free of charge employment services. Meanwhile, the Committee of Social Rights interprets the above provision as a norm obligating the Member States to establish and maintain free employment services. Furthermore, the abovementioned provision may appear to indicate that within Member States there may exist only public employment services, established and maintained by the state. The Committee of Social Rights is of the view that the private sector may also provide the services provided by employment agencies. According to the provision in

58. Conclusions XIX-1, p. 454 (Great Britain)
59. Conclusions XIV-1, p. 793 (Great Britain)
60. Conclusions XIII-1, p. 48; Conclusions XIV-1, pp. 348–349.
61. Conclusions XIV-1, p. 174 (Denmark); p. 506 (Norway).
62. Conclusions V, p. 7.
63. Conclusions IX-1, p. 25 (Great Britain).
64. Conclusions I, p. 8.

question, employment agencies are to provide services for workers. Article 1 § 3 uses the definition of 'worker' as a person seeking employment in the scope of labour relations. People taking advantage of employment services are those who have remained without employment, are capable of employment, and are willing to undertake employment. The definition of 'worker' in this analysed provision is a guideline, as employment agencies will not provide employment services for those who are self-employed.[65]

The employment service sector is charged with providing jobs for individuals who are seeking employment. This is equivalent to providing employers with candidates for employment. These agencies inform those seeking employment of vacant positions and provide employers with the details of possible candidates.[66] Under Article 1 § 3, by definition, these agencies are not responsible for providing vocational training services. Employment agencies and the services they provide may be private or public.[67] The Charter does not place an obligation on Member States to supervise the effectiveness of such agencies in terms of the manner in which jobs are allocated to those seeking employment, or to employers seeking candidates . The Committee of Social Rights pays attention to the research on the effectiveness of these services. It demands information from Member States regarding whether and how governmental administration bodies monitor private employment agencies.[68] The Committee considers that employment agencies should be supervised by governmental administration bodies together with stakeholders,[69] on a local and national level.[70] It obligates Member States to present within its national reports information regarding the number of employment agencies the State has, as well as their methods of organizing. It demands information concerning the number of people who are using these services, including their age, gender, and professional qualifications. The Committee seeks to establish the number of people who are registered in the employment agencies seeking employment, as well as the number of positions that have been filled by those who had sought employment. It wants to know whether national regulations place obligations on employers to provide employment agencies with information regarding vacant work positions. If such regulations are not in place, the Committee seeks to find out how employment agencies receive such information regarding vacant positions. When a state has both private and public employment services, the Committee is interested in familiarizing itself with their coordination and the results of their conduct. Of particular interest for the Committee is the comparison between public and private employment agencies.[71] The Committee of European Communities reports that only 10.5 per cent of those

65. Conclusions I, p. 8.
66. Conclusions I, p. 167 (Ireland).
67. Conclusions III, p. 9 (Austria).
68. Conclusions I, p. 167 (Ireland).
69. Conclusions I, p. 16.
70. Conclusions III, p. 9 (Austria); Conclusions XIV-1, p. 691 (Spain); Conclusions XIV-3, pp. 88–89 (Great Britain).
71. Conclusions XIII-1, p. 58 and following; 221–222; Conclusions XIII-2, p. 235 and following; Conclusions XIII-3, p. 78 and following, 238 and following; Addendum to Conclusions XIII-3, p. 19–20.

seeking employment take advantage of public employment services. Therefore, the Committee concluded that until this rate drops down to 5 per cent, the situation should be considered serious.[72]

Clients of employment services should be charged no fees. These are not charitable organizations; thus, costs associated with their services must be paid for by governmental funds. Such costs incurred by employment service agencies (both private and public) must not be covered by the job seeker or by the employer.[73] Great Britain, as noted by the by the Committee of Social Rights in its fourth supervisory cycle, was in breach of Article 1 § 3, when it allowed for employers to pay for employment agency services. The Committee's ruling allows for an employer to make such payments when seeking to fill positions – including academic and administrative staff, managers, highly specialized technicians and engineers – only when normal, free of charge employment service channels are not available.[74] The position of the Committee has not changed within the following supervisory cycles.[75] In its annual report of the eighth supervisory cycle, the Committee stated that free of charge employment agencies would be jeopardized should they apply their services only to employment demand, without taking into consideration the offer of supply by employers. Considering the fact that some job positions do not follow supply and demand patterns, the Committee has noted that filling such positions is outside the legal regulations of Article 1 § 3. The Committee has modified its earlier position on a general free of charge approach for employers using employment agency services. Instead it has stated there are certain situations when demands for payment from employers using such services can be made, such as for the recruitment of top level position managers.[76] The abovementioned stance was maintained by a report concluding the twelfth supervisory cycle.[77] Article 1 § 3 is thus interpreted by the Committee as guaranteeing standard employment agency services free of charge. A fee for finding candidates should be rare and applicable only to managerial positions, as these fees may assist in the search for appointment of an appropriate candidate for a managerial position. The availability of a candidate to commence work cannot be seen as a reason for an employer to be charged.

Employment services should be freely available regardless of gender,[78] age,[79] trade and profession, including farming[80] and housework,[81] for all persons willing to enter into work relations. Entitlements to free of charge services of employment

72. Conclusions XIV-1, vol.1, p. 351 (Greece).
73. Conclusions IV, p. 10.
74. *Ibid.*, pp. 10–12.
75. Conclusions V, p. 10; Conclusions VI, p. 10; Conclusions VII, p. 11. All former cases apply to Great Britain. Conclusions XIII-3, p. 241; Conclusions XIV-1, p. 762–763 (Turkey).
76. Conclusions VIII, pp. 36–37 (Great Britain).
77. Conclusions XII-1, p. 62 (Denmark).
78. Conclusions III p. 10 (Italy).
79. Conclusions III p. 10 (Denmark, Ireland); Conclusions IV p. 12 (Norway), Conclusions XIII-1 p. 222 (Turkey).
80. Conclusions III p. 10 (Italy).
81. Conclusions IV p. 12 (Italy).

agencies should be equally accessible to citizens of a given state, as well as to citizens of other Member States.[82]

6.1.4. Vocational Guidance, Training and Rehabilitation (Article 1 § 4)

Tasks imposed on Member States by Article 1 § 4 involve providing or promoting appropriate vocational guidance, training and rehabilitation. Authorities are obliged to organize a system of vocational guidance and training and maintain its proper level, as well as to provide a support system for those who intend to take up a new job requiring new skills and abilities, by providing them with necessary preparation. This task is of alternative character – if a state has a private system of vocational guidance, training and rehabilitation and if it works properly, there is no need to organize an identical or similar public system. Member States are, however, obliged to support private systems to make sure their services are in accordance with the rules set by the Committee of Social Rights. Article 1 § 4 has a general scope. It does not specify regulations imposed on Member States. More details can be gathered from Articles 9, 10 and 15. During the first supervisory cycle, the Committee concluded that regulations imposed by Article 1 § 4 are identical to those determined by Articles 9, 10 and 15.[83] Article 1 § 4, as a general regulation, agreed with Articles 9, 10 and 15, which are regarded as specific regulations, noted by the Committee in a ruling stating that a given country abides regulations under the Article 1 § 4, it is implied that regulations of Articles 9, 10 and 15 are also followed by this state. However, due to very detailed regulations of the abovementioned Articles, where Article 9 determines duties of a Member State as far as accessing vocational guidance by other Member State citizens is concerned, Article 10 regulates all matters connected with vocational training and Article 15 ensures the disabled not only have the right to benefit from the entitlements guaranteed by Article 1 § 4, but also includes additional entitlements ensuring the disabled have self-dependency, social integration and the ability to partake in social life. The Committee concluded that abiding by Article 1 § 4 by a given state does not necessarily mean abiding by all specific duties imposed by regulations of Articles 9, 10 and 15.[84] The statement concerning the abiding of some specific duties listed in Articles 9, 10 and 15 does not authorize the Committee to make rulings finding obedience of the state towards general duties formulated in Article 1 § 4. Only fulfilling all the duties regulated by Articles 9, 10 and 15 guarantees a positive ruling of the Committee in terms of conformity of national regulations and every day practise with Article 1 § 4. According to the precedents developed during the first seven supervisory cycles, the Committee considers that a state which does not abide by any of the three abovementioned regulations is considered in violation of the general duty enlisted in Article 1 § 4. Automatism in evaluating the abovementioned duties, consisting of the fact that violating at least one of the three specific duties causes a ruling of violating the general

82. Conclusions XIV-1 p. 72 (Austria), p. 105 (Belgium), p. 213 (Finland), p. 250 (France).
83. Conclusions I, s.16.
84. Conclusions II, p. 6.

duty, reappeared in the twelfth supervisory cycle. However, it became less consistent than during the first seven supervisory cycles. There are cases when, despite the negative ruling in terms of abiding by the three specific duties, the general duty is considered fulfilled.

For example, Finland was found not to have fulfilled its duties regulated by Article 10 § 4 (duty of introducing or supporting long-term measures of special training and rehabilitation of the unemployed), due to a lack of possibilities for other Member State citizens, legal residents on the Finnish territory, to benefit from financial aid. The decision concerning the abiding of the regulations of Article 1 § 4 was postponed until the clarification as to whether other Member States citizens had rights to utilize options of vocational guidance, training and rehabilitation.[85] These are the exceptions from the general rule. Most of the time a positive or negative ruling, or abstaining from taking a position in matters of abiding by the three specific duties (Article 9, 10 and 15) by a Member State, implies the identical ruling concerning fulfilling the general duty determined by the Article 1 § 4.[86] In this latter case, when the Committee abstains from taking a position, it asks Member States to provide it with additional information in order to gain detailed data on measures undertaken in supervisory cycles to organize and promote vocational guidance, training and rehabilitation. Usually a committee ruling is abstained from when there is not clarity regarding whether other states' citizens have access to institutions and devices of vocational guidance, training, and rehabilitation.[87]

A necessary circumstance for an automatic statement of conformity or non-conformity of national regulations and practise with the four provisions (Articles 9, 10, 15) and the general duty (Article 1 § 4), or for abstaining from giving a ruling until the Committee is provided with additional information in the next supervisory cycle, is the ratification of these provisions by a Member State. The abovementioned statement is illustrated by the change in the Committee rulings, which during its first thirteen supervisory cycles took the position that Article 10 § 1 obliges Member States to ensure financial support for the unemployed intending to take part in technical or vocational training. Article 10 § 1 grants the abovementioned entitlement to all persons, including the disabled. During the fourteenth supervisory cycle the Committee changed its mind and stated that the legal foundations enabling the disabled to benefit from financial aid offered by public funds are created by Article 10 § 4. Up to now, countries who have not ratified Article 10 § 4 were accused of violating regulations of Article 10 § 1 based on not providing the unemployed willingly partaking in vocational and technical training or with financial aid, and were automatically held to be out of compliance with the fulfilment of the duty formulated in Article 1 § 4. Since then, the Committee changed

85. Conclusions XIV-2. vol. 1, pp. 213, 238. A similar case occurred during the thirteenth supervisory cycle. Conclusions XIII-3, pp. 92, 190 (Italy).
86. Usually negative rulings are passed in cases of unequal treatment of other Member States citizens. Conclusions XIII-3, p. 90 (Austria), p. 91 (Greece), p. 92 (Malta); Conclusions XIII-4, p. 334–335 (Belgium), p. 335 (Germany); Addendum to Conclusions XIII-3 (Luxemburg's first report), p. 22–23.
87. Conclusions XIV-2, vol.2, p. 627 (Portugal).

its position and agreed that these countries have fulfilled the duties formulated in Article § 4.[88]

A provision of Article 1 § 4 is commonly applicable. Its scope embraces not only employers, but also persons running their own businesses (self-employed).[89] The abovementioned regulation obligates Member States not only to organize and support institutions providing services of vocational guidance, training, and rehabilitation, but also imposes on them equal access services for all interested people.[90] The only case – with the exception of a number of situations mentioned above when there were obstacles in partaking in vocational guidance, training, and rehabilitation by foreigner residing in a country who ratified Article 1 § 4 – of a systematic neglect of duties formulated by the provision in question by a Member State, concerned unequal territorial distribution of services of vocational guidance, training, and rehabilitation.[91] A national report filed by Turkey stated that centres providing vocational guidance, training, and rehabilitation were located in six out of 73 state provinces. The Committee also indicated the limited scope of spending in the field of vocational guidance, training, and rehabilitation.

6.2. The Right to Just Conditions of Work (Article 2)

Article 2 does not include a definition of the term 'conditions of work'. This term is vague. It only encompasses what work the workers are involved in and its conditions.[92] Labour law distinguishes between 'work conditions' and 'conditions of a work agreement'.[93] The first definition is wider in its scope. It encompasses the work environment and the legal basis for the employment process. It is difficult to deduce whether the abovementioned provision may be widely interpreted. On the one hand, it deals with matters, which in a broad context concern work conditions (time of work, days free from work, holidays) as well as with matters concerning the employment process. It enforces employers to inform workers of the essential aspects of the contract or employment relationship (§ 6). On the other hand, Article 2 does not define which of the elements of the contract or employment relationship should be agreed upon. It does not therefore create a legal basis for the division of legal components concerning a work contract into what is regarded as the 'essential subject', that is, what parts the legislation expects the work agreement to entail, and into 'essential entity', parts decided upon independently by both parties to the contract. Assuming Article 2

88. Conclusions XIV-2, p. 109 (Belgium), p. 293 (Germany).
89. Conclusions I, p. 8.
90. Greece. Conclusions XI-1, p. 149, Conclusions, XII-1, p. 68.
91. Turkey. Conclusions XIII-1; Conclusions XIII-3, p. 243; Conclusions XIV-2, p. 739.
92. A. Świątkowski, *La force obligatoire du contract de travail versus le difficultes economiques des enterprises en Pologne*, Yearbook of Polish Labour Law & Social Policy, vol. 4, Kraków 1993, pp. 69 and following.
93. For clarity, in labour law, literature work agreement conditions are referred to as 'components of a work agreement'. *See* A. Świątkowski, *Polskie prawo pracy* (trans: Polish, Labour Law), *Wydawnictwo Prawnicze* (Legal Publications) LexisNexis, Warszawa 2003, p. 160.

does not encompass a wide interpretation of 'work conditions', and instead creates legal foundations for the regulation of national labour laws, it is important to note that this provision exclusively deals with the problem of work time and holidays. The Committee of Social Rights classified this provision in its first supervisory cycle. It defined it as a provision dealing with matters which awake the interest of international and national trade unions, as well as a provision that was first on the agenda for the regulation of laws by the International Labour Organization.[94] From the very beginning of its functioning, Article 2 of the Committee of Social Rights was treated as an accepted norm ensuring workers' safe and hygienic working conditions. The Committee found that if workers are working above the daily and weekly standards of working hours, devoid of rights to daily, weekly and annual rest, they are at a greater risk for accidents at work.[95] Therefore, the Committee regards the practice of Article 2 to be part of the category of provisions which protects the health of workers. This provision, therefore, completes Article 3, dealing with safe and hygienic conditions at work.

Article 2 encompasses solely workers who are under a standard or non-standard work agreement (those employed for a specific period of time, in an incomplete time-frame).[96] It does not offer any protection for the self-employed.[97] It does, however, protect family members who are employed as co-workers in an independently-run agricultural business.[98]

In addition to Article 3 § 1 ESC and Article I § 2 RESC, the responsibilities defined in Article 2 are considered fulfilled in situations when all provisions of Article 2 ESC, as well as Article 2 § 1–5 and 7 RESC, encompass the majority of interested workers. The Committee in the Charter defines the principle of 'majority' as 80 per cent of workers.

6.2.1. The Definition of Reasonable Daily and Weekly Working Hours (Article 2 § 1)

Article 2 § 1 is a norm categorized as a 'dynamic' provision. It requires that the Member States establish what reasonable daily and weekly working hours are, and then shorten the amount of weekly working hours according to productivity growth as well as other factors associated with it. The provision in question, therefore, does not aim at establishing daily and weekly working hour targets. The Committee of Social Rights has not fixed such standards. It took the position that the existing employment standards within Member States (8 hours daily and 40 hours weekly) are responsible for certain social problems, such as the organization of free time.[99] The Committee, however, did not

94. Conclusions I, p. 17.
95. Conclusions XIV-2, vo.1, pp. 364–365.
96. Conclusions XII-2, p. 61 (Malta); Conclusions XIV-2, vol. 1, p. 34; Conclusions XIII-3, p. 249 (Portugal).
97. Conclusions I, p. 8; Conclusions XIII-5, p. 47 (Finland).
98. Conclusions III, p. 12 (Ireland).
99. Conclusions I, p. 18.

specify any particular regulations for Member States in terms of cutting down working hours. It did not leave total freedom in setting weekly and monthly working hour standards, but gave sensible margin guidelines. Determining such weekly and monthly working hours should take into consideration many factors, especially economic and economic-related factors. Other factors connected with work efficiency, according to the Committee, can be listed as follows: work environment, and processes and factors harmful to the health and life of a worker.[100] The Committee thus took the position that weekly and monthly working hour standards will be different in different Member States.[101] According to the Committee, authorities setting working hour standards should take into consideration the unemployment rate. High unemployment rate justifies the shortening of working hours, as it maintains the number of employed on the same level.[102] Shortening of working hours leads to a decrease in remuneration. The case of Ireland is somewhat peculiar. The average Irish working hours at the beginning of the 1990s were 61–62 hours per week. An agreement made by stakeholders and Irish authorities, which required the gradual shortening of weekly working hours by an hour within the next three years, placed special duties on the country. Ireland was trying to fulfil its duties under Article 2 § 1 by granting employees longer paid leave. The Committee criticized the abovementioned practise. It stated that these policies were in breach of Article 2 § 1, which imposes on Member States a duty of gradual shortening of weekly working hours and does not allow substituting this regulation by different techniques, especially based on prolonging paid leave.

As a rule, daily and weekly working hours are longer in countries where efficiency of work is at a lower level. However, the correlation between working hour standards and the level of work efficiency is not obvious. The case of France relying on a 35 hour working week proves that setting working hour standards is often influenced by employer representatives and is not necessarily directly related with the level of work efficiency.

The questionnaire to Article 2 § 1 compiles of a number of questions, allowing the Committee's familiarization with daily and weekly working hour standards, periods of rest and plans of shortening of weekly working hours. According to its practise, the Committee does not recommend a number of hours described by Article 2 § 1 as 'reasonable daily and weekly working hours'. Daily and weekly working hour standards are understood as time when an employee is available for his employer. Thus, working hour standards apply in the case of work on a regular basis, as well as in the case of extra hours.[103] The Article shows cases when daily and weekly working hour standards can be regarded as 'reasonable'. National labour law violates the provision in question when it allows employing workers 16 hour a day and/or 60 hours a week.[104]

100. Conclusions XIV-2, p. 32.
101. Conclusion I, p. 18, Conclusions XIV-2, p. 32.
102. Conclusions I, p. 18; Conclusions II p. 7, Conclusions XIII-1 p. 70; last two cases concerning Ireland.
103. Conclusions XIV-2, p. 32.
104. Conclusions XIV-2, p. 32.

The Committee demanded additional explanation from Member States which allowed exceeding a 48-hour working week, protected under the directive No 104 of 1993 on aspects of work time organization.[105] It reminded Member States that the postulate of 'reasonable' number of working hours should separately apply to daily and weekly standards. Not exceeding the accepted weekly standards does not guarantee a positive committee ruling when daily standards are not met. Setting high weekly average standards automatically causes prolonging of daily standards beyond the limits approved by the Committee. No later than during the first two supervisory cycles, the Committee declared Irish[106] and Italian[107] weekly working hour standards of 64 hours as not in accordance with Article 2 § 1.

The analysed Article 2 § 1 imposes a gradual shortening of weekly working hour standards. However, this provision should not be interpreted as obliging Member States to impose a strict reduction of working hour standards in all weeks of the year, quarters or months. The Committee approves of employers' flexible policies in terms of time management. It allows extending working hour standards in one week of a pay period, on the condition of shortening these standards in another week of the same period. The Committee establishes certain requirements of time management policies in the workplace. The legality of these policies depends on the level of fulfilling the abovementioned requirements. The Committee imposes setting a maximum number of working hours in weekly periods.[108] It prohibits exceeding maximum working hour standards set at the level of 50 hours. It allows the introduction of four and six- month- long wage payment periods. In special cases, it also accepts the extension of this period to 12 months. It requires special conduct from bodies authorized to regulate working hours in cases of extending working hours in some weeks of the pay period. It obligates employers to inform their employees about all changes in the work schedule.[109] It supervises the work of inspectors who monitor abiding work hour standards by employers.

The Member States are the addressees of Article 2 § 1. However, it does not impose an obligation of passing regulations on work hour standards and rules of their reduction. Fulfilling the obligation regulated by the provision in question also takes place in cases of normative agreements, by which stakeholders set reasonable weekly and daily working hours. The Committee accepts customs and ways of conduct directly influencing the working schedule. In cases where working hour standards are regulated in a non-legal way, relevant authorities must ensure supervision of these standards. The Committee does not specify what bodies are responsible for controlling working hours standards. Usually work inspectors execute this function.

---

105. Conclusions XII-1, p. 70 (Iceland), p. 71 (The Netherlands); Conclusions XIII-1, p. 68 (Greece); Conclusions XIII-3, pp. 245–246 (Portugal).
106. Conclusions II, p. 7.
107. Conclusions I, p. 18.
108. Conclusions XIV-2, p. 111 and following (Belgium), p. 329 (Greece).
109. *Ibid.*, p. 34.

6.2.2. Public Holidays with Pay (Article 2 § 2)

The obligation of ensuring that employees have paid holidays embraces only these days which otherwise would be working days. Therefore it does not include holidays falling on free-from-work days, such as Sunday. The provision in question does not determine the number of paid holidays in a year, and nor does the Committee of Social Rights. A Member State should then guarantee paid holidays as the sum of bank holidays and religious holidays accepted by national regulations as free-from-work days. These holidays are free-from-work days according to national labour law regulations, and the wages should be paid as if they were working days. Employing this principle, the Committee regarded states guaranteeing six paid holidays a year (Great Britain) to be equally in compliance with this provision as states guaranteeing 17 holidays (Italy).[110]

The exemption from duty of work on holidays with guaranteed pay is not absolute. Depending on the type of work, employees may be obliged to work on holidays. Duty of work embraces especially those employed in enterprises functioning in a constant cycle.[111] By working during a holiday, an employee acquires the right to an extra day off.[112]Accounting for holiday wages is done on an hourly basis. Employees working full time during a holiday obtain a whole free day. Employees working fewer hours during a holiday obtain as many off-work hours as that which they worked during a holiday.[113] It is not permissible for an employer to grant less off-work time than what has been worked during a holiday.[114] Alternatively, holiday work may be additionally remunerated when a particular employee agrees to it.[115] However, this is regarded as an exception from the rule of recompensing holiday work by an extra day-off. The Committee of Social Rights believes additional pay for holiday work would violate the rule prohibiting requiring any employee to work on holidays.

6.2.3. Two Weeks Annual Holiday with Pay (Article 2 § 3)

Article 2 § 3 guarantees all employees annual holiday with pay, regardless the basis of employment and the type of contract. The Charter sets a minimal period of this leave. The European Social Charter guarantees the right of at least two weeks of paid leave. The Revised European Social Charter guarantees at least four weeks of annual holiday with pay. Annual holiday with pay is the right of every employee. An employee cannot be relinquished of this entitlement or pass it onto another person. As early as the first supervisory cycle, the Committee of Social Rights concluded that the voluntary act of passing this entitlement onto an employer in exchange for additional remuneration

110. Conclusions I, p. 19.
111. Conclusions XII-1, p. 72 (Greece).
112. The case of Greece. Conclusions XII-1, p. 72, XII-3, p. 205, XIV-2, pp. 329–330.
113. Conclusions XII-2 p. 61 (Malta). Employees employed for less than 14 hours a week did not obtain an extra day-off.
114. Conclusions XIV-2, p. 631 (Portugal).
115. Conclusions XIV-2, p. 220 (Finland).

(holiday 'sale') stands in breach of this regulation.[116] The above opinion was repeated in the following supervisory cycles, and those Member States practicing holiday 'sale' for additional remuneration were considered to be in violation of Article 2 § 3.[117] The Committee's rigorous standpoint on these issues sought to protect employees' paid holiday leave.

Article 2 § 3 does not determine factors of acquiring the rights to employee holiday with pay. Therefore it is permissible to acquire the rights to four weeks of holiday with pay, dependent on the period of employment within one workplace, assumed by labour law regulations. During the first supervisory cycle, the Committee determined a 12-month employment period as the maximum amount of time needed to acquire full holiday with pay.[118] Not fulfilling this requirement by an employee enables an employer to shorten the amount of paid holiday, according to the period of employment.[119] The Committee of Social Rights, in its early supervisory cycles, opted for proportional amount of holiday with pay, dependent on the period of employment. It may be assumed that each month of employment grants an employee a 1:12 proportion of the yearly amount of holiday with pay. The Committee also accepted separation of holiday entitlements from periods of employment, in that it approved periods with paid remuneration, not periods of pure employment, as the basis to calculate the number of days of holiday with pay.[120] The latter allowed for the disregard of unpaid leave in periods of employment.

The ban of holiday 'sale' does not deprive an employee of the right to obtain money equivalent for unutilized holidays.[121] An employer, only in cases of resignation, may implement the above solution, when he is not able to grant holidays with pay at a future date. The above case embraces situations when a period of notice is shorter than paid holidays, or when it is not possible for a holidaying employee to obtain a raise, which results in paying him only part of his deserved remuneration.

Article 2 § 3 does not impose on Member States an obligation to grant continuous holidays with pay. The official texts of the Charter were prepared in the official Council of Europe languages: English and French, and a grammatical interpretation of these texts leads to different conclusions. From the French phrase *un congé payé annuel de deux semaines,* it may be concluded that it is obligatory to grant a continuous period of holidays with pay in minimal dimensions determined by the Charter (2 or 4 weeks). However, the English phrase 'two weeks annual holiday with pay' is less clear in this matter.[122] The Committee of Social Rights confined itself to underlining this difference between the official texts of the Charter and did not deal with the issue of continuality of holidays with pay anymore. During the third supervisory cycle, the Committee

116. Conclusions I, p. 170.
117. Conclusions XII-2, p. 62 (Cyprus); Conclusions XIV-2, p. 222 (Finland); XIV-2, p. 503 (Malta).
118. Conclusions I, p. 20.
119. Conclusions VII, p. 14 (Ireland).
120. Conclusions VII, p. 13 (Sweden).
121. Conclusions I, p. 170; Conclusions V, p. 14 (Austria).
122. Conclusions I, p. 170.

addressed a query to Austria, asking what types of employees may be obliged to part with their annual holiday with pay. It expressed hope for a response in regards to this question, as well as with matters of the employee's right to resign from holiday with pay in exchange for additional remuneration.[123] During the following supervisory cycle (the 4th), Austria provided a positive answer to one of the addressed questions referring to the rights of an employee to 'sell' his/her holiday to the employer. The Committee reminded Austria of the decisions undertaken in the first supervisory cycle and concluded Austria to be in breach of Article 2 § 3.[124] It did not re-analyse the problem of employees being allowed to divide their holidays into parts or being forced to utilize holidays in parts.

The Committee is of the opinion that the reason for the existence of a holiday is to allow for the regeneration of physical and mental strength, weakened by labour. In accordance with the above principle, a conviction is formulated that paid holidays are not to be utilized by workers unable to work due to illness. The Committee raised this problem during the first supervisory cycle. It analysed how a worker utilized his holiday, when falling ill during it.[125] However, the Committee was unable to answer questions concerning the interdependency between an illness and the utilization of a holiday. By the twelfth supervisory cycle, the Committee, when referring to the impossibility of forgoing one's holidays, forbade such activity, entitling the worker who is unable to utilize his/her holiday due to illness, to seek the possibility of being able to use the holiday at a later date. Those utilizing the above entitlements are workers who have been unable to take holidays regardless of when the illness took place, inhibiting the utilization of the holiday in whole or in part during a planned period, either before or during the holiday.[126] From this supervisory cycle, the Committee included into the form a standard question, addressing the Member States that are obligated to file reports, which referred to the legal aftermath of the impossibility of a worker to utilize his/her holiday due to the inability to carry out work caused by illness or due to an accident at work.[127] The Committee demanded from all Member States an answer to the above question during all supervisory cycles, concerning the abiding of Article 2 § 3.[128]

---

123. Conclusions III, p. 13.
124. Conclusions IV, p. 16.
125. Conclusions I, p. 20.
126. Conclusions XII-2, p. 62.
127. Form of the report submitted in pursuance of the Revised European Social Charter (in:) European Social Charter. Collected texts, *op. cit.,* p. 308.
128. Conclusions XIII-1, p. 76; Conclusions XIV-2, p. 424 (Italy); Conclusions XIII-2, p. 242; Conclusions XIV-2, p. 117 (Belgium); Conclusions XIII-2, pp. 242–243; Conclusions XIV-2, p. 295 (Germany); Conclusions XIII-3, p. 248 (Finland); XIII-3, p. 250 (Portugal); Addendum to Conclusions XIII-3, p. 24 (Luxembourg); Conclusions XIV-2, p. 182 (Denmark); XIV-2, p. 330 (Greece); XIV-2, p. 365 (Iceland); XIV-2, p. 503 (Malta); XIV-2, p. 759 (Great Britain); Conclusions XVI-2, p. 130 (Czech Republic); XVI-2, p. 196 (Denmark); XVI-2, p. 288 (Germany); XVI-2, p. 328 (Greece); XVI-2, p. 396 (Hungary); XVI-2, pp. 481–482 (Malta); XVI-2, p. 515 (the Netherlands); XVI-2, p. 719 (Slovakia); XVI-2, p. 833 (Spain); Addendum to Conclusions XVI-2, p. 19 (Ireland).

During the thirteenth supervisory cycle, the Committee claimed that according to Spanish labour law regulations, workers do not have the right to demand to utilize holidays at a different day, if unused as prescribed, due to illness. According to the Spanish report, this regulation is a consequence of an agreement between stakeholders who, during collective bargaining agreements, established rigid periods for when holidays may be used according to given years. This is evident with regard to workers who are employed in production employment fields that close down for a given period of time (in accordance with the arrangements made with stakeholders), allocating holidays to all workers involved in the employment. Spanish courts refused those workers seeking to utilize holidays at a different date, due to illness, who were employed in such production fields of employment. The Committee expressed a concern regarding the inability to move one's holiday to a different period from that allocated by the employer, and asked the question whether the above practice was a general one, and in relation to it, whether it was possible to introduce a motion concerning the impossibility of moving an unutilized holiday to a later period.[129] Spain informed the Committee that the decisions handed down by the labour law courts, forbidding workers to utilize holidays at a differing period from what was allocated, were sporadic in their nature, were seen as controversial, and were appealed to the Supreme Court. The Committee once again during the following two supervisory cycles (the thirteenth and fourteenth) sought details concerning the number of workers who, due to illness during the holiday periods agreed to by stakeholders, lost their opportunity of utilizing their holidays, as well as sought information about the Supreme Court's stance on the matter.[130] During the sixteenth supervisory cycle, Spain declared no changes concerning holidays had taken place in the regulations. The Committee therefore recognized that the inability to move a holiday period, to which workers are entitled, to a different time frame, was a breach of Article 2 § 3.[131] Those workers who, due to illness or accident, are unable to utilize the whole or part of the holiday, should have the guarantee of the ability to utilize it at a later date in a capacity of at least two weeks in the yearly calendar. The obligation of Member States is to enable workers to utilize holidays to the minimum extent of what is described by Article 2 § 3 of the ESC or Article 2 § 3 of the RESC, when workers due to illness or accident, are unable to do so in the period prescribed to them by the employer.

The Committee underlined this during the 14th supervisory cycle. Looking at Norwegian legislation which allows workers to utilize holiday periods at a later date, when unable to take holidays during a prescribed period due to illness or accident lasting for at least six days, the Committee saw this as being in accordance with Article 2 § 3, because Norwegian holiday rights guarantee workers 25 days holiday. Therefore a loss of six days of holiday due to illness allows workers to utilize a minimum period of holidays, enforced by Article 2 § 3 of the ESC.[132] The position of the Committee would

129. Conclusions XIII-2, p. 64.
130. Conclusions XIII-1, p. 77; Conclusions XIV-2, p. 670.
131. Conclusions XVI-2, p. 833.
132. Conclusions XIV-2, p. 580.

be different, if Member States ratified Article 2 § 3 of the RESC, which guarantees a four-week holiday period within the year. The obligation to ensure workers the possibility of utilizing their holidays within the minimum standards guaranteed by the Charter (two or four weeks), encompasses all workers employed in full or part-time employment, regardless of the weekly and daily working hour standards.[133] The Committee was particularly interested in the holiday structures of atypical workers. It demanded to receive information concerning the regulations of their holidays and the means of allocating holidays, as well as the possibility of moving an unutilized holiday to a later period.[134] The Committee encountered periodic obstacles in the evaluation of information concerning the possibility of shifting a paid holiday which cannot be utilized by an employee due to sickness or accident. The case of Malta may be presented as an example where falling ill during holiday with pay neither automatically extends the holiday, nor entitles an employee to break this holiday to utilize it afterwards. According to the Maltese regulations, an employee who is taken ill during a holiday with pay is treated exactly the same as a healthy person having a holiday. He is only entitled to continue his sick leave when the holiday period is finished. The Maltese law uses a double legal fiction. First, it recognizes an ill employee as a healthy person who can utilize holiday with pay, and second, it allows an employee to remain on sick leave having already regained work abilities. This is why the Committee concluded the Maltese labour law regulations do not guarantee employers unable to work due to illness or accident the right to utilize the entitled holiday at other times.[135]

6.2.4. Duty to Eliminate Risks for Workers in Dangerous or Unhealthy Occupations and Provide them with Additional paid Holidays or Reduced Working Hours when Possible (Article 2 § 4)

As it is declared in the European Social Charter, Article 2 § 3 obligates Member States to ensure that employees in certain dangerous and unhealthy occupations have additional paid holidays or reduced working hours. This regulation gives Member States the choice in determining which occupations are considered dangerous and unhealthy. The Committee of Social Rights evaluates the lists of dangerous and unhealthy occupations presented by Member States, and in cases of the omission of occupations commonly believed as such, makes a ruling of non-conformity of domestic regulations with Article 2 § 4.[136] The provision in question is strictly connected with Article 3, ensuring employees the right to work in safe and hygienic conditions. In the supervisory process of abiding by Article 2 § 3, the Committee often referred to arrangements and conclusions based on Article 3.[137] Reasoning in the two abovementioned Articles, the Committee classified as dangerous all work that is in contact with

133. Conclusions XIV-2, p. 222 (Finland); XIV-2, p. 502 (Malta).
134. Conclusions XIII-1, p. 74 (Austria); Conclusions XIII-3 p. 249 (Finland); Conclusions XIV-2 p. 365 (Iceland); Addendum to Conclusions XIII-1, p. 77 (Great Britain).
135. Conclusions XVI-2, pp. 481–482.
136. Conclusions II, p. 9.
137. Conclusions IV, p. 18, Conclusions III-1, p. 80 (The Netherlands).

radioactive and toxic substances, connected with the risk of being subject to lead, asbestos, high pressure, noise, high or low temperatures, explosives, works carried out underground, in steelworks, shipyards, and in front of monitors due to radiation.[138] Listing examples of dangerous and unhealthy occupations, the Committee uses the European Union's registers. Framework directives, No 1107 of 27 November 1980 concerning the protection of employees against risks related to being subjected to chemical, physical and biological factors in workplace;[139] No 391 of 12 June 1989 concerning the execution of ventures aiming at the improvement of safety and health protection of employees in workplaces,[140] accompanied by detailed directives,[141] and establishes standards of work protection in safe and hygienic conditions The Committee of Social Rights utilizes the abovementioned standards in the supervisory cycle process of abiding by the Charter's regulations by Member States. The abovementioned standards have no exceptions. A register of work that is dangerous and harmful to the health should be systematically completed. Using similar registers compiled by the European Union institutions for support, the Committee advises Member States to provide information concerning protection against hazards caused by particular factors which were omitted from registers presented by particular countries.[142] Work that is dangerous and hazardous to the health that is undertaken by workers cannot be compensated for by any other means other than what is directed in Article 2 § 4 ESC. In particular, it is impossible to hire personnel in such conditions for higher wages without reducing daily working hours.[143] The first requirement stipulated concerning workers employed in dangerous and hazardous work is the entitlement to longer leave. Further down the list is the reduction of working hours for such employees. Reducing the exposure of the body to physical, chemical and biological factors which occur in dangerous or hazardous labour, reduces the risk of threat. Longer periods of leave allow for the regeneration of the worker's body. Both abovementioned techniques of protecting the health and life of workers exposed to such risks may be implemented simultaneously. Despite the obligation placed on Member States by the usage of the term 'longer paid holidays or limited working hours', Member States may, or rather should, take advantage of the abovementioned measures of protecting the life

---

138. Conclusions V, p. 17, (Italy); Conclusions XII-1, p. 74–75 (Greece, The Netherlands); Conclusions XIII-1, p. 80 (Norway).
139. Polish text published in: A. Świątkowski, H.Wierzbińska, *Dokumenty źródłowe instytucji Wspólnot Europejskich w zakresie prawa socjalnego* (Primary documents of the European Community institutions in matters of social law), Kraków 1999, pp. 475 and following. A. M. Świątkowski, *Bezpieczeństwo i higiena pracy* (Work safety and security), Kraków 2003, p. 302 and following.
140. Polish text: A. Świątkowski, H. Wierzbińska, *op. cit.*, p. 488 and following; A. M. Świątkowski, *op. cit.,* p. 309 and following.
141. Polish text: *Dyrektywy Europejskiej Wspólnoty Gospodarczej dotyczące ochrony pracy* (Directives of the European Economic Community in matters of labour protection), vol. V, Warszawa 1992–1994.
142. During the 14th supervisory cycle Germany became obligated to provide information concerning protection against hazards, such as industrial noise, high temperatures, radiation. Conclusions IV-2, p. 296 (Germany).
143. Conclusions III, p. 14 (Austria).

and health of workers, irrespective of each other. According to the Committee, it is permissible to undertake all measures limiting the risks of being subject to factors listed by Article 2 § f of the ESC.[144] In the earlier supervisory cycle, the Committee anticipated introduced changes by the Revised European Social Charter, which as a priority, obligates Member States to remove the threatening elements associated with work that is dangerous and hazardous for the health, and only when it is impossible to remove or sufficiently reduce such threats, to ensure the cutting down of working hours or provide additional paid holidays. Measures taken to protect the health and life of a worker exposed to the threats of dangerous and hazardous work should complement one another. It is not enough to temporarily restrict the exposure of the worker to dangerous or hazardous factors.[145] In the fifth supervisory cycle, the Committee was convinced that the constant improvement of safety and hygiene in the workplace, as well as the protection of the worker's health against threats caused by processes, conditions and the work environment, should be in line with the reduction of daily and weekly working hours, as well as with the increase of paid holidays.[146] The Committee underlined that the responsibility of reducing work hours and increasing holidays is especially important when there is the existence of danger within the working environment.[147] The goal for which Article 2 § 4 was analysed will be in constant activation mode, unless all dangers for the life and health of workers, brought on by work, by the factors and conditions of work, as well as the working environment, are eliminated. Utilizing the appropriate measures allocated to the Member States, employers are to eliminate, and if impossible, to reduce as much as it is possible, the level of risk workers are exposed to, and to the dangerous and hazardous for the life and health factors.[148]

The Revised European Social Charter, logically associating Article 2 § 4 with Article 3, places paramount importance on the duty of Member States, stakeholders, as well as employers, to remove the risks affiliated with work that is dangerous or hazardous to the health. The Committee of Social Rights underlined that the analysed provision is a standard, which heightens the effects of undertaking measures in an attempt to guarantee workers safe and hygienic working conditions. Arguments provided by Member States concerning the undertakings of particular measures to protect the lives and health of workers employed in dangerous or hazardous conditions were not accepted by the Committee, as there was no improvement of working conditions following the utilization of these measures. It paid heed to the fact that following the obligation to reduce working hours or to increase holidays, in these particular situations, did not ensure a removal or a significant reduction of threats against health or life.[149] The obligation to reduce the working hour standards for

144. Conclusions III, p. 15 (Ireland).
145. Conclusions XIII-2, p. 244 (Belgium).
146. Conclusions V, pp. 15–16.
147. Conclusions VIII, p. 45 (Ireland).
148. Addendum to Conclusions XIII-3, p. 24 (Luxembourg); Conclusions XIII-4, p. 339 (Belgium); XIV-2, pp. 117–118 (Belgium); XIV-2, p. 386 (Ireland); XIV-2, p. 467 (Luxembourg).
149. Conclusions XIII-1, pp. 79–80; XIII-4, p. 202 (the Netherlands).

workers employed in employment that is dangerous or hazardous to the health is a point of reference for the working hour standards existing within a given country. The Committee therefore rejected Austria's arguments claiming it fulfilled its obligations under Article 2 § 4, as it introduced 40 working hour weeks and four weeks of paid holidays. The Committee underlined that the provisions of Articles 1–3 place on Member States obligations of introducing working hour standards as well as minimum paid holidays of four weeks. Article 2 § 4 is the standard in terms of provisions 1–3; that is why it requires for workers employed in conditions that are dangerous or hazardous to the health, shorter than the ordinary daily and weekly working hours, as well as longer than the minimum paid holidays.[150]

6.2.5. To Ensure a Weekly Rest Period (Article 2 § 5)

Article 2 § 5 obligates Member States by placing two types of responsibilities on them. First, it obligates them to ensure one day of rest from work per week. The working week, therefore, wherein workers are obligated to attend their working responsibilities, is comprised of five working days. The sixth day of the weekly calendar is regarded as a day free from work, allocated for rest. The obligation is fulfilled if the majority of workers (i.e. at least 80 per cent) take advantage of this one day free from work.[151] The above responsibility is regarded to be strictly applied. The Charter does not accept any exceptions to this provision. Second, Member States should ensure workers, as is allowable, that the day free from work in each calendar week coincides with the day recognized by tradition or custom in the particular country as a day of rest.[152] In the majority of Member States, the day free from work within the week is Sunday, recognized by tradition or custom in the particular country or region. This regulation is not strictly applied. Depending on the nature of the business run by a particular employer (the hospitality sector) or the specificity of a given branch (medical services), the employer may establish that the day free from work may be a day that does not coincide with the festive day (Sunday or any other day considered to be free from work).[153] However, it does not have a right to make decisions in an arbitrary manner. Member States have the responsibility of monitoring why such decisions have been made. In situations where it has been established that major groups of workers are employed on Sunday and utilize their day free from work on another day of the week, the Committee of Social Rights has the basis to decide that there is a breach of Article 2 § 5 by a given country.[154] The above provision does not place any obligations on the Member States concerning which day should be free from work. National labour laws

150. Conclusions V, p. 17; XII-2, p. 65; XIII-1, p. 78; XIII-3, pp. 199–200.
151. Conclusions I, p. 20.
152. Conclusions XI, p. 55; Conclusions XIII-3, pp. 203–204; Analysing the report filed by the Netherlands, the Committee demanded further information, as it was concerned too many workers were employed on Sunday. Conclusions XIV-2, p. 539.
153. Conclusions XIV-2, p. 239 (the Netherlands).
154. Such instances took place during the 14th supervisory cycle. Conclusions XIV-2, p. 386 (Ireland – 36per cent employed on Sunday); p. 761 (Great Britain – 40per cent employed on Sunday).

leave this matter to stakeholders or employers. They are entitled to appoint a day free from work 'coinciding with' the day traditionally or customarily regarded as a day free from work, and to have their duties fulfilled if they decide to make the preceding day (Saturday) or the following day (Monday) a day free from work, or any other day commonly regarded as a day free from work according to tradition or customs within a country or a region. The Committee of Social Rights takes the position that rules utilized by interpreting Article 2 § 3, the provision obliging Member States to guarantee a minimum four weeks (according to RESC) or two weeks (according to ESC) periods of holiday with pay, also apply to the interpretation of the Article in question. An employee cannot either voluntarily relinquish[155] or 'sell' to a third party[156] his one day free from work within a week. Deferring holidays with pay in time is in accordance with standards established by Article 2 § 5. According to the Committee, this practice is permissible in cases strictly regulated by national labour law. Furthermore, deferring a paid holiday in time cannot exceed the 12 following months. In such a case, an employer is obligated to grant an employee two days free from work respectively.[157] Any employment exceeding 12 consecutive days means, when considering daily working hour standards, an extension of weekly working hours beyond the permissible international limits. Referring to the interpretation of the Committee of Social Rights on Article 2 § 1, infringing on 60 hours of work per week, deferring in time the utilization of a day free from work in the week by the worker, is enough basis to regard the matter as a breach of Article 2 § 5 by a Member State.[158] When accepting the deference of a day free from work to the next week, the Committee takes into consideration the sector the worker is employed in. The Committee treats Article 2 § 5 as a legal basis assisting in the protection of the right to work in safe and hygienic conditions. It attempts to establish whether, for example, reporting to work by an employee for nine consecutive calendar days without the allocation of a rest day during a 60 hour week, which is the practice in the Netherlands, creates a threat for the health of the worker.[159]

The right to a day free from work within the week may be utilized by all workers, those employed in full of part-time employment. Based on Article 33 ESC and Article I § 2 RESC, particular Member States have the right to exclude some categories of employment, for example agricultural or forest workers.[160]

6.2.6. To Ensure Workers are Informed in Written Form of the Aspects of the Work Agreement (Article 2 § 6)

The provision is based on the Council Directive No. 533 of 14 October 1991, concerning the responsibility of the employer to inform the worker about the work

155. Conclusions I, p. 172 (Ireland).
156. As seen: Conclusions XIII-3, p. 253; XIV-2, p. 223 (Finland); XIV-2, p. 503 (Malta).
157. Conclusions XIV-2, p. 387 (Ireland); XIV-2, p. 672 (Spain).
158. Conclusions XIV-2, pp. 668–669 (Spain).
159. Conclusions XIV-2, p. 539.
160. L. Samuel, Fundamental Social Rights. Case law of the European Social Charter, 2nd edition, Council of Europe Publishing, Strasbourg 2002, p. 55.

contract or the employment relationship.[161] Article 2 § 6 places an obligation on the employer to provide information in written form on the essential aspects of the work agreement or the work relationship. The analysed provision does not define these aspects. Applying to Article 2 (2) of the directive No. 533, the employer should inform the employee: who are the parties to the agreement or employment relationship, where is the place of work, what type of work will the employer allocate and the employee carry out, when did employment commence, how does the employer allocate holidays, what is the wage paid and how it will be paid, what are the daily and weekly working hours, and whether and what types of union agreements regulate the conditions of the work agreement. The above information should be given to the worker in written format within two months of commencing employment. In the formula dictating the preparation of national reports, the Committee of Social Rights obligates Member States to provide information regarding the source of a country's labour law, by which the above obligation has been introduced to the domestic laws of a given Member State.[162] It instructs employers to present the content and the manner by which the above provision is defined and how it is utilized and practiced. The responsibility of providing a worker with the information mentioned in Article 2 § 6 rests on all employers, those in the public and in the private sector. There is no exemption from the provision for those employers who have signed a written work agreement with employees. Because work agreements can also be made verbally, the written confirmation of employment and its conditions has a legal force. Article 2(2) of directive No. 533 compiles duties extending beyond a work agreement and factors crucial to the employer. Member States were obliged to ensure that all employees within the first two months of employment are informed about the important parts of the work agreement. Article 2 § 6 does not indicate the exact conduct which must be followed in order to fulfil this duty. Until now, the Committee of Social Rights has not been interested in techniques of implementing this regulation. Fulfilling the abovementioned duty can only be done by Member States that apply administrative penalties and place fines on employers who do not abide by this public and legal obligation.

The Appendix to the Revised European Social Charter authorizes Member States to exclude employees contracted via atypical work agreements from the legal application of Article 2 § 6. Parties can decide upon extinguishing Article 2 § 6 in cases of provisional employees when the total contracting time does not exceed one month. It is also possible to make such exclusions when employment does not exceed eight hours per week, regardless of whether the agreement is made for specified or unspecified periods of time. Exclusions of Article 2 § 6 concerning the abovementioned cases need to be approved by a given Member State. Objective reasons can justify the exclusions of Article 2 § 6 in cases of seasonal and irregular workers. Neither the practise of the Committee of Social Rights, nor the scant literature on the provision in question, allow

161. OJ No L 288, 18.10.1991, p. 32. *See* A. Świątkowski, *Europejskie prawo socjalne* (European Social Law), vol. II *Europejskie prawo pracy* (European Labour Law), Dom Wydawniczy ABC (ABS Publishing House), Warszawa 1999, pp. 79 and following.

162. Form for the reports ... (in:) European Social Charter ... *op. cit.*, pp. 308–309.

for examples to be given in any cases of exclusion by Member States, parties to the Revised European Social Charter.

6.2.7. Protection of Workers Employed in Night Work (Article 2 § 7)

Article 2 § 7 broadens the scope of application in terms of protection, in comparison with the assurance given under Article 8 § 4(a) ESC. It obligates Member States to ensure protection for all workers employed in night work, not only for women (as did Article 8 § 4(a) ESC). Article 2 § 7 broadens the protection of work to men working at night. The original version of this provision (Article 8 § 4(a) ESC) was applicable only to female workers employed in industrial occupations at night. Article 2 § 7 applies to all workers regardless of their sex and employer.

Article 2 § 7 does not legally define the period of night. The Charter leaves this matter to be regulated by Member States. Therefore, a night period is regarded by Article 2 § 7 as night-time by national labour law regulations. Assuming that work during night-time involves an extra burden for workers, Article 2 § 7 obligates Member States to ensure all those working at night to have proper resources according to the nature of work carried out during night hours. In a form drawn up by the Committee of Social Rights, which is used by Member States for the preparation of reports on abiding Charter regulations, there are examples of measures that can be used in order to minimize the burden of night time work. These are as follows: additional breaks, additional holidays with pay, frequent medical check-ups, the possibility of utilizing facilities such as rooms for resting used during breaks, and conditions allowing night-time work to be done during day hours.[163]

6.3. The Right to Safe and Healthy Working Conditions (Article 3)

Member States have been obligated to undertake all measures in order to protect the health and the life of employees. The right to work in safe and healthy conditions is a fundamental human right protected by the recommendations and conventions of the ILO. This right concerns the following issues: avoiding work accidents, safety of loading, unloading and building works, proper protection of machines and devices, protection against radiation, health protection and the organizing of industrial health services.[164] Article 3 refers to Article 2 of the European Convention on Human Rights, a provision protecting the right to live. Article 3 ensures that all persons employed in work – regardless of the type of employment, and whether it is pursuant to a work agreement or self-employment –[165] have the right to physical and psychological

163. Form for the reports ... (in:) European Social Charter, *op. cit.,* p. 311.

164. J. Rosner, *Miedzynarodowa polityka społeczna* (International Social Policies), KiW, Warszawa 1967, pp. 111 and following. Recommendations and convention of ILO on health and safety issues were published in: *Konwencje i zalecenia* (Conventions and Recommendations ...) vol. I and II., Warszawa 1996.

165. Conclusions I, p. 8; Conclusions XIV-2, p. 38.

integrity at work.[166] The Committee of Social Rights accepted a broader definition of the 'worker'. It came to the conclusion that all terms within Article 3 indicate that the international employer (the Council of Europe) had intended to guarantee health protection as well as safe and healthy working conditions.[167] The European Social Charter obligates Member States to legislate provisions concerning safe and healthy working conditions, to ensure means of control, and to consult stakeholders in order to improve the level of health and safety in workplace. As early as during the first supervisory cycle, the Committee stated that a country which committed itself to follow requirements of Article 3 ESC should prove it had legislated provisions concerning health and safety in the workplace. Application of these provisions is of a general nature. It relates to all sectors of the economy, trade, services and others[168] where entrepreneurs employ workers. Government work inspectors execute such provisions effectively. They are authorized to sanction accordingly through the legal civil code, and to administer penalties. States initiate and lead consultations with workers' representatives and workers' organizations, concerning the protection of workers' health within the workplace.[169] Fulfilling the three obligations named in Article 3 means ensuring work conditions that are safe and hygienic for the worker.

6.3.1. According to the European Social Charter

6.3.1.1. The Responsibility to Issue Regulations Dealing with Health and Safety at Work (Article 3 ESC; Article 3 § 2 RESC)

The scope of the above provision is general. It encompasses the following economical spheres: industry, mines (mining industry),[170] trade, transport (road,[171] rail, sea,[172] and air), and agriculture.[173] Member States have the obligation to regulate, according to law, safety and health matters within the workplace in the abovementioned sectors. Article 3 § 1 ESC is not of a standard considered as 'dynamic'. The Charter does not obligate Member States to regulate safety and health at work to a higher or more effective level. It does not dictate to raise the level of protection of health. Considering the constant threats against the safety and health of workers, the Committee of Social Rights came to the conclusion that the process of regulating safety and health at work according to the law is a continuous process. Member States are obliged to systematically review provisions concerning the protection of workers' health, as well as to upgrade them. During supervisory cycles, Member States should meet the obligation of proving that domestic regulations on health and safety issues are

166. Conclusions XIV-2, p. 36.
167. Conclusions II, p. 182.
168. Conclusions II, p. 12.
169. Conclusions I, p. 22.
170. Oil rig platforms on the sea. Conclusions XII-1, p. 81 (Great Britain).
171. Conclusions III, p. 18 (Ireland).
172. Conclusions XI-2, p. 61 (Italy).
173. Conclusions I, p. 22.

kept up-to-date.[174] The Committee, when evaluating whether this obligation is met, will demand statistical data concerning work accidents and occupational diseases.

Legal regulations legislated by Member States with the intention to abide by Article 1 § 3 ESC are meant to protect workers against all kinds of risks recognized by international health standards. The Committee of Social Rights directly refers to directive No 391, legally binding Member States of the European Union, which recommends to adjust the work environment to the requirements and needs of workers, to protect them against harmful impacts and substances, to ensure special care for those subjected to higher risk, and to replace less effective means of health protection with more effective ones. Cases violating Article 3 § 1 discovered by the Committee of Social Rights concern a lack of adequate protection for agricultural workers and their families,[175] self-employed persons,[176] and cottage industry workers.[177]

6.3.1.2. *Obligation to Provide for the Enforcement of such Regulations by Measures of Supervision (Article 3 § 2 ESC; Article 3 § 3 RESC)*

The above provision obligates Member States to organize a system of supervision and control, as well as to enforce the regulations of the Charter. The Committee of Social Rights assumed that violating provisions of Article 3 § 1, namely, not fulfilling the duty of issuing safety and health regulations, automatically leads to violating the duty of Article 3 § 2 ESC. This is logical, because it is impossible to assess whether employers are abiding by non-existing safety and health regulations. Fulfilling the duty of Article 3 § 1 ESC can be legally deduced by checking whether the provision of Article 3 § 2 ESC was enforced with the application of relevant civil, administrative and penalty sanctions.[178] Relation between the provisions of Article 2 § 1 and § 2 ESC can be seen in the obligation of ensuring a means of control over health and safety regulations, that should be legislated under Article 3 § 1. Article 3 § 2 uses the term 'such regulations' *(cés reglements)*. This expression refers to health and safety regulations listed in Article 3 § 1.[179] The responsibility of governmental work inspections is the supervising of employers and assessing whether they are meeting safety and health regulations. It is therefore not possible to accept the Committee's stance, which, during the 14th supervisory cycle, came to the conclusion that there is no direct link between Article 3 § 1 and § 2 supporting the decisions that are handed down according to the provisions and that each section of the provision makes its own demands which should be undertaken irrespectively of each other.[180] Article 3 § 2 places on Member States the obligation to develop controlling mechanisms with strict labour law regulations,

174. Conclusions III, s. 17.
175. Addendum to Conclusions XI-2, p. 14.
176. Conclusions XIII-3, pp. 205–206 (Italy); XIII-3, pp. 206–207 (The Netherlands); XIV-2, pp. 429–430 (Italy); XIII-4, p. 342, (Belgium); XIV-2, pp. 333 and following (Greece).
177. Conclusions XIV-2. p. 123–124.
178. Conclusions I, p. 23.
179. Conclusions XII-1, p. 83, Conclusions XIII-3, p. 209 (Greece), XIII-3, p. 212 (The Netherlands).
180. Conclusions XIV-2, p. 43.

enforcing the protection of health, guaranteeing safety and hygiene at the workplace. In order to establish the level of effectiveness of such control mechanisms, the Committee demands that Member States provide information concerning the number of workplaces, the number of work inspectors, the number of governmental work inspections being carried out dealing with the safety and health of the working conditions within the workplace, the number of safety and health regulation violations taking place, and the number and type of penalties being enforced on employers not abiding by the said provisions.[181] For example, in the case of Portugal from 1996, governmental work inspectors undertook the supervision of a workplace in which only 6 per cent of the work force was employed, and it was decided that Portugal had committed a breach of Article 3 § 2.[182] A negative ruling was also made against Ireland, where there was a cessation of supervision to monitor the adherence to safety and health regulations within the agricultural production sector, and only sporadic monitoring of small places of work.[183] The number of controls taking place and the number of workers employed in sectors monitored by work inspectors, along with the number employed by governmental inspectors, allows the Committee to establish the effectiveness of such control monitoring safety and health regulations.

The objective criteria in anal the effectiveness of adherence to safety and health regulations by Member States is monitored, as mentioned earlier, by the number of accidents or work-related illnesses taking place. The Committee notes the accident rate, as indicated by the number of accidents per 100 workers. It utilizes the statistics entailed in the national reports, as well as ILO information regarding accidents within the workplace, as well as information provided by the European Union.[184] After analysing the reports filed during the fourteenth supervisory cycle by Portugal, the Committee claimed that compared to the previous year, in 1996 the number of accidents occurring within the workplace increased. The rate of accidents also increased (from 3.5 per 100 workers in 1995 to 4.8 per 100 workers in 1996). In the mid 1990s, in Portugal, there was a general increase of work related accidents, as opposed to the normal trend of decrease.[185] The Committee demanded that Portugal provide additional information concerning the reasons for the increase of accidents. Anal the situation from a European Union perspective, the Committee claimed that the highest number of work-related accidents as per 100,000 inhabitants was in Portugal.[186] It therefore pointed out that the ratification of Article 3 meant the acceptance of an obligation to ensure safe and healthy working conditions. The abovementioned obligation should be fulfilled by utilizing well-organized work safety and health services. The obligation of Member States is to organize and support governmental work inspections, an

181. Conclusions VIII, pp. 54–55.
182. Conclusions XIV-2, pp. 641–642.
183. Conclusions X-2, p. 56.
184. Eurostat, Accidents at work in European Union in 1994, Statistics in focus, Population and Social Conditions, 1998; ILO Yearbook of Labour Statistics, 1997.
185. In 1990 the rate of accidents was 6.4 per 100 workers. By 1995 it was 3.5.
186. 7.361, whereas the average in the European Union was 4 539. Conclusions XIV-2, p. 639–640.

institution called to supervise whether employers are following the safety and health regulations within the workplace across all the sectors of the economy. The Committee placed an obligation on the Member States to provide the Committee with regular information concerning the structure of governmental work inspections and the number of inspectors employed, as well as information concerning their competence. Testing the competency of work inspectors across particular Member States, the Committee decided within the majority of national labour law systems, the inspectors have been qualified to directly enforce the following: imposing fines, imposing administrative penalties, temporarily stopping the work of a business if the work is being carried out against safety and health regulations, and closing down a place of work.[187] In the mind of the Committee, the supervision monitoring whether safety and health regulations within the workplace are being met, should be effective. According to the findings accepted by the ILO, this means the method of inspecting employers should be both preventative and repressive.[188]

6.3.1.3. To Ensure Consultation with Stakeholders in Matters of Industrial Health and Safety (Article 3 § 3 ESC)

Member States have the obligation to provide consultations with workers' and employers' organizations on measures intended to improve industrial health and safety. Consultations should be provided 'when necessary'. The above provision encompasses the regulation of rights, principles and procedures of consultations in matters of health and life protection of workers. It obligates the Member States to initiate consultations, as well as to take note of reported conclusions provided by workers' and employers' organizations interested in undertaking such consultations.[189] Independent Member States, therefore, do not decide the necessity of such consultations. This provision places an obligation on Member States to participate in such consultations. Stakeholders do not have this obligation. However, with the technological process, when such decisions are being made concerning the improvement of industrial health and safety, stakeholders really should partake in the process. For this reason, the Committee requires information from Member States regarding the scope and the frequency of such consultations taking place between state authorities and stakeholders.[190] Consultations in such matters should be regularly carried out,[191] at a national level within particular workplaces.[192] The Committee did not demand information to be provided regarding regional consultations. It did not consider them necessary with regards to Article 3 § 3 ESC. The same reasons which dictated that

187. Conclusions XIII-1, pp. 92–93.
188. W. von Richthofen, Labour inspection. A guide to the profession, ILO, Geneva 2002, p. 100 and following.
189. Conclusions I, p. 24.
190. Conclusions V, p. 23; Addendum to Conclusions XI-2, p. 15 (Ireland); Conclusions XIII-1, p. 103 (Ireland); XIII-1, p. 259 (Portugal); Addendum to Conclusions XIII-3, p. 29 (Luxembourg).
191. Addendum to Conclusions XI-2, p. 15 (Ireland).
192. Conclusions XIV-2, p. 46 and following.

some countries are excused from the obligations of organizing consultations at a regional scale, based on Article 6 § 1. On a national scale, the goal of such consultations is to organize a tripartite commission and to work out procedures dealing with precedent-setting decisions in the matter of choosing measures to improve industrial safety and health. At the level of industries, consultations should be carried out on a specialized platform appointed by the workers, whose opinions regarding industrial safety and health and their improvements should reach the employer.[193] Consultations dealing with the improvement of industrial safety and health should reach the majority of workplaces. The Committee takes into consideration that according to some national labour law systems, appointing workers' representatives is dependent on the number of workers. If the minimum standard of employment is established at too high a level, as occurred in Greece, where workers' committees for industrial health and safety (EYAE) were only to be called upon from industries where at least 150 workers were employed, the responsibility of leading such consultations with stakeholders may be conducted within certain industries.[194]

The directive No. 391 of 1981 placed on Member States of the European Union the responsibility of conducting consultations with workers or with their representatives in all matters dealing with industrial health and safety within the work place. These actions include: informing workers about measures undertaken in order to improve industrial health and safety, and a balanced and proper participation of workers' representatives in decisions being undertaken by the employer in matters of health, life, safety and hygiene in the workplace. Directive No. 391 obligates employers to consult with workers' representatives about the following issues: factors that may influence workers' health and work safety in any way; decisions on appointing employees responsible for conducting health protection and minimizing occupational risk in the workplace; any actions regarding health protection and minimizing occupational risk within the workplace; decisions on appointing employees responsible for first aid, medical emergency, extinguishing fire and the evacuation of workers; information on risk evaluation in terms of health and safety as well as health protection, protective procedures, protective equipment, work accidents, ways of enabling workers and their representatives to obtain all relevant information on threats, protective and preventative measures within the workplace; and planning and organizing training in work health and safety, as well as health protection.[195] The obligation of consultancy included in directive No. 381 is broader than the similar obligation formulated in Article 3. For this reason, the Committee during its fourteenth supervisory cycle, addressed the Member States of the European Union and of the European Economic Area, abiding by Article 3 (Denmark, Finland, the Netherlands, Norway, Sweden, and Italy) a question regarding changes brought about by implementing into domestic legal regulations the obligation of consultancy with workers' representatives with regards to

193. *Ibid.*, p. 47.
194. *Ibid.*, p. 48.
195. A.M. Świątkowski, *Bezpieczeństwo i higiena pracy* (Work safety and health), *op. cit.*, p. 192.

measures employed to improve the level of health and safety standards.[196] During the following supervisory cycles, the Committee did not recognize any violation of the obligation to consult with workers' representatives with regards to measures employed to improve the level of health and safety standards by Member States. Ensuring this obligation, which does not require employers to allow workers' representatives into a decision-making process on a partner level, creates no obstacles for Member States. The scope of rights for workers' representatives to obtain information on matters of health and safety within the workplace has been broadened by Article 2 § 3 of the Additional Protocol (currently Article 21 and 22 of the Revised European Social Charter).

6.3.2. According to the Revised European Social Charter

The Revised European Social Charter broadens the scope of consultation that Member States should carry out with stakeholders. These consultations cannot be limited to improving the level of health and safety (Article 3 § 3 ESC), but they should also deal with all actions undertaken in order to ensure efficient access to the right to healthy and safe working conditions. Countries which are parties to the Revised European Social Charter, in consultation with stakeholders, commit themselves to:

Determining, executing and inspecting national policies concerning safety, workers' health and work environment. The most important goal of these policies should be to improve occupational safety and health, as well as to prevent work accidents and health hazards resulting from work, related to work, or occurring in the workplace. The policies should be implemented by first minimizing the reasons for workers' health and life threats deriving from the work environment;

- Legislating provisions concerning occupational health and safety;
- Ensuring enforcement of these provisions;
- Supporting gradual development of occupational health services accessible for all employed persons. Employees should be provided with health-related advice and preventive services.

The Revised European Social Charter gave Article 3 a new meaning. Modelled on the directive No. 391 of 1989, Member States are now obligated to work out policies of work protection and to enforce their postulates. Provisions of occupational health and safety and their execution are meant to ensure adherence to intentions of these policies. Important new elements of this document include: preparing priorities of health protection, drafting guidelines for work protection policies, and bringing about social programmes in order to improve occupational health and safety to avoid work accidents and dangerous factors and processes in the workplace. Article 3 § 1 RESC gained a new meaning, and a new obligation was introduced in Article 3 § 4 RESC. This regulation obligates Member States to support the development of occupational health services.

196. Conclusions XIV-2, pp. 48–49.

6.3.2.1. Policies of Occupational Safety and Health (Article 3 § 1 RESC)

According to the requirements regulated by this provision, Member States are obligated to work out a strategy allowing for the evaluation of the types and the levels of threats to employees' health and life. Policies of work protection should be regarded as an integral part of social policies. Within the confines of social policies, Member States should analyse risks, evaluate threats in the work environment, employ preventative action, monitor protective measures, organize periodical training of occupational health and safety for workers, and ensure professional treatment for victims of work accidents. The obligation of Member States is to constantly and methodically supervise the execution of social programmes. The States are also obligated to evaluate national social policies in terms of work protection periodically.

6.3.2.2. Occupational Health Services (Article 3 § 4 RESC)

The above provision demands that Member States undertake measures to promote the progressive development of occupational health services. Occupational health services should be structured according to the French concept of *médecine du travail*, with preventative and advisory functions. In the Appendix to Article 3 § 4 RESC, it was decided that the definition of functions, organization, and the conditions of such occupational health services are matters which should be left to the Member States. Such states also make decisions regarding the legal regulations and their functioning, such as: acts, executory provisions, collective bargaining agreements, or any other legal matters within that country.

6.4. The Right to Fair Remuneration (Article 4 ESC)

Already during its first supervisory cycle, the Committee of Social Rights was convinced that the right to fair remuneration should be ensured by social rights, and thus regulated by three provisions: the right to work, the right to appropriate work conditions, and the right to safe and healthy working conditions.[197] The above three provisions would be breached if the right to fair remuneration was not ensured. The right to appropriate work conditions in safe and healthy working conditions would lose its significance were there no fair remuneration.[198] The text of Article 4 does not indicate a significant character to the above standard, and provides no indication of how these standards could be connected to the other three provisions of the regulations in Part II. Legal practitioners specializing in labour law regard that the necessary distinguishing element in carrying out work is its remuneration. Remuneration is measured in terms of the type of work carried out and the amount and quality of work services provided, as well as the qualifications and occupational skills of the worker. Remuneration varies according to whether the work undertaken is completed as part

197. Conclusions I, p. 25.
198. *Ibid.*

of relations under the civil law or under economic relations regulated by contract law provisions.[199] In this context it is important to note the Committee's view that remuneration for work should be treated as a guarantee of the realization of the right to work in appropriately safe and healthy working conditions.

Anal employment cases in terms of administrative responsibilities resting on the citizens, i.e., the reserve army or work by prisoners (as part of a prison sentence) the Committee did not regard these as parts of the compulsory work category, as considered by Article 1, but rather work that is not remunerated even in part, as provided for by Article 4. These matters are considered further below. Matters analysed here refer to the basic problem of the definition of 'fair (decent) remuneration'.

6.4.1. Decent Remuneration (Article 4 § 1)

Member States which ratified Article 4 § 1 are obligated to ensure that workers are remunerated in a way that will give them and their families a decent standard of living. Decent remuneration is remuneration enabling an appropriate standard of living. Providing such a definition is substituting one vague term with another. An appropriate standard of living is an expression that has not been defined in labour law or social protection regulations. The Committee of Social Rights, from its first supervisory cycle, was aware of the ambiguity of terms used within Article 4. Almost immediately the Committee noticed that it was impossible to refer to 'decent' remuneration within the Council of Europe, an international organization associating countries so varied in their economic development. As early as the second supervisory cycle, the Committee addressed an important message to Member States who were parties to the Charter. The term 'fair' (decent) remuneration has different meanings. All Member States can interpret it accordingly. Interpretation of this term is directly related to the level of economic development of a particular state.[200]

The Committee sees all Member States as one entity and does not accept diversity in cases of given states.[201] Fair (decent) remuneration is a social policy category, applicable in the exact same manner to all Member States. The rulings of the Committee of Social Rights defining fair (decent) remuneration have had two phases. In both cases the point of reference for defining the term fair (decent) remuneration was the average national remuneration. Initially, the Committee believed that remuneration that did not differ significantly from the average wage would be regarded as fair (decent).[202] However, this attempt to define fair (decent) remuneration was not precise enough. It lacked a percentage relation between remuneration paid for a certain job and the average remuneration for this type of job in a given country. The OECD and the Council of Europe undertook studies,[203] that the Committee familiarized itself with

199. The personal nature of the work and the worker complying to the employer are both elements which can separate work from employment not regulated by labour law provisions.
200. Conclusions II, p. 16.
201. Conclusions IV, p. 31 (Great Britain).
202. Conclusions V, pp. 25–26.
203. J. P. Dalloz, Methods of defining 'decent remuneration', Council of Europe Publishing, Strasbourg 1977.

during the fifth supervisory cycle, and then utilized to draft a more precise definition of fair (decent) remuneration.[204] In a study prepared for the Council of Europe, it was suggested that 68 per cent might be regarded as measurable criteria of fair (decent) remuneration, determining a relation between the remuneration in question and the average remuneration in all of the Member States of the Council of Europe. Therefore remuneration above the 68 per cent rate was considered to meet requirements for fair (decent) remuneration under Article 4 § 1. Any remuneration below this level cannot be qualified as fair (decent). The Committee decided upon utilizing this rate to distinguish remunerations into two categories: fair (decent) remuneration and not fair (decent) remuneration ('decency threshold' approach). Making an attempt to determine measurable criteria for fair (decent) remuneration, the Committee took into consideration not only the nominal value of the wage paid for work (remuneration), but also other benefits with which employees are provided by their employer. The Committee considered this only in cases where the real amount of remuneration received was lower than the 68 per cent rate mentioned above. Member States had the responsibility to provide a fair (decent) rate of remuneration. They had to provide the Committee with details as to how the rate was calculated: realistic remuneration amounts, as well as the average remuneration. They were instructed that in cases when the latter rate was lower than the 68 per cent rate, they should also provide details concerning the material value of various types of social benefits allocated to workers, to the insured as well as to their family members. Amongst these various social benefits named were family benefits, benefits covering part of training/ educational courses, and low levels of tax or tax exemptions for those earning the lowest wage. Article 4 § 1 tells Member States to recognize such legal remuneration (fair-decent) that will ensure workers and members of their families a decent standard of living. Being supported by such guidelines, the Committee prepared separate techniques measuring the rate of remuneration, which were meant to satisfy the material needs of single individuals, married couples, single parents raising one, two or more children, and married couples with children. The Committee measured the value of social benefits and other benefits utilized by families, especially non-nuclear families as well as families with multiple children, to see whether such benefits supplemented the difference between the remuneration received and the average remuneration. Lower wages than the 68 per cent remuneration rate (the 'fair' rate) appeared frequently in reports provided by Member States. The Committee examined cases where economically developed nations did not guarantee to keep fair (decent) remuneration standards, even when considering the definition as understood by Article 4 § 1 – not only incorporating the nominal amount of the pay, but also the material value of social benefits.[205]

The legal and factual basis appropriated by the Committee is evident in the reports prepared by the Member States. They are supplemented by additional opinions and comments made by national organizations representing the interests of employers and workers. The Committee also took advantage of information provided by sources from

204. Conclusions V, p. 25.
205. Conclusions XII-1, pp. 92 and following (Great Britain).

international organizations such as the OECD and the ILO. The above techniques seem to work in situations not requiring maximum precision, as in cases of evaluating bodies such as the Committee of Social Rights for the Charter. In cases of gathering information concerning the rate of remuneration received by workers employed within a given Member State, as well as the average rate of remuneration paid on a national scale by workers employed in various trades and occupations, the Committee did not have enough statistical data. Primarily, the Committee was unable to establish the value of social benefits, which should be taken into consideration when establishing the value of benefits being received by workers and members of their families, where there is no wage recipient within the family. The Committee did not have the technical ability which would have allowed for the above information to be gathered, so it based its information on the statistical data provided by Member States. On more than one occasion, these Member States did not collect some of the above information and were unable to compare them to other indicators.

The first intentions of the Committee, to construct objective measurable rates of remuneration to assist in assessing the standard of living of a worker and his/her family, were not realized. During the thirteenth supervisory cycle, the Committee abandoned the technique of measuring fair (decent) remuneration. Because it did not create an alternate method of measuring the standard of living of a worker and his/her family, in that supervisory cycle, the Committee did not attempt to assess the national labour law standards in matters of remuneration, social benefits ensured by national social security schemes, or in social policies carried out by particular Member States to create the possibility for fair remuneration for workers and to provide them with a decent standard of living.[206]

The method incorporated by the Committee during the next fourteenth supervisory cycle is based on a percentage rate, used for differentiating the categories of fair (decent) remuneration from remuneration which does not ensure workers and their families with a decency threshold approach (an appropriate standard of living).[207] The difference between the new and the former technique establishing the level or remuneration is based on lowering the rate from 68 per cent to 60 per cent, as well as constructing a broader definition of remuneration. Currently remuneration encompasses all cash and non-cash benefits provided to workers by their employers. The level of remuneration comparable to the average rate is the net payable, after the worker makes tax and other insurance payments. To this cash remuneration, with the added non-cash benefits provided by the employer to the worker, there are also added benefits from national social security schemes. A comparison basis with the average wage is the payment and value of social security benefits calculated according to the different technique. The important *novum* when comparing real wages to the average remuneration in a given Member State is the abandonment of calculating the profit per family member. The Committee analyses whether the remuneration is fair (decent) based purely on the remuneration received by one family member in employment. It is of

206. Conclusions XIII-3, pp. 215 and following.
207. Conclusions XIV-2, pp. 49 and following.

no importance how many people within the family are employed and how many family members there are. The basis for this new method of anal the level of remuneration is the net wage, non-cash benefits, and the value of social benefits. If the remuneration of one family member, usually the main bread winner, exceeds 60 per cent of the average domestic remuneration, the Committee claims that the given Member State is fulfilling its obligations under Article 4 § 1.

Even if the remuneration is less than 60 per cent of the average domestic remuneration, Member States may prove that the real wages earned enable workers and their families to fulfil their requirements and provide a decent standard of living. Free education, free medical services, discounts for public transport use and other benefits associated with payable non-cash benefits provided for by the employer for workers, are all taken into consideration by the Committee in the supervisory process of fulfilling obligations under Article 4 § 1.[208] If the material value of the abovementioned benefits supplements the real wages earned, which are less than 60 per cent of the average remuneration within a given country, the Committee is of the view the State fulfils the obligations set by the Charter.

The most reliable evidence of fulfilling obligations under Article 4 § 1 is the establishment of a minimum wage.[209] The following Member States did just that: France, Great Britain, Ireland, Luxembourg, Malta, the Netherlands, Poland, Portugal, and Spain. This method enabled a comparison of the level of minimum wages (net) with the average wage (net) of a given country. If the minimum wage is 40 per cent of the average wage, the Committee claims that the Member State in question is not fulfilling its obligations under Article 4 § 1. A 20 per cent difference between a minimum wage and an average may be supplemented by the material value of benefits and services provided by the employer for the worker.

Summarizing the above arguments concerning fair (decent) remuneration, it is possible to deduce that in the Committee's understanding, a Member State ensures its workers and their families decent remuneration only when it can ensure a minimum wage. The supervisory body is regarded as having met the obligations set by the Charter in establishing a minimum wage and assuring that employers meet this obligation. The basis for this is the non-numerical paragraph of Article 4. The above standard obligates Member States to fulfil the requirements provided by this provision either when completing collective bargaining agreements with stakeholders, or legally when entering into work contracts in accordance with domestic regulations. Minimum wage established by a Member State is one of three abovementioned techniques to standardize domestic labour law regulations with Article 4 § 1. When establishing the minimum wage, Member States take into consideration the costs involved in satisfying the basic needs. Identifying minimum wage with a fair wage that ensures a decent standard of living, creates an uncertainty and questions the Committee's technique in analysing remuneration within Member States. It is possible to view that the method utilized by the Committee in assessing remuneration has been accepted by those bodies abiding by

208. Conclusions XIV-2, p. 52.
209. D. Harris, J. Darcy, *op. cit.*, p. 76.

the Charter, namely the Governmental Committee and the Committee of Ministers. The Council of Europe has failed to provide a decisive critique, authorized to partake in the supervisory process of fulfilling obligations under the Charter. During the debates of the Governmental Committee, two major points were considered: to reduce the real wages rate from 68 per cent to 60 per cent, which is comparable to the average pay, and to move away from the earlier applicable notion of measuring the level of remuneration according to the requirements of a family, and not just the bread winner. It was also pointed out that the newly reduced remuneration rate of 60 per cent, similar to the 68 per cent rate, is arbitrary in nature.[210] The approval of the new technique is undoubtedly caused by the fact that the majority of Member States fulfil the obligations under Article 4 § 1, as they recognize workers' rights to minimum wages.

6.4.2. Additional Remuneration for Overtime Work (Article 4 § 2)

Overtime work should have additional remuneration. Article 4 § 2 discusses a worker's right to an increased rate of remuneration for overtime work. The Committee did not define overtime work. It claimed that work above the standard of working hours (it did not provide those standards; therefore there is a basis to believe that it considers the hours above the daily standard) is work carried out outside the normal working hours or in addition to normal working hours.[211] Overtime work, according to the understanding of Article 4 § 2, is work carried out at night. According to the Committee, carrying out such work requires additional effort from workers, which should be additionally remunerated for.

Article 4 § 2 is generally applicable. It is applicable to workers in full-time employment based on a work agreement not defined by a period of time, as well as to workers in temporary/periodical employment for an unidentifiable period of time. Additional work for this last category of workers is work carried out beyond the shortened daily and working hour standards. To fulfil the obligation of increased remuneration for overtime work, there is no actual place for the carrying out of such work. The right to additional remuneration for overtime hours applies to workers who are carrying out work outside the workplace of the employer. The above argument refers to people working from home.[212] The obligation to additional remuneration is applicable to persons employed in agriculture[213] as well as domestic services employed by individuals.[214] Member States are allowed to denounce a general approach to the obligations set in Article 4 § 2, and the legal basis for such denunciation is found in this provision. It is applicable in certain cases, which the Charter does not specify. The exceptions refer to situations other than those specified in Article 33 ESC. The Committee of Social Rights takes care so the Member States do not use the rights

210. Governmental Committee XIV-2, pp. 220 and the following.
211. Conclusions XIV-2, p. 35.
212. Conclusions XIII-5, p. 54 (Finland).
213. Conclusions XIV-2, p. 479 (Luxembourg).
214. Conclusions XIII-5, p. 168 (Portugal).

provided in Article 4 § 2 *in fine* excessively. The Committee has accepted in practice to exclude from the obligations additional remuneration paid for overtime to those employed in managerial positions[215] as well as those employed in executive organizational units of power and national administration.[216]

Article 4 § 2 does not define methods for introducing this provision into the domestic labour law system. The regulation within the last paragraph of Article 4 instructs Member States how to fulfil their obligations under Article 4 § 1–5 and is applicable to all of the five regulations as parts of the provision in question. Carrying out obligations of additional remuneration for overtime work should be guaranteed either within collective bargaining agreements or through other legal means of establishing remuneration (e.g. statutes, decrees, regulations), or with the help of other sources in accordance with domestic conditions. For example, in Great Britain, the usual custom is to establish all obligations according to standard processes. The Committee analysed a report filed by Great Britain, which, in discussing its implementation of Article 4 § 2, noted 'very widespread expectations among workers that additional work will be remunerated with the higher rates'. The Committee concluded that a custom can be regarded as a source of workers' entitlement to additional remuneration for additional work, creating, as a consequence, enough legal grounds to impose on employers a duty of greater remuneration for the extra hours of work, on the condition that custom law embraces all employed and their employers, and that states efficiently supervise adherence to the obligation by a customary standard.[217] Notions used in the report presented by Great Britain do not create enough legal basis to admit that 'widespread expectations among workers', interpreted by the Committee lawyers as expectations, do not legally enable workers to litigate for additional remuneration for extra hours of work. In connection with the above, the Committee concluded that Great Britain did not fulfil the obligation formulated in Article 4 § 2.

The notion of 'other measures adequate to national conditions', which can be used in order to grant workers employed for extra time greater remuneration, also embraces work agreements. Work agreements are considered to be sources of mutual obligation between the parties in an individual work relationship. Work agreements can regulate work done at extra time, beyond the common daily or weekly standards, and work during night hours, as well as an employer's obligation to pay remuneration calculated on higher rates for additional work. Obligations of one party in a work relationship answer the entitlements of the other. The worker's right to carry out work in extra time answers the employer's right to employ workers in extra time. The employer's obligation to pay remuneration calculated on higher rates for additional work answers the worker's right to demand to be paid additional (greater) remuneration for the work done. A freedom of work agreement guaranteed by labour law cannot not be utilized to regulate other rules of additional employment than those prescribed under Article 4 § 2. If the content of a work agreement contradicts labour law regulations or makes an

215. Conclusions IX-1, p. 41 (the Netherlands).
216. Conclusions XIV-2, pp. 479–480 (Luxembourg).
217. Conclusions XIV-2, p. 773.

employee's situation less advantageous than it would be under labour law regulations, such an agreement has no legal force. The rule of employee's privilege commonly accepted by Member States requires the regulation of matters of additional employment according to a greater rate and disallows parties in work relationships to make exceptions from this rule in work agreements.

This is why, for example, the Committee regarded the conduct of Spain as violating Article 4 § 2 when Spain decided to depart from the rules of remunerating workers employed in extra time and leaving this issue for the interested parties in a work relationship. The Committee concluded such conduct is evident of not abiding by regulations set by Article 4 § 2 by Spain, even though the changed provisions of Spanish labour law compiled clauses guaranteeing that work in extra time should not be remunerated according to lower rates than the ones used for accounting wages of workers employed full time on a regular basis.[218] The Committee claims that Article 4 § 2 allows Member States to regulate rules of remunerating additional work in a most adequate way, according to the practices in a given country. Despite the fact that the Member State may allow stakeholders in collective bargaining agreements, or parties to individual work relations guaranteed by work agreements, to regulate the rules of remuneration for workers employed above daily and weekly standards, or may leave the regulations of the abovementioned issues to be dealt with in other ways – for example, by mutual abiding of commonly accepted customs by all interested parties (stakeholders and parties to individual work relations) – the states are still responsible for not fulfilling the obligations stipulated under Article 4. Member States are not excused in cases of not fulfilling the obligations resulting from the ratified provisions, even when the specificity of domestic labour law regulations excludes the interference of states with issues left for the regulation of stakeholders. Nordic countries may serve as a good example, as the issue of workers' remuneration is regulated by collective work agreements, whereby stakeholders draft the provisions. These countries evade responsibility for not abiding by regulations concerning remunerating workers and deducting wages, arguing that the above sphere was passed onto stakeholders and is regulated by social dialogue. As stakeholders are not international entities of labour law, social security law or social policy, the whole responsibility for not abiding by the regulations and standards set by the Council of Europe must be seen as a Member State's responsibility, as a party to the Charter.

Article 4 § 2 recognizes the right of workers employed in extra time to an 'increased rate of remuneration'. The above provision does not compile any guidelines as to the rates of remuneration and how they may be regarded as 'increased'. The basis for comparison is based on a standard rate of remuneration, which is paid to a worker by an employer for work in regular working hours, namely for work according to the commonly accepted daily and weekly standards of work time. From the textual interpretation of this provision it can be concluded that any rate surpassing the standard rate paid to workers employed according to daily and weekly standards meets the

218. Conclusions XIV-2, p. 682.

requirements of Article 4 § 2 and should be regarded as 'increased'. As it has been mentioned several times before, the Committee does not create models which should be implemented into provisions of domestic labour law by Member States. The Committee only evaluates domestic regulations in terms of their conformity with the standards set by the Charter. This is why analysing the obligation of increased remuneration for workers employed in extra time is sensible. Rulings of the Committee state that domestic regulations, according to which workers employed above the daily and weekly standards of work time obtain remuneration increased by 25 per cent, 50 per cent or 100 per cent, stand in line with the requirements of Article 4 § 2.[219] The Committee accepted, for example, a legal solution in Belgium where additional remuneration for civil service clerks working in extra time was 6.8 per cent higher than the standard, on the basis of which it was calculated.[220] Article 4 § 2 does not mention anything about rules of calculating the additional remuneration for work in extra time. The abovementioned provision orders Member States to accept workers' rights to increased rate of remuneration for work in extra time. Therefore, a rate of remuneration higher than the rate paid for work carried out according to daily and weekly standards of work time meets requirements of Article 4 § 2. Analysing the jurisdiction of the Committee so far, there is no case of a Member State failing to fulfil obligations formulated in Article 4 § 2. Even minimal increases of the rate of remuneration for additional work is regarded, at least up to now, as meeting the requirements formulated in the Charter.

The Committee claims that the increased rate of remuneration mentioned in Article 4 § 2 also encompasses cases of granting time free from work in exchange for additional work of overtime. The Committee replicates the standards established by the ILO in convention No. 1 of 1919 concerning limiting work time to eight hours per day and 48 hours per week in industrial factories,[221] and convention No. 30 of 1930 concerning regulations of work in trade and in offices.[222] It is important to ensure that the time free from work granted in exchange for additional work is longer than the nominal standard of work in extra time. For this reason, France and Belgium were regarded as states not abiding by the obligations stipulated under Article 4 § 2, because France did not determine a conversion rate between time free from work and additional work,[223] and Belgium's civil service clerks employed in extra time obtained in exchange the same amount of time free from work as the amount of time they had worked.[224]

219. Conclusions II, p. 18 (Germany).
220. Conclusions XIV-2, p. 134.
221. Conventions and recommendation ... *op. cit.*, p. 1 and following.
222. *Ibid.*, p. 123 and following.
223. Conclusions X-2, p. 62.
224. Conclusions XIV, p. 134.

6.4.3. The Right of Men and Women to Equal Remuneration for Work of Equal Value (Article 4 § 3 ESC)

Article 4 § 3 orders Member States to recognize the right of men and women to equal remuneration for work of equal value. Despite the fact that the content of this Article stands in line with ILO convention No. 100 concerning equal remuneration for men and women for work of equal value,[225] the provision in question more clearly requires the equal treatment of men and women workers in matters of remuneration for work of equal value. Article 2(1) of ILO convention No. 100 orders Member States to support the establishment of equal rates of remuneration for men and women for equal work, while Article 4 § 3 obligates Member States to accept the rule of equal treatment of working men and women in salary matters. The obligation to undertake particular actions, while accepting the rule of equal treatment of working men and women, involves the necessity of adjusting the regulations and practises to the above rule. From the first supervisory cycle, the Committee emphasized that the execution of this rule needs to be determined by Member States' objective criteria of work carried out by men and women and adherence to these criteria by employers while making a decision upon the remuneration rates.[226] According to the Committee, abiding by the above rule requires Member States to undertake systematic studies analysing different factors that have a legal and practical impact on work carried out by men and women.[227] Examining techniques of evaluating work and remuneration paid to men and women for work of equal value, the Committee pays attention to the equality of wages regardless of the sex, as well as to the conduct of Member States in cases of violating this rule, which is supposed to be constantly adjusting the domestic regulations and practices of a country to the requirements of Article 4 § 2.[228] The rule of equal remuneration of men and women for work of equal value can be put into force differently in different Member States. Implementation of this rule may be passed by Member State onto stakeholders or employers, or left for the judiciary. According to the Committee, however, the only subject responsible for implementing this rule is the state.[229] The rule of equal remuneration for men and women is one of the few regulations of labour law which, according to the Committee, requires involvement of Member States,[230] possibly in a legislative, and definitely in a supervisory phase. The Committee emphasizes the necessity of applying this rule *de jure* and *de facto*.[231]

---

225. *Konwencje i zalecenia* ... (Conventions and Recommendations ...) *op. cit.*, pp. 447–448 and following.
226. Conclusions I, p. 9.
227. Conclusions II, p. 19.
228. Conclusions III, p. 26.
229. Conclusions I, p. 28.
230. Conclusions, V, p. 31; Conclusions VII, p. xvi.
231. Conclusions II, p. 19; Conclusions III, p. xiii; Conclusions VI, p. xv; Conclusions VIII, pp. 67 and following; Conclusions X-1, pp. 60–61; Conclusions Xi-2, pp. 69 and following; Conclusions XIII-2, p. 262 (Germany); Conclusions XIII-4, p. 351; Conclusions XIII-4, p. 350 (Belgium); Addendum to Conclusions XIII-3, p. 32 (Luxemburg).

Article 4 § 3 orders members to equally remunerate workers, regardless of their sex, for work of equal value. The above rule is not limited to equal remuneration for men and women for the same, the like, or identical work. This means that different work having the same value should be remunerated equally, regardless of whether it was a man or a woman who completed it. The basic task of the supervision, monitoring whether this rule is being abided by the Member States, is the evaluation of the remuneration rate criteria and its differences. The Committee claims that criteria used by employers to estimate work should be objective.[232] It is interested in familiarizing itself with ways employed by Member States in determining objective indicators of different work having the same value.[233] During a session on the methods used by Member States in the process of work estimation, the Committee reflected upon introducing a uniform technique allowing all states to make estimations, regardless of the sector of the economy in which workers are employed and whose work was to be estimated. It concluded that it is impossible to find a universal technique which could be used for estimating different types of work.[234] It authorized particular employees discriminated against on the basis of sex (women) to file claims for their work to be estimated, in order to compare their work with the estimation of work carried out by better-remunerated male employees. The Committee as a rule took the position that the processes of work estimation should be restricted to one particular workplace. The rule of equal remuneration for work of equal value had a limited influence, as it did not take into consideration the sector of the economy of a particular workplace.[235] The Committee agreed to exceptions to the above rule only in cases of workplaces where the proportion of employed women was high, making it difficult to compare remuneration of men and women in certain positions.[236] During the first six supervisory cycles (monitoring whether the obligations of Article 4 § 3 were being met by the Member States), the Committee became convinced that none of the Member States had determined objective criteria of work evaluation, which resulted in a ruling stating that none of the Member States followed the regulations under Article 4 § 3. It was not until the seventh supervisory cycle that the Committee noted a significant improvement in these issues within Member States. Changes were seen due to legislating regulations guaranteeing equal remuneration for men and women based on objective indicators of work estimation and remuneration rates, as well as due to the broadening of competences of the national supervisory systems controlling employers and stakeholders in terms of following the above rules of remuneration.[237]

Supervising the usage of objective criteria of work evaluation by Member States, the Committee intended to eliminate workers' discrimination based on sex in the

232. Conclusions I, p. 28.
233. Conclusions IV, pp. 34–35 (Germany, Italy, Sweden); Conclusions V, pp. 32–33; Conclusions X-2, pp. 63–64 (Austria, Spain); Conclusions XII-1, p. 98; Conclusions XIII-1, p. 117 (Greece); Conclusions XIV-2, p. 480 (Luxemburg).
234. Conclusions I, pp. 10–11 (Great Britain).
235. Conclusions XII-1, p. 102 (Norway, The Netherlands).
236. Conclusions XIII-1, p. 120 (The Netherlands); *op. cit.,* p. 121, (Norway).
237. L. Samuel, *op. cit.,* p. 93.

process of remuneration. It underlined cases of direct discrimination where workers were performing the same, like, or comparable jobs, and were differently remunerated, with men earning more than women. It examined whether seemingly neutral criteria of work evaluation resulting in the amount of remuneration for men and women still led to indirect discrimination. Greater availability, readiness to work extra hours, readiness to work at night, and bonuses for physical work are circumstances that, according to the Committee,[238] lead to indirect discrimination, as they create preferences for higher amounts of remuneration for workers accepting work conditions proposed by employers. These workers are mostly men.

Article 4 § 3 prescribes to equally remunerate work of equal value. Applying this rule solely to the same and the like work can be considered a violation of this regulation.[239] Member States who did not distinguish between these categories were judged negatively and obligated to introduce changes into their labour law regulations, replacing provisions guaranteeing equal rates of remuneration for the same and the like work with provisions imposing on employers the duty of ensuring equal rates of remuneration for men and women for work of equal value. The terms 'the same' or 'the like' and 'of the same value' differ significantly. Evaluating a report presented by Turkey based on efficiency – as understood as the relation between labour inputs and the achieved effect, arguing it was the main reason for differentiating between the remunerations – the Committee took the position that the above criterion of differentiating between the remuneration rates did not take into consideration important factors such as the scope of responsibility, occupational preparation, skills, physical and psychological effort, working conditions, etc. As a consequence, the Committee concluded that work efficiency could not be the only criterion for differentiating between work remuneration.[240]

During the eight supervisory cycles, the Committee formulated a rule, according to which Member States are obligated to issue provisions commanding employers to remunerate workers equally for work of equal value.[241] In order to enforce the above rule, it obligated Member States to declare that all clauses violating this rule listed in collective work agreements and work agreements lose their legal power, having no legal consequence.[242] In cases of employers not abiding by the above rule, national labour law regulations should allow for litigation, which once decided, should cease legal power of all agreements standing in conflict with the rule of equal remuneration for workers doing work of equal value.[243] This ruling should result in *erga omnes* consequences. Norwegian labour law regulations, for example, were regarded as being in violation of Article 4 § 3 on several occasions, and labour court jurisdictions invalidated the regulations, only in the cases of the person filing the claim.[244] During such

238. Conclusions XIII-1, p. 126 (Norway); Conclusions IX-1, p. 42 (Denmark).
239. Conclusions VIII, p. 67; Conclusions XI-1, p. 42 (Denmark).
240. Conclusions XIV-2, p. 741.
241. Conclusions VIII, p. 66.
242. *Ibid.*
243. Conclusions XI-1, p. 72 (Norway).
244. Conclusions XII-1, pp. 102–103; XIII-1, p. 121; XIII-3, pp. 219–220.

proceedings to declare the invalidity of agreements, trade unions should posses the right to represent workers. Procedural provisions should allow for class actions by all interested workers. Additionally, the Committee suggested Member States introduce preventive measures in order to avoid applying, aware or unaware, any invalid legal acts bearing no force.[245] Ensuring the rule of equal remuneration for workers regardless of gender should be effective. In doing so, Member States should employ adequate legal measures.[246] Among these measures, the Committee suggested, foremost was litigation based on the rights of aggrieved workers to file claims for the payment of the amount of money not paid by an employer violating the rule of equal remuneration for work of equal value, regardless of who carried it out, a man or a woman. The appeals procedure to a superior court serves the same goal.[247] It should be based on the provisions and references to labour law that the abovementioned guarantee of the enforcement of proper efficient measures employed by Member States in order to monitor whether the rule of equal remuneration for work of equal value is being abided by, does not have legal foundation in Article 4 § 3.[248] The Committee of Social Rights aspires for the provision to be efficiently executed. Declarations are listed in Part I. The catalogue of these declarations does not include workers' rights to equal remuneration for work of equal value. Clause 20 in Part I refers to a worker's right to equal opportunities in matters of employment and occupation, without any gender discrimination. The argument that the abovementioned provision embraces a worker's right to equal treatment in matters of remuneration may be raised; however, it does not stand in line with the European Union[249] and International Labour Organization[250] assurances – one ensuring the rights concerning equal treatment in matters of employment and other concerning rights in matters of remuneration. The international labour law regulations primarily guarantee workers the right to equal remuneration for work of equal value.

Protection of workers' right to equal remuneration regardless of sex is executed by measures of legal protection determined by the Committee. Reinstating a worker who obtained the proper amount of remuneration and was made redundant by an employer is

245. Conclusions XIII-5, p. 255; Conclusions XIV-2, p. 593 (Norway).
246. Conclusions VIII, p. 66.
247. Conclusions IX-1, p. 13; Conclusions IX-2, pp. 10–11.
248. D. Harris, J. Darcy, *op. cit.,* p. 82.
249. Directive No 117 of 10.2.1975 concerning progressing of Member States' legal regulations in terms of equal remuneration for men and women, OJ No. L 45, 19 February 1975, p. 19; Directive No. 207 of 9 February 1976 concerning introducing the rule of equal opportunities for men and women in matters of accessing employment, vocational training, occupational promotions and working conditions, OJ No. 39, 14 February 1976, p. 40. Directive No 207 was replaced by Nr 73 of 23 September 2002 r., OJ L 269, 5 October 2002, p. 15; *See* M. Wanczel, *Równe traktowanie mężczyzn i kobiet* (Equal treatment of male and female employees), Universitas, Kraków 2003.
250. Convention N 100 ILO from 1951 concerning equal remuneration for working men and women for work of equal value, Konwencje i zalecenia ... (Conventions and Recommendations ...) *op. cit.,* pp. 447 and following. Convention No 111 ILO from 1958 concerning discrimination in matters of employment and occupation, Konwencje i zalecenia ... (Conventions and Recommendations ...) *op. cit.,* pp. 552 and following.

considered the most adequate measure.[251] The ruling of reinstatement creates the most desirable situation for a worker. A reactivation of work relations, according to the provisions of Article 4 § 3 namely with remuneration adequate to the type, amount and quality of work carried out, equal to the amount of remuneration paid for a male worker for work of equal value, is the most desirable solution for a female worker. This is also a solution preferred by the Committee. As an exception, the Committee accepts an alternative solution, which is compensation for the unlawful termination of a work agreement with a female worker demanding the proper amount of remuneration. This is a case when work relations cannot be efficiently reactivated or a worker is not interested in regaining a lost work position.[252] An obstacle in efficiently demanding the reactivation of work relations can be the employer's conduct, claiming denial of a legally binding judicial decree for the reinstatement of a worker.[253] In the opinion of the Committee regarding unlawful termination of work relations, this significantly weakens the rule presented above, according to which a worker discriminated against in matters of remuneration in a case of unlawful termination of her work agreement should regain not only her work position, but also due remuneration according to the amount of the work carried out. A worker should be convinced that the court, in a case where her argument is accepted, will order her to be reinstated to her previous position. Otherwise a worker will have no motivation in litigating for due remuneration.[254] A threat of losing a job emerges to be a serious obstacle in asserting pending remuneration entitlements for workers discriminated against on the basis of sex.[255]

In such cases where an employer has terminated a work agreement breaching the contract, the court may make a ruling for damages in favour of the worker, instead of having the worker resume her job. Paying damages has to serve the purpose of compensation and be a deterrent. Analysing the case of Denmark, which established a limit of compensation for a worker having been made redundant to be worth 26 weeks of pay, the Committee came to the conclusion that Danish legislation does not meet the requirements stipulated in Article 4 § 3.[256] It did not alter its position, even when Denmark increased the payment of redundancy to 39 weeks.[257] Analysing Sweden's report, the Committee concluded that damages paid at unlimited levels are seen as appropriate compensation for a worker having been discriminated against, whose legal due process allocates her rights, only when the court is unable to make a ruling due to domestic legislative limitations of reinstating the worker into the former employment. The possibility of such a case may occur when the defendant is a private employer with the right to appeal the court's verdict.[258]

251. Conclusions XIII-5, p. 524.
252. *Ibid.*, p. 525.
253. Conclusions XII-1, pp. 96–97 (Denmark).
254. Conclusions VII, pp. 26–27 (Denmark).
255. Conclusions IX-1, p. 13.
256. Conclusions VII, pp. 26–27.
257. Conclusions IX-1, p. 13; Conclusions X-1, p. 60; Conclusions XI-1, p. 68; Conclusions XII-1, pp. 96–97.
258. Conclusions IX-1, p. 44.

The Charter should ensure effective legal protection for workers against gender discrimination. It is for this reason that in the following supervisory cycles, the Committee underlined the necessity for introducing in domestic labour law legislation a prohibition of terminating work agreements with workers whose legal due course allocates them a right to fair remuneration comparable to the value of work carried out. As an exception, the Committee accepted verdicts of compensation instead of re-employment in cases when work agreements were terminated illegally. It underlined, nonetheless, that the level of compensation should fulfil the two abovementioned requirements; first, to deter private employers from unlawfully terminating work contracts, and second, to provide compensation for the damages entailed by the worker.[259] It is therefore not surprising to note the Committee's negative stance concerning Turkey, who has limited the amount of compensation paid to 24 weeks of pay.[260]

A necessary element of effective protection against gender discrimination is the appropriate allocation of the burden of proof of behaviour, when a worker with whom the employer terminated a work agreement in retaliation for demanding equal treatment concerning remuneration is claiming compensation or re-employment. The Charter does not obligate Member States to describe the reasons for giving notice at work. It is unlikely for an employer who terminates a work agreement with a worker who demands equal treatment in matters concerning remuneration, to inform of the real reason for the termination. A worker demanding his/her rights, when faced with the prospect of litigation, has many obstacles to overcome. A worker is unable to prove that the termination of a work agreement by the employer was done so due to earlier actions – such as demands made for equal pay, and demands not to be discriminated against due to sex.[261] The burden of proof, normally lying with the party suing for damages, is seen by the Committee as having little use in matters concerning the protection of workers' rights demanding equal treatment.[262] The Committee was first to introduce a legal provision, before the European Union did so with their directive No. 80 on 15 December 1997, concerning the burden of proof in cases of discrimination based on sex.[263] It obligated Member States to introduce in their reports dealing with the adherence to Article 4 § 3, information concerning the spreading of the burden of proof, referring to actions undertaken at earlier stages by workers accusing their employers of discrimination based on sex in matters of employment and pay.[264]

In a similar manner as is the termination of a work agreement with workers who are demanding equal pay for equal work, the Committee looked at other sources undertaken by employers in retaliation for actions taken by workers discriminated

259. Conclusions XIII-5, s. 254–255; Conclusions XIV-2, s. 374 (Iceland); XIV-2, s. 480 (Luxembourg).
260. Conclusions XIII-3, pp. 265–266.
261. Conclusions IX-2, p. 39 (Austria).
262. Conclusions XII-1, p. 100 (Iceland).
263. OJ No. L 14, 20.1.1998, p. 6, Polish text in: A. Świątkowski, H. Wierzbińska, *op. cit.*, pp. 362 and following.
264. Conclusions XIII-1, p. 118; Conclusions XIII-3, p. 219; Conclusions XIII-5, p. 256; Conclusions XIV-2, p. 274 (France).

against due to sex: changing the terms of resignation, temporary placements into different positions, decreasing wages, and making changes in working conditions.[265]

6.4.4. The Right of All Workers to a Reasonable Period of Notice for Termination of Employment (Article 4 § 4)

An employer has a right to terminate employment with a worker giving a reasonable period of notice for such termination. The above right of the employer was regulated under Article 4 due to legal consequences. During the period of notice, workers have a right to remuneration. The goal of Article 4 § 4 is therefore to guarantee workers a right to remuneration during the period of notice. The remuneration paid to a worker during the period of notice should also be paid during the period preceding the period of notice given by the employer. Article 4 § 4 is applicable to all work agreements regardless of whether they are standard or non-standard contracts.[266] Spain was regarded as a country not fulfilling its obligations under Article 4 § 4, because temporary work agreements for periods longer than a year were terminated regardless of their length, giving only 15 days notice.[267] It was applicable to workers employed on a trial basis. Analysing Portugal's report, the Committee was of the view that in cases of employment on a trial basis, where the period of employment may be extended to 240 days for employees in managerial positions, the period of notice when terminating a work agreement is dependent upon the agreement made by both individual parties to the contract.[268] There is, however, no obligation to regulate the period of giving notice in cases of self-employment.[269]

Article 4 § 4 does not place an obligation on Member States to make the periods of giving notice uniform for all workers. Differences are acceptable in the period of giving notice for various categories of workers, on the condition that the variety of periods of notice for all the various work categories are regarded as 'reasonable', according to the definition of Article 4 § 4.[270] In general, the Committee accepts variations to the period of notice depending on the nature of the employment, whether it be physical or mental. It does not give consent, as specified by the dynamic approach of Article 4 § 4, for different periods of notice for employees in particular employment for less than 20 years (28 days notice) and above (56 days notice).[271]

A 'reasonable' period of notice, a term used in Article 4 § 4, is neither a universal understanding nor an abstract one. It should be interpreted according to concrete cases analysed in the following supervisory cycles.[272] The Committee never attempted to

265. Conclusions XI-1, p. 43 (the Netherlands); Conclusions XIII-3, pp. 219–220 (Norway); Conclusions XIII-5, p. 270 (Norway).
266. Conclusions XIII-1, p. 124 (Iceland), p. 126 (Great Britain).
267. Conclusions XIV-2, pp. 684–685.
268. Conclusions XIV-2, p. 648.
269. Conclusions I, p. 8.
270. *Ibid.*
271. Conclusions XIII-2, pp. 263–264 (Belgium).
272. *Ibid.*, p. 29.

judge whether a Member State's introduced labour law regulation of a notice period is considered to be reasonable. Referring to earlier arguments disallowing the establishing models of legal institutions by the Committee, during subsequent supervisory cycles monitoring whether obligations under the Charter are being met, the Committee pointed to cases where periods of notice were regulated by a state which could not be regarded as reasonable according to the understanding of Article 4 § 4. The Committee analysed whether the basis for differentiating periods of giving notice according to national labour law, form objective criteria. It is generally accepted that the objective criteria for establishing a period of giving notice are the amount of years worked, either generally or in that particular employment.[273] Already by the fourth supervisory cycle, the Committee came to the conclusion that the term 'reasonable' used in Article 4 § 4, referring to the period of giving notice, is indicative of its dynamic nature and places on Member States an obligation to extend the period of giving notice according to the amount of time worked by the employee for a specified employer.[274] Giving Article 4 § 4 a specific character means the Committee must step away from principles used during the supervisory process, which monitors whether Member States are following the obligations under the Charter, according to which determining the conformity of conduct within the previous supervisory cycles automatically gives the same conclusion in subsequent cycles, in cases where the situation had not changed. The period of giving notice regarded as reasonable in the earlier supervisory cycles could be regarded as 'unreasonable' in the subsequent cycles if the period did not lengthen along with the time of carried out employment for the same employer. The Committee regarded that the legal mechanism for lengthening the giving of notice period, whereby two weeks for a worker having worked two years for the same employer are given, by an additional one week for every year worked up to a maximum of period of notice of 12 weeks, reflects the progressive nature of the obligations under Article 4 § 4.[275] The fulfilment of obligations by Member States under Article 4 § 4 also has an influence on the labour market. The increase in unemployment and the decrease in opportunities of attaining a job should be taken into consideration by Member States when establishing the period of giving notice, which should be lengthened.[276]

Accepting the connection between the periods of notice with the number of years worked for the same employer, the Committee held that it could not approve the following national regulations concerning the period of giving notice:

The period of giving notice of one week for a six-month employment period. A week of giving notice is regarded as 'reasonable' for the first couple of months of employment. During the thirteenth supervisory cycle, the Committee claimed that Portugal had breached Article 4 § 4, since an employer had the right to terminate a work agreement with a worker after working for six months, having a one-week

273. Conclusions IV, p. 35.
274. *Ibid.* Conclusions XIII-2, pp. 263–264 (Belgium); Conclusions XIII-3, p. 267 (Malta).
275. Conclusions XII-1, p. 107 (Great Britain).
276. Conclusions XIV-2, pp. 274–275 (France).

notice period.[277] More importantly, an 'unreasonable' period could not be a one-week period of notice for terminating employment of an employee after working from one month to two years;[278]

A monthly period of notice for a worker having completed one year of employment. The Committee is of the view that Article 4 § 4 is breached by countries which establish the following periods of notice: period of notice of five calendar days in the first year of employment, seven days within the second, 15 days within the subsequent years up to the fifth year of employment, 30 days from five to ten years of employment;[279] six days of notice for workers in less than five years employment, nine days for workers in five to ten years employment, 12 days for workers in more than ten years employment;[280] a week of notice for workers up to one year of employment; two weeks in the next year and eight weeks for workers employed in the same employment for more than five years;[281] a week for workers in up to two years of employment, two weeks for workers in two to five years of employment, four weeks for five to ten years employment, six weeks for ten to 15 years employment and eight weeks for workers employed for more than 15 years.[282]

The minimum length of established period of notice may be lengthened by collective bargaining agreements. The Committee takes into consideration the above possibility and gives it its approval. It does, however, concern itself that such a possibility covers all workers. For this reason the Committee viewed France's report negatively during the fourteenth supervisory cycle.[283] The generalizing approach of collective bargaining agreements should have a strictly obligatory standard. They may not be modified to worsen the position of the worker, neither by the stakeholders nor by any individual party to the work agreement. The above requirements are not fulfilled, for example, by Swedish collective bargaining agreements. It is for this reason that the Committee came to the conclusion that Sweden does not fulfilling the requirements stipulated under Article 4 § 4.[284]

The length of the period of notice cannot be dependant upon the age of the worker. The Committee came to the conclusion that national labour law regulation in Sweden are not in accordance with the requirements set in Article 4 § 4, because based on the collective bargaining agreements for workers in the metal trade, the period of notice for workers who have not reached 30 years of age, regardless of the number of years worked, is one month.[285] The Committee took note that some of these workers had 16 years of employment. The Swedish government explained that the stakeholders who partook in collective bargaining agreements consciously differentiated between the

277. Conclusions XIII-3, p. 267.
278. Conclusions II, p.
279. Conclusions XII-1, p. 104 (Greece).
280. Conclusions I, p. 29 (Italy).
281. Conclusions XIV-2, pp. 513–514 (Malta).
282. Case of Ireland. Conclusions I, pp. 177–178; Conclusions XIII-3, pp. 220–221; Conclusions XIV-2, pp. 397–398.
283. Conclusions XIV-2, p. 275.
284. Conclusions XIV-2, p. 715.
285. *Ibid.*

periods of notice according to the age of the worker and not the amount of time of employment. They believed that the chances for re-employment are proportionate according to the age of a worker. The Committee in part divided its arguments. It agreed that the amount of time of employment and the age of a worker might be regarded as objective criteria for different periods of notice, only when they are both included. As mentioned earlier, the number of years in employment may be regarded as an objective criterion for different periods of notice. However, according to the Committee, the age of the worker alone cannot stand as the deciding criterion in the establishment of a period of notice.[286]

The period of notice commences from the day the employer provides the worker with an appropriate statement concerning an act of will. A reasonable period of notice, as treated by Article 4 § 4, commences from the day the worker becomes familiarized with the employer's announced act of will. It is irrelevant whether the statement made by the employer deals with an individual matter, or whether it forms a part of a larger decision like group termination of contracts.[287] To the abovementioned period, the employer is not subjected to periods preceding the notice to the worker, even when national labour law regulations obligate the employer to announce the work agreement termination (this mainly concerns group terminations) to the trade unions, employment services, or work inspectors.[288] Periods of compulsory consultations preceding a decision with regards to the termination of a work agreement are not included into a notice period, because an employer has not given the written act of terminating a work agreement. This is because the abovementioned consultations can result in changing plans in terms of collective redundancy. Presenting the employee with the employer's notice for the termination of a work agreement is regarded as an announcement in legal terms, as binding both the parties in a particular work agreement. An employer warning a worker about terminating the work relationship, which is to take effect in the last day of the period of notice, is done so to allow a worker to engage into a new work relationship. The Committee takes the position that an employer is obligated to grant a worker some days free from work during the period of notice in order to help him/her seek new employment.[289] During the period of notice, a worker is obligated to carry out work as per usual with the same amount of hours and of the same value as prior to obtaining the notice of termination. However, the Committee claims that an employer has the right to excuse a worker from the abovementioned duty. The Committee's opinion is that the point of the period of notice (warning a worker of a certain event which will occur in the near future, allowing him/her to find a new job) is achieved after informing a worker in writing about the termination of the work relation, and excusing him/her from the obligation of carrying out the work. The essential condition to fulfil the regulations imposed on employers by labour law provisions is the obligation of

286. Conclusions XII-1, p. 106; Conclusions XIII-3, pp. 221–222; Conclusions XIV-2. pp. 715–716.
287. Conclusions XIV-2, p. 513 (Malta).
288. Conclusions IX-1, p. 45 (the Netherlands); Conclusions XI-1, p. 75 (Sweden); Conclusions XI-2, Addendum on Ireland, p. 17.
289. Conclusions XIII-1, p. 124 (Greece).

paying a worker the amount of money equal to the remuneration due, according to the period of notice.[290] The term 'amount' is mentioned and not 'remuneration' because an employer can shorten the period of notice, which results in terminating the work relation before the end of the period of notice, yet an employer is still obligated to pay a worker the amount of compensation equal to the remuneration for the whole period of notice.

Article 4 § 4 does not prohibit employers from terminating work agreements without respecting the period of notice. In the Appendix to the Charter it is explicitly stated that the obligation of introducing sensible periods of notice can by no means be interpreted as a standard prohibiting employers from terminating work agreements without respecting the period of notice, if the reason for the immediate termination of employment is a serious violation. The Appendix to the Charter does not contain a 'serious violation' definition, allowing for the termination of a work relationship without a period of notice. The Committee examines individual cases determining whether there were reasons for the termination of the work relationship without a period of notice.[291]

6.4.5. Deduction from Wages (Article 4 § 5 ESC)

The workers' right to just (decent) remuneration is protected by a provision prohibiting employers to make a deduction from wages for work completed without the employee's authorization. Article 4 § 5 obligates Member States to regulate rules allowing employers to make a deduction from workers' wages. Member States grant permission for making deduction from the remuneration for work. The above-mentioned permission and its scope is commonly accepted and seen as appropriate for particular Member States. The provision in question does not impose any restrictions in this matter for Member States. Conditions and the field of deductions can be regulated by provisions legislated by a given state, in collective work agreements made by social stakeholders, by arbitrary court decisions or in other ways determined by legal mechanisms of establishing work remuneration. They may also be regulated in a different way. Therefore, Article 4 § 5 disallows making deductions from wages which are unauthorized in view of domestic labour law. Under the term 'unauthorized', one should understand deductions not regulated by domestic labour law. The Charter assumes the need for making deductions from remuneration for work. Looking at the rulings of the Committee of Social Rights, there was no case where a Member State *expressis verbis* prohibits employers to make any deductions from workers' remuneration. A lack of regulations in terms of making a deduction from workers' remuneration cannot be regarded as a ban on making a deduction at all. In light of the regulation of Article 4 § 5, it may be perceived as granting permission for making unauthorized deductions. Therefore the provision in question obligates Member States to undertake relevant legislative initiative. Legal regulations resulting from these actions should be

290. Conclusions XII-1, p. 104 (Greece).
291. Conclusions XIII-2, p. 264, p. 513 (Malta).

clear. A general rule listed in Article 36 of the Constitution of the Republic of Italy says that employers have the right to remunerate workers according to the amount and quality of work carried out, ensuring a decent standard of living for an individual and his/her family. The Committee regarded this as inadequate. The abovementioned ruling was clarified by Italy, arguing that under the above clause of the Constitution, the real scope of protection of workers' remunerations is left for the judiciary. The legal system in Italy is not based on precedence. Nevertheless, the Committee asked Italy to provide information on the position of the courts regarding protection of work remuneration. Simultaneously, the Committee presented a view that a more efficient and more likely to be socially accepted – a remuneration, calculated according to the provisions legislated by the state, which is obligated to precisely determine the limits of deductions from remunerations made by employers in cases of employees not meeting employer obligations.[292] Precise legal regulations are intended to protect wages. Lack of such regulations occurred due to negative conclusions of the Committee addressed to Member States in a few subsequent supervisory cycles.[293] The obligation of introducing a regulation, concerning motives and the field of deductions from wages for work made by employers on the basis of either collective agreement or legislated law, cannot be passed onto the involved parties of work agreements, nor to the subjects of a work relationship.[294] The Charter ensures the protection of workers'. Therefore, workers should have the option to utilize legal measures in order to check the legitimacy of their employer's decision about the deductions from their wages that are due.

According to the Committee, the Charter guarantees workers the right to obtain their earned remuneration in full.[295] Neither the Charter, nor the Committee, determines the allowable field of deductions. The above responsibility is given to Member States or may be passed on to the stakeholders. The Committee never analysed the grounds or the scope of permissible deductions from wages. It presented the view that social collections (taxes, social security premiums), a workers' financial obligation in relation to their trade union membership (trade union fees), civil obligations (alimonies), deposits paid by employers to workers, as well as employers' amounts due to damages committed by workers, can be relegated to a category that is regulated by domestic labour law. Additionally, the Committee stated that when regulating rules and the field of deductions from wages, Member States or stakeholders should take into consideration the protection of remuneration, which according to Article 4 § 1, should ensure workers and their families decent standards of living.[296]

292. Conclusions X-2, p. 66.
293. Conclusions XI-2, p. 72; Conclusions XII-2, p. 94; Conclusions XIII-1, p. 124; Conclusions XIII-3, pp. 222–223; Conclusions XIV-3, p. 438.
294. Conclusions XIV-2, p. 399 (Ireland); XIV-2, p. 774 (Great Britain).
295. Conclusions I, s.
296. Conclusions XII-1, pp. 108–109 (Greece); Conclusions XII-1, pp. 127–128 (Norway); Conclusions XIII-3, p. 270 (Turkey); Addendum to Conclusions XIII-3, pp. 33–34 (Luxembourg); Conclusions XIV-2, p. 230 (Finland); XIV-2, p. 399 (Ireland); XIV-2, pp. 481–482 (Luxembourg); XIV-2, pp. 514–515 (Malta); XIV-2, pp. 594–595 (Norway); XIV-2, p. 743 (Norway); XIX-2, pp. 774–775 (Great Britain).

Article 4 § 5 is commonly applied, encompassing workers employed by both public and private sectors, being parties to typical and atypical work relations.[297] The analysed protection standard is not applied to persons running their own business (self-employed).[298] A motion made by Great Britain resulted in a regulation based on a legal fiction listed in the Appendix to the Charter. According to this regulation, Member States meet requirements set by Article 4 § 5 when domestic labour law regulations ensure protection for wage deductions for the majority of workers. It is difficult to determine reasons that this regulation was introduced into the Appendix to the Charter. The clause listed in the Appendix gave the same effect as applying the clauses listed in Article 33 § 2 ESC and Article 1 § 2 RESC. As far as protection against unauthorized deductions from wages by domestic labour law regulations are concerned, workers seem to be the interested party. Therefore, it is sensible to use the same rules of interpretation while interpreting the content of Article 4 § 5 as the ones used to analyse Article 33 § 2 ESC and Article 1 § 2 RESC. This means that in light of the language of Article 4 § 5, a 'significant majority' of workers occurs when there are 80 per cent of persons in work relations in a given country. The above basis for the calculation of the category of workers used by the Appendix to the Charter should be deducted from persons whose legal situation is not defined by national labour law regulations, collective work agreements, or the courts' arbitrary decisions. In the Appendix to the Charter, in the part containing an explanation of the content of Article 4 § 5, the term 'persons' was used for describing a group of subjects (workers), of which the significant majority should be protected against deductions from wages made by employers. Article 4 § 5 is a standard, which applies solely to employees. Some of them may be excluded from the scope of application of collective agreements or courts' arbitrary decisions. Occupational entitlements and rights of this group of workers are subject to domestic labour law regulations legislated by a particular state. Therefore, a 'significant majority' is a term that should be related to all 'persons', also the ones regarded by the final part of the Appendix to Article 4 § 5, as exceptions not encompassed by the law and rulings listed in the Appendix.

6.5. The Right of Children and Young Persons to Protection (Article 7)

6.5.1. Introduction

The general prohibition against employing children issued by the ILO[299] referred to the practice of employing children of kindergarten age. Article 7 § 1 ensures protection for children and young persons during the age of compulsory education.[300]

297. Conclusions XII-2, pp. 94–95; Conclusions XIII-1, pp. 227–228 (Turkey); Conclusions XII-2, p. 267 (Malta); Conclusions XIII-3, p. 270 (Turkey); Conclusions XIII-3, p. 269 (Portugal).
298. Conclusions I, p. 8.
299. ILO convention No 5 of 29.10.1919 concerning determining the lowest children age to be employed in industrial jobs, Konwencje i zalecenia ... (Conventions and Recommendations ...), *op. cit.*, p. 16–17.
300. Conclusions I, pp. 40–41.

Legal protection guaranteed by Article 7 encompasses the following: those at the minimum age of admission to employment (children and young persons); the maximum standards of work time; ban of employment for some types of work and for all work carried out during night hours; the right to just remuneration for the allowed work; annual paid holiday; and regular medical examinations and special protection against physical and moral dangers. The scope of protection ensured by Article 7 is somewhat vague. The Article in question protects children and young people under the age of 18 from direct dangers or indirect dangers resulting from the workplace. Additionally, Article 7 § 10 protects children and young persons from other factors associated with carrying out work and the working environment, and from physical or moral dangers to which children or young persons may be subjected. Supervising whether obligations set by this provision are being met by Member States, the Committee also demands from such states a requisition of information concerning clear prohibitions against employing children, legally permissible hours of employment for young persons, types of jobs in which young persons are able to be employed, regulated principles of employing young persons, and the number of employable young persons are allowed in domestic duties and family businesses. The Committee requires information concerning the controlling mechanisms undertaken by Member States monitoring the employment of young workers.[301]

6.5.2. A Ban on Employing Children Under the Age of 15 Years (Article 7 § 1)

The Charter prohibits the employment of children and young persons under the age of 15 years. It refers to all types of employment, paid or unpaid, in all sectors of the economy, including agriculture and the service sector.[302] It also encompasses jobs organized by individuals as well as relatives of the young person. The prohibition against family relatives employing children or young persons is wide in its scope. It encompasses a wide range of 'help' labour allocated to children by adults, in the course of running the family business. It is also applicable to job activities carried out by the young persons.[303] The Charter does allow for the employment of those children and young persons who are not 15 years of age, only as specific light categories of work, without harming the health and morality of those carrying out such work, and without inhibiting their schooling responsibilities. The exception in Article 7 § 1 places on the Member States the responsibility to draw up and publish such categories of light work, accessible to those who have not yet completed the age of 15 years. The Member States do not have the responsibility to state what types of jobs these are. A lack of such statements means that a particular Member State does not permit exemption from the general rule concerning the employment of young persons under the age of 15 years. The Committee of Social Rights claims it should not be possible to allow for a general

301. Conclusions XIII-2, p. 77.
302. Complaint No. 1/1998 International Commission of Jurists v. Portugal; Conclusions XII-1, p. 133 (Greece); Conclusions XIII-4, p. 291 (France); XIII-4, p. 293 (Italy).
303. Conclusions XIII-4, p. 291 (France).

rule allowing the employment of young persons under the age of 15. It is also impermissible generally to employ young persons under the age of 15 in light labour without prior specificity of such jobs as 'light', established by the Member States.[304] There are no jobs that may be generally categorized as light. In particular, all jobs associated with the service sector run by family businesses are not light labour (hotels, restaurants, farming).[305] For this reason, the employment of children and young persons in positions organized by family relatives, without being safeguarded by Article 7 § 1, is impermissible.[306] Banning such employment encompasses various jobs, regardless of the type of work agreements signed, whether they be work contracts or work experience.[307]

The type of employment of young persons under the age of 15 years, as an exception, should be specified on registers prepared by Member States. They should, in reality, be very light labour, indeed. They cannot cause harm to the physical, moral or educational well-being of the young person.[308] The Committee evaluates the type of jobs where persons under the age of 15 may be employed. Whether such jobs really do belong in the category of light labour is decided by such factors as the amount of hours worked in the given job, the time of day in which the work is carried out (whether it be before school, after school hours, on the weekend or during holiday periods), as well as the amount of time spent on rest.[309] In the opinion of the Committee, it is impossible to include in the category of 'light labour' work which includes the transportation and/or delivery of heavy goods using physically-powered vehicles (such as bicycles).[310] Depending on the nature of the duties carried out in the light labour category, it is impossible to include all work carried out on a farm, work in a forest cutting down and bringing in timber, or breeding pigs.[311] The Committee analysed the type and the nature of specified duties, allowing for the possibility of employing young persons under the age of 15 years. It is permissible, for example, to employ children and young persons in the artistic field, as models in advertising agencies. The Committee demanded as a necessary requirement for such employment that the employer receives permission for employing such individuals, as they are normally not employable.[312] It accepted the type of employment which enriched the practical work experience of the young person, especially when it is directly associated with an apprenticeship or

304. Conclusions I, p. 42; Conclusions II, p. 30; Conclusions III, p. 39; Conclusions IV, p. 53; Conclusions V, p. 56; Conclusions VI, p. 44; Conclusions VII, p. 41; Conclusions VIII, p. 101; Conclusions X-2, p. 80; Conclusions XI-2, p. 82; Conclusions XII-2, p. 119; Conclusions XIII-2, p. 78; Conclusions XIII-4, p. 293; Conclusions XV-2, p. 292.
305. Conclusions I, p. 42.
306. Conclusions VI, p. 44 (France); Conclusions VII, p. 41 (France).
307. First report on certain provisions of the Charter that have not been accepted, p. 17.
308. Conclusions V, p. 55.
309. Conclusions VIII, pp. 101–102 (France, Holland).
310. Conclusions XIII-3, p. 285 (Portugal).
311. Conclusions III, p. 39 (Italy); Conclusions XII-1, p. 133 (Greece).
312. Conclusions XII-2, p. 118 (France); Conclusions XIII-2, pp. 285–286 (Belgium); Conclusions XIII-3, p. 283 (Finland); Conclusions XIII-3 Addendum on Luxembourg, p. 40; Conclusions XIII-4, p. 292 (Sweden);

vocational training. The Committee insisted that the register of light labour allowing for the employment of children under the age of 15 years be completely precise. It was of lesser importance how it was drawn up. Publishing such a register by competent authoritative governmental bodies, administratively or in a format of a collective list prepared on the basis of court or administrative decisions, fulfils the function as specified under Article 7 § 1, on the condition that the chosen method by the Member States to prepare such registers is subject to control, and that the decisions establishing what light labour may be are not made in an arbitrary fashion.[313]

Employed in light labour, young persons who have not reached 15 years of age may not be employed in before-school hours. Work time should be made reasonable. Employment of seven hours daily, five times a week, totalling 35 hours per week, is considered to be excessive.[314] Young persons under the age of 15 years should have one day free from work. They should also be free from work responsibilities for at least half of their holidays.[315]

In particular, the Committee emphasized the necessity of obeying the regulations prohibiting the employment of children and young persons under the age of 15 years. It paid heed to the category creating the highest level of harm, i.e. children whose work responsibility caused the ending of their education before reaching 15 years of age.[316] According to the Committee, the Member States are obligated to undertake vigorous enforcement measures to obey the prohibition of employing children and young persons under the age of 15 years.[317] Children's absence at school was not regarded to be amongst these measures.[318] In a form used by the Committee, as well as by Member States in the preparation of reports concerning the obligations under Article 7 § 1, were questions referring to the activities carried out by state labour inspectors monitoring and supervising the ban of employing children and young persons under the age of 15 years. The Member States were obligated to provide information about the number of confirmed violations of employing children under the age of 15 years, as well as the penalties involved in failing to obey the provision, the level of such employment of children, and the measures and intentions undertaken in rectifying this problem.[319]

6.5.3. A Prohibition of Employing Persons Under the Age of 18 Years in Dangerous or Harmful to the Health Employment (Article 7 § 2)

The Charter provides for a minimum age of admission to employment, 18 years of age, with respect to prescribed occupations regarded as dangerous or unhealthy.

313. Conclusions XIII-3, p. 285 (Portugal).
314. *Ibid.*
315. Conclusions VI, p. 43 (France); Conclusions VIII, p. 103 (Sweden); Conclusions X-2, p. 81.
316. In the opinion of the Committee the most fragile group is children between the ages of 14–15 years. Conclusions X-2, p. 80 (Sweden); Conclusions XIII-1, p. 229 (Turkey); Conclusions XIII-2, p. 78 (Italy); Conclusions XIII-5, p. 185 (Portugal).
317. Conclusions XI-2, p. 82 (Spain); Conclusions XIII-3, p. 286 (Portugal).
318. Conclusions X-2, p. 79 (France).
319. Conclusions XV-2, p. 235–515.

Article 7 § 2 of the ESC orders Member States to set a minimum age requirement for employment. The minimum age set by Article 7 § 1 is 15 years of age.[320] The Committee did not define a general required age for employment higher than the minimum of 15 years. It claimed that establishing such limits is dependant upon the type and conditions of work to be undertaken. It ordered Member States to set such minimum ages as required for employment dependant upon the jobs undertaken by young persons.[321] This provision was changed by the Revised European Social Charter, which sets the minimum age at 18, required for employment in particular occupations and dangerous or unhealthy jobs. This change was inspired by international regulations accepted by the European Union, directive of the Council No. 33 of 22 June 1994, concerning the protection of work of young persons.[322] Analysing the report prepared by Italy, the Committee was of the view that in the following provisions concerning equal treatment of male and female workers, the age of 18 was lowered to 16 years as a minimum age for women employed in jobs where there is a danger of harming the body by benzyl poisoning or by products containing benzyl.[323] The Committee claimed that Italy ratified the ILO convention No. 136 on 2 June 1971, which concerned itself with the protection of health against benzyl.[324] It therefore questioned Italy regarding whether its domestic labour law regulations were congruous with Article 11(2) of the above convention, which prohibits the employment of young persons under the age of 18 years in jobs where they may be exposed to dangers caused by benzyl or benzyl products. Without waiting for a reply, the Committee came to the conclusion that by decreasing the minimum age limit required for the employment in work associated with exposure to dangerous substances, Italy was simply attempting to guarantee equal treatment in the workplace for both men and women. Contravening the standards of the international labour laws, Italy[325] were in breach of Article 7 § 2. Prior to the amendment by the Revised European Social Charter, the Committee supported by Article 7 § 2 ESC decided that 18 years of age is the permissible borderline age for the employment of young persons in dangerous or unhealthy jobs.

Article 7 § 2 obligates Member States to produce a list of dangerous or unhealthy work for young persons. The Committee is of the assumption that dangerous or unhealthy work for young persons may exist within all sectors of the economy, not just in heavy industries. During the third supervisory cycle, the Committee did not accept the arguments presented by Germany, which claimed there were no such jobs in question in trade, transport, hospitality, or gastronomy services. The Committee was of the view that within such sectors, undoubtedly there were jobs dangerous or unhealthy

320. Conclusions I, p. 186.
321. Conclusions XIII-2, p. 81 (Italy).
322. OJ No L. 20.8.1944, p. 12. Polish text in: A. Świątkowski, H. Wierzbińska, *op. cit.*, pp. 439 and following. *See* Explanatory report ... *op. cit.*, p. 164.
323. Conclusions X-2, p. 82.
324. *Konwencje i zalecenia* ... (Conventions and Recommendations ...), vol. II, *op. cit.*, pp. 842 and following.
325. Conclusions XIII-2, pp. 81–82.

for young persons.[326] Accepting the above proposition, the Committee turned to other Member States for their input on whether their lists of prohibited employment for young persons included jobs outside of heavy industry, in agriculture, or family-run businesses. The Committee claimed that these sectors of the economy consist of work demanding heavy lifting, which is carried out in conditions where a worker is subject to factors harmful to health (vibration, noise, chemicals).[327]

As an exception to the rule for disallowing young persons below the age of 18 to enter employment which is dangerous and harmful to the health, the Appendix to Article 7 § 2 of the RESC allows Member States to employ young persons in such occupations when it is necessary for their vocational training. This is allowable on the condition that an employer undertakes special measures for safety and health protection. Member States should determine these measures in advance.

Analogically, as in cases of supervision whereby Article 7 § 1 is being abided by Member States, the Committee demands from Member States the presentation of data on the efficiency of the conduct of work inspectors.[328] An indicator of said efficiency is the information on the number of work-related accidents and occupational diseases amongst young workers.[329]

6.5.4. The Banning of Employment of Children at a School Age in Work Affecting their Education (Article 7 § 3)

Article 7 § 3 complements Article 7 § 1. It is applicable to children and young persons who must attend school despite turning 15 years of age. Comparing Article 7 § 4 and Article 7 § 1 in terms of the scope of application, it can be concluded that that range of protection guaranteed by Article 7 § 1 is broader. Member States are obligated to prohibit the employment of children and young persons below the age of 15 in light labour, which is harmful to their health, morals or education. In cases of young persons over the age of 15, the above ban applies only to work which may interfere with obligatory education. Keeping in mind the contradicting scopes of application of the provisions in question, Member States who did not ratify Article 7 § 1 can be regarded as violating obligations determined by Article 7 § 3, also in cases when they allow employers to employ children and persons under 15 years of age in light labour, making it difficult for them to fully benefit from an obligatory system of education.[330] The goal of Article 7 § 3 is limiting daily work standards for young persons attending schools within an obligatory education system.[331] The analysed provision creates a legal basis for determining maximum daily limits of employment of young persons on days they

326. Conclusions III, p. 39.
327. Conclusions XII-2, p. 120; Conclusions XII-2, p. 287 (Malta); Conclusions, XIII-3, p. 289 (Portugal).
328. Conclusions XIII-5, pp. 66–67 (Finland); Conclusions XIII-5, p. 124 (Luxembourg).
329. Conclusions XV-2, p. 37 (Austria); XV-2, p. 78 (Belgium); XV-2, p. 234 (Greece); XV-2, p. 292 (Italy); XV-2, p. 337 (The Netherlands); XV-2, p. 516 (Spain).
330. Conclusions XIII-2, pp. 83–84 (Austria).
331. Conclusions I, p. 43.

fulfil their educational duties.[332] This provision caused the Committee of Social Rights to determine in what appropriate times young persons can be employed on days when they have educational duties. The Committee disallowed the possibility of employing young persons before undertaking duties connected with education. It ruled against the Netherlands, whose national labour laws allowed children to be employed as newspaper distributors from six o'clock in the morning.[333] It allowed for the employment of young persons after school hours on the condition that it did not cause a negative impact on their education.[334] According to the Committee, employment of four hours per day prevents a young person from fully benefiting from an educational programme.[335] Similar reservations were submitted in cases of the employment of young persons for 25 or 27 hours per week during the school year.[336] The Committee considered excessive any employment engaging young persons for 49 hours, involving time they should spend on studying during the school year.[337] During school holidays it was regarded unacceptable to employ children below the age of 15 for seven hours per day and 35 hours per week, and young persons over the age of 15 for eight hours per day and 40 hours weekly.[338] Analysing the employment of young persons over the age of 15 during periods free from classes (holidays, school breaks, and seasonal holidays), the Committee emphasized that young persons subject to the duty of obligatory education should rest at least half of the time they have free from school.[339] German regulation allowing for the employment of young persons under the age of 15 for four weeks per year were considered contrary to the obligation imposed by Article 7 § 3. The Committee argued that summer holidays last for six weeks, and therefore provisions allowing for the employment of young persons for 75 per cent of the holiday time are conflicting with the protection standards of children and young persons, as guaranteed by the Charter.[340] The point to holidays is to guarantee young persons a rest after a year of studying, in order to allow them to fully benefit from their education during the next school year.[341]

The ban on employing young persons under the age of 15 in work that deprives them of the possibilities of education, should be clear in its layout. Therefore, it is not enough to simply refer to the ratification of ILO conventions by a Member State, one prescribing a ban of children's employment,[342] the other imposing on Member States the obligation of controlling those persons who have the responsibility of educational

332. Conclusions III, p. 40.
333. Conclusions XII-2, p. 85; Conclusions XIII-4, p. 298.
334. Conclusions XI-2, p. 85 (Italy).
335. Addendum to Conclusions XV-2, p. 102 (Malta).
336. Conclusions XV-2, p. 586 (Great Britain and Northern Ireland).
337. Conclusions XV-2, p. 382 (Norway).
338. Conclusions XV-2, p. 549 (Sweden).
339. Conclusions XV-2, p. 382 (Norway); XV-2, p. 587 (Great Britain).
340. Addendum to Conclusions XV-2, p. 38.
341. Conclusions XI-1, p. 92; Conclusions XII-1, p. 136.
342. For instance ILO convention of 25.10.1921 concerning the admission age for work in agriculture, Konwencje i zalecenia ... (Conventions and Recommendations ...) vol. I, *op. cit.*, pp. 34–35.

duty and assessing whether this expectation is being met.[343] Regular class attendance and achieving good grades by a young person who is also working, are not regarded as sufficient evidence that the job is not negatively influential to the process of studying, as one is unable to deduce whether such employment prevents young persons from fully benefiting from compulsory education.[344]

The ban formulated by Article 7 § 3 is of a common nature. It applies to all types of work, including farming work,[345] and work carried out within a household.[346] Any exclusion from applying to this provision must be regarded by the Committee as conflicting with the standards of the Charter. Turkey allowed for the exclusion from the list of prohibited work for those students below the age of 15, the following: work in farming, crafts, construction, and work involving domestic services for individuals. This was judged negatively, and the decisions stated the approach to be conflicting in its nature of national labour law regulations and Article 7 § 3.[347] The ban on work for students below the age of 15 is applicable to all work, regardless of the legal basis of the employment and the relationship between the young person and the persons commissioning the work.[348] The Committee declared Spain in violation of Article 7 § 3, is it allowed young persons at the age of 16, who were still subject to the duty of education, to undertake work for their relatives within their own businesses.[349]

The structure of the ban introduced by Article 7 § 3 can be described as:

- Determining an age limit, which would excuse a young person from the duty of education. The above limit has to be calculated with consideration of a particular age when a young person subject to the duty of education comes of age. Turning that age takes away the status from a young person, who is thus no longer protected by Article 7 § 3;
- Determining maximum daily and weekly standards of work time in periods of education and during holidays.[350]

Summing up the Committee's rulings in matters concerning the adherence to Article 7 § 3, it must be noted that it is forbidden to employ young persons at night-time, in the morning hours before school, for more that a half of a daily standard, and during public holidays and seasonal holidays, as well as for a period longer than half the time of the annual holiday or school break.[351]

343. Conclusions VIII, p. 106 (Austria).
344. Conclusions XI-2, p. 85 (Italy).
345. Case of France: Conclusions XIII-2. p. 84; XIII-4, p. 296; XV-2, p. 192; Case of Austria: Conclusions XIII-2, pp. 83–84; XIII-4, pp. 295–296.
346. Conclusions XII-2, p. 83, Austria.
347. Conclusions XIII-1, pp. 229–230; XIII-3, p. 293; Addendum to Conclusions XV-2, p. 249–250.
348. Conclusions XIII-4, p. 299; Conclusions XV-2, p. 516.
349. Conclusions XIII-2; p. 86; XIII-4, p. 299; XV-2, p. 516.
350. Conclusions XIII-2. p. 83 (Austria).
351. Conclusions VIII, p. 108.

6.5.5. Time of Work for Young Workers (Article 7 § 4)

The working hours of young workers should be shortened. A 'young person' is understood as someone under the age of 16 years, according to the definition in Article 7 § 4 ESC. The same provision in the Revised European Social Charter raises this age definition to young persons under the age of 18 years. Article 7 § 4 is applied to young workers who are under no schooling obligations. This analysed provision regulates the working hour standards of young persons who do not have the responsibility in attending school. It is not applicable to those young persons who are continuing their education without any legal requirement to do so. The young persons who are not encompassed by the scope of the European Social Charter provision are young persons who, before turning 16, finished their compulsory schooling. They are neither protected by Article 7 § 3, nor by Article 7 § 4. The Committee came to the conclusion that there is, without a doubt, room for legal error in the Charter provisions protecting children's and young persons' rights.[352] *Per analogiam* to the situation of this young worker category should be Article 7 § 4, a provision protecting young persons under the age of 16 years who do not have educational responsibilities. Normally this responsibility of education ends at the age of 18. Before reaching this age of maturity, people tend to finish their education at the level of primary and secondary school. They fulfil the educational requirements set by the state. Mimicking views expressed by Article 7 § 4 ESC towards young workers under the age of 18 who completed compulsory education would lead to a faultless opinion concerning the application of Article 7 § 4 RESC in cases where young persons, after having completed compulsory education, but prior to coming of age, have undertaken employment.

The analysed provision takes into consideration the protection of young workers. Shortening of working hours, existing in the case of employment of young persons who are no longer in compulsory education, is required for their mental and physical development. This is particularly necessary for their vocational training needs. Ceasing his/her education at the level that is compulsory does not disallow the young person to continue their vocational education or training. Neither primary school nor secondary school provides a young person with job qualifications. It is for this reason that the usual practice of employing young persons is connected with a work agreement that is based on apprenticeship training or on the preparation for particular employment. This, in turn, places an obligation on the young worker to gain qualifications and knowledge connected with the job. Therefore, shorter working hours should help in achieving such goals. A point of reference to see whether Member States are following the obligations set by Article 7 § 4 is the basic work day (eight hours) and the working week (40 hours). The Committee of Social Rights ruled that the Member States in breach of the provision

352. Second report on certain provisions of the Charter which have not been accepted, 1982, Supervision relating to reports submitted under Article 22 of the European Social Charter (1961), European Social Charter, *op. cit.*, pp. 482–483.

set by the Charter are those who permit young workers to be employed in eight-hour working days and 40-hour working weeks[353] or longer.[354]

The responsibility towards young workers and the shortening of their weekly and daily hours has a general scope of application. It does not mean, however, that all young workers are beneficiaries of this standard. Article 33 § 3 ESC and Article I § 2 RESC, are applicable to Article 7 § 4, creating the basis of finding that Member States comply with the duties established by the Charter, when Article 7 § 4 applied to a significant majority (80 per cent) of interested workers. To form an opinion as to whether the obligation of shortening daily working hours is being met, the Committee turns to Member States for information to be provided concerning the working hour standards, as well as the number of young workers to whom shortening working hour standards apply.

6.5.6. The Remuneration for Young Workers (Article 7 § 5)

Remuneration for young workers should be fair, and other allowances paid to apprentices should be appropriate. The analysed provision regulates the principles of remuneration into two categories of young workers: workers who are employed signing a work agreement, and persons who are employed under a contract preparing them for a future profession – that is, apprentices for whom the job is part of the training undertaken in vocational education. Article 7 § 5 completes Article 4 § 1. The Charter protects all employed from exploitation, regardless of their age or the work contract that they may have signed. However, most importantly, the Charter protects young workers, due to the fact this group is at higher risk of being exploited by employers.[355] Taking into account the level of remuneration and other allowances paid to young workers, the Committee uses the net salary[356] of workers who have come of age in their first year of work as a point of reference. It makes sure that the employers do not lower this salary used as a point of reference in analysing the remuneration and allowances of young workers.[357] It does not accept excuses, such as the argument that lower wages for workers who undertake their first employment, revitalizes the economy and allows for the introduction of a larger number of people onto the labour market who were previously unemployed. The Committee considers this matter according to the perspective of Article 4 § 1 and its standards, which dictate that all workers – regardless of what category they may fall into, and regardless of whether it is their first job or not – have a right to fair remuneration.[358] The remarks made under § 4, as mentioned below,

353. Case of Italy: Conclusions XIII-2, p. 88; Conclusions XIII-4, p. 301; Conclusions XIV-2, pp. 293–294 (Luxembourg); Conclusions XIII-5, p. 124; Addendum to Conclusions XV-2, p. 70.
354. The Committee claimed, that the average weekly working hours in Turkey were: for workers between 12 to 14 years – 40 to 49 hours; for workers between 15 to 19 years – 47 to 48 hours. Conclusions XIII-1, p. 230; XIII-3, p. 296; Addendum to Conclusions XV-2, pp. 250–251.
355. Conclusions XV-2, pp. 340–341 (the Netherlands).
356. Conclusions XV-2, p. 294 (Italy).
357. Conclusions XI-1, p. 28; Conclusions.
358. Case of Spain: Conclusions XIV-2, p. 771; Conclusions XV-2, pp. 589–590.

are applicable when analysing the level of remuneration and allowances for young workers, either in employment or in an apprenticeship. The obligation of Member States is to provide the Committee with reports containing information about the level of remuneration for workers who are of age, having commenced their first employment, as well as the minimum wage paid in specified branches of the economy. Apart from this, Member States are obligated to present information concerning the level of wages paid to young workers, as well as to inform about the type and the value of additional allowances, that are utilized by young workers during their apprenticeships.[359] Apprentices do not remain in the employ of the employer training them. During practical training, jobs that are undertaken for the purpose of the apprenticeship, having a certain value, are advantageous for the employer who prepares such vocational training; therefore, the apprentices have the right to attain appropriate allowances, not to be classified by the state as remuneration. Such allowances, at times referred to as 'scholarships', should be left alone in relation to the wages that are paid to workers who have come of age and are working in their first job. Depending on the wages paid to workers who have come of age, to the young workers, and the appropriate allowances are paid to apprentices as follows: taking as a reference point 100 per cent of net remuneration paid by an employer of a given trade to workers undertaking their first job, remuneration for young workers should be calculated at the level of 75–80 per cent of that amount, whereas young apprentices should obtain from one-third to two-thirds of the remuneration accepted as a basis of comparison for wages and financial benefits. Evaluating national reports, the Committee clearly stated that remuneration lower by 30 per cent, 34 per cent and 40 per cent from the amount of net remuneration paid by an employer to workers of an age entering into the work market is in conflict with the standards established under Article 7 § 5.[360] Wage differences between a net remuneration obtained by a worker of age who is employed for the first time in his/her career and remunerations of young workers, as well as allowances paid to young apprentices by an employer providing training, depends on the professional experience of young workers. In the case of young workers, the difference in the net amount of remuneration should decrease with age and through gaining professional experience. The Committee accepts a 20 per cent difference between the remuneration of workers of age and young workers from the ages of 16 to 18 years. It also approves of a 5 per cent increase of this difference in the case of remunerating young workers under the age of 16.[361]

In the case of young apprentices, the differences in the level of remuneration paid out by employers organizing vocational training, in comparison to wages obtained by workers of age undertaking their first job, should not be bigger that one-third in the first

359. Conclusions I, p. 44; Conclusions VI, p. 52 (France).

360. Case of the Netherlands: Conclusions XIII-1, p. 167; Conclusions XIII-2, p. 91; Conclusions XIII-4, p. 303; Conclusions XV-2, p. 340–341; Case of Luxembourg: Addendum to Conclusions XIII-3, p. 42; Conclusions XIII-5, p. 125; Addendum to Conclusions XV-2, p. 71; Case of Belgium: Conclusions XV-2, p. 80–81; Case of Ireland: Conclusions XIII-4, p. 302–3-3; Addendum to Conclusions XIV-2, p. 16–17; Case of Spain: XIII-2, p. 92; Conclusions XV-2, p. 517–518.

361. Conclusions V, p. 63.

year of training and not bigger than two-thirds of the remuneration obtained by workers of age in the second year of training. The Committee is of the opinion that the maximum length of a training cycle should not exceed two or three years. The period of training professional skills and efficiency of young persons serving their apprenticeships is lower than those of workers of age, who have already been trained. The above disproportions decrease in the course of the training. Establishing the amount of remuneration paid out to young persons benefiting from vocational training organized by an employer, should include the value of this training. There are mutual links between the value of knowledge and practical skills provided for young persons in the process of vocational training, and the amount of remuneration (scholarship) they are entitled to obtain from an employer organizing the vocational training. The value of professional skills acquired during the training should then automatically relate to the amounts of remunerations obtained by young persons in the following stages of training. This is why the difference in remuneration of young apprentices and the initial remuneration of workers of age should not exceed one-third in the first stage and two-thirds in the final phase of training.

Remuneration of young workers and appropriate allowances for young apprentices are legal terms. The practice can be examined after comparing remuneration of young workers and allowances for young apprentices with net remunerations of workers of age who are beginning their professional carrier. These net remunerations cannot be lower than the minimum wages in a particular country.

Article 7 § 5 does not provide us with guidelines on how to establish remuneration for young workers and appropriate allowances for young apprentices. It can occur both by provisions legislated by state or by collective work agreements entered into by stakeholders.[362] As collective work agreements usually regulate conditions of individual work agreements, the amount of remuneration for young apprentices in a period of vocational training is usually specified by provisions legislated by the Member States.

6.5.7. Time of Vocational Training (Article 7 § 6)

In planning a young person's working day, employers must consider the time spent in vocational training by young persons. Article 7 § 6 applies to young workers and young apprentices employed on the basis of work agreements, specifying that the above employment has been undertaken in order to partake in vocational training and professional preparation.[363] Considering time spent by young persons in vocational training and forming part of the working day means that young persons obtain remuneration for time spent in training equal to the amount of remuneration they would be entitled to if they carried out work. They are by no means obligated to catch up on the time spent in vocational training, the time employers have been obligated to pay for, by

---

362. Third report on certain provisions of the Charter which have not been accepted, 1989, Supervision relating to reports submitted under Article 22 of the European Social Charter (1961), European Social Charter, *op. cit.*, pp. 484 and following.
363. Conclusions VIII, p. 116; Conclusions IX-1, p. 63 (Norway).

carrying out extra work.[364] Article 7 § 6 established a rule explicitly expressed by the following citation: 'time spent by young persons in vocational training during normal working hours should be remunerated not recuperated'.[365] It can be concluded from Article 7 § 6 that the necessary condition of judging time spent in vocational training among regular time of work is done by the employer's consent. The Committee of Social Rights declared that the above regulation could not be interpreted as though the employer's consent is considered *conditio sine qua non* of granting a young person the right to remuneration for time spent in vocational training without the obligation of catching up on it. During the fifth supervisory cycle, the Committee concluded that Article 7 § 6 does not provide employers with the imperative rights with regards to making a decision about including or not including time spent by a young person in vocational training, into the total amount of working time binding this person. Including the time spent by a young person in vocational training into a standard of working time occurs automatically, at the employer's will. The analysed provision is interpreted by the Committee as a legal standard allowing employers to determine the time and conditions of utilizing the right of vocational training by a young person and, in turn, the right to have the time spent in vocational training included into a daily standard of working time.[366]

6.5.8. Annual Holiday for Young Persons (Article 7 § 7)

Young workers employed on the basis of a work agreement are entitled to annual holiday with pay. The European Social Charter sets the length of this holiday at three weeks, while the Revised European Social Charter extends this period to four weeks. Holidays are calculated by working days. Their length is directly proportional to the amount of working time. Young workers employed full-time are entitled to three or four weeks of paid holidays per year. Young workers employed part-time acquire a decreased amount of holidays.[367] Young workers whose holiday entitlements are regulated by the European Social Charter, who are employed six days per week, are entitled to 18 days of holidays calculated by working days. Young workers employed five days per week are entitled to 15 days of holidays.[368] In the case of minimum holidays (four weeks), a six-day-a-week employment ensures a worker the entitlement to 24 working days of holiday. In that case, a five-day-a-week employment entitles a young worker to 20 working days of holiday within a calendar year.[369] Accepting the rule *pro rata temporis* by the Charter makes it difficult to enforce the proposition formulated by Belgian labour law regulations, which grant young workers the right to utilize at least three consecutive weeks of holiday between 1 May and 31 October.[370]

---

364. Conclusions V, p. 67.
365. L. Samuel, *op. cit.,* s. 195.
366. Conclusions V. p. 67.
367. Conclusions I, p. 45.
368. L. Samuel, *op. cit.,* s. 196.
369. Conclusions XV-2, pp. 81–82 (Belgium).
370. *Ibid.*, p. 82.

The Revised European Social Charter introduced the same holiday period for both young workers and workers that have come of age. In the European Social Charter, holidays for young workers are longer by one week than those of workers who have come of age (Article 2 § 3). The rules in acquiring holidays for both young and of age workers are similar. The pattern of legal regulation concerning holidays for young workers may be allocated according to the period of employment, subject to the regulations of the national labour laws. A young worker having completed a 12-month period of employment is entitled according to the Committee to have a legal right to a holiday.[371] The Committee emphasized to a greater extent than it does for workers who are of age, the importance of a holiday for the sake of physical and mental health for young workers. For this reason, a young worker is unable to voluntarily transfer his/her holiday onto another worker, even for payment.[372] Young workers should utilize their holidays according to the regulations. If the worker is unable to attend work due to illness which takes place during the worker's holiday period, the holiday period is suspended and utilized at a later date, when the worker has recovered.[373]

Article 7 § 7 is general in its scope,[374] although the most applicable principles are found in Article 33 § 2 ESC and in Article I § 2 RESC. An indication that a Member State abides by the obligations set by this provision is seen when annual paid leave, as prescribed by the regulation set in the Charter, is utilized by at least 80 per cent of young workers.[375] An apprentice or a young worker undertaking vocational training is entitled to uninterrupted rest. Because such workers do not remain in the employment, such rest from vocational training responsibilities is not referred to as paid leave. This type of rest, however, does have the same point as leave.[376]

6.5.9. Banning the Employment of Young Persons in Night Employment (Article 7 § 8)

Member States have the obligation of setting regulations prohibiting the employment of young persons under the age of 18 years, to carry out employment during night hours. This prohibition has a general scope. It is applicable to all young workers, regardless of gender.[377] It encompasses all sectors of the economy, and cannot be limited to employment in heavy industry.[378] Turkey is considered to have breached its obligations set under Article 7 § 8, as the prohibition of employment of young persons during night hours did not take encompass farming and the service sector.[379]

371. Conclusions I, p. 20.
372. Conclusions I, p. 70.
373. Conclusions XV-1, p. 519; Addendum to Conclusions XV-2, p. 176.
374. Young workers also have the right to annual paid leave, when employed in businesses that are run by family members. Addendum to Conclusions XV-2, p. 176 (Slovakia)
375. Conclusions XIII-5, p. 70 (Finland).
376. Addendum to Conclusions XV-2, p. 176 (Slovakia).
377. Conclusions XII-2, p. 130 (Malta).
378. Conclusions XIII-2, pp. 96–97 (Cyprus); Conclusions XIII-5, p. 191 (Portugal).
379. Conclusions XIII-3, p. 305; Addendum to Conclusions XV-2, pp. 252–253.

This policy of disallowing young persons to be employed in night work should encompass the majority of young persons. In the Appendix to Article 7 § 8, it notes that a State fulfils its obligations stipulated by this provision if 'it adapts itself to the spirit of this obligation', and if it ensures in its domestic labour regulations that a significant majority of persons under the age of 18 years will not be employed during night hours. In accordance with the regulation, as part of the Appendix, Member States are obligated to produce information concerning whether Article 7 § 8 is being followed. Not fulfilling the above provision means there is an injunction on the decision being handed down by the Committee with regards to whether domestic labour law regulations practices exist in accordance with Article 7 § 8.[380] Member States, when completing the requirements stipulated by the provision in question, should establish what night-time is, and ensure a clear ban on employing young persons within this timeframe. A necessary requirement for fulfilling the obligation of this provision is to provide in written format the regulations of the domestic labour laws which establish what night hours are, and what the abovementioned prohibition is, as well as include information about how employers are abiding by such a prohibition. Article 7 § 8 does not have any guidelines regarding the definition of what 'night hours' may be. The Committee does not demand for Member States to incorporate both definitions of this period, i.e., one period required for young persons, the other for mature workers. The regulation prohibiting young people from working during what the Committee regards as 'night', a period during which mature workers receive overtime wages, is seen as having fulfilled the obligations. Member States have the right to define the 'night' period depending upon: the possibility of paying a worker who is able to work during the night additional remuneration, and upon the prohibition of employing young persons under the age of 16 or 18 years. An appropriate timeframe ban for employing young persons under 16 years is considered the hours between 7:00 p.m. and 6:00 a.m., and for persons under the age of 18 years, the hours between 10:00 p.m. and 5:00 a.m.[381] State legislation, which forbids the employment of young persons between the hours of 11:00 p.m. and 6:00 a.m., is considered to fulfil the obligations set by the Charter.[382] The prohibition of employing young persons during night hours is not absolute in its nature. Article 7 § 8 authorizes Member States to allow for the employment during night hours of young persons who have not completed 18 years of age, in certain occupations recognized by the State's legislation. The Committee, during its supervisory process, monitoring whether the provision decided upon by a Member State is being met, does not consider the jobs which are exceptions to the prohibition of employing young persons during the night period. It requires presenting information on: occupations and types of work in which young persons can be employed during night-time, on the scope of exceptions from this rule concerning the age of young persons who can be employed during night-time, and the number of hours during

380. Conclusions XV-2, p. 82 (Belgium); Conclusions XV-2, pp. 236–237 (Greece); Conclusions XV-2, p. 519 (Spain).
381. Conclusions XIII-2, pp. 96–97 (Cyprus); Conclusions XIII-5, p. 191 (Portugal).
382. Conclusions XII-2, p. 130 (Malta).

which the above work is allowed to be carried out.[383] Having this data, the Committee is able to control whether the rule of the majority listed in the Appendix to Article 7 § 8 was violated or not.

6.5.10. Regular Medical Control of Young Persons (Article 7 § 9)

Member States are obligated to legislate provisions concerning the health protection of young persons. The abovementioned provisions should introduce the obligation of regular medical control for young persons under the age of 18, employed in given occupations. The obligation of regular medical control of young persons encompasses young workers, young persons running their own businesses,[384] going through professional preparation, attending vocational training, and those carrying out work free of charge by helping out in of a family business.[385] The rule concerns young persons carrying out work that is listed in the domestic labour law regulations. The Charter leaves the drafting of such a list of these occupations and types of work to Member States. The Committee familiarizes itself with registers drawn up by Member States and evaluates them in terms of the number of occupations and types of work listed in the register, and also in terms of the availability of out of work medical services, or a place where the learning of trade, professional preparation or vocational training takes place.[386] The Committee finds it important that regular medical control is performed for the largest possible number of young workers, and not only restricted to young persons employed in work exposing them to dangerous substances[387] or in selected occupations or types of work. The Committee demands that Member States do not present information only on some medical examinations, but that they provide information on all examinations performed in the occupations and types of work listed by the domestic labour law regulations.[388] There is no reason for the organization of medical control in some sectors of the economy or services. Article 7 § 9 imposes on Member States the obligation of preparing registers of occupations where regular medical control of young employees is necessary. Occupations and types of work encompassed by the obligation of regular medical control are located in different sectors. Therefore, there are not sufficient grounds to exclude particular sectors of the economy from the abovementioned obligation. Regular medical control should also apply to young persons employed in particular types of work in agriculture, craft and trade.[389]

Medical control should be performed very regularly.[390] Performing a medical examination before making a hiring decision about a young person and conducting

383. Conclusion I, p. 46.
384. Conclusions XIII-2, pp. 99–100 (Spain).
385. *Ibid.*; Conclusions XIII-4, p. 3120; Conclusions XV-2, pp. 519–520.
386. Conclusions VI, p. 58 (Great Britain).
387. Conclusions III, p. 46 (Germany).
388. Conclusions VI, p. 58 (Great Britain).
389. Case of Turkey: Conclusions XIII-1, pp. 232–233; Conclusions XIII-3, pp. 306–307; Addendum to Conclusions XV-2, p. 254.
390. Conclusions II, p. 37.

a further medical control a year from the date of signing a work agreement or agreement of learning a trade only, does not meet requirements set by Article 7 § 9.[391] Medical examinations of young persons should be performed in regular intervals of time, for example, annually.[392] Organizing medical controls in longer intervals, for instance, medical controls of young sailors performed once every two years, was considered by the Committee as not fulfilling the obligation established by Article 7 § 9.[393] Performing regular medical controls of young persons is an obligation that can be substituted by way of consultations. Regulations existing in one of the Member States leaving young persons the decision whether they want to go through a medical examination or not was regarded by the Committee as conflicting with the standards established by the Charter. Medical control of young persons is an important aspect of social protection of young persons, and the decision to carry it out cannot be left to the good will of the interested subjects.[394] Sweden was considered a state that did not meet the requirements formulated in Article 7 § 9, because its national report does not explicitly state whether medical examinations of young persons are performed systematically and are obligatory in certain intervals of time, or solely precede an employer making a hiring decision concerning a young person.[395] Member States are obligated to provide information proving that regular medical controls of young persons' health are performed as a practice.

The Charter does not impose on Member States the obligation of organizing a separate health service system, accessible only for young persons. Existing health service units, as referred to in Article 7 § 9, can carry out regular medical controls.[396] The Committee demands, however, that doctors are informed who is responsible for performing such controls on young persons as patients, and that doctors are provided with detailed instructions on performing such examinations.[397]

6.5.11. Special Protection of Children and Young Persons Against Physical and Moral Dangers (Article 7 § 10)

The objective scope of Article 7 § 10 is significantly broader than the objective scopes of the nine described provisions. As early as during the first supervisory cycle, the Committee declared that the goal of Article 7 § 1–9 is to ensure children and young persons protection against the dangers created by work, work factors and processes and work environment.[398] Article 7 § 10 takes it a step further, imposing on Member States the obligation of guaranteeing children and young persons legal protection against all dangers of a physical and moral nature, which they can be subject to not only the

391. Conclusions VI, p. 57 (Germany).
392. Conclusions XIII-2, p. 99 (Italy).
393. Conclusions X-1, p. 89 (Sweden).
394. Conclusions VI, p. 99; Conclusions XV-2, p. 551 (Sweden).
395. Conclusions XV-2, pp. 550–551.
396. Conclusions VIII-2, p. 119.
397. *Ibid.*, pp. 120–121.
398. Conclusions I, p. 41.

workplace, but also in all aspects of life.[399] First of all, Member States are obligated to ensure children and young persons protection against dangers resulting directly or indirectly from the work carried out. Because such protection against these dangers is ensured for children and young persons by other provisions (Article 7 § 1–9), the Committee demands that Member States provide the broadest range of information on physical and moral dangers in families, in school, in local communities and in the work environment, from the day the children start their education to the moment of coming of age.[400]

The Committee demands information on the types of dangers and protective measures undertaken by Member States in terms of the following: drugs, alcohol, tobacco and other stimulants, sexual abuse, venereal diseases, corporal punishments, involvement in crime, forced begging, etc.[401] As protection of children and young persons against neglect, violence and abuse is guaranteed by Article 17 § 1(b), the Committee during its fifteenth supervisory cycle made a division of issues evaluated according to Article 7 § 10 and Article 17 RESC, employing the following criteria. Within the confines of Article 7 § 10, the Committee examines whether Member States ensure children and young persons are protected against: physical and moral dangers in the work environment and outside of it; whether they are protected from sexual abuse; and whether they are protected from forced begging. During the supervision, the Committee assesses whether Member States are abiding by Article 17, and also deals with the situation of children and young persons in light of regulations existing in Member States, their entitlements to utilize social services, and protection against ill treatment and abuse.[402]

6.6. The Right of Employed Women to Protection (Article 8)

The aim of this provision is to allow female workers to efficiently fulfil their maternity duties without fear of losing employment. During the first supervisory cycle on whether Article 8 was being followed, the Committee stated that the provision in question guarantees a female worker protection in the period of maternity and protects a woman's body against dangers deriving from work factors and processes and the work environment.[403] In matters concerning maternity protection, Article 8 guarantees pregnant female workers maternity leave and financial entitlements during this leave (§ 1), deems it unlawful for an employer to give a woman notice of dismissal during the period from the time she notifies she is pregnant (§ 2), ensures nursing mothers who are working the right to take time off during work for this purpose

399. Conclusions XII-1, p. 31.
400. Conclusions V, p. 73.
401. Conclusions VIII, p. 122 (The Netherlands); Conclusions X-1, p. 90 (Great Britain); Conclusions XII-1, p. 31; Conclusions XIII-2, p. 300 (Luxembourg).
402. Conclusions VIII, s.122 (The Netherlands); Conclusions X-1, s. 90 (Great Britain); Conclusions XII-1, s. 31; Conclusions XV-2, pp. 26–27 (Luxembourg).
403. Conclusions I, p. 49.

(§ 3), regulates the employment in night work of pregnant women, women who have recently given birth and women nursing their infants (§ 4), prohibits the employment of pregnant women, women who have recently given birth and women nursing their infants in underground mines as well as in all dangerous, unhealthy and arduous work, and imposes on Member States the obligation of undertaking appropriate measures to ensure the protection of rights in terms of employment for this group of women (§ 5). The provisions of Article 8 are complex. The Article consists of standards belonging to the category of individual labour law (protection of work relation stability, protection of female workers), and to the category of provisions of social security law (maternity leaves and financial entitlements obtained by women during such leave). This monograph discusses social rights protected by the Charter. Keeping in mind the close interdependence of workers' and social rights for women employed in the period preceding giving birth and in the period of maternity, it is reasonable to divide the area into three categories: individual workers' rights, collective workers' rights and social rights regulated by provisions of social security law.

Article 8 entails the circumstance of women being parties to work relations.[404] Its legal protection encompasses all women employed on the basis of work agreements for both defined and undefined amounts of time,[405] full time or part time.[406] It applies to women workers employed in household works,[407] even if they are an employer's relatives.[408] It applies to women employed in the public service, or on the sea,[409] regardless of whether they are citizens of a Member State. The Charter imposes on Member States the obligation of equal treatment of the citizens of other Member States who are parties to the Charter, and are legally residing on the territories of other states. Foreigners legally employed on the territory of Member States have standard workers' rights and entitlements. The abovementioned rule applies to women workers during the period of maternity.[410] Women running their own businesses are excluded from the range of protection guaranteed by the provision in question. During the first supervisory cycle, the Committee considered ensuring protection for women who were not parties to work relations. However, it concluded that the content of Article 8 gives no reason for broadening the interpretation of this provision to include protection for women active in professional life, albeit not parties to work relations. Article 8 § 1 imposes on Member States an obligation to guarantee legal protection for 'employees'. Section 2 of Article 8 prohibits 'employers' from handing women a 'notice of dismissal'. It uses

404. Conclusions I, p. 53.
405. Conclusions XIII-4, p. 73.
406. For example employment for 3 days a week. Conclusions XIII-4, pp. 85–86 (The Netherlands); Conclusions XV-2, p. 345; Conclusions XIII-1, pp. 174–175 (Ireland).
407. Conclusions XIII-4, pp. 85–86 (The Netherlands); Conclusions XIII-4, pp. 93–94 (Austria); Conclusions XIII-4, pp. 96–97 (Italy); Conclusions XV-2, p. 345 (The Netherlands).
408. Case of Malta: Conclusions XIII-2, p. 304; Addendum to Conclusions XV-2, pp. 108–109.
409. Case of Greece: Conclusions XIII-1, p. 178; Conclusions XIII-4, p. 96.
410. Case of Greece: Conclusions XI-1, p. 103; Conclusions XII-1, p. 148; Cases of Malta: Conclusions XII-2, p. 137; Conclusions XIII-2, pp. 306–307; Conclusions XIII-4, pp. 84–85; Addendum to Conclusions XV-2, p. 110.

terms of clear content for labour law specialists, which are used only while analysing legal relations regulated by provisions of labour law – work relations.[411]

6.6.1. Maternity Leave (Article 8 § 1)

Member States are obligated to ensure female workers maternity leave. The Committee interprets this obligation as an obligation to regulate the right to maternity leave contained in provisions legislated by a Member State.[412] This is despite the fact that in some Member States where systems of labour law and social security law are based on precedence, the Committee takes the position that the provision in question of Article 8 § 1 does not excuse these states from legislating provisions establishing the obligation of ensuring female workers the right to maternity leave and confirming the right of women workers to take advantage of such leave.[413] A Member State that regulates maternity leaves by collective work agreements or by custom does not fulfil the obligation established by the analysed provision.[414] For example, the Committee did not accept Ireland's argument that Article 8 § 1 does not give female workers a subjective right to maternity leave, but only orders Member States to provide women workers utilizing such a leave with financial entitlements. According to the Committee, Article 8 § 1 obligates states to guarantee female workers paid maternity leave or leave, during which a female worker would have the right to obtain benefits either from social security (maternity benefits) or from public funds. Article 8 § 1 ensures female workers the right to stop working when pregnant and giving birth, and guarantees reinstating a worker with all her professional duties after the period of maternity. Ireland, a state which did not guarantee female workers the right to be reinstated into their previous positions after maternity leave, was regarded to be non-compliant with Article 8 § 1.[415]

Article 8 § 1 ESC orders States to guarantee pregnant workers the right to maternity leave for at least 12 weeks. The same provision of the Revised European Social Charter imposes on Member States the obligation to give female workers 14 weeks of maternity leave. All workers who give birth to a child are entitled to maternity leave, either for 12 or 14 weeks. The length of maternity leave cannot be shortened in cases when an employee does not inform her employer about her intention to take maternity leave.[416] Giving birth to a stillborn baby does not influence the length of

411. Conclusions I, pp. 49–50.
412. Conclusions II, p. 39 (Great Britain).
413. Conclusions III, p. 49 (Great Britain).
414. Case of Great Britain: Conclusions III, p. 48; Conclusions IV, p. 66; Cases of Ireland: Conclusions V, p. 76.
415. Conclusions V, p. 76.
416. Maltese labour law regulations established a sanction, according to which when a pregnant worker did not inform an employer about planning maternity leave three weeks in advance, before the commencing date of the planned break, the length of the leave was shortened to five weeks after giving a birth. The Committee regarded this provision as conflicting Article 8 § 1 of the Charter; Conclusions XIII-2, p. 104;Addendum to Conclusions XV-2, pp. 108–109; The Maltese authorities declaration stating that this provision is not used in practice had no influence on Committee's decision.

maternity leave. The Committee declared that a Member State limiting the length of maternity leave to one month in the case of a stillbirth violates Article 8 § 1.[417] The same applies to a premature birth. Granting a female worker less than 12 weeks of maternity leave guaranteed by Article 8 § 1 ESC in the case of premature delivery created grounds for the Committee to make a negative ruling against the Netherlands, for example.[418] Maternity leave should be utilized in periods preceding giving birth to a child and directly following this event. Member States have been obligated to ensure female workers the right to maternity leave 'before and after giving birth'. Analysing the above provision, the Committee considered whether Member States should divide this break into two periods, one to be utilized by workers before the childbirth, and the other to be utilized after the childbirth. It also debated the scope of workers' entitlements to utilize maternity leave. During the first four supervisory cycles, the Committee claimed maternity leave is an entitlement for a worker who can decide upon its utilization.[419] The above view was presented based on information concerning inadequate financial benefits obtained by workers utilizing maternity leave. According to the Committee, workers who are in difficult material situations should have the right to resign from a significant part of maternity leave and come back to work earlier, or the right not to utilize maternity leave at all. However maternity leave helps to achieve three socially important goals: it allows for a woman's preparation for childbirth, it enables a woman to establish a psychological bond with a child, and it enables a woman's system to regenerate (mentally and physically). Total or partial resignation from the right of utilizing maternity leave is contradictory to the goals that maternity leave is meant to achieve. For this very reason, during the fifth supervisory cycle, the Committee declared that maternity leave should be obligatory, at least throughout a part of the minimum 12-week period.[420]

The above ruling created a problem for Member States, as the Committee did not precisely determine the part of maternity leave that is obligatory, and which part the worker can reject. Sweden, for example, introducing parental leaves by provisions legislated in 1976, gave the Committee a reason for inquiry that took place during the sixth supervisory cycle. The Committee asked Sweden about the following: the nature of this parental leave, the mother's right to pass a part of the leave onto a male partner, and the plausible obligation of utilizing maternity leave by a woman who does not take personal care of a child up to the 29th day after childbirth.[421] The questions were intended to determine the scope of plausibly utilizing maternity leave by a woman worker entitled to maternity leave. Seeking patterns of establishing the obligation of utilizing maternity leave, the Committee took advantage of the regulation of

---

417. Case of Greece: Conclusions XII-1, p. 148; Conclusions XIII-1, p. 173.
418. Conclusions XII-1, p. 149.
419. Conclusions I, p. 50; Conclusions IV, p. 66 (Great Britain).
420. Conclusions V, p. 76 (Sweden). The above view was presented in accordance with Article 8 § 1 ESC. It has relevant application to reports on abiding of Article 8 § 1 RESC, with a reservation that in such a case, a female worker is obliged to utilize a part of minimum 14 weeks of maternity leave period.
421. Conclusions VI, p. 62.

Article 3(a) of the ILO convention No. 3 of 29.10.1919 – a rule prohibiting a female worker to undertake work within six consecutive weeks after giving birth.[422] During the eighth supervisory cycle, the Committee decided that a worker who gave birth to a child should utilize at least six weeks of the maternity leave to which she is entitled.[423] Therefore, maternity leave is the type of entitlement that can be taken advantage of by an interested female worker. The above statement does not refer to six weeks of maternity leave, which a worker should utilize after childbirth and which must be granted by an employer.[424] There is no exclusion from the obligation of utilizing a minimum of six weeks of maternity leave directly following childbirth.[425] Member States were obligated to introduce this rule into their domestic labour law regulations.[426] Not complying with this obligation resulted in a negative ruling passed by the Committee against Denmark,[427] Ireland,[428] and Great Britain.[429] The same consequences resulted from granting female workers the right to shorter leave than the minimum of four or five weeks, which should be granted after the childbirth.[430] The obligation of granting a female worker at least six weeks of maternity leave is intended to protect the mother and the child. On the one hand, it makes it impossible for an employer to put pressure on a female worker to come back to work directly after giving birth: on the other, it opposes female workers interested in immediately returning to work, having made a decision to arrange childcare by another. Among the following three options: the obligation of utilizing maternity leave by a female worker to its full length, utilizing six weeks of maternity leave after giving birth, and authorizing a worker to decide what length of maternity leave she wants to utilize, the Committee decided to accept a solution which reconciles conflicting interests of interested parties: female workers, newborn babies, and employers. A female worker must utilize six weeks of maternity leave directly after giving birth, and must personally use this leave. She cannot renounce this part of maternity leave by passing this entitlement onto a man – the father or a guardian, or onto another woman – a proper caretaker.

During maternity leave, a worker should obtain financial allowances. Article 8 § 1 imposes on Member States particular financial obligations. It prescribes that a worker on maternity leave should be obtaining remuneration for work (paid holiday), and appropriate allowances from social security (maternity benefits) or from

---

422. *Konwencje i zalecenia* ..., t. I, *op. cit.*, pp. 7–9.
423. Conclusions VIII, p. 123. The majority of votes passed the ruling. A different view was presented by F. Fabricius (*op. cit.*, pp. 233 and following). He argued that it is impossible to prove from Article 8 § 1 of the Charter that Member States authorities are obligated to force a worker who gave birth to a child to utilize six weeks of her maternity leave against her will. The above opinion was shared by S. Billum Stegard, Conclusions XII-1, pp. 253–254.
424. Conclusions XIII-5, p. 195 (Portugal).
425. Conclusions VIII, p. 125.
426. Conclusions XV-2, pp. 123–124 (Denmark); XV-2, p. 552 (Sweden); XV-2, p. 593 (Great Britain).
427. Conclusions VIII, p. 124; Conclusions XIII-4, pp. 76–77.
428. Conclusions III, p. 48.
429. Conclusions III, p. 49; Conclusions IV, p. 66.
430. Conclusions XIII-5, p. 194 (Portugal); Addendum to Conclusions XV-2, p. 108 (Malta).

public funds. The Committee takes the position that the above regulation of financial obligation leaves the Member States the choice of the most adequate technique of funding financial allowances paid during maternity leave.[431] The Member States can choose one of the abovementioned techniques presented in the analysed provision, or may create their own combinations of these techniques: combining the obligation of paying a part of the remuneration by an employer with maternity allowances, or supplementing the whole amount due to a worker.[432] The Charter does not determine the amount of allowances that should be paid out to employers during the period of maternity leave. It only mentions that allowances paid by social security or public funds should be 'adequate'. The Charter does not specify the amount of remuneration paid to a female worker during maternity leave, which creates a basis for the Committee to evaluate individual cases. In the abovementioned first supervisory cycle dealing with the obligations of non-ratified provisions, the Committee emphasized that Article 8 § 1 should be treated equally to regulations of labour law, guaranteeing a holiday with remuneration equal to the standard remuneration paid to a given worker during the carrying out of the work.[433]

The Committee started evaluating financial allowances paid to female workers during maternity leave from the sixth supervisory cycle. It stated that allowances equal to 40 per cent of the weekly remuneration for work (giving the amount from 14–50 Irish pounds) cannot be considered adequate.[434] Cases of allowances paid to women workers earning less than 30 Irish pounds a week, as well as allowances obtained by agriculture workers, were treated the same.[435] Generally, the Committee declared that allowances paid during maternity leave being 80 per cent of a standard remuneration meet the requirements established by the Charter. Lower allowances were not regarded as adequate, unless they approached 100 per cent of net remuneration or spanned between 84–90 per cent of the previous remuneration for work. The Committee took the position that allowances paid to female workers during maternity leave meet the requirements set by the provisions when they are as concurrent as possible with remuneration obtained by female workers in the period of employment.[436] The amount of financial allowances paid during maternity leave is dependant upon the basic amount, which is regulated by provisions of social security law. As a rule, this basic amount is subject to limitations. National provisions of social security law set a limit, above which remuneration is not taken into consideration while calculating allowances paid to female workers during their maternity leaves. Using this technique of calculating allowances paid to female workers during their maternity leaves, the Committee wanted to find out whether and in what ways domestic provisions of labour and social security laws

431. First report on certain provisions of the Charter which have not been accepted, 1981, Supervision relating to reports submitted under Article 22 of the European Social Charter (1961), European Social Charter, *op. cit.,* p. 480.
432. Conclusions VIII, p. 124 (Germany); Conclusions X-1, p. 93 (Greece).
433. First report, *op. cit.*
434. Conclusions VI, p. 61.
435. Conclusions XIII-4, p. 82.
436. Conclusions XIII-4, p. 72 (Denmark).

compensate female workers utilizing maternity leave allowances calculated according to the lower basis than their standard work remuneration.[437] Comparing the amount of financial allowance paid to female workers utilizing maternity leave to the amount of remuneration paid to these workers in the period of employment preceding the commencement of maternity leave, the Committee stated that some Member States[438] established the maximum amount of allowances, regardless of the basis of calculating of the abovementioned allowances. The Committee found that maternity allowances in France did not exceed 58 per cent of monthly wages paid to workers employed in managerial positions in workplaces.[439]

After making these statements concerning one Member State, the Committee became interested in the situation of other workers earning above the maximum limits as a basis used for calculating allowances paid to workers during maternity leave. It aimed to find out the number of workers obtaining allowances not corresponding with the amount of their remuneration, as well as the reason for such amounts of allowances (the difference between the amount of standard remuneration and the amount of allowances obtained during the period of maternity leave).[440] One of the three possibilities formulated in the analysed provision relates to maternity benefits as to financial allowances paid by the system of social security, which is interestingly the most common way of regulating financial allowances paid to workers utilizing maternity leave; thus, the Committee was interested in familiarizing itself with national provisions of social security law granting entitlements to the abovementioned benefits, such as the length of insurance policy[441] or the obligation of paying the insurance premiums.[442] The Committee declared that when acquiring entitlements to maternity allowances is dependent upon a woman's employment from two to five years before childbirth, and upon paying insurance premiums in the period of 180 to 200 days, two years prior to childbirth; this must be regarded as conflicting with the standards established by the Charter.[443] A similar ruling was made against the requirement of employment with a particular employer for a period of two years as a condition of acquiring the right to maternity benefits,[444] as well as the requirement of employment with a particular employer for a period of 12 months as a condition of obtaining entitlements to maternity leave.[445] Less firm requirements of acquiring entitlements for a female worker who gave birth to a child, such as the requirement of employment with a particular employer for the period of six months as a condition of obtaining entitlements to the above allowances,[446] were not criticized by the Committee.

437. Conclusions XII-2, p. 134 (France).
438. Belgium, the Netherlands, Ireland. Conclusions XIII-1, p. 174; Conclusions XIII-2, p. 303.
439. Conclusions XII-2, p. 134.
440. Conclusions XIII-4, pp. 76 and following.
441. Conclusions XIII-1, p. 172.
442. Conclusions XV-2, p. 197.
443. Conclusions XV-2, pp. 239–240 (Greece); p. 522 (Spain).
444. Conclusions VI, p. 62 (Great Britain).
445. Conclusions II, p. 39(Sweden).
446. Conclusions XIII-5, p. 130 (Luxembourg).

The Committee examined premises by which domestic labour law regulations condition the acquirement of entitlements to maternity leave and benefits, and insisted on Member States providing information on female workers who do not meet the abovementioned requirements or obtain allowances of insufficient amounts. Especially, it insisted on presenting data on entitlements of such workers taking advantage of additional benefits of social security.[447]

6.6.2. Prohibiting the Termination of Work Agreements with Pregnant Women (Article 8 § 2)

The European Social Charter prohibits employers to dismiss or terminate a work agreement during a female worker's absence due to maternity leave. It classifies a termination of a work agreement during this protective period as unlawful. The protective period embraces solely the period of maternity leave a worker utilizes. The Committee took the position that it would have been more advantageous for workers *de lege frenda*, if the special protection of work relation lasted all through the pregnancy and the period of maternity leave.[448] The above position was achieved by the Revised European Social Charter, which ensures the special protection of work relations from the day of informing an employer about the pregnancy up to the termination of the period of maternity. The Committee claims that a Member State meets the requirement imposed by Article 8 § 2, even when maternity leave is shorter than the minimum period determined by Article 8 § 2, which creates the legal basis for determining whether the latter provision is being followed.[449] Not fulfilling the obligations set by Article 8 § 1 does not automatically mean non-fulfilment of obligations set by Article 8 § 2. Special protection of work relations during the period defined by national labour law regulations should be ensured by Member States for all female workers. The rule of majority enlisted in Article 33 § 2 ESC and Article I § 2 RESC cannot be applied.[450] Negative rulings made by the Committee concern cases when Member States exclude from the scope of protective regulations some categories of female workers who are employed part time,[451] in household service employed by individuals,[452] female workers from small workplaces where the total employment does not exceed 20 workers,[453] and workers employed on merchant ships.[454]

Prohibiting the giving of notice and terminating a work agreement during the protective period regulated by Article 8 § 2 ESC was not absolute. Even though the Appendix to the European Social Charter did not list cases excluded from the

447. Addendum to Conclusions XV-2, p. 20 (Cyprus).
448. First report on certain provisions of the Charter, which have been not accepted, *op. cit.*
449. Conclusions VI, p. 63 (Austria).
450. Conclusions IV, p. 67 (Austria); Addendum to Conclusions XV-2, p. 111 (Malta).
451. Conclusions XIII-4, p. 97 (Malta).
452. Conclusions I, p. 51 – Conclusions XIII-4, p. 96–97 (Italy); Conclusions III, p. 49-Conclusions XIII-4, p. 93–94 (Austria); Conclusions XV-2, p. 523 (Spain).
453. Addendum to Conclusions XV-2, p. 22–23 (Cyprus).
454. Case of Greece: Conclusions XIII-1, p. 178; Conclusions XIII-4, p. 96; Conclusions XV-2, p. 241.

application of this provision, the Committee during all supervisory periods beginning from the first presented the view that domestic labour law regulations can introduce exceptions from the rule prohibiting termination of work agreements in the protective period. It allowed for the possibility of terminating a work agreement in the protective period in cases of behaviour or actions performed by a worker deemed offensive or inappropriate to the standards of the workplace, justifying terminating a legal bond by an employer; ceasing entrepreneurship by an employer, and termination of the period for which a work agreement was signed.[455] The Committee stated that terminating a work relation in the protective period could be justified by 'sudden', 'objective', and 'serious' reasons.[456] The experiences of the Committee were taken into consideration by the Revised European Social Charter, where its Appendix stated that prohibiting the termination of a work relation with a female worker whose work relation is encompassed by special protection of stability, is not of absolute character. As an example it lists reasons for terminating a work agreement mentioned by the Committee in rulings made during previous supervisory cycles, when debating the abidance of Article 8 § 2 ESC by members states. Exceptions from the rule of special protection of stability of work relations should be interpreted strictly. According to the Committee, the policy of collective redundancy does not justify including into the group of dismissed employees female workers encompassed by special protection of stability of work relations. In cases of collective redundancy, the dismissal of pregnant workers is acceptable when the reason for this dismissal lies in the closing of their workplace.[457] The case of taking over a workplace by another employer is treated analogically. The conversion within the employing party is not the same as liquidation, even though the employer passing on a workplace ceases entrepreneurship.[458]

The Committee regards Article 8 § 2 as a standard supplementing the provision of Article 8 § 1, legislated in order to ensure female workers efficient protection during maternity. The aim of Article 8 § 2 is to guarantee female workers financial stability and ensuring the protection of a lasting work relationship.[459] Prohibiting the giving of notice terminating a work agreement in the protective period includes filing acts of will by employers, as well as legal consequences of earlier acts of will informing of dismissal, received by female workers in the period preceding the commencement of the protective period. The above classification of acts of employers' will and their legal character in terms of terminating a work agreement requires a more detailed explanation. It is not clear whether the ban on giving notice in the protective period causes that unlawful notice of an employer to have no legal consequences or, despite its illegality, whether it results in the termination of a work relation. Jurisdiction of the Committee concerning this issue is vague. On the one hand, the Committee presents the view that

455. Conclusions I, p. 51.
456. Conclusions XIII-1, p. 179 (the Netherlands); Conclusions XIII-2, p. 215–216 (Spain); XIII-4, pp. 98 and following; Addendum to Conclusions XIII-3, p. 49 (Luxembourg).
457. Conclusions XIII-4, p. 99 (Spain); Conclusions XIII-5, p. 197 (Portugal).
458. Addendum to Conclusions XV-1, p. 181–182.
459. Conclusions VII, p. 54.

despite violating the ban of terminating work agreements in the protective period, termination of work relations eventuates. In that case the necessary condition for reactivating the unlawfully terminated work relation is for the protected female worker to initiate court proceedings aimed at reinstating her to the previous position.[460] During the thirteenth supervisory cycle, the Committee made a ruling stating that a work agreement with a woman who is pregnant cannot be terminated during the protective period. Prohibiting the giving of notice terminating a work agreement at will with a pregnant woman and prohibiting the termination of work agreements before the commencement of the protective period if the above notice would evoke legal consequences in the protective period, both strengthen the provision of special protection of stabilizing work relations. The Committee claims that an unlawful notice given by an employer results in suspending the course of the notice period for the duration of the period of special protection of stability of the work relation.[461] Therefore, there are sufficient grounds to state that the employer's actions, which would have legal consequences in the protective period, are not binding. Hence, it does not result in the consequences intended by an employer. Since the notice does not eventuate in terminating a work relationship, there is no basis to present views on the necessity of reinstating an unlawfully dismissed female worker to her previous position as an efficient way to resolve this issue. The Committee does not notice the emerging inconsistency. It takes the firm position that decisions upon reinstating a dismissed female worker who is pregnant should be a general rule. The exceptions from this rule can only be legislated by Member States in special circumstances. In these cases, decisions upon reinstating should be replaced by compensation. The amount of this compensation should be as high as the trouble the employer has caused, and should compensate a female worker for the loss of employment during the protective period.[462] The Committee claims that compensation has two functions: repressive and compensative. It gives a list of Member States who do not follow this rule, as they have not introduced the rule of reinstating female workers dismissed in the protective period: Belgium,[463] Cyprus,[464] France,[465] Greece,[466] and Luxembourg.[467] Some of these states grant

460. Conclusions XII-2, p. 140 (Cyprus); Conclusions XIII-2, p. 307–308 (Belgium); XIII-2, p. 308–309 (Malta); Conclusions XIII-3, p. 314 (Finland); XIV-2, p. 157; XIV-2, p. 200 (France).
461. Conclusions XIII-4, pp. 92–93. The Committee negatively judged regulations of labour law in Slovakia where a protected female worker can make a declaration upon not utilizing the construction of suspending the period of notice. Addendum to ConclusionsXV-1, p. 181 and following.
462. Compare to the ruling invoked in footnote 541.
463. Conclusions XV-2, p. 89.
464. Addendum to Conclusions XV-2, pp. 22–23.
465. Conclusions XV-2, pp. 199–200.
466. Conclusions XIII-1, p. 178; Conclusions XIII-4, p. 96; Conclusions XV-2, p. 241.
467. Conclusions XIII-5, pp. 131 and following. During the fifteenth supervisory cycle, the Committee stated that the situation of pregnant women had changed. Female workers were granted the right to litigate to be reinstated with the help of the head of the court of labour law, in cases of finding out that the notice of the agreement is legally invalid. All announcements made by employers stating termination of a work agreement with a pregnant woman are legally invalid. Addendum to Conclusions XV-2, p. 75.

female workers unlawfully dismissed from work compensation which was not regarded by the Committee as sufficient: Belgium – six months; Finland – from three to 24 months.[468]

Special protection of the stability of women's work relations does not change the character of the work agreement for the specified amount of time. While it is true that in the period when a fixed agreement is in force, pregnant female workers and female workers on maternity leave benefit from special protection of stability of work relations, neither pregnancy nor maternity leave ensures protection against the termination of a work relationship as a consequence of time passed subjected to by the agreement.[469]

6.6.3. Time Off Work for Mothers Nursing their Infants (Article 8 § 3)

Member States that ratified Article 8 § 3 are obliged to ensure that female workers nursing their infants have time off work. The above obligation is of a general nature. The Committee examines whether this entitlement to take breaks during work to nurse infants is organized for female workers employed in agriculture[470] and in household service by individuals.[471] It allows for non-regulated breaks from work for female workers carrying out work at their own homes.[472] Its view is that in the case of piece-work jobs, female workers can independently decide upon the number and the length of breaks needed for nursing infants. The Committee emphasized that employers are obligated to pay female workers taking nursing breaks remuneration equal to what they would obtain for carrying out work. Breaks for nursing infants are treated by the Committee jurisdiction as part of the working day, during which female workers retain the right to remuneration equal to what they would obtain for carrying out the work.[473] Therefore, domestic labour law regulations allowing employers to demand that female workers catch up for the time spent on breaks for nursing infants or regulations authorizing employers to deduct a part of the remuneration paid for work that has not been carried out due to nursing infants breaks, are in conflict with the standards established by the Charter.[474] The Committee states that Member States are obligated to introduce into their labour law regulations standards allowing for female workers nursing infants to utilize paid time off during work. It is not enough, according to the Committee, to introduce the above obligation based on the argument of an employer taking care of his/her employees, especially when there is a lack of specific legal regulations in establishing collective labour agreements.[475] Mothers nursing their infants should be entitled to

---

468. Conclusions XV-2, pp. 156–157.
469. Conclusions XII-2, p. 139; XIII-2, pp. 213–214 (Austria); Addendum to Conclusions XIII-3, p. 49 (Luxembourg); Addendum to Conclusions XV-2, p. 22 (Cyprus), p. 111 (Malta).
470. Conclusions XIII-4, p. 101 (France), p. 103 (the Netherlands).
471. Conclusions IV, p. 67 (Italy).
472. Conclusions XV-2, p. 300 (Italy).
473. Conclusions I, p. 51 (Italy); Addendum to Conclusions XIII-3, p. 49 (Luxembourg); Conclusions XIII-4, p. 104 (Sweden); Conclusions XV-2, p. 200 (France).
474. Conclusions IX-1, pp. 71–72.
475. Case of the Netherlands: Conclusions X-1, p. 97; XI-1, p. 107; XIII-1,p. 180.

utilize breaks for nursing during their working day.[476] The above obligation is not fulfilled by Member States that employ alternative measures, such as part-time employment, or exemptions from the obligation of carrying out work without the right to remuneration.[477] The Committee gave particular attention to the Swedish report of 1978 when, instead of breaks for nursing infants, parental 'leave' of two hours a day was introduced.[478] This Swedish regulation is an intermediate solution between part-time employment of mothers raising small children and an entitlement to utilize parental leave. When taking breaks during the day, female workers were not guaranteed remuneration. Therefore, the Committee concluded that the abovementioned regulation violated the standards set by the Charter and emphasized that the Member States should ensure paid breaks from work for female workers nursing infants.[479] Article 8 § 3 does not specify either the number or the length of time taken off work spent for nursing infants. Neither does it regulate the period of time when female workers are entitled to utilize the above breaks. The Committee requires from the Member States information concerning the above matters and states the obligation of the provision in question is met by Member States that ensure that working mothers have two 30- minute breaks from work per day. A necessary condition of compliance is providing a day nursery or room where female workers can nurse their infants. In cases of not ensuring female workers such a possibility in the workplace or in its proximity, employers are obligated to enable mothers to utilize two breaks from work, each one hour long.[480] Regulations according to which workers nursing infants are entitled to two 45-minute-long breaks[481] and of one one-hour-long break[482] were regarded as compliant with the international standards established by the Charter. Taking into consideration one of the cases, the Committee became convinced that an hour break from work for nursing infants could be divided into two equal parts or replaced by a 30-minute-shorter working day.[483] Despite the accepted rule, there is still a need to evaluate domestic legal regulations on an individual basis. This was a ruling made by the Committee during the tenth supervisory cycle, drastically different for the interested disadvantaged parties (breastfeeding women and infants) from the standards approved during the first supervisory cycle. The right to utilize breaks from work for nursing infants by a worker lasts for nine months,[484] or no longer than past the time that the baby reaches one year of age.

---

476. Conclusions XIII-4, p. 104 (Sweden).
477. Conclusions XIII-2, p. 309; Conclusions XIII-4, pp. 374–375; Conclusions XV-2, p. 89.
478. Conclusions XIII-4, p. 104; Conclusions XV-2, p. 554.
479. Conclusions XIII-4, p. 104.
480. Conclusions I, p. 51 (Italy), p. 191 (Germany); Conclusions XIII-3, p. 315 (Portugal).
481. Addendum to Conclusions XIII-3, p. 49 (Luxembourg).
482. Conclusions V, p. 78 (France).
483. Addendum to Conclusions IX-2, p. 22 (Spain).
484. *Ibid.*

6.6.4. Obligation to Regulate Rules of Employment Concerning Female Workers Employed at Night-Time in Industrial Occupations (Article 8 § 4(a) ESC)

The European Social Charter orders Member States to regulate the rules of employment concerning female workers employed at night-time in industrial occupations. Article 8 § 4(a) ESC includes legal protection of all women, not only pregnant women and women on maternity leave. Regulating the rules of employment concerning female workers employed at night time in industrial occupations, Member States are obligated to consider whether establishing provisions for women's work protection will not be in conflict with the obligation of equal opportunities for all workers, regardless of sex, and the prohibition of discrimination in the field of employment.[485] Supervising over the compliance to the above provision, the Committee remarked that Member States were not obligated to introduce the banning of women's work at night-time, but only to regulate the rules of such work in terms of law. Legal regulations of the employment at night-time, which is not defined by the Charter, may apply to all categories of workers regardless of sex. Provisions of domestic labour law should determine the rules of employment (concerning men and women) at night time, allow for carrying out work in industrial workplaces in cases justified by the requirements of production or the job organization. In the case of employing female workers at night-time in industrial workplaces, Member States should specify additional requirements such as: acceptance of work inspectors, breaks from work, days free from work at night-time, and the obligation of shifting a female worker to daily work in case of medical problems.[486] The aim of these regulations is to decrease the negative impact of employment at night-time on a female worker's body and her family life.[487]

The range of protection for women's work at night-time encompasses all industrial jobs. According to the Committee, the obligation of regulating the employment of female workers at night did not relate to jobs of a non-industrial nature carried out by female workers in industrial workplaces.[488] The Committee paid special attention in examining the rules of employment of female workers at night-time in cases of pregnant workers, workers who have recently given birth to a child, or workers nursing infants.[489] It stated that international standards should force Member States to regulate the employment of women covered by special protection at night-time, or even to introduce a ban on the employment of such women at night-time.[490] The arguments of the Committee were taken in by the Revised European Social Charter.

485. Conclusions XII-1, pp. 22 and following.
486. Conclusions XV-2, p. 242 (Greece), p. 349 (Austria), p. 436 (the Netherlands and Poland), p 486 (Portugal).
487. Conclusions X-2, p. 97; Conclusions XII-1, p. 22–23.
488. Conclusions I, p. 192.
489. Conclusions XII-2, p. 145 (France), p. 146 (Italy); Conclusions XIII-1, p. 181 (Greece); Conclusions XIII-2, p. 218 (Italy), p. 310 (Belgium), p. 312 (Malta); Conclusions XIII-4, p. 106 (France).
490. Conclusions XIII-4, p. 107 (Greece), p. 109 (Italy); Conclusions XIII-5, p. 199 (Portugal).

6.6.4.1. *Duty of Regulating the Rules of Employment at Night-Time Concerning Pregnant Women, Women who have Recently given Birth to a Child, or Women Nursing their Infants (Article 8 § 4(a) RESC)*

Provisions of Article 8 § 4(a) RESC are replicating the regulations introduced by the ILO convention No. 171 of 6 June 1990,[491] concerning work at night-time and by the directive of the Council No. 85 of 19 October 1992, concerning the implementation of measures intended at improvement of health and safety in the workplace for pregnant female workers, workers who have recently given birth to a child, and workers nursing their infants (the tenth individual directive according to Article 16(1) of directive 89/391/EEC).[492] International treaties mentioned above provide protection for female workers in relation to maternity.[493] Comparing the ranges of the analysed provision worded by the European Social Charter and the Revised European Social Charter, it has to be noted that Article 8 § 4(a) RESC provides protection for all female workers taking advantage of the special protection during the period of maternity, regardless of the place of their employment and the type of work they carry out. Article 8 § 4(a) ESC applies to all female workers employed in industrial occupations.

In light of Article 8 § 4(a) RESC protection is ensured for workers who inform an employer about the state of pregnancy, workers who have recently given birth to a child, as well as workers nursing their infants. Labour law regulations in Member States compile legal definitions of these three categories.[494] Legal limitations upon including men to utilize the right to protection on the basis of Article 8 § 4(a) does not have a discriminative character. Female workers not benefiting from special protection in relation to the state of pregnancy, childbirth or breastfeeding an infant are comprised of protection guaranteed by Article 2 § 7 RESC on equal grounds with men.

6.6.4.2. *Prohibiting the Employment of Women (Article 8 § 4(b) ESC)*

Member States are obligated to implement provisions prohibiting the employment of women in underground mining, as well as carrying out other jobs inappropriate for women because of their dangerous, unhealthy, or arduous nature. The Committee debated whether the ban on the employment of women in underground mining is of a general nature. Analysing the official texts, the Committee became convinced that according to the French version of Article 8 § 4(b) ESC, women are not allowed to undertake any work in underground mining, while according to the English version, they must not do mining work underground. Therefore, prohibition based on the interpretation of the above provision in its French version is broader.[495] However, the Committee ultimately utilized the English version. It became convinced that the above provision is compliant with the requirements established by the ILO convention

491. *Konwencje i zalecenia* ..., t. II, *op. cit.,* pp. 1265 and following.
492. OJ No L 348, 28.11.1992, p. 1. Polish text: A.M. Świątkowski, H. Wierzbińska, *op. cit.,* pp. 414 and following.
493. Explanatory report to the Revised European Social Charter, European Social Charter, *op. cit.,* p. 165.
494. *Ibid.*
495. Conclusions VI, p. 65 (Great Britain).

No. 45 concerning the employment of women in underground work in all types of mining legislated on 4.6.1935,[496] which, as a rule of exception, allows for the occasional employment of women underground as doctors and nurses or in other work not demanding physical activity. It concluded that female workers can be employed in underground mining work, which is not considered inappropriate for women because of its dangerous, unhealthy or arduous nature, other than connected with the direct extraction of minerals.[497] Hence, there are no legal obstacles, moreover it is recommended – with regard to equal opportunities and the prohibition of gender discrimination – to employ female workers underground in work of medical, managerial or other natures, not connected with mining, as well as in mines where minerals are not excavated from the underground.[498] Article 8 § 4(b) ESC does not regulate the conditions of the employment of women beyond the excavating industry.[499]

Examining national reports, the Committee concluded that two of the Member States did not comply with the prohibition of employing women underground, namely Italy, which overruled the ban of employment of women underground as long as women were not pregnant,[500] and Ireland.[501] In both cases, the Committee made negative rulings. It did not take into consideration explanations of the two Member States that referred to international documents prescribing equal treatment of workers regardless of gender, as well as the practical insignificance of the analysed issue.[502]

Article 8 § 4(b) ESC prohibits employing female workers in all other work inappropriate for women because of its dangerous, unhealthy or arduous nature. Introduction of the prohibition on employing women was left to be evaluated by the Member States. The Committee interprets the provision in question as a basis for legislating such bans on women's employment in work that is dangerous for a pregnant woman's health, *nasciturusa* and infants.[503] Such dangers are created by work which exposes a worker to the impact of chemical substances and factors (such as lead, asbestos, ionizing radiation) or demands heavy lifting.[504] Analysing the reports of Member States, the Committee complies with the standards established by the directive 92/85/EEC.[505]

6.6.5. Prohibiting the Employment of Pregnant Women, Women who have Recently given Birth or who are Nursing their Infants in Underground Mining and all other Work of Dangerous, Unhealthy or Arduous Nature (Article 8 § 5 RESC)

Remarks of the Committee were utilized at the drafting of the new provision of Article 8 § 5 RESC. This new standard orders Member States to establish the

496. *Konwencje i zalecenia* ... (Conventions and Recommendations), vol. I, *op. cit.*, p. 187.
497. Conclusions X-2, p. 97 (Italy).
498. Conclusions XII-2, p. 147 (Malta); Conclusions XIII-1 (the Netherlands).
499. Conclusions XII-2, p. 147 (Malta); Conclusions XIII-1, p. 184 (the Netherlands).
500. Conclusions XIII-2, p. 217; XIII-4, pp. 110–111.
501. Conclusions III-1, p. 183; Addendum to Conclusions XV-2, p. 22.
502. Case of Italy where there was only one mine employing a few women. *See* L.Samuel, *op. cit.*, p. 233.
503. Conclusions X-2, p. 97–98.
504. L.Samuel, *op. cit.*, p. 234–235.
505. *See* A.M.Świątkowski, Bezpieczeństwo ..., *op. cit.*, p. 243 and following.

prohibitions on the employment of female workers in underground mining and all other work considered to be of dangerous, unhealthy or arduous nature during the protective period: in pregnancy, directly after giving birth, or during breastfeeding. It imposes on Member States the obligation of undertaking adequate actions in order to protect female workers employed in work which should not be carried out by them. Article 8 § 5 RESC is a standard which, during the special period, protects female workers against all types of risk brought on by work, work factors and processes, and by conditions in which work is carried out, especially the work environment.[506] The new obligation introduced by Article 8 § 5 commands Member States to legislate provisions ensuring female workers in their protective period, who are employed in work they should not carry out, the entitlement to request to be relocated to another position with guaranteed remuneration for work of the same amount or – in the case of an impossibility of providing them with work to a different position – the entitlement to be excused from carrying out prohibited types of work. During the period of being excused from carrying out prohibited type of work, female workers utilizing the right to special protection should be ensured to entitlements guaranteeing adequate financial benefits, compensating them for lost wages. The period of notice should be included into the work tenure, according to domestic labour law regulations. It is the basis for acquiring and retaining entitlements to workers' benefits and to determine their scope in an individual case.

6.7. The Right to Vocational Guidance (Article 9)

Article 9 is a dynamic provision. Member States are obligated to independently organize advising services for all persons interested in choosing or changing his/her occupation or, alternatively, to support actions undertaken by public organizations in order to establish such services. The point of the analysed legal regulation finds expression in ensuring a free of charge access to vocational guidance according to individual predispositions and characteristics of the labour market.[507] Member States have full freedom in organizing institutions carrying out vocational guidance. Domestic systems of vocational guidance can be organized within the confines of commonly accessible systems of education, or in courses teaching particular qualifications or occupational skills, in order for workers to acquire new skills, which will help them enter the labour market.[508] The important element is to ensure common access to institutions of vocational guidance. These services should be available for schoolchildren, university students and adults.[509] First of all, institutions of vocational guidance should serve

506. Conclusions 2003, vol.2, pp. 385–386 (Romania). During this supervisory cycle the committee postponed the decision in cases of: Bulgaria, Romania and Slovenia. In cases of France and Italy the Committee stated congruousness of the national labour law regulations with the standards established by Article 8 § 5 RESC.
507. Conclusions IV, p. 69.
508. Conclusions XIII-3, p. 31.
509. Conclusions I, p. 53; Conclusions XIV-2, p. 55.

the disabled and other particular social categories (women, young persons, the unemployed, foreigners) whose needs are more difficult to satisfy.[510]

Article 9 is a standard obligating Member States to satisfy needs related to the organization and promotion of vocational guidance 'as needed'. Therefore, the objective scope of this duty is dictated by the situation of the national labour market. The interdependency between the situation of the national labour market and the duty of organization and promotion of vocational guidance is direct. The higher the unemployment rate, the more serious the duty is of organization and promotion of institutions of vocational guidance.[511] The above rule was used by the Committee in consecutive supervisory cycles. The increase of unemployment inspired the Committee to address the Member States' questions concerning expenses on vocational guidance and the number of institutions of vocational guidance advising persons intending to change their job or to undertake employment.[512]

Article 9 imposes on Member States the obligation of ensuring free of charge vocational guidance. The way of executing the above duty does not matter. It may occur via public or private institutions. The services provided by these organizations should not be financed by persons seeking employment or intending to acquire new occupational qualifications. The Committee took a firm position about the payment for vocational guidance. It ruled negatively against Dutch legal regulations, according to which services of vocational guidance were delivered to the interested parties to an essential extent and with the possibility of charging for the services in 'hard cases'.[513]

The Committee demanded from Member States presenting data on the organizations and conduct of such vocational guidance services. It was interested in familiarizing itself with the organizational structure, the number of workers in these services, their funds, and the number of persons to whom help was given.[514] Taking into consideration the above data, the Committee made a negative ruling against Turkey, as the small number of persons employed within the vocational guidance services, their uneven geographical distribution, and inadequate financial resources did not guarantee general access to the services provided.[515] According to the Committee, services of vocational guidance should be organized in regions of the highest unemployment rate.[516] The small number of workers employed in the vocational guidance services sector has a direct negative impact on the evaluation of adherence to the requirements of Article 9 by a Member State.[517] It also imprints negative consequences on the social perception of the activity of the abovementioned services. It makes citizens of a given Member State, as well as citizens of other Member States that are parties to the Charter, notice that a particular State does not fulfil obligations formulated under Article 9.

510. Conclusions XIII-2, p. 314 (Belgium); Conclusions XIII-3, p. 318 (Finland).
511. Conclusions I, p. 53.
512. Conclusions XIII-5, p. 77 (Finland).
513. Conclusions XIV-2, p. 255.
514. *Ibid.*
515. Conclusions XIII-1, pp. 234–235.
516. Conclusions XIII-2, p. 219 (Italy).
517. Conclusions XIII-3, p. 318 (Finland).

Member States should try to prove in front of the Committee that they ensure or support the conduct of institutions dealing with vocational guidance for schoolchildren, youth, and adults. Not fulfilling the above duty results in – in the case of not fulfilling the same duty as in previous supervisory cycles – a ruling stating that a given Member State does not abide by the standards regulated by the Charter.[518]

6.8. The Right to Vocational Training (Article 10)

The Charter is one of the first international treaties ensuring the common right to vocational training for citizens of a given Member State, as well as to citizens of the parties. Recommendations of the ILO regulate the above right only fragmentarily. They declare the right to undertake vocational training in: agriculture,[519] the construction industry,[520] vocational training[521] and vocational guidance,[522] occupational education of sailors,[523] vocational training in agriculture,[524] and vocational training of fishermen.[525] With the exception of recommendation No. 117 concerning vocational training[526] and No. 150 concerning the role of advising services and occupational education in development of human resources,[527] the remaining of the abovementioned recommendations limit themselves to fragmentary regulation of vocational training of selected occupations. Within the European Union, the issues related to vocational training are regulated by the two decisions[528] and one recommendation of the Council.[529] The Charter's position in the hierarchy of international law sources is high.[530] The provision of Article 10 ESC consists of four paragraphs. They impose on Member States the obligation of organizing or/and supporting the following:

- Common vocational and technical training;
- Free access to higher technical and university education (§ 1);
- System of apprenticeship (§ 2);

518. Conclusions 2003, vol.1, p. 265 (Italy).
519. No 15. Legislated during the 3rd session of ILO in 1921.
520. No 56. Legislated during the 23rd session of ILO in 1937 , *Konwencje i zalecenia* ... (Conventions and Recommendations ...), v. I, *op. cit.,* p. 255.
521. No 57. Legislated during the 25th session of ILO in 1939.
522. No 60. Legislated during the 25th session of ILO in 1939.
523. No 77. Legislated during the 28th session of ILO in 1946 ; No 137. Legislated during the 50th session of ILO in 1970.
524. No 101. Legislated during the 39th session of ILO in 1956.
525. No 126. Legislated during the 50th session of ILO in 1965.
526. Legislated during the 46th session of ILO in 1962 .
527. Legislated during the 60th session of ILO in 1975.
528. No 63/266/EEC of 2 April 1963 r. concerning establishing common rules of mutual policy in terms of vocational training, OJ No 63, 20 April 1963, p. 1338; No 94/819/EEC of 6 December 1994 introducing a programme of actions executing the policy of the European Community in terms vocational training, OJ No L.340, 29 December 1994, p. 8.
529. Nr 93/404/EEC z 30 June 1993 r. concerning the access to persistent vocational training, OJ No L.181, 23 July 1993, p. 37
530. Conclusions I, p. 55.

- Vocational training for adults (§ 3);
- And access to utilizing vocational training (§ 4).

The Revised European Social Charter introduced additional obligations of ensuring and supporting special measures of training and reintegration of the long-term unemployed. This provision was marked as § 4, while § 4 ESC was marked as § 5 RESC.

The scope of obligation of providing and/or supporting vocational training on all levels, including university courses, is of a general nature. It comprises citizens of Member States, migrants, citizens of other states, parties to the Charter,[531] young persons and adults, educated and uneducated, nonworking persons, unemployed persons, those carrying out work according to work relation agreements, as well as those running their own businesses.[532] According to the Committee, some of the aforementioned social groups should utilize the right to vocational training according to preference rules. This concerns persons who experience above-average obstacles in finding employment: the disabled and immigrants. The opinion of the Committee is that privileged treatment of these persons does not prompt the accusation of discrimination by the remaining beneficiaries of the right to vocational training.[533] In the light of legal regulations introduced by Article 10 § 4 RESC, privileged treatment can also apply to the long-term unemployed.

Article 10 is classified as a dynamic standard of international labour law. Enforcement of the duty regulated by this provision is related to the needs of labour markets occurring in particular Member States. The Committee emphasizes that the unemployment rate cannot be considered as a main or as the only indicator of executing duties imposed on Member States by the analysed provision. The unemployment rate is the most obvious indicator. Another important factor in determining the scope of duty of providing and/or supporting vocational training on all levels is the demand for a particular type of work.[534] The latter means that the Member States should organize and/or support vocational training on various levels and respond to the changing demand of labour market as well as to the expectations of different social groups in the age of professional activity. Under the term 'vocational training' used in Article 10, the Committee understands the entirety of duties imposed on Members States related to enabling all persons interested in acquiring education, from primary school to university, increasing occupational qualifications and occupational reorientation. According to the Committee, the right to vocational training is the entitlement that should be available during the course of life for all social categories considered as potentially professional active groups: students, young persons, educated and uneducated, employed and unemployed.[535] European societies are learning societies in their nature.

531. Conclusions XIII-3, p. 32 and following.
532. Conclusions XIV-2, p. 59.
533. Conclusions I, p. 81.
534. Conclusions XIII-3, p. 37.
535. Conclusions XIV-2, p. 59.

The above classifications obligate Member States to undertake constant efforts in order to organize and/or support initiatives aimed at increasing the level of knowledge, skills, and occupational qualifications of all interested subjects. The execution of the abovementioned duty is considered the most crucial and the most efficient measure of preventing social exclusion.

6.8.1. The Obligation to Provide or Promote the Technical and Vocational Training and of Granting Facilities for Access to Higher Technical and University Education (Article 10 § 1)

Member States who ratified the above provision are obligated to provide all interested persons, including the disabled, with technical and vocational training and to grant facilities for access to higher technical and university education. It does not imply that the above training has to be organized by the State. Article 10 § 1 obligates the Member States that do not want to provide technical and vocational training themselves, to support technical and vocational training provided by private institutions. In the case of higher technical and university education, Article 10 § 1 orders a Member State to grant facilities for access to higher technical and university education existing in a given State. During the first supervisory cycle, the Committee became convinced that the essence of duties listed in the analysed provision is comprised of the following: providing, promoting and granting access to units and institutions providing technical and vocational training from the basic to the advanced level.[536] Article 10 § 1 has the common range. All citizens of a particular Member State and citizens of other States who ratified the Charter, should be provided with vocational training. However, this entitlement is not of an absolute nature. Member States were obligated to provide or promote technical and vocational training 'as needed'. The 'need' in a particular Member State is determined by that State. The Committee exists to verify the above evaluations. It demands that Member States present information concerning the undertaken actions in order to provide all interested persons with technical and vocational training. It orders the presentation of information concerning the number of persons who utilized the above option.[537] The Committee particularly insists on delivering data on the number of immigrants coming from other Member States, parties to the Charter, who partook in technical and vocational training.[538] It is interested in measures undertaken in order to prevent discrimination against immigrants in terms of technical and vocational training.[539] The preference treatment is accepted in case of disabled persons. Despite the fact that disabled persons should experience privileged treatment in matters concerning technical and vocational training as it is prescribed by the analysed provision, the Committee states that these preferences should be spread over all types of training, including higher technical and university education, which

536. Conclusions I, p. 55.
537. Conclusions II, p. 42 (Denmark).
538. Conclusions IV, p .71 (Germany).
539. Conclusions V, p. 81 (France).

is mentioned in the final part of the provision in question.[540] Access to higher technical and university education should be granted according to democratic rules, based solely on individual merit.[541] Attending university and studying is enabled by scholarships and other measures of financial help. The Committee is interested in knowing about the benefits provided for interested persons by Member States for those undertaking higher technical and university education.[542] Familiarization with domestic systems of vocational training obligates Member States to provide detailed information about the organizations, division of tasks between various educational bodies and institutions, conduct of these institutions, and ways of financing them. The Committee demands this information to be presented regularly.[543]

Providing and/or supporting vocational training by a Member State should be performed in consultation with stakeholders. According to the Committee, this reservation does not imply passing duties set by Article 10 § 1 of the Charter onto tripartite committees, consisting of representatives of employers and workers, debating under the chairmanship of the states.[544] Stakeholders should participate in the planning of educational institutions and bodies and achieving statutory goals by these organizations. In the cases of Great Britain and Turkey, the Committee stated trade unions were incidentally involved in the planning of technical and vocational training happening within the conduct of governmental bodies.[545] Institutions providing technical and vocational training should be evenly spread over the territory of a State, so all parties interested in utilizing their services could have equal access. In the case of Germany after the unification, the Committee stated that there were significant differences between Eastern and Western provinces in terms of density of training institutions.[546] It obliged Germany to eliminate the above disproportion. Training institutions should be organized in order to ensure the maximum utilization of their services by persons interested in undertaking technical or vocational training. The necessary condition for the execution of this rule is the proper proportion between learners and teachers. The increase of persons undertaking training accompanied by a stable number of teachers resulted in the Committee's reaction,[547] when examining the level of state expenses on technical and vocational training. The Committee considered the proportion of state expenses on technical and vocational training in the whole state budget as an important indicator of actions undertaken by Member States in order to meet the obligations determined by Article 10 § 1.[548]

Article 10 § 1 orders Member States to organize recruitment procedures for higher technical and university education as solely based on individual merit. The obligation

540. Conclusions II, p. 43; Conclusions III, p. 54 (Norway).
541. Conclusions I, pp. 55–56.
542. Conclusions II, p. 42 (Denmark).
543. Conclusions XIII-3, p. 33.
544. Conclusions XII-1, p. 165 (Great Britain).
545. Conclusions XIV-2, p. 748 (Turkey); XIV–2, p. 779 (Great Britain).
546. Conclusions XIII-2, p. 319; XIII-4, p. 382.
547. Conclusions XIV-2, p. 234 (Finland).
548. Conclusions XIV-2, p. 349 (Greece).

of granting access to higher technical and university education to all faculties,[549] not only faculties leading to particular occupational qualifications such as law and medicine, orders Member States to provide financial benefits (scholarships, allowances, loans) for persons studying, as well as to eliminate all barriers in accessing education. The requirement to obtain a work permit before entering into a vocational training agreement[550] or applying for a scholarship was regarded to act as an obstacle. The Committee declared that the right to apply for financial assistance during education and training is treated as a necessary condition of ensuring learning persons the right guaranteed by Article 10 § 1 to utilize vocational training.[551] In response to the restrictions introduced by Germany in terms of applying for financial help by persons studying or attending vocational training, the Committee was obliged to determine whether Germany fulfils the obligations imposed by Article 10 § 1. Germany argued that the duty of granting financial aid to persons attending vocational training is not regulated by Article 10 § 1 ESC, but by Article 10 § 4 ESC, which was not ratified by Germany. They reasoned that Article 10 § 4 ESC is the detailed provision to Article 10 § 1 ESC (*lex specialis*).[552] By a three-to-four majority of votes,[553] the Committee decided that providing measures of financial aid for those learning and studying is the necessary element of executing the right to vocational training. In view of this decision, Germany was considered a State violating the obligations of Article 10 § 1. During the following supervisory cycle, the Committee changed its position on this matter. It concluded that the duty of granting financial aid to learning persons should be evaluated within the supervision over the enforcement of Article 10 § 4 ESC, not Article 10 § 1 ESC as it had been so far.[554] This is because this particular issue is more strictly connected with § 4 of this provision. The negative ruling against Germany was overturned. The Committee stated that Germany had not violated Article 10 § 1. During the twelfth supervisory cycle, the Committee, debating in a partly changed structure,[555] concluded that the view on the Member States' duty of facilitating the utilization of vocational trainings presented during the seventh supervisory cycle[556] concerns granting financial aid.[557] It adjourned the decision in response to the German report, requesting data on the scope of financial aid for students and those attending vocational training. During the following supervisory cycle, the Committee declared that approximately 2 per cent of those learning or studying in Germany benefit from the financial aid provided by the state.[558] Rejecting the previously presented German

549. Conclusions XIII-3, p. 37.
550. Conclusions VII, p. 59 (Germany).
551. Conclusions VIII, p. 136.
552. Conclusions IX-2, pp. 103 and following.
553. W.F. de Gaay Fortman (the Netherlands), F. Fabricius (Germany) i T. Öhlinger (Austria) voted against.
554. Conclusions X-2, p. 103 (Germany).
555. With the presence of new members: S. Grévisse (France), S. Billum (Sweden), D. Harris (Great Britain) and T. Jaspers (the Netherlands).
556. Conclusions VII, p. 59; Conclusions VIII, p. 136.
557. Conclusions XII-2, p. 154.
558. Conclusions XIII-2, pp. 320–321.

arguments explaining the legal qualifications of the duty of granting financial aid to persons learning or studying, the Committee unambiguously stated that the above duty should be regarded as the material warranty for the entitlement to benefit from vocational training at all levels for the interested subjects.[559] However, during the following supervisory cycle, the new structure of the Committee decided that the opinions expressed during the seventh and the eighth supervisory cycles should be altered, and the fulfilling of the duty of granting financial aid to persons learning or studying should be evaluated while supervising Article 10 § 4.[560] Evaluating the German report, the Committee was obliged to state that Article 10 § 1 ESC does not impose on Member States the duty of granting financial aid to persons learning or studying. This obligation is derived from Article 10 § 4, which was not ratified by Germany. Eventually, the Committee concluded Germany had not violated Article 10 § 1.[561]

The right to technical and vocational training, as well as to higher technical and university education, should be equally utilized by citizens of a particular country and citizens of other Member States. Cases of unequal treatment of citizens of Member States, signatories of the Charter, were detected by the Committee during these supervisory cycles, when the Committee held the position that granting financial aid to persons learning or studying is a duty formulated in Article 10 § 1. The Committee stated that discriminatory practises concerning the granting of financial aid to persons learning or studying, employed by Belgium against citizens of Turkey, conflicted with Article 10 § 1.[562] The Finnish regulation that introduced the requirement of two years of residency as the necessary condition for acquiring the right to financial aid for persons learning or studying, was considered to be a manifestation of discrimination.[563] In the eleventh supervisory cycle, Greece was evaluated negatively by the Committee. It was regarded as a state in violation of the provision, as it made the right of a foreigner to partake in vocational training dependent upon being born and being a permanent resident of the territory of Greece.[564] It was not until the Greek regulations changed and Greece declared equal access to technical and vocational training, as well as to higher technical and university education, for Greek citizens and for citizens of other Member States, parties to the Charter, when the Committee changed its jurisdiction towards this country.[565] In 2003, the Committee detected one case of national labour regulations conflicting with Article 10 § 1 RESC. Slovenia had not provided citizens of other Member States with equal access to vocational training. It conditioned the option of utilizing vocational training on work permits for an unspecified period of time.[566] The exception from the above rule was introduced for citizens of those Member States,

559. Conclusions XIII-4, p. 383 (Germany).
560. Conclusions XIV-2, p. 62 (General introduction).
561. *Ibid.*, p. 314–315.
562. Conclusions XIII-4, p. 382.
563. Conclusions XIII-5, p. 81.
564. Conclusions XI-1, p. 112; Conclusions XII-1, p. 161–162; Conclusions XIII-1, p. 185; Conclusions XIII-3, p. 155.
565. Conclusions XIV-2, p. 349.
566. Conclusions 2003, vol. 2, pp. 472–473.

parties to the Charter, which were bound with Slovenia by international multilateral agreements on facilitating vocational trainings.

6.8.2. The Duty of Providing or Promoting a System of Apprenticeship for Young Persons (Article 10 § 2)

Member States that ratified the above regulation are obligated to provide or promote a system of apprenticeship for young persons (boys and girls) or to provide or promote other systemic arrangements for training young persons in their various employments. The Committee defined an apprenticeship, during the first supervisory cycle, as a mixed system of training, a combination of theoretical and practical aspects. An apprenticeship is not intended solely to acquire practical skills. It is a complex system based on full, coordinated and systematic vocational training.[567] It may occur in the formalized legal form, according to which training is understood strictly in terms of vocational training. Vocational training can also be comprised of apprenticeships, served by older students of technical und academic faculties such: pedagogical science, medicine, dentistry, and law.[568] The Committee evaluates whether systems of vocational training existing in Member States meet the requirements of the analysed provision. It monitors the actions undertaken by Member States in order to provide youth with systematic vocational training; the number of persons who can enrol for training;[569] the number of persons who partook in vocational trainings;[570] the types of the offered vocational trainings; financial support for persons attending trainings;[571] and the number of persons who completed training, taking into consideration their sex[572] and geographical location.[573] Foremost, the Committee supervised the obeying of the rule of equal opportunities for citizens of Member States. It continued to hand down negative rulings against States that restricted the entitlement of foreigners to utilize financial aid during apprenticeships,[574] demanding the acquisition of a work permit or a certificate excusing them from the above obligation.[575] It did not accept the explanation from the Member States, which provided information on the results of the above protective actions intended at the future protection of national labour markets concerning a small minority, approximately 5 per cent of the whole working population, hence smaller than the 20 per cent accepted according to the rule of majority formulated in Article 33 § 2 ESC and Article I § 2 RESC. The Committee declared that excluding less than 5 per cent of foreigners out of 100 per cent of citizens who had been

567. Conclusions I,. p. 57.
568. Conclusions III, p. 55.
569. Conclusions XIV-2, p. 97 (Austria); p. 200 (Denmark).
570. Case of Spain: Conclusions XII-2, pp. 159–160; Conclusions XIII-3, p. 167.
571. Conclusions I, pp. 56–57.
572. Conclusions XIV-2, p. 749 (Turkey).
573. Conclusions XIII-3, p. 240 (Turkey).
574. Conclusions XIII-4, p. 386 (Germany).
575. Case of Austria: Conclusions VIII, p. 138–139; Conclusions XIII-3, p. 162; Conclusions XIV-2, pp. 97 and following.

deprived of the entitlement to serve apprenticeship is, in fact, excluding 100 per cent of foreigners residing in the territory of other Member State. This is why the rule of majority cannot be applied to all members of a particular social category. Therefore, the regulations of domestic labour law were regarded by the Committee as conflicting with Article 10 § 2, although a given Member State treated work permits as a 'pure formality'.[576] Identical rulings were handed down in the case of Greece, which also required a work permit from participants in vocational training,[577] whilst Ireland[578] and Malta privileged its own citizens in accessing vocational training.[579]

6.8.3. Vocational Training for Adult Workers (Article 10 § 3)

The duty of Member States is to guarantee or provide adequate trainings for adult workers. Special facilities for the retraining of adult workers needed as a consequence of technological development and new trends in employment, should be provided by Member States. The obligation stipulated under Article 10 § 3 has a relative nature. Providing or promoting vocational trainings and adequate training for adult workers should be organized as necessary. The Committee believes that particular Member States decide themselves whether the above necessity applies. During the early supervisory cycles, the Committee took the position that the margin of freedom for Member States in terms of making decisions upon promoting and providing vocational training should be limited. It is usually determined by the unemployment rate existing in given Member States. According to the Committee, Article 10 § 3 imposes special duties on Member States where unemployment is high.[580] The Committee made a negative ruling in the case of Italy, which neglected to provide training for adult workers. According to the Italian report, the percentage of unemployed utilizing the option of vocational training was minimal.[581] The situation in the aforementioned countries looked similar during the second supervisory cycle.[582] Influenced by the negative rulings of the Committee, Great Britain and Italy changed the policy of vocational training for adult workers, which let them obtain positive decisions of the Committee in terms of abiding by regulations formulated in the analysed provision during the following supervisory cycle. Gradually the Committee became convinced there was no direct correlation between fulfilling the obligation of promoting and providing adequate training for adult workers and the unemployment rate. It concluded that what is protected by Article 10 § 3 is vocational training for adult workers as a virtue *per se,* which, generally analysing, plays an important role in the process of evaluating

576. Addendum to Conclusions on Luxembourg, p. 56 and following; Conclusions XIV-2, p. 486 (Luxembourg).
577. Conclusions XII-2, p. 156–157; XIII-2, p. 220; XIII-3, p. 165; Addendum to Conclusions XIII-3, pp. 56 and following.
578. Conclusions XIV-2, p. 404.
579. Conclusions XIII-2, p. 323; Conclusions XIII-3, pp. 165–166.
580. Conclusions I, p. 58 (Italy, Great Britain).
581. *Ibid.*
582. Conclusions II, p. 43 (Italy), p. 44 (Great Britain).

the chances of adult workers within the labour market: adult workers who want to work, who want to apply for jobs. The Committee ordered the Member States to prepare reports concerning the number and geographical location of public and private institutions of vocational training dealing with adult workers, especially ones who are unemployed; permanent centres of upgrading skills for persons of particular occupations (doctors, dentists, lawyers, etc.), craftsmen, merchants, etc.; and actions undertaken by administrative bodies in order to promote these institutions.[583] It observed disproportion between the number of vocational training institutions and their localization and the unemployment rate in particular Member States.[584] On the one hand, vocational training contributes to the increase of mobility of persons seeking employment and migrating for employment purposes;[585] on the other hand, vocational training provided by employers enables workers to undertake new responsibilities, giving employers a reason for not leaving and extending their work relations with the same workers, but with higher professional qualifications.[586]

The Committee paid special attention to Member States which fulfilled the duty of providing or promoting actions aimed at vocational trainings for adult workers in social groups vulnerable to changes in the labour market: women, the unemployed, migrant workers, and citizens of other Member States. Evaluating national reports, the Committee emphasized that in some countries the participation of women in programmes of vocational training is low, especially training obtaining with professional qualifications essential for carrying out works dominated by men. In relation to the above, the Committee emphasized the need for privileged treatment for women applying for participation in vocational training, which, once accomplished, increases the chances of a woman to carry out work within occupations traditionally regarded as 'male'.[587] Despite the previously certified lack of direct correlation between professional training and the rate of unemployment, the Committee demanded from the Member States the reasons that a significant part of the unemployed are not included in training.[588] It presented the opinion that unemployed persons, especially those who remain without employment for the period of one year, should be included in special programmes of vocational training and upgrading skills. It noted that in some countries such programmes had been drafted and were executed.[589] The experience of the Committee was taken into consideration by Article 10 § 4 RESC: a standard which orders Member States to undertake special measures of professional training and reintegration of the long-term unemployed.

During each supervisory cycle, the Committee demanded from the Member States information concerning programmes of vocational training for adult workers, and for

583. Conclusions V, p. 84 (France).
584. Case of turkey: Conclusions XIII-1, pp. 240–241; Conclusions XIV-2, p. 751.
585. Conclusions XIII-3, pp. 34–35 (Denmark).
586. *Ibid.*, Ireland, Iceland.
587. Cases of: Spain, Ireland, Portugal, Sweden and Turkey. General introduction to Conclusions XIII-3, p. 35.
588. Conclusions XIV-2, p. 237 (Finland).
589. Spain, Ireland, Portugal, Sweden, Great Britain. General introduction to Conclusions XIII-3, p. 35.

citizens of other Member States. The lack of such information resulted in postponing a ruling on the compliance of national regulations and practices with the requirements of the Charter.[590] During its supervisory session, the Committee held the position that excluding or limiting the rights of foreigners, citizens of other Member States, parties to the Charter because of their national identity, is a case of discrimination and must be considered as a violation of Article 10 § 3.[591] It pursued a goal of encouraging the Member States to apply the same requirements in accessing vocational training for adult workers for their own citizens and citizens of other Member States, parties to the Charter. Evaluating the case of Germany, which introduced the requirement of a particular work tenure for candidates to vocational training for adult workers (three years for qualified workers and six years for unqualified), the Committee made attempts in order to determine whether the work tenure from different Member States is respected in this requirement. After a positive answer, the Committee declared that requirements for candidates to vocational training for adult workers were not conflicting with the analysed provision of Article 10 § 3.[592] The above position was repeated in the case of Denmark.[593] The Committee negatively evaluated the legal regulation existing in Austria, which allowed for utilizing vocational training for adult workers by foreigners from Member States, other than members of the European Economic Area according to the availability of places, not engaged by citizens of the privileged states.[594] It also stated that introducing the requirement of residency as a condition to accessing vocational training for adult workers was not in accordance with the standards of the Charter.[595] It took the identical position towards work permits as a condition of accessing vocational training in some Member States;[596] however, debating on a different case, the Committee concluded that the final legal evaluation of such a requirement depends on the condition of obtaining a work permit in the light of national labour law regulations and on practise of applying this provision, namely on comparing the number of issued permits with the number of negative decisions. It also

590. During five consecutive supervisory cycles – the eighth, ninth, tenth, eleventh and twelfth – the Committee postponed making a ruling in case of Austria. Conclusions VIII, p. 142; Conclusions IX-2, p. 69; Conclusions X-2, p. 106–107; Conclusions XI-2, p. 13, p. 105; Conclusions XII-2, p. 160. It demanded information on the possibility of participation of immigrants in trainings organized for Austrian citizens. The Committee opposed the policy of providing vocational trainings for a country's own citizens and foreigners according to different rules. During the fourteenth supervisory cycle, the Committee postponed making a ruling in case of: Belgium (Conclusions XIV-2, pp. 144 and following); Denmark (XIV-2, pp. 200 and following); Finland (XIV-2, pp. 235 and following); Ireland (XIV-2, pp. 405 and following); Malta (XIV-2, p. 521); Portugal (XIV-2,pp.655–656); Turkey (XIV-2, pp. 750 and following) and Italy (XIV-2, pp. 444–445). During the following supervisory cycle in 2003, the Committee postponed making a ruling in the case of Italy (Conclusions 2003, vol.1,p.274) .

591. Conclusions 2003, vol.2, p. 478 (Slovenia).

592. Conclusions V, p. 84; Conclusions VI, p. 73.

593. Conclusions XIV-2, p. 202.

594. Conclusions XIII-2, p. 221.

595. Conclusions XIV-2, p. 103 (Ireland).

596. Conclusions XIV-2, p. 521 (Malta).

concluded that when a Member State made a decision upon granting a work permit on the basis of objective criteria, not having been guided by citizenship of candidates, and granted work permits to an adequate number of foreigners, there was no legal basis for the negative ruling to be made.[597]

6.8.4. Special Measures for the Retraining and Reintegration of the Long-Term Unemployed (Article 10 § 4 RESC)

Because of the limited possibilities of reintroduction of the long-term unemployed into the labour market, the new provision was added to the Charter, the provision that imposes on Member States the duty of providing or promoting special measures for the retraining and reintegration of the long-term unemployed.[598] The supervision over abiding of this duty took place for the first time in 2003. Amongst six Member States who delivered their reports,[599] two states[600] did not ratify Article 10 § 4 RESC. Therefore, the Committee supervised over abiding of this provision by four remaining Member States. In two cases[601] it declared compliance of the national conduct with the standards established by the Charter. Slovenia drafted seven employment programmes enabling the unemployed, especially persons under the age of 26, to acquire professional qualifications and employment. One of these programmes marked by number '5000' is addressed to young persons who are missing professional preparation or obtained qualifications, which are not demanded by the labour market. 60 per cent of persons benefiting from this programme were women. The programme enabled them to obtain secondary education. Due to acquired professional qualifications, over 20 per cent of persons previously regarded as long-term unemployed found employment.[602] Better results of training programmes were ascertained in Sweden. 35 per cent of persons taking part in the special programme 'Activity Guarantee' found employment.

The long-term unemployed are persons remaining without employment for a period longer than a year. Italy does not apply this definition of long-term unemployed. Three employment programmes for the long-term unemployed were addressed to workers from 16–32 years old, remaining without employment for at least 24 to 30 months. None of the programmes significantly reduced unemployment. The Committee emphasized that in Italy the percentage of long-term unemployed is the highest in Europe. For this reason, it declared that Italy did not meet the obligations formulated in Article 10 § 4 RESC.[603] The Committee also critically evaluated the French report. Relating to independent sources, it prescribed the French to undertake more efficient measure of professional elicitation of the long-term unemployed.[604]

---

597. Conclusions XIV-2, p. 488 (Luxembourg).
598. Explanatory report to the revised European Social Charter, European Social Charter, *op. cit.*, p. 166.
599. Bulgaria, France, Romania, Slovenia, Sweden, Italy.
600. Bulgaria and Romania.
601. Slovenia, Sweden.
602. Conclusions 2003, vol.2, p. 480 (Slovenia).
603. Conclusions 2003, vol.2, p. 275–276.
604. According to the information delivered in the French report, 40 per cent of the long-term unemployed embraced by governmental programmes undertake employment within a period of six months from the date of the completion of training. According to the data of EC Joint Employment Reports

6.8.5. The Duty of Encouraging Actions Facilitating Vocational Trainings (Article 10 § 4 ESC; Article 10 § 5 RESC)

The analysed provisions lists the duties imposed on Member States that ratified one of the paragraphs of Article 10. They are obliged to employ appropriate measures aiming at:

- Reducing or abolishing any fees or charges for apprenticeships (§ a);
- Granting financial assistance in appropriate cases for persons serving apprenticeships (§ b);
- Including supplementary training in normal working hours. The Charter introduces two conditions to include the time of training in the time of work: first, undertaking training during the period of employment; second, vocational training should be undertaken at the request of the employer (§ c);
- Adequate supervision, in consultation with social stakeholders, over the efficiency of apprenticeship of young workers and adequate protection in general (§ d).

The above list is only an example. The Committee, in its previous prevailing practise, did not extend supervision over different cases not mentioned in the above list. In a form used in preparation of national reports by Member States, the set of questions relate directly to the benefits mentioned in (a)–(d) of the analysed provision.[605] The Committee is interested in obtaining an answer whether fees for serving apprenticeship are charged in Member States, what the amount of these charges is, and what actions are undertaken in order to reduce or resign from charging fees. It pursues a goal of obtaining information concerning the prevailing system of financial assistance for persons serving apprenticeships. It is interested in being aware of types of allowances (scholarships, loans, credits, others), and of the nature of these allowances. It makes an attempt to determine the conditions of acquiring the entitlements of the above allowances, their amounts, and the period they are obtained in. It pays special attention to abiding by Member States the rule of equal treatment of its own citizens and citizens of other Member States. It orders the Member States to deliver information concerning actions undertaken in order to include vocational training undertaken during the period of employment at the request of the employer, in normal working hours. It also obligates the Member States to describe the supervisory techniques introduced in consultation with employers' and workers' organizations to ensure workers' rights to attend vocational training.

In the majority of cases, the Committee adjourned its decision with regards to whether the analysed provision in question was being followed by Member States.[606]

1999–2001 the indicator of professional elicitation of the long-term unemployed came to 23 per cent. Conclusions 2003, vol.1, p. 142. The Committee postponed making a ruling until the above discrepancy is clarified.

605. Form for the reports ..., *op. cit.*, s. 335.

606. Conclusions XIII-1, pp. 241–242 (Turkey); Conclusions XIII-2, pp. 327–328 (Belgium); Conclusions XIII-3, pp. 337 and following (Finland Portugal); Addendum to Conclusions XIII-3, pp. 60 and following (Luxembourg); Conclusions 2003, vol. 1, pp. 276–278 (Italy); Conclusions 2003, vol.2, pp. 594–596.

The reason for this adjournment was a lack of information provided about the introduction of measures by a given Member State dealing with workers' vocational training.

Financial aid for those partaking in vocational training should be ensured in appropriate cases (Article 10(5)(b)). The Committee came to the conclusion that this definition encompasses cases whereby participation in vocational training would have been impossible had it not been for the financial assistance.[607] The scope of this obligation refers to various types of vocational training considered by Article 10 § 1–3. In all cases referred to in these provisions, subjects authorized to make a decision upon granting a financial assistance to persons serving apprenticeships utilize the freedom of material evaluation of these persons. Article 10 § 1–3 cannot be the basis to impose on Member States the duty of granting financial assistance to all persons serving an apprenticeship.[608] The duty of providing persons serving apprenticeships with financial assistance is independent from the duty of reducing or abolishing any fees or charges for apprenticeships.[609] In relation to evaluative language used twice in Article 10 – once in Article 10 § 1 'as necessary', and again in the analysed provisions of Article 10 § 4 ESC and § 5 RESC (b) 'in appropriate cases', the Committee decided that all matters concerning the provision of vocational training financed by Member States on all levels, from the basic training and apprenticeship to the higher technical and university education, will be analysed in the supervisory processes over Article 10 § 4 ESC and § 5 RESC.[610] Financial assistance in the form of scholarships, grants, loans and credits should be utilized to different expenses related to the participation in vocational training, not vocational training fees. Participation in vocational training is an entitlement, and not an obligation. Therefore, the regulation of national labour law depriving the unemployed of benefits in case of not accepting the option of vocational training turns into a duty of legal nature for this group. For this very reason, the Committee was interested in obtaining information on balancing the labour market with the individual expectations of the unemployed in matters of undertaking employment.[611] The opinion of the Committee reflects the entitlement of undertaking employment according to education, professional qualification and individual predispositions. Member States of the Council of Europe should attempt provide workers the opportunity of freely choosing the place and type of work by those able to undertake employment, wanting or looking for employment. The threat of losing unemployment benefits, due to refusing to take employment offered by an employment agency or failing to carry out specified vocational training, in order to attain certain trade qualifications that are at the time required within the domestic labour market, is in contradiction to the principle

607. Conclusions XIII-1, p. 242 (Turkey).
608. Conclusions XIV-2, p. 62.
609. Conclusions XIII-3, p. 339.
610. Conclusions XIV-2, p. 62.
611. Case of Great Britain: Conclusions XII-1, p. 172; Conclusions XIII-3, pp. 177–178.

of the freedom to work. Despite its doubts, the Committee did not conclude that Great Britain was violating Article 10 § 4 ESC. It concluded that a typical example of violating the standards established by the given provision is evident in the discriminatory treatment of citizens of other Member States, who are parties to the Charter. Amongst the countries that do not meet the standards specified by the provision in question are Austria,[612] Belgium, Greece,[613] Finland, France, and Slovenia. None of the mentioned States[614] ordered for less favourable treatment of foreign nationals in matters concerning financial assistance for those wanting to undertake vocational training. All the mentioned States specified the requirement of residency within the territory of the given Member State for those who are attempting to undertake vocational training, in order to be able to seek financial assistance. Turkish citizens in Belgium under the age of 21 have to prove a five-year residency within the territory of the State, as well as a five-year period of study within Belgian educational institutions.[615] Finland demands that foreign nationals seeking financial grants and scholarships, with the exception of citizens of Member States of the European Union and the European Economic Area, reside within Finland for at least a period of two years continuously.[616] France, in addition to the identical requirements, requires that taxes be paid within that same period of residency within its territory.[617] Slovenia grants financial assistance for those undertaking vocational training based on possession of a work permit. Permits are granted to those residing in Slovenia for a period of eight years.[618] The Committee reminds the Member States that the introduction of residency requirements within the territory of a given Member State, as a condition for being able to receive financial assistance for those wanting to undertake vocational training within the territory of another Member State, is regarded as indirect discrimination. It is forbidden. Member States that have introduced such requirements are in violation of Article 10. In all the abovementioned cases, the Committee rendered decisions that the mentioned Member States violated the obligations stipulated under the provision in question. In cases where Member States did not provide the relevant information dealing with foreign nationals of other Member States seeking financial assistance during vocational training, the Committee adjourned its decisions dealing with the legal situation of the said foreign nationals.[619]

612. Conclusions XIII-2, p. 221.
613. Conclusions XI-1, p. 171; Conclusions XIII-3, p. 175.
614. This is with the exception of Belgium, which regards citizenship as a necessary condition for being able to receive financial assistance for those undertaking vocational training. Conclusions III-4, pp. 386–388; Conclusions XIV-2, pp. 146–147.
615. *Ibid.*
616. Conclusions XIII-5, pp. 84–85; Conclusions XIV-2, pp. 237–238.
617. Conclusions 2003, vol. 1, p. 144.
618. Conclusions 2003, vol. 2, p. 483.
619. Conclusions XIV-2, pp. 352–353 (Greece); pp. 406–407 (Ireland); pp. 657–658 (Portugal); pp. 752–753 (Turkey); pp. 445–446 (Italy).

6.9. The Right to Equal Opportunities and Equal Treatment in Matters of Employment without Discrimination on the Grounds of Sex (Article 20 RESC)

Article 20 obligates Member States to employ the rule of equal opportunities and equal treatment in matters of employment without discrimination based on sex towards workers and candidates for work.[620] This regulation is modelled on the legal regulation introduced by the Council's directive No. 207 of 9 February 1976 concerning equal treatment of men and women in accessing employment, vocational training and professional promotion, as well as working conditions.[621] This provision orders the Member States to recognize the right to equal opportunities and equal treatment in matters of employment, to prohibit the discrimination based on sex within the abovementioned issues, and to undertake adequate measures to guarantee the enforcement of the abovementioned provision in the following areas:

- Accessing employment, protection against terminating a work agreement, professional reintegration.
- Vocational training, upgrading professional skills, changing occupation, professional re-adaptation.
- Working conditions, conditions of employment, including remuneration.
- Path of professional career, including promotions.

The objective range of the right to equal treatment is broad. It encompasses categories of rights regulated by the directive No. 207 and the directive No. 117 of 10 February 1975 concerning the legislation of Member States in terms of employing the rule of equal remuneration of men and women.[622] The range of legal protection guaranteed by this provision is large.[623] It encompasses nearly all categories of issues regulated by the labour law, including those, previously described:

- Article 1 § 2 (prohibiting the discrimination in work relations);
- Article 4 § 3 (the right to equal remuneration of men and women for work of the equal value;
- Article 8 (the right of female workers to protection during maternity);
- Article 9 (the right to vocational guidance);
- Article 10 (the right to vocational training).

---

620. P. Koncar, *Kwestia równouprawnienia kobiet i mężczyzn w Europejskiej Karcie Społecznej* (Equality between men and women in the Revised European Charter), In: *Dorobek Rady Europy* (European Social Charter Towards ...), *op. cit.,* pp. 22 and following.
621. OJ No L 39, 14.2.1976, p. 40, *see* A.M. Świątkowski, H. Wierzbińska, *op. cit.,* pp. 333 and following.
622. OJ No L 45, 19.2.1975, p. 19, *see* A.M. Świątkowski, H. Wierzbińska, *op. cit.,* pp. 329 and following; *see* also M. Wandzel, *Równe traktowanie* ... (Equal Treatment ...), *op. cit.,* pp. 21 and following.
623. Equality between men and women in the European Social Charter: study compiled on the basis of the case law pf the Committee of Independent Experts, Council of Europe Publishing, Strasbourg 1999.

Despite the fact that all the abovementioned regulations obligate the Member States to guarantee to abovementioned rights without discrimination on the basis of sex, Article 20 imposes on Member States additional duties.[624] According to the Committee,[625] a Member State that ratified Article 20 is obligated to: introduce into its national labour law regulations the rule of equal opportunities and equal treatment in matters of employment as well as establishing the prohibition of discrimination of workers on the basis of sex; to undertake adequate measures in order to guarantee the efficient protection of workers' right to equal treatment; to prepare special programmes for the enforcement of the policy of equal treatment, and to undertake proper actions in order to enact it.[626] Alike duties are not imposed by the abovementioned Articles. Additionally, the Committee emphasized the different objective ranges of the provisions in question: Article 20 and Article 1 § 2, 4 § 3, 8, 9, and 10.[627] The provision of Article 1 § 2 disallows the differentiation of workers on the basis of unlawful criteria, not only on the basis of sex. The provision of Article 4 § 3 applies to work of the equal value. Therefore, the objective scope of Article 20 is significantly larger.[628] The provision of Article 8 guarantees entitlements not accessible by all workers. The provisions of Article 9 and 10 order the equal treatment of 'all persons'. Article 20 is a special standard. It orders Member States to guarantee the equal treatment of workers regardless of sex within all categories of issues regulated by individual provisions of labour law, as well as selected aspects of social policies, such as the policy of employment and the policy of promoting workers. The term 'conditions of work and employment' has many understandings. It relates to all rights and situations of persons benefiting from and within the confines of work relations, with the exception of social security and other benefits for the unemployed, pensioner allowances and allowances due to the death of the sole breadwinner in the family.[629] These allowances can be excluded by Member States from the objective scope of this provision on the basis of the authorization listed in the appendix to Article 20. The exclusion of applying Article 20 in matters of social security is possible after filing a relevant notification at a proper time by a Member State. In the period till such a notification is filed, Member States are obliged to follow the rule of equal treatment in matters of social security. On this basis, the Committee demanded from Sweden presenting data on numbers of men and women employed part-time who were not entitled to obtain social security benefits such as: the unemployment benefit, health pension, and retirement pension.[630] After having familiarized itself with the information provided by Sweden, the Committee concluded that the provisions of Swedish social security law discriminate against women indirectly, because workers employed part-time, whose employment does not exceed three hours

624. Conclusions XIII-5, p. 253.
625. Conclusions XIII-3, p. 429.
626. Conclusions XIII-3, p. 429.
627. Conclusions XIII-5, p. 253
628. Explanatory report to the 1988 Additional Protocol, European Social Charter, *op. cit.*, p. 130.
629. *Ibid.*
630. Conclusions XV-2, pp. 575 and following.

per day or 17 hours per week, are not covered by insurance in case of losing the job. The significant majority of workers employed part-time are women.[631] Swedish regulations concerning benefits in case of unemployment condition the entitlement of insurance coverage on the employment of at least 17 hours a week. Workers who do not meet this requirement are entitled to apply for financial assistance from social security, if they were employed for at least 75 hours per month.[632] Because of the indirect discrimination in matters of social protection for women, the Committee in both 2002 and 2004 supervisory cycles made rulings upon the discrepancy between national regulations of social security law in Sweden and the standards established by the Article 20. A similar ruling was issued in the case of Cyprus.[633] Provisions of social security law existing in this country entitle a woman to obtain a family benefit only in the case of her husband's death. The right of a female worker to a retirement pension and other social security benefits is dependent on whether her husband is in receipt of such benefits. This in turn results in a woman's inability to support herself. The above differentiation between insured men and women in their range of social benefit entitlements was recognized by the Committee as a case of discrimination on the basis of sex, which violates the Article 20.

Legal measures that Member States are obligated to undertake under the provision in question include authorization of judicial bodies and labour courts to overrule or recognize as not binding all provisions of law and clauses of collective and individual work agreements violating the rule of equal treatment of workers regardless of sex.[634] In order to meet this obligation, the Member States should introduce special measures preventing discriminating actions against workers that may possibly be undertaken by the State, stakeholders or parties of individual work agreements. Amongst these measures the Committee lists: ruling upon the common invalidity (*erga omnes*) of provisions and clauses violating the rule of equal treatment of workers regardless of sex; and the entitlement of trade union organizations to litigate on behalf of an individual worker, intervening into the ongoing proceedings initiated by the discriminated workers, as well as registering class actions on behalf of workers interested in the court's verdict upon the invalidity of regulations violating the rule of equal treatment of workers regardless of sex.[635]

Within the confines of enabling workers to utilize the right to equal opportunity and equal treatment in matters of employment and professional occupation without gender discrimination, Member States are obligated to assure the adequate (material-legal and procedural) measures of workers' legal protection, for those workers who are the victims of discrimination on the basis of sex.[636] The Committee demands that

631. Conclusions 2004, vol.2, p. 594. In 2000 77.3 per cent of workers employed part time were women. Comparing the percentage of employed part time and full time, 36.3 per cent employed part time were women, 10.9 per cent were men. *See* Conclusions 2002, p. 260.
632. Conclusions XIII-5, p. 274; Conclusions 2002, p. 260.
633. Conclusions 2004, vol.1, pp. 123 and following.
634. Conclusions XIII-3, p. 429.
635. Conclusions XIII-5, p. 255.
636. Conclusions XIII-3, p. 429; Conclusions XIII-5, p. 255.

Member States introduce procedural facilities for the process of proving cases of discrimination being necessary to reinstate rights of the discriminated workers that have been violated. The Committee employs the rules established by the directive of the Council No. 80 of 15 December 1997 concerning the onus of proof in cases of gender discrimination.[637] According to this directive, persons considering themselves aggrieved as a result of a violation of the rule of equal treatment within work relations by their employer, and who prove before the court or other relevant judicial body that events forming the ground for the case of direct or indirect discrimination took place, are exempt from giving evidence of the facts of discrimination. The sued employer is obligated to give evidence that the rule of equal treatment of workers regardless of sex was not violated. The employer has to prove the said discrimination did not take place, and that differentiating between workers resulted from objective criteria, and not on the basis of the worker's sex.[638]

In the case of the termination of labour relations as a result of registering a complaint by a worker asserting the rule of equal treatment within labour relation had been violated, or applying for benefits he or she is entitled to as a victim of discrimination, it should become a common practice to reinstate unlawfully terminated labour relations, as well as granting compensation for the period the worker remained without a job. Only when it is not possible to make a ruling upon reinstating a worker into the previous position, the Committee allows for the granting of compensation for unlawfully terminated labour relations. It notes that this compensation should be adequate, meaning it will repair all losses caused by the employer to the illegally dismissed employee. It also should serve the repressive function for the employer to be aware of the financial consequences.[639] The right to utilize adequate legal measures should encompass all aggrieved workers, regardless of the sector of employment (private or public) complaining about employers not abiding by the rule of equal treatment in labour relations and matters of professional occupation.[640]

The Committee interprets Article 20 according to the guidelines listed in the directive No. 207. It distinguishes indirect and direct discrimination. It argues that the rule of equal treatment of workers means the lack of any discrimination, direct as well as indirect, on the basis of sex in labour relations and matters of professional occupation. It gives the following example of indirect discrimination: less favourable conditions of employment (lower remuneration) for part-time workers amongst whom the majority represents one social category, distinguished on the grounds of sex (women).[641] Indirect discrimination is the case when the employer does not remunerate

637. OJ No L 14, 20.1.1998, p. 6. A.M.Świątkowski, H.Wierzbińska, *op.cit.*, pp. 362 and following.

638. Conclusions XIII-5, p. 256; Conclusions 2004, vol.2, pp. 495–496 (Romania).

639. Conclusions XIII-3, p. 429; Conclusions XIII-5, p. 256. In 2004 the Committee decided that Swedish employers who made redundant workers demanding the rule of equal treatment are obligated to pay a compensation of 10,000 to 60,000 Swedish kronas (1.096 krona – 6.578 Euro). The Committee requested information whether, apart from the compensation, national regulations of labour law allow for cash penalties. Conclusions 2004, vol.2, p. 594

640. Conclusions XIII-5, p. 266 (the Netherlands).

641. Conclusions XIII-5, p. 274 (Sweden).

part-time workers proportionally to daily or weekly wages of full-time workers. For example, he pays workers employed for the half of the standard of weekly norm 40 per cent of what full-time workers obtain. The excuse given by employers – arguing that differentiating of remuneration between workers employed full-time and part-time can be explained by the limited availability of the latter – is regarded by the Committee as untrue should disproportion between men and women in the two above systems of work organization be discovered. The obligation of assuring workers the protection against indirect discrimination in matters of employment and professional occupation imposes on the Committee the duty of supervising regulation of labour law binding in Member States, as well as practices. Therefore, the Committee requests that the Member States deliver detailed information on:

- The situation of men and women on the labour market;
- Numbers of employment;
- Part-time and full-time, taking into consideration the criteria of sex; and the number of unemployed and self-employed within these two social categories (men and women). Member States are obligated to provide information on the number of men and women in active employment age. The above information is to allow the Committee to review national labour markets and establish the position in matters of equal treatment of workers regardless of sex;
- Access to and participation in vocational trainings for men and women. The Committee is especially interested in obtaining data on the opportunity for women to acquire professional qualification for jobs traditionally regarded as 'male;'
- Differences between the conditions of employment for men and women employed at identical, similar or comparable jobs existing in practice. First, The Committee is interested in familiarizing itself with the differences in the remuneration of men and women employed in identical, similar or comparable jobs. It obligates Member States to deliver information on the amount of basic and minimal remuneration, all other benefits paid by employers in cash, regularly or sporadically, as well as material benefits and bonuses of the job to which workers are entitled.[642] In order to enable the Committee to make a comparison of men and women in terms of remuneration for work, all data mentioned above should take sex into consideration;
- Practical differences in the 'path of career' for men and women employed in different sectors of the economy;
- Social programmes introduced in order to ensure equal treatment for men and women in matters of employment and professional occupation.[643]

In cases when the Member States did not utilize the option created by the Appendix to Article 20 and did not exclude matters concerning social security from

---

642. Explanatory report to the 1988 Additional Protocol, European Social Charter, *op. cit.*, p. 130.
643. Conclusions XIII-5, p. 256–257.

the application range of this provision, the Committee requested presenting the situation of men and women in terms of matters regulated by social security law as well.[644]

The Appendix to Article 20 also gave the legal ground to create the two anti-types in national regulations of labour law. First, the Appendix to Article 20 does not consider the provision on the protection of a female worker's body and labour relations during pregnancy and maternity leave as a case of discrimination in employment. Second, the obligation of equal treatment of workers and the prohibition on discriminating against them on the basis of sex does not create a legal obstacle to undertake measures leading to the decrease of the actual inequalities between men and women in labour relations. The Appendix to Article 20 authorizes Member States to run the policy of privilege towards previously discriminated social categories distinguished on the ground of sex.[645] Member States have been authorized to exclude from the rule of equal treatment of workers regardless of sex particular types of jobs and occupations which, due to their character or conditions, may be given only to persons of one sex. The Member States that utilize the above option are not obligated to enlist within binding regulations the list of occupations available for one sex. In cases when the Member States decide to prepare and publicly advertise the lists of jobs prohibited for women, the Committee requests to see such lists and postpones the ruling on conformity of national labour law regulations and Article 20 to the subsequent supervisory cycle.[646]

Supervising whether Article 20 has been obeyed by the Member State, the Committee considered national labour law regulations of the Netherlands,[647] Norway,[648] France,[649] Ireland,[650] Lithuania,[651] and Italy[652] as being in accordance with the provision in question. In the case of Italy, a positive ruling was subject to the provision of information on the elements of remuneration used as the basis of comparison of men's and women's wages, as well as material-legal measures of protection of workers demanding equal treatment and registering complaints regarding discriminative acts of employers.[653] The Committee postponed a ruling in the case of Finland.[654] It demanded information on actions undertaken in order to overrule the clauses of collective and individual work agreements contradicting the rule of equal treatment. It also asked about the possibility of obtaining a ruling on reactivating a labour relation with workers who were made redundant because of registering a complaint concerning discriminating treatment by an employer. It was interested in gathering information on

644. Conclusions XIII-5, p. 259 (Finland); XIII-5, pp. 266–267 (the Netherlands).
645. Conclusions XIII-5, p. 256.
646. Conclusions 2004, vol.1, p. 197.
647. Conclusions XV-2, pp. 376 and following.
648. Conclusions XV-2, pp. 401 and following; Conclusions 2004, vol.2, pp. 440 and following.
649. Conclusions 2002, pp. 58 and following; Conclusions 2004, vol.1, pp. 250 and following.
650. Conclusions 2004, vol.1, pp. 293 and following.
651. Conclusions 2004, vol.2, pp. 390 and following.
652. Conclusions 2002, pp. 103 and following; Conclusions 2004, vol.2, pp. 325 and following.
653. Conclusions XIII-5, pp. 261 and following; Conclusions XIV-2, pp. 452–453; Conclusions XV-2, pp. 324 and following.
654. Conclusions XIII-5, pp. 257 and following; Conclusions XV-2, pp. 178 and following.

executing the rule of equal treatment of workers regardless of sex practiced in all the fields listed in Article 20: first, access to employment, protection against redundancy and vocational reintegration; second, vocational guidance and training, re-qualification, professional re-adaptation; third, conditions of employment, working conditions, remuneration; and fourth, career, policy of promoting workers.[655] It wanted to know the proportion of men and women employed part-time and full-time,[656] and about the programmes of equalizing professional chances of social categories previously discriminated on the labour market prepared by the national authorities.[657] It enquired whether Member States introduced restrictions in accessing police and army services,[658] and dangerous work jobs.[659] It demanded detailed and comprehensive answers. It wanted to familiarize itself with the results brought about by introducing programmes of equal treatment of workers by Member States. It postponed making a ruling in the case of Slovenia, who informed about introducing three programmes introduced in order to promote the rule of equal treatment: 'positive programme' allowing for the active policy of preference employment for persons so far discriminated in matters of employment and professional occupation; 'encouraging programmes' aimed at employers to stimulate employment of persons of a particular sex; and 'promoting programmes' emphasizing the necessity of abiding by the rule of equality in employment prohibiting discrimination in matters of employment on the grounds of sex.[660] The provision of Article 20 is regarded by the Committee as a progressive standard obligating Member States to undertake systematic actions within the four fields listed in this regulation, the fields regulated by labour law and formed by social policy. In the case of not utilizing the option delivered by the Appendix to this provision, these actions should also include the introduction of maintenance and strengthening of the rule of equal treatment of workers regardless of the sex in matters of social security.

6.10. The Right to Protection in Cases of Termination of Employment (Article 24)

The Revised European Social Charter ensures workers protection in cases when their employment is terminated (Article 24).[661] The norms of protecting workers' rights were introduced by the Revised European Social Charter[662] modelled on international

655. Conclusions XV-1, pp. 172 and following.
656. Conclusions 2002, p. 160 (Romania).
657. Conclusions 2002, p. 219–220 (Slovenia).
658. Conclusions 2004, vol.1, p. 123 (Cyprus).
659. Conclusions 2004, vol.1, p. 197 (Estonia).
660. Conclusions 2004, vol.2, p. 548.
661. A.M.Świątkowski, *Ochrona praw pracowników w razie restrukturyzacji zakładu pracy i w innych przypadkach* (Protection of Employee Rights in the Case of Restructuring of their Employer and in Other Cases), in: *Dorobek Rady Europy* ... (European Social Charter. Towards Common Application of the Revised Charter) *op. cit.,* pp. 44 and following.
662. Provisions in the Revised European Social Charter referred to as RESC. Provisions in the European Social Charter referred to ESC.

regulations, such as the ILO conventions and recommendations or on the directives of the European Union. Amongst the ILO conventions and recommendations which became the prototypes for the introduction of legal regulations of Article 24, the following need to be mentioned: convention ILO No. 158 concerning work agreement termination by the employer[663] and the recommendation No. 166 concerning the same matter.[664]

The ILO convention No. 158 deals with the termination of a work agreement by an employer as a standard labour law clause in the contract. The premise for terminating such an agreement by an employer must be a valid reason, such as a lack of skills of the employee, their conduct, or a valid reason based on the operational requirements of the workplace or any of its areas (Article 4). The ILO convention lists reasons which cannot be legally recognized as reason validating the termination of the work agreement (Article 5 & 6). An impartial body monitors the decisions for termination handed down by an employer (Article 8). Those workers who have had their employment terminated have the right to appeal to such a body in order to be informed of the reasons for their termination. The onus of proof lies on the employer in providing the valid reasons as to why the work agreement was terminated (Article 9). The impartial body should be empowered to propose reinstatement of the worker, or should be empowered to order payment of adequate compensation or such other relief as may be deemed appropriate (Article 10). The ILO convention No. 158 enforces that workers whose employment is to be terminated shall be entitled to a reasonable period of notice or compensation at least in part for the loss of employment (Article 11). The employers who are exempt from the above provision are those whose workers have displayed serious misconduct – misconduct of such a nature that it would be unreasonable to require the employer to continue his employment during the notice period.

The normal practice of the Council of Europe is to adopt the standards of the International Labour Organization or the European Union, as their own. Despite the fact that in 1961 the European Social Charter did not accept, for obvious reasons, the standards existing in the European Union or the standards of the European Committee of Social Rights, a body called upon to supervise whether Member States were following the obligations of the Council of Europe set by the European Social Charter, it does so now using the current standards of the European Union. It is for this reason that all Member States of the Council of Europe (46 countries), including in it the number of those who have ratified the Revised European Social Charter (9 countries), should be aware of the necessity to contract national labour laws

663. Passed during the 68th session of the ILO General Conference 2 June 1982 Convention No.158 comes into force on 23 November 1985, ratified by 33 Member States. Poland does not ratify this convention. *See Konwencje i zalecenie Międzynarodowej Organizacji Pracy* 1919–1994 (Conventions and Recommendations, ILO 1919–1994), vol. II (1967–1994), *Wydawnictwo Naukowe* PWN (Publisher), Warszawa 1996, pp. 1084 and following; Lists of ratifications by Convention and by Country, International Labour Conference 91st Session, Geneva 2003, p. 187; Application of International Labour Standards 2004 (II), International Labour Conference 92nd Session, Geneva 2004, p. 80.

664. Undertaken during the 68th session of the General Conference ILO 2 June 1982, Conventions ... *op. cit.*, pp. 1090 and the following.

according to the standards accepted as obligatory by the European Committee of Social Rights, therefore by the standards of ILO as well as the European Union.

Article 24 RESC hopes to ensure workers with sufficient legal protection in cases where their agreements may be terminated. The preservation of the permanence of labour relations is protected by the following guarantees:

- The obligation to provide the worker with a valid reason for the termination of the employment. Such reasons validating the termination of a work agreement are connected with the conduct or the capacity of the worker (reasons concerning the worker) or reasons that are based on the operational requirements of the undertaking, the establishment, or service (reasons concerning the employer);
- Ensuring that all workers who have their employment terminated without a valid reason have a right to adequate compensation or other appropriate relief;
- The right of a worker to appeal to an impartial body, which will determine the reasons for the termination.

Despite the three separate obligations placed on Member States, Article 24 RESC is regarded as a standard which should be abided by in its entirety by the Member States that ratified the RESC. The regulations stipulated under paragraph (a) and (b), as well as the last unlettered paragraph of Article 24, are not separate in their nature, and do not allow Member States to choose which of those paragraphs they would prefer to abide by, to fulfil the required quota of 16 out of 31 Articles or 63 out of 98 paragraphs of the RESC.

Article 24 RESC ensures the protection of workers' rights in cases of work agreement termination by the employer or due to the employer's initiative.[665] Such legal protection ensured by the provision in question may also be utilized by workers have terminated their work agreement by consent of both parties, even if the termination was initiated by the employer. The Addendum to Article 24 fulfils a significant requirement, and that is it how Article 24, i.e. a general standard, is not applicable in particular categories of workers specified in the Addendum. The Addendum authorizes Member States to exclude from legal protection during termination of employment, wholly or partially, the following categories of workers: those employed on a temporary basis or on a contractual basis where the aim of the employment is to fulfil particular requirements of the job, those employed on a probationary basis, as well as those employed on a casual basis. This list is exhaustive in its nature. Member States do not have the right to expand upon this list in the Addendum to Article 24. The European Committee of Social Rights, a supervisory body monitoring the obligations under the European Social Charter of 1961 and the Revised European Social Charter of 1996, was of the view that Italy was not abiding by the obligations set in Article 24, as the list of exclusions was expanded to the following categories of workers: those employed in senior positions in employment service agencies, domestic help, those employed in professional sports, employees who are aged 60 years or more and entitled to social

665. Addendum to the Revised European Social Charter.

security benefits in the case of old age, and those laid-off as part of a group.[666] The European Committee of Social Rights concluded that the situation in Cyprus was not in conformity with Article 25 RESC on the ground that Cypriot labour law excludes from protection against dismissal employees who have not completed a continuous period of 26 weeks with their employer regardless of the employee's qualifications.[667] The European Social Rights Committee has undertaken efforts to decrease the categories of workers excluded from the protection of the law during termination instigated by their employers. In the report produced by Bulgaria, it is impossible to deduct information concerning those who are employed on a temporary basis and the level of legal protection received during the termination of their work agreements. Because of this, the European Committee of Social Rights decided not to pass judgement concerning Bulgaria's labour law compatibility with Article 24 RESC, and instead obligated Bulgaria to respond to the questions produced regarding whether workers who are signed to atypical work agreements utilize from the same rights guaranteed to those workers who are employed in full time employment without an established period of duration of the employment, and whether a necessary requirement for receiving legal protection during termination is that one completed their probationary period in full.[668] Establishing the above criteria is necessary for the European Committee of Social Rights when deciding whether Bulgarian labour law is in accordance with the standards stipulated under Article 24 RESC. At the same time, the Committee points out the necessity for equal treatment of all workers regardless of the basis of employment (typical or atypical work agreements).

The European Committee of Social Rights draws the attention of Member States to provisions in both Social Charters of the Council of Europe, which demand the enforcement of increased worker rights protection and forbid the termination of work agreements based on the following reasons: participating in trade union activities (Article 5), as well as partaking in worker representative organizations (Article 28), taking part in legal strike actions (Article 6 § 4), maternity leave (Article 8 § 2), disability (Article 15), and family responsibilities (Article 27). Some of the provisions in the Social Charters (namely Article 1 § 2, Article 4 § 3) forbid the discrimination of workers, and especially forbid the termination of work agreements based on the legally prohibited criteria (Article 1 § 2, Article 4 § 3, Article 20).[669] The Revised European Social Charter also supports the European Committee of Social Rights stance. In paragraph 3 to Article 24 of the Addendum to this Charter, there are six reasons, which do not constitute validity when terminating a work agreement. They are:

a) Trade union membership or participating in trade union activities outside working hours or with the consent of the employer within working hours;

666. Conclusions 2003, vol. 1 (Bulgaria, France, Italy), Council of Europe Publishing, Strasbourg 2003, pp. 319 and following.
667. Conclusions 2005, vol.1 (Bulgaria, Cyprus, Estonia, France, Ireland, Italy, Lithuania), Council of Europe Publishing, Strasbourg 2005, p. 111.
668. Conclusions vol. 1, *op. cit.*, p. 81.
669. *Ibid.*, p. 423 (Romania); p. 533 (Slovenia).

b) Seeking office as a workers' representative undertaking responsibilities (either acting or having acted in) in such a body;
c) The filing of complaints or the participation in proceedings against an employer involving alleged violations of labour law regulations;
d) Illegal premises of discrimination, i.e. Race, colour, sex, marital status, family responsibilities, pregnancy, religion, political opinion, national extraction or social origin;
e) Maternity or paternity leave;
f) Temporary absence from work due to illness or injury.

These specified reasons, which do not validate the termination of a work agreement, are only examples. This is indicated by the term in particular in the Addendum to Article 24 RESC.[670] Utilizing the abovementioned possibilities, the European Committee of Social Rights sought information from Romania as to whether there were labour law regulations in existence within the country that would ensure workers protection against the termination of work agreements for such reasons as exercising their civil liberties.[671]

Member States regulate their own grounds for terminating work agreements. Member States usually utilize one of two legislative methods: standard contractual clauses or expressed terms. In the first supervisory cycle monitoring whether Member States were abiding by the obligations of Article 24 RESC in 2003, the Committee of Social Rights was of the view[672] that the first technique of protecting the right to work within the above provisions, was administered by French legislation. The French labour law code authorizes employers to terminate a work agreement in cases where there are objective and serious reasons (sec. L 122-14-3).[673] The second legislative technique is applied by Romania's labour law code, which stipulates 12 valid reasons for terminating a work agreement[674] and by Bulgaria's labour law code, in which the valid reasons for terminating a work agreement are divided into three categories:

- Trivial but frequent instances or serious offences made by the worker whilst carrying out work duties (Article 126, 187, 190): being late to work by one hour, three times during a one month period, or leaving work early by an hour; absence from work for the following two days; taking advantage of the employer's trust and disclosing confidential information; passing on false information with regards to the cost, weight or quality of the commodity or service (this is applicable to workers employed in the trade and services sector);

670. *Ibid.* D. Harris, J. Darcy, *op. cit.,* p. 273.
671. Conclusions vol.1, *op. cit.,* p. 424.
672. The reasons for the abovementioned provisions were not part of the report prepared by French authorities, rather they were discussed in a labour law textbook by J. Pellissier, J. Supiot, A. Jeammaud, *Droit de Travail*, Dalloz (20th edition), Paris 2000.
673. Conclusions vol. 1, *op. cit.*, p. 190 and following (France).
674. European Committee of Social Rights. Revised European Social Charter. Conclusions 2003 – Volume 2 (Romania, Slovenia, Sweden), Council of Europe Publishing, Strasbourg 2003, pp. 421–422 (Romania).

- A loss of skills due to health or disability, as stated by a medical practitioner (Article 325);
- Remanding the worker into custody (Article 330 § 1).[675]

Estonia's labour law code divides the valid reasons for the termination of work agreements by employers into grounds concerning the employee (Article 86 § 4–12)[676] and according to the reasons of the market, concerning the employer (Article 86 § 1–3).[677] A non-typical regulation was established by the Lithuanian legislature. The Lithuanian labour law code provides the reasons with which the termination of a work agreement by an employer cannot be validated. Amongst these stipulated reasons is the participation of a worker's misconduct breaching the regulations of the workplace. The abovementioned legislative technique obligates the Committee of Social Rights to formulate specific questions for Lithuania regarding work agreement termination by an employer in such cases as the justifiable absence at work.

Analysing the general clause as well as the specifically defined cases, which according to national labour law regulations validate the termination of work agreements by employers, the Committee of Social Rights aims to familiarize itself with the litigation process of applying these provisions. Its view is dependent on the compliance or non-compliance of the above legislative techniques with the standard of workers' rights protection established by Article 24 RESC. As in the cases of France, Romania and Bulgaria, the Committee did not provide a ruling, withholding its decision until the filing of the next reports in the following supervisory cycle (in 2007) by the Member States in question, concerning the information of applying the provisions regarding the protection of workers from the termination of work agreements.

In cases where there is a termination of a work agreement without a valid or serious reason, Article 24(b) RESC pressures Member States of the Council of Europe to obligate employers to compensate the worker or provide him or her with other appropriate relief. As is made obvious by the Addendum to Article 24 RESC, the legal basis for compensation to which a worker is entitled when there is no valid reason for the termination of a work agreement, may be regulated by national labour law provisions, such as acts and statutes depending on their jurisdiction, by collective agreements, or by other measures acceptable by the given country. Article 24 RESC is another provision of the Social Charters, which establishes the principles associated with compensation for damages protected by the legal regulations of the European Social Charters. The European Committee of Social Rights has worked on its position with regards to this issue during its supervisory cycles which monitor whether Member

675. Conclusions 2003, vol.1, *op. cit.*, pp. 76–77.
676. Such as: inability to carry out the required work (§ 4), inappropriate fulfillment of work responsibilities during the probationary period (§ 5) violating employee responsibilities (§ 6), losing the trust of the employer (§ 7), inappropriate conduct (§ 8), a long-lasting inability to carry out work duties (§ 9), age (§ 10), employing a part-time worker in the place of a full-time worker (§ 11), and worker's access to corruption (§ 12).
677. Liquidation of a company (§ 1), bankruptcy (§ 2), group lay-offs (§ 3).

States to the Council of Europe are abiding by the obligations of equal treatment, forbidding discrimination based on sex at the workplace, regulated by legislation. According to the opinion of the Committee, national legislation dealing with social rights should ensure that the injured has the possibility to regain his/her employment. In cases where the termination of the work agreement has not been sufficiently validated, there should be a possibility of reinstatement to the previous work position, as well as compensation for the various financial damages entailed during the unsubstantiated lay-off period.[678] Only in cases where it is impossible to reinstate the worker to the same position, other forms of compensation for damages are permissible. Compensation received instead of being reinstated into a former position, should primarily deter an employer from breaching labour law regulations protecting workers, and secondly should compensate the worker for losing his/her employment. National legislation may also introduce further sanctions for employers who are guilty of violating workers' labour rights.[679] In cases where there has been unequal treatment of workers and discrimination against them, the Committee of Social Rights advises the introduction of supplementary sanctions. In these arguments it has been stated that the Committee of Social Rights will interpret Article 24 RESC in an identical manner as it does other Social Charters, which protect workers from discrimination based on sex.[680] Poor rulings made by the European Committee of Social Rights may have the opportunity of redemption through the above hypothesis. In the case of Bulgaria, for example, the Committee ruled that Article 24 was violated, as the maximum amount of compensation that may not exceed a 6-month remuneration amount, cannot be seen as an adequate method in calculating damages for an unwarranted termination of a work agreement.[681] A non-typical method of regulation in the Lithuanian labour law code, accepted under Article 297 § 4, obligates the court to make a ruling in cases of unwarranted work agreement termination, in favour of compensation in an amount equal to the normal remuneration to which a worker would be entitled, if he/she remained in the employment from the day of the contract termination to the day of the court ruling. This poses many problems for the Committee. The amount of compensation is obviously dependent upon the speed with which litigation may be carried out. On the one hand, paying compensation for the entire period the worker is left unemployed is an efficient deterrent mechanism sanctioning the employer, if the compensation is a high amount, for breaching regulations governing work agreements. On the other hand, efficient running of the court system has a direct influence on lowering the amount of compensation paid. Taking note of the latter point, the Committee will request information concerning the amount of compensation calculated by the courts for workers who have lost their employment due to unwarranted work agreement terminations. Depending on the details or lack thereof provided, the Committee would hand down a ruling during the following supervisory cycle, which may be

678. Conclusions XIII-5, p. 256.
679. *Ibid.*, p. 256.
680. D. Harris, J. Darcy, *op. cit.*, p. 273.
681. Conclusions 2003, vol. 1, *op. cit.*, p. 82.

against Lithuania, due to the predicted lack of specific information, which would help in analysing the pros and cons of such compensation. A ruling of the European Committee of Social Rights is on the way to ensuring protection for workers who have had their work agreements terminated without valid reasons, to help them regain employment, as well as guaranteeing them compensation calculated from the day of the illegal termination of the work agreement until a decision is passed down by the court or some other body, concerning the reactivation of the work contract. If there is an exception and work may not be reinstated, compensation may be paid to cover the damages, and should, as specified by the Committee, prove to be as onerous to the employer who is paying it, as it is beneficial to the worker who has been discriminated against at the workplace and lost his/her wages. It is therefore a necessity that the compensation be of a higher amount than the remuneration, calculated from the day the work agreement is illegally terminated to the day of the judgment being passed.

A worker, who has had his/her work agreement terminated by a breach of provisions protecting against such termination, has a right to appeal to an impartial body. Neither Article 24 RESC, nor the Addendum, names such impartial bodies authorized to deal with appeals concerning unwarranted work agreement terminations. In the documents treated in the legislative process as *traveaux preparatoire* by the Revised European Social Charter, Article 8(1) of the ILO convention No. 158 was named as a standard in which the names of impartial bodies dealing with appeals of workers who have had their work agreements illegally terminated, were included.[682] Such bodies, in particular, are courts, arbitration tribunals, and commissions. National labour law regulations determine the period limitations, in which a worker who has had his/her work agreement terminated may file an appeal to an impartial body. In accordance with the regulation stipulated in Article 8(2) ILO convention No. 158, failing to keep the appeal period specified, is an indication that the worker has relinquished his/her right to appeal against the termination of the work agreement.

It is highly probably to assume that the European Committee of Social Rights will utilize the ruling handed down during the supervisory cycle of the European Social Charter. Article 13(1) ESC obligates Member States to supervise, via independent bodies, the decisions made by administrative institutions dealing with the refusal to allocate social and medical benefits. A similar manner is adopted by the Committee of Social Rights in Article 5 ESC, when dealing with the registration of trade unions or employer organizations.[683] Verifying the position of the supervisory bodies monitoring administrative and quasi administrative institutions, the Committee attempts to analyse the manner with which members of such bodies are appointed and the length of their candidature, and also researches the level of independence of such bodies from national administration.[684] In cases where such bodies show they cannot fulfil the required conditions to establish their independence, based on the collected data concerning the above preliminaries, the Committee then must turn to states, seeking additional

682. D. Harris, J. Darcy, *op. cit.*, p. 273, footnote 1738.
683. Conclusions I, p. 64.
684. Conclusions XIII-4, p. 55.

information with regard to control procedures applicable to administrative bodies existing within the given country and analysing the country's reports concerning the obligations under the Social Charter. The Committee regards the rulings handed down by supervisory bodies monitoring the decisions of administrative and quasi administrative institutions in matters of registration of employee and employer organizations (trade unions and other representative organizations), decisions made with regards to the refusal or the allocation of social and medical benefits, as rulings which should be handed down by a truly independent body. If such rulings handed down by supervisory bodies over the decisions made by administrative and quasi administrative institutions, may be appealed on accusations based on merit, and the judiciary and the arbitration tribunal has the jurisdiction to deal with such matters substantively and look over the content of the supervisory body's decisions, it is obligated to function according to rigid provisions, and cannot hand down an arbitrary decision concerning the rulings made by such supervisory bodies. There is a basis for concluding the impartiality and the independence of such supervision over decisions made by employers who terminate work agreements.[685]

6.11. The Right of Workers to the Protection of their Claims in the Event of the Insolvency of their Employer (Article 25)

The Revised European Social Charter ensures workers protection in cases of insolvency of their employer (Article 25).[686] The Revised European Social Charter, modelled on the regulations of the international conventions and recommendations, the ILO and the directives of the European Union, introduced the standards of workers' rights protection in cases where the employer becomes insolvent. Amongst the conventions and the recommendations of the ILO which formed the prototype for the regulations introduced by Article 25, the following should be noted: convention of the ILO No. 173 dealing with the protection workers' claims in cases of insolvency of their employer[687] and the ILO recommendation No. 180 concerning the protection of workers' claims in cases of insolvency of their employer.[688]

The ILO Convention No. 173 dealing with workers' claims in cases of insolvency of their employer, concerns the state of the insolvency (Article 1), legally defines the protection of workers' claims employed by insolvent employers (Article 6, 7) as well as regulates the way by which payments of such claims are made by insurance institutions (Article 9, 12).

685. Conclusions XIII-4, *op. cit.,* p. 56.

686. A.M.Świątkowski, *Ochrona Praw Pracowników.* ..., (Protection of Workers' Rights), *op. cit.,* pp. 64 and following.

687. Passed during the 79th session of the General Conference ILO 3 June 1992. Convention No. 173 came into force on 8 June 1995, ratified by 15 Member States. Poland did not ratify this convention. *See* Conventions ..., *op. cit.,* p. 1281 and following; Lists ..., *op. cit.,* p. 203; Application ..., *op. cit.,* p. 84.

688. Passed during the 79th General Conference ILO 3 June 1992 r., Conventions ..., *op. cit.,* pp. 1286 and following

The standards of protection of workers' rights were established by the European Union. Looking at the matter globally, these are standards considered to be higher than average. The Directive 2002/74/EC contains the definition of a insolvent employer, it determines the scope of property and assets of the insurance institutions which in turn settle the workers' claims, it regulates – irrespective of property and assets – the principles of establishing trust funds, which may settle the amount due for workers.

Article 25 RESC obligates Member States to the Council of Europe, ratifying the part of the Charter, to ensure the protection of workers' claims, which have resulted out of a work agreement or from insecure labour relations due to employer insolvency. The goal of this provision is to ensure protection for workers and their claims in cases of insolvency of their employer. The European Social Charter does not define insolvency. In the Appendix to RESC, Member States became authorized to define their meaning of insolvency. They may do so independently or to put the matter into practice (Article 25(2)). Looking at the Member State reports dealing with Article 25 RESC, the Committee of Social Rights took note of Slovenia's report, which protects workers' claims that are not settled by employers who have commenced bankruptcy proceedings, or are legally bound to undergo economic restructuring of the bankrupted company. The Committee of Social Rights questioned Slovenia as to whether the settling of property claims encompasses cases where the employer ceased business activities prior to commencing bankruptcy proceedings.[689] In accordance with Article 1(1) and (2) of the ILO convention No. 173 and Article 2(1) of the Council and Parliament of Europe of 23 December 2002, directive No. 74 (2002/74/EC), the state of bankruptcy is also declared, if a competent body announces that the assets and property of the employer are not sufficient to cover the debts to creditors.[690] The Committee adapted the abovementioned wide definition of insolvency in the process of assessing Slovenia's report and adjourned its decision in the matter of whether the national laws of the country are in accordance with Article 25 RESC.

Article 25 RESC does not obligate Member States that have ratified the Article and the standards, to choose any out of the familiar techniques of protecting the solvency of asset and property claims of workers by an insolvent employer. It leaves for Member States the choice of familiar techniques, such as calling upon insurance institutions, which guarantee to cover workers' claims in cases of employer insolvency, or to choose alternate efficient methods of protecting such claims.

According to the jurisdiction of the Committee of Social Rights, the technique of protecting worker's claims against insolvent employer is of minor importance. The Committee emphasizes, however, that the legal protection of these claims should be efficient, regardless of the technique employed.[691] The case of Bulgaria indicates that

---

689. Conclusions 2003, vol.2, *op. cit.,* pp. 535–536.
690. A. Świątkowski, Directive of the Parliament and Council of 23. November 2002 No. 74 (2002/74/EC) re: the protection of workers' claims in cases of insolvency of the employer, '*Studia z Zakresu Prawa Pracy i Polityki Społecznej*', (Studies in Labour Law and Social Policy) Rocznik 2003/2004 (Year 2003/2004), Kraków 2004, pp. 14–15.
691. Conclusions 2003, vol.1, *op. cit.,* p. 83 (Bulgaria).

the protection of workers' claims must be adequate. Bulgarian insolvency law states that workers' claims are fulfilled as fourth in priority. The first three positions on the list of debts of an insolvent employer are three other claimants, which emerged during the insolvency procedures. In reality, therefore, workers' claims are listed on the first position before the insolvency proceedings begin. Evaluating this system, the Committee concluded that workers' claims could not be characterized as being in a privileged position in comparison with other claimants of the insolvent employer. According to the Committee, the Bulgarian legislation does not meet the standards established by Article 25 RESC.[692] This does not mean that the introduction of a privileged system of fulfilling workers' claims by insolvent employer is, as a rule (treated by the Committee as inadequate, thus contrary to the Article 25 RESC), a technique of assuring a worker's claim. The directive 2002/74/EC mentioned above follows the directive No. 987 (80/987/EEC) issued by the Council on 20.10.1980 concerning the unification of the legislation of Member States in terms of workers' protection in the case of employer's insolvency,[693] and imposes on the European Union Member States the obligation of bringing into being an institution guaranteeing the payment of financial benefits to which workers are entitled.[694] However, the ILO Convention No. 173 lists the techniques of protecting workers' claims indicating the superiority of the technique, which prioritizes these claims amongst other liabilities of the insolvent employer (part II, Articles 5–8). Additionally, the ILO Convention No. 173 proposes to protect workers' claims by the guaranteeing institution (Articles 9–13). Originally, Article 25 RESC was drafted after the legal regulations binding in the European Union and ILO of those days and consisted of the two techniques assuring fulfilment of claims put forward by workers employed by insolvent employers.[695] In the final version of this provision, it was agreed that the privileged technique of fulfilling workers' material claims is one of many techniques of protection of financial benefits. At the same time, the Council of Europe allows Member States to apply other measures of protection of workers' claims on the grounds of work agreement or labour relations not fulfilled by insolvent employers, aside from the technique verified by the European Union of fulfilling workers' material claims not fulfilled by insolvent employers by the assuring institution, whose assets are independent from the capital of entrepreneurs. The Committee of Social Rights evaluates the efficiency of these measures.

The Appendix to RESC (Article 25 § 1) authorizes Member States to exclude particular groups of workers from the protection guaranteed by Article 25. This authorization is addressed to the 'proper authorities'. This term should be understood as governmental bodies relevant in regulating legal conditions of particular occupations. Depending on the scale of the regulation, this authorization applies to legislative bodies, able to regulate legal conditions of workers in the whole of the country or bodies of

---

692. *Ibid.*, p. 84.
693. *See* A. M. Świątkowski, Restrukturyzacja ... (Restructuring ...), *op. cit.*, pp. 268 and following.
694. A. Świątkowski, *Dyrektywa Parlamentu* ... (Parliamentary Directives), *op. cit.*, pp. 21 and following.
695. D. Harris, J. Darcy, *op. cit.*, pp. 274–275.

governmental administration in charge of certain occupations and professions only. The authorization was granted to the 'proper authority'. Interpreting Article 25 § 1, the Appendix to RESC states this term should also include stakeholders entitled to shape conditions of employment and remuneration for particular occupations within the collective work agreements or other normative documents. The exclusion from the force of provisions ensuring workers' material claims on the ground of labour relation not fulfilled by the insolvent employers cannot be a common practice. It may encompass only particular groups of employees. Categories of workers, whom Article 25 RESC can protect, can also be overruled due to the nature of the labour relations. Working papers enlist, modelled on the ILO Convention No. 173, workers of public administration as well as workers of small workplaces employed in managerial positions as categories of workers. Member States ratifying the Article 25 RESC can exclude from legal protection of claims made by workers in cases of insolvency of employer.[696] According to the rule of majority applied during the supervisory cycle over abiding the provisions of the European Social Charter by Member States, and also employed by the Committee of Social Rights, provisions ratified by particular States should be applied to at least 80 per cent of workers employed within the given State. Before making a decision upon restricting the application of Article 25 RESC, the Member States are obligated to run consultations with stakeholders, i.e. organizations of workers and employers. The employers for workers of public administrations are particular on the State agendas. Allowing for the exclusion of this category of workers from the protection given by Article 25 RESC, the Charter expresses trust to the State as the employer, assuming it is not going to declare insolvency. In cases of workers of small workplaces employed in managerial positions, the reason for their exclusion is the conviction that workers employed in managerial positions are, because of their positions implying the proper proportion of remuneration, in possession of allocated savings, which guarantee covering of their expenses in the case of employer's insolvency. The Committee of Social Rights regarded the above exclusions as being in accordance with the standards of legal protection established by Article 25 RESC.

Taking advantage of the possibility of the above exclusion, Sweden broadened categories beyond the guaranteed protection onto workers to co-owners of a workplace being a part of the insolvent's assets.[697] The necessary condition of not applying Article 25 RESC is the initial date of entering into the ownership, not exceeding six months from the date of declaring insolvency, individually or being a member of the closest family, a significant part of the property being a part of the insolvent's assets. Guarantees determined under the Article 25 RESC do not apply, in Sweden or elsewhere, to members of the family of the insolvent entrepreneur.[698]

The Appendix to the Revised European Social Charter enlists three categories of workers' material claims, which should be fulfilled in case of the employer's

696. *Ibid.*, p. 275.
697. Conclusions 2003, vol.2, s.632.
698. *Ibid.*

insolvency (Article 25 § 3). The order is random. It can be explicitly concluded from the statement of the Article 25 § 2, which simply says that workers' claims being the main subject of Article 25 must include at least:

- Workers' claims on the ground of remunerations for work for a given period of time before insolvency was declared or – depending on legal regulations of the particular state – from the day the labour relation was terminated, if the abovementioned event took place in the period preceding insolvency. The length of this period cannot be shorter than three months in the system where the technique of fulfilling workers' material claims in the first order before other outstanding claimants of the insolvent is in force. In the case of employing the technique of protection of workers' material claims by the assuring institution, material benefits cannot be lower than the workers' remuneration paid in the period of eight weeks before insolvency was declared or from termination of labour relation in the period preceding insolvency (Article 25 § 2);
- Workers' claims on the ground of paid holidays workers are entitled to on the basis of employment in the year when insolvency took place or labour relation terminated (Article 25(2));
- Workers' claims on the ground of liabilities not fulfilled by the employer in the periods of employment listed in the Appendix to the Article 25 § 1 RESC.

The Appendix to the Article 25 RESC allows the Member States of the Council of Europe to limit workers' material claims included in either one or another system of assurance: protected within the privilege or ensured by the assurance institutions (Article 25 § 4). Limitation is only possible by legal standards legislated by the State, normative acts being at the rank of bills or executive provisions. It is not acceptable for stakeholders to introduce such limitations. The Appendix to Article 25 RESC does not directly describe the extent to which Member States can restrict the range of guarantee of material claims not fulfilled by the insolvent employers. However, it gives an important guideline, according to which the extent of guaranteed protection of the material claims in the system of privilege or of the institution of guarantee should be set to the 'socially accepted' extent (Article 25 § 4). The provision in question establishes the legal ground for the Committee of Social Rights to evaluate the range of protection in particular Member States. The Committee's practices give no guidelines for what reasons should be taken into consideration while analysing the extent of the guaranteed compensation when they are lower in the amount than the remuneration or other financial liabilities listed in the Appendix to the Article 25 RESC, due to three-months or eight-week periods preceding an employer's insolvency or termination of labour relation before the date of declaring insolvency. There was only one case when the Committee ruled the Swedish system of limiting the benefits compensating the worker's material claims not fulfilled by the insolvent employers, established at the level of 100,000 Swedish kronas (equivalent of 10,966 Euros), was sufficient. It guarantees workers protection at an adequate level, meeting, therefore, requirements established in the Appendix to the Article 25

§ 4 RESC.[699] Swedish regulations guarantee the protection of workers' material claims by privilege. They do not create any restrictions in terms of the amount of the compensation, which is paid before other claimants of the insolvent employer. Having in mind the protection of the State's financial system and in order to prevent possible abuse, Sweden introduced the abovementioned limit within the guaranteed worker's compensation if not fulfilled by the insolvent employer. As the Swedish report did not compile the information on the periods when the claims were protected by the privilege, the Committee, having stated the conformity of Swedish regulations with the standards established by Article 25 RESC, requested the presentation of this data during the subsequent cycle.[700]

The Appendix to the Article 25 § 3 RESC does not determine the amount of workers' material claims on the grounds of labour relations protected by privilege or by the assurance institution. The Member States of the Council of Europe present the range of guarantees in their reports. It can be concluded from the report delivered by Slovenia that three legal acts legislated between 1997 and 2000[701] determine the obligation of the guarantee fund to compensate workers' material claims not fulfilled by the insolvent employer in the period of three months before the labour relation terminated in the amount not exceeding three minimum state-guaranteed monthly remunerations. The financial equivalent for paid leave which has not been utilized in the calendar year the insolvency took place, is also paid by the abovementioned fund, being the amount not exceeding half of the minimum state-guaranteed monthly remuneration. When severance pay for those workers having had their work agreements terminated for reasons concerning the workplace is not paid out by the insolvent employer, it is compensated for by the State assurance fund in the amount of one State-assured minimum monthly wage.[702] The Committee of Social Rights takes the position that the range of material benefits not paid out by the insolvent employers in Slovenia is in accordance with the requirements set in Article 25 RESC. Accepting the abovementioned national legal regulations, the Committee requested that Slovenia provide confirmation of their own approach to the legal situation in terms of protecting workers' material claims in cases of employer's insolvency.[703]

France is a state where the system of labour law employs the two techniques of guaranteeing the protection of workers' claims not fulfilled by insolvent employers. The remuneration for the last 60 days not exceeding the double monthly basis of the insurance premium not paid by insolvent employer is prioritized in the process of paying out the claims of insolvent employers out of their assets. The labour code imposes on employers the obligation of insuring responsibility for unfulfilled workers'

---

699. Conclusions 2003, vol. 2, p. 632.
700. *Ibid.*
701. No 25/1997; No 80–3784/1999; No 22/2000; No 103–4344/2000; *ibid.*, p. 535.
702. *Ibid.*, p. 536.
703. *Ibid.* In addition, the basic obstacle of the Committee work has to be brought to attention being the vague editing of reports on abiding the ratified provisions of the Revised European Social Charter by Member States.

material claims. The range of responsibility of the insurance company for covering liabilities of insolvent employers, based upon the binding regulations, collective as well as individual work agreements, cannot exceed the amount of 13 times the monthly basis of the insurance premium in cases of unemployment (*plafond* 13). The range of responsibility of the insurer for fulfilling other entitlements of workers on behalf of the insolvent employer cannot exceed the amount of four times the monthly basis of the insurance premium in case of unemployment (*plafond* 4).[704] The Committee of Social Rights stated conformity of the national system of labour law in France with the requirements listed in the Article 25 RESC. It obligated the French to explain the relation between the material benefits compensated by the insurer within the two abovementioned programmes '13' and '4'.[705] Article 25 RESC does not introduce new legal solutions. Standards of protection of workers' claims not fulfilled by the insolvent employer introduced by this regulation stand in line with the standards binding globally (the ILO Convention No 173) and regionally (the European Union). Member States of the Council of Europe associated within the European Union (France, Slovenia, Sweden, Italy), out of whom only Slovenia ratified the 3rd part of the ILO Convention No. 173, whose reports on abiding the obligations of Article 25 RESC were analysed by the Committee of Social Rights in 2003, did not experience any difficulties with proving that their national regulations of labour law did not conflict with the standards established by Article 25 RESC. The Committee of Social Rights negatively evaluated Bulgaria, a State that is not a member of the European Union and did not ratify the ILO Convention No. 173, but did ratify Article 25 RESC, as Bulgaria did not guarantee workers' claims not fulfilled by an insolvent employer the priority status against other claimants of the insolvent employer.

6.12. The Right to Dignity at Work (Article 26)

The Article 26 protects dignity of workers. It was formed in order to counteract harassment, sexual harassment and mobbing in workplaces.[706] The Council of Europe used the experiences of the European Union. The guidelines of the European Commission from 27.11.1991 concerning the protection of men and women at work[707] classifies all kinds of improper behaviour with sexual connotation, or as grounds for violating the dignity of a woman or a man in the workplace. It regards such actions as not acceptable and partially comparable to the rule of equal treatment of workers in the interpretation of the directive No. 207 of 1976. Article 26 does not produce a legal definition of sexual harassment. The Committee of Social Rights defines sexual harassment as behaviour violating the sphere of privacy or psychiatric balance, which defames the dignity of the worker, which interrupts carrying out the

704. Conclusions, vol.1, *op. cit.*, pp. 199–201.
705. *Ibid.*, p. 200.
706. *See* P. Koncar, *Kwestia Równouprawnienia* ... (Equality Between ...), *op. cit.*, pp. 32 and following.
707. 92/131/EEC, OJ No L 49, 24.2.1992, p. 1. *See* H. Wierzbińska, A. M. Świątkowski, *op. cit.*, pp. 369 and following.

duties of the job, and which contradicts socially accepted patterns of conduct within labour relations.[708] The definition of sexual harassment approved by the Committee varies from the definition of sexual harassment listed in the Commission's recommendation No. 131 and its Appendix, where the code concerning the prevention of sexual harassment was published. Article 1 of the recommendation No. 131 sees sexual harassment as determined by all kinds of behaviour with sexual connotation and all kinds of behaviour based on sex, which is inappropriate, defaming and offensive for the person to whom it is applied. The above definition worked as a blueprint during the editing of Article 26 RESC. Sexual harassment, in light of this provision, would be behaviour based on sex or on sexual connotations, which is not accepted and which violates the dignity of the person to whom this conduct is addressed. Classifying a given behaviour as an act of sexual harassment, whether the behaviour is performed by a superior or by a work colleague, makes no difference.[709] The Committee of Social Rights has broadened the above definition. It pays attention to actions violating the sphere of privacy, unwanted and disapproved by a victim of the prohibited conduct. The basic characteristic of such sexual harassment is that the prohibited behaviour is felt to be undesired by the person to whom it is addressed. Sexual interest becomes sexual harassment when a person, being the addressee of such behaviour, regards it as insulting. The undesirable nature of such behaviour is a very important characteristic, distinguishing sexual harassment from friendly behaviour, which is welcome and reciprocated. It is not a necessary condition of an act of sexual harassment that the alleged perpetrator is more highly ranked within the workplace hierarchy than the victimizing. Sexual harassment is not directly connected with using power to achieve a goal, which is not forbidden in itself. Cases of sexual harassment were found even where the initiators of the undesirable sexual behaviour were other workers with no labour ties with a victim, or where the initiators were third parties not entering into labour relations with a victim (clients, representatives of other workplaces). In the Appendix to Article 26 RESC, it was decided that fulfilling the obligations determined by this provision does not impose on Member States the obligation of legal regulation of harassment and sexual harassment. Supervising the reports delivered by Member States, the Committee was also interested in obtaining information concerning whether national labour law regulations give legal definitions of sexual harassment.[710]

The above position was interpreted by three members of the Committee as an attempt to obligate the Member States to prepare legal definitions of sexual harassment.[711] The lack of obligation to legally define sexual harassment does not mean that there is an opposition to constructing such a definition. The French labour law code defines the act of sexual harassment as 'order, threat, compulsion or any other pressure applied to a worker in order to achieve sexual advantage' (Sec. L122–46).[712] French

708. Conclusions 2003, vol.1, p. 85 (Bulgaria).
709. Explanatory report to the revised European Social Charter, European Social Charter, *op. cit.*, p. 171.
710. Conclusions 2003, vol.1, p. 85 (Bulgaria).
711. S. Evju, R. Birk and K. Grillberger expressed a dissenting opinion. Conclusions 2003, vol.1, p. 95.
712. Conclusions 2003, vol.1, p. 202.

labour law regards sexual harassment as the use of supremacy by the harasser on the subject, the harassed victim. The above definition does not depart from the definition of sexual harassment as an unwanted act, since the order, threat, compulsion or any other pressure applied is not acceptable to the victim subjected to the power play that is used by the aggressor.

Article 26 § 1 RESC obligates Member States to take appropriate measures to promote awareness of the harm sexual harassment may cause at the workplace. These Member States should support and promote information and prevention. They should also undertake all appropriate measures to protect workers from sexual harassment. This obligation is interpreted by the Committee as a basis upon which the Committee can demand from Member States annual reports concerning the introduction of domestic legislation protecting workers against sexual harassment. The European Committee of Social Rights concludes that the situation in Moldova, for example, is not in conformity with Article 26 § 2 RESC, since neither Moldavian legislation nor any other regulatory or administrative measures provide for the necessary preventive and reparatory means to protect individual workers against harassment directed against them at the workplace, and there is no indication in the Moldavian report of any practical application of the existing laws by public authorities or courts that would provide such protection.[713] During the first supervisory cycle dealing with the compliance of Article 26 § 1 RESC, the Committee concluded that Member States were utilizing one of the two models of protection of the rights of workers from sexual harassment. Member States were seen to either render separate regulations prohibiting harassment or were seen to analyse the act of sexual harassment in other widely defined categories of dealing with prohibition. The former model is utilized by the French and Swedish. In France, victims of sexual harassment within the workplace have the right to take part in mediation or to file criminal charges. The perpetrator of the act may be sentenced to a period of one year imprisonment and be subjected to a fine. The injured party has a right to seek compensation as well as demand to be reinstated to his or her former employment position.[714] Swedish employers are forbidden from harassing their employees and are obligated to develop guidelines to the procedures required, should sexual harassment charges be brought. Victims of sexual harassment may directly file claims against their offenders as well as their employers in labour courts, as well as in criminal jurisdictions. They may also benefit from the assistance provided by the ombudsman in matters of equal treatment in labour relations and in trade unions.[715] A different method, using the already existing regulations, which treats sexual harassment as a civil law matter, as well as an act forbidden by the criminal code protecting the personal inviolability of the worker, is used in Bulgaria, Italy and Slovenia. Using the already existing regulations to counter sexual harassment means that the Committee is interested in the various types of legal sanctions which may be used, in order to examine their effectiveness.[716] States which introduced

713. Conclusions 2005 (Moldova, Norway, Romania, Slovenia, Sweden), vol. 2, p. 496.
714. Conclusions 2003, vol. 1, pp. 202–203.
715. Conclusions 2003, vol. 2, pp. 633–634.
716. Conclusions 2003, vol. 1, p. 86 (Bulgaria); pp. 324–325 (Italy); Conclusions 2003, vol. 2, pp. 537–538 (Slovenia).

separate legal measures to counteract sexual harassment within the workplace gained the approval of the Committee, which considered such measures to be in compliance with Article 26 § 1 RESC. Those States that have been making use of legal implementations already in existence to combat sexual harassment, have to provide the Committee with complete information, whilst the Committee postpones handing down any decisions.

The Committee does not regard a sexual harassment act within labour relations as an act discriminating against gender in itself. In the opinion of the Committee, sexual harassment is regarded as an act violating the principles of equal treatment of workers. This is because it creates more or less favourable grounds for the treatment of workers, straying from the acceptable norm. The Committee therefore monitors whether Member States are fulfilling the set obligations of informing about, and preventing sexual harassment. Good examples of fulfilling such obligations by the Member States are widespread information and advertising campaigns, and the preparation and distribution of publications dealing with the harm caused by sexual harassment.

Article 26 § 2 RESC orders Member States to undertake actions informing and preventing against harassment of workers, which is not sexual in its nature. Member States have the obligation to counteract against other forms of harassment and mobbing. This obligation was introduced thanks to an application made by Sweden. The point of this regulation is to protect workers from hostile, insulting and offensive behaviour by their superiors or by other workers, which violates the recipient's dignity, within or in connection to the workplace. Examples of such behaviour include: a systematic exclusion of workers from discussions dealing with labour organizations in which other workers are involved, provoked by the employer's dislike or hatred; or refusing to inform the worker about the duties involved in his/her position.[717] The Committee interprets Article 26 § 2 as a standard, which obligates Member States to create 'friendly' working environments. Fulfilling the above obligation, some States introduced particular regulations, despite the fact the Appendix to Article 26 RESC did not demand for this to occur, which forbid psychological harassment of workers (this definition encompasses certain actions undertaken or tolerated by employers), which may result in the marginalization of the discriminated against employee.[718] The effect of such psychological harassment is worsened by the conditions of work, exerting negativity on the rights and the dignity of the workers. This causes deterioration of health as well as threatens the workers future within the employment.[719] Workers who are victim to psychological harassment should use those legal measures which are available to victims of sexual harassment within the workplace.

6.13. The Right of Workers with Family Responsibilities to Equal Opportunities and Equal Treatment (Article 27 RESC)

The ILO convention No. 156 of 3 June 1981 formed a prototype for Article 27, dealing with equal opportunity and treatment of workers of both sexes. These included those

717. Explanatory reports ..., *op. cit.*, p. 172.
718. Conclusions 2003, vol. 2, p. 635 (Sweden).
719. Conclusions 2003, vol. 1, p. 204 (France).

workers having family responsibilities.[720] Also taken into consideration in the prototype were the recommendations of the ILO No. 165, also passed on 3 June 1981 during the 67th session of the General Conference ILO, international documents obligating Member States to allow those having family responsibilities (being employed or seeking to gain employment), to carry out or attain such employment without discrimination (as much as it is possible), without compromising their family responsibilities. This standard was established in order to ensure the effective availability of workers' rights (of both sexes), in particular those having family responsibilities, to equal opportunity and treatment as well as to be equally treated with other workers. The goal of Article 27 RESC is to protect against discrimination based on sex and to ensure equal treatment of both men and women who are carrying out family responsibilities with those who are not. The Appendix to Article 27 RESC defines workers 'having family responsibilities' as workers of both sexes with family responsibilities in relation to their dependent children, as well in relation to other members of their immediate family who clearly need their care or support. The European Committee of Social Rights found that the situation in Lithuania is not in conformity with Article 27 § 1 of the RESC, on the ground that fathers who are not single are discriminated against with regard to part-time work. Article 46 of the Lithuanian Act on Safety and Health at Work states that a part-time schedule must be agreed to by an employer only upon request of a pregnant female, a nursing mother, a woman or single parent raising a child or children under 14 years of age, or a disabled child under 16 years of age, or a person nursing a sick family member. The European Committee of Social Rights noted that there is no legal obligation to agree to part-time work for a father who is not single.[721]

The Charter obligates Member States to define clearly, within the domestic legislation, the persons who are encompassed by the regulations (dependent children or other members of the immediate family), and to undertake measures aimed at creating equal treatment and opportunity within employment for those persons executing child rearing responsibilities. Those who are caring for dependent children as well as other members of their immediate families, who clearly need their care or support, should have their right to equal opportunity in employment ensured by the obligated Member States. Those who are preparing for, entering, participating in or advancing in economic activity and are restricted by family responsibilities, also should have this right of equal treatment ensured. Article 27 RESC is comprised of three paragraphs. Paragraph 1 obligates Member States to undertake the following measures in an attempt to:

- Enable workers with family responsibilities to enter and remain in employment, as well as to re-enter employment after an absence due to those responsibilities, including measures in the field of vocational guidance and training;
- Take account of their needs in terms of conditions of employment and social security;

720. Conventions and recommendations ... vol. II, *op. cit.,* pp. 1063 and following.
721. Conclusions 2005, vol. 1, pp. 397–398.

- Develop or promote services, public or private, in particular child day-care services and other childcare arrangements.

Supervising the compliance to Article 27 RESC, the Committee is particular about Member States fulfilling the obligations stipulated under Article 1 § 1 and 3, as well as Article 10 § 4. Not fulfilling at all or inappropriately fulfilling the obligations specified in the provisions in question renders a judgment of non-compliance with Article 27 § 1 RESC. During the first supervisory cycle, Member States did not pay heed to the differences evident between Article 27 § 1 RESC and Articles 1 § 1 and 3, as well as Article 10 § 4 RESC. It was for this reason that the Committee obligated the Member States to provide information regarding techniques that were actively appropriated in employment policies, which could be introduced to the labour market and enabled the equal employment for those who have family responsibilities. Member States are obligated to ensure workers with family responsibilities particular assistance in gaining employment. Because of the responsibilities that must be met, such workers have difficulties in establishing good labour relations, as the breaks in employment caused by family care responsibilities usually lead to the worker experiencing a delay concerning the newest technological developments. Workers who have family responsibilities do not have the ability to keep up with the advancements occurring within their field of employment.[722]

One of the techniques that is implemented to help workers with family responsibilities to carry out their work duties on equal grounds with other employees, are flexible working hours (working part-time or working from home). Member States are obligated to inform workers with family responsibilities of such employment possibilities. In the Committee's view, Article 27 RESC is not a standard, which orders Member States to take into consideration the particular requirements certain workers with family responsibilities may have. The provision in question obligates Member States to grant those workers with family responsibilities the right to make demands regarding the betterment of their employment conditions in a manner comparable to the conditions of other employees.[723]

The obligation to take into consideration the needs of workers with family responsibilities in matters of social security means the inclusion of time spent taking care of family responsibility during working hours, into their superannuation and insurance funds. Typical questions dealing with the needs of workers who are taking care of dependent children and other immediate family members, include circumstances upon which social security benefits are dependent, as stated in domestic legislation.[724] With regards to the States that have ratified Article 16 RESC, the standard protecting the right of the family to social, legal and economic security, the monitoring of fulfilling the obligations stipulated under Article 21(1)(c) RESC (the organization of children's

722. Conclusions 2003, vol. 2, p. 637 (Sweden).
723. Conclusions 2003, vol. 1, p. 328.
724. From the reports submitted in pursuance of the Revised European Social Charter, European Social, European Social Charter, *op. cit.*, pp. 368–369.

day-care) is also exercised by complying with Article 16 RESC. Monitoring over the compliance of this provision, the Committee draws attention to whether Member States ensure workers who are rearing children social security benefit entitlements, which allow for the availability of resources should the carer fall ill and such entitlements become necessary.[725]

Article 27 § 2RESC obligates Member States to issue regulations concerning parental leave. The entitlement to such leave should be allocated to the parents of a child. The point of such parental leave is to enable working parents to care for their children without having to terminate a working agreement. During parental leave, workers are exempt from work duties. The loss of remuneration is fully covered by social security benefits.[726] The measure of parental leave and the circumstances with which one acquires such leave, are regulated by the Member States. During the first supervisory cycle, monitoring over the compliance of Article 27 § 2, the Committee claimed that all the regulations of all the Member States are in compliance with the standards established by the Charter. This decision was handed down based on various legal systems. In accordance with the standards established by the Charter, domestic regulations were recognized ensuring paid parental leave as an entitlement for parents until their child reaches the age of two,[727] for a period of one year until the child turns 3,[728] or for a leave of 10 months, until the child reaches the age of eight.[729] In some cases, parental leave may be renewed. The maximum period for parental leave cannot exceed three years.[730] A necessary requirement to acquire parental leave is to remain with the same employer for a period of one year,[731] or to be covered by the general insurance and superannuation fund for a period of six months during the previous 12 months, or for a period of 12 months during the last 24 months.[732]

The interpretation of Article 27 § 2 RESC is in compliance with the standards established by the Council directive of 3 June 1996, concerning the framework of parental leave structured by UNICE, CEEP and ETUC/CES.[733] This directive ensures women and men workers the right to parental leave due to a child being either born or being adopted, in an attempt to enable the parents to exercise personal care over their child for a period of at least three months. Taking advantage of such parental leave cannot mean that family responsibilities alone may be a basis for an employer to terminate employment. The Committee treats Article 27 § 3 RESC as a standard forbidding the termination of a work agreement by an employer with his/her employee

725. Conclusions 2003, vol. 1, p. 206 (France); p. 329 (Italy); Conclusions 2003, vol. 2, p. 638 (Sweden).
726. On parental leave *see* A. Świątkowski, *Urlopy Opiekuńcze* (Maternity Leave), ZN UJ, Warszawa-Kraków 1981; Tenże, *Urlop Wychowawczy* (Parental Leave), ZN UJ, Warszaw-Kraków 1985.
727. Conclusions 2003, vol. 1, p. 89 (Bulgaria); Conclusions 2003, vol. 2, p. 427 (Romania).
728. *Ibid.*, (France).
729. Conclusions 2003, vol. 1, p. 329 (Italy).
730. Conclusions 2003, vol. 1, p. 206 (France).
731. *Ibid.*
732. Conclusions 2003, vol. 2m p. 427.
733. 96/34/EC, OJ No L 145, 19.6.1996, p. 4. *See* A. Świątkowski, H. Wierzbińska, *op. cit.*, pp. 424 and following.

based on the utilization of parental leave.[734] The Committee demands from Member States information regarding the termination of employment with workers who have family responsibilities.[735] Article 27 § 2 RESC is a standard which complements the prohibition on terminating employment without a valid reason, citing Article 24 RESC. This provision however, may not be regarded as *superfluum*.[736] Article 24(a) RESC established the prohibition on terminating employment without valid reason connected with the worker's capacity or conduct. Article 27 § 2 RESC strengthens this prohibition. It demands from Member States the assuredness that family responsibilities alone will not stand as a valid reason for terminating a work agreement. This is an indication of the obligation Member States took on after ratifying the above provision, which forbids the termination of employment of a worker by an employer for carrying out family responsibilities.

734. Conclusions 2003, vol. 2003, p. 542 (Slovenia).
735. Conclusions 2003, vol. 1, p. 207 (France).
736. Distinct without valid reason and irrelevant. D. Harris, J. Darcy, *op. cit.*, p. 278.

CHAPTER 7 THE REGULATION OF SOCIAL RIGHTS THROUGH COLLECTIVE LABOUR LAW

7.1. The Right to Organize (Article 5)

Article 5 is a standard issued to promote the freedom of workers and employers to form local, national or international organizations for the protection of their economic and social interests. This provision ensures interested workers and employers the right to join already existing organizations representing their interests. It also guarantees workers and employers who do not wish to join such organizations the freedom from compulsory membership in such organizations. The solid judicature of the Committee of Social Rights is completely dedicated to the protection of workers' rights to organize and to join organizations representing their interests. Up until now, the Committee has not engaged itself with issues concerning employers' rights to organize or join organizations representing their interests. Article 5 refers to the regulation accepted in the ILO convention No. 87 of 17 June 1948, concerning the right to freedom of association and the protection of organizations' rights,[1] which ensures workers and employers equal rights without the need to attain prior permission for the establishment and membership of an organization (Article 2). The cited provision of Article 2 of the ILO No. 87 convention does not define the types of organizations that workers may join. However, it has become accepted that most organizations established to represent and protect the working, economic and social interests of the workers, are trade unions. Neither the ILO No. 87 convention nor Article 5 has given any legal grounds for the international protection of workers' and employers' organizations that have been established for political purposes. The universally practiced political affiliations of trade unions formed a basis to pass a resolution concerning the independent running of trade organizations during the 35th session of the General Conference ILO in 1952.[2] The ILO resolution warned those trade unions that decided to form political parties or those that took up political activity (within a constitutional framework) to meet economic or the

1. Conventions and recommendations ..., vol. I, *op. cit.*, pp. 353–355
2. ILO Proceedings, International Labour Conference, 583, 35th Session (1952)

undertakings' interests prior to fulfilling their statutory obligations or the functions of a trade union (social and economic interests protection). An evident lack of reservations in Article 5 concerning the right of workers to associate and join trade unions is frequently debated, especially when it concerns the ease with which workers can establish organizations other than trade unions.[3] The Committee of Social Rights never took upon itself the issue of whether to evaluate whether Member States complied with Article 5 with regards to organizations other than trade union organizations representing the economic and social interests of workers.

Article 5 obligates Member States not to impair the freedom of workers and employers to organize. Despite the unambiguous definition of the obligation, the Committee interprets Article 5 as a standard that imparts to Member States certain positive obligations. To this end, the law should protect the right to form coalitions, which encompasses the freedom of employees to associate and organize, within a trade union as well as the rights of employers within an organization. Member States are therefore obligated to pass legislation ensuring full freedom of association for workers.[4] Even though the Committee examines the practices of abiding by the regulations set in the Charter, in this case the necessary requirement for the conformity of collective labour law of Member States is the issue of specified regulations and adapting them into practice. A decision regarding the inability to fulfil obligations stipulated under Article 5 may be handed down in the event that particular Member States do not issue regulations concerning the principles of associating in trade unions and employers' organizations as well as in cases when non compliance with the regulations is evidenced.

Article 5 specifies two obligations, one negative and one positive. The addressees of these obligations are the Member States. The negative obligation requires Member States not to violate or to restrict freedom of association. This means that governmental administrative bodies may not issue actions that may infringe the freedoms in question.[5] State governmental and administrative bodies should neither forbid nor order workers to form trade unions or to join already existing union organizations. Member States cannot set demands that must be fulfilled in order to form an organization. Trade unions and employers' organizations should take advantage of their autonomy. A Member State and its bodies should refrain from interfering in the internal issues of an organization representing economic and social interests of the parties to labour relations (collective and individual).[6] The decisions handed down by the Committee mentioned below include examples mentioning behaviour that is compliant and non compliant with the standards established by Article 5. These cases are not exhaustive and do not cover the whole array of permitted and prohibited behaviour. The primary crux of the negative examples is that Member States may

3. D. Harris, J. Darcy, *op. cit.*, p. 93.
4. Conclusions XI-1, p. 78 (Iceland).
5. Conclusions I, p. 31.
6. The right to organize and to bargain collectively (2nd edition), Council of Europe Publishing, Strasbourg 2001, p. 12.

not enact legislation that disrupts workers from utilizing their right to associate in trade unions.[7]

The positive obligation is expressed in the general requirement that Member States undertake actions, especially in issuing appropriate legislation, that will ensure workers the full possibility to associate in and join trade unions and that will ensure such organizations the freedom to act and to be protected from employers.[8]

Member States have the right to restrict the freedom of association in trade unions, through the power of the police. The Charter, for example, gives the right to exclude from the Article 5 provision professional soldiers (members of armed forces). In contrast, however, Member States cannot deprive police officers of the right to associate. In Article 5 there was a deliberate inclusion of the differentiation between competent authorities of Member States with regards to their authority to restrict the rights of association for persons in the armed forces (military organizations) as compared to the rights of association for employees of the Member States' police forces (paramilitary organizations). The last sentence of the provision in question includes language authorizing Member States to describe in domestic regulations the principles of association and the scope of how these principles can be applied to the armed forces. The scope of applying such principles of freedom of association to the armed forces is only in force if a Member State does not exclude, under Article 5, the professional armed forces from the right to associate or the right to form organizations. In contrast, with respect to the police forces in Member States, organize the freedom to associate as stipulated under Article 5 remains in force. Article 5 grants authority over the extent of the guarantees provided for police officers wishing to organize to Member States. Article 5 differs from convention No. 87 ILO, upon which it was formulated. In Article 9(1) of the cited convention, Member States are authorized to specify in domestic legislation, to what level such assurances, as envisaged by the convention, would be applicable to the police and the armed forces.

7.1.1. Forming Trade Unions

The right to form trade unions is assured to workers regardless of the status of such workers' labour relations and regardless of whether or not a worker is self-employed.[9] This right applies to civil servants a well.[10] Membership of a civil servant, or of a citizen of one Member State legally inhabiting the territory of a different Member State, or of a migrant worker, cannot be a valid reason to diversify the above provision.[11] The restrictions on the freedom to organize specified elsewhere than in Article 5, may be introduced by a Member State through general principles stipulated under Article 31 (1) ESC or under Article G(1) RESC. The ability to enact these restrictions is crucial

7. Conclusion XII-1, p. 116.
8. Conclusions I, p. 31; Conclusions XIII-3, p. 108.
9. Conclusions I, p. 8.
10. Conclusions I, p. 31; Conclusions II, p. 184; Conclusions VI, p. 29 (Cyprus).
11. Conclusions I, p. 79.

for the proper functioning of a democratic society and its ability to protect the rights and freedoms of others or to protect public order, national security, public health and good customs. This is further discussed in Chapter 5 of the monograph.

Workers take advantage of forming trade unions and joining organizations. This is an indication of the workers' independence in deciding what type of trade union to form or to which organization to belong.[12] Member States must issue legislation ensuring such freedom of choice in deciding the above and must enact legislation inhibiting other entities (such as state authorities, or trade unions themselves) from influencing workers in their decision making process. This issue is exemplified by the case of Denmark, in which domestic legislation restricts the right of trade unions to negotiate collective work agreements within the maritime sector representing workers who are citizens of Denmark and who are employed on ocean vessels that are registered in Denmark. According to the Committee, granting trade unions the right to negotiate collective work agreements for their members is one of the major reasons for association. The refusal to grant such rights for particular organizations causes workers to allocate their membership elsewhere. Thus, restricting such activities is a contradiction to the freedom to form and join organizations.[13]

Member States, citing domestic labour legislation, are obligated to make demands of workers who are committee members of trade organizations. Such demands may be twofold. On the one hand, domestic labour legislation may require workers to join trade unions based on a membership criteria of a particular category of employment. The labour law regulations in Cyprus, that restricted the freedom of association of workers (for example those employed in specific workplaces), were regarded as non-compliant with Article 5.[14] Workers do not have the obligation to join already existing trade organizations within their workplace. A legal requirement for civil servants to be members of a particular trade union, whose membership is limited exclusively to public civil servants, was deemed in violation of Article 5.[15] They should have been permitted to take advantage of the freedom to form different trade unions.[16] The Committee is of the view that the pluralism within trade organizations is a legal and organizational result of the organizations' freedoms as ensured by Article 5. It accepts the concept of trade union pluralism and does not believe that the existence of many trade organizations within the workplace inhibits trade union movements.[17] The workers' act of taking advantage of such freedom either to join an already existing trade union within the workplace or to form a new one cannot be regarded as non-compliant with the standards established under Article 5.[18]

Member States may elect to establish formal demands to be fulfilled by workers forming a new trade union. Such demands include registration, the payment of fees as

12. Conclusions II, p. 184.
13. Conclusions XII-1, p. 111; Conclusions XVII-1, vol. 1, p. 126.
14. Conclusions XI-2, p. 74.
15. Conclusions II, p. 184 (Cyprus).
16. Conclusions XII-2, p. 97.
17. Conclusions VII, p. 31.
18. Conclusions XIII-1, p. 129–130.

well as stipulations regarding a minimum number of members. The Committee regards some of these requirements in compliance with the standards established under Article 5. Some, however, are considered excessive. Settling such discrepancies between domestic collective labour law and international standards and deciding whether there is compliance or non-compliance on behalf of the domestic legislation, is dependent upon the scope and the definition of the demands made by Member States. A trade union should accept a defined number of members, workers, the self-employed or the unemployed. Article 5 does not define the minimum number of members necessary for a trade union to form and to be able to protect the economic and social interests of its members. The Committee of Social Rights does not stipulate how many members should be associated in an organization for this organization to be regarded as a trade union. It renders judgments concerning the compliance and non-compliance of domestic demands with Article 5, regarding the number of members within a trade organization. Considering the reports filed by Member States, the Committee determined that Polish legislation requiring a minimum of 10 members for a trade union formed by workers to be recognized complies with international standards.[19] Demands that the number of workers in a trade union be 30,[20] 500,[21] or 2000,[22] however, have not been considered compliant. Negative judgments were handed down regarding demands concerning requirements stipulating the number of members in worker and employer organizations compared to the overall number of those having the right to join a trade union. This refers to the precondition for a trade organization to have 10 per cent membership,[23] employers' organization 25 per cent membership,[24] and the federation of workers' organizations 30 per cent.[25] The Committee made one exception to this rule. Setting excessive minimum member counts as a condition of registering either workers' or employers' organizations does not breach Article 5 standards, as a registering body cannot refuse registration based on an insufficient number of members.[26] In reality therefore, it is possible to set a required minimum (not excessive) number of members as a condition of registering a trade union, on the condition that it is not a necessary requirement for the existence of the trade union.

The obligation to register an organization complies with Article 5, as long as domestic labour law ensures such an organization sufficient protection (administrative and legal) during the registering process.[27] In accordance with the standards based on Article 5, fees upon registration are payable by workers' and employers' organization

19. Addendum to Conclusions XV-1, p. 108–109.
20. Conclusions 2004, vol. 2, p. 342.
21. Conclusions III, p. 31 (Ireland).
22. Conclusions XIII-3, p. 272 (Portugal).
23. Conclusions XIV-1, pp. 654–655 (Portugal).
24. Conclusions XIII-3, p. 272 (Portugal); Conclusions XIV-1, vol. 2, pp. 654-655; Conclusions XV-1, vol. 2, p. 469.
25. Conclusions XIII-5, p. 172.
26. Conclusions XIV-1, pp. 654–655.
27. Conclusions II, p. 184.

as long as they are not too exorbitant. The fees must also be validated objectively and cover the registration costs.[28]

Some states' legal systems permit a registered trade union to carry out certain functions for which it was created. These include negotiating collective labour agreements, after the organization attains representative status. Such status can be achieved after being granted a licence to carry out negotiations on behalf of the workers in matters related to employment conditions and ages as well as reaching collective labour agreements. If a condition of registering a trade union is the requirement of a minimum of 1000 members as well as paying significant fees (e.g., 20,000–60,000 Irish pounds), the Committee recognizes such requirements as restrictions and deems such domestic collective labour law as violating international standards stipulated under Article 5.[29]

7.1.2. The Freedom of Trade Unions to Regulate their Internal Organizational Affairs

Trade unions have broad autonomy. The Committee usually regards acts by Member States that interfere with the internal organizational matters of trade unions, as being in breach of Article 5.[30] The Committee holds that a Member State law or policy that restricts the freedom of a union organization to dictate its internal organizational structure, that determines the requirements for membership in a union organization, that determines its disciplinary methods (of members) or that denies membership in such an organization is non-compliant with the standards stipulated under Article 5.[31] The freedom of trade unions regulating their internal organizational affairs may, in certain cases, collide with state regulations that deal with equal treatment, anti-discrimination and protection of rights. It may, therefore, appear that state intervention may be justified in matters concerning the treatment of members by the authorities of the trade union, ensuring trade union members the right to sue in court based on the violations that breach obligatory regulations of such a union. Nonetheless, the principle ensuring a trade union's autonomy stands against such interference. The institutions that are entitled to supervise the actions of a trade union are other, overriding, trade unions. Therefore the regulations established by Member States should be treated as a threat to the autonomy of a trade union as should the interference into internal organizational affairs of a trade union.[32] In legal systems where the actions of a

28. Conclusions IV, pp. 40–41; Conclusions XII-2, p. 99; Conclusions XV-1, vol. 2, p. 629.
29. Case of Ireland: Conclusions III, p. 31; Conclusions XIV-1, vol. 2, pp. 654–655; Conclusions 2004, vol. 1, p. 263.
30. Conclusions II, p. 23.
31. Case of Great Britain: Conclusions XII-1, p. 115; Conclusions XIII-3, p. 109; Conclusions XIV-1, vol. 2, p. 797; Conclusions XV-1, vol. 2, p. 629; Conclusions XVII-1, vol. 1, p. 513. British collective labour law as criticized by the committee is analysed by A. Świątkowski, Wspóczesne brytyjskie prawo pracy (Contemporary British Labour Law) (in:) Prawo pracy państw obcych (Labour Law of Foreign States), Ed. M. Matey, vol. III, Ossolineum, Wrocław-Warszawa 1989, pp. 334 and following.
32. Conclusions XIII-1, pp. 137–138.

trade union do not require supervision of the lower trade union structures, the state may include into its regulations the legal guarantees for members of union organizations. State legislation protecting members of trade unions from potential violations of their rights by authorities of such unions, is seen by the Committee as excessive and as constituting state interference into the internal organizational affairs of a trade union.[33]

Trade unions have the right to specify the way and the means by which they elect their representatives. For this reason, it is deemed a contravention of Article 5 if state regulation stipulates that the election of trade union officials is available only to those who are at that moment employed within the given workplace, sector or undertaking.[34] On the other hand, it is considered a violation of international standards for trade unions to introduce demands calling for the filling of positions associated with the representation of the trade union to be comprised of citizens of a given Member State only, or from a Member State chosen by the trade union,[35] making such positions to be held by foreign nationals be dependent upon the period of their stay and employment within the given country,[36] or specifying the limit of such positions which may be filled by foreign nationals.[37] The Committee did not accept arguments that filling such positions with foreign nationals would cause citizens of other Member States to become acquainted with the labour relations of the given country in which they would be carrying out trade union functions. In countries where the above restrictions concerning the election process for foreigners are established by trade unions, citizens of the European Union have non-restricted rights to be able to carry out trade union functions.[38]

Authorities of trade unions have the right to administer fully the property of the union organization.[39] This also applies to the ability to accumulate trade union funds. Granting employers the right not to deduct union fees from workers (members of trade unions) wages may be regarded as restricting the income of trade organizations.[40] Fines, however, do not have the same application when administered by competent authorities or administrative bodies, implemented when trade unions breach regulations concerning the organization of strikes and protests. The Committee does not regard monetary penalties and asset liability imposed for illegal strikes that are organized by trade unions, as a way to reduce the property of trade unions.[41]

Member States have the right to establish some demands aimed at the protection of rights and freedoms of others and for the purpose of serving as protection of public

---

33. Conclusions XVII-1, vol. 1, p. 512 (Great Britain).
34. Case of Cyprus: Conclusions XII-2, p. 96; Conclusions XIII-1, p. 127.
35. Case of Finland: The positions of trade union representatives within industry sectors were reserved for citizens of that country, or to citizens of other Nordic countries. Conclusions XIV-1, vol. 1, p. 215; Conclusions XV-1, pp. 198–199.
36. Conclusions VI, p. 30 (France).
37. *Ibid.*
38. Conclusions XIV-1, p. 74 (Austria); Conclusions XIV-1, p. 492 (Luxembourg); Conclusions XIII-1, p. 131 (Denmark).
39. Conclusions XIV-1, vol. 2, p. 796.
40. Conclusions XIII-1, p. 137 (Great Britain).
41. Conclusions X-2, p. 68 (France); Conclusions XV-1, vol. 2, p. 629.

order. Based on these principles, the Committee decided that in accordance with Article 5, regulations imposed by Member States that demand from trade unions to observe confidentiality requirements during elections of representative officials, to make resolutions in strike matters and manage collective actions as well as to develop 'political funds' out of trade union budgets are permitted.[42]

Trade unions have the freedom to start federations or confederations of unions as well as centralized international unions. The Committee regards the various forms of restricting this right by Member States as contravening Article 5. The case of Cyprus is an example in which state authorities issued regulations restricting the joining of a pre-existing trade union federations or confederations and established a criteria to which trade unions had to refer when electing to start trade union federations or confederations. The Committee held that trade unions have the right to form superior trade union structures that they deem appropriate. It also pointed out that trade unions have the freedom to select the trade union federations or confederations that they wish to join. Member States do not have the right to define the ways (trade, territorial or professional) by which certain trade unions form their organizational structures (federations or confederations).[43]

7.1.3. The Right of Workers to Join a Trade Union or Elect Not To

Member States are obligated to issue regulations to establish the protection of workers' rights to elect whether they will or will not join a trade union.[44] The Committee examines whether Member States fulfil such obligations. If such rights are sufficiently declared, the Committee sees to it that such regulations are in force.

7.1.3.1. The Right to Join a Trade Union

Workers have the right to join trade unions freely selected by themselves.

A union organization may not be included in this provision, as a worker must seek permission to join such an organization. Therefore Article 5, which guarantees workers hoping to join a trade union the right to choose the organization to which they would like to be members. This provision is not to be treated as a standard ensuring such rights. Trade unions take advantage of autonomy, and thanks to such autonomy, they may regulate the intake of members. The right to join a trade union is therefore understood by the Committee as a right prohibiting Member States from establishing the conditions a person must fulfil before joining a given union. At first, the Committee was of the opinion that Member States could not make the above right dependent upon the workplace of a person wanting to join a particular trade union or to demand that a person to be of particular employment.[45] In the following supervisory cycles, the

42. Conclusions X-1, p. 68 (Great Britain).
43. Case of Cyprus: Conclusions II, p. 184; Conclusions III, p. 31; Conclusions XII-2, p. 97; Conclusions XIII-1, pp. 129, 133.
44. Case of Ireland: Conclusions XIII-1, p. 133; Conclusions XIII-3, p. 100.
45. Conclusions XI-2, p. 74 (Cyprus).

Committee came to the conviction that Member States have the right to establish the rules upon which workers will base their Charter rights of having the freedom to select the trade union they wish to join. Member States may not restrict workers' rights to freely elect the trade union.[46] Evaluating the legality of the actions of Member States that have decided to determine through their labour law criteria (according to which trade unions may be formed) depends upon the union plurality within the confines of the work, trade or profession. A necessary requirement to execute the right of unconstrained choice of union organization by a worker in a situation where the state has determined a set of criteria for forming trade unions (industrial, trade, territorial or professional), is the existence within the undertaking of at least two union organizations, from which workers may elect to join one. During the supervisory process, the Committee concluded that Article 5 is breached if the following occurs:

- The legislator approves the introduction of a clause disallowing a worker employed in the position of a foreman to enter into a trade union where his subordinates are also members;[47]
- An advantageous position of higher earnings is granted to workers who are not members of a given union organization or a trade union[48] or to members of a trade union that is authorized to negotiate collective labour agreements.[49]

7.1.3.2. The Right not to Join a Trade Union

Article 5 does not forbid trade unions to form agreements with employers concerning the sole employment of members of a given union organization. However, the Committee, in line with the European Tribunal for Human Rights,[50] during the first supervisory cycle handed down the judgment that Article 5 encompasses also the 'negative' aspect of union freedom and protects workers from the obligation of joining a trade union. The Committee also stated that all requirements establishing that workers must form an association with trade unions, are to be regarded as non-compliant with the international standards stipulated under Article 5.[51] Despite this unambiguous position against domestic collective labour law that makes employment dependent upon trade union pre-entry or post-entry closed shop, the Committee initially was unable to establish the compliance or non-compliance with Article 5 of British statutes concerning trade unions and labour relations in 1974, that included the provision that the termination of a work agreement by the employer with a worker is

46. Conclusions XII-2, p. 97; Conclusions XIII-1, p. 129.
47. Conclusions II, p. 23 (Sweden).
48. Case of Great Britain: Conclusions XIII-3, p. 108; Conclusions XIV-1, p. 798; Conclusions XV-1, p. 631.
49. Case of Denmark: Conclusions XII-1, p. 111; Conclusions XIII-1, p. 131; Conclusions XIII-3, p. 97; Conclusions XIV-1, p. 178; Conclusions XV-1, pp. 144–145; Conclusions XVII-1, vol. 1, p. 128.
50. *Young, James and Webster v United Kingdom* decision handed down on 13 August 1981, Series A, No. 44 (1982); 1982. 4 EHRR, p. 39 concerning Article 11 Convention on the Protection of Human Rights.
51. Conclusions I, p. 31.

validated if the worker has failed to join a trade union. The legal basis for the Committee's doubt was the Appendix to Article 1 § 2 ESC, a standard seeking the neutral interpretation of Article 1 § 2 ESC, a provision that demanded that Member States protect the right of workers to earn a living in an employment freely selected by them. In the Appendix to the European Social Charter, an obligation was stipulated not to interpret Article 1 ESC as a prohibiting or as an allowing provision for the introduction of a union security clause.[52] It should be pointed out that in the Appendix to Article 5, a similar clause was also introduced. The Committee took the decision rendered by the European Tribunal of Human Rights in the case of Young, James and Webster into consideration during its 7th supervisory cycle.[53] The Committee did not express its opinion with regards to the Appendix to Article 1 § 2 ESC being accepted into Article 5. It came to the conclusion that Article 5 should be interpreted by the standard listed in the Appendix to Article 1 § 2, and that it does not provide sufficient legal grounds to state that the so called 'negative' aspect of trade union freedom lies beyond the frames of the regulation under the Article 5. In the ruling, the Committee stated that the obligation of trade union membership always collides with the 'spirit' of Article 5. Placing the two aspects of trade union freedom (negative and positive) was heralded as a ruling made by the Committee in the following, eighth supervisory cycle. In this ruling, the Committee did not refer to the 'spirit' of Article 5; the explicit language of this provision leaves no doubt that negligence in terms of regulating the workers' right to make a free decision upon joining or refraining from joining a trade union or establishing any legal sanction in relation to this on the site of Member States should be regarded as violating the freedom of trade unions. The Committee applied the language interpretation of Article 5. Additionally, it noted that the broadening interpretation of the Appendix to Article 1 § 2 ESC is not in accordance with the fundamental freedom protected under Article 5.[54] The ruling was not held unanimously. In opposition were Fritz Fabricius[55] and the chairman of the Committee Andreas N. Loizou.[56] They expressed the opinion that the Appendix to Article 1 § ESC applies to Article 5. There are not enough grounds to analyse the clause of 'closed shop' in context of Article 5.[57] Great Britain reported on adjusting their regulations to the international standards established by the Committee, which allowed the Committee assembled on its ninth supervisory cycle to rule that the British regulations conformed to the provisions of the Article 5.[58] The Committee, however, reserved the right to change this verdict should cases of employees who were made redundant due to the refusal of joining trade unions be discovered. Because, in the following 10th supervisory cycle, there were cases of employment termination, that were included in

52. *Ibid.*
53. Conclusions VII, pp. 32–33.
54. Conclusions VII, p. 77.
55. Professor of law, University of Bochum.
56. Judge of the Highest Court of Cyprus, Conclusions VIII, pp. 223 and following.
57. *Ibid.*, p. 230.
58. Conclusions IX-1, pp. 48–49.

the category of not being in accordance with British labour law, the Committee postponed its ruling and demanded that Great Britain present additional information concerning the reasons for such terminations.[59] The case of Great Britain exemplifies the extent to which the Committee pays attention to the scope of Article 5, a provision ensuring workers union freedom in both negative and positive aspects. Under the influence of the decisive position of the Committee, Great Britain altered their regulations and introduced a record of employers who terminate work agreements with their employees based on the fact they are or are not members of a trade union.[60] As of now, the Committee is of the solid view that the 'negative' freedom of association may take advantage of the protection of Article 5. Such a lack of protection by a Member State of workers not joining a trade union cannot be seen as compliant with Article 5.[61] Accepting the standpoint as an entry point to the interpretation of Article 5, the Committee views those Member States that have not implemented legislation protecting such workers, as being in contravention of international standards. In particular the Committee rendered a decision of non-compliance with Article 5 regarding a provision of the Danish labour law of Denmark, to allow the termination of a work agreement with a worker who refused to join a given union organization, even though, when the work agreement was being signed, the worker had the knowledge that trade membership was a crucial element for the continuance of employment.[62] The Committee held demanding that a worker join a particular trade union to be a breach of Article 5. Similarly, cases in which stakeholders were allowed to give their opinion in matters concerning the termination of employment of workers who had decided not to take up trade union membership were not in accordance with international standards, based on the provision of Article 5.[63] The history of closed shop clauses has not come to its completion. During the last supervisory cycles, the Committee handed down a series of decisions about the non-compliance of domestic labour law regulations with Article 5 in Denmark,[64] the Netherlands,[65] Ireland,[66] and Sweden[67] due to their inclusion of such a clause. In the case of France, the Committee handed down a decision about the non-compliance of domestic labour law regulations with international standards for implementing forbidden practices of employing members of the CGT trade union in the printing industry.[68]

59. Conclusions X-1, p. 69.
60. *Ibid.*, p. 79.
61. Conclusions XI-1, p. 78.
62. Conclusions XI-1, p. 77; Conclusions XII-1, p. 110; Conclusions XIII-1, p. 130; Conclusions XIV-1, vol. 1, p. 177; Conclusions XV-1, vol. 1, pp. 142–143.
63. Conclusions XI-1, pp. 78, 133; Conclusions XIII-3, pp. 97, 99, 107; Conclusions XV-1, pp. 240–241, 325–326, 413, Addendum to Conclusions XV-1, p. 23.
64. Conclusions XVII-1, vol. 1, p. 128.
65. Conclusions XVII-1, vol. 2, p. 314.
66. Conclusions 2004, vol. 1, p. 263.
67. Conclusions 2002, p. 233; Conclusions 2004, vol. 2, p. 564.
68. Conclusions XIII-1, p. 131; Conclusions XIII-3, pp. 97-98; Conclusions 2002, p. 31; Conclusions 2004, vol. 1, p. 217.

Other cases of violating the 'negative' trade union freedom are evident where the right to financial benefits in the event of a loss of employment (unemployment benefits) is dependent upon whether the worker was a trade union member,[69] when there are obligatory membership limits established for a given trade organization,[70] or when a trade union is authorized to act as an employment agency.[71] In this last situation, the closed shop clause is a basis for one of the major collective complaints, filed in 2002 by the Workers Confederation to the Committee against Sweden.[72] After conducting a public hearing on 31 March 2003, the Committee handed down a decision against Sweden for approving stakeholder practices that allow for pre-entry closed shop clauses in collective work agreements. On the basis of this decision of the Committee, the Committee of ministers, on 26 September 2003, passed a resolution[73] confirming Sweden's non-compliant behaviour with the international standards.

Also non-compliant with Article 5 is the obligation for workers who are not associated within an organization to contribute membership fee payments that are equal to those paid by actual members. The Committee regards this obligation as a substitute of the closed shop clause.[74] A trade union, however, does have the right to charge fees from workers who are not members of a trade organization for services rendered, such as monitoring whether employers are making wage payments in accordance with the terms of a collective agreement.[75]

7.1.4. The Freedom to Carry Out Trade Union Activities

Workers typically join trade unions in order to have their economic and market interests represented and protected. A workers' organization, which has a trade union feature, should be able to carry out such functions. The freedom of trade union activities requires the existence of the right to negotiate collective labour agreements, which determine the working conditions and workers' wages for its members and non-members; the right to carry out trade union activities within the workplace territory; and the right to hold meetings. Among the provisions that guarantee the right of association and the right to freely carry out trade union activities by statute are provisions forbidding employers to discriminate against workers who are trade union members, or who are engaged in trade union activities as well as provisions which forbid employers to order workers to carry out duties that are not being completed by other employees

---

69. Conclusions XI-1, p. 78.
70. Case of Belgium: Conclusions XIII-2, p. 268; Conclusions XIV-1, vol. 1, p. 106; Conclusions XV-1, vol. 1, p. 74.
71. Case of Sweden: Conclusions XIII-3, p. 107; Conclusions XIV-1, vol. 2, pp. 730 and following; Conclusions XVI-1, vol. 2, p. 559.
72. Complaint No.12/2002: Confederation of Swedish Enterprise v. Sweden. List of registered collective complaints (as from 1 January 2005), European Social Charter. Collected texts (5th edition), Strassbourg 2005, p. 513.
73. ResChS (2003) 1, *Ibid.*
74. Conclusions 2002, p. 131 (Romania).
75. Complaint No. 12/2002, Collective complaints, *op. cit.*

who are on strike. These issues are connected with the rights, which are ensured by Article 6. The Committee decided to deal with these issues during the supervisory cycle monitoring the compliance of Article 5. It concluded that the right of trade unions to negotiate in collective labour agreements is a crucial ground for ensuring trade union freedom regulated by Article 5.

7.1.4.1. Negotiating Collective Labour Agreements

The Committee emphasizes the right of workers to organize in trade unions is not a complete right in itself. Workers form trade unions or join already existing ones because they want their interests protected and have available negotiators at the ready to talk terms about the collective labour agreements, work and wage condition.[76] In such circumstances, where domestic labour law regulations restrict the rights of trade organizations to negotiate collective labour agreements, it may be deduced that the fundamental labour law grounds are violated, as there is a breach of the freedom to join a trade union.[77] The interconnection between collective labour law foundations and Article 5 should be obvious. In order to comply with international standards, which stipulate the limits of trade unions' freedom, under Article 5, a necessary requirement of conducting a dialogue with stakeholders, has to be met (as is stipulated under Article 6 § 2).[78] Member States have the right to make demands upon which the negotiating rights (collective labour agreements) of a trade union are dependent. The Committee viewed the issuing of a licence by a state for a trade union to be able to carry out negotiating activities (in collective labour agreements) only if it fulfils a minimum membership requirement (at least 500 or 1000 members), as non-compliant with the right of trade union freedom.[79] The same view was appropriated for the increase of administration fees payable for a licence (20,000 – 60,000 Irish pounds)[80] and for the requirement to pay an amount that is dependent upon the number of members (5,000 Irish pounds for 20,000 members; 15,000 Irish pounds for more than 39,000 members).[81] Ireland attempted to protect its domestic regulations, pointing out that such high demands are implemented to increase a trade union's position when acting prior to the signature of a collective work agreement. The authorities argued that due to the increased amount of existing trade unions, some organizations were too weak and therefore were unable to evoke sufficient pressure in the negotiation of work and wage conditions as well as during collective labour agreements negotiations. The Committee did not accept these arguments. It claimed trade union pluralism is a typical phenomenon within the Irish union movement. An increased amount of trade unions does not weaken unions as long as they continue to have rights to develop horizontal or

76. Conclusions I, p. 31.
77. Conclusions IV, p. 39; Addendum to Conclusions XI-2, p. 19 (the Netherlands).
78. Conclusions VI, p. 36.
79. Conclusions III, p. 30 (Ireland).
80. *Ibid.*
81. Conclusions II, p. 22 (Ireland).

vertical structures.[82] Regional, national, federal and confederate trade unions, as well as trade unions representing the interests between the undertakings themselves, constitute unions of trade unions. The Committee was not against the introduction of licences for negotiating purposes and establishing fees for administrative costs and services. It regards that standards of collective labour relations are complied with if every trade organization seeking a negotiating licence actually receives one, unless public security is against it (*l'ordre public*). Administrative fees taken from trade organizations seeking permission to undertake negotiating activities involving employers and establishing collective labour agreements are permissible if such fees will cover the costs involved in issuing the licence.[83] The Committee is of the view that negotiating licences should be issued automatically to all trade unions. Depriving a trade union of a licence for negotiating purposes in collective labour agreements, because domestic labour regulations which demand confidentiality during given resolutions are not met, is in breach of Article 5.[84] A lack of negotiating rights in collective labour agreements undermines the existence of a trade union. For this reason, the Committee decided that the Irish labour law regulations which granted a negotiating licence to trade unions only if there was disclosure concerning the amount of members, whilst eliminating those unions having less than the required amount, was in breach of Article 5.[85] The same reasoning was applied to the increase of administrative fees for trade unions, with regards to stipulations regarding the amount of members. The Committee is of the view that the introduction of an obligatory negotiating licence to reach collective labour agreements, and collecting administrative fees for issuing permission to enable social dialogue (which is one of the stakeholders' responsibilities), is superfluous and that it violates the basis for the freedom to associate in trade unions in contravention to Article 5.[86] For example, Article 5 was held to be violated by the Danish regulation related to the registering of sea vessels and forbidding maritime trade unions to negotiate work and wage condition for the workers who were neither citizens of Denmark nor permanently residing in Denmark. The Committee decided the exclusion of such workers who are members of the trade union, from the scope of collective labour relations created a serious violation of the right to associate, as it deprives trade unions of the right to represent and protect the interests of their members.[87]

The Committee similarly recognized as non-compliance with union freedom, British labour regulations, which permitted employers to offer advantageous employment conditions for workers who would not form trade unions or join already existing ones.[88] An identical view was propounded regarding restrictions imposed on

82. Conclusions VII, p. 31; Addendum to Conclusions XIII-3, p. 100.
83. Conclusions IV, p. 39.
84. Case of Ireland: Conclusions XIII-1, p. 133; Conclusions XIII-3, p. 100.
85. Conclusions IV, p. 40.
86. Addendum to Conclusions XI-2, p. 19; Conclusions XIII-3, p. 100; Conclusions XIV-1, p. 23; Addendum to Conclusions XV-1, vol. 1, p. 14.
87. Conclusions XII-1, p. 119; Conclusions XIII-1, p. 131; Conclusions XIV-1, pp. 177–178.
88. Conclusions XIII-3, pp.108–109; Conclusions XIV-1, vol. 2, p. 798; Conclusions XV-1, vol.2, pp. 630–631.

stakeholders who sought arbitrary processes during collective labour disputes. According to collective labour laws in Malta, a minister representing one of the two stakeholders, in leading the negotiating process had the right to present before the industrial tribunal dispute certain issues. These dispute issues were binding in their nature, forbidding stakeholders from negotiating this problem for a year.[89] The Committee's position was that such restrictions on stakeholders during negotiating collective labour agreements and in leading collective labour disputes, are in conflict with the rights of competent trade organizations and undermine the freedom of association for workers in trade union in breach of Article 5. This decision was handed down during the Committee's supervision over the compliance of Member States of Articles 6 § 2 and 3, indicating a relationship between those regulations and Article 5. The Committee also declared that restrictions placed on one stakeholder during collective negotiations by Member States, are to be considered as violating trade union freedom.

In the abovementioned decisions it is not possible however to conclude that there is non-compliance of domestic collective labour regulations with Article 5, which creates criteria for establishing representative status of a trade union. During the 6th supervisory cycle, the Committee decided that the introduction by a Member State of objective criteria for evaluating whether there trade organization may be regarded as a representative one, cannot be seen as a breach of Article 5.[90] Representative status, according to the Committee, is dependent upon fulfilling certain required and verifiable criteria. It obligated Member States to present such criteria. During the individual supervisory cycles, it examined whether the criteria were known earlier by the trade organization, whether they were subject to control of an independent body or whether such control was systematically carried out.[91] The Committee aspired to establish whether a trade union, which does not have representative status, was not devoid of certain competencies with regards to the interests and protection of rights of its members.[92]

7.1.4.2. Carrying Out Trade Union Activities on the Territory of the Workplace

A necessary requirement for carrying out statutory activities by a trade union is the possibility to enter the grounds of the area employing members of the given trade organization. Examining a report filed by Germany during the 11th supervisory cycle, the Committee claimed that trade unionists who were no longer employed by the employer (who employed other members of the trade union) had no right to enter the grounds of the plant.[93] The Committee demanded clarification. In the following

89. Conclusions XIII-2, p. 270; Conclusions XIII-3, p. 102; Conclusions XV-1, vol. 1, p. 402.
90. Conclusions VI, p. 29.
91. Conclusions XIV-1, vol. 1, p. 43; Conclusions XV-1, vol. 1, p. 40 (Austria); p. 79 (Belgium); p. 144 (Denmark); p. 198 (Finland); pp. 247–248 (France).
92. Conclusions XV-1, vol. 1, p. 79 (Belgium); p. 144 (Denmark); p. 248 (France).
93. Conclusions XI-2, pp. 75, 98.

supervisory cycle, information was presented indicating that the trade unionists took advantage of a restricting right to enter the grounds of the plant, in which other members were employed. The ruling from 1972 *Betriebsverfassungsgesetz* mentions cases in which trade unionists were granted permission to enter the grounds of a workplace where at least one member of the given trade union is an employee. A taxing amount of such cases does not encompass the issues, in which trade unions are most interested in, i.e. the issue of recruiting non-member workers into the trade organization and the issues of information and advice. In those places of work where no members of a trade union are employed, unionists would be able to apply for the right of entry. The Constitutional Tribunal made the above rights of entry dependent upon coming into force in appropriate legal regulations. It did not exclude that the above rights may be accepted in the future exclusively for trade unions with representative status.[94] Because this cited act from 1972 was not applicable to workplaces employing less than 5 workers, to minority religious organizations and charitable institutions, the Committee demanded that Germany present information regarding the practices of the regulations concerning trade unionists' access to work grounds. Germany refused to provide such information, as they believed that the above matter could not be considered based on Article 5. The Committee propounded a different approach for considering this issue, concluding that Article 5 ensures workers the right to form trade unions, to join existing trade organizations and to refrain from participating in union activities. This cited provision also encompasses the right of trade unions to carry out their statutory requirements and tasks. Allowing trade unionists to enter the grounds of a workplace, a workplace employing both trade union members and non-members, is an important means of protecting the economic and social interests of the workers.[95] Accordingly, the Committee concluded that in performing this right trade union activists should take into consideration the employers' rights and interests such as the necessity to keep a fully functioning workplace, the requirement to abide by security and health regulations in the workplace and the obligation not to disclose information regarded as confidential.[96] The Committee incorporated the judgment of the Federal German Labour Court handing down a decision on 25 March 1992, that the representatives of 'representative' trade unions take advantage of the right to enter the grounds of the that workplace. Whether the trade union is 'represented' within the workplace is a deciding factor if in the given workplace there should be at least one member of the trade organization that is employed within that workplace. Basing its argument on this principle, the Committee decided the German labour law is responsible for the standards stipulated under Article 5 and demanded information from Germany concerning the practices of applying the act of 1972.[97] The problem of allowing access to trade unionists onto workplace territory and having access to the workers is an issue, which Member States should explain in their annual reports presented before the Committee

94. Conclusions XII-2, p. 98.
95. *Ibid.*
96. *Ibid.*
97. Conclusions XIII-4, pp. 355–356; Addendum to Conclusions XV-1, p. 22.

dealing with the fulfilment of the obligations stipulated under Article 5.[98] Only on two occasions (the 14th and 15th supervisory cycles) did the Committee demand from Member States information concerning the right of trade unionists to have access to the grounds of the workplace.[99]

Connected to the right of trade union representatives to enter the grounds of the workplace is the right to organize meetings by the trade union with worker and member participation. Despite the information provided by certain Member States, the Committee did not conclude that there were violations of international standards based on Article 5, and instead had doubts about the possibility of police officers making use of this right[100] and about the ability of state administrative bodies to suspend the availability of this right.[101] The Committee did not further occupy itself with the details of situations where trade unions had the right to organize meetings on the grounds of a workplace. It rendered one opinion concerning the fulfilment of obligations by Finland stipulated under Article 5. It exemplified how Finland requires employers employing at least 10 workers to make available (entailing no costs) an area within the workplace for purposes of holding trade union meetings after working hours.[102]

7.1.5. Legal Guarantees Ensuring Workers to Freely Associate in Trade Unions

7.1.5.1. Prohibiting Discrimination of Workers Based on their Trade Union Membership and Participation in Trade Union Activities

Article 5 is interpreted by the Committee as a standard obligating Member States to ensure workers legal protection against employer discrimination based on trade union membership and/or participation in trade union activities. Such prohibition of discrimination is regarded by the Committee as an assurance for workers to freely associate in trade unions. The scope of this protection should be applied generally. For example, Austria's labour laws therefore cannot be seen as compliant with the international standards, as they exclude from such protection workers in small workplaces where employment is less than 5 workers.[103] Issuing regulations forbidding employers to discriminate against workers for reasons of trade union membership is not a valid reason for concluding compliance of domestic labour laws of Member States with international standards. The Committee asks whether such prohibited behaviour by an employer under Article 5, should entail a penalty. The Committee is interested in determining whether there are any penalties for discriminatory behaviour of employers

98. Question D, Form for the Reports Submitted in Pursuance of the Revised European Social Charter (1996), European Social Charter. Collected texts (5th edition), Council of Europe Publishing, Strasbourg 2005, p. 325
99. Conclusions XIV-1, pp. 295-296; Conclusions XV-1, p. _.
100. Case of Cyprus; Conclusions X-2, p. 67; Conclusions XI-2, p. 74.
101. Conclusions III, p. 30 (Austria).
102. Conclusions XIV-1, p. vol. 1, p. 215.
103. Addendum to Conclusions XV-1, pp. 14–15.

violating such workers' rights or whether the injured worker receives compensation. It makes clear that Member States that have ratified Article 5, are obligated to undertake measures to reinstate the initial rights or ensure compensation for the injured discriminated against workers.[104] According to the Committee, Member States should ensure that workers who are discriminated against due to their trade union membership or participation, receive compensation equal to the amount of remuneration from the period of terminating the work agreement until the labour court renders a judgment about the reinstatement of the worker to his/her previous position. Because Bulgarian and Irish labour law regulations, for example, do not ensure legal protection against such discrimination, the Committee decided that these countries do not fulfil the obligations under Article 5.[105] Employers do not have the right to demand lists of members from trade unions. In cases of providing an employer such a list by a trade union or in the case of when an employer gains such information, the Committee demands from Member States assurances, that workers who were found on that list did not experience repressive actions by their employers.[106] Examining Finnish reports, the Committee questioned whether there was a case of discrimination in the carried out actions that were beyond labour law regulations. The report showed that in Finland, a council worker for a period of carrying out the responsibilities of a trade union representative within the workplace had his/her right to take part in council elections suspended. Taking into consideration the potential conflict of interests, the Committee was convinced this prohibition of being able to carry out both functions is not in accordance with Article 5.[107]

Article 5 ensures the protection of rights workers who are members and non-members in trade unions. The provision obligates Member States to issue appropriate regulations and carry out suitable measures in an attempt to protect workers who have not joined a trade union or those who joined a trade organization without having representative status, against discrimination.[108]

7.1.5.2. A Prohibition Against Allocating Workers Duties, Which are not Being Fulfilled by Workers Participating in a Legal Strike Action

The compliance of domestic collective labour regulations with international standards is monitored by the Committee when analysing the reports concerning the fulfilment of obligations stipulated under Articles 5 and 6. In situations of collective action carried out by stakeholders, the point of reference for establishing legislation and practices is Article 6 § 4. The Committee also indicated the importance of those obligations stipulated under Articles 5 and 6.

---

104. Case of Austria: Conclusions XX-2, p. 101; Conclusions XIII-2, p. 271; Conclusions XV-1, vol. 1, p. 39.
105. Conclusions 2004, vol. 1, pp. 34, 37-38 (Bulgaria); p. 263 (Ireland).
106. Conclusions XIII-1, p. 136 (Great Britain); Case of France: Conclusions XIV-1, vol. 1, pp. 254–255; Conclusions XV-1, vol. 1, p. 243.
107. Conclusions XX-1, pp. 197–198.
108. Addendum to Conclusions XI-2, p. 19 (Ireland); Conclusions XIV-1, vol. 1, p. 414.

Workers form trade unions and join such unions to have their economic and social interests protected. A strike is a last resort option used to protect such interest regulated by collective labour law. Similarly, cases of restricting trade union rights to carry out negotiations in achieving collective labour agreements as well as employers undertaking actions restricting the after-effects of a strike, are also treated by the Committee as non-compliant with trade union freedoms, protected under Article 5. These conclusions were appropriated in the case of Germany, which allowed council employers to employ council clerks to carry out duties which were not being fulfilled by workers taking part in a legal strike (including manual labour workers). Employing 'strike-breaker' clerks, council employers limit trade union freedom for the workers who strike. An additional rationale for disallowing employer interference in the workers' right to associate in trade unions was that the council clerks and those workers who were legally striking were all members of the same trade union.[109] Because the right to employ 'strike-breakers' is in accordance with trade union freedom in Germany according to its Constitutional Tribunal, the Committee adjourned its judgment. In the following supervisory cycle, the Committee took note of the decision handed down by the German Constitutional Tribunal, which claimed non-compliance of the practices not regulated by the existing legislation with constitutional principles of trade union freedoms.[110] Because this case, at first instance, concerns the principles of undertaking collective actions by trade unions, especially in reference to organizing strikes, the Committee concluded that such instances should be analysed during the supervisory processes, according to Article 6 § 4 and that its compliance should be enforced by Member States.

7.1.6. Union Freedom and the Right to Associate in Trade Unions for Certain Categories of Workers

The Committee pays particular attention to the way in which domestic labour laws are regulated as well as to the practices used when attempting to administer the international standards established by Article 5 to the following workers: civil servants, police officers, professional soldiers and foreigners who are citizens of a Member State. As mentioned earlier, Article 5 creates a legal basis for restricting trade union freedoms for two categories of the employed, police officers and professional militia. In the latter category, Article 5 even allows for the complete exclusion of the right to associate for the armed forces. A large number of judgments handed down by the Committee in such matters are indicative that Member States are expanding their restrictions and excluding trade union freedoms, which may be regulated by domestic collective labour laws into different categories of employment, such as civil servants and migrant workers (citizens of Member States parties to the Charter).

---

109. Conclusions XII-2, p. 99.
110. Conclusions XIII-2, p. 269.

7.1.6.1. Trade Union Freedom for Civil Servants

With the exception of police officers and professional military personnel, the remainder of the employment categories can take advantage of unrestrictive rights of association in trade unions.[111] These rights are also applicable to civil servants.[112] The Committee is of the view that the various restrictions imposed on the freedom of trade unions in the case of civil servants are in breach of Article 5. This view related particularly to Member State demands wanting civil servants to form or join trade organizations, which were compiled strictly of employers in the civil sector.[113] Because of the specificity of employers (state organizational units) and the nature of the employment duties (collecting information, preparing and handing down decisions state authorities and administrative bodies), the Committee permitted the implementing of a few restrictions based on Article 31 § 1 ESC, on the trade union freedom of civil servants. This is illustrated by the case of the British Government Communications Headquarters (GCHQ) in Cheltenham. The Committee received information that Great Britain deprived more than 7000 civil servants working in connection with a military centre of communication, of the right to association in trade unions.[114] From the details presented by the British, it may be deduced that the given centre of communication was carrying out duties concerning public security. The Committee agreed, citing Article 31 § 1 ESC, that such restrictions on the right to form and join trade unions was permissible in such particular cases and adjourned its decision.[115] Great Britain permitted the workers in question to form a staff federation, which was registered as a trade union whose members were civil servants and employees of GCHQ. The federation was authorized to negotiate the conditions and wages of its members. Taking into consideration the above circumstances as well as the fact that these employees did not have an obligation to join a trade union, the Committee concluded the restrictions implemented on this category of workers was not a violation of Article 31 § 1.[116] It claimed that there was a lack of legal grounds to conclude the domestic labour laws were non-compliant with Article 5.

The Charter, however, does not permit Member States to exclude or limit trade union freedoms of all civil servants. It also allows for the exclusion of rights of association for judges and civil servants in managerial positions.[117] It is against depriving civil servants of their rights to take part in trade union functions.[118] Because of the need to protect public order and national security within democratic societies, the

111. Conclusions I, p. 31.
112. Conclusions II, p. 184.
113. *Ibid.*
114. Conclusions IX-1, p. 49.
115. Conclusions X-1, pp. 68–69.
116. *Ibid.*, p. 80.
117. Conclusions 2004, vol. 2, pp. 455–456 (Romania).
118. Conclusions XVII-1, vol.2, pp. 376, 378 (Poland). *See* A.Świątkowski, *Scope rationae personae* of Article 5 of the European Social Charter (The Right to organize) and Its Application to Poland [w:] Facing the European Union-Challenges for Polish Law, Archivum Iuridicum Cracoviense, vol.XXXV-XXXVI, Kraków 2002-22-3, pp.88 and following.

Committee accepted the restrictions on trade union freedoms for some civil servants, especially those who are part of the authority and administrative hierarchy in political decision making positions. This is the only permissible basis for allowing such restrictions and depriving certain civil servants from their right to organize are Article 31 § 1 ESC and Article E § 1 RESC.

7.1.6.2. *The Right of Police Officers to Organize*

Member States may introduce restrictions for police officers regarding the right to organize in trade unions. They cannot however, wholly deprive police officers of forming trade unions or becoming their members.[119] Depriving police officers of their right to organize is a breach of Article 5.[120] The Committee supervises Member States and determines whether they are compliant with Article 5, allowing police officers to organize. In the second supervisory cycle the Committee decided that domestic labour laws, which forbid the police to form their own trade unions or forbid the police to join organizations through their own choosing, are not in accordance with Article 5.

A breach of Article 5 by domestic labour laws is also apparent when such regulations force police officers to join trade unions that are chosen by the state.[121] This is a violation of trade union freedom. The above approach by the Committee was undertaken in subsequent supervisory cycles.[122] Limitations on trade union freedom are not reduced even when those trade unions, which are chosen by the state for police officers to join, have the right to negotiate in work and wage conditions of the workers. The Committee believes that the assurance of the chosen trade union rights is not determined simply because it has the power to negotiate in collective labour agreements.[123] In the case of police officers, restricting trade union freedoms may cause domestic labour legislation to include regulations for trade organizations formed by the police only to have other police officers as members.[124] The above trade union freedom limitations are permissible due to the particular duties police officers are obliged to fulfil. The limitations placed on the police and their right to associate in trade unions is the restriction on associating in national and international trade unions (federations and confederations).[125] Member States have the right to stop police trade unions from joining other trade organization structures, which have other workers as members.[126] The Committee accepted Member State regulations, which allowed police officers to form and join not trade union, rather professional associations' federations accepting

119. Conclusions I, p. 31.
120. Conclusions II, p. 22; Conclusions III, p. 30.
121. Conclusions II, p. 22.
122. Conclusions III, p. 30; Conclusions XII-2, p. 100 (Malta); Conclusions XIII-2, p. 268 (Belgium).
123. Conclusions II, p. 22.
124. Conclusions X-2, pp. 68-69; Conclusions XIII-3, p. 106 (Spain).
125. Conclusions VIII, p. 80 (Italy); Conclusions IX-1, p. 49 (Great Britain); Conclusions XIII-3, p. 106 (Spain).
126. Conclusions XV-1, vol. 2, p.359 (Italy).

only police officers as members.[127] A necessary requirement for fulfilling the obligations under Article 5 is for police to form trade unions. Appointing representatives authorized to represent the interests of the police officers (even according to democratic procedures), was considered by the Committee as non-compliant with international standards. The community of police officers does not fulfil legal expectations simply by being regarded as a professional association federation.[128] A necessary condition for the existence of an association is the voluntariness with which one can make a decision to join a trade union or organization. The Committee was against cases in which trade union membership for police officers was obligatory.[129]

Professional associations of police officers may be regarded as quasi trade unions, is they fulfil some of the fundamental functions of a trade organization such as holding meetings as well as having the right to negotiate with the police employers about employment and salary conditions.[130] Limitations on trade union freedom for workers and the police calls for Member States to have the necessary rights of regulating the conditions of association for the police into trade organizations to which police officers have the right to join, substituting the professional associations. All cases of non-compliance with Article 5 therefore are those where the state excludes police officers the right to associate in trade organizations or forcing membership to take place.

7.1.6.3. Union Freedom for Professional Militia

Professional solders are not considered to be workers by labour law. They are tied to the army through administrative (official) relations. However the law does not exclude professional militia from taking advantage of the assurance established by the Article 5. It may be concluded from the said provision international guarantees of union freedom apply to professional solders if the scope of application of the Article 5 in relation to professional solders is determined in national labour law or if there is a legislated regulation stating the said provision does not apply to professional militia at all. The situation looks analogically to that of the police force. The Committee stated: 'the third sentence of the Article 5 allows a Member State to limit or entirely deprive professional militia of union freedom'.[131] The position of the Committee expressed during the supervisory process of abiding Article 5 was repeated in rulings made by the Committee acting as a quasi judicial body dealing with collective complaints[132] in the cases *European Federation of Employees in Public Services v. France,*[133] *European*

127. Conclusions II, p. 23.
128. Conclusions VI, p. 31 (Italy).
129. Conclusions X-1, p. 68; Addendum to Conclusions XI-2, p. 20 (Ireland).
130. Conclusions X-2, p. 67; Conclusions XIII-3, p. 237 (Portugal).
131. Conclusions I, p. 31; Conclusions III, p. 30; Conclusions XIII-2, p. 268.
132. A. Świątkowski, Quasi jurysdykcyjna funkcja Komitetu Praw Społecznych Rady Europy (Quasi judicial function of the European Committee of Social Rights of the Council of Europe), PiP Nr 9, 2004, pp. 46 and following.
133. Complaint No. 2/1999. The complaint was registered on 13 August1999 and concerned violating the Article 5 and 6 in relation to professional militia. The committee accepted the complaint to

Federation of Employees in Public Services v. Italy,[134] *European Federation of Employees in Public Services v. Portugal*.[135] The applicant, international federation of trade unions (EFEPS) argued that three Member States, France, Italy and Portugal, violated Article 5 and 6 because they did not guarantee their professional militia the right to associate in trade unions as well as the right to negotiate in collective work agreements. The Committee referred to the rulings made during the following supervisory cycles monitoring the abiding of the Article 5, stating that the third sentence of Article 5 allows Member States to deprive professional militia of the right to associate in trade unions entirely. It emphasized the international federation of trade unions registering the collective complaints against three Member States had not provided arguments that could have changed the Committee's position towards the freedom of union of professional militia. The only contentious issues within the interpretation of the Article 5 concerning professional militia were those dealing with the background of the right of Member States to deprive persons employed in paramilitary organizations, of the right to associate in trade unions, e.g. gendarme in France,[136] officers of civil guard in Spain,[137] and Security of Internal Affairs and the Intelligence Agency in Poland.[138] The Committee was interested in the legal status of the above listed organizations. Regarding them as military organizations automatically excused the deprivation of the right to associate in trade unions imposed on the officers of these organizations.

7.1.6.4. The Right of Migrant Workers, Citizens of a Member State, to Organize

Citizens of Member States, parties to the Charter, take advantage of the right to organize in a trade union in a manner permissible to them by the regulations specified by the given country that are applicable to its own citizens (Article 19(4)(b)). The Committee sought information from Member States concerning the regulations dealing with equal treatment of Member State citizens in issues regarding trade union membership.[139] Further, during the 14th supervisory cycle the Committee took an interest in what kind of approaces were taken by foreigners (citizens of a Member State) within trade unions legally employed and living on the territory of another Member State.[140]

---

recognition on 10 February 2000 and on 12 December 2000 made a ruling stating France did not violate Article 5 and 6 of the Charter. The Committee of Ministers of the Council of Europe approved of the above verdict on 7 February 2001 ResChS (2001)2.

134. Complaint No. 4/1999. The complaint was registered on 13.8.1999. The Committee accepted it to recognition on 10 February 2000. The Committee's ruling on 12 December 2000, approved by the Committee of Ministers on 7.2.2001 ResChS (2001)3. The content of the verdict as in the case No. 2/1999.
135. Complaint No. 5/1999. The content and the dates of decisions as in the cases Complaint No. 2/1999 and Complaint No. 4/1999.
136. Conclusions XV-1, vol. 1, p. 249.
137. Conclusions XV-1, vol. 2, p. 512.
138. A Świątkowski, Scope ..., *op. cit.*, pp. 94 and following.
139. Conclusions XV-1, vol. 2, p. 512.
140. Conclusions XIV-1, vol. 1, p. 45.

In a questionnaire addressed to Member States was the Question A concerning the rights of foreigners, members of another Member State, to form trade unions, join to already existing trade organizations as well as carrying out trade union functions.[141] From the reports filed by the Member States, it may be concluded, that in some Member States citizens of other Member States (with the exception for the contracting parties to the European Economic Area EEA), do not take advantage of the right to stand for election in representative body elections within the workplace[142] as well as in bodies recognizing wage claim disputes of workers and in matters of social security.[143] The Committee decided that depriving foreigners of the right to stand for elections, who are legally employed within the given Member State, is in breach of Article 5. It did not however claim there is non-compliance in cases of depriving foreigners of the right to sit representatives in recognizing wage claim disputes and as representatives of workers' interests. Establishing equality within workplace relations is part of the state's responsibility, which is capable of restricting the scope of persons authorized to deal with equality within the field of its own citizens.[144]

The following domestic labour laws have been considered by the Committee as non-compliant with Article 5: prohibiting citizens of other Member States from forming trade unions in the country where they are legally employed;[145] making the right to stand elections be dependent upon a period of 5 years employment within the given country;[146] allowing citizens of other Member States not to take up more than 1/3 of the managerial positions with a trade organization. In the opinion of the Committee legally binding restrictions upon the amount of foreigners permitted to function in managerial positions within trade unions creates doubts about the representation of the trade union. In certain cases this inhibits the process of forming trade organizations within the workplace and in industrial sectors employing migrant workers.[147]

7.2. The Right to Bargain Collectively

7.2.1. Introduction

Article 6 promotes social dialogue between stakeholders: representatives of workers and employers. Four paragraphs of the regulation govern various aspects of legal relations between stakeholders. The first three paragraphs cover the relations between stakeholders in the time of social peace: consultations, negotiation of normative

141. Form for the reports submitted in pursuance of the Revised European Social Charter, European Social Charter, *op. cit.*, pp. 317–318.
142. Case of Austria: Conclusions XIII-3, p. 96; Conclusions XIV-1, vol. 1, p. 74; Conclusions XV-1, vol. 1, p. 42. Case of Luxembourg: Conclusions XIV-1, vol. 2m p. 492; Addendum to Conclusions XV-1, p. 45.
143. Conclusions XV-1, vol. 1, p. 249 (France); Addendum to Conclusions XV-1, p. 23 (Germany).
144. The right to organize ..., *op. cit.*, p. 45.
145. Case of Turkey: Conclusions XIII-3, p. 414; Conclusions XIV-1, vol. 2, p. 780.
146. Conclusions VI, pp. 30, 121.
147. *Ibid.*, p. 30.

agreements, primarily collective agreements; solving collective labour disputes by means of peaceful methods: conciliation and voluntary arbitration.[148] The last, fourth paragraph of Article 6 specifies the techniques for conducting collective actions by stakeholders – parties to collective labour disputes. Article 6 § 4 is the first legal standard of international labour law that guarantees the right to strike.[149]

Similarly to Article 5, Article 6 applies to foreigners and citizens of Member States to the Council of Europe legally residing and employed in other Member States. Contrary to Article 5, Article 6 has not introduced any limitations or exceptions with respect to exercising the stakeholders' right to bargain collectively. Certain limitations in taking collective actions are admissible for the sake of protecting public order, national security, public health or good practice.

7.2.2. Joint Consultations between Workers and Employers (Article 6 § 1)

Article 6 § 1 imposes on Member States the obligation to promote joint consultations between workers and employers. The analysed provision does not grant stakeholders 'the right to consultations'.[150] It obliges Member States to promote such consultations. This obligation is absolute in its nature. It is not dependent upon the opinion expressed by the individual Member States as in the case of being obliged to promote, where necessary and appropriate, voluntary negotiations with a view to regulate the terms and conditions of employment by means of collective labour agreements. The Committee of Social Rights has a broad interpretation of such consultations. Joint (*paritaire*) consultations with stakeholders cover a variety of relations between such stakeholders that are based on the principles of equality.[151] In accordance with the analysed provision, Member States are obliged to encourage stakeholders to initiate mutual relations and communicate on all the issues within the area of their interest. The consultations may be conducted directly by the interested parties or they may involve representatives of Member States. Consultations conducted within the framework of the so-called 'tri-lateral commissions' by stakeholders and organized by the Member States, headed by competent ministers of labour and social policy meet the requirements arising from 6 § 1.[152]

Member States are obliged to promote joint consultations. This obligation signifies that some specific, positive steps should be taken when a stakeholder fails to initiate mutual relations independently.[153] When stakeholders show an initiative and take a voluntary and independent step to encourage negotiations on all matters falling within the scope of their interest, the Member States should refrain from taking any actions that could discourage stakeholders from such social dialogue.

148. Conclusions I, p.34.
149. *Ibid.*
150. *See* judgement of the European Human Rights Tribunal on: National Union of Belgium Police, 279 Eur.Ct.H.R. (ser.A) (1975).
151. Conclusions IV, p. 43.
152. Conclusions V, p. 41; Conclusions XVII-1, vol.2, p.355 (Aruba).
153. Conclusions 2004, vol.2, p. 457 (Romania).

Article 6 § 1 leaves the Member States relatively large freedom of evaluation of the relations between stakeholders. Nevertheless, the approach to such freedom adopted by the Member States is subject to the control of the Committee of Social Rights. The Committee does not accept explanations of Member States outlining that some appropriate actions were undertaken in order to prompt stakeholders towards mutual relations and social dialogue, if such efforts did not bring about a positive result due to a lack of interest on the part of the parties in question or due to an aggressive attitude of the representatives of trade unions.[154] The Committee stressed that Article 6 § 1 introduces an absolute obligation to take appropriate measures with a view to promote joint consultations of stakeholders.[155] In reality therefore Article 6 § 1 is interpreted by the Committee as standard which obligates Member States to ascertain particular results. Postponing a judgment with relation to the compliance of a Member State to the obligations arising from Article 6 § 1 is the best-case scenario in justifying situations where efforts have been made towards prompting stakeholders to enter into direct relations and to run joint consultations presented by Member States.[156] In accordance with the practice followed so far, the Committee is interested in reading the regulations underlying joint consultations of stakeholders and how they are applied practically. [157] The particular practice that is of some interest to the Committee, is the case when joint consultations of stakeholders are not based on the legal regulations introduced by the state. [158]

Article 6.1 does not identify any entities authorized to conduct the consultations. Joint consultations should be conducted 'between workers and employers'. In the consultations, workers are typically represented by trade unions. However, the provision analysed herein should not be approached as a legal standard, which grants a monopoly for conducting consultations with employers to trade unions. The Committee does not investigate whether other representative bodies, apart from trade unions have been authorized to represent workers. However, it is interested to learn what bodies representing workers take part in the consultations with employers and the entities, where trade unions do not operate.[159] The Committee advised Ireland that the Joint Labour Committees formed in some sectors, primarily in the agricultural sector, competent in maters of regulating remuneration, do not allow for the participation of workers' representatives in joint consultations in the manner described in Article 6 § 1.[160] Furthermore, the Committee raised some doubts whether regulations authorizing workers to express suggestions on the matters connected with managing

154. Conclusions I, p. 35 (Italy, Great Britain); Conclusions III, p.33 (Italy); Conclusions IV, p. 44 (Italy); Addendum to Conclusions XV-1, p.115.
155. Addendum to Conclusions XI-2, p.22–23 (Ireland).
156. Addendum to Conclusions XV-1, p. 24.
157. Conclusions XIII-3, p. 113 (Ireland), p. 114 (Malta), p.274 (Portugal).
158. The case of Great Britain: Conclusions XIII-1, p. 141; Conclusions XIII-2, p. 275; Conclusions XIII-3, pp. 116-117; Conclusions XIV-1, p.801; of Malta: Conclusions XV-1, p. 405.
159. The case of the United Kingdom: Conclusions XIII-1, p.141;Conclusions XIV-1, p.801; Conclusions XIII-2, p.273 (Belgium); Conclusions XIII-3, p. 274 (Finland).
160. Conclusions II, p. 25; Addendum to Conclusions XI-2; Conclusions XIII-3, p.113.

establishments to their employers conform with the requirements towards consultations as construed by the provisions of 6 § 1.[161]

The scope of the matters subject to joint consultations covers all issues of interest to stakeholders: work efficiency, work safety and hygiene, conditions of employment, working hours, vocational training, any matters in connection with organization of work and management of establishments and social security of workers.[162] The above specification of the matters indicated for joint consultation of stakeholders is presented by way of example. As stakeholders enjoy equal status during their joint consultations, the consultations should be conducted on any economic, professional and social matters within the scope of their mutual interests.

Joint consultations should be conducted at all levels: national, regional and in-house level. In smaller countries, the Committee did not require stakeholders to conduct consultations at a regional level.[163] However it heightened the importance of such consultations within the workplace,[164] both in the public and private sectors. In such cases, the obligation to conduct joint consultations is deemed fulfilled when representatives of workers employed on the basis other than employment contracts have the right to express their opinion at the stage preceding the issuance of regulations governing any formal work relations and in the process of application of these regulations by employers.[165] Any work relations initiated on the basis of employment contracts in offices and other public sector workplaces are governed by the same rules that are applicable to private enterprises. Because of the specifics of joint consultations in public sector workplaces, the Committee requested that Member States provided it with information on the techniques used in the consulting process used by stakeholders in state offices and other public sector workplaces.[166] Consultations should be conducted in all sectors, including agricultural sectors[167] and should involve all workers. In the case of Article 6 § 1, the principle of 'the great majority' is introduced by the provisions of Article 33 § 1 ESC and Article I § 2 RESC. The self-employed have been excluded from the scope of obligations to promote joint consultations.

161. Conclusions XVII-1, vol.2, p.286 (Malta).
162. Conclusions I, pp. 34–35; Conclusions IV, p. 43; Conclusions V, p. 42; Conclusions VII, pp.35–36; Addendum to Conclusions XI-2, pp.22–23 (Ireland).
163. The case of Malta: Conclusions XIII-2, p. 274; Conclusions XIV-1, p. 528.
164. Consultation XII-2, p.104 (Malta); Consultation XIII-3, p. 274 (Finland); Conclusions XIV-1, vol.1, p.153 (Cyprus), p.179 (Denmark); Conclusions 2002, p.132 (Romania).
165. Conclusions III, p.33 (Germany).
166. Conclusions V, p.42 (France); Conclusions XI-2, p. 77 (Spain); Conclusions XIII-3, p.114 (Malta); Conclusions XIII-3, p.275 (Portugal); Conclusions XIII-5, p.59 (Finland); Conclusions XIV-1, vol. 1, s.418 (Ireland); Conclusions XV-1, vol.2, p.635 (United Kingdom); Conclusions XVII-1, vol.2, p. 355 (Aruba).
167. Conclusions II, p. 25 (Ireland); Conclusions 2004, vol.1, p. 144 (Estonia).

7.2.3. Collective Labour Agreements (Article 6 § 2)

Article 6 § 2 is a voluntary standard, with respect to collective bargaining and collective labour agreements.[168] It not only imposes on Member States the obligation of accepting negotiations of stakeholders in collective labour agreements, but also obliges the states to actively promote negotiations of employment, remuneration conditions and entering into collective labour agreements.[169] Therefore, the obligation stipulated in Article 6 § 2 is composed of two sections. The second section of the obligation, i.e. an active promotion of negotiation of collective labour agreements, applies when stakeholders do not make an independent and spontaneous agreement as to the negotiation techniques applicable when entering into collective labour agreements.[170] Member States are obliged to provide detailed information on the procedures applied in the process of negotiating collective labour agreements as well as on their effects, on the number of finalized collective labour agreements, on the number of workers covered by collective labour agreements and on the number and type of organizations authorized to represent interest of workers and employers when negotiating collective labour agreements.[171] Supervising Member States' conformity with the provisions of Article 6 § 2, the Committee made conclusive remarks in certain cases, where these states intervened, in a manner that restricted the freedom to negotiate collective labour agreements enjoyed by stakeholders. The right to negotiate conditions of employment and salaries and the freedom to enter into collective labour agreements is inherent in the freedom to associate enjoyed by workers. For this reason, any of the abovementioned cases involving violations of the freedom to form trade unions, guaranteed by the provisions of Article 5, are deemed to conflict with the provisions of Article 6 § 2. Issuing a judgement on the non-compliance of national regulations with the provisions of Article 5 is equal to the non-compliance with the provisions of Article 6 § 2. It is worth remembering the judgment of non-compliance of requirements to issue permissions to bargain collectively and to enter into collective labour agreements with the provisions of Article 5.[172] Similarly, the Committee automatically concluded that any requirements related to candidates or workers (the 'closed shop' clauses) that violate the freedom to associate in trade unions arising from legal regulations or provisions of collective labour agreements were in breach of Article 6.2.[173] Some writers question the grounds for the abovementioned interpretation of the provisions of Article 5 and 6 § 2.[174] The closed shop clause, which is in conflict

168. The judgement of the European Court of Human Rights on Swedish Engine Drivers Union, 20 Eur. Ct.H.R. (ser A) (1976).
169. Conclusions I, p.35.
170. *Ibid.*
171. *Ibid.*; Conclusions III, p. 34 (Austria, Cyprus, Denmark); Conclusions XIV-1, vol.1, p. 384 (Iceland); Conclusions XV-1, p.146.
172. Conclusions III, s.35 (Ireland); Conclusions XIV-1, p. 179 (Denmark), p.419 (Ireland), p. 530 (Malta).
173. Conclusions XIV-1, p. 257 (France); Conclusions 2004, vol.1, pp. 264–265 (Ireland).
174. D. Harris, J.Darcy, *op. cit.*, p.102.

with Article 5, does not constitute an automatic breach of the provision of Article 6 § 2 if trade unions, associating all workers employed in a workplace in accordance with the principle of common obligation, enjoy the freedom to negotiate conditions of employment, remuneration and entering into collective labour agreements. However, the situation differs when trade unions enjoy the right to negotiate collective labour agreements for only some workers employed by a given employer, but exclude others. The case of Denmark, which prohibited citizens of other Member States (except for the citizens of the members of the European Economic Area), employed in sea navigation from accessing trade unions and prohibited trade unions from negotiating conditions of work and pay for the workers, reflects a direct relationship between the freedom to associate in trade unions and the freedom to negotiate collective labour agreements. The conclusion that Denmark breached the provisions of Article 5 automatically justifies the Committee's conclusion on the non-compliance of national labour law regulations with Article 6 § 2.[175] However, the Committee has a very decisive and consistent view on a bilateral dependency between the freedom of association in trade unions and the freedom to negotiate collective labour agreements. In the Committee's opinion, any breach of the provisions of Article 5 may automatically serve as the basis for issuing a judgement on non-compliance of a Member State with the standards established in Article 6 § 2.[176]

Member States are obliged to promote, whenever required and appropriate, negotiations between stakeholders on collective labour agreements. Article 6 § 2 empowers Member States to assess the need for negotiating collective labour agreements. Workers' conditions of employment may be regulated in a manner other than through collective labour agreements. The Committee assesses whether any departures from the principle of entering into collective labour agreements are justified. Undoubtedly, conditions of employment offered to the workers employed by the private sector should be negotiated by stakeholders and introduced in collective labour agreements they enter into. A prohibition to negotiate collective labour agreements,[177] regulating more favourable conditions of employment and pay on an individual basis for workers, who refuse to be represented by trade unions negotiating collective labour agreements on behalf of their employer, is considered to violate the standards of Article 6 § 2.[178] The Committee holds that any restriction of the freedom to negotiate collective labour

175. Conclusions XI-1, p. 72.

176. The case of Denmark: Conclusions XIII-1, pp.142–143; Conclusions XIII-3, p.118; The case of Malta: Conclusions XIII-1, pp.142-143; Conclusions XIII-3, p.118; The case of the Great Britain: Conclusions VI, p.36; Conclusions XIII-1, p.145; Conclusions XIII-2, p. 277.

177. Conclusions XII-1, p.120–121; Conclusions XIV-1, vol.1, p.384–385.

178. Conclusions XIII-3, pp.127–129; Conclusions XVII-1, vol.2, p.516 (Great Britain). The Committee referred to the judgement of the European Count of Human Rights of 2nd July 2002, the case: *Wilson and the National Union of Journalists, Palmer, Wyeth and the NURMTW, Doolan and others v. United Kingdom*. In the judgment, the Court adjudicated that permitting an employer to use the means of financial motivation in relation to employees in exchange for their resignation from representation of their interests during negotiations of collective labour agreements is in conflict with Article 11 of the European Convention on Human Rights Protection.

agreements by the organizations representing workers employed by private employers is not in compliance with the provisions of Article 6 § 2. Some exceptions from the aforementioned rule may be introduced on the basis of Article 31.[179] The Committee concluded that Member States had the right to impose certain restrictions on the right to negotiate collective labour agreements by stakeholders, in particular in matters connected with pay rises, especially in grave economic circumstances.[180]

However, the abovementioned restriction of the freedom to negotiate in collective labour agreements may be imposed by a Member State authority after in-depth consultations with all interested entities, trade unions and employers in particular. The reasons for imposing the abovementioned restrictions should be presented to stakeholders and should be of an extraordinary nature. Member States do not have the right to increase remuneration limits for workers who are covered under collective labour agreements.[181] Member States should convince stakeholders that because of exceptional circumstances, restricting the freedom to negotiate in social agreements is necessary to rectify the situation.[182] The restrictions may be imposed for a precisely determined period, required for the re-establishment of regular conditions, where collective labour agreements serve as the basis for regulating work and pay conditions of workers.[183] In the case of the Netherlands, where the authorities restricted the freedom to negotiate collective agreements for a period of 6 months, the Committee concluded that the Netherlands complied with the above regulation, conditional upon the taking of appropriate steps towards ensuring workers an appropriate standard of living.[184] However, in its conclusion on Ireland, where the authorities limited the pay of workers employed in navigation of ferries by 10 per cent as a result of a strike announced in 1993, the Committee established that Ireland did not comply with the Charter through the intervention in the freedom to negotiate collective labour agreements[185] and in the same decision, it concluded that the decision of the state authorities suspending the freedom to negotiate collective labour agreements and the freedom to set wages by the state authorities equipped with appropriate legislative powers, falls into the margin of the power enjoyed by the states, authorized to make decisions on the basis of Article 31 § 1 ESC and Article I § 2 RESC introducing restrictions in the enjoyment of the rights ensured by the Charter aimed at protecting the rights and freedom of other persons and the public order.[186] The Committee issued negative conclusions in the case of Denmark, where, acting in accordance with special regulations issued solely for the purpose of ending collective labour disputes in 1985 and 1987, the government extended the validity period of collective labour agreements.

179. Conclusions X-1, p.72; Conclusions XII-1, p.123.
180. General Introduction to Conclusions VIII, p. 11; Conclusions IX-1, p. 53; Conclusions XIV-1, vol.2, pp. 734–735.
181. Conclusions VIII, p.11.
182. Conclusions IX-1, p.53.
183. Conclusions X-1, p. 72; Conclusions XII-1, p. 123.
184. Conclusions XII-1, p. 122-123.
185. Conclusions XIV-1, pp. 385 and following
186. Conclusions XV-1, vol.1, p. 333.

The Committee concluded that the abovementioned interventions prevented stakeholders from freely negotiating in collective labour agreements and a breach of the provisions of Article 6 § 2 was established.[187]

The prohibition of any interference with the freedom to negotiate in collective labour agreements in the private sector also applies to the generalization of collective agreements. This term is commonly used in collective labour law for the act of extending a collective labour agreement to employers who are not covered by the agreement, by the bodies of a Member State competent in labour law matters. Reading the report presented by the Netherlands, the Committee concluded that the generalization of a collective labour agreement by virtue of an administrative decision of a competent minister (of social affairs) represented the unlawful intervention of Member States in the freedom to negotiate collective labour agreements violating Article 6 § 2.[188] The report presented by the Netherlands in the subsequent supervisory cycle informed that a employer, who enters into a collective labour agreement has the right to request for his exclusion from the obligation to follow the provisions of a sectoral or nationwide collective labour agreement, where the validity and effectiveness of the agreement has been extended by virtue of a regulation issued by a competent minister of labour. The Committee concluded that the abovementioned case did not constitute a breach of the freedom to negotiate collective labour agreements established on Article 6 § 2.[189]

The Netherlands do not respect the division of trade unions into representative trade unions, i.e. trade unions empowered to negotiate collective labour agreements and other trade unions, not empowered to enter into collective agreements. As collective labour agreements have not been given any specific legal priority, they do not occupy any position in the hierarchy of labour law sources negotiated by stakeholders. Therefore, no dependency exists between in-house and in sector or in national collective labour agreements. Execution of a collective agreement by an employer justifies an application for excluding such employer from the obligation to abide by the provisions of other (sectoral or national) collective labour agreements.

The Committee adopted the conclusion by the majority of votes (10:3). Three members of the Committee dissented.[190] They stressed that the obligation to promote a mechanism for voluntary negotiations formulated in Article 6 § 2 could not be limited to the state's acceptance of a spontaneous process of negotiating collective labour agreements by stakeholders, but signified the obligation to create a harmonious system for entering into collective labour agreements. This signifies that, if stakeholders fail to reach a normative agreement – a collective labour agreement, Member States have the right to oblige the stakeholders to observe the collective labour agreement indicated by the state. The Member State should build a system of collective labour agreements at all levels, including the national, regional and in-house level. Collective labour agreements executed at a lower level should correspond to the agreements executed on

187. Conclusions X-1, p. 72; Conclusions XII-1, p. 118.
188. Conclusions XVI-1, vol.2, p. 444.
189. Conclusions XVII-1, vol.2, p. 317.
190. J-M. Belorgey, N. Aliprantis i P.Koncar. *As above*, pp. 343–344.

higher levels. In accordance with the hierarchy of sources of negotiable labour law, the criteria for determining the validity of collective labour agreements, whose rank is lower in the same hierarchy, is their conformity with collective agreements ranking higher in the hierarchy. In the opinion of the authors of the *votum separatum*, the dissenting opinion, a departure from the abovementioned rule, is justified by extending the validity of a sectoral or national collective labour agreement to the partners obliged to observe in an in-house agreement only. There are no legal grounds justifying acceptance of this concept. Article 6 § 2 obliges Member States to promote techniques for voluntary negotiations between stakeholders. However, in accordance with the provisions, Member States are not obliged to create a hierarchic structure of collective labour agreements. When an in-house collective labour agreement executed on a voluntary basis collides with the empowerment of a competent state authority to extend the validity and effectiveness of a sectoral or national collective labour agreement, priority should be given to the principle of voluntary negotiation of collective labour agreement by the entities interested (representatives of workers and competent employer) in entering into such agreement.

Another example of the collision of a national regulation with the standards introduced by virtue of Article 6 § 2, was presented in the justification of the Committee's conclusion on Poland,[191] where the principle was introduced by Article 2417 § 1 of the Labour Code. The Constitutional Tribunal of the Republic of Poland decided that the Polish Constitution violated this principle, as well as Article 6 § 2 and the convention No. 98 ILO. In accordance with the principle, after a collective labour agreement expires, its terms would be automatically renewed until the stakeholders entered into a new collective labour agreement.[192] The automatic extension of the validity of a collective labour agreement that expired with the elapse of the period, for which it was entered, is in conflict with the obligation to promote the mechanisms for voluntary negotiations between employers and employees' organizations imposed on Member States.

On the basis of the clause on promoting 'where necessary and appropriate, the mechanisms for voluntary negotiations', the Committee accepts Member State interventions in negotiations of work conditions and wages by workers employed directly by state administration and state authorities' organizational units. A limitation of the rights of workers' representatives to negotiate in collective labour agreements with employers – state administration and state authorities organizational units – applies solely to workers who are not employed on work contracts. Theories vary within Member States, about work relations that are entered into directly with the state administration and state authorities organizational units. The Committee did not analyse the grounds for entering into formal work relations. However, it stressed the inequity of the parties entering into such relation. Subordination of a clerk to his employer – an organizational unit of the state administration and state authorities – justifies the independent regulation of employment conditions and wages by the employer.

191. Conclusions XVII-1, vol.2, p. 380.
192. Judgement of the Constitutional Tribunal of 18.11.2002 (The Journal of Laws of 196, item 1660).

In formal work relations, the rule preventing representatives of civil servants from negotiating collective labour agreements with their employer is generally accepted.

However, the Committee does emphasize that, in the case of civil servants, Member States must guarantee the participation of representatives of civil servants in the process of creating the regulations issued by employers in order to determine their employment conditions.[193]. This obligation of consultation in conditions of employment and wages with workers' representatives is also applicable to police officers.[194]

The Committee is not satisfied with the information presented in the national reports showing that police trade unions have the right to express their opinions on acts of law determining conditions of employment and wages, and instead demands the presentation of evidentiary data of the influence of policy trade organizations on the content of regulations issued by a state authorized to regulate the conditions of employment and wages for the police.[195]

For workers employed in the public sector who are not employed directly by state authorities and administrative units, the Committee has adopted an indirect position. It arrived at the conclusion that the situation of these workers is rather specific. Whilst their remuneration is financed from the state budget, their traditional level of wages in the sector reflects the level of wages received by workers in the private sector. In the conclusions issued for the report presented by the Netherlands, the Committee presented the trends prevailing in wage policy in the sector by using the phrase 'trend follower sector'.[196] As the funds which finance the wages of workers in this sector remain at the disposal of the state, the Netherlands decided to authorize the administrative bodies authorized to set or raise wage limits for stakeholders negotiating collective labour agreements. The Committee concluded that the problem of negotiating collective labour agreements in this sector should be solved by way of consultation and negotiations conducted by the interested parties: stakeholders and state authority agencies.[197] It signifies that stakeholders negotiating collective labour agreements should consult agencies of Member States. In such cases, the process of negotiating in collective labour agreement is very complex. For example, the Committee seems to approve a case when a competent labour minister is authorized to raise wage limits negotiable in collective labour agreements executed by stakeholders on the condition of broad consultations with the organization representing workers' interests, are carried out prior to issuing a decision binding the negotiating parties.[198] Collective labour agreements executed on such grounds may be described as 'trilateral' in opposition to 'bilateral' normative agreements. Use of such terms is justified when specific

193. Conclusions III, s.34 (Germany); Conclusions IV, p .45 (Austria); Conclusions X-2, p 73 (Spain); Conclusions XIV-1, s.299 (Germany); Addendum to Conclusions XV-1, s.155-156 (Poland).
194. Complaint No.11/2000, Council of Europe of Police Trade Unions against Portugal. Conclusion of the Committee of 21st May 2002, the Resolution of the Ministers' Council of 17 July 2002, ResChS (2002) 5. European Social Charter, Collected texts (5th edition), Strasbourg 2005, pp. 512–513.
195. Conclusions XVII-1, vol.2, p. 381 (Poland).
196. Conclusions IX, p. 53.
197. Conclusions IX-1, p. 54.
198. Conclusions X-1, p. 73.

Member States are involved in the process of negotiating collective labour agreements.[199]

The obligation to promote negotiations of collective labour agreements does not apply to the self-employed.

7.2.4. Mediation and Arbitration (Article 6 § 3)

Member States are obliged to promote the establishment and use of appropriate techniques for the out of court settlement of collective labour disputes. In Article 6 § 3 such techniques have been labelled as 'conciliatory', naming 'voluntary arbitration' as an example. The Committee believes that these techniques can be introduced into the legal systems of Member States and applied, subsequently, when utilizing a law introduced by the Member State, and in normative decisions and collective labour agreements executed by stakeholders, or in practice.[200]

Member States are obliged to promote peaceful methods of settling collective labour disputes. Therefore, if the procedure for settling collective labour disputes is regulated independently and spontaneously by stakeholders, there is no valid legal ground for the Member States to intervene in such matters.[201] The Committee requires that the mechanism for the peaceful settlement of collective labour disputes introduced to domestic legislative systems and practice provides the freedom of judgement for stakeholders, in disputable cases, and to the chosen persons or institutions.

Conciliatory techniques for settling such labour disputes should be independent from both stakeholders and from the agencies of state administration. In particular, the above applies to social arbitrage, which should be organized in a manner which prevents a Member State from influencing the outcomes of the arbitration decisions. For this reason, the Committee believes that domestic regulations governing collective labour law should not provide any instructions, indicate any guidelines or suggest any criteria to be followed by the arbitration commission or an arbitrator when handing down a judgment.[202] Moreover, peaceful techniques of settling collective labour disputes should not be replaced by labour court proceedings.

The above argument is illustrated by the case of Slovenia. Slovenian law allows courts to appoint an arbitrator or a higher arbitrator when parties to a collective labour dispute or one of the parties refuses in indicating the arbitrator or is delayed in fulfilling the above obligation, which it has voluntarily accepted.[203] It is equivalent to a violation

199. Conclusions 2004, vol.1, pp. 145–146 (Estonia).

200. Conclusions I, p.37. The Committee concluded that France lacks the regulations governing conflict-free mechanisms for the settlement of collective labour disputes in local government institutions. In practice, employers – local government administration agencies – were appointing mediators to recognize collective labour agreements, the Committee refused to issue a conclusion on non-compliance with the standards set in Article 6 § 3 of the Charter on the part of the French authorities. Conclusions XV-1, vol. 1, pp. 253–254.

201. *Ibid.*

202. Conclusions XIV-1, vol.1, p. 388.

203. Conclusions 2002, p. 186.

of Article 6 § 3, when one of the authorizing parties of the collective disputes (chiefly the employer) takes the dispute to court.[204] In addition, national collective labour law regulations provide no legal grounds for authorizing the party to choose the bodies authorized to try collective labour disputes: arbitration or court proceedings.[205]

Article 6 § 3 has been included in the regulations aimed at inspiring stakeholders by Member States to enter into collective labour agreements. The Committee primarily believes that collective disputes should have been settled by peaceful methods such as conciliation proceedings and social arbitration during the application of collective labour agreements.[206] Contrary to individual disputes, which arise from the application of individual provisions of labour law, collective labour disputes are disputes which relate to interests rather than rights. Depending on the subject matter, disputes arising from the interpretation of provisions of collective labour agreements should be classified as collective or individual disputes. Collective disputes arising from the interpretation of such provisions of collective labour agreements, which create obligations, are tried in accordance with the legal mechanisms regulated by the collective labour agreement. Therefore, the obligation to support peaceful mechanisms to settle disputes, which may arise between stakeholders in the process of negotiating or in the process of entering into collective labour agreements, is broader and it includes the obligation of peaceful settlement of collective disputes irrespective whether stakeholders negotiate a collective labour agreement or attempt to amend its provisions. Only a so-called 'social peace clause', as described below, voluntarily introduced to a collective labour agreement, can prevent trade unions from requesting that the employer offered different conditions of work and wages, that are more favourable than those regulated by the effective collective labour agreement, to the workers represented by a given trade union. In such collective labour relations, stakeholders may be bound by the provisions of a collective labour agreement or such an agreement which is not in force or is not accepted by a trade union. Any disputes about interests, i.e. about granting more favourable rights to workers and duties to employers with respect to wages and work conditions are, in essence, collective labour disputes. The Committee departed from the view that Article 6 § 3 could only apply to conciliatory proceedings and social arbitration directly related to a collective labour agreement, in that it solely is applied to collective disputes that may arise in the process of negotiating collective labour agreements by stakeholders[207] and concluded that, on the basis of Article 6 § 3, Member States are obliged to promote legal mechanisms for the peaceful settlement of all collective labour disputes.[208] The previous restrictive interpretation of Article 6 § 3 was based on the statement forming a part of the introduction to Article 6. Initially, the Committee believed that Member States were obliged to promote the development and undertaking of appropriate mechanisms of conciliation and voluntary arbitration for

204. Conclusions 2004, vol.2, p. 515 (Slovenia).
205. Conclusions 2004, vol.2, p. 346–347 (Lithuania).
206. Conclusions V, p. 45.
207. Conclusions V, p. 46 (Italy).
208. Conclusions XIV-1, p. 616 (Norway).

settling collective disputes 'with a view to exercise the right to collective negotiations effectively'. As late as during the 14th supervisory cycle that the Committee changed its view and concluded that, on the basis of Article 6 § 3, peaceful methods of settling collective labour disputes were commonly applied.

Common employment of peaceful techniques in the process of solving collective labour disputes should be the goal of all deliberations. Conciliation proceedings and social arbitration should be introduced by Member States with a view to settling collective labour disputes of workers in the public sector.[209] During a number of supervisory cycles, the Committee made negative conclusions concerning Malta, due to an absence of the peaceful techniques required for the settlement of collective labour disputes in the public service sector.[210] The situation changed during the 15th supervisory cycle. In the report on the application of the provisions of Article 6 § 3, Malta included some information on the introduction of conciliation techniques in the public sector. To examine the abovementioned amendments of domestic regulations of the collective labour law, the Committee postponed its conclusion on the observance of Article 6 § 3 by Malta.[211]

Two examinations of the new peaceful settlement system of collective disputes of the public sector workers in Malta did not bring about any amendment of the conclusions on non-compliance of national collective labour regulations with the international standards regarding the settlement of collective labour disputes. Conciliation proceedings are conducted by a committee set up on the basis of the principle of parity (four members representing employers – the authorities and their bodies/agencies and four members representing the trade unions representing the largest groups of workers involved in the collective dispute).

A collective labour dispute is settled by a unanimous decision of the conciliation commission. In the absence of unanimity, the chairman of the commission is required to refer the case within two months to the industrial tribunal for settlement. Before determining the compliance or non-compliance of the domestic regulations with the provisions of Article 6 § 3, the Committee requested some additional information on the subject of the competences of the conciliation commission to be provided by Malta.[212] It did not pay much heed to it, as decisions handed down by the industrial tribunal have an implicating nature for all parties involve in a collective labour dispute. The Committee is against the principle of voluntary social arbitration.

The Committee's conclusions on the mandatory arbitration with its decisions binding both parties to a collective labour dispute established by Member States are stabilized. Any introduction of mandatory arbitration procedure without the consent of

---

209. Conclusions V, p. 46 (France); Conclusions VIII, pp. 92–93 (Denmark), p. 93 (Iceland).
210. Conclusions XII02, pp. 110–111; Conclusions XIII-2, pp. 279-280; Conclusions XIII-3, p. 132; Conclusions XIV-1, p. 530. Due to the absence of procedures for peaceful settlement of collective disputes of public sector workers in Bulgaria, the Committee concluded on non-compliance of collective labour law regulations with Article 6 § 3 of the Charter. Conclusions 2004, vol.1, p. 42.
211. Conclusions XV-1, p. 407.
212. Conclusions XVII-1, vol. 2, p. 289

the interested parties cannot be considered as complying with the provisions of Article 6 § 3, unless it is limited to the exceptional cases specified in Article 31 § 1 ESC or Article G § 1 RESC.[213] The Committee obligates Member States to indicate the extent to which the obligation of observing the arbitration procedure is required for the protection of rights and freedoms of other persons or for the protection of the public order, national security, public health or good practice. A reference to the 'humanitarian interest' as the basis for submitting a petition for trying a collective dispute by social arbitration after 20 days of a strike have elapsed[214] served as the basis for postponing its conclusion and demanding a presentation of some additional information on possible threats to legal and public order, health or good practice, which could, for example, justify the apparent breach of international standards, from Romania.[215]

The case of Norway, which, on several occasions, took advantage of the regulation permitting reference of a collective labour dispute to arbitration for settlement in order to prevent trade unions from conducing a strike of workers employed on the North Sea oil rigs, prompted the Committee of Ministers towards adopting a resolution on non-compliance of the actions taken by the Norwegian government with the international standards for the reasons of exceeding the authorizations formulated in Article 31 § 1 ESC and a breach of Article 6 § 3 and 4.[216]

In accordance with the existing conclusions, the Committee examined the practice of appropriating domestic labour law regulations. In the case of Portugal, for example, the Committee concluded a compliance of its domestic labour law regulations with Article 6 § 3 regardless of the obligation of arbitration imposed by regulations applicable in that country. However, the Committee established that the abovementioned regulations are non-enforceable. The state authorities failed to prepare a list of arbitrators that should be agreed upon by stakeholders. [217]

7.2.5. Right of Workers and Employers to Collective Action (Article 6 § 4)

Article 6 § 4 guarantees all stakeholders the right take part in collective actions in the case of a labour dispute.[218] This provision ensures that both parties to the labour dispute (both workers and employers) are granted the right to take part in collective action.

---

213. Conclusions XII-2, p.110 (Malta); Conclusions XIII-1, p. 152 (Norway); Conclusions XIII-3, p. 133 (Norway); Conclusions XIII-3, p.278 (Portugal); Conclusions XIV-1, vol. 1, p. 387 (Iceland); Conclusions XIV-1, vol.2, p. 616–617 (Norway); Conclusions XV-1, vol.1, p. 44-46 (Austria); Conclusions XV-1, vol.2, p. 430 (Norway).
214. The case of Romania. Conclusions 2002, p. 134.
215. Conclusions 2004, vol.2, p. 458–459.
216. RChS (93)2. Zob. The right to organize ..., *op. cit.*, p. 61; L. Samuel, *op. cit.*, p. 149.
217. Conclusions XVII-1, vol.2, p. 418.
218. *See* T. Novitz, International and European Protection of the Right to Strike, Oxford Monographs on Labour Law, Oxford University Press, Oxford 2003, pp. 125 and following, p.211 and following; A.M.Świątkowski, European Social Charter: The right to strike, Managerial Law, vol. 47, No.6, 2005, p. 285 and following.

It was not mentioned explicitly what type of collective action is permitted to be taken by all sides to the collective labour relations. However, in the case of the workers, it was specified they had the right to all types of collective action, including the right to strike. The general regulation of stakeholders' rights to participate in collective action when there are cases of conflict of interests constituted the legal basis for the European Committee of Social Rights to extend its scope of protection of social rights in cases of collective labour disputes. The Committee's rulings concerned the idea of collective action, the definition of a legal strike, the legal restrictions concerned in the utilization of the right to organize strikes, the procedural requirements required to carry out and pursue legal collective action and the legal consequences of collective action for workers. The Committee also undertook the steps for the legality of collective action taken up by employers.

7.2.5.1. Collective Action

Article 6 § 4 does not indicate any specific collective actions that may be undertaken by the workers in order to protect their interests, except for the right to strike. The Committee did not analyse nor discuss those collective actions, which can be organized based on Article 6 § 4. Instead, the Committee was only interested to learn about the types of collective action that are considered legal by the domestic collective labour regulations of a given country.[219] It demanded to know from certain Member States why domestic collective labour laws prohibited certain categories of workers, such as state officials, from partaking in a particular collective action, permitting them only the right to strike.[220]

Since the first supervisory cycle, the Committee has taken the view that Article 6 § 4 ensured stakeholders the right to carry out collective action. This provision states *expressis verbis* the right to strike, which workers may utilize in the case of a conflict of interest. Although the provision in question did not clearly state that in the case of conflict of interest, have the right to carry out collective action, and the Committee pointed out that the lockout was the basic if not the only mean of protecting the employers' interests against the excessive demands made by the trade unions representing the workers.[221] It is somewhat difficult to determine whether Article 6 § 4 ensures stakeholders the right to exert pressure on the other party or parties to the collective labour relation, in order to regulate the work conditions and the wages for the workers, who are represented in such collective labour relations by union organizations, meeting the demands of the trade unions. The rulings of the European Committee of Social Rights, primarily deal with strikes organized by the workers. It should be assumed that the international collective labour law standards of the Council of Europe,

219. Conclusions XV-1, vol.1, p.81 (Belgium), p.121 (Cyprus).
220. Conclusions XIV-1, vol.1, p.21; Conclusions XV-1, vol.1, p.202; Conclusions XV-1, vol.2, p. 477 (Portugal), p. 520 (Spain).
221. Conclusions I, pp. 38–39.

do not respect the rule of equality when it comes to exerting pressure, which may be executed by stakeholders engaged in collective labour disputes.

A necessary requirement in carrying out a collective action in a collective labour relation is the conflict of interest between stakeholders. In accordance with generally binding labour laws, the Committee believes that the right to organize collective labour actions cannot exist in cases where there is a difference of opinion amongst stakeholders with regards to the interpretations and practices of applying the binding labour law regulations or provisions of collective agreements. According to the Committee, this point of view continues to hold weight even if stakeholders were to unanimously introduce into their collective agreements, provisions allowing for discrepancy of opinion to form a necessary requirement justifying the organization and for the carrying out collective action.[222]

7.2.5.2. A Legal Strike

Article 6 § 4 does not classify strikes into legal and illegal categories. It only regulates the workers' right to undertake legal collective action, including the right to strike. It therefore provides the grounds for such classifications. In accordance with the understanding of the provision, a legal strike is one that falls into the scope of an analysed standard. A strike is a collective action organized by workers in order to exert pressure on the employer who regulates the conditions of work and the wages. The aim, therefore, of a strike is to create more favourable conditions of employments and better wages. Strikes may be organized by workers in order to protect the workers' interests against the actions of the employer. Strikes and other forms of collective action cannot be organized if their aim is to protect the interests of workers who are employed by other employers, or to protect the rights of customers or consumers.[223] A conflict of interest between workers and the employer is therefore a requirement in order for a legal strike to be able to be organized.[224]

The provisions of Article 6 § 4 and Article 5 are closely interrelated. Collective action and strikes may be organized to meet the same goals, protecting both economic and social interests. In order to achieve such goals, workers may join trade union organizations. The Charter does not protect the other interests of workers that are unrelated to their economic and social interests. Strikes induced by politics, for example, do not enjoy legal protection since Article 6 is a norm, which ensures effective regulations for collective negotiations between stakeholders, whilst political issues cannot be negotiated through a collective agreement.[225]

Workers organize in trade unions, negotiate with employers and carry out collective action to ensure their economic and professional interests are protected. On this basis, the legal protection ensured by Article 6 § 4 does not protect strikes

222. Conclusions I, p. 38.
223. *Ibid.*
224. Conclusions XV-1, vol. 2, pp. 637–641 (Great Britain).
225. Conclusions II, p. 27.

when they are organized to support the interests of other groups of workers. The Committee of Social Rights has not taken a stand regarding to the legality of solidarity strikes organized by one trade union in support of another union, which demand to be recognized by the Member States and employer organizations. By referring to the jurisdiction of the ILO Trade Union Freedom Committee (Rights Committee), which does not ensure protection for solidarity strikes organized to support the demands made by other trade unions attempting to gain recognition, the European Committee of Social Rights inferred that strikes aimed at protecting interests of the union, which is responsible for organizing the strike, enjoy the legal protection guaranteed by Article 6 § 4.[226]

Workers are entitled to organize strikes with the goal of protecting their economic, social and union related interests. Such interests do not have to be directly related to the negotiations aimed at entering into a collective agreement.[227] The boundary of the Committee's jurisdiction in matters of legality concerning strikes organized and not in direct connection with the entering into collective agreements, has not changed since the initial supervisory cycles monitoring the compliance by Member States. The Committee has handed down decisions concerning the failure of some domestic collective labour regulations meeting the requirements of Article 6 § 4. It was of the view that some Member States considered the organization of a strike, which did not exert pressure on employers in connection with the negotiating of collective agreements to be illegal.[228]

This was viewed by the Committee as a violation of Article 6 § 4. The Committee claims that domestic collective labour regulations, which forbid workers from organizing strikes which are unrelated to the negotiations of collective agreements neglect the reality that stakeholders also negotiate in order to enter into other normative agreements. According to the Committee, any negotiations aimed at regulating any issues that may evoke the interest of stakeholders, should be treated as collective negotiations, as understood by the provision of Article 6 § 4. This is true irrespective of whether such negotiations are supported by domestic collective labour regulations .[229] An example of a legal strike is an action organized by workers in order to exert pressure on the employer to comply with the health and safety regulation requirements and the protection of the health of the workers.[230]

Legal strikes can be organized by all workers irrespective of their membership in trade unions. Granting a monopoly according to the domestic collective labour law regulations, to a trade union organization for organizing collective actions, is a breach

226. Conclusions XVII-1, vol. 2, p. 290 (Malta).
227. Conclusions II, p.28; Conclusions III, p.96; Conclusions XII-1, p.129.
228. Case of Germany: Conclusions XIII-2, p.282; Conclusions XIV-1, vol.1, p.310; Addendum to Conclusions XIV-1, pp.27-28; Conclusions XVII-1, vol.1, p. 206; Case of Iceland: Conclusions XIII-3, p. 135; Conclusions XIV-1, p.390; Conclusions XV-1, p.335. Case of Finland: Conclusions XV-1, vol.1, p.203; Conclusions XVII-1, vol.1, p.170; Conclusions XV-1, vol.1, p. 153 (Denmark); Conclusions XVII-1, vol.1, p.103 (Czech Republic).
229. Conclusions IV, p. 50.
230. Conclusions II, p. 28.

of the international labour law standards established by the European Committee of Social Rights. The Committee opined that it is in the best interest of both workers and employers to negotiate the work conditions and wages through collective labour agreements and other such normative agreements. Both sides also have the right to exert pressure on the other party in collective agreements. Irrespective of trade union membership, workers have the right to organize and partake in strikes, which are neither supported nor organized by trade unions. The Committee views the right to strike as a guarantee of an effective of collective negotiations by workers.[231]

The Committee's judgments with regards to the opportunity to exercise the right to organize strikes, are not uniform. Firstly, the Committee ruled domestic collective labour law regulations, which would allow for the right to organize a legal strike dependent on the decisions of either the trade unions or other organizations representing the workers' interests in the workplace where the majority were not represented by trade unions, were in compliance with Article 6 § 4.[232]

However the Committee soon changed its position, and all subsequent cases where such domestic collective labour regulations within Member States legalized strikes only on the premise that they would be organized by trade unions, were seen as a non-compliance of domestic laws with international standards.[233] The Committee's position was that a group of workers, who had no legal status, had a right to organize a legal strike.[234] The Committee soon adopted a differing position with regards to this issue. Whist assessing the reports presented by Sweden and Finland, states where collective labour law regulations legitimize a strike on the basis that the strike is organized or approved by a trade union (if the strike is organized by workers who are not members of trade union, the strike has to be carried out under the care of trade union patrons), the Committee concluded that domestic collective labour law regulations did not create a particular hindrance for workers to form trade union organization. Therefore, in those Member States that have long lists of prerequisites and requirements for the establishment of a trade union, the right to organize and participate in a legal strike may depend on the way such collective actions are manoeuvred by trade unions.[235]

If the validity of such collective actions as is a strike, forces workers to be dependant upon the requirements of domestic collective labour when intending to form trade unions in order to be able to organize a strike, the Committee must evaluate the domestic labour law regulations. The Committee's ruling regarding the compliance of Member States with Article 6 § 4, therefore depends upon the conclusions made from the analysing of Article 5. The subject matter of such analysis concerns cases solely

231. Conclusions IV, p.50; Conclusions XV-1, vol.1, p.204.
232. Case of Portugal: Conclusions XIII-3, pp. 280–281; Conclusions XIII-5, pp. 179–180; Conclusions XIV-1, vol.2, p.662.
233. Conclusions XVII-1, vol.2, p. 420 (Portugal); Conclusions 2002, p. 237 (Sweden); Conclusions 2004, vol.2, pp.350-351 (Lithuania).
234. Conclusions XV-1. Citing: The right to organize …, *op. cit.*, p. 65.
235. Conclusions XV-1, vol. 1, p. 204 (Finland); Conclusions XV-1. vol. 2, p. 566 (Sweden).

dealing with the compliance of Member States to the standards established under Article 5.

Among the domestic labour law regulations complying with the international standards based on Article 5, the Committee chooses those which have the least amount of requirements to be fulfilled by workers intending to establish a trade union organization. If domestic labour law regulations do not hinder workers from establishing a trade union with the intention to strike, the Committee believes that granting a trade union a monopoly in supervising over a collective action is in accordance with Article 6 § 4. Domestic regulations that include requirements for the establishment of a trade union that are difficult to fulfil, are seen by the Committee as inconsistent with Article 6 § 4. This is exemplified by a scenario in which a trade union is the only institution allowed to organize a strike.[236] For example, prior to handing down a decision with regards to Portuguese collective labour law regulations, which allow for trade unions only to organize strikes, and the compliance of such laws with Article 6 § 4, the Committee examined legal requirements concerning workers' rights to establish trade unions as well as how those requirements are put into practice. The Committee focused mainly on how long it took to register a trade union.[237] It also analysed whether a minority of workers employed by the one employer and who do not belong to a trade union nor are represented by a trade union organization, can organize a legal strike in order to protect their rights.

Public service employees also have the right to organize legal strikes. Article 6 § 4 does not limit this right. However, by the first supervisory cycle, the Committee decided that domestic labour law regulations which would impose such restrictions, as verified by the reasons stipulated under Article 31 § 1 of the European Social Charter, would not be inconsistent with international standards. The Committee identified the following groups of public servants that may be restricted in organizing strikes: policemen, professional servicemen, the judiciary, high-level public administrators[238], firemen and prison warders.[239] The Committee regarded the exclusion of all public servants from the right to organize strikes as a breach of Article 6 § 4. The protection of rights stated under Article 31 § 1 of the Charter forms the basis for such exclusions on the following bases: protection of rights and liberties, public order, national security, protection of public health and customs. The exemption from the right to organize strikes concerns the category of public servants whose tasks (falling within the scope of administration and authority of the state) are related to the protection of the principles enumerated under Article 31 § 1 of the European Social Charter. The Committee found that Iceland was consistent with Article 6 § 4 in accordance with Article 31 § 1 when they drew up a list of all public sector workers deprived of the right to organize strikes.[240] The Committee demanded however, that the information

236. Addendum to Conclusions XV-1, pp. 28–29 (Germany).
237. Conclusions XV-1, vol. 2, pp. 477–478.
238. Conclusions I, pp. 38-39; Conclusions II, p. 187 (Cyprus); Conclusions III, p. 36.
239. Conclusions V, p. 48 (France); Conclusions XIII-2, p. 282 (Malta).
240. Conclusions XV-1, vol. 1, p. 122.

concerning the criteria, with which this list was dependent upon, should be produced. The Committee became aware that before the list was prepared, the state authorities consulted trade unions and permitted a trade union to appear before a labour court seeking an injunction concerning the addition of a certain category of public servants to the list. The Committee handed down a decision stating the Icelandic labour laws were consistent with international standards.[241]

At first the Committee maintained that Member States having ratified Article 6 § 4 could not effectively make a declaration concerning the exclusion of certain categories of public servants from the scope of the application of the provision in question.[242] The Committee found that a complete exclusion of certain public servants in Germany[243] from having the right to organize strikes, violated Article 6 § 4.[244] After the Netherlands, having ratified Article 6 § 4, objected to the inapplicability of this regulation to public service officials, the Committee concluded (as all Member States accepted the objection) that under Article 20, Member States were entitled to exclude certain categories of public servants from the scope of Article 6 § 4.[245]

On 28 September 1961, Germany declared it would not apply Article 6 § 4 to public officials. The Committee, however, regarded that this declaration had no legal basis.[246] It did, however, change its views after having examined the legal validity of the objections put forth by the Dutch. It came to the conclusion the 1961 declaration could be treated as a reservation for the exclusion of the abovementioned categories of workers (public servants) from the provision of Article 6 § 4.[247] In summary of the argument presented, proving the Committee's tendency to changing its attitude towards the organization of strikes in the public sector, the exclusions and restrictions of rights may:

> Be justified only by the reasons stipulated under Article 31 § 1 of the European Social Charter. The Committee maintains the limitations, which extend beyond the scope of the general clause established under Article 31 § 1 of the European Social Charter is inconsistent with international standards.[248]relate only to some public servants. Barring all public servants from the right to organize symbolic strikes, especially prohibiting the right to public servants who are employed by work agreements in the government sector,[249] and to those employed in privatized public institutions (such as in the postal system or the railways)[250] is a breach of Article 6 § 4.

241. *Ibid.*
242. Conclusions I, pp. 184–185 (Germany).
243. German state officials – *Beamte*. *See* T. Novitz, *op. cit.*, pp. 307 and following.
244. Case of Germany: Conclusions III, p. 336; Conclusions IV, pp. 48–49; Case of Denmark: Conclusions XIV-1, vol. 1, p. 180; Conclusions XV-1, vol. 1, p. 153; Conclusions XVII-1, vol.1, p. 134; Conclusions 2004, vol. 1, p. 149 (Estonia).
245. Conclusions VII, p. 39.
246. Conclusions I, pp. 184–185.
247. Conclusions VII, p. 39.
248. Conclusions 2004, vol. 1, p. 97 (Cyprus).
249. Conclusions 2004, vol. 1, p. 46.
250. Conclusions XVII-1, vol. 1, p. 207 (Germany).

7.2.5.3. Restricting the Right to Strike

The right to strike is not absolute. In the Appendix to Article 6 § 4, Member States were authorized to regulate, to a reasonable extent, the application of the right in question in a way that each further restriction of the law could be justified only by the circumstances stipulated either in Article 31 § 1 ESC or Article G § 1 of the Appendix to ESC. The right to strike may be restricted by: collective agreements, regulations established by Member States and by the judicial decisions of courts.

7.2.5.3.1. Restricting the Right to Strike in Collective Labour Agreements

Pursuant to Article 6 § 4, the restriction to strike imposed by the stakeholders in a collective agreement complies with international standards. Parties to the negotiation of collective agreements have the right to introduce the so- called 'social peace clauses', binding the workers' representatives, signatories of collective agreements, to voluntarily refrain from any collective actions, including strikes, for as long as the collective agreement is in force. The voluntarily incorporated provision in a collective agreement by all parties, excluding or limiting the right to strike, complies with Article 6 § 4.[251] A social peace clause binds only those workers who are represented by a trade union that has signed a particular collective agreement.[252] Workers, members of a trade union bound by a social peace clause – must refrain from collective actions only in matters covered by the collective agreement. The same principle applies to trade unions that are signatories to collective agreements. Trade unions may refrain from carrying out collective actions whilst a collective agreement is in force.[253] In such cases, the Committee attempts to establish whether the signatories to the agreement have introduced the exclusion of the right to strike during the period when a collective agreement is in force, knowingly and voluntarily.

7.2.5.3.2. Restricting the Right to Strike, as Introduced by the Domestic Legislation of Member States

Member States enact regulations on collective bargaining. The legality of a strike is conditional on the fulfilment of certain procedural requirements by the organizers of a strike action that are introduced by the Member States. State intervention during the workers' process of carrying out their right to collective action (including a strike), consists of:

- Restrictions on the amount of entities entitled to organize strikes;
- Establishing formal requirements which need to be met before a legal strike may proceed;

251. Conclusions I, p. 38; Conclusions VIII, p. 98 (Sweden); Conclusions XV-1, vol. 2, p. 521 (Spain).
252. Conclusions VII, p. 40 (Sweden); Conclusions XIV-1, vol. 2, p. 619 (Norway).
253. Conclusions XV-1, vol. 2, p. 432 (Norway); Conclusions XV-1, vol. 2, p. 521 (Spain).

- Introducing the obligation to exhaust all possible avenues of arbitration before declaring strike action;
- And introducing the obligation to ensure the continuity of operation within certain workplaces.

The right to introduce procedural requirements concerning strikes cannot be considered equivalent to the prohibition of collective actions and strikes.[254]

7.2.5.3.3. Restricting the Amount of Entities Entitled to Organize Strikes

No Member State guarantees all workers the right to strike. Generally a precondition for a lawful strike is the establishment of a trade union organization. Some Member States restrict the participation of trade unions that are not considered to be representative of the workers, from the right to organize a strike. This requirement, that only representative trade union organizations have the right to organize strikes, is evident, for example, in the French labour law. Only the most representative trade unions can call strikes in the public sector. Whether a trade union is representative is determined not only by the level of membership, but also on the results achieved in a ballot carried out at a given workplace concerning various trade organizations and voting on the union that is considered to be the most fitting representative of the workers. All workers employed by a given employer may participate in such a ballot. The Committee believes that the above restriction on the right to strike is in breach of Article 6 § 4.[255] Workers have the right to carry out collective actions including strikes, regardless of whether they are unionized.[256]

7.2.5.3.4. Procedural Requirements needed Prior to the Commencement of a Legal Strike

According to the Committee, a requirement, which makes the decision to go on strike conditional on the approval of the executive committee of a trade union[257] or of the majority of workers,[258] is considered to violate international standards. It is a breach of Article 6 § 4 to carry out a ballot amongst workers who are employed by an employer against whom the strike is being organized, making voting obligatory with regards to the undertaking of a strike action.[259] The case of Great Britain is unique in this respect, since in the earlier supervisory cycles, the Committee held that Member States had the right to impose on the strikes organizers an obligation to carry out a secret ballot

254. Conclusions XII-1, p. 128 (Iceland).
255. Case of France: Conclusions 2002, p. 35–36; Conclusions 2004, vol. 1, p. 220.
256. Case of Romania: Conclusions 2002, pp. 135, 137; Conclusions 2004, vol. 2, p. 461.
257. Conclusions 200, vol. 1, p. 97 (Cyprus).
258. In the case of Romania 50per cent of workers. Conclusions 2002, p. 137; Conclusions 2004, vol. 2, p. 461. Whereas in the care of Lithuania 75per cent of workers. Conclusions 2004, vol. 2, p. 461.
259. Conclusions XV-1, vol. 2, p. 641 (Great Britain).

amongst the workers over a planned strike action.[260] The Committee found the requirements imposed by the British to be too strict and too complicated. Trade unions intending to organize strikes were obliged to notify the employer, at least 7 days in advanced, of the planned strike ballot[261] and to provide a list of workers participating in the ballot.[262] The Committee concluded that such requirements were in breach of Article 6 § 4, on the assumption the said requirements were introduced with the view to enable the employer to exert pressure on the workers entitled to call on the strike.

The Committee did not, however, question the compliance of the domestic regulations with the international standards regarding the notice period required when there is a planned strike action. The Committee opined that in the case of a planned collective action, particularly a strike action, notice periods help to calm down the emotions and help to allow the parties to consider is the details involved in organizing a strike. The literature on collective agreements refers to such notice periods as *'cooling off periods'*, a term effectively justifying their purpose of being introduced by the Member States. The Committee claims that the obligation to notify an employer of the planned collective action in advance cannot be considered a restriction on the right to strike.[263]

However, the length of the notice period may be restrictive. The Committee, by definition, does not establish a model of legal solutions and therefore does not specify what notice periods are in line with international standards. It only assesses the labour legislation enacted within the Member States. The Committee handed down the following decision concerning Member States imposing extended notice periods. When domestic labour law requires prolonged notice periods (lasting for several weeks) prior to the commencement of planned strike actions, especially on the request of the employer or a public administrative body, and also requires the plan to be presented to a court or an arbitration tribunal, the Committee sees this as a violation of Article 6 § 4.[264]

7.2.5.3.5. Compulsory Referral of Collective Disputes to an Arbitration Tribunal

Some Member States make it compulsory for collective dispute cases to undergo arbitration. The purpose of such a procedure is to defer a collective action or a strike. Compulsory arbitration stipulated under the legislation of Member States is permissible if it serves to protect the rights and liberties referred to in Article 31 § 1 ESC or in Article G § 1 RESC. Such restrictions placed upon the right to strike, however, should not be excessive.

260. Conclusions II, p. 187, Conclusions XIV-1, vol. 1, p. 389 (Iceland).
261. Conclusions XII-1, p. 131; Conclusions XIV-1, p. 805; Conclusions XV-1, vol. 2, p. 639.
262. Conclusions XV-1, vol. 2, 639.
263. Conclusions I, p. 38.
264. Conclusions XIV, vol. 1, p. 157; Conclusions XV-1, vol., p. 123.

The timeframe with which such restrictions are utilized should be limited. Under no circumstances should such restrictions exceed that which is needed to return the situation to normal.[265] If there is an absence of the circumstances that are stipulated under Article 31 § 1 ESC and Article G § 1 RESC, the Committee may conclude domestic labour legislation of Member States is noncompliant with international standards in the following situations: if state authorities prolong the existence of a collective agreement that is in place (generalization)[266] and when there is an imposition of compulsory arbitration before a trade union is entitled to pass a resolution to call a strike.[267] A similar stand was adopted in cases where collective disputes had to be referred by trade unions to mediation[268], in cases when the mediation period was extended by Member States to thirty days[269] or when the mediator was authorized by way of a ballot to suggest a resolution of the collective dispute in a way the mediator saw most appropriate, and not in a way presented by a trade union representing workers. The mediator is bound by the position taken up by the trade union. However, when more than one trade union participates in a dispute on behalf of the workers, each having the right to propose different methods of solving the dispute, Danish labour law authorizes the mediator to decide whether several solution proposals are to be considered as a whole for voting purposes (*linkage rule*). This procedure was considered by the Committee as a violation of Article 6 § 4.[270]

7.2.5.3.6. The Obligation to Ensure Continuous Operation of Certain Workplaces

Member States may restrict the right to strike with regards to workers employed in private employment, in order for the rights and liberties as are stipulated under Article 31 § 1 ESC and Article G § 1 RESC be protected. The Committee is adopting the same approach that it adopted in relation to workers engaged in public services and the interpretation of Article 6 § 4. The scope of restrictions on the right to strike for workers employed in the private sector depends upon the level of services provided to local communities by such workers. The Committee views that the restriction to the right to strike is permissible only in situations when the cessation of work within such a workplace constitutes a serious danger for the existence of a given community.[271]

When reviewing the restrictions on the right to strike imposed by Member States, the Committee examines whether such restrictions apply to workers employed in areas that are crucial to local communities, and whether, instead of restricting the right to strike, it would be possible to oblige the striking participants to provide necessary

265. Conclusions X-1, pp. 74–75.
266. Case of Denmark: Conclusions XI-1, p. 87; Conclusions XII-1, p. 127.
267. Case of Norway: Conclusions XI-1, pp. 89–90; Conclusions XII-1, p. 130; Conclusions XIII-1, pp. 158–159; Conclusions XIV-1, pp. 622-623; Conclusions XV-1, p. 432.
268. Conclusions 2002, p. 136 (Romania).
269. Conclusions XVII-1, vol. 1, p. 103 (Czech Republic).
270. Conclusions XVII-1, vol. 1, pp. 132, 134 (Denmark).
271. Conclusions I, p. 38.

services. The Committee opposes the idea that Member States reserve the right to define the minimum range of services, which would be provided during a strike action.[272] It also emphasizes the manner in which such restrictions must be introduced. Special attention is drawn to ensuring that strike organizers are entitled to appeal against the decisions handed down obliging workers to provide continuous operation of a workplace during the period of a strike.[273]

Based on the Committee's conclusions, the following factors justify the introduction of such restrictions to the right to strike: the scope, the length of the strike and the importance of the workplace and the services it provides to the local community, which is carrying out a strike.[274] In cases where a strike could have irremediable effects on the life of a local community, the Committee opined that the restrictions imposed on the right to strike, were in line with international standards. When such restrictions however, encompassed various workplaces within various sectors of the market or when they were too broadly defined, the Committee ruled that they were in violation of international standards.[275] The Committee claimed that the default on the obligation stipulated under Article 6 § 4 is related to the provision Article 1 § 2, which violates the prohibition against forced labour that is stipulated under that provision.[276]

To ensure the continuity of operation within a workplace, some Member States replace the striking workers with strike-breakers. The Committee has dealt with three such cases. Cases in Germany have twice served as a basis for disparate conclusions of the Committee. Initially, the Committee held that the replacement of workers striking in public workplaces, employed on work agreements and civil servants being appointed, was in compliance with international standards, provided there was no breach of Article 31 § 1 ESC.[277] In the following supervisory cycle, the Committee ruled that the decision of the German Constitutional Tribunal, allowing for the replacement of striking workers with new employees was unlawful, and was in breach of Article 6 § 4, since such a claim could not be grounded by Article 31.[278] The Committee has not changed its position in this respect, as seen in the rulings handed down recently with regards to Slovenia.[279]

---

272. Conclusions XVII-1, vol. 2, p. 420 (Portugal).
273. Conclusions XII-2, p. 114; Conclusions XIII-1, pp. 156-157; Conclusions XIII-3, p. 137; Conclusions XV-1, vol. 2, p. 480.
274. Case of Portugal: Conclusions XIII-3, p. 281; Conclusions XIII-5, p. 181; Conclusions XIV-1, vol. 2, p. 663; Conclusions XV-1, vol. 2, p. 479; Conclusions XV-1, vol. 2, pp. 367–368 (Italy); Conclusions XV-1, vol. 2, p. 523 (Spain); Addendum to Conclusions XV-1, p. 30 (Germany).
275. Case of Portugal: *See* The Right to Organize ... *op. cit.*, p. 71; Conclusions 2004, vol. 1, p. 46 (Bulgaria), which declared the unlawfulness of strike in the public health care, in the power industry and in the telecommunications sector. Conclusions 2004, vol. 2, p. 351 (Lithuania) – due to the ban of strikes in power plants and in the gasworks.
276. Conclusions XIV-1, vol. 1, p. 110 (Belgium); p. 158 (Cyprus).
277. Conclusions XII-2, pp. 113–114.
278. Conclusions XIII-2, p. 282.
279. Conclusions 2004, vol. 2, p. 282. The decision was deferred until information was provided, concerning the legal consequences of the unlawful dismissal of employees by employers during a lawful strike.

7.2.5.3.7. The Legal Consequences of Collective Action with Regards to Individual Work Agreement

Participation in a lawful strike should not bring about any negative legal consequences for workers.[280] Whilst analysing the reports of Member States, the Committee generally concluded the Member States had accepted or regulated legal solutions provided for the legal consequences for the participation in a strike in cases related to the termination of employment contracts, to the loss of remuneration and civil liability or even criminal responsibility.

7.2.5.3.7.1. Strike and the termination of a work agreement

During the first supervisory cycle the Committee concluded that participation in a lawful strike action cannot result in the termination of a work agreement and cannot justify the dissolution of such a contract [281] Legal regulations of Member States, which do comply with the above principle, are also in breach of Article 6 § 4. Due to the differences in labour law provisions of various Member States with regards to the termination and restoration of work agreements, the Committee concluded that labour regulations which provide for the automatic termination of a work agreement in the event of a strike, but also oblige the employer to reinstate all of the participating workers post strike completion, are compliance with international standards. The Committee believes that if those who are participating in a strike and who have their employment terminated, are then reinstated to their former positions after the strike has ended, none of their acquired rights impaired, and that such formal termination is not regarded as a breach of the Charter.[282] When considering their decision concerning the consequences of a strike on individual work agreements, the Committee requested the Member States to provide information confirming that their domestic labour legislation ensure the existence of a legal relationship between the parties in the individual work contract when there is a strike. The Committee also requested information showing legislation ensuring that workers must be reinstated and ensuring that their acquired rights are not impaired.

The Committee takes the view that a strike action should not yield any negative legal consequences with regards to individual work agreements. The Committee therefore ruled against Great Britain and Ireland whose domestic labour law, based on the common law, regards a strike as a breach of workers' obligations under a work agreement and therefore in turn gives an employer the right to dismiss a worker immediately and every employee participating in such a collective action.[283] The ruling handed

280. *See* A. Świątkowski, Swoboda podejmowania akcji zbiorowych a prawa obywatelskie, ekonomiczne i socjalne regulowane prawem pracy (Freedom to collective action and for civic, economic and social rights to be regulated by labour law), Studia z Zakresu Prawa Pracy i Polityki Społecznej (in: Studies in Labour Law and Social Policies), Kraków 1995, pp. 135 and following.

281. Conclusions I, p. 39.

282. *Ibid.*; Conclusions II, p. 29 (Norway); Conclusions XII-2, p. 116.

283. G.S. Morris, T.J. Archer, Collective Labour Law, Hart Publishing, Oxford-Portland Oregon 2000, p. 519 and following.

down by the Commission against the British[284] and the Irish[285] whose labour law legislation was not in compliance with Article 6 § 4 as the regulations provided the employer with the freedom to choose whether he/she would reemploy their striking workers. The British labour law regulations allowed an employer to dismiss all workers taking part in a strike and to reemploy workers selectively three months after the dismissal. The Committee concluded that the certainty entailed in the termination of a work agreement for workers partaking in a strike, accompanied by the uncertainty as to who is going to be reemployed, constituted a serious threat to the right to organize and participate in strike action, protected under Article 6 § 4.[286] The Committee reached a similar conclusion concerning certain provisions of Danish labour law, which did not ensure reinstatement of the workers dismissed on the grounds of participation in a strike action.[287] As a result of the Committee's conclusions, the provisions discriminating against the participants of lawful strikes have been changed. The Committee was interested in information, whether there are any practical examples of unequal treatment by employees involved in strike actions.[288]

7.2.5.3.7.2. Strike action and the right to fair remuneration

Wages are paid for work performed. During a strike, workers do not work and are therefore, not entitled to a salary. Therefore, Member States, without violating international standards, may grant employers the right to deduct from employees' salaries amounts due for the periods when workers were not at work due to the strike action. The Committee has adopted the view that such deductions should be proportional to the length of the strike, but in principle, such deductions also function as penalties.[289] The Committee declared the French labour provision allowing employers to deduct from workers' salaries (engaged the public sector receiving monthly wages) 1/30th of their wage per day of the strike action, regardless of whether the strike lasted the whole day or only one hour, to constitute a breach of Article 6 § 4.[290]

7.2.5.3.7.3. Strike: civil liability and criminal responsibility

During the first supervisory cycle, the Committee decided that domestic labour legislation providing for civil liability (for damages) and criminal responsibility for unlawful acts committed during a strike, cannot be considered as a violation of

284. Conclusions XIII-1, p. 160; Conclusions XIV-1, vol. 2, p. 804; Conclusions XV-1, p. 638. On the basis of the decision issued by the Committee of Social Rights, the Committee of Ministers of the Council of Europe adopted two recommendations addressed to the authorities of Great Britain: No. RchS(93)3, No.RSChS (97)3.
285. Conclusions XIV-1, vol.1, p. 422; Addendum to Conclusions XV-1, p. 18.
286. Conclusions XI-1, p. 90; Conclusions XIII-3, pp. 144–145; Conclusions XIV-1, p.804; Conclusions XV-1, pp. 638–639.
287. Conclusions XIV-1, vol.1, p.181; Conclusions XV-1, vol.1, p.156.
288. Conclusions XV-1, vol.2, p.619 (Norway).
289. Conclusions XIII-1, p. 153.
290. Conclusions XIII-1, p.154; Conclusions XIII-3, p.135; Conclusions XIV-1, vol.1, p.258; Conclusions 2002, p.36.

Article 6 § 4.[291] In the case of Member States where the legal system is based on the common law, the organizers and participants of lawful industrial actions are granted immunity from civil liability and criminal responsibility for the consequences of any events during strikes.[292] The restrictions imposed on the above rule led the Committee to the conclusion that these domestic provisions constitute a breach of international standards. Although employers participating in lawful strikes were absolved from civil liability and criminal responsibility,[293] in the Irish legislation, participation of civil servants in a lawful strike action was classified as an offence against the state.

Similarly this view was propounded in the case of merchant seamen. Under Irish criminal law, a strike action of merchant seamen constitutes a breach or neglect of duty or even an act of criminal conspiracy.[294] The Committee has taken the view the above-cited provisions constitute an impediment of the effective execution of the right to strike by merchant seamen. The Committee reasoned that public authorities are only entitled to establish procedural requirements regulating the exercise of the right to collective action and that any wholesale restriction on this right could only be justified according to the relevant conditions laid down in Article 31 § 1 ESC.[295]Although the provisions subject to which participation in a lawful strike action by civil servants and seamen were acts prohibited by criminal law, had no practical application, the Committee noted that the maintenance of such provisions constitutes a serious threat to the right to strike.[296]During the following supervisory cycles, the Committee was informed of provisions constituting the basis for the Committee's negative opinion with regards to Irish compliance with international standards of the protection of the right to strike, had been repealed.[297] Irish law does not provide immunity from civil liability and criminal responsibility for participating in a strike action organized by a trade union, which does not have the status of a representative organization. Domestic labour legislation, which gives employers the right to dismiss the striking employees, is in breach of Article 6 § 4.[298] The Committee concluded that keeping such provisions in force, under which only trade unions holding a negotiating licence are entitled to carry out collective action, including strikes, was a violation of the provisions under Article 6 § 4.[299] As pointed out earlier, the Committee was of the opinion that a group of employees who are not members of a trade union have the right to organize a lawful

---

291. Conclusions I, p. 39.
292. *See* A.Świątkowski, Uprawnienia, wolności, przywileje, obowiązki i immunitety w prawie związkowym (Rights, liberties, privileges, responsibilities and immunities in trade union law), Studia Iuridica, vol. 23, Warszawa 1992, pp. 159 and following
293. Addendum to Conclusions XI-2, p. 26.
294. The Conspiracy and Protection Act of 1875. This Act was amended to The Merchant Shipping (Miscellaneous Provisions Act) 1998.
295. Conclusions II, p.27; Conclusions X-1, pp.74-75; Conclusions X-2, p.75; Conclusions XI-1, p.76; Addendum to Conclusions XI-2, p.26; Conclusions XIII-1, p.156; Conclusions XIII-3, p.136
296. Addendum to Conclusions XI-2, pp.24–26; Conclusions XIII-1, p.156; Conclusions XIII-3, p.136.
297. Addendum to Conclusions XV-1, p. 27.
298. Conclusions 2004, vol. 1, p. 265.
299. Conclusions XIII-1, p. 156; Conclusions XIII-3, p. 136.

strike. Therefore depriving such workers of immunity from civil liability and criminal responsibility for participating in a lawful action is not in compliance with the international protection standards.[300]

Although the Committee did not actually deal with the cases of compliance with international standards of industrial action taken up by workers wanting to protect the economic and social interests of employees employed by other employers, it nonetheless stated that excluding those workers from liability for striking in a legal collective action against an employer, although have been formally employed by an intermediary company, is a violation of the right to strike protected under Article 6 § 4. A similar stand was adopted in the case of an industrial action carried out in order to protect employees hired by a different intermediary company than the striking employees, although working for the same employer.[301]

The immunity from civil liability and criminal responsibility for participating in a lawful strike should be granted to all workers, regardless of trade union membership. The Committee believes the Member States should ensure legal protection of all workers involved, either as organizers or as participants, in a lawful industrial collective action.[302] The exclusion from this protection of striking workers who are not members of a trade union is incompatible with international standards protecting the rights of the workers.[303]

The Committee also dealt with the liability of the strike organizers and concluded the power of the state to impose excessive financial sanctions for the violation of the procedural requirements regarding collective action constitutes a breach of Article 6 § 4. Under Swedish labour law, the failure to give requisite notice of a collective action may yield a fine between 30,000 and 100,000 Swedish Krona (SEK; 3301 – 10,831 euros) and litigation for the violation of a postponement order (discussed in detail in the subsequent paragraph) may entail liability ranging from a minimum 300,000 SEK (33,008 euros) up to a maximum of one million SEK (108 310 euros).[304]

7.2.5.4. Restrictions to the Right to Strike as Imposed by the Courts

In some Member States, courts have the power to restrict the right of workers to strike. In such cases, the Committee found itself competent to review the rulings of domestic labour courts with regards to their compliance with the international standards set by the Charter.[305] During the following nine supervisory cycles, the Committee did not make a use of this power. By the 11th supervisory cycle, the Committee assessed the judicature of the Danish courts with regards to their compliance with Article 6 § 4 and with Article 31 § 1 ESC. This move was consequent to the judgment handed down by the Netherlands Supreme Court on 30 March 1986,

300. Conclusions XIV-1, p.422; Addendum to Conclusions XV-1, p.27.
301. Case of Great Britain: Conclusions XII-1, pp.131-132; Conclusions XIII-1, pp. 159–160; Conclusions XIV-1, vol.2, p. 805; Conclusions XV-1, vol.2, p. 637.
302. Conclusions 2004, vol. 2, p. 405 (Norway).
303. Conclusions XVII-1, vol.1, p. 135 (Denmark).
304. Conclusions 2002, p.237; Conclusions 2004, vol.2, p. 566.
305. Conclusions I, p. 38.

which ruled that the above mentioned provisions were directly applicable to the Dutch labour law.

The Committee was of the opinion that allowing direct applicability in domestic regulations Article 31 § 1 ESC lead to a situation where the provisions of an international treaty create a legal possibility to restrict the right to strike. Based on this principle, the Committee's interest in the rulings handed down by national courts dealing with collective labour relations is justified.[306] While examining the judgments of the Dutch courts, the Committee came to the conclusion that in order to protect financial interests of third parties (consumers, clients) and employers, the courts had been imposing restrictions on both the duration and the measures taken in collective actions initiated by the workers. The Committee claimed, on the basis of Article 31, that the protection of economic interests of third parties could only be taken into consideration in exceptional cases. The Committee also required information regarding the individuals and entities who made requests before the courts to have the measures and the duration of a collective action limited and whether it was possible to appeal against the judgments of first instance courts in this field.[307] In the absence of sufficient information with regards to the appeal avenues against interim judgments concerning restrictions of duration of lawful collective actions, the Committee postponed its conclusions concerning the compliance by the Dutch court with Article 6 § 4 during the following two supervisory cycles.[308] The failure of Member States to submit information requested by the Committee, thereby forcing the Committee to postpone its conclusions in three subsequent supervisory cycles, constitutes sufficient grounds for the Committee to declare that the domestic legislation of certain Member States violates international standards. Having received the required information, the Committee stated the Dutch courts' power to determine whether a strike was premature, as confirmed in the judicial practices and rulings of the Netherlands Supreme Court,[309] and that the Netherlands restricted the right to strike, in violation of Article 6 § 4.[310]

The Committee has found similar examples of court-imposed controls over industrial actions in Belgian reports to be unlawful. Although the power to monitor the lawfulness of industrial actions is not formally granted to the Belgian courts, the judges have the right to assess the behaviour of workers participating in such actions. Even if a strike or a picket line is lawful from a formal point of view, courts may decide workers participating in a lawful collective action are guilty of criminal behaviour. The Committee observed the above right afforded to Belgian courts, allows such courts to assess collective action, and therefore causes judges to be the determiners over whether a strike is appropriate, consequently deciding its legality. The outcome of such rulings results in the restriction of the right to strike.[311]

306. Conclusions XI-1, p. 88.
307. Conclusions XIII-1, p.158; Conclusions XIII-3, pp. 139–140.
308. Conclusions XIV-1, pp.555-556; Addendum to Conclusions XV-1, pp.93–94.
309. Judgment of 28 January 2000 cited in Conclusions XVI-1, p. 471.
310. Conclusions XVII-1, vol. 2, p. 320.
311. Conclusions XVI-1, pp. 71 and following; Conclusions XVII-1, vol.1, pp. 68–69.

7.2.5.5. *Lockouts*[312]

Article 6 § 4 also provides employers the right to take industrial action. It ensures them the right to institute a lockout, which, in the Committee's opinion exists as the major if not the only form of employers' collective action concerning collective labour relations.[313] Since the employers' right to institute lockouts has not been explicitly formulated in Article 6 § 4, the Committee has come to the conclusion that the right in question is not on an equal footing to the workers' right to strike, under the Charter.[314]

This conclusion may seem rather risky – the fact Article 6 § 4 does not in any way authorize Member States to enact regulations concerning the right of the employer to lockouts should not be used as evidence supporting the claim that the Charter does not protect the right to lockouts as it does the right to strike. The absence of any legal basis in the domestic labour legislation for regulations concerning the procedure for executing the right to lockouts does not justify, in the Committee's opinion, the statement a Member State does not comply with international standards if the right to lockouts is not explicitly recognized in its domestic legislation.[315]

The Committee is of the view that judicial bodies of Member States may be granted authorization to impose certain restrictions on the employers' right to lockouts.[316] In its decisions, the Committee does not apply the principle of equal means to be used by the parties in collective work agreements (who, in a period of social peace, are defined as stakeholders), i.e. by employers and employees, to exert pressure on each other. The Committee does not regard Article 6 § 4 as an international labour law standard established with a view to ensure and maintain balance with regards to collective work agreements.[317]

The Committee does not impose on Member States any obligation to explicitly recognize the employers' right to institute lockouts. Notwithstanding, it believes that domestic labour legislation that determines that a lockout is a tortious act punishable by a fine imposed on an employer who makes use of an illegal form of exerting pressure, violates international standards.[318] Also, domestic legislation where lockouts are considered to be a breach by employers of a work agreement is considered to be in non-compliance with international standards. An exception may be the Committee's decision on the non-compliance of domestic labour law with Article 6 § 4, resulting

312. For the legal definition of a lockout and the consequences of a lockout in collective and individual work agreements *see* A.Świątkowski, Lokaut. Studium stosunków przemysłowych, Studia z Zakresu Prawa Pracy i Polityki Społecznej (Lockouts. Studies in industrial relations, Studies in Labour Law and Social Policies), Kraków 1996, pp. 31 and following.
313. Conclusions I, p. 38.
314. Conclusions VIII, p. 95.
315. Conclusions II, p. 187 (Cyprus).
316. Conclusions VIII, p. 95.
317. A.Swiatkowski, Balance of Economic Weapons During Collective Labour Dispute (in:) Liber Amicorum Reinhold Falbeck, Lund 2005, p. 607 ff.
318. Case of Italy: Conclusions III, p. 38; Conclusions VI, p. 40; Conclusions IX-2, pp. 48–49; Conclusions XV-1, vol. 2, p. 367.

from the absence of regulations legitimizing the right to lockouts in such legislation.[319] The Committee regards lockouts as deliberate actions taken by employers in cases of *force majeure*. In the Committee's conclusion, lockouts are regarded as a lawful method of protecting employers' interests threatened by collective industrial action initiated by workers.[320] Therefore, the Committee approves of defensive lockouts.[321] However, it has not expressed an opinion on the compatibility of defensive lockouts with international standards.

7.3. The Right to Information and Consultation (Article 2 Additional Protocol of 1988; Article 21 RESC)

Article 21 obligates Member States to undertake or to encourage measures enabling workers or their representatives to attain information concerning the financial and economic situation of the undertaking employing them and to be consulted on proposed decisions, which could substantially affect their interests.[322] Foremostly, employers should consult with their workers or with their representatives about the decisions, which may seriously influence the level of employment within their industry. The right to information and consultation introduced by the Additional Protocol into the European Social Charter in 1988 (Article 2) was a prototype for the directive No. 14 of the European Parliament and the Council on 11 March 2002 (2002/14.EC), which formulated the basic grounds for information and consultation amongst the workers of the European Community.[323] The prototype for Article 21 RESC (Article 2 Additional Protocol of 1988) is a directive project of the Vredelinga community dedicated to the processes of information and consultation in industries.[324] In contrast to the European Union directive, neither Article 2 of the Additional Protocol nor Article 21 RESC considers workers' rights or their representatives' to information concerning their employers, as personal rights available to each employed individual. The analysed provisions of the Charter are treated as a standard, which may be utilized by labour collectives or by their representatives.

The analysis of the Committee's judgment allowed for the formation of the hypothesis that Article 21 RESC is also considered as a legal standard, which certain employees may utilize. The Committee, which not only supervises the compliance of domestic labour legislation with the international standards established by the Charter,

319. Case of France: Conclusions V, p.48; Conclusions VI, p.39.
320. Conclusions IX-2, pp. 47–48 (France); pp. 48–49 (Italy).
321. Addendum to Conclusions XV-1, p. 27 (Germany).
322. *See* R. Birk, Prawo pracowników do informacji, konsultacji i współudziału w podejmowaniu decyzji w Poprawionej Europejskiej Karcie Społecznej (Workers' right to information, consultation and participation in the Revised European Social Charter) (in:) Dorobek Rady Europy … (European Social Charter Towards Common …), *op. cit.*, pp. 92 and following.
323. OJ L.80, 23.3.2002. In Polish writings *see* S.Koczur, P.Korus, Dialog społeczny – prawo pracowników do informacji i konsultacji (Social Dialogue – the right of workers to information and consultation), Universitas, Kraków 2003, pp.153 and following.
324. Directive on Information and Consultation Procedures for Employees, 1980 OJ (C 197), p.3.

decided the right to information and consultation should be ensured by domestic legislation which would allow its beneficiaries effective use. To guarantee this result, the regulation present in domestic labour legislation must allow for an independent body to deal with claims and complaints that may arise from the inability to make use of such a right to information and to the consultation by workers who have attained such a right.[325] This above entitlement should be ensured to workers and their representatives.[326] The right should not be limited to bodies, which in turn pursue those employers who are violating provisions concerning information and consultation.

In certain situations, the beneficiaries whose right to information and consultation has been breached, should be able to file a claim seeking damages.[327] In the view of the Committee, penalties imposed should support civil liability claims and should pay for damages and annul decisions[328] carried out by employers without consulting and informing the workers or their representatives. Having in mind the protection of employers' rights who have acted criminally or in a white-collar crime capacity, which resulted in penalties imposed on the employer for breaching the obligation to inform and consult the workers or their representatives, the Committee desired to receive information concerning the decisions handed down by courts or work inspectors.[329] It demanded information from Member States, stipulating which particular workers or organizations have the right to litigate and file claims against employers who have breached domestic legislation stipulating the obligation of information and consultation with workers or their representatives under Article 21 RESC.[330] The position of the Committee, is demonstrated in its demand to receive from Bulgaria and Romania detailed information concerning the entities entitled to file claims, regulated by labour law, in the case when an employer breaches the obligation outlined under Article 21 RESC, sought its information by way of questionnaire, whether the above provision is guaranteed to all workers or solely to their representatives. The Committee holds that these rights must be afforded to particular workers, and not, only their representatives.

In executing the plan for information and consultation, Member States should either independently formulate provisions dealing with the principles of information and consultation by industries with workers or their representatives or encourage stakeholders to define the above principles in collective labour agreements or in other normative agreements. Informing and consulting about matters stipulated under Article 21 RESC, does not require legislative action. It may, depending on the individual customs of particular Member States concerning collective labour relations, be ensured by the judiciary or may also be customary in nature. The undertaken methods of regulating information and consultation by each Member State through employers,

325. Conclusions XIII-3, p. 440.
326. Conclusions XIII-5, p. 288 (Sweden).
327. Conclusions XIII-5, p. 278 (Finland).
328. Conclusions 2003, vol. 1, p. 311 (Italy).
329. Conclusions XVI-2, vol.1, p. 365 (Greece); Conclusions XVI-2, vol.2, pp. 594–595 (Norway).
330. Conclusions 2003, vol.1, p. 72 (Bulgaria); Conclusions 2003, vol.2, p.420 (Romania).

workers or their representatives should be effective and adequate.[331] To determine whether such mechanisms dealing with information and consultation for workers and/or their representatives are effective, the Committee demands detailed information concerning the established procedures of the issue at hand.[332] Article 21 RESC obligates Member States to undertake or encourage measures, which will ensure workers or their representatives the right to information and consultation. This obligation is considered to be fulfilled, when the existing regulations within a country are established by the state, negotiated by stakeholders, the judiciary or the binding customs, and that warrant employers to inform workers or their representatives, or both.[333] The word 'or' included in the analysed provision does not demand Member States to utilize only one or the other option – to inform and consult workers or their representatives.

This does not indicate, however, the right to information and consultation of workers changes its nature and becomes dependent upon whom the employer is informing and with whom the employer is consulting the matters stipulated under Article 21 RESC, a right which can be utilized by either individuals or by particular workers or by their representatives.

The beneficiaries of this provision are the workers. This provision allows workers to utilize the right to information and consultation either individually or collectively. In the latter case, the workers' representatives usually carry out this right. In the case where a workplace failed to organize representation, the state or the stakeholders may establish that an employer will be obligated to inform the workplace of the matters raised in Article 21 RESC. Consulting with a group of workers may function according to various legal-admin formats, such as a referendum.

Neither the obligation to inform nor the obligation to consult with workers and/or their representatives within the workplace deprives the employer from carrying out decisions in matters stipulated in Article 21 RESC. The employer has the right to inform workers and/or their representatives. He also has the right to consult with the workers, their representatives and with the workplace about intended decisions. The state and stakeholders decide which of the above options will be carried out. There are no law-based barriers, which might hinder all the options from being executed. In such cases, whereby the report has indicated that the trade union, an authorized body, is responsible for receiving the information from the employers, and stating its opinion in the name of the workers, the Committee demands that Member States produce information concerning the laws protecting information and consultation of workers who are not represented by a trade union.[334] In particular, the Committee is interested in attaining information dealing with the guarantees of the right in question for workers who are citizens of other Member States and, thus, parties to the Charter.[335]

331. Explanatory report to the 1988 Additional Protocol, European Social Charter., *op. cit.*, p. 132.
332. Conclusions 2003, vol.1, pp. 71–72 (Bulgaria); Conclusions 2003, vol.2, p.419 (Romania).
333. *Ibid.*, p. 131.
334. Conclusions 2003, vol.1, pps.71-72 (Bulgaria); Conclusions 2003, vol.2, p. 625 (Sweden).
335. Conclusions 2003, vol. 1, p. 72.

In the Appendix to Article 21 RESC it was stipulated that a representative in the Charter, is a body entitled to representative status due to domestic regulations. If the other authorized bodies from the side of the workers partaking in the consultative process happen to be entities other than trade union entities, the Committee requests gain information about their legal status, and in particular interested in its ability to attain information, whether it falls under the protection of the law ensuring independence in work relations with the employers.[336] Workers' representatives are bodies that are recognized as such by domestic labour laws. As is evident by the regulations included into Article 2 of the Additional Protocol of 1988, the prototype for the definition of workers' representative bodies is Article 3 of the ILO convention No. 135 dealing with the protection of workers' representatives in industries and allocating them certain conveniences, during the 56 sessions of the General Conference ILO of 2 June 1971.[337] The technique of electing workers' representatives and the level of conducting consultations (the level of the workplace, at the local, regional and national levels) was left for Member States to address, who in turn were authorized to pass on the decisions in serious matters to the interested parties, i.e. the stakeholders.[338] Consultations are not carried out at the same level as the decision making level within the workplace.[339] Workers' representative bodies, in the understanding of the given provision, may be trade unions and/or advisory councils.[340] In most Member States, the representative function is fulfilled by trade unions. With regard to such unions, the Committee attempts to ensure Member States abide by the principle that all trade organizations, without exception regardless of their status (representative or non-representative) are treated equally.[341]

Article 21 RESC obligates Member States to inform and consult with workers employed in industries. In the Appendix to the Additional Protocol of 1988 an industry was redefined as a 'set of tangible and intangible components, with or without legal personality, formed to produce or provide services for financial gain and with power to determine its own market policy'. The right to information and consultation set forth above applies solely to those workers who are employed in an industry as defined by the Additional Protocol of 1988. In a situation when an industry has an established organizational structure, an industry by definition of the provision in question is an organizational unit with the purpose of producing goods or rendering services.[342] The scope of the effect of the provision of Article 21 RESC encompasses solely the employers not in the public sector. The terms 'produce goods', 'provide services' used to identify the entities who are encompassed by the provision in question suggest that public sector

336. Conclusions 2003, vol. 1, p. 71 (Bulgaria).
337. *Ibid.*, pp. 131-132. *See* Conventions and recommendations ..., *op. cit.*, vol. II, pp. 836–837.
338. *Ibid.*, Conclusions XIII-3, p. 447 (Sweden).
339. *Ibid.*
340. Conclusions XIII-3, p. 443 (the Netherlands).
341. Conclusions XIII-3, p. 447 (Sweden).
342. Explanatory report ..., *op. cit.*, p. 133.

workers are also encompassed by the provision.[343] The scope of the effect of these public undertakings' is carried out by public administrative bodies.[344]

Article 21 RESC allows Member States to exclude from the scope of application of this provision those undertakings, which employ a small number of workers. The Committee regards the exclusion of undertakings employing 20,[345] 50[346] or even 100[347] workers is in accordance with the international standards. Regardless of the amount of workers employed by the undertakings, which may be excluded from the scope of application of the above provision, are undertakings, which are established and organized by associations and religious organizations.

Further, undertakings which are carried out by organizations inspired by ideals or by moral viewpoints or by approaches subject to legal protection by the legislation of Member States, may be excluded from the scope of Article 21 RESC to such a point as it is necessary to protect the reason as to why the undertaking was established in the first place. Excluded from the encompassing obligation of Article 21 RESC are undertakings that function solely for educational, artistic or charitable purposes.[348]

Article 21 RESC is a standard on which the principle of the 'majority of interested workers' (Article 7 § 2 Additional Protocol of 1988) is based. It indicates that a Member States fulfils its applicable obligations specified by the provisions of the Charter (i.e., if such a matter includes information and consultation) if 80 per cent of the workers use their right to information and consultation.[349] In the understanding of this provision the 'interested workers' are all those employed in undertakings that utilize the right to information and consultation. To the category of those employed in undertakings, which form the basis for calculating the amount of workers, Member States should guarantee the right to information and consultation workers who are not included or employed in the public sector or in small undertakings to which Article 21 RESC cannot be applied on the grounds of domestic legislation or established collective labour agreements.

Employers should be obligated to inform workers and/or their representatives, regularly or within a reasonable timeframe. Member States and stakeholders may choose how frequently employers should inform and consult with their workers concerning matters stipulated under Article 21 RESC. Depending on how the obligation to inform and consult is regulated, employers may be obliged to provide information and seek opinions from workers and/or their representatives in regular, previously established intervals (monthly, quarterly, half-yearly or even annually[350] or if required from time to time). Domestic labour legislation or the standards, which are negotiated by stakeholders, should specify the frequency of the consultations.[351]

343. Conclusions XIII-5, p. 284 (Norway).
344. Conclusions XV-1, pp. 176–177 (Denmark).
345. Conclusions XIII-5, p. 270 (Finland).
346. Conclusions XVI-2, vol. 1, p. 363 (Greece).
347. Conclusions XVI-2, vol. 2m p. 594 (Norway).
348. D. Harris, J. Darcy, *op. cit.*, p. 246.
349. Conclusions XIII-3, p. 442 (Finland).
350. Case of Finland: *Ibid.*, p. 441; Conclusions XIII-5, p. 277.
351. Conclusions 2003, vol. 1m p. 71 (Bulgaria).

This analysed provision provides the legal grounds for certain obligations and for how these legal obligations are to be carried out in a legal framework. The frequency of fulfilling these obligations is dependent upon the necessity of the employer to offer information to the workers and/or their representatives. The information should be transmitted to the workers and/or their representatives in an accessible fashion. Because Article 21 (1)(a) RESC demands employers to inform their workers and/or their representatives about the economic and financial situation of the workplace, in which the workers are employed, as well as about the planned decisions, which may have an impact on the workers interests, employers should provide such information in an accessible fashion so that it may be understood by individuals who have not completed any specialist education.[352]

Consultations regarding planned planed decisions by the employer should be conducted in ‘good time’ (Article 21 (1)(b) RESC). Aside from the provisions which regulate the obligation of employers to inform and consult workers and/or their representatives, there is also the strict labour relationship. Therefore employers have the obligation to consult with the workers and/or their representatives in matters that are included within the scope of information. This includes the financial and economic situation of the workplace in which the workers are employed. The interdependency between the obligation to inform and the obligation to consult is very particular. Employers should inform the workers and/or their representatives of all matters concerning the financial and economic situation of the place of employment.

However, employers are only obligated to consult about those financial and economic matters, which form a part of the planned decisions and that may in turn, affect the interests of the workers. Consultations should be carried out before the employer makes any decisions whose consequences may have a serious effect on the employment in the industry. The Charter analysts present the following examples of such decisions: liquidation of the workplace, transferring the production sector or its services to another region,[353] and changing the production profile.

The obligation to consult should be fulfilled by the employer in such a way that all parties taking advantage from this entitlement may accomplish positive benefits. Such consultations will not be effective if they are conducted at a late period so much so that the decision makers are unable to take into account the views and proposals of the workers and/or their representatives. In informing workers and/or their representatives about proposed decisions and also inviting them to express their opinions in such matters, the employer should enable consultative contemplations and expression of opinion. However, certain information may not be released to the workers and/or their representatives if such information when disclosed would cause the workplace grave damage. The employer decides which information will be disclosed.

An employer should be conscious of the fact the failure to disclose certain information to workers and/or their representatives may violate the obligation specified under Article 21 § 1 RESC. Judicial bodies or those administrative institutions

352. D. Harris, J. Darcy, *op. cit.*, p. 247.
353. *Ibid.*

equipped to deal with labour matters (work inspectors) that have been mentioned in the introduction of this section, are delegated to analyse the reasons for the employer's refusal to provide information or the employer's disallowance of workers and/or their representatives' opinion to be taken into account concerning matters specified in the provision. The necessary requirement for the effectiveness of the consultation is the availability of crucial and important information concerning the economy and financial situation of the workplace, before the employer can reach any decision.[354] Employers who fear the disclosure of certain details may be detrimental to the workplace may oblige workers and/or their representatives to maintain duties of confidentiality.

7.4. The Right to Take Part in the Determination and Improvement of the Working Conditions and Working Environment (Article 3 Additional Protocol of 1988 and Article 22 RESC)

This provision was enacted to ensure workers utilized effectively the right to participate in the determination and improvement of the working conditions and the working environment within the workplace.[355] In order to achieve this effectiveness, Member States are obligated to undertake or support measures, which will enable workers and/or their representatives to partake in the following improvements to the workplace: working conditions, work organization or working environment, protection of health and safety, organizing social and socio-cultural services, as well as supervising the practices that are used to comply with the provisions in such matters.

This regulation places upon Member States similar obligations to those established in Article 2 Additional Protocol of 1988 as well as Article 21 RESC. The obligatory conditions are identical in this provision. In Article 22 RESC, the same terms were utilized as in Article 21 RESC. In both provisions Member States were obligated to undertake or specify measures, which would lead to the attainment of the desired goals. In the case of Article 22 RESC, the effect of these measures should enable workers and/or their representatives to partake in the determination and improvement of the working conditions and the working environment in the workplace.

With regards to the other terms used in the provision such as 'the undertaking', 'workers' representatives', they carry the same connotations as in Article 21 RESC. Article 22 RESC therefore encompasses solely employees of an undertaking. It is not applicable to civil services. However it is applicable to undertakings, which are run by administrative bodies. Despite the fact that it is more difficult to derive from Article 22 RESC the assurance concerning the guarantee of rights to particular workers to partake in the determination and improvement of the working conditions and working environment, the Committee examines whether compliance with this provision has been secured by claims filed either by the interested workers or by their representatives.[356]

354. Explanatory report to the 1988 Additional Protocol, *op. cit.*, p. 133.
355. R. Birk, Prawo pracowników do informacji ... (Rights of Workers to Information ...), *op. cit.*, pp. 102 and following.
356. Conclusions XIII-3, p. 440.

If there is a possibility, Member States are obligated to ensure the defendant employer the ability to appeal the decision.[357] Member States are obligated to enable workers and/or their representatives to partake in the decision making process carried out by the employer in matters concerning the improvement of the working conditions and the working environment, as well as in organizing work, in issues concerning health and security protection at the workplace, organizing social matters and meeting the socio-cultural needs of the workers. Member States are also obligated to enable workers and/ or their representatives to oversee the employers' compliance of the provisions in question. The right of the workers to partake in the determination and improvement of the working conditions and the working environment in the undertaking does not entitle them to make decisions with regards to these matters. Article 22 RESC demands Member States enable workers to take part in such decisions.

This does not mean however that workers and/or their representatives have according to the provision, the right to make decisions together with the employer in the matters stipulated in points *a* to *c* of the provision in question nor are they authorized to voice their objections with regards to the decisions made by the employers.[358] The results of the workers and/or their representatives determining and improving the working conditions, namely, the organization of work and the working environment, protecting health and safety in the workplace, organizing social services as well as fulfilling the socio-cultural needs of the workers, cannot be identified with negotiating and reaching collective work agreements. The element raised in Article 22 RESC is often the subject of negotiations conducted by stakeholders and is regulated by the collective labour relations or by other agreements of stakeholders.[359]

By signing collective labour agreements, the workers' representatives do not automatically partake in the determination and improvements of the work conditions and work environment conditions. However, Member States that ratified Article 22 are obligated to ensure that workers and/or their representatives, have access to legal avenues (other than collective labour agreements) resulting in the determination and improvements of the work conditions and work environment conditions, as well as to supervising the compliance of those provisions concerning these issues.

In the Additional Protocol of 1988, in which Article 3 was included, repealed by Article 22 RESC, it was decided the provisions of this Protocol are not in breach of the provisions of the Charter (Article § 1 Additional Protocol 1988).[360] In view of this it is possible to conclude the provisions of Article 22 RESC do not breach the either provision § 1 nor § 2 of Article 6 RESC.

In relation to Article 3 Additional Protocol 1988, there were differences introduced to Article 22 RESC. Article 3 § 2 Additional Protocol allowed for Member States to solely exclude from the scope of application of this provision undertakings in which the amount of employers does not reach the limit specified in the domestic legislation

357. Conclusions XIII-5, p. 293 (Finland).
358. Explanatory report to the 1988 Additional Protocol, *op. cit.*, p. 134.
359. *Ibid.*
360. *Ibid.*

or in its practices. Article 22 RESC does not include such an approach. In light of this provision, workers and/or their representatives have a right to contribute to the improvement of the working conditions in all sectors of the industry regardless of the amount of workers employed.

Contributing to the improvement of working conditions, the health and safety of the workplace and the improvement of social matters within the workplace, takes on the form of an institutional structure with a commission overlooking the above matters. Generally, workers' representatives delegate managerial trade union organizations to work with such commissions. The Committee desires to receive information regarding how workers' interests are protected and regarding the identities of the members of trade unions.[361]

Member States do not provide information in relation to the contributions made by workers' representatives concerning the improvement of the work conditions and the organization of work and the working environment.[362] The same attention may be paid to the definition of socio-cultural issues within the undertaking and fulfilling such socio-cultural needs of the workers,[363] despite the fact that, in Article 3 of the Additional Protocol of 1988, it was suggested that fitting under the definition were all socio-cultural matters, which aid in the convenience of the following: social assistance, sporting grounds, available areas for mothers feeding their young, libraries, and holiday camps for children.

There are no set indications as to how to carry out the procedure of decision making with regards to these issues. Postponing its ruling in matters of domestic labour law compliance with international standards, the Committee obligated the given Member States to present detailed information regarding to the issues in question. The most developed techniques of contributions by workers' representatives are seen in the area of improving the protection of health and safety within the workplace. Usually, Member States obligate employers to create security and health commissions. Parts of such a commission are workers' representatives selected by the trade organizations. This is the most widely used technique incorporated by the Member States obligated by Article 22 (b) RESC.[364]

Article 22 (b) RESC does not influence the rights and obligations of a Member State in the area of health and safety responsibilities within the workplace. Workers' and/or their representatives' present input in the monitoring of the compliance of their employers of the obligations stipulated under Article 22 (a)(b)(c) RESC. Compliance with this Article does not absolve employers (or their representatives) from their obligations to improve working conditions, the organization of work, the protection of the working environment, the protection of health and safety within the workplace as well as fulfilling the social and cultural needs of the workers. The commissions created

361. Conclusions XVI-2, vol. 1, p. 184 (Czech Republic); Conclusions XVI-2, vol. 2, p. 819 (Slovakia); Conclusions 2003, vol. 1m p. 73 (Bulgaria); p. 313 (Italy).
362. Conclusions XVI-2, vol. 1, p. 184 (Czech Republic).
363. *Ibid.*, p. 185; Conclusions 2003, vol. 1, p. 75 (Bulgaria); p. 313 (Italy).
364. Conclusions XIII-3, p. 453 (Sweden).

by the employers (including workers' representatives), which monitor the employer compliance of obligations under the Charter cannot free the employers of their duty to fulfil such obligations, but rather assist in improving the supervisory institutions within the workplace.[365]

7.5. The Right of Workers to Information and Consultation in Collective Redundancy Procedures (Article 29 RESC)

Article 29 RESC obligates Member States to introduce regulations, which obligate employers to inform and consult workers' representatives about the collective redundancy procedures.[366] The cited provision was structured on the model of part III (Article 13-14) of the ILO convention No. 158 as well as on European Union directives 75/129/EC, 92/56/EC and 98/59/EEC, which was issued in order to bring closer the various Member State legislation dealing with collective redundancy. These international regulations, upon which Article 29 RESC was structured, obligate consultations to take place before a decision by the employer is made concerning collective redundancy. Article 29 RESC includes specific standards comparatively to Article 21 RESC, which obligate Member States to ensure that employers regularly inform the workers' representatives about the economic and financial situation of the workplace as well as to consult with workers about planned workplace decisions, which may be influential on the workers' interests.

Consultations in matters in collective redundancy procedures should be carried out in 'good time'. The goal of such consultations is to understand the position of the workers' representatives in the planned collective redundancy. A necessary requirement for the consultations to be effective is to provide the workers' representatives with all appropriate information dealing with the causes upon which the collective redundancy is based, as well as how the redundancy is planned, and the selection criteria for choosing which employees will be made redundant during the collective proceedings (and the sequence with which following employees will be let off). The European Committee of Social Rights considers that in order for there to be an adequate dialogue between employer and workers' representatives on ways of avoiding redundancies or limiting their number and mitigating their effects, all relevant documents must be supplied before the consultation starts. To this end, prior information must cover not only the reasons, the time period and the category of workers concerned, but also must include proposed social measures, criteria for dismissals and the order of dismissals. If the information provided to workers' representatives is too restricted, the Committee considers that the situation is not in conformity with Article 29 RESC.[367] An employer planning to institute collective redundancy proceedings should inform workers' representatives, in writing, stating the above information.

365. Conclusions XIII-3, p. 453 (Sweden).

366. A. M. Świątkowski, Ochrona prawa pracowników ... (Protection of Workers' Rights ...) *op. cit.*, pp. 82 and following.

367. Case of Lithuania: Conclusions 2005, vol.1, pp.404–405.

Article 29 RESC does not define the term 'collective redundancy'. This term was also not defined by the Appendix to the RESC. The Committee of Social Rights is of the position, that the case of collective redundancy is evident when during a given period, regulated by domestic labour legislation, and a group of employees have their work agreements terminated for reasons not associated with the given employees.[368] The Committee, when defining collective redundancy, took into consideration the concept of *acqui communitaire*. This accepted definition is broader than that of Part III of the ILO convention No. 158 (Article 13(1), Article 14(1)). The cited ILO convention, in its understanding of 'collective redundancy', takes into consideration redundancies made due to economic, technological, structural or other such similar reasons. The amount of workers and the period with which the collective redundancy takes place, are regulated by Member State domestic labour law legislation.

During one of the completed control cycles, finalized with an annual report and accepted by the Committee of Ministers in 2003, the Committee of Social Rights analysed 6 such state reports, which dealt with the compliance of standards established by Article 29 RESC.[369] In one of the cases, the Committee determined that domestic labour legislation did not comply with the demands stipulated under Article 29 RESC.[370] One of the reports exemplified compliance.[371] The remaining four decisions concerning the presented reports were adjourned and the Committee sought further information from those countries.

One country that complies with the international standards stipulated under Article 29 RESC is France, where the domestic labour law legislation regards collective redundancies as redundancies executed by the employer due to economic reasons, affecting at least two employees within a period of 30 days. Before making a decision involving such redundancy, the employer is obligated to consult with workers' representatives and such consultations must be carried out within a workplace employing at least 50 workers. In small plants where there are more than 11 workers employed, there is an obligation for the appointment of workers' representatives. In workplaces where the workers do not have the obligation of appointing their representatives, the employer must carry out consultations with the workers whom he intends to lay off, as part of the collective redundancy.

The French labour code specifies the scope of information that must be presented to workers' representatives by the employer. The workers' representatives must be informed about the reasons for the redundancies. The information must specify the type of reasons (economic, financial or technical) responsible for the collective redundancy. The workers' representatives must be informed about the amount of workers and the categories of employment from which the collective redundancies will derive. They also have to be made aware of the selection criteria for the laying off of workers during

368. Conclusions 2003, vol. 1, *op. cit.*, pp. 92, 210, 332; Conclusions 2003, vol. 2, *op. cit.*, p. 429, 546, 640.
369. Reports filed by Romania, Slovenia, Sweden, Bulgaria, France and Italy.
370. Romania. Conclusions 2003, vol. 2m *op. cit.*, pp. 429–431.
371. France. Conclusions 2003, vol. 1, *op. cit.*, pp. 210–213.

the collective redundancy process. The workers' representatives also must be familiar with the order of the redundancies. The employer also must inform the representatives of the period in which the collective redundancy process will take place. In order for workers' representatives to become familiarized with the structure and scale of the collective redundancy, the employer should inform the workers of the amount of typical and atypical work agreements that the workers have signed within the workplace.

Workers' representatives are obligated to inform the employer about their opinion in relation to the collective redundancy. The responsibility of the employer is to carry out an analysis of the workers' representatives' positions and to familiarize workers' representatives with any of the decisions made. The Committee of Social Rights underlined that Article 29 RESC obligates employers to 'inform and consult' with workers' representatives in cases where there is a planned collective redundancy. The goal of this process is to avoid collective redundancies or, if impracticable, to limit the extent of collective redundancies. Furthermore the employer does not satisfy his duties in the consultation process by merely providing workers' representatives with information, or allowing them to take a standpoint, or (as it is in France) obligating the employer to inform the workers' representatives with details concerning the decision of the collective redundancy. The Committee believes that consultations with stakeholders should employ a legal format of 'balanced social dialogue'. It, therefore, cannot be a case of merely presenting and receiving information.[372] The Committee obligated the French to provide more detailed information in the following supervisory cycle, concerning the scope of dialogue, before an employer in France renders decisions regarding matters of collective redundancies.

The French labour law code regulations order those employers who intend to lay off at least 10 workers within 30 days, to provide the appropriate institutions, which monitor labour law compliance, a copy of the same information provided to workers' representatives. Such competent authorities, like national workplace inspectors, do not examine the reasons for collective redundancy decisions. They only control the procedure, which takes place before the decision is made. Independent from the functions carried out by such administrative supervisory institutions prior to when a final decision is handed down, workers' representative bodies have the right to appear in court seeking an injunction for the information to be provided by the employer concerning the collective redundancy. Unless the obligations set by domestic labour regulations are met, meeting the various standards stipulated under Article 29 RESC, the court may grant an injunction that will suspend the collective redundancy process. Employers' obligation to carry out consultations with workers' representatives with regards to collective redundancy is also protected by penal provisions. Workers' representatives who are not fully informed by the employer about the planned redundancies are regarded as aggrieved parties. Violating the obligation to inform and consult such representatives about planned group redundancies by an employer creates a situation in which workers' representatives are unable to carry out their own statutory obligations.

372. Conclusions 2003, vol. 1, *op. cit.*, p. 212.

Such a violation by the employer carries a maximum sentence of 1year imprisonment and/or a fine of 3811 euros.

The legal right protected by Article 29 RESC is the social dialogue between the employer and the workers' representatives before any final decision is made about collective redundancies. Information and consultation serve as a legal basis for the above dialogue, and are necessary to limit or even avoid collective redundancies. In such cases, where collective redundancy cannot be avoided, the social dialogue carried out by the partners within the workplace may help to minimize the potential harm arising from the inevitable consequences of such an action. This may occur via the provision of certain social benefits provided for by the employer who will be obligated by the workers' representative to provide assistance for those workers who will suffer the collective redundancy. The scope of such assistance is usually established by the social pact, which is often an effect of the social dialogue, carried out by the social partners. Article 29 RESC refers to such assistance in the form of redeployment or the reintegration of the workers who are being made redundant.

The remainder of the reports differs from the obligations stipulated under Article 29 RESC. The Romanian report indicates that the information an employer provides to workers' representatives is limited. It is limited the reasons provided for the collective redundancies as well as to the numbers of workers who will made redundant. It does not provide any information about the legal consequences involved when collective redundancy procedures are not followed.[373] The Slovenian[374] and Bulgarian[375] reports inform about the change in collective law regulations and about how those changed laws are adapted to the standards stipulated under Article 29 RESC. In accordance with the informal rigueur accepted by the Committee during supervision and assessment of the annual domestic reports, the information justifies the adjournment of a decision being made against Bulgaria's and Slovenia's existing labour regulations concerning the procedures involved in collective redundancy situations, and left until the next supervisory cycle.

The Committee of Social Rights examines not only the existing regulations within Member States of the Council of Europe, but also their practices and how they are applied. For this reason the Committee is able to adjourn its decision until all the information concerning the actions committed prior to a collective redundancy are provided. In the case of Sweden, the Committee was interested to determine whether the trade unions involved were entitled to file claims for compensation in court from employers who did not fulfil their obligations to consult about their intention to carry out collective redundancies, and if they were entitled did they take advantage of this right.[376]

---

373. Conclusions 2003, vol. 2, *op. cit.*, pp. 430–431.
374. *Ibid.*, pp. 546–547.
375. Conclusions 2003, vol. 1, *op. cit.*, pp. 92–93.
376. Conclusions 2003, vol. 2, *op. cit.*, pp. 642–643.

A more interesting case is that of Italy. The Italian report stated that, in addition to the penal consequences involved for employers who do not fulfil their obligation to consult with workers' representatives about the intended collective redundancies, such collective redundancy action by force of law is transformed into individual work agreement terminations.[377] The Committee demanded clarification. Collective redundancy is a summing up of individual terminations. The scope of workers' protection against the termination of their work agreements is Article 24 RESC. This provision does not demand for consultations to be carried out between employers and workers' representatives, due to the fact that in individual terminations, there is no need for social dialogue to occur, as is required in collective redundancies.

7.6. The Right of Workers' Representatives to Protection (Article 28 RESC)

Article 28 RESC has a functional nature. It was introduced in order to enable workers' representatives to carry out their functions and statutory goals within the workplace. Member States that ratified Article 28 RESC are obligated the ensure workers' representatives effective protection against acts prejudicial to them by employers, especially actions which may cause their dismissal based on their status or activities as workers' representatives within the workplace.[378] They are also obligated to facilitate workers' representatives in the carrying out of their statutory functions. Article 28 RESC is comprised of two standards. The addressees of these two standards are Member States of the Council of Europe. They should ensure particular protection of the functions carried out by workers' representatives. Article 28(a) RESC deals with this element. Member States are also obligated to afford facilities for workers' representatives to carry out their functions promptly and efficiently (Article 28(b) RESC). Article 28 RESC is modelled on the ILO convention No. 135. The wide scope of protection provided by this provision needs to be underlined. Article 5 of both Social Charters ensuring workers the right to organize in trade unions, is interpreted by the Committee of Social Rights as a standard ensuring the increased protection of the right of the workers' representatives protection and obligating Member States to afford such facilities, so that the workers' representatives are able to carry out their functions.[379]

7.6.1. An Obligation to Ensure Workers' Representatives the Protection of Endurance in the Undertaking

The Committee of Social Rights underlines the necessity of ensuring workers' representatives the protection of endurance in the undertaking. It is possible to increase the

377. Conclusions 2003, vol. 1, *op. cit.*, p. 334.
378. A. M. Świątkowski, Ochrona praw pracowników ... (Protection of Workers' Rights ...), *op. cit.*, pp. 74 and following.
379. L. Samuel, *Fundamental Social Rights. Case Law of the European Social Charter,* 2nd edition, Council of Europe Publishing, Strasbourg 2002, pp. 118–119.

scope of the protection inherent in the undertaking of workers' representatives through the mechanism of the Committee decisions based on Article 5 RESC. This provision protects the rights of workers who are active within trade unions and forbids any discrimination based on such trade union activity, by the employers in any of the decisions made concerning labour relations (signing, changing or terminating work agreements).[380] Increased protection of all workers carrying out functions within trade unions must be ensured, and not only to workers of employers employing more that the amount of workers stipulated by domestic legislation. The Committee of Social Rights, on many occasions, emphasized that the domestic labour regulations, which excludes any of the workers from the protection of endurance in the undertaking due to being employed in a workplace of less than five workers, are not in compliance with Article 5 RESC.[381] Workers and trade unionists, should take advantage of the protection of their rights regardless of the trade union they represent (representative and authorized to reach collective labour agreements or others without such legal status).[382] The Committee of Social Rights continues to examine whether workers' representatives take advantage of this protection of rights in light of domestic labour legislation. The Committee demands additional information from Member States when it is evident that such protection is used.[383]

It is important to mention that the Committee is not content with information which shows that such protection is solely applicable to workers who are trade unionists. Article 28 RESC obligates Member States to protect workers' representatives. Aside from trade unionists, workers who are active in organizations other than trade union organizations representing workers should receive the increased protection. In such cases when, as in the report filed by Romania, a Member State issues information dealing only with particular rights of workers who are members of trade union organizations, the Committee adjourns its decision and demands further information concerning the legal situation of workers who are active in other than representative trade union organizations within the workplace.[384]

The Committee is interested in situations in which workers are members of health and safety committees, and in which workers are members of general assemblies of workers within the workplace, owned by the state treasury.[385] It is of the position, in light of the legal regulation established by Article 28 RESC, that the definition 'workers' representatives' has no international meaning encompassing solely those organizations that are authorized by domestic labour legislation to represent the interests of the workers and protect their rights. On the other hand, the position of the Member States is that a given labour legislation only authorizes a trade union to represent

380. *The Right to Organize and Bargain Collectively*. Study drawn up on the basis of case law of the European Social Charter. 2nd edition, Council of Europe Publishing, Strasbourg 2001, p. 35.
381. Case of Austria: Conclusions XI-2, p. 73; Conclusions XIII-3, p. 96; Conclusions XIV-1, pp. 73–74; Conclusions XV-1, p. 39.
382. Addendum to Conclusions XV-1, pp. 14–15.
383. Case of France: Conclusions XIV-1, vol. 1, pp. 254-255; Conclusions XV-1, vol. 1, p. 243.
384. Conclusions 2003, vol. 2, p. 428.
385. Case of Bulgaria: Conclusions 2003 vol. 1, p. 91.

workers' interests and to protect their rights and is binding in nature. In such a case, the Committee of Social Rights has no basis for further examination of reasons why solely a trade union or other representative organization is authorized to represent workers' interests or protect their rights.

The Committee of Social Rights does not express itself about the particular scope of protection of rights of a representative team within a workplace carrying outs is functions. It is of the conviction that any form of rights protection especially concerned with the protection of lasting labour relations that may be moving away from the protection regulations established by a given Member State yet benefiting the worker, is in accordance with the standards stipulated under Article 28 RESC. The protection of lasting labour relations should be a major concern of those workers who are representing the interests of workers and are protecting their rights. The increased protection therefore is not applicable to workers who are not carrying out their responsibilities stipulated in their work agreement.

7.6.2. The Obligation to Afford Workers' Representatives Facilities to carry out their Statutory functions

A necessary condition for workers' representatives to appropriately carry out their functions and statutory goals is for employers to allow workers' representatives entry onto the work plant and allow them to organize meetings within the workplace. Article 5 RESC guaranteed trade unions these rights. The Committee of Social Rights claimed that the obligation of an employer to allow representatives of union organizations access to the workplace is not strict. In examining the methods of allowing workers' representatives to access the workplace, the Committee must take into consideration some of the employer demands such as the necessity of assured management of the workplace, the protection of confidential information and the obligation to protect the health and safety of every person within the workplace.[386] During the 12th and 13th supervisory cycle, the Committee concluded that Germany ensured trade unionists limited access to the workplace in such cases when the workplace employs only one or a few members of the particular union organization.[387] During the 15th supervisory cycle the Committee changed its position. It concluded that the right to access onto the grounds of a workplace should apply to workers' representatives of trade union. Regardless of the type of workplace (whether it is public or private) and the amount of workers employed (over or under 5 workers) workers' representatives of union organizations gained the right of access onto the grounds of a workplace in order to be able to carry out trade union activities.[388]

A direct connection of the rights of the workers' representatives being able to enter the grounds of a workplace is to be able to organize meetings. The questionnaire prepared by the Committee, which is to be used as a basis for Member States in

386. Conclusions XII-2, p. 98.
387. Conclusions XII-2, p. 98; Conclusions XIII-2, p. 269.
388. Addendum to Conclusions XV-1, p. 22.

preparing reports and then used by the Committee to examine domestic standards to the international model established by Article 28 RESC, contains questions concerning the ease with which workers can organize as well as the limitations of being able to take advantage of this right. Despite this question, the Committee of Social Rights did not concern itself[389] with the matter of trade union meetings being organized within on the grounds of a workplace. For this reason, the official publication regarding Committee decisions included an official lack of position in this matter.[390] In reality, however, the Committee indeed was concerned with this matter. Examining the case of Finland, the Committee concluded that an employer employing more than 10 workers must make available (under control) room and facilities within the workplace for after-hours trade union meetings.[391]

Despite the minimum experience of the Committee concerning the accessibility of room and facilities within the workplace for after-hours trade union meetings, this right must be made available to other workers' representatives' organizations to be able to carry out meetings. Depending on the type of property, some workers' representative bodies are regarded as (especially in Central and Eastern Europe) as bodies managing the workplaces, especially those where the owner is the state treasury. In such cases, the workers' representative bodies carry out a managerial function. They are authorized to independently define their own rights in matters associated with the fulfilment of their statutory functions and are active within the scope of the regulations. Therefore the Committee of Social Rights has legal rounds for carrying out examinations concerning the compliance of domestic labour law regulations with the international standards established under Article 28 RESC.

389. During the 3rd supervisory cycle the Committee concerned itself with the accusations of destabilization of trade union meeting in Austria. Conclusions III, p. 30.
390. The right to organize . . . , *op. cit.*, p. 34.
391. Conclusions XIV-1, vol. 1, p. 215.

CHAPTER 8 THE REGULATION OF SOCIAL RIGHTS THROUGH SOCIAL SECURITY LAW

8.1. The Right to Protection of Health

The right to protection of health is a fundamental human right.[1] The scope of application of Article 11 is broad. Initially, the Committee was of the opinion the obligations specified by the provision in question could be analysed inclusively. The obligations within the provision comprise three points:

- Elimination of causes of ill health (point 1).
- Advice and educational facilities for the promotion of health (point 2).
- The prevention of diseases (point 3).

They should be adhered to strictly. It is for this reason that during the first supervisory cycle, the Committee determined that Member States must provide relevant information proving that an organized system of health protection ensures the following: general access to health services, particular health care for certain social groups (mothers, children, and the aged), possibility of education in the protection of health, preventing and fighting against possible epidemics, financing the predominant health care costs.[2]

Analysing the reports filed during the first supervisory cycle, the Committee determined that it is impossible to make global conclusions about health care systems. Even though the three points of obligations set for Member States in Article 11 are interdependent, they should be analysed separately when examining whether Member States are fulfilling the obligations in matters concerning prevention, advice and education and prevention of epidemics.[3] The Committee also concluded that, when analysing the level of health services, it is important to examine the amount of members of a population who have access to basic health care, to examine whether preventative

1. B.C.A. Toebes, *The Right to Health as a Human Right in International Law*, Antwerpen-Groningen-Oxford, 1999, *passim*.
2. Conclusions I, p. 59.
3. *Ibid.*

measures are less developed in some states than the health care system in those states, and whether there are inadequacies in health care for the aged.[4] The Committee specified priorities for Member States and pointed to inadequacies in their health care systems.

These health care priorities of the Committee changed. Taking into consideration external factors, the Committee, according to Article 11, concerned itself with the protection of the natural environment. It took the view the state of the environment had a deciding significance in the effects on health prevention.[5] It underlined the interdependency between the standard of living in a society and the health of a society.[6] It interpreted the right to health care protection broadly. It was of the view that effective health care protection requires Member States to undertake preventative measures, which include the curing of illnesses and the rigorous abidance of hygiene standards.[7] It examined health policies of Member States.

Considering the increased costs of health care, the Committee pointed out the necessity of instituting preventative measures,[8] in particular ensuring effective protection from industrial noise,[9] atmospheric contamination,[10] exhaust fumes pollutants,[11] sewerage,[12] and AIDS.[13] The Committee claims that the protection of health cannot be treated in isolation from other social rights ensured by the Charter. Foremostly, the Committee referred to particular at-risk social groups, namely expectant women, infants, children and the aged.[14]

The Committee considers the development of awareness and responsibility about the state of the environment and its association with the protection of health, within society as essential. To achieve such goals, the Committee pointed to the need of health care education within schools,[15] the development of education,[16] and the carrying out medical research[17] in matters concerning health protection. Objective restrictions in an attempt to fight against certain illnesses meant that the Committee paid serious attention to the analysis of preventative measures initiated by Member States, in an attempt to minimize the dangers associated with alcohol, smoking tobacco, drug use, exposure to HIV,[18] and the effects of asbestos.[19]

---

4. *Ibid.*, pp. 59–60.
5. Conclusions IV, p. xvi; Conclusions V, p. xviii.
6. Conclusions VI, p. xiii.
7. Conclusions VIII, pp. 12–13.
8. Conclusions IX-1, p. 16.
9. Conclusions XIII-4, p. 391 (Belgium).
10. Conclusions X-2, pp. 27–28.
11. Conclusions IX-2, p. 13.
12. Conclusions X-1, p. 110 (Italy).
13. Conclusions IX-2, pp. 12–13.
14. Conclusions X-2, p. 25.
15. Conclusions III, p. 58 (Cyprus).
16. Conclusions XI-1, p. 31.
17. *Ibid.*, pp. 34; Conclusions XI-2, pp. 40–41.
18. Conclusions XII-1, p. 34 and following; Conclusions XII-2, p. 32 and following.
19. Conclusions XIII-4, p. 116; Conclusions XIV-2, pp. 40–41.

The decisions handed down by the Committee dealing in matters of health protection are eclectic.

A positive aspect of the Committee, with regards to such issues, is its quick reaction to any dangers that may appear and endanger humanity, such as AIDS, the Chernobyl catastrophe, the Creutzfeld-Jacob virus as well as other phenomena departing from European standards such as a high infant mortality rate[20] and a high level of road death tolls.[21] The inclusion of very general terms in the provision such as 'as far as possible' of Article 11 obligating Member States in matters concerning health protection, means that, when comparing with the standards established by the Committee concerning the level of some rights, affecting individual liberties such as the right to works and other rights affecting collective bodies (right to organize) labour laws, the Committee's meaning is weaker in the area of health care.

8.1.1. The Obligation to Eliminate the Causes of Ill Health

Article 11 obligates Member States to take measures of eliminating, as far as possible, the causes of ill health. In order to meet such obligations, Member States must organize a general system of medical health care services.[22] Even though most of the Member States have fulfilled such conditions, in order for the above demand to be regarded as met,[23] the Committee, during the 2004 supervisory cycle of complying with Article 11 out of the six examined states,[24] only considered Sweden as having instituted social policies concerning health care protection that were in accordance with international standards.[25] In contrast, in the case of Romania, the Committee ruled non-compliance with Article 11(1), because of the high rate of infant mortality (21.6 mortalities for 1000 births) as well as the high rate of women dying during child birth (43.3 deaths for 100,000 cases).[26] In the remaining situations the Committee adjourned its decisions and demanded that Member States produce further details. In the last supervisory cycle the Committee did not present any positive conclusion on compliance about any of the 12 examined states[27] with Article 11(1) RESC. The Committee, for example, concluded that the situation in Bulgaria, Moldova and Romania is not in conformity with the Article 11(1) RESC because of the manifestly too high maternal and infant mortality rates.[28]

---

20. Conclusions XIII-1, pp. 243–244 (Turkey); Conclusions 2003, vol. 1, p. 48 (Bulgaria); p. 147 (France); Conclusions 2003, vol. 2, p. 390 (Romania).
21. Conclusions XIII-3, p. 343 (Portugal).
22. Conclusions I, p. 59; Conclusions XIII-4, p. 119 (Iceland).
23. Addendum to Conclusions XV-2, p. 25.
24. Bulgaria, France, Italy, Romania, Slovenia and Sweden.
25. Conclusions 2003, vol. 2, pp. 597–599.
26. *Ibid.*, p. 390
27. Bulgaria, Cyprus, Estonia, France, Ireland, Italy, Lithuania, Moldova, Norway, Romania, Slovenia and Sweden.
28. Conclusions 2005, vol. 1 (Bulgaria), p. 27. According to World Health Organization data the mortality rate in Moldova for children aged between 0 and 5 years was from 23 (girls) to 32 (boys) per 1,000 live

In order for the above obligations by Member States to be fulfilled, the following matters need to be analysed: payment of health care fees, time spent waiting for medical assistance, and the amount of medical personnel. The Committee is of the view that health care is the fundamental obligation of Member States (state or local). Disproportion between public and private health care institutions in Member States, by transferring medical responsibilities onto private health care institutions causes alarm and the Committee is forced to demand clarifications from Member States.[29]

Basic health care services should be made available for free. Payments for additional medical services should be dependent upon the affluence of the patient. A lack of an obligation to incur the costs for medical services should be correspondent to a shortening of the time spent for providing specialist medical assistance. Even though some Member States underwent a shortening of time spent waiting for medical assistance,[30] and also a decrease in the percentage of people waiting for medical assistance more than a year,[31] the Committee concluded there is still a dangerous tendency amongst Member States where the hospital waiting list increases, and the amount of hospital beds decrease.[32] This relationship is regarded by the Committee as the main obstacle of Member States in fulfilling the obligations stipulated under Article 11.[33]

Analysing the level of health protection within Member States, the Committee points to the geographical lay out of medical facilities and their accessibility for the inhabitants of Member States, especially those living in villages and isolated regions.[34] It uses the following factors in its analysis: budget allocated for health care services, the proportion of such spending per inhabitant, the amount of deaths due to certain illnesses (e.g. cardiovascular, AIDS, cancer), the average life expectancy for men and women, the rate of infant mortality, and female deaths during child birth.

8.1.2. Health Advice and Education

A point of reference for establishing the level of health advice and education in Member States was the assertion concerning the fragmentation and the inadequately systematic organization of health advice and education.[35] This critical analysis was

---

births. The mortality rate for children less than 1 year of age amounted to 14.7 deaths per 1,000 live births. The Committee considers that this is particularly high, although it notes a decrease over recent years. Conclusions 2005, vol. 2, p. 447, 450. In Romania the rate of infant mortality amounted to 17.3 death per 1,000 live births, while the maternal mortality rate was 22 deaths per 100,000 live births. Conclusions 2005, vol. 2, p. 599, p. 601. Second reason for the negative conclusion in the case of Romania was manifestly inadequate living conditions in certain psychiatric hospitals.

29. Conclusions XV-2, p. 492 (Portugal); Addendum to Conclusions XV-2, p. 115 (Malta); Conclusions 2003, vol. 2, p. 488.
30. Great Britain from 45 to 35 days. Conclusions XV-2, p. 598.
31. Great Britain from 20 per cent to 3 per cent. *Ibid.*
32. The Committee considered the factors of the World Health Organization for developing countries: 3 beds per 1000 inhabitants. Addendum to Conclusions XV-2, p. 257.
33. Conclusions XV-2, p. 127 (Denmark).
34. Addendum to Conclusions XV-2, p. 257 (Turkey).
35. Conclusions I, p. 60; Conclusions II, p. 189 (Cyprus).

later improved. In the last supervisory cycle, only one Member State was considered to be compliant with the obligations stipulated under Article 11(2),[36] although none of the Member States received a negative judgment. The Committee demanded additional information concerning health education in schools,[37] and about the creation of social awareness[38] about the current health dangers and their prevention and about the responsibility of regular medical check-ups.

The Committee noted the necessity to inform children and the wider community about the dangers caused by a pathological life style.[39] It refers to the necessity of introducing the following educational subjects: sex education and health care. It requires Member States to produce information regarding whether such educational subjects encompass information regarding the dangers involved from smoking, excessive alcohol consumption, drug addiction and unprotected sex.[40] It takes into consideration whether the above information is presented as part of a programme of creating awareness within society about the dangers associated with pathological behaviour.[41] It does not accept generalized statements.[42] The Committee demands that Member States produce concrete details about the amount of hours allocated in schools for health care subjects, the amount of students taking health education, the amount of organized programmes promoting a healthy lifestyle, and on the amount of money spent by the state on such health advice, health education and the promotion of it. It also seeks information about the free of charge obligatory health check-ups in schools, how frequently they are carried out, on the amount of students examined and on the amount of medical personnel available within the schools assisting in the conduct of these examinations.[43]

8.1.3. Prevention of Epidemic and Endemic Diseases as well as Accidents

Analysing the reports of Member States concerning the compliance of Article 11(3), the Committee has concentrated on two categories. The first are social policies concerned with the counteractions against dangers, which can be prevented; and the second is the category of effective preventative measures. The Committee is of the view that the necessary requirement in carrying out successful social policies concerned with the counteractions against dangers is the protection of the natural environment. Carrying out such policies may only be achieved with the organization of appropriate programmes as well as by allocating necessary funds for such programmes.[44] The Committee demands from the reports compiled by Member States, detailed information regarding

---

36. Conclusions 2003, vol. 2, pp. 600–601 (Sweden).
37. Conclusions III, p. 59 (Austria); Conclusions XV-2, p. 97 (Belgium).
38. Conclusions XV-2, pp. 208–209.
39. Conclusions 2003, vol. 1, p. 285 (Italy); Conclusions 2003, vol. 2, pp. 394–395 (Romania).
40. Conclusions X-2, p. 111 (Spain); Conclusions XIII-3, p. 346 (Finland); Conclusions 2003, vol. 1, p. 52 (Bulgaria).
41. Conclusions XIII-4, p. 126 (Greece).
42. Conclusions 2003, vol. 2, p. 488.
43. Addendum to Conclusions XV-2, p. 199 (Slovakia).
44. *Ibid.*, p. 201; Conclusions XV-2, p. 452 (Poland).

programmes against air pollution,[45] water contamination,[46] asbestos exposure during work,[47] radiation,[48] cancer causing factors, industrial noise and toxic factors (especially tobacco and alcohol).[49] It demands information about programmes propagating a healthy eating lifestyle.

One of the preventative measures that the Committee monitors carefully are vaccination programmes needed to fight against viral diseases.[50] Such programmes should cover at least 90 per cent of the community.[51] If such programmes are not created, and if the conditions are not met, the Committee automatically regards a Member State to be in non-compliance with Article 11(3).[52] The Committee demands that Member States ensure that health care is organized within schools, and that school principles are involved in providing regular health care check-ups of the students,[53] that there are programmes in force to ensure health care protection in cases of epidemics within the country, and that such programmes are accessible for all inhabitants of Member States.[54]

Article 11(3) increased the above obligations to include the prevention of accidents. This section is not solely applicable to workplace accidents, but also encompasses accidents within the transport sector, especially accidents involving children[55] as well as deadly accidents.[56]

In some situations, the Committee rendered judgments about the non-compliance of Member States and their inability to fulfil the obligation stipulated under Article 11(3). Three such judgements were handed down for not providing vaccination programmes for the amount of people required.[57] One was for an inadequate campaign against smoking.[58] During the last supervisory cycle the Committee, in one of the cases, ruled about the compliance of domestic practices with the standards introduced by Article 11(3).[59] In the remaining five cases, the Committee adjourned its rulings and asked for additional information from the Member States.[60]

45. Conclusions VIII, p. 147 and following; Conclusions 2003, vol. 1, pp. 53–54 (Bulgaria); pp. 151–152 (France); pp. 286–288 (Italy); Conclusions 2003, vol. 2, pp. 395–396 (Romania); pp. 491–492 (Slovenia).
46. Conclusions XV-2, p. 462 (Poland); Addendum to Conclusions XV-2, p. 262 (Turkey).
47. Conclusions XIII-4, p. 116.
48. Conclusions XII-1, p. 174; Conclusions XII-2, p. 166; Conclusions XV-2, p. 214; Addendum to Conclusions XV-2, pp. 51–52.
49. Conclusions XV-2, pp. 101–102.
50. Conclusions 2003, vol. 1, p. 57 (Bulgaria); p. 155 (France); pp. 288–289 (Italy); Conclusions 2003, vol. 2, p. 397 (Romania); p. 493 (Slovenia).
51. Conclusions XIII-4, p. 138 (Great Britain).
52. Conclusions X-2, p. 111 (Spain); Conclusions XIII-5, p. 138 (Luxembourg); Conclusions XV-2, pp. 103–104 (Belgium); Addendum to Conclusions XV-2, pp. 264–265 (Turkey).
53. Case of Cyprus: Conclusions III, p. 60; Conclusions IV, p. 78.
54. Conclusions XIII-3, p. 350 (Portugal); Conclusions XIII-5, p. 138 (Luxembourg).
55. Conclusions 2003, vol. 1m p. 56 (Bulgaria).
56. *Ibid.*, p. 155 (France); p. 289 (Italy).
57. At least 90 per cent of the community. *See* footnote 48 and 49.
58. Conclusions XV-2, pp. 252–253 (Greece).
59. Conclusions 2003, vol. 2, p. 605 (Sweden).
60. Bulgaria, France, Romania, Slovenia, Italy.

8.2. The Right to Social Security (Article 12)

8.2.1. Introduction

The standards of social security within Europe are determined by three international organizations: the European Union, the Council of Europe and the International Labour Organization.[61] Officially, the European Union is an international organization, which issues regulations coordinating domestic social security systems within Member States. The regulations of the original communitarian rights (Article 42 of the Treaty of Rome) obligated the Council of Europe to ensure that insured individuals who are mobile within the European Union vicinity have the right to accumulate their various insurance periods even though the domestic social security regulations existing within given Member States of the European Union may acquire an increase in social security benefits. It also orders citizens of Member States the right to use the benefits paid out by a particular state social security institution, regardless of the place of residency within the European Union of the beneficiary.

This obligation is ensured by the decree of the Council (No. 1408 of 14 June 1971) in matters of applying systems of social security for workers, those who are self-employed and their families moving within the territory of the Community, and by another decree (No. 574) establishing the way in which to fulfil decree No. 1408.[62] Differing from the regulations of European labour law, which establish standards in matters applicable only to some of the institutions of individual labour rights, the European social security law coordinates the separate domestic systems of social security within Member States.

European Union institutions do not stipulate social security standards. However, completely independently, two models of social security (Bismarck and Beveridge) upon which domestic systems are based on, show certain similarities. The assimilation of state social security institutions in Member States of the European Union was a

61. A. Świątkowski, Rola i znaczenie europejskich standardów zabezpieczenia społecznego dla polskiego ustawodawstwa na XXI wiek (The Role and Importance of European Social Security Standards for Polish Legislature in the 21st Century), Polityka Społeczna 2005 (Social Policies 2005), No. 3, p. 9 and following.

62. *See* Prospects of social security coordination, ed. P. Schoukens, Acco Leuven/Amersfoort 1997; Rozporządzenie Rady Wspólnot Europejskich w dziedzinie zabezpieczenia społecznego z komentarzem T. Bińczyckiej-Majewskiej (Orders of the European Community Council in social security with the commentary by T. Bińczyckiej-Majewskiej) ZUS, Warszawa 1995; Idem, Koordynacja systemów zabezpieczenia społecznego w Unii Europejskiej (Coordinating social security systems in the European Union), Zakamycze, Kraków 1999; R. White, EC Social Security Law, Longman, Harkowa 1999; A. Świątkowski, Europejskie prawo socjalne (European Social Law), vol. III. Europejskie prawo ubezpieczeń społecznych (European social security law), Dom Wydawniczy ABC, Warszawa 2000; Y. Jorens, B.Schulte, The Implementation of Regulation 1408/71 in the Member States of the European Union, European Journal of Social Security, 2001, vol. 3/3, p. 237 and following; A. Giżejowska, A. Świątkowski, Zabezpieczenie społeczne (Social security), Uniwersitas, Kraków 2003; F. Pennings, Introduction to European Social Security Law, Intersentia, Antwerp-Oxford-New York 2003; Idem, European Union. International Encyclopedia of Laws, Social Security Law – Suppl.42, Kluwer Law International, The Hague 2003.

product of the need for coordination, stipulated by the decree of the Council of Europe No. 1408/71. Member States of the European Union came to the conclusion that successful coordination of separate domestic systems of social security is possible when such systems possess similar traits. The standards of social security existing within Member States of the European Union were issued by the various Member States. Domestic social security systems are based upon the consolidation of insurance. They encompass protections against various risk factors such as illness and maternity, disability, old age, death of the provider for the family, work related accidents and industrial illnesses, loss of employment, and an increase in family members. The factors of acquiring, maintaining and increasing the security benefits as well as the level of such benefits are completely regulated by domestic social security systems.

The Council of Europe and the International Labour Organization have very different roles in establishing the standards of social security within Europe. These organizations pass regulations, which include social security standards.[63] The right to social security and assistance are regarded as fundamental human rights.[64] According to such regulations, the Council of Europe has passed the European Social Charter of 1961 as well as the Revised European Social Charter of 1996.[65] Poland is a signatory of the former Social Charter. The following argument will concentrate on standards of social security established within the European Social Charter of 1961. These standards are correspondent to the global standards, established by the Convention No. 102 passed during the 35th session of the ILO on 4 June 1952, dealing with the minimal standards of social security.

8.2.2. The Scope of Social Protection

The Charter does not provide a legal definition for social security. It declares protection in the following fields: health (Article 11), social security benefits

63. Under the auspices of the Council of Europe the following international treaties deal with social security: European Interim Agreement on Social Security Schemes Relating to Old Age, Invalidity and Survivors along with the Protocol and the European Interim Agreement on Social Security Other than Schemes for Old Age, Invalidity and Survivors along with the Protocol. These treaties were passed on 11 December 1953. They came into force on 1 July 1954 and 10 October 1954. Poland did not ratify these documents. After passing the European Social Charter in 1961, 16 April 1964 the European Code of Social Security along with the Protocol was accepted. The law came into force on the 17 March 1968. Poland did not ratify this document. On the 14 December 1972 the European Convention on Social Security and Supplementary Agreement was passed. It came into force on the 1 March 1977. Poland did not ratify this convention. Passing the European Convention on Social Security the ILO convention No. 118 passed on 6 June 1962 was cited during the 46th General Conference of the ILO. In 1990 the Revised European Code of Social Security was passed. The Code is available for ratification from 6 November 1990.
64. M. Mikkola, Social Rights as Human Rights in Europe, European Journal of Social Security, Kluwer Law International 2000, vol. 2, No. 3, p. 259 and following.
65. European Social Charter. Collected texts (4th edition), Council of Europe Publishing, Strasbourg 2003; S. Evju, The European Social Charter (in:) The Council of Europe and the Social Challenges of the 21st Century, Bulletin of Comparative Labour Relations, ed. R. Blanpain, vol. 39, Kluwer Law International, The Hague/London/Boston, p. 19 and following; A. Świątkowski, Karty społeczne ... (Social Charters ...), *op. cit.*, p. 36 and following.

(Article 12), social and medical care (Article 13), and social welfare services (Article 14). In addition, it ensures protection for people who are disabled (Article 15) and ensures social, legal and economic protection for the family (Article 16). The broadest scope of its protection is set forth in Article 12:

- Obligating Member States of the Council of Europe to establish and maintain a system of social security (point 1);
- Defining a minimum level of social benefits (point 2);
- Obligating members states to endeavour to raise progressively the system of social security to a higher level (point 3);
- And obligating the authorities to ensure equal treatment in respect of social security rights regardless of their citizenship (point 4).

In establishing the social security standards, the Committee of Social Rights points to the effectiveness of domestic social security systems. Social benefits should be appropriate, meaning that they should ensure that the insured and his/her family are able to provide for the poorer member of society.[66] The Committee accentuated this aspect due to the tendency of increased costs of managing social security systems within Member States as well as a tendency in reducing the expenditure allocated for social security benefits.

In establishing the European standards of social security, the Committee did not attempt to define 'social security'. It did not allude to the attempts made by Member States to separate social security systems from social protection systems or social assistance in terms of financing the benefits involved. Within the confines of Article 12, the Committee analysed domestic systems ensuring financial benefits as well as social assistance for persons in need. The concept of 'social security' was treated by the Committee, as a 'socially advanced technique of social protection', confined also to (regardless of the source of financing such benefits, e.g. by way of premiums or not) social assistance.[67] The Committee was not interested in the legal nature of paying out the social security benefits for those insured. Instead, it examined the development of domestic social security systems within Member States, taking into consideration the scope of subjects, type and level of paid benefits in the case of the insured risk coming to fruition.[68] It was concerned mostly with the reasons for which the social benefits were allocated and with the conditions required to be met in order for such benefits to be received.

Article 12 has a broad definition of 'social security'. It encompasses general, obligatory, voluntary and complimentary systems of security based on the payment of voluntary premiums of those insured, financed either fully or partially from state funds, the ensured parties' financial benefits or social assistance for those insured, affected by circumstances limiting or affecting their means of earning a living.

---

66. Conclusions XII-1, p. 32 and following; L. Samuel, *op. cit.*, p. 283 and following.
67. Conclusions VII, p. 74 (France).
68. Conclusions XIII-4, p. 37 and following.

The primary position within the European system of social security standards is filled by the circumstances of the insured individuals, which are considered to be the risk of putting livelihood at risk or the risk of limiting the ability of such individuals to self sufficiently support themselves or their families. Such risks include illness, disability, pregnancy, old age, death, unemployment, and work related accident or industrial illness.

8.2.3. An Obligation to Establish a System of Social Security (Article 12(1))

Member States are obligated to establish or maintain a system of social security (Article 12(1)). In the opinion of the Committee, the general description of a 'system' of social security[69] assumes the application of social security provisions protecting citizens as well as those legally residing on the territory of a Member State, against certain risks. This is a necessary condition in deciding whether domestic social security regulations form a 'system' of social security in the understanding of Article 12(1), which guarantees protection against the majority of risks protecting the majority of the community.[70] A system of social security does not have to protect against all forms of risk.[71] Not all social security laws may be considered as compliant with the standards established in Article 12(1). Cyprus, for example, did not fulfil the requirements of a 'system' because of the serious loopholes in the conditions that should have been fulfilled by persons seeking social security benefits, and also due to the low level of such benefits.[72] The shortcomings were not of a serious nature, as they were ratified within one of the supervisory cycles. As stated previously, in the fourth supervisory cycle, the Committee declared that the social security laws in Cyprus fulfil the obligations established by Article 12(1). There is no country within Europe that may be accused of violating Article 12(1).

8.2.4. An Obligation to Maintain a System of Social Security at an Appropriate Level (Article 12(2))

Article 12(2) obligates Member States to maintain

> A national social security system at an 'appropriate' level, at least appropriate to the demands set by the ILO convention No. 102, dealing with minimum standards of social security.[73]

---

69. Conclusions I, p. 62.
70. Conclusions XIII-4, p. 37.
71. Despite the lack of social security in cases of illness, pregnancy, social benefits in Cyprus, the Committee of Social Rights declared the system of social security in Cyprus is in accordance with Article 12(1) of the Charter. Conclusions IV, p. 81.
72. Conclusions III, p. 62.
73. Conventions and recommendations ... vol. 1, *op. cit.*, Pracy, p. 462 and following. Convention No. 102 ILO came into force on 27 April 1955. 40 countries ratified it. Poland did not ratify this convention. *See* Lists of Ratification by Convention and by Country, ILO, Geneva 2003, pp. 122–124.

A point of reference for the Committee in terms of the Charter, are standards established by the ILO. In its first version, Article 12(2) ESC obligates national social security systems to be retained at a level as defined by the European Code of Social Security.[74] Countries intending to ratify the ILO convention No. 102 are obligated to accept at least 3 parts out of 9 of this convention, including at least one part dealing with unemployment benefits (part 4), retirement (part 5), benefits due to workplace accidents or industrial illnesses (part 6), disability pensions (part 9) or benefits allocated due to death of the provider within the family (part 10).

A country ratifying the Code of Social Security is obligated to accept at least six out of 9 parts of the Code modelled on the ILO convention No. 102. Part 2 deals with medical care and is treated in two sections. Part 5 regulates benefits for the retired and is made up of three sections. In reality, ratifying the two mentioned parts and any other third part fulfils the requirement when ratifying six out of nine parts of the Code. The European Code of Social Security is treated by the Committee as a point of reference in cases of supervising Member States of the Council of Europe and their compliance of the Revised European Social Charter of 1996.[75]

Countries forming the Council of Europe do not have the obligation to ratify the ILO convention No. 102. In the case of ratifying this convention, the compatibility of domestic social security systems with the standards of ILO is controlled by the Committee of Experts of the ILO. The Committee of Social Rights of the Council of Europe fills the 'intermediate' supervisory function[76] in monitoring the compliance of the standards established by Article 12(2). It usually looks to the position of the Committee of Experts of ILO for support.[77] The Committee of Social Rights is not connected to the stance of the Committee of Experts of the ILO. It may therefore occur that the negative position of the Committee of Experts of the ILO does not influence the opinion of the Committee of Social Rights.[78] Member States of the Council of Europe could ratify more than the required amount of parts of the ILO convention No. 102, and the ILO Committee Experts can simultaneously negatively assess a domestic social security system.[79]

---

74. L. Samuel, *op. cit.*, p. 287; D. Harris, J. Darcy, *op. cit.*, p. 157.
75. The Committee of Social Rights on two occasions handed down negative rulings about the social security system in Greece (Conclusions XIV-1, p. 352) and Italy (Conclusions XIV-1, pp. 461–462). In the case of Greece it concluded non-compliance of benefits allocated due to workplace accidents and industrial illness with the international standards established by the European Code of Social Security. In the case of Italy there was non-compliance in the area of retirement and family benefits.
76. Conclusions XIII-4, *op. cit.*, p. 38.
77. In the case of Austria, Cyprus and Spain, the Committee of Social Rights of the Council of Europe took an identical stance as that of the Committee of Experts of ILO. Conclusions I, p. 62; Conclusions IV, p. 82 (Austria); Conclusions II, p. 19 (Cyprus); Addendum to Conclusions IX-2, pp. 31–32 (Spain).
78. During the 14th supervisory cycle the Committee concluded that the Italian social security system fulfills the obligations set in the ILO convention No. 102 in two of the domains. It did not hand down a negative ruling; it demanded further information about fulfilling the obligations stipulated by the convention in other domains of social security. Conclusions XIV-1, *op. cit.*, pp. 461–462.
79. Conclusions I, *op. cit.*, p. 62.

A domestic social security system may be regarded as being in accordance with the standards stipulated by the ILO convention No. 102, even though a given country may not have ratified the convention. However, ratifying the ILO convention No. 102 is not a necessary requirement for fulfilling the demands made under Article 12(2) of the European Social Charter.[80] Evaluating the domestic social security systems from the point of view of compliance of the minimal standards of the ILO convention No. 102, the Committee of Social Rights points to the value and the effect of social security laws within Member States. It also draws attention to the level of those insured and employed or residing within a Member State and how they are encompassed by such laws, and focuses on the protection ensured to them at least in three of the categories of social and economic risk.

In situations when Member States do not ratify the ILO convention No. 102, the Committee of Social Rights independently examines whether each domestic social security system is in compliance with the requirements stipulated in the convention. It, therefore, demands that Member States produce additional information. The Committee, for example, adjourned its decision in the case of Poland and whether the country's social security system was in compliance with Article 12(2).[81]

8.2.5. An Obligation to Endeavour to Raise Progressively the System of Social Security to a Higher Level (Article 12(3))

Article 12(3) obligates Member States to undertake measures to improve progressively their domestic social security system. The dynamic understanding of this obligation means that during a period of recession, when Member States reduce their spending on social concerns, the factors of entitling social security benefits become much more rigorous.[82] The earlier decisions, as seen in Poland, become verified and make social security benefits (such as unemployment benefits) dependent upon new requirements such as the inability to retrain oneself in a new profession or a lack of any employment offers.

Article 12(3) is a legal norm establishing social security standards. In Article 12(3), there is an indeterminate term. Member States are obligated to take measures in improving domestic social security systems. An obligation of these authorities is to raise the level of these systems and inform the Committee about the measures taken.[83]

---

80. The Committee was of the view that Finland, even though had not ratified the ILO convention No. 102, still fulfilled the requirements made under Article 12(2) of the European Social Charter, because it ratified other ILO conventions, which regulate social security issues. Conclusions XIII-3, p. 354.
81. The Committee initially analysed the types of risks as well as scope of social security regulations. It did not voice any reservations with regards to the amount of social security benefits. It demanded additional information concerning the amount of persons insured and entitled to medical benefits and in what type of periods the above entitlements would be possible. It adjourned its decision with regards to the amount of family social security benefits as well as to the persons entitled to benefits in the case of the death of the breadwinner within the family. Addendum to Conclusions XV-1 (Poland).
82. D. Harris, J. Darcy, *op. cit.*, p. 159.
83. Conclusions I, p. 62; Conclusions XIII-4, pp. 141–142.

The Committee examines the results in each supervisory cycle by looking at the level of social security within each Member State as compared to the last supervisory cycle. The primary basis for conducting such analysis is the ILO convention No. 102. Further, the Committee determines a level of social security standard that is higher than the one established by the convention. The rationale for the Committee's handed down is that a domestic social security system, which does not fulfil the minimum standard requirements established by the ILO convention No. 102, contravenes Article 12(3).[84]

The standard established by Article 12(3) requires Member States of the Council of Europe to undertake constant efforts to improve their social security systems. The Committee indicates ways in which this can be achieved. Domestic social security systems should, for example, aim to increase range of beneficiaries, and to increase the level of social security and ensure social protection against other types of risk. The main idea of the Committee is clear. The Committee is an institution establishing the European standards of social security, aiming at a 'broader and fuller protection of social rights'. It is a body, which, foremostly, accentuates the effects of protecting social security rights. Having this in mind, it underlines the necessity to undertake constant measures (even if on a small scale), which will improve the level of social protection. Raising the level of social security benefits,[85] especially well above the increase in living costs,[86] making preparations for ratifying the European Code of Social Security,[87] ratifying the protocol of this Code,[88] are all indicators treated by the Committee of Social Rights showing that a Member State is compliant with the requirements made under Article 12(3).

The standards established by the Committee take into consideration outside circumstances such as major economic and population factors and the costs involved in managing a social security entity, as well as the increase of an ageing population in Europe. When stipulating the standards of social protection, the Committee does consider outside restrictions affecting the level of such protection. Not losing track of its aim, namely, achieving a high level of social security, which will allow a Member State to ratify the Protocol of the European Code of Social Security, the Committee has accepted the idea of introducing changes into domestic social security systems. It is interested in the scope of such changes as well as in their nature. It wanted to become familiar with the reasons propagating such changes.

The Committee signalled the Member States that it is open to various changes introduced to the social security systems, even if these changes will limit the subjective and the objective scope of the states' social security regulations. It wanted to become familiar with the effects of the introduced changes and, thus, demanded information concerning the assurance of alternative methods of social protection for those affected

84. Conclusions II, pp. 191–192; Conclusions III, p. 63 (Cyprus); Conclusions IV, p. 82 (Austria).
85. E.g. maternity benefits in Italy. Conclusions III, p. 64.
86. Conclusions IV, p. 83.
87. Measures undertaken by Danish authorities. Conclusions IV, p. 83.
88. European Social Charter, Conclusions X-1, Council of Europe Press, Strasbourg 1995, p. 113 (the Netherlands).

by such changes.[89] The dynamic nature of Article 12(3) is not an obstacle for the reformation of domestic social security systems, when necessary. An example of this is a restriction on the financial expenditure on social benefits such as benefits for the retired due to an increase in ageing population,[90] as long as it does not affect the effectiveness of social protection due to social and economic risks of all those insured. However, examining the actions undertaken by the Dutch, who attempted to transfer the costs of social benefits payable to those unable to work due to illness in the first weeks of the illness (from two to six weeks, depending on the size of the workplace) onto the employers, the Committee concluded such an action to be not in accordance with Article 12(3). It was of the view that this provision obligates Member States (those who have ratified it) to make efforts in improving social security regulations. In the view of the Committee, the Dutch actions were not in accordance with the idea of social security participation, which, either by way of premiums or taxes, depending on the system, contributes to the social security scheme, which then pays for sickness benefits. This participation is connected to various forms of risk stemming from a variety of health dangers as well as to the management of funds deposited from which benefits are paid to those insured who are unable to work due to illness. In its conclusion, the Committee states the Dutch actions were not compliant wit the standards established by Article 12(3).[91]

The Committee similarly regarded the changes introduced by Norway to unemployment benefits negatively. Making unemployment entitlements to social security benefits dependent upon accepting any form of job offer, even if not appropriate to the professional skills, the experience, qualifications and education of the unemployed, as well as his/her family situation, is regarded by the Committee as non-compliant with Article 12(3), which aims to improve the situation of domestic social security systems.[92] In the case of Poland, the decision was adjourned as to the compliance of Article 12(3) and the actions undertaken to restrict the amount of unemployment benefits. Poland's stipulation of economic reasons causing the loss of rights to unemployment benefits, as well as making the length of time in which such benefits may be received dependent upon the unemployment levels within each region, as well as the discrepancy between the average monthly earning and the unemployment benefit, caused the Committee to depart from the opinion of the OECD, since the unemployment benefits in Poland are being paid out in the form of social assistance.[93] The Committee adjourned its decision concerning the compliance of Polish employment measures and actions taken against unemployment with Article 12(3), and demanded additional information from Poland, which would enable it to form a position on the scope, the level and the amount of unemployment benefits.

89. Conclusions XIII-4, pp. 143–144.
90. Case of Belgium: Conclusions XVI-1, vol. 1, p. 86. Prof. J. Nickless, Trends and Development in Old-age Pension and Health Care Financing in Europe During 1990s, Council of Europe, Series 'Trends in Social Cohesion', No. 2, Strasbourg 2002, pp. 9 and following.
91. Conclusions XIV-1, vol. 2, pp. 561–562, 565.
92. Conclusions XV-1, p. 441.
93. OECD, Economic Survey, Poland, 1998; Addendum to Conclusions XV-1 (Poland).

8.2.6. An Obligation of Equal Treatment of Those Insured (Article 12(4))

Article 12(4) obligates Member States to provide equal treatment to all insured individuals regardless of their citizenship. As part of this obligation, the Member States should take measures[94] in an attempt to ensure equal treatment to the citizens of the given Member State in matters concerning the granting, retention and resumption of social security rights by such means as the accumulation of insurance or employment periods completed under legislation existing within another Member State. The obligation of the Member States is to ensure that the insured citizens of other Member States receive the right of accumulation of insurance under the social security legislation existing within that Member State, regardless of changing place of residency within the territory of a Member State that is a party to the Council of Europe.

Member States who have ratified Article 12(4) do not have the obligation to appropriate bilateral or multilateral agreements ensuring equal treatment of all those insured. They must ensure that the citizens of other Member States receive equal treatment based on the legislation of that given Member State. The Committee came to the conclusion that Article 12(4) allows Member State the choice one of three methods of ensuring equal treatment of all those insured: through bilateral agreements, through multilateral agreements or through unilateral regulations. This conclusion was reached after analysing the reports of the Member States that did not have signed agreements about migrant workers.[95] It later stated that regardless of whether or not Member States have an agreement with regards to migrant workers, Member States have the choice of one of the methods in Article 12(4).[96]

Article 12(4) has a general application to citizens of all Member States regardless of whether such Member States have ratified this standard or not.[97] The principle of reciprocity existing in international public law is not applicable in this case.[98] The scope of Article 12(4) is also applied objectively. This provision is applicable to all social benefits, with the exception of social assistance and health care regulated by Article 13, regardless of their scope and form of financing. It is therefore applicable to social benefits payable by general social security systems (obligatory and voluntary), as well as to benefits financed by premiums of the insured and/or the insurer, or to benefits financed by the funds allocated by central or local budget authorities.[99]

---

94. For example issuing regulations ensuring equal treatment to those insured regardless of their citizenship of one of the Member State, party to the Council of Europe. Conclusions XII-2, p. 178; Conclusions XIII-2, p. 118 (France).
95. Conclusions VII, p. 73 (Austria); Conclusions XIII-2, p. 117 (Cyprus); Conclusions XIII-2, p. 121 (the Netherlands).
96. Conclusions XIII-2, p. 122 (Norway).
97. Those countries that have not ratified the Article 12(4) but ratified the Charter European Social Charter of 1961 are: Croatia, Latvia, Malta, Hungry and Great Britain. Those countries that have ratified the Revised European Social Charter of 1996 but have not ratified Article 12(4) of the Charter are: Armenia, Bulgaria and Sweden.
98. Conclusions XIV-1, p. 667.
99. Conclusions XIII-4, pp. 42–43.

In addition to Article 12(4), it was decided that bilateral or multilateral agreements could contain certain conditions, upon which equal treatment application may be premised. Such conditions of attaining social security benefit rights may exist, regardless of citizenship and the financial input into the insurance (by way of premiums or taxes based on the period of residing within that Member State).

This provision formed the legal basis for the Committee of Social Rights' development of the supervisory processes over the compliance of domestic social security systems. The Committee considered whether the introduction of residency conditions into treaties and international agreements would be discriminatory to an insured party who is not a citizen of the given Member State in which social security claim has been filed, even if such a condition is general. It refers to the citizens of a given country as well as to the other Member States of the Council of Europe. The Committee reserved for itself the right to examine the conditions implemented.

The Committee concluded that there needs to be a proportion maintained in the conditions between the international agreements and the benefits ensured by the domestic social security systems.[100] Basing its decision on the above principle, the Committee stated that the requirement of residing within a given country for a period of 5 years for a citizen of another Member State, party to the Council of Europe, in order to attain the right to pension benefits, is discriminatory for that citizen in whose country the same requirement entails 3 years of residency for claiming such benefits.[101] Social security regulations are discriminatory when the right to pension entitlements by the insured who is a citizen of a given state, is dependent upon his/her residency on the territory of that given state for a period of 10 years between the age of 10 and 65 years of age as well as for a period of 5 years directly prior to retirement age (67 years)[102], for 20 years after turning 40 years of age or for 35 years after reaching the age of 18.[103] Belgium's regulations requiring proof of residency of 5 years for citizen of other Member States, seeking social security family benefits, were similarly regarded as displaying unequal treatment.[104]

One year of residency, however, was regarded as fair and not in breach of equal treatment requirements, for those citizens of other Member States of the Council of Europe seeking family benefits.[105] After examining the reports filed by Member States, the Committee drew attention to the fact that the condition for residing on the territory of a given country where the insured is seeking social security family benefits be applicable to the parents or the legal guardians and not to the children.[106] The countries, in which family benefits are paid only in cases where the insured parents and the children are residing within the territory of the given country, are considered to be

100. Conclusions XIII-3, p. 358 (Finland); Conclusions XIV-1, p. 191 (Denmark).
101. Conclusions XIII-3, p. 358 (Finland).
102. Conclusions XIV-1, vol. 1, p. 191 (Denmark).
103. Conclusions XV-1, p. 126 (Cyprus).
104. Conclusions XV-1, p. 88.
105. Conclusions XIV-1, vol. 1, p. 189 (Denmark).
106. Conclusions XIII-4, p. 44.

in violation of Article 12(4) and its specified obligation of equal treatment. It is an indication the policies carried out are indirectly discriminating against the insured who are citizens of other Member States, that are parties to the Council of Europe[107] and not being members of the European Union.[108] The differences in livelihood costs between Member States of the Council of Europe justify the differences in paid social security benefits, for children of the insured who are not citizens of the given country in which their children are living in and where the costs of maintenance are much lower.[109]

The Committee views the exclusion of citizens of Member States of the Council of Europe (different than EU members), on the basis of domestic social security regulations, as direct discrimination, violating equal treatment principles of the insured under Article 12(4).[110]

Article 12(4) orders that identical criteria must be used when analysing the insurance rights of citizens from Member States forming the Council of Europe, regardless of their citizenship, in all matters dealing with social security. The cited provision indicates that it is applicable when retaining the rights attained under the regulations of domestic social security legislation of other states of the Council of Europe. The insured, citizens of states other than those states in which they attained their social security rights, have the right to seek a transfer of their social security funds by an insurance institution and have them paid out elsewhere.[111] The Committee decided that the model applied in the legal regulations of the European Union,[112] with the exception of unemployment benefits,[113] is that all other social security benefits paid out in any Member State of the Council of Europe to citizens of other Member States are transferable.[114] In the case of 7 countries[115] the Committee decided that domestic social security systems do not comply with the standards stipulated under Article 12(4). In two other cases[116] it adjourned its opinion, seeking further information

107. Conclusions XIV-1, p. 467 (Italy).
108. Decree 1408/71 (Article 73) as well as the European Tribunal of Justice orders social security institutions to pay family benefits for children of the insured residing within a different Member State of the European Union (*Bronzino*, ECJ 22 Feb 1990, case 228/88, 1990 ECR, p. 551). *See* F. Pennings, *Case Law. Social Security Law*, International Encyclopaedia of Laws, Kluwer Law International, The Hague, London, Boston, 1999, pp. 1919–1920; A. Świątkowski, *Europejskie ...* (*European ...*), *op. cit.*, p. 415.
109. Conclusions XIV-1, pp. 314–315 (Germany).
110. Conclusions XIV-1, p. 268 (France).
111. D. Harris, J. Darcy, *op. cit.*, p. 164.
112. A. Świątkowski, *Europejskie ...* (*European ...*), *op. cit.*, p. 505 and following.
113. Conclusions XIV-1, p. 630 (Norway).
114. Addendum to Conclusions XV-2, p. 22 (Ireland); Committee of Social Rights decided that France forbidding the transfer if disability pensions and family benefits of Maltese and Slovakian citizens violates Article 12(4) of the European Social Charter. Conclusions XV-1, p. 126.
115. Conclusions XV-1, pp. 49–50 (Austria); Conclusions XV-1, p. 88 and following (Belgium); Conclusions XV-1, p. 126 (Cyprus); Conclusions XV-1, p. 49–50 (France); Addendum to Conclusions XV-2, p. 22 (Ireland); Conclusions XIV-1, pp. 667 and following, XV-1, p. 22 (Turkey); Conclusions XIV-1, pp. 768 and following, XV-1, pp. 599–600.
116. Addendum to Conclusions XV-1, pp. 35 and following (Germany); Addendum to Conclusions XV-1, p. 130 and following (Poland).

to clarify the doubts about the compliance of domestic social security systems with Article 12(4).[117]

8.2.7. Summary

Articles 12–17 establish the standards of social security. Among these provisions, particular importance must be paid to Article 12, which reflects a broad understanding of social security. Establishing and maintaining social security systems is an obligation of all Member States forming the Council of Europe. These countries have the obligation to improve their domestic social security systems. The standards used in order to examine the compliance of such system for Member States (that have ratified the European Social Charter, the ILO convention No. 102 or the Revised European Social Charter), are those established by the European Code of Social Security. The Committee of Social Rights has oversight as to whether theses standards are followed by domestic social security systems.

The analysed provisions, especially the standards established by Article 12(4) of both Social Charters of the Council of Europe, are regarded, as the most broadly understood principles of social protection on the European Continent.[118] These principles are applicable to all citizens of Member States of the Council of Europe, regardless of their place of residency. Article 12(4)(b) of the European Social Charter is a legal standard, which may initiate a transfer of insured citizens between Member States of the Council of Europe. In cases of states belonging to the European Union, the Committee of Social Rights demands reports containing information about the current application of social security standards, about the transfer of the insured out of countries who are not part of the European Union as well as information about their legal situation in matters concerning the granting, maintaining and resuming social security rights by such means as the accumulation of insurance completed under the legislation of other Member States of the Council of Europe. The following chapter dealing with the experience of the Committee of Social Rights in matters concerning the establishment and the following of standards of social security within Europe, also examines the thesis of accepting and aspiring to the realization of high and effective

117. The Committee of Social Rights demanded proof that social security payments attained under the social security regulations existing with members states of the Council of Europe, can be classified as social security payment rights under the governance of Polish social security law for citizens of Member States of the Council of Europe. Poland formed bilateral agreements with the following countries: Belgium (agreement 26 Nov 1965, full scope of benefits, with the exception of unemployment benefits), France (agreement 9 June 1948, full scope of benefits, with the exception of unemployment and family benefits), Germany (agreement 8 Dec 1990, full scope of benefits, with the exception of unemployment, family or death of the breadwinner benefits), Slovakia (agreement 5 April 1948, full scope of benefits) as well as the European Community (treaty 16 Dec 1991), Addendum to Conclusions XV-1 (Poland).

118. W. Beck, L. van der Maesen, A. Walker (eds), *The Social Quality of Europe*, Kluwer Law International, The Hague-London-Boston 1997, pp. 79 and following; D. Pieters (ed), *European Social Security and Global Politics,* Kluwer Law International, The Hague-London-New York 2001, p. 3 and following.

standards of social security protection by the Council of Europe.[119] Examples of decisions handed down by the Committee of Social Rights with regards to Germany and Poland, two countries with developed social security systems that have had decisions adjourned in matters concerning the compliance of their regulations with European standards of social security, exemplify that the obligations set for Member States are high and that the role and meaning of European social security standards is serious.

8.3. The Right to Social and Medical Assistance (Article 13)

8.3.1. Introduction

Article 13 has become the norm for introducing the concept of social assistance in Europe. The intention of current legislation has been to move away from the original concept of social assistance, a departure from identifying social assistance with welfare benefits that are provided on a charitable basis through administrative bodies for the poor.[120] When interpreting Article 13, the Committee unanimously agreed that the law allows a person subjective rights to monetary and/or resource services.[121]

The approach to social and medical assistance needed to be altered to eradicate the social stigma associated with people who use such welfare benefits. Article 13, rather than referring to 'the poor' uses the term 'without adequate resources'.[122] Persons in need benefiting rightfully from such social or medical assistance should not be restricted from utilizing their political and social rights (Article 13, paragraph 2).[123] After analysing reports made by the Member States, the Committee is of the view that subjective rights in relation to social and medical assistance are guaranteed when: social and medical assistance is guaranteed for all those in need, when services are allocated when considered appropriate, and when persons who are refused assistance have the right to appeal to an independent body.[124]

The right to social and medical assistance is universal and should be enjoyed by all eligible citizens of the Member States of the Council of Europe, residing legally within member territory. Initially, the Committee monitored whether the governments of individual Member States fulfilled their obligations under Article 13 with respect to citizens of other Member States who also ratified the Article 13, paragraph 4. From the thirteenth supervisory cycle onwards, the Committee changed its position on the matter, and began to monitor the compliance of Member States' who had not ratified Article 13, paragraph 4 with Article 13, paragraphs 1, 2 and 3.[125] Article 13,

119. M. Mikkola, Prawo do zabezpieczenia społecznego w Europie – prawem człowieka i prawem podstawowym (Social Security in Europe – a Human Right and a Basic Right), (in:) Dorobek Rady Europy ... (European Social Charter Towards ...), *op. cit.*, p. 118 and following.
120. Conclusions I, p. 64.
121. Conclusions XIII-4, p. 54.
122. *Ibid.* Conclusions I, p. 54.
123. *Ibid.* Conclusions XIII-4, pp. 58–59.
124. Conclusions XVI-2, vol. 2, p. 787 (Slovakia).
125. Conclusions XIII-4, pp. 60–61.

paragraph 4 imposes an obligation on Member States (those who have ratified) to treat equally citizens of other Member States 'staying legally on their territories' according to the obligations imposed by the European Convention of Social and Medical Assistance on 11 December 1953.[126] The annexure to Article 13, paragraph 4 stipulates that those states, who have failed to ratify the above Convention, may, instead, ratify Article 13, paragraph 4, provided that they treat citizens of other Member States in a manner that is pursuant to the provisions of the above Convention.

The right to medical and social care is regulated by a separate article. It is distinct in its character from the right to social security stipulated by Article 12. Those Member States that have ratified Article 13 are not obliged in any way by the provisions stated in Article 12. The same applies in reverse, and those Member States that are under obligations to Article 12 are not automatically obliged to abide the laws of Article 13. In its conclusion, the Committee in its thirteen supervisory cycle, remarked upon the dependency between social security rights and social and medical assistance.[127] Even though both concepts are closely related to the idea of social welfare, it is possible for Member States to abide only by one of the two articles stipulated by the Charter.

8.3.2. The Responsibility to Provide Adequate Social and Essential Medical Assistance (Article 13)

Article 13, paragraph 1 obligates Member States to ensure that any person without adequate resources or the ability to secure such resources either through their own efforts or through other sources (such as benefits given under a social security scheme), is granted adequate assistance, and, in cases of illness, the necessary care. The right to social and medical assistance is granted to those who do not have 'adequate resources' and who are unable to seek such resources from elsewhere. The Committee has not defined what constitutes the 'adequate resources', upon which countries are dependant, when developing their welfare services laws.

It is a practice for Member States to provide social and medical assistance to those whose income is lower than the minimum wage and does not cover the cover the costs of living. Through its decisions, the Committee accepts this general practice. Given the different levels of living standards among the Member States, the Committee does not demand information regarding minimum income or costs of living. It does however, demand information from its Member States, about procedures which determine such levels of standard of living[128] and information regarding the criteria used in assessing such standards.[129] The Committee also examines whether the Member States performing the above assessments account for national, regional and local conditions.[130]

126. Preliminary Documents of the Council of Europe ..., *op. cit.*, pp. 83–84.
127. Conclusions XIII-4, p. 35.
128. Conclusions I, p. 66.
129. Addendum to Conclusions IX, p. 33 (Spain).
130. Conclusions XIII-4, pp. 56–57.

It follows the Recommendation of the Council of the European Union 92/441, which determines adequate resources required. This, in turn, obligates EU Member States to consider the protection of human dignity and to determine the minimum standards of living using the cost of living indices and price levels.[131] Effective from the sixteenth supervising cycle, and all subsequent cycles, as a point of reference, the Committee, in assessing persons without adequate resources and having the right to social assistance, accepted half the required average monthly income in a given country as an acceptable standard. Whenever social assistance benefits are determined at a level that is lower than half the average monthly income of Member States, the Committee issues a warning about the failure to comply with obligations set out in Article 13, paragraph 1.[132] When determining the level of financial resources of a particular population, the Committee also considers additional benefits, which supplement the minimum wage, like unemployment benefits and other cash benefits under the social security system.[133] If the benefits remained at a permanent level, the Committee would be interested if they were subject to indexation.[134] It required from Member States data regarding the level of social assistance expenditures.[135]

The right to social and medical assistance is reserved for persons who are not able to secure adequate resources from sources other than social security. Article 13, paragraph 1 used welfare benefits as an example of social security. Persons without sufficient resources will not acquire the right to social assistance benefits, if they can effectively receive a supply of financial resources from their family, who is subject to alimony under family law.[136]

A right to social assistance is a subjective right. Therefore, national social assistance legislation should determine eligibility criteria for persons with insufficient

131. Council Recommendation 92/441 on Common Criteria Concerning Sufficient Resources and Social Assistance in Social Protection Schemes, OJ 1992 L.245, p. 46.
132. Conclusions XVI-2, vol. 2, p. 788 (Slovakia provides benefits at a level lower than 25 per cent of the average wage); Conclusions XVII-1, vol. 1, p. 176 (Finland – social assistance benefits amount to 374.92 euros, 50 per cent of the average monthly wage is 619 euros); p. 109 (the Czech Republic – benefits equivalent to 72 euros, 50 per cent of the average monthly wage is 132 euros); p. 76 (Belgium – benefits 550 euros, 50 per cent of the average monthly wage is 645 euros); Conclusions XVII-1, vol. 2, p. 294 (Malta – benefits at a level of 53 per cent); p. 327 (the Netherlands – benefits at a level of 2 452 euros per year, poverty level below 6 663 euros per year); p. 425 (Portugal); p. 524 (Great Britain – benefits equivalent to 690 euros per month, 50 per cent of the monthly wage of 738 euros); Conclusions 2004, vol. 1, p. 70 (Bulgaria – benefits equivalent to 19 euros, 50 per cent of the monthly wage of 45 euros), p. 177 (Estonia – benefits equivalent to 32 euros, 50 per cent of the average monthly wage – 79 euros); Conclusions 2004, vol. 2, p. 373 (Lithuania – benefits equivalent to 39 euros per month, 50 per cent of the average monthly wage – 78 euros); p. 483 (Romania – benefits equivalent to 4.3 euros per month, 50 per cent per of the monthly wage – 19 euros).
133. Conclusions XIV-1, p. 85 (Austria); p. 537 (Malta); p. 632 (Norway); Conclusions XVII-1 vol. 1, p. 77 (Belgium); p. 176 (Finland); Conclusions XVII-1, vol. 2, pp. 294–295 (Malta); p. 425 (Portugal).
134. Conclusions 2002, p. 94 (Italy).
135. Conclusions XIII-4, p. 57.
136. Conclusions XIII-1, p. 188; Conclusion XIII-2, p. 128 (Greece).

resources, seeking assistance. The process of granting such assistance should also be regulated, and the principles of refusing grants clearly defined.[137]

Decisions made by authorized bodies dealing with grants or refusals of social assistance benefits should be subject to control by an independent appeals tribunal. This implies that decisions regarding social assistance cannot be made arbitrarily. National legislation under social security law should therefore establish a criterion regarding this decision making process.[138] The criteria should be uniform. The Committee passed decisions addressing the failure of Member States to comply with Article 13, paragraph 1, in cases where there were no clear guidelines set for administrative bodies in dealing with the decision making process involved in granting social assistance.[139] The rulings of the Committee regarding Member States' failure to abide the rules set out in Article 13, paragraph 1 were not influenced by the Member States, since the scope of arbitrary rulings affects less than 1 per cent of society.[140] The failure to regulate the criteria involved in the decision making process in Greece was determined by the Committee to be a failure to provide social assistance to those without adequate resources.[141]

The Committee interprets Article 13, paragraph 1 as a standard for international social security law, obligating Member States to establish a social assistance system. Such national social assistance legislation should, in its scope, cover all citizens within each Member State as well as those citizens who are living legally on the territory of another Member State. Under such obligations, a social assistance system protecting those requiring its aid,[142] would not be in violation of international standards if the national social security law would reserve some benefits to particular categories of people (like the disabled and the elderly), allocating such rights also to those without sufficient resources.[143] On the other hand, it is not compliant with international standards to grant social assistance rights exclusively to selected categories of people (the disabled, the elderly without rights to pension benefits, single parents raising their children, people above 65 years of age who are not insured) and subjecting the rights of those who do not have adequate resources.[144]

Despite the obligation to establish national eligibility criteria for the right to social assistance benefits, Member States' governments may formulate their own general directives, and regional and local authorities may establish more specific criteria

137. Conclusions X-1, p. 116 (Iceland); Conclusions X-2, p. 11; Conclusions XI-2, p. 119 (Spain); Conclusions XII-I, pp. 188–189; Conclusions XIII-1, p. 188 (Greece); Conclusions XV-1, p. 376 and subsequent (Italy); Conclusions XVI-2, vol. 1, p. 432 (Hungary); ConclusionsXVII-1, vol. 1, p. 110 (Czech Republic).
138. Conclusions XIII-1, p. 188 (Greece); Conclusions XIII-3, p. 361 (Finland).
139. Case of Greece, Conclusions XIII-4, pp. 177–179; Conclusions XIV-1, pp. 35–360.
140. Conclusions XIV-1, p. 809 (Great Britain).
141. Conclusions XVII-1, vol. 1, p. 248.
142. Conclusions IV, p. 88 (Italy); Conclusions X-2, p. 121 (Spain); Conclusions XIII-3, pp. 362–363 (Portugal); Addendum to Conclusions XIII-3, pp. 73 (Luxembourg).
143. Case of Spain: Conclusions XIII-3, p. 362–363; Conclusions XIII-5, p. 224.
144. Conclusions XIII-4, pp. 177–179 (Greece).

requirements, upon which social assistance benefits are dependent. However, if local authorities do utilize this discretion, the Committee demands from Member States information about the use of such discretion. In particular, the Committee is concerned about legal opportunities for claims to be brought to independent bodies against decisions that are rendered with respect to social assistance benefits.[145] An independent body, by definition, is a court (dealing with administration, public insurance or labour). If appeals against decisions made regarding social assistance benefits, are dealt with by institutions other than judicial bodies, the Committee is called upon: to choose members for an appeals institution, to formulate how such members are chosen, to decide how long they will serve their duties, to determine what qualifications are demanded from them and to decide who monitors its conduct and its members' independence from the welfare institutions, according to its statutes.[146]

The Committee saw a discrepancy between a Member State's own labour laws and Article 13, paragraph 1, when a given Member State did not pass its decisions regarding social assistance benefits to other independent tribunals. Such an independent tribunal cannot be seen, according to law, as a governmental administrative institution (e.g. a Ministry) or a council.[147] However, such an independent body will retain its status of independence even when employing civil servants and functioning accordingly with administrative channels, if a given Member State grants such a body autonomy in its decision making process.

An example of such an independent institution is the *Social Welfare Appeals Office*, employing civil servants who are called upon by a given minister, e.g. *the Minister for Social Welfare.* To ensure competency within such an independent institution, recognition of appeals is required. The Supreme Court of Ireland ruled that those civil servants whose role it is to supervise according to law the decisions made regarding social assistance benefits, should remain 'free and unrestricted'.[148] Citing this case as a precedent, the Committee ruled that if such a body is entitled to acquire evidence, to make decisions and allow for them to be appealable – it fulfils the requirements of an independent body. Without breaching international standards, the authority of such a body should be able to recognize complaints and to allow appeals against decisions made regarding social assistance benefits.[149] In cases of ambiguity, the Committee demands that Member States present the decisions made by the bodies supervising matters dealing with social assistance benefits.[150] It also demands information regarding the number of appeals made.[151] It is also interested whether those intending to

145. Conclusions XIII-4, p. 56; Conclusions 2002, p. 245 (Sweden); Conclusions XVII-1, vol. 1, p. 110 (Czech Republic).
146. Conclusions XIII-1, p. 189 (Iceland); Conclusions XIII-4, p. 175 (Denmark); p. 182 (Iceland); p. 184 (Ireland); p. 189 (Norway); Addendum to Conclusions XIII-3, p. 71; Conclusions XIV-1, pp. 504–505 (Luxembourg); Conclusions 2004, vol. 2, p. 483 (Romania).
147. Conclusions XIII-2, p. 127 (Greece).
148. *McLoughlin v Minister of Social Welfare,* 1958. in Conclusions XIV-1, pp. 429–431.
149. *Ibid.*
150. Conclusions XIII-3, p. 362 (Finland); p. 364 (Turkey); Conclusions XIII-4, p. 172 (Austria).
151. Conclusions XVI-2, vol. 2, p. 789 (Slovakia); Conclusions XVII-1, vol. 2, p. 487 (Turkey).

appeal the decisions concerning social assistance benefits, have the possibility to utilize specialist legal aid.[152] The Committee accepts the rulings of those appeal bodies supervising social assistance decisions, even if these bodies cannot be regarded as objective or independent, given they are subject to the next level of judicial jurisdiction.[153]

The Committee believes the independent appeal body authorized to process appeals against the decisions on social assistance benefits, shall have the following characteristics:

- The appeal body should be empowered to exercise subject matter control over the decisions appealed against;
- The appeal body should have an objective opportunity to determine whether the body that issued the decision appealed against acted in compliance with the criteria laid down in the effective legislation on the matters referring to the statement that the person applying for social assistance benefits does not have adequate resources through his/her own efforts from other sources – if a decision on granting social assistance benefit has been made it should be able to check the correctness of determining the benefit level.[154]

Introducing the above criteria is an indication that Member States are responsible for the authorization of an appeals body that looks into the decisions made regarding social assistance benefits and to monitor the legitimacy of such appeals based on the evidence collected. The appeals body has the power to determine the legibility of claims through the evidence collected. Such a supervisory system rules out arbitrary rulings over requests for social assistance benefits. The Committee also conducts research into whether such appeals bodies dealing with social assistance benefits decisions, are carrying out their responsibilities.[155] In such cases the Committee demands the following information:

- The organization of social assistance;
- Types of assistance, the bodies allocating such assistance;
- The categories of people who can use such assistance;
- The amount of people who are taking advantage of medical and social assistance;
- The level of such service, the level of funds allocated for such services;
- The facilities with which national legislation guarantees social assistance benefits;
- And the criteria used in undertaking such decisions regarding social assistance benefits.[156]

---

152. *Ibid.*; Conclusions XVI-2, vol. 1, p. 432 (Hungary).
153. Conclusions XIII-4, p. 56, p, 175 (Denmark); p. 182 (Iceland); Conclusions XIV-1, pp. 632–633 (Norway).
154. Conclusions XIII-4, p. 56.
155. Conclusions XIII-5, p. 97 (Finland); Conclusions XIV-1, .126 (Belgium); Conclusions XV-1, p. 44 (Iceland), p. 447 (Norway).
156. Conclusions XIII-4, pp. 56–57.

Member States may neither limit nor condition the fulfilments required in exercising the right to social and medical assistance. During its analysis of Member States' reports, the Committee has found the following irregularities in national social assistance systems:

1. The rights to social assistance benefits are subject to the period and conditions of residence in a certain Member State or in the territories of certain regions of a single Member State.[157] As far as social assistance benefits were concerned, the Committee decided there was a lack of compliance between national legislation and international standards, when national legislation appropriated such rights according to terms of residency in particular Member States (e.g. for 6 months,[158] 1 year[159], 3 years[160], 5 years[161] or 10 years.[162] However, this does not mean that Member States do not have rights to introduce conditions on social assistance benefits according to residential terms. Entitlement to social and medical assistance benefits is given to those who are unable to attain resources from elsewhere, who are associated with a given country claiming in it the above benefits. It is for this reason that the Committee changed its approach, in light of the case of Great Britain's, and ruled that the *Habitual Residence Test – HRT* used by Great Britain in determining a person's residential details, is in accordance with Article 13, paragraph 1.[163] The goal of this test is to establish the relationship of a person seeking social assistance benefits with Great Britain. Because British regulations do not require a clearly defined period of time of residence on either British or Northern Ireland's territory, and because decisions verifying circumstances made by administrative bodies regarding social assistance benefits are determined objectively, the Committee ruled that the British regulations comply with international standards despite the residential requirement to live on British territory even if for a brief period of time when applying for social assistance benefits. The Committee considered the fact that because people move easily within the European Union, British administrative authorities did not refuse social assistance benefits to those who initially lived on British territory, then moved and then returned to reside in Britain again.[164]

157. Case of Spain: Conclusions XIII-4, pp. 189–190; Conclusions XIV-1, p. 170; Conclusions XV-1, p. 531; Conclusions XVII-1, vol. 2, pp. 455–456.
158. Conclusions XIII-2, p. 127 (Greece); Conclusions XV-1, p. 344 (Iceland).
159. Conclusions XIV-1, p. 193 (Denmark); Conclusions 2004 vol.1, p. 281 (Ireland).
160. Case of France; Conclusions XIV-1, p. 272; Conclusions 2004, vol.1, p. 236.
161. Case of Great Britain: Conclusions II, p.49; Conclusions XIV-1, p. 809; Conclusions XV-1, pp. 644–645; Conclusions XVII-1, vol. 2, pp. 525–526; Conclusions 2004, vol. 2, pp. 374–375 (Lithuania).
162. Addendum to Conclusions XIII-3, pp. 71–72 (Luxembourg).
163. Conclusions XIV-1, p. 810; Conclusions XVII-1, vol. 2, pp. 525–526.
164. *Ibid.*, 526, case of *Robin Swaddling v Adjudication Officer*, Case C-90/97, 1999 E.C.R. 1075.

2. Excluding from eligibility for social assistance benefits young people below 25 years of age[165] or 30 years of age.[166] The Committee has decided that allocating a lower level of social assistance benefits for younger people may be seen as evidence of legislative contradiction between national regulations and Article 13, paragraph 1.[167] This decision has therefore introduced a legal barrier in attaining social assistance benefits for those who have not reached the eligible age according to national requirements. A prerequisite to acquire the right to social assistance benefits is a person's lack of adequate resources and the inability to attain such resources by the person applying for such benefits. Young people who are studying may apply for scholarships or loan schemes. Therefore, in principle they are not qualified to rights of social assistance benefits. Despite the fact the Committee debated twice on this matter, it failed to adopt a position.[168]

   The above rights of the persons applying for social assistance benefits are dependant upon the employment or training proposals made for them by appropriate administrative authorities. The Committee believes social assistance of a State allocated to people who do not have adequate resources should not be limited to paying them cash benefits. The objective of social assistance should be to enable those individuals without adequate resources, to participate, to a universally accepted extent, in the life of a community. Therefore, exercising the right to social assistance benefits should indeed be dependent upon the acceptance of employment or vocational training offers, especially if the proposal of such employment or training will enable the individual to return to a normal life. Accordingly, this will be viewed as compliant with international standards.[169] When analysing the case where a prerequisite to the acquisition of the right to social assistance benefits by a person below the age of 24 was to accept a job selected by the administrative body[170], the Committee demanded an explanation regarding the connection between the right to social assistance benefits and the obligation to accept the proposal for such a job. Information was required regarding the extent of this connection, as well as to explain the dependency between the right to social assistance benefits and an obligation to register as an unemployed person without adequate resources.[171] The Committee is interested in examining, if and for which purpose such conditions are established, as well as what conditions are set by Member States' governments for the persons applying for social assistance benefits. In particular, the Committee is determined to seek out the legal consequences involved when

165. Case of France: Conclusions XIV-2, p. 272; Conclusions 2002, p. 48; Conclusions 2004, vol. 1, p. 236; Conclusions XVII-1, vol. 2, p. 456.
166. Case of Luxembourg: Addendum to Conclusions XIII-3, p. 73; Conclusions XIV-1, p. 504 and following; Addendum to Conclusions XV-1, p. 64.
167. Conclusions XIV-1, pp. 193–94 (Denmark).
168. Case of Finland: Conclusions XIII-5, p. 98; Conclusions XIV-1. p. 123.
169. Conclusions XIV-1, p. 52.
170. Conclusions XVII-1, vol. 1, p. 177 (Finland).
171. Conclusions XVII-1, vol. 2, p. 328 (the Netherlands).

an individual refuses to accept such conditions when applying for social assistance benefits.[172]

3. Unequal treatment of own and foreign citizens. Decisions regarding non-compliance with national social security legislation and Article 1, paragraph 1, were issued when the Committee came to realize that an inequality of treatment of citizens of other Member States existed by certain Member State governments. It is not relevant whether the discrimination takes place during the acquisition rights to social assistance benefits or during the renewal of rights acquired earlier.[173]

Article 13 Paragraph 1 obligates the Member State governments to provide those in need and without adequate resources not being able to secure such resources through their own efforts, appropriate assistance. According to the Committee, social assistance for those without adequate resources must not be simply reduced to financial aid – benefits and allowances.

Comments made regarding social assistance apply also to medical assistance and care for the sick, who do not have adequate resources. The implementation of the right to medical assistance and doctor's care may have a legal form of purpose-specific financial benefits that will be utilized by those in need to pay for medical services, otherwise, when necessary, granting them the right to free-of-charge doctor's services.[174]

8.3.3. Ensuring That Those who Receive Social and Medical Assistance are not Discriminated Against (Article 13, Paragraph 2)

Article 13, paragraph 2 obligates Member States to ensure political and social rights for those who benefiting from social and medical assistance. During its first supervisory cycle, the Committee emphasized that those benefiting from social and medical assistance cannot be treated as second class citizens, simply because they are not able to support themselves. Benefiting from social and medical assistance cannot stand in the way of a citizen's political and civil rights.[175] The Committee did not define which civil and political rights are protected in the case of those benefiting from social and medical assistance. For example it referred to: the right to stand for election, the right to hold public office, and the right to run for a public service position.[176] The Committee did not determine whether the right to benefit from social and medical assistance negatively affects the utilization of political and economic rights; hence the

172. Conclusions XIV-1, p. 52.
173. Case of Denmark: Conclusions XV-1, p. 166; Conclusions XVII-1, vol. 1, p. 148; Case of Spain in the part dealing with medical assistance: Conclusions XIII-4, p. 191; Conclusions XIV-1, p. 712; Case of Malta: Conclusions XIII-4, pp. 187–188; Conclusions XIV-1, pp. 537–538; Conclusions XV-1, p. 411; Case of Germany: Conclusions XIV-1, pp. 322–323; Addendum to Conclusions XV-1, pp. 40–41; Conclusions XVII-1, vol. 1, p. 214.
174. Conclusions XIII-4, p. 57.
175. Conclusions I, p. 64.
176. *Ibid.*, p. 67; p. 203 (Ireland).

scope of these laws protected by Article 13, paragraph 2 is unknown. According to written reports it is established that, among the social and economical rights protected by law, are those social and economical rights guaranteed by the Charter. Beyond those social rights guaranteed by the Charter, the Committee defined that the right to privacy is also guaranteed by Article 13, paragraph 2.[177]

The Committee claims that Article 13, paragraph 2 is violated when Member States restrict, in an obvious manner, the political and civil rights of those benefiting from social and medical assistance.[178] A poignant example of the law regulation contradicting Article 13, paragraph 2 is a rule forbidding those benefiting from social and medical assistance to apply for a position in local government, during the period of assistance and 12 months thereafter.[179]

The rule may be understood in a particular case of a conflict of interest, which provoked the Committee's ruling, seen by the clash of local Irish legislation and international standards. The case involved a person benefiting from social assistance who applied for a job with the social welfare department. The Committee clearly stated that benefiting from social and medical assistance could not by definition, restrict any political or social rights of citizen and legal residents of any Member States. The Committee, when interpreting Article 13, paragraph 2, did not limit its research to the determination of whether those benefiting from social and medical assistance are discriminated by law. The Committee analysed whether Member States introduced regulations, which would allow such discrimination.

It was proven, that the Danish Constitution of 1953 gives an employer the right to limit those benefiting from social and medical assistance. According to the Danish Constitution, minor laws can regulate the scope of usage of political rights by those benefiting from social assistance.[180] The Committee did not rule that the Danish Constitution violated Article 13, paragraph 2. It did, however, obligate the State to present detailed information on the regulations restricting political and social rights of those benefiting from social and medical assistance. It was a common exercise for the Committee to familiarize itself with those codes and practices guaranteeing equality to those benefiting from social assistance. The Committee was not satisfied by declarations formulated by constitutions or international treaties.[181] Rather, it demanded information regarding the equal treatment of those benefiting from social and medical assistance.[182] However, when information was not provided, it did not make any rulings against the local regulations.[183] The Committee prolonged its final decisions, until such information was attained from the officials of the Member States.[184]

---

177. Conclusions XIII-1, p. 324 (Germany); Conclusions XIV-1, pp. 324–325.
178. Conclusions I, p. 67.
179. *Ibid.*, p. 203 (Ireland).
180. Conclusions XIII-4, p. 195.
181. Conclusions XVII-1, vol. 2, p. 295 (Malta).
182. Conclusions 2004, vol. 2, p. 484 (Romania).
183. Conclusions 2002, p. 152 (Romania).
184. Conclusions XVI-2, vol. 1, p. 433 (Hungary).

The Committee gave detailed attention regarding cases of indirect discrimination against those benefiting from social assistance. Usually, this applies to the homeless. Introducing permanent residency as a condition for obtaining social assistance is regarded by the Committee as a discriminatory practice. This is because the above condition affects negatively and solely those who are benefiting from social and medical assistance.[185]

The principle ensuring that those who receive social and medical assistance are not discriminated against is also applied to citizen of other Member States. Notwithstanding, the Committee is aware that political, economical and social regulations differ between Member States, depending on the period of residency in a particular state.[186] Applying for social assistance or benefiting from it cannot be a fundamental reason for deportation of persons without adequate resources or the ability to sustain themselves from other sources by Member States.[187]

Analysing documents provided by Member States, the Committee, on only one occasion, declared that contradictions exist between local regulations and standards regulated by Article 13, paragraph 2. It occurred in the already mentioned case in Ireland where regulations prohibited those who benefit from social assistance to run for public office.[188]

8.4. The Right to Advice and Necessary Assistance (Article 13, Paragraph 3)

Member States should organize a system of social assistance (public or private services) that would allow everyone to obtain advice and personal help as may be required to prevent, to remove, or to alleviate personal or family deprivation. According to the Committee, Member States should perform all necessary tasks to help those in need. Article 13, paragraph 3 is dynamic in character. On the one hand, it obligates Member States to organize efficient help for those who need it. On the other, it leads to a situation where demand for the above mentioned help would decrease and then disappear.[189] Article 13, paragraph 3 is regarded by the Committee as guaranteeing the fulfilment of responsibilities formulated by Article 13, paragraph 1.[190] Duty of ensuring social and medical assistance is executed, among others, by a system of advice and help for those without adequate resources or means of supporting themselves.

Scope of application of Article 13, paragraph 3 is covered by the scope of application of Article 14, a regulation giving rights to benefit from social assistance. Analysing the connection between the abovementioned regulations, the Committee concluded Article 13, paragraph 3 obliges Member States to organize a system of

185. Conclusions XV-1, p. 167.
186. Conclusions XII-4, pp. 61–62.
187. Case of Denmark: Conclusions XIII-4, p. 61; Conclusions XV-1, p. 166.
188. Conclusions XV-1, p. 412.
189. Conclusions I, p. 64; Conclusions XIII-4, p. 55.
190. Conclusions XIV-1, p. 52.

advice and social assistance for those in need, while Article 14 forces Member States to organize a specialized net of social assistance services. For this reason the Committee estimates independently the way in which Member States fulfil their freely accepted obligations. A positive opinion made by the Committee on fulfilling one of the obligations does not automatically mean a positive opinion of fulfilling the other.[191]

Member States that ratified both regulations can organize two separate systems of social assistance, one assisting only those who do not have adequate resources to support themselves, the other assisting all parties interested. They can also organize one common system of social assistance services advising persons without adequate resources.[192] The differences between the social assistance services providing required help, referred to the abovementioned regulations, rely upon the division of allocated services (according to Article 13, paragraph 3, advice is exclusively given) as well as upon a group of beneficiaries. According to Article 13, paragraph 3, those who do not have adequate resources to support themselves are entitled to advice and personal help. If a Member State does not report properly on how the social assistance is organized, the Committee insists on answers to questions whether proper social services providing advice and help for those without adequate resources and means of supporting themselves, were organized.[193]

Article 13, paragraph 3 does not define the scope of application of advice and personal help for those without adequate resources and means of supporting themselves, and who find themselves or their families in danger. It has to be noted that advice and personal help should embrace housing issues, social welfare benefits, and the possibility of taking advantage of social services.[194] The Committee interprets the analysed regulation in a broader manner. It forces the Member States to ensure that those who do not have adequate resources to support themselves have access to advice and personal help in all issues regarding social and medical assistance regulated by Article 13.[195] The Committee is also interested in the scope of services provided based on the analysed regulation of Article 13, paragraph 3.[196] In the case of personal help, it is important to determine whether persons in need can rely on the assistance of a nurse, house assistance, meal services, drivers, and means of transport when hospitalization is required.[197]

Advice and personal help should be provided at an adequate level and should also be readily accessible to those who need them. The Committee monitors the number of available personnel and the qualifications of the personnel providing such services.[198]

---

191. Conclusions I, pp. 64–65.
192. Conclusions XIII-4, p. 59; Conclusions XIV-1, pp. 86–87 (Austria).
193. Case of Romania: Conclusions 2002, p. 152; Conclusions 2004, vol. 2, p. 485.
194. D. Harris, J. Darcy, *op. cit.*, p. 173.
195. Conclusions XIII-4, p. 59; Conclusions XIV–1, p. 743 (Sweden).
196. Conclusions XVII-1, vol. 2, p. 296 (Malta).
197. Conclusions XV-1, p. 93 (Belgium); Addendum to Conclusions XV-1, p. 105 (the Netherlands).
198. Conclusions XIII, p. 59; Conclusions XV-1, p. 167 (Denmark); p. 345 (Iceland); pp. 381–382 (Italy); p. 412. (Malta); Addendum to Conclusions XV-1, pp. 164–165 (Poland); Conclusions XVI-2, vol.1, p. 148 (Denmark); p. 434 (Hungary); Conclusions 2002, p. 204 (Slovenia).

In special instances, the Committee demands information from Member States, regarding the amount of personnel assisting in services advising those in need of matters of housing.[199] It requires funds information for the abovementioned services as well as details concerning the expenses made for such purposes.[200] It is also interested in researching the ability of access to social assistance and help service centres for those in need. It is, for this reason, that the Committee requires information regarding geographical location of public or private institutions providing such advice and assistance to people in need.[201]

Article 13, paragraph 3 does not allow Member States' to enact or maintain legislation in which social circumstances govern the acquisition of assistance and personal help. The Committee researches conditions of access to the abovementioned services.[202] It regards that States' regulations dealing with rights of local protection cannot be based on the period of residency in a particular Member State. On more than one occasion, the Committee unanimously decided against regulations passed by Member States where rights to take advantage of advice and personal help for persons who do not have adequate resources to support themselves, were dependent on the period of residency in a particular Member State.[203]

Above all, the Committee wants to provide protection for citizens of other Member States – that are parties to the international treaty that is the Charter – residing in other Member States.[204] The Committee ruled against German regulations regarding social protection, verified by Article 13, paragraph 3. Germany did not guarantee rights to access advice and assistance for the citizens of Member States, which did not belong to the European Union or the European Economic Area, allowing for such decisions to be made by social assistance services.[205] Article 13, paragraph 3 obliges Member States to provide those in need with adequate advice and assistance. It does not allow Member States to define such conditions for accessing the abovementioned services by such Member States. The Committee is interested in familiarizing itself with the conditions of accessing the services,[206] most probably in order to underline discrepancies with the Charter.

Article 13, paragraph 3 obliges Member States to provide those in need with advice and personal help, which may be necessary for improving personal or family

199. Conclusions 2004, vol. 1, p. 180 (Estonia).
200. Conclusions XIII-4 p. 59; Conclusions XVII-1, vol. 1, p. 111 (Czech Republic); p. 148 (Denmark); Conclusions 2002, p. 95 (Italy); Conclusions 2004, vol. 1, p. 113 (Cyprus); p. 180 (Estonia); Conclusions 2004, vol. 2, p. 379 (Lithuania); p. 534 (Slovenia).
201. Conclusions 2004, vol. 1 p. 113 (Cyprus); p. 180 (Estonia); Conclusions 2004, vol. 2, p. 534 (Slovenia).
202. Conclusions 2004, vol. 1, p. 73 (Bulgaria); p. 180 (Estonia).
203. Conclusions XIV-1, pp. 325–326 (Germany); Conclusions XVII-1, vol. 2, p. 296 (Malta); Conclusions 2002, p. 204 (Slovenia); Conclusions 2004, vol. 2, p. 379 (Lithuania).
204. Conclusions XIII-4, p. 62; Conclusions 2002, p. 204 (Slovenia); Conclusions 2004, vol. 2, p. 534 (Slovenia).
205. Conclusions XIV-1, pp. 325–326; Addendum to Conclusions XV-1, p. 42.
206. Conclusions 2004, vol. 1, p. 73 (Bulgaria); Conclusions 2004, vol. 2, p. 534 (Slovenia).

situations of a person who does not possess adequate resources. The analysed regulations encroach on the protective sphere legislated by Article 16 guaranteeing a family the right to social, legal and economical protection. The Committee did not consider the relations between Article 13, paragraph 3 and Article 16. It appears that Article 13 paragraph 3 guarantees an individual the right to access to advice and personal help in a situation when taking advantage of such help can improve the living standards of the person entitled to the abovementioned benefits or its family. Simultaneously, Article 16 imposes on Member States responsibilities in supporting the protection of family life in economic, social and legal spheres.

Execution of duties formulated by Article 13, paragraph 3 can be carried out by public or private charity organizations. The Committee approves both ways of proving services guaranteed by Article 13, paragraph 3. It also accepts advisory legal partnerships as well as co-ordinations of such services executed by public sectors and charity organizations.[207]

8.5. The Responsibility to Treat Own and Foreign Citizen on Equal Footing (Article 13, Paragraph 4)

Member States are obliged to apply provisions of Article 13, paragraphs 1, 2, and 3 towards citizens of other countries that are legally residing on their territories. The Committee stated that the analysed regulation Article 13, paragraph 4 broadened the scope of application of Article 13, paragraphs 1, 2 and 3 because it entitled legal residents of particular Member States to social and medical assistance.[208] Foreigners, who are citizens belonging to other Member States, are entitled to access, social and medical assistance at the same level as citizens and permanent residents of a particular territory. Since the thirteenth supervisory cycle, the Committee has demanded that Member States produce reports of compliance of Article 13, paragraphs 1, 2 and 3, regarding their treatment of citizens of other Member States.[209]

Article 13 paragraph 4 is considered to be the standard in international treaties, obligating Member States to guarantee citizens of other Member States temporarily residing on foreign territories, the right to social and medical assistance, as well as those protected under Article 13 paragraph 1, 2 and 3. Hence, the abovementioned responsibility includes the protection of tourists and students coming from other Member States.[210] Broadening the categories of beneficiaries of social and medical assistance under Article 13 has decreased the range of entitlements for citizens of other Member States temporarily residing on the territories of other Member States. The Committee stated, according to Article 13, paragraph 4, that Member States are obliged to ensure adequate social and medical assistance.[211]

---

207. Conclusions XIII-4, p. 62; Addendum to Conclusion XV-1, p. 165 (Poland).
208. Conclusions II, p. 51 (Norway); Conclusions XIV-1, pp. 53–54.
209. Conclusions XIV, p. 55.
210. Conclusions XIII-4, p. 62.
211. Conclusions XIV-1, p. 55.

The abovementioned term is regarded by the Committee as a duty to provide help in cases of emergency. The scope of this help includes providing shelter, food supplies, clothing as well as ensuring medical assistance. The above interpretation of Article 13, paragraph 4 is limiting in nature. The analysed regulation compels Member States to provide equal treatment to citizens of other Member States in all matters regulated by Article 13, paragraph 1, 2, and 3. These regulations are not limited to providing assistance solely to cases of emergency for people in need without adequate resources.

The scope of responsibilities of Member States is regulated by the European Convention on Social and Medical Assistance, ratified in Paris on 11 December 1953.[212] Article 13, paragraph 4 compels those Member States that ratified this document to apply Article 13, paragraphs 1, 2, and 3 towards their own citizens and citizens of other Member States – that are parties to the Charter, in accordance with the European Convention on Social and Medical Assistance. Member States of the Council of Europe who are not parties to European Convention on Social and Medical Assistance, however, but who have ratified Article 13, paragraph 4, are obliged to treat citizens of other Member States pursuant to the standards set forth in the abovementioned Convention.[213] Used within the jargon of the European Convention on Social and Medical Assistance, the term 'assistance' is defined broadly as all types of assistance seen by regulations existing within Member States, which are 'granted under the laws and regulations in force in any part of its territory under which persons without sufficient resources are granted means of subsistence and the care necessitated by their condition' (Article 2(a)(i)). Excluded from this obligation of assistance are non-premium benefits and benefits for war veterans.

Article 1 of the European Convention on Social and Medical Assistance reinstates the obligation of equal treatment of foreign and domestic citizens. Therefore, there is a lack of legal basis for limiting interpretation of Article 13, paragraph 4. Particular heed is taken by Central and Eastern European countries when applying responsibilities under Article 13 paragraph 4.[214] The abovementioned concerns are not without reason and are due to the existence of a multitude of rulings in Central and Eastern Europe, where other Member States' citizens were discrimination against in cases of social and medical assistance.[215]

212. Polish text published in: *Podstawowe Dokumenty Rady Europy* ... (Primary Documents of the Council of Europe), *op. cit.*, p. 83.

213. Annexure to Article 13, paragraph 4 of the Charter.

214. This article was not ratified by Armenia, Azerbajdzhan, Bulgaria, Cyprus, Estonia, Lithuania, Moldova, Poland, Romania, Slovakia, Slovenia. Tables of accepted provisions. Situation at 1 January 2005 (in:) European Social Charter. Collected texts (5th Edition), *op. cit.*, pp. 85, 90.

215. Cases of: Austria (Conclusions Xii-1, p. 196; Conclusions XIII-2, p. 139); France (Conclusions XVI, p. 91; Conclusions 2002, p. 49; Conclusions 2004, vol. 1, p. 237); Greece (Conclusions XI-1, p. 133; Conclusions XIII-2, p. 138); Spain (Conclusions XIV-1, p. 714); the Netherlands (Conclusions XV-1, pp. 572–573; Conclusions XVII-1, vol. 2, p. 329); Malta (Conclusions XIII-2, p. 349; Conclusions XIII-4, p. 208; Conclusions XIV-1, p. 539; Conclusions XV-1, p. 412); Germany (Addendum to Conclusions XV-1, pp. 42–43); Portugal (Conclusions XIV-1, pp. 674–675; Conclusions XVII-1, vol. 2, p. 426; Conclusions XV-1, p. 491); Great Britain (Conclusions XIV-1, pp. 811–812; Conclusions XV-1, p. 648).

8.6. The Right to Benefit from Social Welfare Services (Article 14)

8.6.1. Introduction

Article 14 should ensure the effective exercise of the right to social welfare provided for by Member States. This provision entails legal guarantees. The goal of the protection of this provision is to ensure the effective exercise of the right to benefit from social welfare services. 'Social welfare' is not defined by Article 14, nor is it indicated how 'benefits ensured by social welfare services' should be understood. In the first supervisory cycle the Committee defined the above terms by encompassing them into all services of a welfare character provided by social work services. The aim of such services is to enable the beneficiaries to adapt to social changes.[216]

The Committee came to the conclusion that, at a certain point, Article 13 and Article 14 intercept. After closer analysis of both provisions, it concluded that between both standards of the provisions there are actual differences. These differences are contained within the objective and subjective scope of such Articles as well as within the aim of the comparative provisions. The provision in question does not have a restricted scope. Article 13 is applicable solely to persons finding themselves in a difficult personal or family situation. The scope of services also differs (provided for by Member States that have ratified similar provisions). Under Article 14, Member States are obligated to encourage the participation of organizations in the establishment and maintenance of such services. On the other hand, Article 13 obligates Member States to provide material assistance for those in need of it.[217]

Articles 13 and 14 also have different goals for Member States to achieve. The Committee, regards Article 14 to be part of the 'dynamic' category. Article 13 however, ensures that those persons in need, without adequate resources, have the right to benefit from social welfare services. The comparable provisions supplement one another. Member States ratifying both provisions are obligated to independently organize welfare services or support such services provided by non-governmental organizations. Such services should ensure material assistance for those in need. Comparing the scope of obligations stipulated by both provisions, the Committee concluded that fulfilling the requirements of just one of the comparative provisions does not guarantee a positive decision concerning the fulfilment of the obligations specified in the other provision. Member States fulfilling their obligations under Article 13 by ensuring material assistance for those without adequate resources may be regarded as not fulfilling the obligations under Article 14.[218] Non-compliance of Article 13 cannot be automatically regarded as non-compliance of Article 14.[219] A Member State may either support or organize social welfare services and not ensure those in need with advice and personal assistance in order to prevent, to remove or to alleviate personal or family want. This result is possible, given the broad scope of

216. Conclusions I, p. 69.
217. *Ibid.*
218. *Ibid.*, pp. 65, 69; Conclusions VIII, p. 170 (Iceland); Conclusions XII-1, p. 256 (Turkey).
219. Conclusions I, p. 65.

Article 14, as well as the differentiating nature of the comparable provisions (Article 14 and 13).[220]

Even though Article 14 is general in its application, the Committee specified a few social categories, which allocate an order of priority for individuals seeking to benefit from the right to social welfare services. These categories include the elderly, those who are single, disabled, ex-prisoners, the youth, women who are victims of violence, drug addicts, alcoholics, work migrants and their families, and political asylum seekers. These persons have an order of priority to receive social welfare services. These are categories of people who are marginalized the most, as well as excluded from society due to demographic (ageing population) and custom (decrease in the number of couples getting married, increase in divorce rates) changes.[221] The Committee underlined the dynamic nature of Article 14, a provision obligating Member States to react to social changes. It obligated the Member States to provide information within their reports about the measures undertaken to satisfy the needs of social groups requiring social welfare services. It drew attention to the necessity of allocating such services in a way that is accessible to all members of society requiring assistance, regardless of their residency.

8.6.2. The Obligation to Promote or Provide Social Welfare Services (Article 14 § 1)

The right to benefit from social welfare services is a subjective right. The Committee that Member States produce details concerning the possibility of benefiting from this right by all persons legally residing within the territory of a given Member State, as well as by those citizens of another Member State that is party to the Charter.[222] It examines whether the above entitlements may be reached judicially,[223] and whether a refusal to grant such rights may be appealed in a court of higher jurisdiction.[224]

Article 14 obligates Member States to promote or provide social welfare services. This obligation may be fulfilled in such a way as is regarded most appropriate by a given Member State. Social welfare services may be organized by charitable institutions, or by administrative, governmental or local institutions. The Committee demands Member States to produce information that will show, regardless of how such services are organized, that the services are rendered in a professional and effective manner. In particular, regarding services that are rendered by private institutions, the Committee

220. Conclusions VIII, p. 170 (Iceland); Conclusions XIII-1, p. 372 (Turkey).
221. Conclusions XII-1, pp. 38–40.
222. Conclusions XV-2, p. 278 (Iceland); pp. 363–364 (the Netherlands); p. 502 (Portugal); Conclusions XVI-2, vol. 1, p. 168 (Czech Republic); p. 436 (Hungary); Conclusions 2003, vol. 1, p. 60 (Bulgaria); Conclusions 2003, vol. 2, p. 495 (Slovenia).
223. Conclusions I, pp. 70–71.
224. Conclusions XV-2, p. 313 (Italy); p. 458 (Poland); p. 609 (Great Britain); Conclusions 2003, vol. 1, p. 60 (Bulgaria).

wanted to be sure that such services are appropriate and are generally accessible,[225] whilst Member States are regularly supervising them.[226]

The Committee has identical expectations in cases where the social welfare services were decentralized and where the welfare services were entrusted to local bodies.[227] The Committee is of the opinion that social welfare services should be located in places that will ensure the general accessibility to the services provided, and that the bodies in charge of making decisions should be in the lowest possible grade.[228] It, for example, obligated Bulgaria to explain the accusations made by the Helsinki Committee branch within the country, about Bulgaria's inappropriate localization of social welfare housing.[229] The Committee drew attention to the issue of whether social welfare services as well as the bodies managing such institutions are abiding by the appropriate regulations, and especially whether they are ensuring those intending to benefit or are benefiting from social welfare services the right to privacy.[230] Article 14 ensures that those who are considered to be in need of social welfare services, receive the right to benefit from such services. A person capable of making such a decision is someone who is authorized. Neither charitable organizations, nor national or local government (which organize the existence of such social welfare services) have the right to decide, or allocate certain persons authorized to decide in such services. The Committee was interested to know whether those persons who were ordered to undergo drug rehabilitation had the right of appeal to an independent body.[231]

The criteria for indicating the effectiveness of social welfare services are the amount of funds allocated for such services, the amount of offices and the amount of personnel working in such services.[232] The Committee demanded that Member States present current information about the criteria in question. It wanted the Member States to be able to indicate, in their national reports, what type of social welfare services are financed by the national treasury budget.[233] It demanded confirmation that the social welfare services rendered are open to all those entitled.[234]

---

225. Conclusions XII-1, pp. 201–202 (Great Britain); Conclusions XII-2, p. 91 (Malta).
226. Conclusions XIII-5, p. 102 (Finland); p. 230 (Portugal); Conclusions XVI-2, vol. 1, p. 168 (Czech Republic).
227. Conclusions XV-2, p. 64 (Austria); p. 167 (Finland); p. 313 (Italy); p. 364 (the Netherlands); p. 565 (Sweden).
228. Conclusions XI-2, p. 125 (France); Conclusions XII-1, p. 201 (Great Britain).
229. Conclusions 2003, vol. 1, pp. 61–62.
230. Case of the Netherlands: Conclusions XII-1, p. 201; Conclusions XIII-4, p. 220; Conclusions XV-2, p. 364.
231. Case of Norway: Conclusions XIII-4, p. 211; Conclusions XV-2, pp. 396–397.
232. Case of Turkey: Conclusions XIII-3, p. 372; Conclusions XIII-4, p. 222; Addendum to Conclusions XV-2, p. 266 and following; Conclusions XVI-2, vol. 1, p. 168 (Czech republic); Conclusions 2003, vol. 2, p. 496 (Slovenia)
233. Conclusions XV-2, p. 65 (Austria); p. 136 (Denmark); p. 458 (Poland); Conclusions XVI-2, vol. 1, p. 168 (Czech Republic); p. 438 (Hungary); Conclusions 2003, vol. 2, p. 496 (Slovenia).
234. *Ibid.*, p. 535 (Spain).

In cases where Member States were unable to provide such information, the Committee adjourned its decisions.[235]

8.6.3. The Participation of Voluntary Organizations Providing Social Welfare Services (Article 14 § 2)

Article 14 § 2 obligates Member States to encourage the participation of individuals and voluntary organizations in the establishment and maintenance of social welfare services. Similar to Article 14 § 1, § 2 is dynamic in its nature. In supervising the compliance of the provision in question by Member States, the Committee seeks information about the measures undertaken by Member States to encourage individuals and voluntary organizations providing such services. The measures undertaken by Member States cannot be restricted to simply providing financial assistance to individuals and voluntary organizations interested in providing social welfare services.[236] The Committee nonetheless demands information about the funds allocated from the national budget for individuals and voluntary organizations providing social welfare services.[237]

From the first supervisory cycle, the Committee demanded information concerning the measures carried out by given Member States in order to increase the amount of individuals and voluntary organizations providing social welfare services.[238] The input of individuals and voluntary organizations regarding social welfare services does not mean that such entities are responsible for taking over all functions associated with such services. The obligations stipulated under Article 14 § 2 are fulfilled by the Member States, enabling individuals and voluntary organizations to take part in state provided social welfare services. Article 14 § 2 does not demand from Member States that they transfer various authoritative functions to individuals and voluntary organizations in matters associated with independently carried out social welfare services.[239] The Committee, rather, demands that Member States, that have ratified the above provisions, provide information about the measures taken to encourage individuals and voluntary organizations to carry out social welfare services and regarding the amount of funds allocated by the stats to support such actions.[240] It also demands Member States to provide information dealing with concrete measures undertaken by individuals and voluntary organizations when providing social welfare services.[241]

---

235. Addendum to Conclusions XV-2, p. 55 (Germany).
236. Conclusions XIII-4, p. 420 (Belgium); Conclusions XV-2, p. 168 (Finland); p. 256 (Greece); p. 314 (Italy); p. 503 (Portugal); p. 535 (Spain).
237. Conclusions XVI-2, vol. 1, p. 169 (Czech Republic); Conclusions 2003, vol. 1, p. 63 (Bulgaria).
238. Conclusions I, p. 71; Conclusions III, p. 72; Conclusions 2003, vol. 1, p. 291 (Italy).
239. Conclusions IV, p. 95 (Sweden).
240. Conclusions XV-2, p. 535 (Spain); Addendum to Conclusions XV-2, p. 88 (Luxembourg).
241. Addendum to Conclusions XV-2, pp. 216–217 (Slovakia)

8.7. The Right of Persons with Disabilities to Independence, Social Integration and Participation in the Life of the Community (Article 15)

8.7.1. Introduction

Article 15 ESC is made up of two parts. This provision obligates Member States to take measures to provide persons with disabilities with guidance, education and vocational training (§ 1) as well as to support persons with disabilities in finding employment (§ 2). The Revised European Social Charter broadened the objective scope of this provision. Member States that ratified Article 15 RESC are obliged to carry out the necessary measures to ensure disabled persons with independence, social integration and participation in the life of the community. Member States must promote full social integration and participation in the life of the community (§ 3).

The Community established the legal framework of the provision during the first supervisory cycle.[242] Article 15 provides disabled persons with the right to full inclusion into community life, in a civic sense as well as in an employment understanding. The Committee took note that, for a long period, disabled persons were treated by legal social security regulations within Member States as persons needing only resources to retain a basic standard of living. Disability pensions as well as other social benefits (unemployment benefits, financial assistance) paid out to disabled persons were regarded as being on the same level as benefits paid to persons (regardless of age) unable to support themselves.

During World War II however, out of necessity due to the benefits received by Great Britain, the approach of Member States to disabled persons who were of an employable age, changed. The social policies during this time, with regards to disabled persons ceased to exist. The experiences gained during World War II exemplified that disabled persons of an employable age who are properly trained could independently function within the community.

The aim of Article 15 is to enable disabled persons to partake in community life, to gain independence, attain employable qualifications in order to be financially independent. Interpreting Article 15 the Committee decided § 1 and § 2 are strictly interconnected.[243] It claimed that integration within the work sector means that it is necessary for disabled persons to integrate within the life of the community. This stance is still valid and has been strengthened by Article 15 RESC, which treats education and vocational training as well as accessibility to employment for disabled persons as necessary factors for the full integration and full participation in the life of the community (§ 3).

The imperative aim of Article 15 is to ensure that disabled persons are able to gain independence through employment and are able to financially support themselves. Through the other provisions (Article 1 § 4 and Articles 9 and 10), the Charter ensures

242. Conclusions I, p. 72.

243. Conclusions XIV-2, pp. 62–63.

the right to guidance and vocational training. In Article 15, these rights have been raised to the level of a subjective right encompassing the disabled only. The provision in question obligates Member States to take measures in increasing the chances of employment for disabled persons. The separately regulated rights of disabled persons is an indicator for Member States to treat this group independently and favourably in order for them to be able to regain their independence and functioning within society.[244]

With regard to this matter, the Charter takes advantage of the experiences available from the International Labour Organization, which handed down the following decree No. 88 dealing with adult vocational training as well as disabled persons vocational training, during the 33rd session of the general Conference of the ILO in 1950, and No. 99 dealing with the adjustment and rehabilitation into the workforce of the handicapped passed on 1 June 1955.[245] It orders Member States to provide disabled persons with vocational training (§ 1), and ensure them assistance in entering the labour market (§ 2)[246] as well as to support them in full integration into the life of the community (§ 3). The Committee interprets Article 15 as a standard, which obligates Member States to reach the desired outcomes. Measures taken by the Member States in matters regulated by Article 15 § 1 and 2 should be effective. Article 15 is treated as a dynamic standard, which obligates Member States to undertake new measures to enable a fuller realization of integration of disabled persons. The Committee rendered a decision concerning the non-compliance of domestic practices with Article 15, for not being able to attain the desired results.[247]

The Committee treats Article 15 as a standard guaranteeing human rights protection – the right to dignity regardless of the disability. According to the Committee, the protection of the rights of disabled persons in matters dealing with guidance, education and vocational training (§ 1) as well as with employment (§ 2) is the best example of 'real' dependency between the protection of social rights and each human right to dignity.[248]

The protection of rights of disabled persons to independence, social integration and participation in community life, should be ensured by Member States as well as by stakeholders. Their responsibility is to take various necessary measures, which will allow disabled persons to partake within the labour market and in community life on an equal footing with those who are not disabled.[249]

---

244. *Ibid.*, p. 63.
245. Conventions and recommendations ... vol. 1, *op. cit.*, pp. 504 and following. The literature analysed that the Charter in a les decisive manner than the ILO No. 99 ruling, orders authorities of Member States to take measures to introduce into the labour marker disabled workers. *See* The European Social Charter and International Labour Standards, International Labour Review, vol. 84, 1961, p. 373.
246. Conclusions I, p. 72.
247. Conclusions I, p. 73 (Norway); p. 208 (Ireland).
248. Conclusions XIV-2, p. 64.
249. *Ibid.*, p. 63.

Article 15 does not contain a legal definition of disability with respect to the rights to independence, social integration and participation in community life borne by disabled persons who are citizens of Member States, legally residing within a state that is a party to the Charter. The Committee's position is that the Charter, which is modelled on the ILO convention No. 159 passed on 1 June 1983, dealing with the vocational rehabilitation and employment of disabled persons,[250] leaves the definition of disability open to the legislation of each Member State.[251] The definition of disability should take into consideration not only medical factors but also the social aspects.[252] In accordance with the approximations made by the European Union, only 10 per cent of the European population is disabled in the age group considered to be employable.[253]

Both the physically disabled and the mentally disabled are included into the category of disabled persons.[254] The Committee was forced to reanalyse the subjective scope of disabled persons, whose right to independence, social integration and participation in the life of the community, is legally protected due to the discrepancy of the two official languages of the Charter (French and English). In the English text of the provision there is no doubt that the persons entitled to the right are *disabled persons*. The type of disability, whether it is physical or mental, is of no relevance. In the French text of the provision, Article 15 stipulates the persons entitled to the rights are physically disabled persons (*personnes physiquement diminuées*). Despite such discrepancies, the Committee along with other commentators of the Charter, basing their arguments on historical analysis, agree that the right to the protection guaranteed by Article 15 is available to all disabled persons regardless of their type and source of disability.[255]

The Committee is clear in its stipulation that Member States are bound by the obligation of equal treatment of disabled persons regardless of whether they are citizens of a given Member State, in which they are legally residing or whether they are citizens of other Member States, that are parties to the Charter. Member States, which introduce the requirement of residing within a Member State for a specified period (2, 4 or 5 years) as a condition for a disabled person to attain the rights specified under Article 15 are regarded as being in violation of the provision by the Committee.[256] Other cases of unequal treatment of disabled persons being able to take advantage of the right ensured by Article 15, whether they are citizens or foreigners in a particular Member State, were regarded as non-compliant by the Committee.[257] These cases

250. Conventions and recommendations ... vol. 2, *op. cit.*, p. 1096 and following.
251. *Ibid.*, p. 64.
252. Conclusions XVI-2, vol. 1, p. 51 (Austria); p. 316 (Germany); Conclusions XVI-2, vol. 2, p. 653 (Poland); p. 796 (Slovakia).
253. *Ibid.*
254. Conclusions 1, p. 208 (Germany); Conclusions XIV-2, p. 62.
255. D. Harris, J. Darcy, *op. cit.*, p.183 and footnote 1142.
256. Conclusions XI-1, p. 137 (Denmark 2 years), pp. 139–140 (Great Britain – 4 years); Conclusions XIV-2, p. 148 and following (Belgium – 5 years). The residency requirement was waived in Denmark. During the following supervisory cycle the Committee decided that the Danish regulations are in accordance with Article 15 of the Charter. Conclusions XII-1, p. 204.
257. Conclusions XIV-2, pp. 63–64 (Denmark); pp. 241–242 (Finland).

show that discrimination of citizens of other Member States in matters dealing with vocational training[258] as well access to employment is prohibited.[259]

The Committee, for example, considered the case of Great Britain and its actions as discriminatory. The right of disabled persons to take advantage of vocational training and assistance in finding employment was dependent, in Great Britain, upon whether these persons were allowed access to the country in order to take advantage of British welfare services. Only foreigners, citizens of other Member States that are parties to the Charter, could take advantage of the rights entailed for the disabled under Article 15, if, according to British customs regulations, they were accepted into the country for purposes of rehabilitation, vocational training and guidance.[260] Disabled children of such persons were exempt from the restrictions placed on making use of the rights under Article 15, when they came of age during their residency with Great Britain.[261] Taking into consideration the Committee's criticism, Britain overturned its regulations by providing disabled children, citizens of other Member States, the possibility of taking advantage of the right to guidance, education and vocational training on the same conditions as applicable to British citizens.[262]

Article 15 contains no indicators in the part dealing with ways of protecting the right of the disabled to independence, social integration and participation in the life of the community. The Committee, further, does not define for Member States a social policy model, which should be put into use with regards to the disabled. Member States should provide details within the reports dealing with social policy systems, which guarantee the disabled the right to independence, social integration and participation in the life of the community. The Committee examines whether the measures taken by Member States ensure disabled persons the receipt of such rights.[263] It draws attention to whether Member States taking such measures allow access for disabled persons into the life of the community on the same grounds that are applicable for other members of society, who are temporarily out of work. The Committee is of the view, that such types of action should take place in other Member States, in which the dominating practice prevailing is to employ disabled workers in separate workplaces adjusted to their abilities.[264] The Committee decisively moved away from examining matters dealing with the integration of disabled persons into the life of the community. In the place of the old practice of 'separate but equal' the Committee began to form a principle

258. Conclusions XVI-2, vol. 1, p. 225 (Denmark); Conclusions XVI-2, vol. 2, p. 866 (Spain); Conclusions 2003, vol. 1m p. 163 (France); p. 295 (Italy); Conclusions 2003, vol. 2, p. 402 (Romania); p. 502 (Slovenia).
259. Conclusions XVI-2, vol. 1, p. 54 (Austria); p. 99 (Belgium); p. 172 (Czech Republic); p. 360 (Greece); p. 472 (Iceland); Conclusions XVI-2, vol. 2, p. 547 (the Netherlands); p. 593 (Norway); p. 657 (Poland); p. 799 (Slovakia); p. 868 (Spain); Conclusions 2003, vol. 1, pp. 296–297 (Italy); Conclusions 2003, vol. 2, p. 405 (Romania); p. 506 (Slovenia).
260. Conclusions VII, p. 84; Conclusions VIII, p. 177; Conclusions IX, p. 91; Conclusions X-1, p. 126.
261. Conclusions XI-1, pp. 139–140.
262. Conclusions XII-1, p. 207.
263. Conclusions XIV-2, p. 69.
264. *Ibid.*, p. 64.

according to which disabled persons should be treated equally with others when of the employable age and are in want of work and are seeking employment.[265] The former concept of including disabled persons into the life of the community lead to the elimination out of generally accessible workplaces. The new concept, which is used by the Committee, is based on the establishment of equalized opportunities for the disabled competing with the non-disabled, so that they may partake in the life of the community with the same equal rights as the non-disabled. The Committee is against creating alternative labour markets. It refers, instead, to the creation of possibilities for the disabled to enter an already existing labour market. It underlines the necessity of taking extra measures in order for disabled persons to gain professional qualifications allowing them to compete on the labour market with non-disabled persons.

8.7.2. Guidance, Education and Vocational Training of Disabled Persons (Article 15 § 1)

Article 15 § 1 obligates Member States to take necessary measures in order to ensure the disabled with guidance, education and vocational training by way of generally accessible educational institutions.[266] In situations where this is not possible, specialist institutions, in either the private or public sectors should provide such services.[267] The Committee should monitor whether Member States are fulfilling their obligations. In the questionnaire prepared by the Committee, used as a basis by Member States when preparing reports with regards to the obligations set by Article 15 § 1, questions have been included dealing with the following: measures taken by Member States in order to fulfil their obligations under the provisions, the amount of institutions providing services in guidance, education and vocational training for the disabled, the amount of placements available for the disabled within these institutions, the amount of disabled taking part in education, the amount of professional personnel, the criteria used when deciding a disabled person's application for education, the type of educational and vocational training programmes, and educational techniques.[268]

The Committee is interested in evaluating the educational methods used and the adapting the educational methods to the types of disability.[269] According to the Committee, the opinion of the effect of the rehabilitation is judged by the employment availabilities for the disabled. A specialist working in strict proximity with a disabled person who wants to regain their ability to carry out employment should make such an opinion known.[270] Educational and vocational training programme for the disabled

265. Conclusions XVI-2, vol. 2, p. 505 (Malta); p. 657 (Poland); p. 797 (Slovakia).
266. Conclusions XVI-2, vol. 1m pp. 51–52 (Austria); p. 96 (Belgium); Conclusions 2003, vol. 1m p. 159 and following.
267. Cumulating disabled children within special schools forms a basis for the non-compliance of domestic regulations with international standards. Conclusions 2003, vol. 2, p. 402 (Romania).
268. Form for the reports ... *op., cit.*, p. 343 and following.
269. Conclusions III, p. 74; Conclusions XIV-2, pp. 64 and following; Conclusions 2003, vol. 2, p. 609 (Sweden).
270. *Ibid.*, pp. 65–66.

should satisfy the individual needs of the disabled. Specialist training should be treated as a preparation for further education for all those seeking to gain additional professional qualifications. Teachers instructing disabled persons should be familiar with their particular needs and demands. Vocational training for the disabled should be conducted according to their needs, yet, at the same time, providing disabled persons with the qualifications and ability which will allow them to enter the labour market along with those who are not disabled.

8.7.3. Promoting the Access to Employment for Disabled Persons (Article 15 § 2)

Member States are obligated to promote access to employment for the disabled through all measures possible. Monitoring Member State compliance with this provision, the Committee seeks information regarding measures taken by Member States, the amount of disabled persons employed within particular years in open workplaces or in specialist positions created for such disabilities, initiatives made to encourage disabled persons to form their own businesses and the role filled by private organizations in social policies enabling the disabled to work.[271]

The Committee is not always content with the information provided. It pays particular attention to determining whether Member States take intensive measures in order to promote disabled persons into the 'open' labour market. In accordance with the dominating social policies of fully integrating disabled persons into the community, the Committee pays particular attention to specialist measures taken by Member States enabling disabled persons to be employed in workplaces that have always employed fully able workers. It encourages preferential measures towards disabled persons by employment agencies (such as reserving certain positions for the disabled, introducing quotas within workplaces of more than 20 workers for hiring disabled persons, subsidizing industries that offer positions for the disabled, and lowering public insurance premiums and taxes).

The provision in question has a dynamic nature. Monitoring the measures carried out by Member States, the Committee pays partial attention to whether the policies treating disabled persons more favourably within the labour market do not become discriminatory against those who are able. This refers to the obligation of employing a certain percentage of disabled persons in workplaces hiring more than 20 workers (quota system). The Committee rendered a decision that Article 15 § 2 does not obligate Member States to issue orders requiring the employment of a specified amount of disabled persons.[272]

The Committee attempts to establish whether Member States, where the quota system has been introduced, saw a change for disabled persons within the domestic labour market.[273] The introduction of compulsory quotas by some Member States for

271. Conclusions I, pp. 73–74; Conclusions III, p. 76. *See* P. Tuset del Pino, La contrataciõn de trabajadores minusválidos, Arazadi Editorial, Pamplona 2000.

272. Conclusions II, p. 54; Conclusions IV, p. 99 (Ireland).

273. Conclusions XIV-2, p. 357 (Greece); In the case where the number of disabled persons on the labour market decreases, the Committee demands information from authorities of Member States clarifying

disabled workers, carry as much as 2 per cent,[274] 3 per cent,[275] even 6 per cent[276] of disabled out of the total of the employed. The Committee approves such a technique promoting the employment of the disabled. In all cases, in which the method of supporting the employment of the disabled has been introduced, an additional question concerning legal sanctions has to be asked with reference to those employers who have an obligation of employing disabled persons yet choose not to abide by it.

In legal systems in which the disabled are employed in separate workplaces or in special positions, the Committee examines whether the Member States take measures to allow access for the disabled to enter generally open workplaces.[277] It attempts to establish equilibrium amongst the disabled in 'open' and 'closed' workplaces.[278] Violating such proportions by outweighing the employment of disabled persons within the separated 'closed' workplaces may cause the Committee to hand down a decision about the non-compliance of domestic regulations with Article 15 § 2.[279]

The Committee analyses the conditions of employing disabled persons.[280] It compared the remuneration packages of the disabled with those of the able bodied employees.[281] It demands information about the disabled workers' right to associate.[282] It attempts to establish whether disabled workers take advantage of the protection of the longevity of their work agreement.[283] Confirming cases of discrimination of disabled workers or not providing them with particular protection against the termination of work relations by the employer justifies decisions handed down, referring to the non-compliance of a Member State with the international standards expressed under Article 15 § 2.[284]

Between 2001 and 2003 the Committee concluded that only two Member States (Great Britain[285] and Sweden[286]) had domestic regulations that were in accordance with the international standards under Article 15 § 2.

---

the reasons for such a reduction as well as information about the measures taken stop the process of deprecation. Conclusions XVI-2, vol. 2, p. 797 (Slovakia).

274. Conclusions XVI-2, vol. 2, p. 506 (Malta).
275. *Ibid.*, p. 798 (Slovakia).
276. Conclusions 2003, vol. 1, p. 165 (France).
277. Conclusions XVI-2, vol. 1, pp. 227 and following; Conclusions XVI-2, vol. 2, p .799 (Slovakia).
278. Conclusions XVI-2, vol. 1, pp. 53–54 (Austria); pp. 87–98 (Belgium); Conclusions XVI-2, vol. 2, p. 657 (Poland).
279. Conclusions XVI-2, vol. 2, pp. 797–799 (Slovakia).
280. Conclusions XVI-2, vol. 2, p. 799 (Slovakia).
281. Conclusions XVI-2, vol. 1, p. 319 (Germany); Conclusions XVI-2, vol. 2, p. 656 (Poland).
282. Conclusions XVI-2, vol. 1, p. 319; Conclusions XVI-2, vol. 2, p. 656 (Poland).
283. Conclusions XVI-2, vol. 1, p. 54 (Austria); p. 99 (Belgium); p. 172 (Czech Republic); p. 473 (Iceland); Conclusions XVI-2, vol. 2, p.547 (the Netherlands); p. 799 (Slovakia).
284. Conclusions XVI-2, vol. 1, p. 229 (Dania); p. 357 (Greece); Conclusions XVI-2, vol. 2, p. 593 (Norway); p. 865 (Spain); Conclusions 2003, vol. 1, pp. 296–297 (Italy); Conclusions 2003, vol. 2, p. 405 (Romania); p.506 (Slovakia).
285. Conclusions XVI-2, vol. 2, pp. 946–948.
286. Conclusions 2003, vol. 2, pp. 611–612.

8.7.4. Promoting the Full Social Integration and Participation in the Life of the Community of Disabled Persons (Article 15 § 3 RESC)

Member States have an obligation to promote the full social integration and participation of disabled persons in the life of the community.[287] Article 15 § 3 RESC is a dynamic standard. It obligates Member States to initiate and carry out positive measures, which will enable the goals of the provision to be achieved. Member States must enable disabled persons to gain access to transport, housing, cultural activities and leisure. Disabled persons should have technical aids to overcome communication and mobility barriers. According to the Committee, measures taken by Member States in order to fulfil the obligations cannot be carried out in isolation, and instead they should supplement each other. Consultations with regards to such measures should be carried out with the representatives of the disabled.[288] The Committee is of the opinion that Article 15 § 3 RESC is a provision forbidding the discrimination of disabled persons. Not being able to fulfil the above obligations means that the Committee can hand down a decision about the non-compliance of domestic regulations with international standards.[289] The Committee demands reports about the following: consultations with representative organizations of the disabled, technical measures taken for disabled persons to overcome barriers in public transport, and housing, and access to cultural activities and leisure, communication. The Committee is interested in receiving information dealing with the legal status of sign language, access to public transport for the disabled, and the finances allocated by Member States for various aids to be made available for the disabled to be used freely and limitlessly. Examining the compliance of Article 15 § 3 RESC of four domestic reports[290] during the first supervisory cycle, the Committee did not hand down any decision about the compliance of domestic regulations with international standards.

8.8. The Right of the Family to Social, Legal and Economic Protection (Article 16)

The Charter regards the family as a fundamental unit of society. In order to ensure the family the necessary conditions for full development, Article 16 of the Charter obligates Member States to take measures to ensure legal, social and economic protection for the family. The provision in question has a broad scope. It obligates Member States to initiate and carry out various measures, which will form social policy

287. *See* Framework of Integration Policies, Council of Europe. Directorate of Social Affairs and Health, Strasbourg 2000; M. Menédez, F.M. Fernandez Lies, La protección de las personas y grupos vulnerables en el Derecho Europeo, Madrid 2001; Promoting the Policy Debate on Social Exclusions From a Comparative Perspective, Council of Europe Publishing, Strasbourg 2002.

288. Conclusions 2003, vol. 1, p.168 (France); p. 297 (Italy); Conclusions 2003, vol. 2, p. 507 (Slovenia); p. 613 (Sweden).

289. Conclusions 2003, vol. 1, p.299 (Italy); Conclusions 20003, vol. 2, p. 510 (Slovenia).

290. France, Slovenia, Sweden and Italy. Bulgaria and Romania did not ratify Article 15 § 3 RESC.

protecting the family, harmonize such measures as well as to adapt them to the already existing pro-family measures existing within the given country.[291]

In Article 16, the following measures have been stipulated for Member States to follow and to ensure legal, social and economic protection for the family: social and family services, fiscal arrangements and taxation benefits, encouraging housing developments appropriate to family needs, and the allocation of benefits for young married couples. These measures are examples only and are not exhaustive. The provision in question obligates Member States to take various measures ensuring full development for the family unit.

During the first supervisory cycle the Committee obligated Member States to present information dealing with the following: domestic systems dealing with family social security, benefits and exemptions for families with multiple children from public responsibilities, social services, assistance and care for families rearing children, legal property protection, family housing developments, and financial assistance for families in need.[292] The Community hands down decisions of compliance or non-compliance with international standards stipulated by Article 16 of Member States, based on the information gathered from the reports presented.

The provision in question is dynamic in its nature. The Committee is of the view that Member States are obligated foremostly to indicate, which measures have been taken to ensure development for families. The Committee is, therefore, interested, to a lesser degree, in the results attained from administering such measures.[293] It rendered a decision of non-compliance on Member States, to the international standards under Article 16, that provided an insufficient level of material benefits to families and children.[294] Member States are therefore obligated by the decisions handed down by the Committee for establishing general social security systems for families and their children[295] and to ensure that families receive the proper benefits, at an appropriate level.

The right of the family to social, legal and economic protection has no normative meaning. Article 16 defined obligations for Member States to fulfil and attain the specified goals, i.e. creating necessary conditions for the family so it can fully develop. Based on such reports, an authorized entity, such as the family, has no right to file claims against Member States in terms of social security. Article 16 is therefore a provision, which establishes the provisions under the aegis of the Member States.

The Committee, during the first supervisory cycle, was of the opinion that the above understanding of the family's right to social, legal and economic protection, is

291. Conclusions I, p. 75.
292. *Ibid.*
293. Conclusions XIV-1, p. 56.
294. Conclusions XVII-1, vol. 1, p. 253 (Greece); Conclusions XVII-1, vol. 2, p. 394 (Poland); p. 464 (Spain); Conclusions 2002, pp. 153–154; Conclusions 2004, vol. 1, p. 75 (Bulgaria); Conclusions 2004, vol. 2, p. 491 (Romania)
295. The Committee handed down a decision with regards to Turkey and its inability to comply with the standards under Article 16 of the Charter due to its failure to develop a family social security system.

entitled to approval because attaining the above goals is possible not by individual measures (even when they have a legal status of dealing with claims), but rather through centralized measures carried out by the Member States. In reality, therefore, the provision of guaranteeing a family the protection in order for it to develop is ensured by pro-family policies, which should be carried out by the Member States.[296]

Article 16 obligates Member States to create and sustain conditions, which are necessary for the full development of a family. Deducing from the decisions rendered by the Committee, it may be concluded that such conditions are met when Member States fulfil the following: ensuring parents equal legal status, allocating to parents and guardians the required family and social benefits, providing fiscal arrangements to the family, and allocating sufficient social services and family housing.

Equal rights and responsibilities of parents should be guaranteed. This refers to property and parental rights, with an emphasis placed on paid parental leave.[297] The Committee is of the opinion that Member States, that do not abide by the above principles, discriminate against one of the parents (in property cases it is usually the woman, in terms of child rearing it is usually the man), and therefore do not abide by the standards established under Article 16.[298]

Three Member States were viewed as being discriminatory against parents by not ensuring equality. Two, namely Malta[299] and Turkey[300], were found to be in violation by giving the male the status as the 'head' of the family, authorized to manage the family property. Great Britain was seen to be discriminatory, as it did not ensure women in Northern Ireland equal rights along with the men to manage joint family property.[301] Due to the Committee's influential decisions, family rights provisions were changed in some Member States. Men were granted parental rights in divorce cases, by being given child rearing holidays, termed as parental leave from the moment that equality was given to both men and women.[302]

Article 16 names two types of social benefits deemed necessary for the development of a family, namely family benefits and social benefits. The Committee understands family benefits as encompassing family allowances. Social benefits on the other hand for family purposes include services such as family counselling services, home-help

296. Conclusions I, p. 75.
297. Conclusions XIII-3, p. 59; Conclusions XIV-1, p. 332 (Germany).
298. Conclusions XIII-2, p. 27.
299. Conclusions XII-2, p. 204. In the following supervisory cycle the Committee was of the opinion that the civil code in Malta was altered in such a way as to ensure spouses equal rights. Conclusions XIII-2, p. 362
300. Conclusions XIII-3, p. 384. *See* the recommendations of the Committee of Ministers addressing the Turkish authorities. CM Recommendations R ChS (98)4.
301. Conclusions XVII-1, vol. 2, p. 530. Great Britain was regarded during the fifth supervisory cycle, as a Member State not complying with the standards stipulated under Article 16 of the Charter, as the allocation of family benefits was dependent upon the full-time employment of one of the parents, namely the male. Conclusions V, p. 111.
302. Conclusions X, p. 130 (the Netherlands); Conclusions XIII-2, pp. 28–29; pp. 150–151 (Ireland); Conclusions XIII-2, p. 230; Conclusions XIV-1, p. 216 (France); *See* L. Samuel, *op. cit.*, p. 355.

services, children's holiday homes, family holiday homes and childcare services.[303] Due to the various services provided, the Committee requires that the Member States provide information (based on Article 16) with regards to the level of family benefits paid and the conditions, which need to be met before such benefits may be received. Because Member States have the right to choose provisions within the Charter to abide by, the Committee was forced to determine, which out of the two conflicting provisions, Article 12 or Article 16, demands information from Member States concerning family benefits. The problem arose whilst Denmark was establishing social security regulations and the necessary elements required for being able to receive family benefits. In accordance with the report provided by Denmark, such benefits are paid out only when one of the parents of the child as well as the child are Danish citizens or have been legally residing on Danish territory a year prior to when the benefits are to be paid out. Family benefits are paid out thanks to social security benefits, which are referred to in Article 12. Under this provision Member States are authorized to establish the necessary requirements needed to be met before one is able to receive social security, especially contributory benefits (meaning benefits which are directly connected to the payments made by either the employer or the employer and the worker combined). On the other hand, in light of the decision handed down by the Committee, Article 16 does not permit the introduction of regulations in domestic social security systems, which would condition in any way the receivership of family benefits (especially citizenship requirements of a given Member State or residency requirements within that state). Denmark argued that family benefits are not contributory in nature. They are regarded as non-contributory benefits. Payments made for such benefits come from other state treasury budgets. For this reason Article 16 should be interpreted in support of Article 12 § 4 and therefore allow for the Member States to introduce conditions for social security entitlements to be dependent upon requirements irrespective of the contributory system. In the Appendix to Article 12 § 4, it was clarified that the introductory paragraph to the provision 'and subject to the conditions laid down in such agreements' means that, in cases of non-contributory benefits, Member States (that are parties to the Charter) may require the completion of a prescribed period of residency before granting such benefits to citizens of other Member States. The Committee decided that family benefits are part of the family allowances that are provided through social security, a necessary source for the full development of the family. The Committee alluded to Article 12, a provision that orders the establishment and maintenance of a social security system. It noted that one of the conditions for fulfilling the requirements established by the provision in question is to organize and maintain a social security system in accordance with the requirements set up by the ILO convention No. 102 or by the European Code of Social Security.

The Committee views that the introduction into domestic social security systems of assurances of paying out family assistance, according to the international treaties, for those unable to work (thus realizing three out of the nine factors named in the ILO

303. Form for the reports ... *op. cit.*, p. 347.

convention No. 102), as well as the obligations established by Article 12 are met. Family benefits are just one of the nine types of property assistance named in the ILO convention No. 102. Member States therefore may elect not to take on the obligation to introduce family benefits into the domestic social security regulations.

Despite the above decision, there is a lack of evidence in establishing decrees about the non-compliance of Member States with the obligations set under Article 12. The Committee is of the view that the obligation specified under Article 16 is particular in its nature, in comparison to the general obligations specified under Article 12. Because the European Code of Social Security allows Member States to establish 6 month residency requirements within the territory of a Member State before granting an individual the right to non-contributory social security benefits, the Committee was viewed the Danish social security regulations as non-compliant with the international standards based on Article 16.[304]

Family benefits should be of a sufficient level and should be protected against inflation.[305] The level of family benefits should also reflect the costs of living standards. These benefits, on a collective level reflect the right of a family to economic protection. The Committee negatively regarded those Member States that paid out family benefits equal to 2.45 euros[306] and 4 euros[307] per month. Taking into consideration living costs, the above family benefit amounts cannot be regarded as sufficient entitlements assuring a family (the core unit of society) full development.

Family benefits should be made available to all families in which children are raised. The above obligation is not fulfilled when only certain families are ensured the right to family benefits (e.g. those families where the breadwinner is employed in the public sector or under a collective labour agreement) and such conditions are seen by the Committee as non-compliant with Article 16.[308]

Similar decisions were rendered in situations where it was obvious that a Member State had set criteria for eligibility for family benefits at such a level that the majority of families raising children could not meet.[309] Conditions that yield this result are seen as the general non-compliance by domestic regulations with international standards established by Article 16.[310] Family benefits should be paid out to families for the duration of time in which children are unable to support themselves; and, instead, are being financially supported by their parents. Generally, family benefit entitlements should be made available until the coming of age day. In the case of children continuing with university studies and being supported by parents, such benefits should be made

---

304. Conclusions IX-1, p. 95; Conclusions X-1, p. 129; Conclusions XI-1, pp. 143–144; Conclusions XIII-1, pp. 198–199; Conclusions XIII-2, p. 148; Conclusions XIV-1, pp. 198 and following.
305. Conclusions XIII-2, p. 63; p. 149 (Greece); p. 154 (Norway); Conclusions XIV, p. 575 (the Netherlands); p. 745 (Sweden).
306. Conclusions 2002, pp. 153–154 (Romania).
307. Conclusions 2004, vol. 1, p. 75 (Bulgaria).
308. Conclusions XIII-3, p. 382 (Turkey) The Committee of Ministers passed a Turkish resolution in the matter in question. CM Recommendation R ChS (98) 4.
309. Conclusions XVI-2, p. 803 (Slovakia).
310. Conclusions XVII-1, vol. 2, p. 464 (Spain).

available until the age of 25 or 26 years of age. Taking into consideration the above standards, the Committee unanimously passed a negative decree with regards to the social security regulations of Lithuania, which granted family benefit entitlements for children until the age of 3.[311]

Examining the level of social services provided for families, the Committee looks at the following: the scope, the amount, the quality and the availability of such services.[312] It was interested in whether the costs of the above services were accessible to less well off families.[313]

An important social pro family policy element is the exemption and relief in public duties. In the form prepared by the Committee, which forms a basis upon which Member States model their reports, questions were included dealing with certain tax exemptions for families raising children.[314] Commencing from the 14th supervisory cycle, the Committee did not seek information from Member States dealing with the tax exemption issue in question. Examining the Spanish reports, it took note at the low level of family benefits, which could not be accepted in justifying tax exemptions for families with multiple children.[315]

The subject of family housing is another area that is of importance to the Committee. The Committee sought reports from the Member States dealing with family housing conditions in which children are being raised. It was interested in the built up areas of family housing.[316] Housing should meet the requirements and should be equipped with the necessary amenities (electricity, water, heating) necessary for families.[317] Appropriate housing is housing with defined parameters, which should not be less than the minimum requirements within a given Member State.[318]

Article 16 encourages Member States to erect housing for families. The above obligation is understood as carrying out housing initiatives by state institutions or administrative bodies of Member States as well as supporting private businesses in undertaking such actions to meet their commercial goals.[319] In the opinion of the Committee, Article 16 is the basis upon which information demands can be made on Member States concerning details of housing rental costs as well as the accessibility to loans and mortgages for the purchase or the building of houses for young and not too well off families.[320] The provision in question also forms a legal basis for protecting

311. Conclusions 2004, vol. 2, p. 384.
312. Conclusions III-2, p. 155 (United Kingdom); Conclusions XIV-1, p. 91 (Austria); p. 135 (Belgium); p. 365 (Greece); Conclusions XV-1, p. 220 (Finland); p. 309 (Belgium); Conclusions XVI-2, p. 441 (Hungary).
313. Conclusions XIV-1, p. 278 (France).
314. Form for the reports ... *op. cit.*, pp. 334–335.
315. Conclusions XVII-1, vol. 2, p. 464.
316. Conclusions XIII-2, pp. 43–44; Conclusions XVI-2, p. 441 (Hungary).
317. Conclusions XII-1, p. 30; Conclusions XIII-3, p. 381 (Portugal); p. 382 (Turkey).
318. Conclusions XIII-2, p. 42.
319. *Ibid.*, p. 43; p. 153 (Italy).
320. Conclusions IV, p. 102 (Norway); Conclusions XIII-2, p. 155 (Great Britain); Conclusions XIV-1, pp. 132–133 (Belgium).

tenants against eviction. The Committee obligated Member States to pay particular attention to the situation of poor families affected by an above-average unemployment problem, who do not have enough resources to cover the rent, and are therefore open to eviction.[321] It also dealt with exceptional cases. It rendered a decision concerning Turkey's inability to fulfil the obligations stipulated under Article 16. Turkey's security forces carried out compulsory evictions of persons, under the pretext of terrorism, residing in southeast Turkey.[322]

Article 16 also ensures families the right to social, legal and economic protection. The provision in question contains legal definitions of the term 'family'. The Committee accepted the definition provided in the report handed down by the Netherlands in 1996, stating that the 'family is a social group comprised of one or more adults (of age) responsible for the raising of one or more children'.[323] This broad definition encompasses all families as well as homosexual relationships raising children. The Committee does not demand from Member States to legally recognize relationships of homosexuals. It only obligates such Member States to ensure social, legal and economical protection for these relationships, which according to domestic legal regulations carry the family status.[324]

In defining the scope of entities legally protected under Article 16, the Committee points out that the changes occurring in society means the idea of the nuclear family unit made up of two adults of the opposite sex raising children, is undergoing alterations due to the increase in divorce rates, the widespread management of property by persons not remaining in the marriage and the entrusting of grandparents with the care of children of single parents.[325] The Committee is of the opinion that a lack of a legal definition of family with Article 16 creates a possibility for a functional debate of this provision to such an extent as the moral standards of the European continent allow. It draws attention to the fact that neither the provision in question nor other Charter provisions provides a legal basis for distinguishing between adult persons in joint household maintenance, either in a marriage or in a non-married situation.[326] It does, however, point out that the protections of certain rights under Article 16 are available only to persons forming a family and remaining married. The Committee is concerned with property rights, which are available solely for persons remaining in a marriage.[327]

321. Conclusions XIII-2, p. 44.
322. Conclusions XIII-3, p. 383. *Votum separatum* from the above Committee decision made by D. Harris, *op. cit.*, p. 465 Emphasis was placed on Article 13 of the Charter and the possibility of restricting social rights in exceptional situations. The European Tribunal Of Human Rights declared that the destruction of homes by security forces is a violation of Article 8 of the European Convention of Human Rights. *Akdivar v Turkey* 1996 Eur. Ct. H.R. IV-1192.
323. Conclusions XIV-1, p. 574.
324. D. Harris, J. Darcy, *op. cit.*, p. 186, footnote 1154.
325. Conclusions XIII-2, pp. 25–26.
326. *Ibid.*, p. 27.
327. *Ibid.*

Article 16 obligates Member States to ensure protection for single parents raising children.[328] Regarding violence within the family as a pathological occurrence, the Committee was interested in gaining information with regards to actions taken by Member States of certain Member States to counteract such pathological family behaviour.[329]

The Charter orders Member States to provide equal treatment to its own citizens and to foreigners of other Member States that are parties to the international treaty. Equality and the prohibition of discrimination are applicable to the social, legal and economic protection of a family legally residing within the territory of another Member State. The Committee emphasizes to Member States that the above principles of equality are applicable to their own citizens as well as to the citizens of other Member States. Cases do not exist whereby citizens of other Member States receive privileged treatment whilst residing on the territory of another Member State.

It is usually the case for Member States to introduce more difficult criteria for foreign nationals attempting to access specified family entitlements. The Committee considers such instances and passes non-compliance judgments of domestic regulations with international standards established by Article 16 when:

- The right to family benefits is only assured to a state's own citizens;[330]
- The right to family benefits is dependent upon residency for a given period of time as specified by domestic regulations,[331] unless this condition does not remain in any way linked to social security sought out by citizens of another Member State.[332] A period of residency within a given Member State as a condition for attaining the right to family benefits out of social security, should be proportional to the benefits, which are sought by a citizen of another Member State, party to the Charter;[333]
- Granting the right to family benefits to citizens of only certain Member States (i.e., those entering the European Union or the European Economic Area or states that are part of certain bilateral agreements);[334]
- Introducing various conditions before family benefits are granted for a Member State's own citizens and for foreign nationals of other Member States, that are parties to the Charter.[335]

328. Conclusions XIII-3, p. 156 (Great Britain); Conclusions XIV-1, p. 132 (Belgium); p. 133 (Germany).
329. Conclusions XIV-1, p. 434 (Ireland).
330. Conclusions 2002, p. 207 (Slovenia).
331. Conclusions XIV-1, p. 131 (Belgium); p. 236 (Finland); p. 330 (Germany); p. 474 (Italy); Conclusions 2004, vol. 2m p. 384 (Lithuania).
332. Conclusions XIV-1, p. 58.
333. *Ibid.* Applying the above measure, the Committee decided that the period of residency for 6 months or for period of one year, as a condition for attaining the right to family benefits, is in accordance with Article 16 of the Charter. Conclusions XIV-1, p. 199 (Denmark); p. 746 (Sweden).
334. Conclusions XIV-1, pp. 56–57 (Austria); p. 332 (Germany); p. 541 (Malta); Conclusions XV-1, pp. 95 and following; pp. 276–277; pp. 307–308; pp. 347–348; Addendum to Conclusions XV-1, p. 38; Conclusions XVII-1, vol. 1, p. 45 (Austria); p. 219 (Germany); Conclusions 2004, vol. 2, p. 539 (Slovenia).
335. 15 years for the French and 20 years for the Turkish. Conclusions XV-1, pp. 276–277.

The Committee did not conclude upon the grounds required to establish non-compliance of domestic regulations with Article 16, in cases where a Member State introduces conditions upon which family benefits are granted, based on the residing children receiving benefits that are passed on to their parents.[336]

A particular case deals with the discrimination of families of a Member State's own citizens, namely the ethnic Roma minority. The Committee, in all cases of unequal treatment of ethnic minorities, ruled that the subject Member State was in non-compliance with the standards established under Article 16.[337]

8.9. The Right of Children and Young Persons to Social, Legal and Economic Protection (Article 17)

8.9.1. Introduction

Article 17 is a standard that is subject to change. The European Social Charter protects the economic and social interests of mothers and children. In the Revised European Social Charter, Article 17 underwent changes and was further broadened. It excluded mothers from its scope of protection, yet encompassed young persons along with children. The scope of protection was expanded to ensuring legal protection to both children and young persons. Both classes were granted the right to free primary and secondary education. Both versions of Article 17 (the 'new' and the 'old') are legally binding. Therefore, the following analysis will deal with both Social Charters and Article 17. With the exception of mothers, who are not protected by Article 17 RESC, Committee decisions dealing with children under Article 17 ESC have not lost their validity under Article 17 RESC.

8.9.2. The Right of Mothers and Children to Social and Economic Protection (Article 17 ESC)

Article 17 ESC obligates Member States to carry out necessary and appropriate measures to establish or maintain appropriate institutions or services that will ensure social and economic protection for mothers and children. Member States are obligated to ensure that mothers and children receive social and economic protection, when required. This is an indication that Member States are not obliged to provide such protection if non-governmental organizations or charitable institutions provide such protection at a required level.[338] Sources of protection mentioned in Article 17 ESC encompass both institutions (such as children's homes, preschools, kindergartens, schools and educational and development centres)[339] and services (assistance, advice).[340] With reference

336. Conclusions XIV-1, p. 332 (Germany).
337. Conclusions XVII-1, vol. 1, p. 253 (Greece); Conclusions 2004, vol. 1, p. 79 (Bulgaria); Conclusions 2004, vol. 2, p. 491 (Romania); p. 539 (Slovenia).
338. Conclusions I, p. 77 (Italy).
339. Conclusions XIII-2, p. 166 (Great Britain); Conclusions XIII-5, p. 238 (Portugal).
340. Conclusions III, p. 80.

to all of the expressions within Article 17 ESC, the Committee obligated all Member States to present detailed information in their reports regarding the following: solutions incorporated within each given Member State to ensure that mothers and children receive social and economic protection, the scope of economic assistance for women before and after they give birth, the legal procedure used in establishing parental rights, the level of legal protection given to single mothers, the level of legal protection for orphans and homeless children, adoption procedures, and approaches taken with regards to juvenile offenders.[341]

The legal protection provided by Article 17 ESC encompasses all mothers, including single mothers, as well as children.[342] The protection is granted to two already mentioned categories, not solely due to their mutually binding relationship, but also regardless of it.[343] Article 17 ESC does not entail legal definitions. In particular, it does not express a maximum age for when a protected entity ceases to be regarded as a 'child' in the understanding of the provision. Taking into consideration the connection between Article 17 and Article 7 ESC, the Committee initially interpreted that a 'child' remains a child until the age of fifteen.[344]

Article 7 ESC forbids the employment of children who have not finished the age of fifteen. The United Nations Convention on the rights of children[345] and the European Convention on carrying out the rights of the children[346] defines the child as a person who has yet not competed the age of 18, unless domestic regulations specify a different age of maturity. In the understanding of Article 17 ESC, a 'child' is, therefore, a person who has not reached an age of maturity. The provision in question ensures social and economic protection for children born into legal marriages and to those born outside of them.[347] In the case of children being born out of wedlock the Committee is particularly concerned with the protection of their property. After earlier attempts were made to introduce an obligation to look after the economic interests of children born out of wedlock,[348] the Committee (due to the social changes that have taken place) unanimously took the view that it is necessary to make all rights of children equal (including property rights) regardless of whether children are born in wedlock or out of it.[349]

The European Convention on the legal status of a child born out of wedlock on 15 October 1975 was a source of influence for the Committee.[350] Initially, the

341. Conclusions I, p. 77; Conclusions III, p. 80.
342. Conclusions I, p. 77; Conclusions XIII-2, p. 26.
343. D. Harris, J. Darcy, *op. cit.*, pp. 193–194.
344. Conclusions I, p. 42.
345. New York 20 Nov 1989, Bills Register from 1991, No. 120 pos. 526, Bills Register from 2000, No. 2, pos. 11.
346. Strasbourg 25 Jan 1996, Bills Register from 2000, No. 107, pos. 1128.
347. Conclusions XIII-2, p. 159 (France); p. 365 (Malta).
348. Conclusions III, p. 80.
349. Conclusions XIII-2, p. 36.
350. Came into force in 1978. Ratified by 12 Member States of the Council of Europe. *See* D. Harris, J. Darcy, *op. cit.*, pp. 195, footnote 1233.

Committee decided that Article 17 ESC forms a legal basis to demand that those Member States that ratified the provision undertake measures to ensure equal rights for children born in or out of wedlock. The Committee, however, concluded that Article 17 ESC ensures solely economic and social protection for mothers and children. In contrast to Article 16 ESC (standard ensuring a family social, economic and legal protection), Article 17 ESC does not ensure mothers and children legal protection. The Committee, basing its arguments on the elements of Article 17 ESC, decided that it is impossible to exclude legal protection from economic and social protection for mothers and children, by a provision attempting to regulate the legal status of these persons. Therefore legal protection cannot be omitted when analysing the social and economic situation of mothers and children.

The right to inheritance and the legal situation of children born out of wedlock has a direct influence on the social situation and the economic position of this category of persons. Even though Article 17 ESC does not expressly define itself as 'the right to legal protection for mothers and children', the Committee is of the view that the 'law does not only reflect social and economic facts but also manages them through the regulation of legal and economic relations'.[351] Due to the inability to carry out a true separation between the law and social and economic repercussions of regulations, Article 17 ESC was interpreted as obligating Member States to ensure that mothers and children receive social, legal and economic protection.[352] In the version that was accepted by the Revised European Social Charter, Article 17 ensures children and young persons social, legal and economic protection.

Expectant mothers and women having just given birth are also protected under Article 17 ESC. Pregnancy, as well as child rearing responsibilities carried out by mothers, obligate Member States to ensure that mothers receive medical care and financial stability.[353] Legal protection for mothers is ensured regardless of their marital status. Member States should not just simply stop at forbidding discrimination of unwed mothers by way of changing legislation, but rather, should take measures to ensure that these mothers receive proper care and assistance.[354] The Committee expanded the scope of protection ensured by Article 17 ESC to single parents raising children. Even though the said provision ensures legal protection to mothers, under the definition of 'single parents', the Committee includes also fathers who are raising children on their own.[355] It did not, however, pass a judgment about the non-compliance of domestic regulations with the international standards established by Article 17 ESC in countries where the legislation did not ensure single fathers raising children social, legal and economic protection.

351. Conclusions IV, p. 103.
352. D. Harris, J. Darcy, *op. cit.*, p. 196
353. Conclusions III, p. 80.
354. *Ibid.*
355. Conclusions XIII-2, p. 31.

8.9.3. The Right of Children and Young Persons to Social, Legal and Economic Protection (Article 17 RESC)

The protection guaranteed by Article 17 RESC encompasses the right of children and young persons to grow up in an environment, which encourages the full development of their mental and physical capacities. Member States are obligated to undertake either directly, or in cooperation with public or private organizations, all appropriate and necessary measures to:

- Ensure (taking into account the rights and duties of parents) that children and young persons have medical care, assistance, education and training, which they may require. Having this in mind, Member States should establish and/ or maintain adequate institutions and services (educational and developmental institutions, schools);
- Protect children and young persons against negligence, violence or exploitation;
- Provide protection and allocate special aid from the state for children and young persons temporarily or definitely deprived of their family support;
- Ensure free primary and secondary education for children and young persons and to encourage them to regularly attend school.

The Committee regards Article 17 (both the European Social Charter and the Revised European Social Charter versions) as a basis for forming international standards in establishing the status of children and young persons. In particular, the Committee is concerned with the issues associated with establishing the family relationships of children, with the protection of orphans and homeless children, with the protection of children and young persons against violence, with the right of children and young persons to due process, and with the processes dealing with juvenile offenders. The Committee is also of the view that children have the right to seek information about their biological parents as well as to keep in contact with both their biological and their adopted parents.[356] It is of the view that all interested parties in adoption procedures (biological parents, those preparing the adoption and the child) have the right to participate in such procedures.[357] Those preparing the adoption should take advantage of the same rights that are granted to the child.[358] Orphans and homeless children should have specialized protection suited to their needs.[359] Member States are

356. Conclusions XV-2, p. 66 (Austria); p. 139 (Denmark); p. 220 (France); p. 567 (Sweden). Biological parents giving up a child for adoption have identical rights. Conclusions XIII-2, p. 163 (Ireland); p. 364 (Belgium). Judgments passed by the Committee in cases dealing with the rights of biological parents in adoption procedures are based on the precedent of the European Tribunal of Human Rights decision in the case *Keegan v Ireland* Ser. A No. 291 on 26 May 1994. The Tribunal decided that carrying out adoption procedures without the knowledge and permission of the biological father of the child is a violation of Article 8 of the European Convention of Human Rights.
357. Conclusions XV-2, p. 109 (Belgium).
358. Conclusions XII, p. 217; Conclusions XIII-2, p. 365.
359. Conclusions XIII-2, p. 38.

obligated to ensure that such children experience a similar standard of living to what they would have had should they have lived with their parents.[360]

Protection of children and young persons against violence, negligence and exploitation encompasses protection against physical violence, sexual exploitation within the family and outside of it, and protection against alcohol consumption and drug use. The Committee has obligated Member States to provide information dealing with cases of violence, negligence and the exploitation of children and young persons. It obligates authorities to establish services providing care for victims of violence and to inform the community that such services are being provided.[361] Article 7 § 10 also provides legal protection against physical and moral dangers that children may be exposed to through violence, substance abuse and sexual exploitation. The Committee is of the view that the objective ranges of Article 17 and Article 7 § 10 crossover only partially. The Charter, however, does not contain legal principles in situations of such crossover. For this reason, the Committee demands from Member States information about physical and moral dangers facing children and young persons, when preparing reports about the compliance of Article 7 § 10 and Article 17.[362] The obligation to double-up the reports is only relevant when a Member State has ratified one of the two provisions.[363]

In terms of protecting children and young persons against violence, the Committee pays close attention in particular to corporal punishment. The UN Committee for the Rights of the Child forbids corporal punishment,[364] as does the European Tribunal of Human Rights[365] and the Committee of Ministers of the Council of Europe.[366] Based on the collected international documents and decisions, the Committee is of the view that corporal punishment has no educational value.

Article 17 demands that Member States introduce legislation forbidding corporal punishment in primary and secondary schools, in educational and developmental institutions, within the home and other locations. The Charter, as viewed by the Committee, obligates Member States to issue bans on corporal punishment as well as criminal and civil sanctions on anyone violating the provisions against corporal punishment.[367] Those Member States that do not abide by the above regulations are deemed to be in violation of the international standards of human rights.[368] Collective complaints were made against those Member States that did not forbid the use of corporal

360. Conclusions III, p. 80.
361. Conclusions XIII-2, p. 157.
362. Form for the reports ... *op. cit.*, p. 327, p. 350.
363. Albania, Azerbaijan and Cyprus did not ratify Article 17 § 2 RESC. They did however ratify Article 9 § 10. Denmark, Hungary, Iceland and Latvia did not ratify Article 7 § 10 ESC. They ratified Article 17. *See* European Social Charter ... 5th edition, *op. cit.*, pp. 84–85; pp. 89–90.
364. CRS/C/15/Add. 38. *See* L. Samuel, *op. cit.*, p. 374.
365. *Ibid.*, *A v United Kingdom*, 23 Sep 1998.
366. *Ibid.*, Recommendation No. R (90) 2.
367. Conclusions XV-2, pp. 27 and following.
368. Conclusions XVI-2, vol. 2, p. 661 (Poland); p. 807 (Slovakia); Conclusions 2003, vol. 1, p. 178 (France); Conclusions 2003, vol. 2, p. 413 (Romania); p. 515 (Slovenia).

punishment,[369] and the Committee rendered the domestic regulations of such states to be non-compliant with international standards. Those Member States that did not provide information dealing with the banning of corporal punishment against children and young persons had their decisions adjourned by the Committee.[370]

Article 17 RESC obligates Member States to ensure access to the courts. The Committee demands information from Member States about whether children and young persons may partake in civil litigation processes, especially in cases filed against parents or legal guardians.[371] In cases where parents have been stripped of their parental authority or where children or where young persons have been placed into juvenile correctional centres, the Committee seeks information from Member States concerning the administrative decisions made in such cases and whether they are based on established regulations, which are subject to monitoring criteria. The Committee has voiced its preferences for court access, for example, in situations where a child is to be placed in a children's home or in a foster home. Ideally, Member States should elect to administer the latter option. In cases where a decision has been made to place a child in a children's home, Member States should ensure that the child is placed in a children's home that is closest to where the biological parents or legal guardians reside. Siblings should be placed within the one location. Children placed in foster care or into children's homes should have legal protection and access to adequate support. Their individual rights should be respected.

Juvenile offenders should have access to due process, and should have the same access to the legal rights that are available to adults.[372] Deterring measures carried out against criminal behaviour cannot be utilized in cases of very young offenders.[373] The court process should be carried out much faster when young offenders are involved. As a rule, young offenders should not be placed into detention unless the offence committed is serious in its nature. Imprisonment as a form of deterrence should be applied in moderation. Young offenders should not be placed into detention with adult offenders.[374] In cases of full-time custody sentences, the periods of imprisonment should not be lengthy.[375] The protection of young offenders in custody is based on the principle of limiting their depravities.

Article 17 RESC obligates Member States to ensure that children and young persons receive free primary and secondary education. The responsibility of the

369. Complaint No. 17/2003 *World Organization Against Torture (OMCT) v Greece*; Complaint No. 18/2003 *World Organization Against Torture (OMCT) v Ireland*; Complaint No. 19/2003 *World Organization Against Torture (OMCT) v Italy;* Complaint No. 20/2003 *World Organization Against Torture (OMCT) v Portugal*; Complaint No. 21/2003 *World Organization Against Torture (OMCT) v Belgium.* European Social Charter 5th edition ... pp/ 514 and following.

370. Conclusions XV-2, p. 112 (Belgium); p. 537 (Spain); pp. 614 and following (Great Britain).

371. Conclusions XIII-2, p. 157.

372. *Ibid.*

373. Criminal responsibility cannot be assumed in cases where the child is either 7, 11 or 15 years of age. Conclusions XIII-2, p. 162; Addendum to Conclusions XV-2, p. 271 (Turkey).

374. Conclusions XIII-5, p. 143 (Luxembourg).

375. Conclusions XVI-2, vol. 2, p. 661 (Poland).

Member States is to ensure that this obligation is being followed. The Committee renders decisions with regards to non-compliance of the obligations set under the Charter, when there is a large number of children and young persons not being able to take advantage of this obligation,[376] as well as when a Member State does not ensure children and young persons an integrative educational system.[377]

8.10. The Right of Elderly Persons to Social Protection (Article 4 Additional Protocol, Article 23 RESC)

Article 4 of the Additional Protocol to the European Social Charter as well as Article 23 RESC ensures elderly persons the right to social protection. The Charter is the first international treaty to implement such a right and legally protect this right.[378] The provision in question belongs to the 'dynamic and fundamental' rights of social security.[379] Member States that ratified these provisions, are obligated to adopt or encourage, either directly or in cooperation with private or public organizations, appropriate measures that will in particular[380] enable the elderly to remain full members of society for as long as possible, and to enable them to choose their life-style freely and to lead independent lives in their familiar surroundings. Those elderly persons who are living in nursing homes should have adequate support ensured by the state, should have their privacy protected and should be able to participate in decisions concerning their living conditions.

Member States have full freedom to elect measures and sources that will enable the elderly to fully participate in the life of the community. The elderly cannot be eliminated from the life of the community and cannot be ostracized due to their age. The right to partake in various sectors within society cannot be made dependent upon the age of an elderly person, whether they be retired or professionally active, or whether they may have full legal capacity or be *diminutio capitis*.[381] Due to the increasing ageing society within Europe and to the increase in social security benefits, the provisions in question are among the most important standards in the Charter.

The provisions establish the living standards for persons unable to independently support themselves.[382] Elderly persons should be protected against discrimination.[383]

376. Conclusions 2003, vol. 2, p. 413 (Romania).
377. *Ibid.*, p. 515 (Slovenia – which introduced separate schools for the Roma ethnic minority).
378. Conclusions XIII-3, p. 455.
379. *Ibid.*
380. The use of the words 'in particular' means that the mentioned measures within the provisions are not exhaustive in their nature of obligations for Member States. *See* Explanatory report to the 1988 Additional Protocol (in:) European Social Charter, *op. cit.*, p. 135.
381. *Ibid.*
382. Conclusions XIII-3, p. 455.
383. The Committee attempted to establish whether Member States issued regulations banning discrimination based on age. Conclusions XVI-2, vol. 1, p. 186 (Czech Republic); Conclusions XVI-2, vol. 2, p. 822 (Czech Republic); Conclusions 2003, vol. 1, p. 186 (France); p. 314 (Italy); Conclusions 2003, vol. 2, p. 528 (Slovenia).

Member States are also obligated to ensure that the elderly (as much as it is possible) receive adequate resources to be able to lead a decent life and to be able to play an active part in public, social and cultural life. In the appendixes to Article 4 of the Additional Protocol as well as Article 23 RESC, it was clarified that the term 'for as long as possible' in which Member States should fulfil their obligations, 'refers to the elderly person's physical, psychological and intellectual capacities'. As long as an elderly person is capable of participating in the life of the society, Member States should take measures to enable the elderly to maximize such participation. Resources for the elderly should be 'adequate' if they are to be used in order to achieve such goals. This term should be interpreted in the same manner as in Articles 12 and 13. The Committee decisions cited in parts 2 and 3 of this chapter establish the level of social protection that Member States should ensure for the elderly.[384] 'Adequate' resources are those that can ensure that an elderly person will sustain a decent standard of living. The Committee attempts to examine whether Member States can ensure the elderly an adequate standard of living, by analysing the level and structure of the budget spent on social security entitlements and social services.[385] It demands information about the relationship between pensions and retirement funds and the average remuneration,[386] about health care costs and the price of medicine,[387] about the type, range and amount spent on social services (such as rehabilitation centres, and about the quality and availability of nursing homes, home care and assistance, public transport discounts) for elderly persons.[388]

The Committee views the right of the elderly to social protection as a subjective right. It is applicable to all elderly persons, regardless of their citizenship (citizens of Member States, that are parties to the Charter), legally residing on the territory of any of the Member States of the Council of Europe.[389] If a Member State does not fulfil the above obligations, an elderly person has the right to file a suit. The Committee examined whether domestic social security regulations ensure the elderly the right to file claims to an independent body, when they are refused their social benefit rights and access to social care regulated by Member State social security legislation.

The provisions in question do not contain legal definitions of an elderly person. Based on Committee decisions, it is possible to deduce that an 'elderly person' is a person who has attained a retirement age, as is established by domestic social security law. In Member States of the Council of Europe, it is still widely accepted to

384. Explanatory report to the 1988 Additional Protocol ... *op. cit.*, p. 135.

385. Conclusions XIII-5, pp. 303 and following.

386. *Ibid.*, p. 305 (Italy).

387. Conclusions XIII-3, p. 461 (Sweden).

388. *Ibid.*, p. 461.

389. In the opinion of D. Harris and J. Darcy, *op. cit.*, p. 251, footnote 1641 – the legislation in domestic social security regulations, where there are residency conditions (of 5 years) to live within the territory of a given Member State as a requirement for being able to be granted to the right to a pension, may form a basis for the non-compliance of domestic regulations with international standards. The Committee did not pass such a judgment even though it concluded some Member States (Finland) had introduced such conditions. Conclusions XIII-5, p. 304.

differentiate between the insured retirees according to their sex. There is also a tendency to extend this age. The Committee is aware this tendency has evolved in an attempt to decrease public social security funds. In accordance with common practice, the Committee does not specify an age limit for being active in a professional sense for both men and women. It continues to express its opinions about the information received dealing with Member State laws extending the retirement age and increasing periods of employment, filed by the Member States. It demands from such authorities, details concerning such particulars.[390] Without the specificity of an acceptable retirement age, the Committee will, at some stage, conclude that in cases where the retirement age is increased, some Member States will be seen as violating social security protection standards specified by the provisions by the Charter. For social protection rights to eventuate, as assured by Article 4 of the Additional Protocol, as well as by Article 23 RESC, Member States are obligated to ensure in their domestic social security legislation a minimum retirement age between 60 to 65 years.[391]

A social security system should ensure the elderly the ability to freely choose their lifestyle and to lead independent lives in their familiar surroundings for as long as they wish and are able to function in this capacity. The Committee examines whether Member States ensure that elderly persons receive appropriate housing.[392] In cases where the elderly are unable to support themselves by their own means, the Committee demands from Member States information about the range of social assistance made available for the elderly to help them do so. Member States may suggest various forms of legal solutions and organizations for those interested in receiving such services. These include: nursing homes, home care institutions, and care and assistance provided for by the state or due to local budget allocations.[393] Analysing the level of care for the elderly in home care institutions, the Committee pays close attention to the standard of services provided. Beneficiaries should have their privacy protected.[394] They should also be able to participate in decisions concerning their living conditions in the institutions where they reside.[395] Institutions providing social care should ensure a high level of services.[396]

8.11. The Right to Protection Against Poverty and Social Exclusion (Article 30)

The goal of Article 30 is to obligate Member States to organize cohesive social policy concepts to fight poverty and social marginalization.[397] The provision in question

390. *Ibid.*
391. Such retirement age limits exist in Member States of the European Union. *See* Social Protection in the EU Member States and the European Economic Area, Officer for Official Publications of the European Communities, Luxembourg 2001, pp. 262–265.
392. Conclusions XIII-5, p. 308 (Italy).
393. Conclusions XIII-3, p. 458 (Finland); p. 462 (Sweden).
394. Conclusions XIII-5, p. 305 (Finland); p. 317 (Sweden); Conclusions XIV-2, p. 451 (Italy).
395. Conclusions XIII-5, p. 305 (Finland).
396. *Ibid.*, p. 317 (Sweden).
397. Explanatory report ... *op. cit.*, p. 173.

obligates Member States to take measures, which will grant access to poverty stricken persons as well as to those deemed to be 'socially marginalized' to employment, housing education, culture, social assistance and medical care. The goal of Article 30 is not to obligate Member States to double up on measures taken with regards to other provisions of the Charter, namely Articles 12 and 13. Rather, the primary concern of Article 30 is to obligate Member States to take measures within the framework of an overall and coordinated approach to fight against the onset of poverty and social exclusion is the primary concern for those who drafted Article 30.

This provision contains various social-policy related undertakings. The Committee *Charte-Rel* views that a complex, multi-facetted approach to poverty and social exclusion will strengthen the legal protection of social rights guaranteed by other provisions of the Charter.[398] Article 30 obligates Member States to coordinate, promote and execute social programmes fighting against poverty and social exclusion as well as to supervise the measures taken to execute such programmes, and when necessary, adapt them to changing situations.

Introducing this new provision into the Charter, the Council of Europe and its Member States tried to deduce whether life in poverty or in social exclusion is in conflict with the principle of human dignity. The Committee is of the opinion that the provision in question obligates Member States to prioritize social policies which deal with fighting against poverty and social exclusion, as well as to take measures, which will enable all or make it easier for all, regardless of their social status to take advantage of the available social rights and to monitor the actions taken in order to encourage authoritative bodies, state and local administration, non-governmental institutions, stakeholders, charity organizations, and representatives of social interest groups to execute programmes that fight poverty and social exclusion.

Among the range of obligations placed on Member States by Article 30, these states must integrate their actions in eradicating poverty and social exclusion.[399] Measures initiated by Member States should promote the effective access to social rights, especially the rights to employment, housing, education, training, cultural benefits and social and medical assistance. Measures are taken by Member States to promote should include increasing information about social rights, fighting socio-cultural barriers by making use of such rights, and improving the procedures, which would make such undertakings more efficient.[400] The provision question does not mention about the obligation of providing financial assistance to those in need. Provisions Article 12 and 13, mentioned earlier, already fulfil such necessary obligations.

Actions, which should be undertaken by the Member States, may, although should not have to, cause financial burdens for a particular Member State. Examining the reports presented by the Member States, which have ratified the provision in questions,

398. F. Vandamme, The Revision of the European Social Charter, International Labour Review, 1994 No. 133, Issues 5–6, pp. 635 and following.

399. Conclusions 2003, vol. 1, p. 214 (France); p. 335 (Italy); Conclusions 2003, vol. 2m p. 548 (Slovenia); p. 644 (Sweden).

400. *Ibid.*

the Committee has concentrated on measuring social pathology (poverty and social exclusion). It examines whether the social programmes utilized by Member States are appropriate to the current social conditions. It monitors whether Member States are abiding by their obligations under Article 30 and pays close attention to whether Member State actions are indeed 'adequate'.[401]

Article 30 obligates Member States to 'ensure the effective exercise of the right to protection against poverty and social exclusion'. The basic principles of the understanding of 'poverty' and 'social exclusion' in the provision in question are defined within a document explaining the legal regulations introduced to the Revised European Social Charter.[402] Poverty is a state, which affects people within a generation cycle of welfare benefits as well as individuals who are temporarily placed in a difficult financial situation.[403] Member States usually measure poverty by the income held by an individual, compared to the monthly remuneration average. The poverty boundary is met when the monthly income is less than 50 per cent[404] or 60 per cent[405] of the average.

In support of the above indicator (based on percentages), some Member States take into consideration unconditional factors to establish the state of poverty. In France, for example, people who are earning less than or equal to 560 euros per month are included into the 'poverty' category. Each additional dependent adult residing with the person of the said earnings is taken into consideration when analysing the poverty level, with a deduction of half of the above earning. Children under the age of 14 are taken into consideration with a measuring of 0.3 of the 560 euros earnings. A family comprised of two adults and two children with a monthly income of less than 1184 euros is considered to be living in poverty.[406]

'Social exclusion' or 'marginalization' are interchangeable terms when describing marginal poverty for those who have found themselves in such a situation, when due to unfortunate circumstances, they are unable to access social security entitlements. Such terms are also used to describe persons who do not find themselves in poverty, but have somehow become devoid of certain social rights and services due to long term illness, family break-up, violence, imprisonment and/or addictions (alcohol, drugs).[407] Member States are examining whether various indicators of individual situations exasperated by financial difficulties, consumption restrictions, delayed payments and problems with housing, should be included into the social exclusion category.[408]

During the first supervisory cycle of Member States abiding by the obligations set under Article 30, the Committee examined the reports of four states.[409] In all cases, the

401. *Ibid.*
402. Explanatory report ... *op. cit.*, p. 174.
403. *Ibid.*
404. Conclusions 2003, vol. 1, pp. 214–215 (France).
405. *Ibid.*, p. 336 (Italy).
406. *Ibid.*, p. 215 (France).
407. Explanatory report ... *op. cit.*, p. 174.
408. Conclusions 2003, vol. 1, p. 215 (France).
409. France, Italy, Slovenia and Sweden. Two other states in this cycle (Bulgaria and Romania) did not file reports, as they did not ratify Article 30 of the Charter.

Committee adjourned its decision and demanded further information from the such Member States, dealing with the coordination of various social programmes introduced in order to fight poverty and social exclusion.

The Committee is of the opinion that the primary goal of Article 30 is not to introduce separate social programmes to ensure those who are socially excluded or in poverty social rights, but to adapt such social programmes to the needs of those living in poverty. The obligation of the Member States is to identify the deprived social groups as well as the geographical regions where there is a concentration of poverty and a high level of social exclusion. The Member States that ratified Article 30 should present, in their reports to the Committee, that they are able to coordinate various social programmes addressed to various categories of persons regarded as socially excluded and show such programmes can eradicate poverty. As mentioned earlier, no Member State (not even Sweden where there is only 9 per cent of the population living under the poverty line, the lowest in Europe – much lower than the 15 per cent existing within the initial 15 EU members[410]) has been able to achieve a positive ruling about the compliance of the international standards under Article 30.

In their reports, Member States present a variety of incentives to improve the situation of particular social groups. These social groups include the elderly, the disabled, the ill, women, young persons and ethnic minorities. Separate provisions protect social rights of these groups and the social categories. As was already mentioned, the Committee does not demand a doubling up effect of measures taken by the Member States to enable the said social groups gain rights ensured by the Charter. Rather, it demands the provision of information detailing the methods incorporated to organize, by the Member States, various social policy sectors to achieve the effects mentioned in Article 30 and gain an 'overall and coordinated approach' to poverty and social exclusion, the most severe aspects of social pathology.

France and its many, well prepared, appropriately funded[411] and positively regarded social programmes, was close to receiving a positive ruling. Despite the reduction in unemployment levels, the state institution called upon to monitor the level of poverty and the scale of social exclusion, and concluded, that the above programmes in a small way, limited the scale of poverty. The positive outcomes were noted in the case of social groups affected by the lowest level of social exclusion.[412] The Committee concluded that the small effects of the large-scale social programmes indicate France's inability to undertake measures as an 'overall and coordinated approach' with regards to the impeding social issues of poverty and social exclusion.

Article 30(b) has a dynamic nature. It obligates Member States to review, as far as possible, the anti social exclusion measures and to adopt them to the current situation. The introduction of this clause, which obligates the Member States to react to the

410. Conclusions 2003, vol. 2, p. 645.
411. During a period of 3 years expenses for programmes dealing with social exclusion reached 7.8 million euros. Conclusions 2003, vol. 1, p. 216.
412. *Ibid.*, p. 218.

changes in the social and economic situations, also obligates Member States to create institutions, to monitor such social processes on a national, regional and city scale.[413]

Member States organize and finance such observations of social change and processes. Such observations are made by administrative bodies, by non-governmental institutions, by stakeholders, by research institutions as well as by representatives of social groups who are marginally excluded. Member States have elected similar monitoring measures to control anti social exclusion programmes, despite the fact that the reasons for the regulation contained within Article 30 establish the type of institutional organization monitoring the social processes.

Member States called upon observers of social change and processes to analyse Member States' performance. Analysing the reports about the functioning of such observers, the Committee demanded information concerning the tendencies evolving into poverty and social exclusion, the professional qualifications of persons fighting poverty and social exclusion, the social groups and categories most affected by poverty and social exclusion, and the practices of Member States and their coordination of anti-social exclusion social programmes. The Committee wants to deduce what specialist branches of society may be best used to work out a general, coordinated and effective social policy to fight poverty and social exclusion.

8.12. The Right to Housing (Article 31)

The provision in question was issued in order to ensure citizens of Member States, both foreign citizen and those of a said Member State, receive the right to housing. Member States are obligated to undertake the following measures designed to promote access to housing (Article 31 § 1); to prevent and reduce and eliminate homelessness (Article 31 § 2); and to make housing accessible to those without adequate resources (Article 31 § 3). The Committee is of the view that Article 31 § 1 obligates Member States to ensure all those authorized (citizens of a given state or other Member States) receive the right to housing and requires Member States to promote access to housing of an adequate standard.

Member States are obligated to specify how they understand the term 'housing of an adequate standard' under Article 31 § 1. The Committee defines minimum requirements for the above term. According to the Committee housing 'of an adequate standard' means structurally sound housing outfitted with amenities that are not overpopulated and that are protected against eviction.[414]

Secured amenities means housing with electricity, sewage and water, heating and that do not pose any health and life threats for the inhabitants. Housing that is not overpopulated is housing, which does not contain an excessive amount of people and where the parameters are not less than 20 square metres. Housing that is protected

413. J. Niessen, Diversity and Cohesion: New Challenges for Integration of Immigrants and Minorities, Council of Europe. Directorate of Social Affairs and Health, Council of Europe Publishing, Strasbourg 2000.

414. Conclusions 2003, vol. 1, p. 211 (France).

against eviction means housing where its inhabitants cannot be forced to leave without due procedure.[415] The Committee is of the view that these standards should be applied to various forms of housing including the newly built and those needing renovations.

Inclusive in its monitoring of whether the given provision is abided by, the Committee examines whether the existing domestic regulations within Member States obligate their internal authorities to ensure adequate housing for those who need it, and whether domestic regulations ensure tenant rights guaranteed by rental agreements. The right to housing is treated by Article 31 as a basic human right. This right ensures the beneficiaries the right to freely select which housing to live in. Housing selection should be limited housing that fulfils the 'adequate' requirements. Deducing from the reports presented by the Member States, it appears that in some economically developed European countries, approximately 4.2 per cent of housing does not fulfil the standards accepted by the Committee as established by Article 31 § 1.[416]

Protecting the lessee from the lessor means that the lessee should have the right to demand that the lessor abide by the appropriate housing regulations and provide the lessee with residency that is up to the specified standards, or require the lessor to adapt the residency to the standards specified. During the period when the residency is being adapted to the standards according to the residency regulations, the lessor should provide the lessee with alternate housing. According to the Committee, not fulfilling such obligations means that the lessee may commence court proceedings and demand the residency reach a suitable standard within a specified period of time. If the above is not met, the lessee has the right to have his/her rent reduced as well as be able to terminate the tenancy agreement.[417]

Article 31 § 2 obligates Member States to prevent and limit homelessness. This provision is dynamic in its character. The Committee examines the process made by given Member States, which have undertaken twofold efforts to gradually reduce homelessness. The ultimate goal of the provision in question is to completely eradicate this adverse societal occurrence. The Member States are not obligated to undertake efforts that would eradicate homelessness completely. They should however, take various measures to eliminate it gradually. The Committee regards homeless persons as those without permanent homes and adequate living standards. Temporary housing availability is not regarded as fulfilling the obligations under Article 31 § 2, even if the temporary accommodation fulfils the requirements under Article 31 § 1.[418] Providing the homeless with temporary housing is regarded as a first step in fulfilling the obligations under Article 31 § 2.

---

415. *Ibid.*
416. *Ibid.*, p. 223. More than a million homes in France lack amenities. In Italy 6 per cent of homes do not have adequate amenities. Further, approximately 3 million homes lack safe structural construction. *Ibid.*, p. 343.
417. *Ibid.*, p. 225 (France).
418. *Ibid.*

Preventative measures should be taken by the Member States in order to gradually eliminate homelessness. Firstly, they are obligated to note the persons who form part of the social category that have lost their homes, and to provide them with particular protection. In the scope of preventative measures, the Member States should ensure those individuals without adequate resources, government housing with lower rent rates. The Committee is interested in the situation of the governmental housing market. It seeks information with regards to the supply and demand of governmental housing, the conditions that need to be fulfilled by those seeking such accommodation, and the waiting period required to obtain such housing. Local and state administrations are responsible for providing such governmental housing. The Committee is interested in gaining information about the measures taken to encourage the private sector in building and renting out low rental housing for less well off sectors of society.

An important element of the social policies counteracting homelessness is a total ban of evicting those who do not have adequate resources for paying the rent or utility costs or those who are residing without any legal title. The Committee is of the opinion that, before a body makes an eviction decision, there needs to be a court proceeding and a clarification process. Those who are being evicted should have the opportunity to defend their rights and should be notified of the eviction prior to the eviction. Residential regulations should include the prohibition of evicting at night and in winter. Those who are being evicted should have alternative accommodation provided to them. Eviction that is carried out in non-compliance of the above requirements should be regarded as illegal, and those who have implemented such evictions should be penalized. Moreover, victims of such illegal evictions should receive compensation for their losses.

From the reports presented by Member States, it is possible to deduce that the above directives of eviction are not being followed. For this reason, the Committee seeks further information dealing with the measures taken by Member States to protect the right to housing. In three out of four cases,[419] it has adjourned its decisions about the compliance of Member States' domestic regulations with the international standards established under Article 31 § 2. These states filed in 2003 reports about their adaptation of their domestic regulations with the requirements of Article 31 § 2.

In the case of Slovenia, the Committee rendered non-compliance of the domestic regulations with the international standards under Article 31 § 2, due to the discrimination of other foreign nationals of other Member States. The Slovenian report indicated that the possession of Slovenian citizenship is a requirement for being able to receive government housing.[420] In contrast, even though the Italian report indicates that the possession of Italian citizenship (or citizenship of a country, whose citizens have the right to apply for governmental housing) is a requirement for being able to take part in a social programme, which establishes the rules in being able to access government housing, the Committee adjourned its decision and deemed the clarification of this

419. *Ibid.*, p. 232 (France); *ibid.*, p. 348 (Italy); Conclusions 2003, vol. 2m p. 655 (Sweden).
420. Conclusions 2003, vol. 2, pp. 560–561.

situation dependent upon the legal status of citizens of other Member States seeking the right to governmental housing.[421]

Article 31 § 3 obligates Member States to ensure that the price of housing is accessible to those without adequate resources. The Committee is of the view that housing is available only when the lessee is able to pay the rental costs without lowering his/her standard of living. Rental costs include the deposit, the bond, the rent and utility costs. Taking these factors into consideration, the Committee is of the view that based on Article 31 § 3, Member States are obligated to take measures to lower the value and costs of housing utility as well as to ensure those without adequate resources, housing benefits. In accordance with this principle, the Committee demands from the Member States details concerning the costs of building governmental housing as well as the level of population having an income that is lower than the minimum wage within a given country. The Committee attempts to gather information about whether there are social groups that do not have the independent means of covering the cost of rent and utility payments of governmental housing. Regardless of the results of the above analysis the Committee attempts to establish whether Member States ensure individuals and their families, who cannot meet such costs, social entitlements in the form of housing benefits. It formulates the rules for paying out the payments, for providing financial security, for guaranteeing the rights of individuals who reside in such housing, and checks how citizens of other Member States are treated when attempting to receive such benefits.[422]

421. Conclusions 2003, vol. 1, pp. 346–347.
422. *Ibid.*, pp. 235 and following

CHAPTER 9 RIGHTS OF CITIZENS OF OTHER STATES – PARTIES TO THE EUROPEAN SOCIAL CHARTER

9.1. The Right of Nationals to Engage in Gainful Occupation in the Territories of Other Countries (Article 18)

9.1.1. Introduction

The expansion of the European Union (EU) has had a direct impact on the meaning of the provision in question. Article 18 is applicable solely to matters associated with gainful occupation by citizens of one Member State in the territory of another state that is a member of the Council of Europe. The free flow of workers between EU Member States means that Article 18 is of greater importance for citizens who are employed within the EU yet are citizens of states who do not belong to the EU or the European Economic Area (EEA). The Article in question applies also to cases in which citizens of the 25 states that form the EU, as well as the three additional states, which along with EU members form the EEA, are employed in states that belong to the Council of Europe yet do not belong to the EU. The right to engage in gainful occupation or self-employment protected by Article 18 obligates Member States to the following:

- To apply existing employment regulations to citizens of other Member States in a spirit of liberty (§ 1);
- To simplify the existing formalities and to reduce or abolish chancery dues and other charges (administrative and others) payable by foreign workers attempting to gain employment or by their employers (§ 2);
- To liberalize the regulations governing the employment of foreign workers (§ 3);
- To recognize the right of their nationals to leave the country to engage in a gainful occupation in the territories of other Member States (§ 4).

The Committee is of the opinion that the right to engage in gainful employment in the territory of another Member State is solely applicable to citizens of Member States party to the Charter.[1] A source of doubt concerning the validity of the above argument carried out during the first supervisory cycle is evident in the Appendixes to the Charter, which clearly specify 'the persons covered by Article 1-17 ... include foreigners only in so far as they are nationals of other Parties lawfully resident or working regularly within the territory of the Party concerned ...' The doubts, based on the citation above, centred around whether Articles 18 and 19 protects the rights of foreigners who are not citizens of Member States that are party to the Charter. Article 18 does not specify whether the persons whose rights are protected must be citizens of other Member States party to the Charter or whether they may be citizens of other states that are not party to the Charter. The Committee, when examining the application of the provision in question to citizens of Member States, took a two-fold approach. Firstly, it decided that the right to occupation within the territory of another Member State, party to the Charter, is applicable only to citizens of Member States that are party to the Charter.[2] This conclusion is not obvious. It cannot be disregarded, however, since the text of Article 18 is clear. Member States, party to the Charter, are obligated to apply the rulings of Article 18 § 1-4 in order to enable their own nationals to carry out an occupation within the territory of another Member State that is party to the Charter. Member States are obligated to deal with their own citizens. The scope of application of Article 18 encompasses citizens of Member States party to the Charter who are attempting to undertake employment or self-employment within another Member State party to the Charter. This is also the stance of the Committee. Secondly, Section 18 of Part I clearly states that the right to gainful occupation within the territory of another Member State is given to 'citizens of both sides'. Part I formulates the human rights protected by the Charter. These rights are further developed in Part II of this international treaty. Similar to other provisions, Article 18 applies to citizens of all Member States party to the Charter, regardless of whether they have ratified the provision of the international treaty.[3] It applies, therefore, to Albania, Estonia, Norway, Hungary and Latvia, all countries that have not ratified the provision. Article 18 refers to the protection of employee rights. The Committee understands this as the protection of workers and self-employed individuals.[4]

The provision in question does not ensure protection of the right to enter the territory of another Member State, party to the Charter. It encompasses the protection of the right to gainful occupation within a different country. The term 'a different Member State' is understood by the Committee to be the territory of that state as well as structures located beyond territorial waters that are the property of the Member State, such as oil rig platforms on the North Sea.

Article 18 § 1-3 is part of the dynamic category.[5] It obligates the Member States to achieve the following goals: to liberally apply existing regulations (§ 1); to simplify

1. Conclusions I, p. 79.
2. Conclusions I, p. 79.
3. Conclusions XIII-2, p. 172 (Spain).
4. Conclusions XIII-4, p. 319 (Ireland); p. 321 (Great Britain).
5. Conclusions II, p. 59.

existing formalities and reduce or abolish charges payable (§ 2); and to liberalize the regulations governing the employment of foreign workers (§ 3). The dynamic nature of the provision has its boundaries. It specifies goals that should be met thanks to the adaptation of domestic practices (§ 1) and domestic regulations (§ 2-3) to the international standards protecting human rights established by Article 18 § 1-3. After given Member States have achieved the goals specified in the provision in question, the Committee expects further information in reports dealing with the lack of implemented changes to the standard practices and existing regulations. Full compliance of domestic legal systems with the international standards stipulated under Article 18 will be reached if foreigners and citizens of other Member States party to the Charter are treated equally to nationals (of the country in which they are employed) by the Member State in which they are working. Article 18 does not require that migrant workers be treated similarly to the state's own nationals. The Committee did, however, base the standards on Section 18 of Part I. The social policy declaration in Section 18 includes a clear statement that a citizen from each party has the right to carry out an occupation within the territory of another Member State 'according to the principles of equality with the nationals of the latter'. The Committee is of the opinion that the above statement is the 'letter and the spirit' of the provision.[6] The dynamism of the provision in question is also evident in its interpretation. The Committee's stance is that the Member States party to the Charter have the obligation to take measures to gradually bring closer the legal position of foreign nationals to that of their own citizens, so that the rights of the former are more like the rights attained by the citizens of the given state.[7] The Committee is not in favour of full equality for citizens and foreign nationals in matters of occupation and self-employment. It accepts the restrictions established by particular Member States based on economic and social circumstances. It obligates Member States that have introduced limitations to the freedom of undertaking employment and self-employment by foreign nationals and citizens of other Member States to prove that the grounds for the restrictions involve economic and social circumstances.[8] The Committee directs itself according to the regulations in Section 18 Part II, that order that the treatment of foreign nationals in Member States be equal with the treatment of their own citizens. The part that declares the right of a Member State to introduce limitations with regard to equal treatment of foreign nationals with its own citizens dictates that it is acceptable only if there are 'serious economic and social reasons'. The following paragraphs describe examples of Committee decisions, which, despite the general rules, view the granting of permits for a limited time for particular employment by an employer specified in a permit (legally and factually), as 'binding' a worker. This may be seen as in accordance with the protection of human rights that, due to economic and social circumstances, limits the freedom of foreign nationals to undertake employment and permits them to take up specific employment, in particular professions and specializations, in the geographical

6. Conclusions II, p. 60.
7. *Ibid.*
8. Conclusions II, pp. 59–60; Conclusions XIII-1, p. 262.

confine specified by the state.[9] 'Serious economic and social reasons' means that in the practice of abiding by the obligations under Article 18 ensuring foreign nationals of Member States the right to freely carry out gainful occupation within the territory of another Member State, the Committee sanctions limitations placed on foreign nationals' rights to employment and self-employment. These rights are based on other factors that are partly covered by other provisions such as Article 31 § 1 ESC and Article G § 1 RESC. 'Serious economic and social reasons' may, depending on the situation, be regarded as reasons that limit the right of an individual to carry out employment wherever it is most suitable for him/her, as ensured by Article 18. This may occur when the above limitations are necessary for the protection of rights and liberties of other persons (especially for all the citizens of the given state, for the protection of public interest, national security, public health and good customs). These are all legal grounds for limiting human rights, even though some are not 'serious economic and social reasons'. The term 'serious economic and social reasons' is applied differently to labour law and social policy needs, and exemplifies a fusion of the general clause of Article 31 § 1 ESC and Article G § 1 RESC about 'public interest'. The effect reached by the Committee referring to Section 18 Part I, could be attained by taking advantage of Article 31 § 1 ESC or Article G § 1 RESC.[10] 'Serious economic and social reasons' as a ground for limitations is also grounds for refusing to grant permits for carrying out an occupation during an economic crisis in the country.[11]

Limitations on the right to carry out gainful occupation freely within the territory of another Member State, party to the Charter, can only be applied as an exception to the accepted and practiced rules of treating foreign nationals and one's own citizens equally.[12] Allowing for differentiation between the rights of foreign nationals and a state's own citizens due to 'serious economic and social reasons', cannot be applied solely to foreigners and citizens of other Member States party to the Charter. The Committee ruled that Ireland and Great Britain did not adapt to the international standards of protecting the right to freely carry out gainful occupation in another Member State, because the domestic legislation favoured British and Commonwealth citizens, who at large were not members of the Council of Europe, party to the Charter.[13] The provision in question does not permit the Committee to tolerate regional relationships, even when they extend beyond the European boundaries. Limitations on liberal policies and employment regulations of foreigners cannot be applicable solely to citizens of other Member States that are applying for work and residency permits within the territory of another Member State, party to the Charter. As was mentioned earlier, Article 18 does not regulate entry permits. As such, the limitations placed on a liberal approach to

9. Conclusions III, p.85 (Ireland); p. 86 (Great Britain).
10. D. Harris, J. Darcy, *op. cit.*, pp. 204–205.
11. Conclusions IV, p. 107 (Denmark).
12. Conclusions IV, p. xv.
13. Conclusions III, p. 85 (Ireland); p. 86 (Great Britain); Conclusions IV, p. 111 (Great Britain). An analogous case occurred in Scandinavian countries. Citizens of these countries forming the 'Nordic labour market' were treated more favourably than the citizens of the remaining Member States. *See* case of Denmark: Conclusions XII-1, pp. 225–227.

citizens of other Member States gaining residency and work permits contradicts the right to undertake employment in a different Member State.[14]

The Committee reserves for itself the right to examine whether exclusion due to serious economic and social reasons based on Article 31 § 1 ESC or Article G § 1 RESC is valid. Leaving margins of appreciation for the Member States, the Committee is able to examine such reasons and the scope of the exclusions. The Committee does not consider, referring to the above indicators, that economic and social reasons justify the exclusion from international standards citizens of small Member States (e.g. Austria and Cyprus).[15] When examining the reports filed by Member States concerning the fulfilment of the obligations stipulated by Article 18, the Committee demands further information concerning the following: the legal and factual criteria used for making decisions about granting permission or refusing the right to employment based on a work agreement or carrying out self-employment; the number of applications filed for the above and the number of decisions made granting permission; the number of applications filed by citizens of Member States and the number of foreigners, citizens of other Member States, permitted to carry out gainful employment in another Member State; the number of citizens of other Member States and the number of citizens of countries that are not members of the Charter, who have received permission to work within the territory of a given Member State; details concerning formalities preceding a decision in the matter of granting permission to carry out gainful occupation within a given Member State; and the period of validity for such permission as well as information about the situation of the individual, who has had his/her permission expire.[16] Furthermore, the Committee was interested in receiving information about whether it was possible to file applications and receive permission while abroad and further information about the procedure of extending the work permit once it is granted.[17] The Committee also attempted to establish whether there is a connecting interdependency between the granting of permission to stay within a given Member State and carrying out gainful employment within that state. The Committee holds the view that the most influential factor in the matter of work permits is the administrative body dealing with the rights of residency within a given state. Losing the right to remain within a given Member State has an adverse effect on the ability to take advantage of the right to carry out gainful occupation. Losing the right to gainful occupation usually lead to the withdrawal of a right to remain within a given Member State.[18] Taking this consideration, the Committee demanded further information from the Member States concerning the procedures dealing with these practices.

---

14. Conclusions XIII-1, p. 204 (Sweden); Conclusions XIII-2, pp. 371–372 (Germany); Conclusions XIII-4, pp. 319–320 (Sweden).
15. Case of Denmark, which according to serious economic and social reasons introduced limitations against citizens of Cyprus and Austria. Conclusions IV, p. 108; Conclusions XII-1, p. 226.
16. Conclusions II, pp. 61–62.
17. Conclusions V, p. 118; Conclusions VIII, p. 197.
18. Conclusions XIII-2, p. 168.

9.1.2. An Obligation to Apply the Existing Regulations in a Spirit of Liberty (Article 18 § 1)

Article 18 § 1 obligates institutions functioning according to domestic legislation to adopt a liberal interpretation. The provision in question does not establish an obligation for Member States to liberalize domestic legal systems. Such an obligation was established by Article 18 § 3. The Committee is of the view that Article 18 § 1 is a standard that holds more importance for administrative practices than for the position of the law. Even rigorous legislation, interpreted according to the directives of the Article in question, does not give the Committee a legal ground to issue decisions about the non-compliance of Member States with the standards stipulated under Article 18 § 1. In the case of Great Britain, permission for undertaking occupation was granted for a strict period of time, for a specified occupation for a given employer who could not employ British citizens. Every change of employment required a further permission grant. In this case, such rigorous regulations were non-compliant with the standards established under Article 18 § 3. Yet such a case does not provide the Committee with the grounds to voice its complaints, since British administrative bodies dealing with employment were granted the right to apply the existing regulations liberally, and the permission to continue the work had thus far been renewed without difficulty. After four years, foreign nationals were excused from renewing their permission grants for working and living in Great Britain.[19] A similar decision was rendered in the case of Greece.[20] Allowing administrative bodies that apply domestic regulations a large margin of interpretation means that the subject of examination for the Committee is how these state bodies deal with the power they are granted. The Committee compares the decisions to grant permission to carry out gainful employment with the number of applications filed.[21] It takes these factors into consideration to evaluate whether the administrative state bodies apply the required regulations in accordance with Article 18 § 1 liberally.[22] A systematic refusal to grant permission to work to a citizen of a Member State wishing to extend his/her time abroad in another Member State is considered by the Committee as a restrictive interpretation of regulations.[23] Legalizing migrant workers' stays residing within the territory of a given state, for purposes of employment, is an example of a liberalized interpretation of domestic regulations.[24]

---

19. Conclusions III, p. 86.
20. Conclusions X-1, p. 137.
21. Conclusions VIII, p. 197; Conclusions XII-2, p. 210; Conclusions XIII-1, p. 263 (Turkey); Conclusions XIII-2, p. 369 (Belgium).
22. Conclusions IV, p. 109 (Austria); pp. 110–111 (Great Britain); p. 112 (Ireland); Conclusions VII, p. 94 (France); Conclusions VIII, p. 194 (Germany); p. 197 (Ireland); p. 200 (Great Britain); Conclusions IX–1, p. 101 (Sweden); Conclusions XII-1, p. 220 (Denmark); 221 (Iceland); Conclusions XIII-3, p. 393 (Finland). In the decision rendered during the 2003 supervisory cycle, the Committee over-analysed the Swedish report that claimed that in 2001 there were 6 542 applications filed for a permission to work, out of which 4 684 were granted. The Committee claimed Sweden functioned in accordance with the standards established under Article 18 § 1 of the Charter. Conclusions 2003, vol. 2, p. 621.
23. Conclusions VI, p. 114 (Sweden).
24. Conclusions XII-2, p. 210 (Italy).

Aside from the Turkish case (where legislation prohibits foreigners to be employed in more than 20 different types of professions and trades, and Turkey does not leave administrative bodies the freedom to interpret employment of foreign nationals regulations, a violation of Article 18 § 1),[25] the Committee had doubts as to whether Member States function in accordance with the international standards and therefore adjourned its decision and sought further information intended to evaluate whether administrative bodies interpret domestic regulations liberally.[26]

9.1.3. Simplifying Existing Formalities and Reducing or Abolishing Administrative Fees (Article 18 § 2)

Article 18 § 2 is a dynamic standard,[27] with certain objective limitations. The limit of the obligation to simplify existing formalities means to achieve a state in which necessary formalities are retained that must be fulfilled by foreign workers wanting to undertake employment in a different Member State. Abolishing administrative fees for granting work permits limits the process that should be carried out by the Member States obligated to abide by the provision in question. The range of obligations established in the provision in question is similar to the obligations introduced to Article 18 § 3. Article 18 § 2 orders the Member States to simplify the existing formalities, while Article 18 § 3 obligates these states to liberalize the regulations. The Committee supervising whether the above provisions are being followed came to the conclusion that the range of these provisions overlap, despite the fact that they establish different obligations. Simplification of existing formalities usually indicates an earlier completed liberalization of regulations.[28] It is possible to deduce from the above argument that there is a cause-and-effect dependency between the obligations stipulated under Article 18 § 2 and 3. A liberalization of the regulations provides the basis for simplifying formalities. It is, however, possible to simplify formalities that need to be liberalized. In cases where Member States have ratified both comparable provisions, there is no difficulty in monitoring their compliance with the provisions. The border between formalities that should be simplified and the regulations that should be liberalized no longer exists. Problems arise in situations where Member States ratify just one of the two standards. This has occurred in Moldavia, Romania and Slovenia. These countries ratified Article 18 § 2 RESC but did not ratify Article 18 § 3 of this Charter. In terms of the European Social Charter, Austria, the Czech Republic, Malta, Poland and Slovakia ratified Article 18 § 2 ESC but did not ratify Article 18 § 3. In such cases, it is important to divide precisely the obligations undertaken by these countries that have ratified one out of the two named provisions in that they obligate themselves

25. Conclusions XIII-3, p. 397.
26. Conclusions XV-2, p. 114 (Belgium); pp. 226–227 (France); p. 319 (Italy); pp. 370–371 (the Netherlands); pp. 570–571 (Sweden); Addendum to Conclusions XV-2, p. 37 (Ireland); Conclusions 2003, vol. 1, p. 180 (France); p. 305 (Italy); Conclusions 2003, vol. 2, pp. 517–519.
27. Conclusions II, p. 9.
28. Conclusions III, p. 83.

to simplify the existing formalities dealing with the employment of foreign nationals (i.e. Article 18 § 2) and citizens of other Member States. They did not obligate themselves to liberalize the domestic regulations dealing with the employment of foreigners within their own country. It is therefore clear that the obligation specified under Article 18 § 2 is easier to fulfil. As such, the obligation differs from that regulated by Article 18 § 3. The Committee did not concern itself with the essential differentiation between the ranges of obligations established by the two provisions. Based on the decisions rendered by the Committee, it is possible to form the opinion that Article 18 § 2 concerns itself with the procedural requirements carried out before making a decision permitting foreign nationals to undertake employment (e.g., the obligation of documenting all decisions, whether they be ones of refusal or permission), while Article 18 § 3 deals with property rights regulations (e.g., the reasons for refusing or granting permission to undertake gainful employment).[29] Analysis of the Committee's decisions shows that the approach of dividing up the subject matter of the two comparable provisions is correct. Steps taken to simplify the existing formalities encompass the following: abolishing entry visas;[30] extending the validity period of permits from one year to four[31] or five[32] years; issuing permits for employment based on the conclusion of the employer or (if already applied) based on the interested worker;[33] and no longer requiring reports to be filed by prospective employers wanting to employ foreigners and citizens of Member States.[34]

Member States that required foreign workers to hand in their work permits annually or forced foreigners to leave the given Member State and terminate their work agreements for reasons not associated with themselves were regarded as not complying with the standards established by Article 18 § 2.[35] [36] Non-compliance was also evident when Member States made the issuing of work permits dependent on the presentation of documents showing no criminal record, financial independence, state of health, scope of insurance, or being in possession of property.[37] Member States that obligate foreigners wanting to open up their own businesses to file applications through diplomatic departments of the country in which the business will function and further grant permission for such ventures depending on the assent of three ministries (ministry of foreign affairs, ministry of the interior as well as the trade ministry)[38] were also non-compliant with the established standards. The Committee generally handed down

29. *See* D. Harris, J. Darcy, *op. cit.*, p. 208.
30. Conclusions IX-1, p. 99 (Iceland).
31. Conclusions XII-1, p. 225 (Great Britain).
32. Conclusions X-2, p. 142 (Spain).
33. Conclusions XII-2, pp. 211–212 (Germany).
34. Conclusions XII-1, p. 224 (Sweden).
35. Case of Germany: Conclusions X-2, p. 141; Conclusions XIII-2, pp. 371–372; Conclusions XIII-4, p. 436. In the opinion of the Committee, repeating the identical procedure for renewing work permits, is not necessary.
36. Conclusions XII-1, p. 223 (Iceland).
37. Conclusions XVI-2, vol. 2, pp. 810–811 (Slovakia).
38. Case of Italy: Conclusions XV-2, p. 320; Conclusions 2003, vol. 1, pp. 306–307.

decisions about the non-compliance of domestic regulations with the international standards when the procedure carried out prior to granting permission was deemed too difficult while the permit required to carry out gainful occupation was seen as restrictive (i.e., when a particular employer, place of employment, type of work, is valid for a particular period and getting such a permit is made dependent upon the supply and demand of the labour market).[39]

Article 18 § 2 also obligates Member States to reduce or abolish administrative fees and other charges placed on migrant workers or their employers. The provision does not specify which charges and fees should be abolished or reduced. The practices of the Committee indicate that the charges include those associated with the issuance of permit grants as well as the taxes imposed by Member States on those wanting to open their own businesses within the territory of another Member State. It is not possible to deduce from Article 18 § 2 alone that the abolishment of all charges is necessary. The decisions handed down by the Committee indicate that small administrative fees for work permits does accord with Article 18 § 2. The Committee also accepts fees taken by employers or deposits taken by administrative authorities, that are low enough to allow a foreign worker arriving from another Member State (usually placed quite far geographically from the place of the gainful occupation) to cover the costs of a return trip home.[40] The Committee rejected the charging of administrative for applications filed to receive permission to carry out gainful occupation.[41]

9.1.4. Liberalization of Regulations (Article 18 § 3)

Article 18 § 3 also presents a dynamic standard. The provision does not obligate Member States to liberalize regulations concerning the employment of foreigners and citizens of other Member States during the period of one supervisory cycle. Member States are obligated to take measures in order to achieve the goal of liberalizing the said regulations. During particular supervisory cycles, the Committee examines the progress attained. Article 18 § 3 is a standard that obligates Member States to take systematic ongoing measures in order to substitute the existing regulations with provisions that are less restrictive with regard to the employment of foreign nationals. The dynamic nature of the provision in question has its limits, however; the achievement of the stated goals means that further liberalization of the regulations is no longer possible. The obligation of the Member States that have reached such goals is to sustain them.[42] Until the ideal state is reached, the Committee has instructed that the problem of domestic regulations be solved either by elimination or by change. Such regulations include: prohibitions on changing employment where work permits authorize only the performance of those actions for purposes of the employer specified

39. Conclusions XIII-2, pp. 174–175 (Greece).
40. Conclusions IV, pp. 107–108 (Austria); Addendum to Conclusions XIII-3, p. 89 and following (Luxembourg).
41. Conclusions XV-2, p. 72 (Austria); p 175 (Finland).
42. Conclusions II, pp. 60–61; Conclusions III, p. 84 (Ireland).

in the permit;[43] prohibiting the change of an employer within the first year of work abroad;[44] demanding a work permit prior to the entry onto the territory of the other Member State;[45] continuing to demand that a citizen of another Member State who has been granted a work permit abide by the same legal requirements that applied during his/her first employment;[46] giving preference for employment to the citizens of the Member State in which a foreigner is applying for work[47] and conditioning the grant and validity of a work permit on whether the foreign national interested in working abroad is a legal holder of valid residence permit.[48] The following regulations require change: those implementing a complete ban on employing foreign nationals of other Member States;[49] those limiting the rights of migrant workers, citizens of other Member States, to change employers or workplace;[50] those that condition the granting of a work permit for a citizen of another Member State on 'valid professional reasons',[51] character references,[52] or on a specified amount of money invested.[53]

Article 18 § 3 does not obligate Member States to abolish regulations limiting the employment of citizens of other Member States completely. It obligates them to relax such restrictions gradually. It recommends acting according to the rules: the longer the period of stay of a foreign national who is a citizen of another Member State, the fewer the restrictions placed on extending his/her work and residency permit.[54] Cases of positive decisions handed down by the Committee in terms of actions taken by the Member States to liberalize regulations concerning the employment of foreign nationals encompass the following: granting work permits to family members of a migrant worker;[55] extending the validity of a work permit for a period of 5 years;[56] taking measures to assimilate migrant workers into the local society;[57] permitting a migrant worker to look for employment elsewhere when he/she becomes unemployed;[58] excusing young workers who are undertaking their first employment from certain formal

43. Conclusions II, p. 60; Conclusions III, p. 84 (Ireland); Conclusions V, p. 117 (Denmark); p. 119 (Germany); Conclusions X-1, p. 141 (Denmark); Conclusions XIII-2, pp. 174–179 (Greece); Conclusions XIII-3, p. 403 (Turkey); Addendum to Conclusions XIII-3, pp. 91–92 (Luxembourg).
44. Conclusions II, p. 85 (Sweden); Conclusions III, p. 84 (Denmark); Conclusions XII-1, p. 223 and following (Iceland); Addendum to Conclusions XIII-3, pp. 91–92 (Luxembourg).
45. Case of Denmark: Conclusions V, p. 117; Conclusions VI, p. 110; Conclusions X-1, p. 141; Conclusions VI, p. 114 (Sweden).
46. Conclusions III, p. 86 (Great Britain); Conclusions X-2, pp. 140–141 (Germany).
47. Conclusions V, p. 117; Conclusions VI, p. 110 (Denmark); Conclusions VIII, p. 198 (Spain).
48. Conclusions X-1, p. 141 (Denmark).
49. Conclusions VI, p. 111 (France); p. 112 (Germany).
50. Conclusions V, p. 119 (Germany).
51. Conclusions XII-1, p. 225 (Denmark).
52. Case of Ireland: Conclusions XIII-4, p. 319; Addendum to Conclusions XV-2, pp. 41–42.
53. 200 000 pounds in Great Britain. Conclusions XIII-4, p. 320; Conclusions XV-2, pp.621–622.
54. Conclusions II, p. 60.
55. Conclusions VIII, p. 196 (France).
56. Conclusions X-2, p. 143 (Spain).
57. Conclusions XI-1, p. 154 (Great Britain).
58. Conclusions IX-1, p. 154 (Great Britain).

requirements prior to the granting of a work permit.[59] The provision in question obligates Member States to take measures ensuring 'to such a point as it is possible' that the situation of the migrant worker is comparable to that of the Member State's own citizen.

9.1.5. The Right of the Nationals of a Member State to Leave the Country to Engage in Gainful Occupation in the Territory of another Member State (Article 18 § 4)

The freedom to move in an attempt to find work or embark upon self-employment is a core principle for the Council of Europe. Article 18 § 4 addresses the Member States and the citizens who want to take up employment in the territory of another Member State. It defines the relationship between the Member States and their own nationals. Along with the warning specified by Article 31 § 1 ESC and Article G § 1 RESC, it prohibits the Member States to restrict their own nationals from taking advantage of the right in question. With the exception of one negative decision handed down concerning Turkey,[60] the Committee has not rendered any judgments about the non-compliance of domestic regulations with the international standards established by this provision, even though Member States have refused their own citizens the right to leave their motherland for the following reasons: failing to fulfil their public duties (i.e., pay their taxes);[61] committing a serious crime;[62] an ongoing court process and court order prohibiting the individual from leaving the country;[63] failing to complete compulsory military service;[64] failing to file for bankruptcy and not fulfilling the legal responsibilities associated with bankruptcy;[65] violating the regulations of the permissible export of foreign exchange currency;[66] and being unable to independently support oneself.[67]

The Committee is of the opinion that a citizen who has been refused the right to leave the country by his/her Member State should have the right to file a complaint to the court or another independent body. Moreover, after analysing the reports filed by the Member States regarding compliance with the standards of Article 19 § 8, the Committee was concerned with regard to the procedural guarantees for migrant workers and their family members.

---

59. Conclusions XI-2, p. 140 (Austria).
60. Addendum to Conclusions XV-2, pp. 277–278. The basis for handing down the decision about Turkey's non-compliance of the obligations under Article 18 § 4 of the Charter was the refusal of the general clause of 'security reasons' used by the authorities as a ground for refusing to grant passports to Turkish citizens wanting to find employment abroad.
61. Conclusions XIII-3, p. 405 (Turkey).
62. Conclusions XIII, p. 86 (Austria); Conclusions XI-1, p. 154 (Greece).
63. Conclusions XIII-2, p. 183 (Spain).
64. *Ibid.*
65. Case of the Netherlands: Conclusions VIII, p. 201; Conclusions IX-1, p. 155.
66. Conclusions XI-1, p. 155 (Iceland).
67. Conclusions XIII-5, p. 113 (France).

9.2. The Right of Migrant Workers and their Families to Protection and Assistance (Article 19)

9.2.1. Introduction

Article 19 is modelled on the ILO convention No. 97 dealing with migrant workers, passed on 9 June 1942 during the 32nd ILO General Conference.[68] Similar to the convention, Article 19 obligates Member States to organize an appropriate institution, or to ensure that one is called upon, to assist migrant workers by providing free information about their legal position in a country in which they have undertaken employment. Member States are obligated to ensure that migrants who are legally residing on the territory of the given Member State receive the same rights granted to their nationals in matters such as: remuneration, joining trade unions, housing, social security, taxation, insurance payments and premiums, and in taking out claims, a process regulated by labour and social security laws. The goal of Article 19 is to provide migrant workers with information and to ensure them a legal status that is equal to that of the nationals of the given Member State in which the migrant worker is working. During the first supervisory cycle, the Committee came to the conclusion that Article 19 is a standard that does not restrict itself to ensuring migrant workers rights equal to those of nationals. Article 19 obligates Member States to ensure that migrant workers receive preferential treatment on the labour market as well as in matters concerning social security.[69] Simply ensuring equal rights and treatment for migrant workers through domestic regulations does not ensure an equal position in the labour market. According to the Committee, equalizing the situation in the labour market for migrant workers and citizens will only happen if certain measures are taken by the Member States.[70] From the very first supervisory cycle, the Committee was adamant about connecting the principles of equal treatment of workers regardless of their citizenship with policies of priority treatment of citizens of any Member States who decided to undertake occupation in the territory of another Member State.

Article 19 applies to citizens of one Member States who emigrated in order to gain employment in another Member State. The scope of the protection does not apply to citizens of states who are not part of the Council of Europe.[71] This protection of rights is relied upon by citizens of Member States who are legally residing in the territory of another Member State for the purpose of employment. In light of Article 19 (similar to Article 18), the term ‘territory of Member States’ is applicable to oil rigs situated beyond the territorial waters yet under the supervision of a given Member State of the Council of Europe.[72]

---

68. Conventions and recommendations ... *op. cit.*, vol. 1, p. 413 and following.
69. Conclusions I, p. 81.
70. Conclusions V, p. 123.
71. Conclusions I, p. 81.
72. Conclusions IV, p. 113; Conclusions VI, p. 121 (Germany, Norway); Conclusions VII, p. 205 (Norway).

Article 19 comprises 10 paragraphs in the ESC and 12 paragraphs in the RESC. The first three paragraphs of this provision were passed during a time when migrant work was regarded as a collective, either organized by the authorities of those states that were interested in accepting new workers or by employers. By collectively migrating, care during travel was ensured. Migrant working patterns have undergone changes. It is no longer a collective movement; instead it has taken on individualistic characteristics, and travel times between emigrating and immigrating countries have been reduced. The Committee came to the conclusion that these patterns have forced Article 19 § 1-3 to be interpreted in a different light, as well as Article 19 § 4-10 ESC and Article 19 § 4-12 RESC. In the view of the Committee, the current fundamental understandings are reserved under Article 19 § 4-10.[73] Similar to Article 18, Article 19 is important for workers who have decided to undertake employment by migrating out of EU and EEA countries to other EU or EEA countries or to the remainder Council of Europe states. The provision in question is not applicable to migrant workers that are not part of the EU or the EEA.

9.2.2. Free Assistance and Information and an Obligation to take Steps against Misleading Propaganda Relating to Migrant Work (Article 19 § 1)

Article 19 § 1 obligates Member States to maintain or to organize free services to assist migrant workers. In particular, such services should inform migrant workers about the possibility of employment or self-employment and such services should take steps against misleading propaganda information with regard to this matter. The Member States have the right to choose whether they decide to empower non-governmental organizations with information concerning the obligations or whether they engage governmental institutions instead. Member States may independently organize services to publicize the possibility of hiring migrant workers within the labour market of a particular Member State. They may also commission these types of services to non-governmental institutions such as trade union headquarters.[74] Information services should be provided before, during and after the migratory process between Member States of the Council of Europe. Such information should be provided to migrant workers free of charge. This type of information should be 'adequate'. To a lesser degree the Committee was concerned with the subject matter of the information being provided. It was more interested in how the information was passed on to those interested. It was of the opinion that it should be passed on to individuals who are envisaging emigration in order to pursue a gainful occupation in their mother tongue.[75] The range of this information should also include information about the living and working conditions within the other Member State (work training, working conditions, living conditions, social security, social and housing services).[76]

---

73. Conclusions XIV-1, p. 59.
74. Conclusions IV, p. 114 (Germany).
75. Conclusions III, p. 87 (Cyprus).
76. L. Samuel, *op. cit.*, p. 403.

The main issue was with the scope of information and assistance provided. During the first two supervisory cycles the Committee was of the view that Member States had the obligation to maintain such information services to provide information about the possibility of migrant work between all Member States. Examining Ireland's report, that showed that its citizens predominantly immigrated to Great Britain, the Committee changed its opinion and decided that a Member State fulfils the obligations under Article 19 § 1 if it ensures specialist services required for the provision of information for those wanting to enter a Member State for the purpose of labour.[77] The change in the migratory patterns means that Member States are obligated to change their information policies dealing with migrant work issues.[78] The obligation to provide assistance and information for migrant workers is understood by the Committee as an obligation that evolves along with the changes occurring in this field and is needed in order to inform people who are interested in relocating between Member States in line with the most popular migratory trends.[79]

Article 19 § 1 obligates the authorities of Member States to take all appropriate steps against misleading information relating to emigration and immigration. This refers to any propaganda material. The decisions passed by the Committee dealing with such propaganda have undergone changes. First, the Committee demanded that Member States prohibit the printing of material bearing false information.[80] It then changed its position on this matter and demanded that Member States (despite a lack of appropriate regulations) react against practices that are in violation of Article 19 § 1.[81] It further declared that even though Article 19 does not obligate Member States to introduce regulations prohibiting misleading propaganda in matters of migration, if such regulations were to exist they would indeed counteract activities deemed unacceptable by the Charter.[82] The Committee further developed this idea and decided that effective counteractions against misleading propaganda is facilitated if a state's legal system, includes legislation prohibiting discrimination based on race, ethnicity, nationality and religion. The introduction of regulations prohibiting the spreading of misleading information based on stereotypes, according to which migrant workers are seen as more of a threat than crime, alcoholism and drugs, would cause, according to the Committee, an increase in the effectiveness of abiding by the obligations under Article 19 § 1.[83] The Committee noted that some Member States introduced criminal sanctions for not reacting to misleading propaganda relating to emigration and immigration.[84] It obligated the authorities of Member States that have not introduced such prohibitions to

77. Conclusions III, p. 87–88.
78. Conclusions XIII-3, p. 408 (Turkey).
79. *Ibid.* Conclusions XIII-2, p. 185 (Ireland).
80. Conclusions II, p. 195 (Cyprus).
81. Conclusions IV, p. 113 (Austria).
82. Addendum to Conclusions XV-1, p. 172 (Poland).
83. Conclusions XV-1, p. 59 (Austria); p. 129 (Cyprus); p. 261 (France); p. 311 (Greece); p. 388 (Italy); p. 455 (Norway); p. 588 (Sweden); Addendum to Conclusions XV-1, p. 91 (the Netherlands); p. 172 (Poland).
84. Conclusions XV-1, p. 653 (Great Britain); Addendum to Conclusions XV-1, p. 57 (Luxembourg).

show what measures they have taken in fighting racism and xenophobia,[85] because by failing to introduce such regulations prohibiting the spread of misleading propaganda information relating to emigration and immigration, they are not abiding by the international standards.[86] The Committee has attempted to obligate Member States to introduce criminal sanctions for violating the standards under Article 19 § 1.[87] The Committee is equally interested in preventative measures. It has ordered Member States to provide information about the educational programmes for civil clerks dealing with emigration and immigration. In particular, the Committee is interested in gaining information about whether civil servants are informed about the necessity of an immediate reaction against cases of racism and xenophobia.[88]

With the exception of Turkey, the Committee has not rendered a judgment about the non-compliance of domestic regulations with Article 19 § 1. It positively regarded those authorities of Member States who decided to publish information for migrant workers and their families in various languages about the possibility of employment and work conditions and about living condition and social security.[89] The Committee positively regarded the development of boards (developed by the authorities of Member States) dealing with migration, where the board members are migrant workers' representatives.[90]

9.2.3. Facilitation of the Departure, the Journey and the Reception of Migrant Workers and their Families (Article 19 § 2)

Two obligations were introduced in Article 19 § 2. Member States from which immigrants originate and to which they emigrate are obligated (each within their own jurisdiction) to take appropriate measures to facilitate the departure, journey and reception of migrant workers and their families. They are also obligated to provide migrant workers and their families within their own jurisdiction with appropriate services for health and medical attention and with good hygienic conditions during the journey. The provision in question ensures certain rights for migrant workers as well as their family members regardless of whether they are travelling in an organized group or individually.[91] Authorities of Member States should not simply treat migrant workers as if they were citizens of that given state. States that accept migrant workers should provide them with favourable treatment.[92] In light of this, authorities of Member States should take

85. Conclusions 2004, vol. 1, p. 187 (Estonia).
86. Conclusions XVII-1, vol. 2, p. 494 (Turkey).
87. Case of Spain: Conclusions XII-2, p. 217. During the 14th supervisory cycle the Committee positively noted that the criminal code of Spain in 1995 included the regulation about the spread of misleading information relating to emigration and immigration and deemed it banned. Conclusions XIV-1, p. 718.
88. Conclusions 2004, vol. 1, p. 187 (Estonia); Conclusions 2004, vol. 2, p. 540 (Slovenia).
89. Conclusions XII-1, p. 231 (the Netherlands); (Norway); Conclusions XII-2, p. 217 (Germany); (Italy).
90. Conclusions XV-1, p. 222 (Finland)
91. Conclusions I, p. 214.
92. Conclusions III, p. 88.

care of the migrant workers and their families on the day of their arrival to the country of work as well as during their first weeks of stay.[93] The authorities should provide assistance in the following: housing, health care during an illness and assistance during a lack of financial sources.[94] Immigrants should undergo medical tests not only as a precaution to protect members of the society they are about to join, but also to protect their own health.[95] The Committee seeks from the authorities of Member States information about the health care provided to migrant workers and their families after reaching the country in which they will be working. It adjourned its decision about the compliance or non-compliance of domestic regulations and practices with international standards in cases where Member States did not provide adequate information.[96] It demanded information about the possibility of educating children of migrant workers,[97] vocational training for the migrants and language studies for them and their families.[98]

The provision in question obligates Member States to take the aforementioned steps in order to assist migrant workers and their families. The Committee is of the view that these obligations are deemed to be satisfied when the authorities of Member States accepting migrant workers pass on the various obligations to the employers. The Committee holds that a Member State may not be freed from its obligations of assuring care for migrant workers and their families during their stay in the host country. Passing on the various obligations to the employer does not free a Member State from its obligations to assure support for the migrant worker in exceptional cases. Authorities of Member States therefore have the obligation to monitor employers who have accepted the responsibilities of assisting migrant workers and their families during the first weeks of their stay.[99] Regardless of whether state institutions or the employers fulfil the obligations under Article 19 § 2, the Committee makes sure that the reports filed by Member States contain not only administrative information but also details about the social and humanitarian aspects of assistance for migrant workers and their families during their departure, their journey and their first period of stay in the host country.[100] The Committee does not demand that the authorities of Member States provide migrant workers with certain institutions. General social services capable of dealing with the needs of the immigrants and their families fulfil the requirements under Article 19 § 2.[101]

Another obligation under Article 19 § 2 placed on Member States is to ensure migrant workers and their families appropriate health and medical attention as well as

93. Conclusions IV, p. 115; Conclusions XIII-3, p. 410 (Portugal).
94. Conclusions IV, p. 116.
95. *Ibid.*, p. 115 (Austria); Conclusions XV-1, p. 130 (Cyprus); Addendum to Conclusions XV-1, p. 58 (Luxembourg).
96. Conclusions XIV-1, p. 137 (Belgium).
97. Conclusions IV, p. 117 (Great Britain).
98. Conclusions V, p. 125; Conclusions VIII, p. 205 (Italy); Conclusions XIII-2, p. 189; Conclusions XV-1, p. 130 (Cyprus).
99. Conclusions IV, p. 117 (Great Britain); Conclusions XIII-3, p. 413 (Turkey).
100. Conclusions I, p. 83; Conclusions V, p. 126 (France).
101. Conclusions XIII-5, p. 114 (Finland).

good hygienic conditions during the journey. The scope of this obligation includes the journey between the country of the migrants and the host countries to which they are emigrating. Authorities of Member States should ensure migrant workers protection during the journey.[102] The obligation of ensuring medical care was introduced during a time when there was large-scale group migration. The Committee was of the opinion that there was a direct link between migration and medical care. A reduction in the migratory scale means a reduction in the obligations under the provision in question.[103]As with the obligation of assistance and care for migrant workers and their families, authorities of Member States should be aware of the changes in migratory patterns and adapt to them. An increase in migratory patterns means that the obligation to provide health and medical care during the journey should also increase.[104] The Committee is of the opinion that the above obligation is truly activated during organized group migration. This does not mean, however, that the authorities of Member States no longer have the obligation to ensure migrant workers assistance and care when they are travelling individually. The Committee logically deduces that a larger migratory group obligates the authorities of Member States to increase their efforts in providing assistance and care. The decision in the case of Cyprus indicates that singular examples of individuals and their families migrating between Member States for employment purposes is not a basis for non-compliance of domestic regulations with Article 19 § 2 if the Member State does not ensure the migrating workers and their families sufficient care and assistance during their journey or upon arrival in their host country.[105]

During the last few supervisory cycles, the Committee adjourned its decisions with regard to the compliance of domestic regulations with international standards in the case of Slovenia.[106] Even though during the last supervisory cycle, the Committee declared compliance of the Slovenian regulations with the international standards established under Article 19 § 2,[107] in order to understand the situation better, in 2004 it demanded from the authorities particular details about the special measures taken to provide assistance and ensure care for migrating workers and their families during their journey and in the initial period of their stay within the host state. It also wanted to know which entities are responsible for the health and medical care assured to migrants during their journey.[108]

---

102. Conclusions I, p. 83.
103. Conclusions II, p. 64 (Italy); Conclusions III, p. 89 (Ireland); Conclusions IV, p. 116 (Cyprus). During the fifth supervisory cycle the Committee decided Cyprus was not in violation of the obligations set under Article 19 § 2 of the Charter because the very small percentage of migrating individuals meant specialist care and assistance during the journey to the host country was not necessary. Conclusions VI, p. 126.
104. Conclusions IV, p. 115 (Cyprus); Conclusions XIV-1, p. 367 (Greece).
105. Conclusions XV-1, p. 438 (Ireland); p. 456 (Norway).
106. Conclusions 2004, vol. 2m p. 541.
107. Conclusions 2002, pp. 208–209.
108. Conclusions 2004, vol. 2m p. 541.

9.2.4. Cooperation Between Social Services of Emigrating and Immigrating States (Article 19 § 3 of the Charter)

Member States should support the cooperation between social services, public and private, in emigrating and immigrating states. The methods to achieve such cooperation under Article 19 § 3 are left for Member States to choose. One such method may be the utilization of a legal representative from the Member State from which persons are migrating as well as a representative from the state to which the workers are emigrating. Consulate and diplomatic posts may have liaison officers dealing with protection, care and assistance for migrant workers and their families.[109] The duty of a liaison officer may be to establish the rules of cooperation between social services and emigrating and immigrating states. The Committee is interested in understanding these techniques and requests information on these issues from the Member States.[110] The goal of the cooperation between social services is to protect the rights and interests of the migrants within their host country as well as to ensure the state's own citizens the same protection in a state to which they immigrate. Article 19 § 3 also applies to repatriates[111] but does not apply to the influx of workers and their family members coming into the states of the Council of Europe from third party states.[112] The Committee emphasized that Article 19 § 3 protects the rights of two specified categories of migrant workers.[113] It requires that the Member States provide information about the cooperation of social services in order to ensure migrant workers protection that is available to the state's own nationals and to foreign nationals.[114] The point of protecting one's own nationals, who have immigrated to other Member States for employment purposes, is to ensure them the protection of the rights that would be granted to them by being employed in their mother country.

The range of services provided by social services cannot be limited to the provision of social benefits from social security.[115] The Committee's understanding of 'social services', that should be coordinated by social service posts includes benefits provided by public and private organizations to facilitate migrating workers and their families in adapting to new work, housing and living conditions within another state as well as to facilitate contact between them and their families back home.[116]

---

109. German authorities introduced such liaison officers to deal with the migrant workers coming into Germany for employment purposes. Conclusions I, p. 215.
110. Conclusions XIV-1, pp. 165–166 (Cyprus); pp. 280–281 (France); p. 337 (Germany); Conclusions XV-1, p. 224 (Finland).
111. Conclusions XIII-1, p. 268 (Turkey).
112. Conclusions III, p. 91 (Great Britain); Conclusions XIII-2, p. 191 (Ireland).
113. In unclear situations, for example in the case of protecting migrant workers with permanent residency status, the Committee demands from the authorities of Member States additional information that will be used to establish the scope of protection and conclude whether persons who lack such a status are legally protected. Conclusions 2004, vol. 2, p. 386 (Lithuania).
114. Conclusions I, p. 81; Case of Norway: Conclusions XIII-4, p. 261; Conclusions XIV-1, p. 639; Conclusions XV-1, p. 457; p. 103 (Belgium); Case of Slovenia: Conclusions 2002, p. 209; Conclusions 2004, vol. 2m p. 541; Conclusions 2004, vol. 1, p. 189 (Estonia).
115. Conclusions VIII, p. 207; Conclusions XIII-4, p. 261 (Ireland).
116. Conclusions III, p. 91 (Ireland); Conclusions IV, p. 117 (Austria); Conclusions VIII, p. 206 (Ireland); Conclusions XIII-3, pp. 410–411 (Finland). The Committee is interested in gaining information about

Cooperation should be carried out by social services, public institutions[117] or private organizations[118] or through common institutions called upon by the states and non-governmental institutions acting independently [119] or in cooperation with international organizations such as International Social Services (ISS).[120] Member States have the obligation to support such cooperation. If the cooperation is organized solely by non-governmental institutions, Member States are obligated to supervise it. Member States cannot be absolved from carrying out these obligations simply because the cooperation is organized by private services.[121] As opposed to the obligations under the previously mentioned provisions of Article 19, Member States are obligated to support the cooperation of social services regardless of the scale of migratory workers.[122] A reduction in the level of migration for employment services may influence only the methods of cooperation of social services, in that systematic cooperation may be substituted by irregular cooperation. Article 19 § 3 establishes the obligation to support the cooperation between emigrating and immigrating states. There is no need, therefore, for such cooperation to take place between social services of Member States where there is no migratory flow of workers. A reduction in the number of migrant workers, therefore, impacts upon the methods incorporated by social services. Regardless of the cooperation techniques implemented (permanent or temporary), Member States have the obligation to inform the Committee of all the forms of cooperation implemented by social services.[123]

The provision in question indicates that Member States have the obligation to support social service cooperation as is appropriate. This understanding brought about the exchange of opinions between Ireland and the Committee during the third supervisory cycle. Irish authorities argued that the cited Article 19 § 3 forms a basis for Member States to determine whether there is a need to support cooperation between social services of emigrant and immigrant countries. The Committee did not share this opinion. It concluded that Article 19 § 3 does not leave room for debate with regard to the obligation of all Member States to support the cooperation of social services between immigrating and emigrating countries. The term 'as appropriate', according to the Committee, refers to the methods and techniques used in such cooperation. Due to the existing differences between social service structures within various Member States, cooperation may take place according to the most appropriate methods (public or private social services or their conglomerates).[124] The Committee is interested in gaining information about the legal possibilities of cooperation by social services

fulfilling the alimony obligations of family members who are left in the country of origin. Conclusions 2004, vol. 1, p. 189 (Estonia)

117. Through consulates. Conclusions VIII, p. 206 (Italy).
118. Conclusions XI-1, p. 158 (the Netherlands).
119. Conclusions XIII-2, pp. 190–191 (Greece).
120. Conclusions II, p. 66 (Great Britain).
121. Conclusions IV, pp. 118–119 (Great Britain); Conclusions IX-1, p. 106 (the Netherlands).
122. Conclusions III, p. 91 (Norway); Conclusions IV, p. 118; Conclusions XIII-2, p. 191 (Ireland).
123. Conclusions VII, p. 101 (Norway).
124. Conclusions III, pp. 90–91.

carried out by private institutions, especially when reports from the authorities of Member States indicate that such cooperation is carried out by public institutions.[125]

The Committee rendered a judgment about Norway's non-compliance with Article 19 § 3, as its authorities showed in their filed report that no measures had been taken to promote cooperation between Norwegian public and private institutions and appropriate foreign institutions in other Member States. The Committee reached a conclusion that the obligation of Norwegian authorities to ensure care and social assistance to migrant workers and their families does not apply to their own nationals living abroad. It reiterated that the goal of the provision in question is to ensure social protection for all migrant workers, including a state's own nationals.[126] During the following supervisory cycle, the Committee concluded that the Norwegian authorities provided information about the legal international possibilities of measures taken by social services functioning within Scandinavia, namely in Denmark and in Sweden. Cooperation between social services of these countries takes place according to multilateral regional agreements. The Committee obligated Norwegian authorities to provide particular information about this cooperation and adjourned its decision.[127]

9.2.5. Member States' Obligation not to Treat Migrant Workers Less Favourably than their Own Nationals (Article 19 § 4)

Member States must ensure that migrant workers who are residing within the territories of particular Member States are not treated less favourably than their own nationals in the following matters: remuneration and other employment and working conditions (19(4)(a)); membership in trade unions and enjoyment of the benefits of collective bargaining (19(4)(b)); and accommodation (19(4)(c)). The provision in question was modelled on Article 6 § 1 of the ILO convention No. 97, dealing with migrant workers. It was revised on 8 June 1949.[128] The beneficiaries of this provision are foreign nationals of Member States, party to the Charter. A condition of being able to attain this right and to continue being able to remain within the given Member State is to be in possession of a work and residency permit. A foreign national who has either lost his residency permit or entered a Member State's territory by violating entry regulations has no status of legal residency within the territory of another Member State. The term 'territory' also applies to oil rigs on the sea, under the management of a given Member State.[129] The legal protection assured by this provision encompasses citizens of all Member States, including those that have not ratified the provision.[130] By requiring that the treatment of migrant workers who are citizens of other Member States, be 'not less favourable (than?) that of their own citizens', Article 19 § 4 refers to

125. Conclusions XVII-1, vol. 2, p. 397 (Poland).
126. Conclusions XIV-1, pp. 638–639.
127. Conclusions XV-1, pp. 456–457.
128. Conventions and recommendations ... *op. cit.*, vol. 1, p. 413 and following.
129. Conclusions VI, p. 121 (Germany, Norway).
130. Conclusions VIII, p. 209 (Spain).

other provisions that obligate the authorities of a given Member State to abide by the provisions that regulate employment conditions, remuneration, training, membership in trade unions as well as accommodation conditions (Articles 1–4, 5, 9, 15, 16). Migrant workers should not be treated worse than the nationals of a given state. However, this does not carry the same connotation as equal treatment. Even though Article 19 § 4 does not introduce the obligation of equal treatment of migrant workers and nationals, the Committee is of the view that the provision forbids discriminatory practices in matters concerning employment, remuneration, trade union membership, rights gained due to collective labour agreements and accommodation. In order for domestic regulations to be regarded as fully compliant with international standards under Article 19 § 4, it is not enough for the authorities of Member States to prove that migrant workers are not discriminated against in the fields specified under sections a–c of the provision. Member States are obligated to prove that discrimination has no place in domestic legislation, and its practices, that regulate working conditions, remuneration, membership in trade unions, the possibility of taking advantage of collective labour agreements and accommodation.[131] The Committee is of the opinion that the Member States are obligated to issue anti-discrimination legislation. A Member State that does not discriminate against foreign workers who are citizens of other Member States fulfils its obligation under this provision.[132] According to the Committee, the obligation of issuing legislation to ensure migrant workers' rights must be 'in so far as such matters are regulated by law or regulations or are subject to the control of administrative authorities'. The cited provision is interpreted as prohibiting the usage of existing domestic legislation to differentiate between worker situations based on citizenship (i.e., between the nationals of a given Member State and foreign nationals of Member States party to the Charter). It also prohibits various administrative bodies and state authorities from applying any such existing legislation differentiating between its own citizens and foreign nationals.[133]

The Committee is of the view that Article 19 § 4 is one of the most important provisions of the international treaty, issued in order to ensure social and economic rights.[134] Even though abiding by the international standards of protecting migrant workers' rights depends upon the number of migrant workers or to which Member States the flow is generated, the Committee is of the view that Article 19 § 4 should be followed by all Member States that ratified the provision regardless of the number of people emigrating and immigrating.[135] Article 19 § 4 is of particular importance during recession. An increase in demand for labour within national markets obligates Member States to protect the rights of foreign workers, who have remained within a given Member State for employment purposes. An increase in the unemployment level is a direct link to negatively affecting the employment of migrant workers.[136]

131. Conclusions II, p. 68.
132. *Ibid.*, p. 67.
133. D. Harris, J. Darcy, *op. cit.*, p. 221.
134. Conclusions XIV-1, p. 59.
135. Conclusions V, p. 129 (Cyprus); p. 130 (Italy).
136. Conclusions IV, p. 119.

Article 19 § 4 specifies the fields in which foreign nationals of other Member States cannot be treated less advantageously than the nationals of a Member State in which the migrant workers are working. The first field deals with remuneration and other employment and working conditions. According to the Committee, the term 'remuneration' means financial benefits directly or indirectly associated with employment and the job. Two understandings are taken into consideration here, since they exist adjacently to each other in Article 19 § 4. In this context, 'remuneration' refers to the guaranteed wage assured to: the worker who is not working but is in vocational training,[137] the worker who is changing his/her place of work and undertaking employment in a field recommended by the employer,[138] the worker who is receiving wages guaranteed to him after the employer has terminated work agreements (for reasons not associated with the employees),[139] and the worker entitled to family benefits. In the latter case, the Committee heightens the importance of treating migrant workers no less favourably than a Member State's own nationals. The loss of employment places a foreign national at a disadvantage. For this reason the Committee calls upon the authorities of Member States to undertake particular measures to counteract the discrimination of foreign nationals.

Neither the Committee nor the Charter defines working and employment conditions. This category incorporates all issues associated with workers' rights as well as those undertaking employment according to different agreements that are not regulated by labour legislation. From the decisions handed down by the Committee, it is possible to deduce that this also includes accessibility to vocational training for workers and other employed persons,[140] protecting the longevity of a work agreement of workers who are called into military service,[141] and rules of employing workers over-time during days that are free from work and at night as well as rules of employing women and young persons.[142] The Committee rendered a decision about the non-compliance of Germany's labour law regulations, that excluded migrant workers from the protection of rights ensured to workers who are called into military services, with the standards established under Article 19 § 4.[143] Initially the Committee did not concern itself (with respect to this provision), about the principles of hiring foreign nationals.[144] It changed its position however and decided that making employment (including the civil servant sector) dependent upon citizenship of a given Member State is a violation of the standards under Article 19 § 4.[145]

137. Conclusions III, p. 92.
138. *Ibid.*, p. 94.
139. Conclusions IV, p. 119.
140. Conclusions VII, p. 103 (Great Britain).
141. Case of Germany: Conclusions XIII-2, p. 380; Conclusions XIII-4, pp. 443–444; Conclusions XIV-1, p. 337–338; Addendum to Conclusions XV-1, p. 49; Conclusions XVII-1, vol. 1, p. 222.
142. D. Harris, J. Darcy, *op. cit.*, p. 222.
143. *See* decisions cited under footnote 557. The regulations prohibited employers terminating work agreements with workers called into military service.
144. Conclusions IV, p. 119 (Cyprus).
145. Conclusions VIII, p. 208 (Norway).

Foreign nationals should not be treated less favourably than the nationals of a given Member State in matters concerning trade union membership, being active within a trade union, holding a position within a trade union as well as taking advantage of the rights ensured by collective labour agreements. Article 19 § 4 holds any trade union membership rights based on citizenship in a given Member State non-compliant with the standards.[146] This concept has been extended to various workers' representative bodies including workers' councils, bodies representing workers' interests and taking into consideration their rights as well as other official bodies of representative stakeholders (industrial tribunals, arbitration courts, social security institutions etc).[147] Decisions about the non-compliance of domestic regulations due to the violation of the above rules were rendered with respect to Turkey, Finland and Luxembourg. Turkish labour law forbade foreign nationals from joining organizational committees set up by workers in an attempt to form trade organizations.[148] In Finland migrant workers were disallowed from being selected as trade union representatives within the workplace.[149] In Luxembourg, foreign nationals of other Member States, with the exception of European Union members, did not have the right to be representatives of a trade organization within the workplace.[150]

The Committee was also concerned with the second element, presented in Article 19 (4)(b), that forbids Member States from treating migrant workers less favourably than their own nationals in matters concerning the enjoyment of the benefits of collective bargaining. It did not confirm any cases of discrimination of migrant workers within collective bargaining agreements.

The Committee paid much attention to the last obligation ensuring migrant workers and their families the same treatment in matters concerning accommodation, Article 19(4)(c). During the first supervisory cycle, the Committee decided that the conditions underlined in the introduction to Article 19 § 4 dealing with the legal residency of migrant workers within the territory of a Member State refers only to the workers and not to their families. However the illegal entry and/or residency of family members of migrant workers within the territory of a Member State does not free the authorities of Member States that accept migrant workers from abiding by Article 19(4)(c).[151]

The text of the provision in question ensures migrant workers and their families access to communal housing subsidized by the Member States. Examining the situation of migrant workers in a foreign Member State, it was decided that this element of the provision is of prime importance.[152] Consequently, the Committee handed down a decision about the non-compliance of this obligation in cases where Member States: excluded foreign nationals from the category of those having the right to apply for

146. Conclusions XIII-3, p. 418.
147. Conclusions XIV-1, p. 45.
148. Conclusions XIII-3, p. 418; Conclusions XIII-4, p. 268; Conclusions XIV-1, p. 780; Conclusions XV-1, p. 612.
149. Conclusions XV-1, p. 225; Conclusions XVII-1, vol. 1m p. 495.
150. Addendum to Conclusions XV-1, p. 59.
151. Conclusions I, p. 84.
152. *Ibid.*

communal housing,[153] made the granting of the abovementioned rights dependent upon the availability of the same rights for their own nationals living within another Member State,[154] limited financial aid for construction for their own nationals,[155] created exceptions solely for citizens of EU and EEA Member States,[156] and made dependent housing rights for migrant workers and their families upon the period of residence within the territory of another Member State.[157] Introducing conditions of residency in a Member State or in the geographical region of that state, for nationals and foreign nationals (citizens of other Member States), is a case of indirect discrimination. Their ability to fulfil such conditions is much lower than that of the nationals within that state. The Committee granted exceptions to this rule only when the number of migrant workers who are citizens of other Member States who could be discriminated against was slight.[158]

The standard of communal housing allocated to migrant workers cannot be lesser than the standard of similar housing allocated to the state's own nationals.[159] Article 19(4)(c) prohibits less favourable treatment of citizens of other Member States who are attempting to rent or purchase private property for accommodation purposes.[160] Only security reasons[161] and change in real estate allocation may justify the different treatment of citizens of other Member States.[162]

9.2.6. Equal Treatment of Citizens of other the Member States in Tax Matters (Article 19 § 6)

Article 19 § 6 obligates Member States to treat foreign workers who are citizens of other Member States equally in matters of taxation, insurance premium and other public contributions paid by workers in the employment arena. The Committee

153. Conclusions XIII-2, p. 198 (Italy); Case of Slovenia: Conclusions 2002, p. 210; Conclusions 2004, vol. 2, p. 542.
154. Conclusions XIV-1., p. 477 (Italy).
155. Conclusions XIII-3, p. 413 (Portugal).
156. Conclusions XIV-1, p. 819 (Great Britain).
157. Case of Norway: Conclusions V, p. 123; Conclusions XI-1, p. 159; Conclusions XIII-1, pp. 207–208; Conclusions XIII-2, pp. 194-196; Conclusions XIII-4, p. 266; Conclusions XIV-1, p. 640; Conclusions XV-1, p. 458. Case of Italy: Conclusions XIII-2, p. 193; Conclusions XIII-4, p. 265; Conclusions XIV-1, pp. 477–478. Committee changed its decision with regards to Italy during the 15th supervisory cycle. The Committee decided that Article 40 of the directive No. 286 from 25 July 1998 ensured citizens of other Member States equal rights with Italian citizens with regards to communal housing rights. Case of Spain: Conclusions XI-2, p. 147; Conclusions XII02, p. 222; Conclusions XIII-2, pp. 194–196; Conclusions XIV-1, p. 719; Conclusions XV-1, p. 545. Spanish authorities argued that foreign nationals living in Spain are mainly retirees and tourists. Case of Great Britain: Conclusions XIV-1, pp. 821–822; Conclusions XV-1, pp. 655-657; Conclusions XVII-1, vol. 1, p. 536.
158. Conclusions XII-1, p. 234 (Norway); Conclusions XIII-2, p. 49; p. 195 (Spain).
159. Conclusions IX-2, p. 98 (France); Conclusions XIII-2, p. 379 (Belgium).
160. Conclusions IV, p. 121 (Norway).
161. Conclusions XI-1, p. 159 (Greece).
162. D. Harris, J. Darcy, *op. cit.*, p. 223, footnote 1444.

interprets this provision as a ban on introducing higher or additional taxes for foreigners. The Committee classified the imposition of a 0.5 per cent tax on all foreigners working in Italy by the Italian authorities as violating the international standards established by this provision.[163] The Committee did not accept the arguments of the Italian authorities that the above tax contributes to the fund covering the costs of a journey back home for one who cannot afford such expenses. The Committee expressed its firm opinion that tax can by no means be imposed on foreigners who are not citizens of the Member States of the EU. In 2000, the Italian authorities lifted this obligation. Since then, the Committee has not come across a case where additional taxation of citizens of one Member State employed in the territory of another Member State of the Council of Europe was imposed. However, it has dealt with cases of exemption in paying a part of the tax used for the costs of supporting under-age children. According to the report delivered by the German authorities, workers who support under-age children are entitled to claim back a part of the paid tax. The above entitlement encompasses only children living within the territory of Germany. Given the situation that children of migrant workers who are citizens of other Member States usually do not live with their parents in a state of temporary residence, the Committee came to the conclusion that regulations issued by the German authorities *de facto* discriminate against foreigners.[164] Currently, this case would have to be classified as a typical example of indirect discrimination. Seemingly equal regulations applied to employed persons – a State's own and foreign citizens – discriminate against the latter. The German authorities, influenced by the Committee's position, decided to change tax regulations and release all workers supporting children from paying a part of the tax. However, the exempted amount still differs depending on whether a child lives in Germany or in another Member State. Taking into consideration the costs of living in a particular Member State, the scope of the tax exemption varies from one-third to two-thirds of the amount to which workers whose children live in Germany are entitled.[165] The regulations do not provide for a bigger exemption in the case of states where the costs of living are apparently higher than in Germany (unclear sentence). The Committee did not deal with this matter although it positively regarded British authorities who exempted from tax travel expenses associated with re-emigrating workers.[166]

Despite the fact that Article 19 § 5 deals only with the obligation of equal treatment of migrant workers in matters of taxes and contributions, it does not apply only to cases concerning the obligation to fulfil public employment related contributions by foreigners working in the territory of another Member State. Within the confines of this provision, the Committee also evaluated obligations imposed on employers. Analysing the Swedish report, the Committee stated that the authorities of this state impose on employers the obligation of participating in costs of language training for foreigners. The Committee concluded that keeping this obligation in force may lead to

163. Conclusions XIII-4, pp. 198–199; Conclusions XIV-1, p. 478; Conclusions XV-1, pp 390–391.
164. Conclusions X-2, pp. 148–149; Conclusions XI-2, pp. 148–149.
165. Conclusions XII-2, p. 223; Conclusions XIII-2, pp. 381–382.
166. Conclusions XII-1, p. 237.

practical discrimination of migrant workers because an employer, having the choice of hiring a Swedish national or a migrant worker, would employ the former because the employer would not have to pay extra fees. This is another example of indirect discrimination, proving that employers intending to reduce the cost of employment would enter into labour relations with workers who speak Swedish. The significant majority within this category would be citizens of Sweden.[167] The Swedish authorities appreciated these arguments and lifted the employers' obligation to contribute to the costs of language tuition for migrant workers – citizens of other the Member States temporarily employed in Sweden in 1986.

9.2.7. Facilitating the Family Reunion of Migrant Workers (Article 19 § 6)

Separation of migrant workers from their families during periods of employment in other Member States does not accord with the spirit of the Charter.[168] The Charter imposes on the obligation of facilitating the reunion of families of migrant workers to the extent possible. Article 19 § 6 is related to Article 16, the international standard guaranteeing the protection of family rights. In the Appendix to the European Social Charter a family of a migrant worker, a citizen of another Member State, has not been defined. It was only noted that a family consists of at least a wife and children under the age of 21 who are financially supported by a migrant worker. There were futile efforts undertaken by the authorities of some of the Member States to grant the right to a reunion with a husband (not only a wife). It was not until the Appendix to the Revised European Social Charter that the term 'wife' was replaced with 'spouse'. However, the Committee interprets Article 19 § 6 ESC as granting a husband the right to settle in a Member State where his wife is employed.[169] This entitlement does not apply to parents and other relatives of a migrant worker employed on the territory of another Member State, however.

The differences between the Revised European Social Charter and the European Social Charter in terms of age definitions of children granted the right to settle in a Member State where their father or mother is employed has contributed to many difficulties in the practice of determining whether Member States are abiding by the analysed provision of Article 19 § 6. In the Appendix to the Revised European Social Charter, the right to settle in a host Member State where a migrant parent (mother or father) is employed, was granted to non-married children who are financially supported by migrant workers (male or female workers) and who, according to the regulations of the country of their intended emigration, are not of age. The Member States, party to the European Social Charter, started applying a rule introduced by the Revised European Social Charter and legislating provisions prohibiting children who have come of age to enter the country. In Europe, one attains maturity by turning 18. The controversy

167. Conclusions VII, p. 104.
168. Conclusions XIII-2, p. 58.
169. Conclusions IV, p. 124.

centred around children of migrant workers between 18 and 21 years of age. The Committee stated that the Member States that ratified the European Social Charter are obligated to abide by its regulations.[170] However, it did not order the introduction of a provision into the national system guaranteeing the right to settle in a Member State to children of migrant workers who according to the regulations of a certain Member State are of age but have not turned 21. The Committee predicated that the authorities of these states should give evidence that they are following the standards established on the basis of Article 19 § 6 ESC. According to the established practice, the Committee examines whether provisions and the application thereof in practice in Member States are in accordance with the relevant international standards. In the case of the age limit of a child being financially supported by migrant workers as a direct reason for the family reunion and settling in a state where the child's mother of father is employed, not excluding from this right children between the age of 18 and 21 who were allowed to settle in other Member States plays an important role.[171] A Member State that meets the requirements determined in Article 19 § 6 ESC is a state that regards children as underage persons, if it does not deny the right to settle for children of migrant workers who are of age, according to the binding legal regulations in a given country. The Committee examined in detail the case of Great Britain where the regulations differentiated the right of children of migrant workers to reunite with parents (mother or father) employed in the given country. The British authorities, bound by the European Social Charter, decided that attaining maturity, i.e., turning 18 years of age, is the limit for children of migrant workers to utilize the right guaranteed by the Article 19 § 6. The exception was made for non-married daughters of migrant workers who were not yet 21. Taking into consideration the contradicting provisions and the practices towards children of male migrants, the Committee declared that Great Britain abides by the standards established by the Article 19 § 6 ESC.[172] From the reports delivered by the British authorities it can be concluded that despite the limiting of the age of male children of migrant workers to 18 years, the British immigration authorities demonstrate good will in applying the standards established in Article 19 § 7 ESC and are prompt to make positive decisions in cases of male children of migrant workers, between 18 and 21 years of age. Persons who were denied the right to settle in Great Britain can appeal to the immigration department. The Committee adjourned its ruling, because the British authorities did not deliver the required statistical data on the number of men between 18 and 21 years applying for the right of residency in Great Britain in relation to the intention of living with a family residing within the given state.[173] The Committee stated that there were no applications made by children of

170. Conclusions XIV-1, p. 94 (Austria); p. 104 (Belgium).

171. Conclusions XII-1, pp. 229–230 (Sweden); Case of Austria: Conclusions XIII-2, p. 200; Conclusions XIV-1, p. 94. Case of Great Britain: Conclusions XIII-2, pp. 204–205; Conclusions XIV-1, p. 823; Case of Portugal: Conclusions XIII-3, p. 418; Conclusions XIV-1, pp. 681–682.

172. Conclusions VII, p. 106; Conclusions VIII, p. 216; Conclusions XI, p. 152.

173. Conclusions XII-1, p. 240.

migrant workers by men between 18 and 21 years to the British immigration offices. The Committee obligated the British authorities to deliver data and information addressing families being able to utilize the right to a reunion. [174] From the report presented by the British authorities it can be concluded that potential beneficiaries of this entitlement had been improperly informed about the possibility of a reunion guaranteed by Article 19 § 7 ESC. Among other pieces of improper information, the British authorities stated that the right to settle in the given country applies to sons of migrant workers who live alone in difficult conditions in their country of origin. The Committee concluded that the above information was aimed to discourage men between 18 and 21 years of age to apply for the right to settle in Great Britain within the confines of a reunion of families of migrant workers.[175] The Committee also took into consideration that British authorities accepted the possibility of permitting the reunion of migrant workers families by allowing for men between 18 and 21 years to settle in Great Britain on the condition that the participants of these reunions do not apply for financial benefits from public funds. Based on information received from the British authorities, the Committee declared Great Britain had not provided the data proving the conformity of the immigration practice with the standards set on the basis of Article 19 § 6 and explicitly stated Great Britain did not fulfil the obligations established by the provision in question.[176] The Committee ruled upon the contradicting nature of national regulations and the standards set on the basis of Article 19 § 6 in all cases in which it was detected that the authorities of the Member States, party to the Charter, did the following: set the age limit of children of migrant workers under 21 years of age;[177] did not present data proving that despite the age limit, in practice, migrant workers' children of both sexes have the right to settle on the territory of other Member States that employ their mother or father;[178] introduced additional requirements such as the obligation of applying for a permit of residency for children up to 14 years of age within the territory of a given Member State within a year from the legalization of residency of migrant workers, citizens of other Member States once employed without a required permit;[179] introduced the obligation of applying for permission to bring in another child within a year of the family reunion of the first family member (spouse or child);[180] introduced limits on the number of children who can be brought to the country of residency of

---

174. Conclusions XIII-3, p. 205.
175. Conclusions XIII-4, p. 279.
176. Conclusions XIV-1, pp. 823–824; Conclusions XVII-1, vol.2, pp. 536–537.
177. Austria – 19 years. Conclusions XV-1, pp. 62–63; Conclusions XVII-1, vol.1, p. 50; Belgium – 18 years. Conclusions XIII-2, pp. 382–384; Conclusions XIII-4, p. 446; Germany – 16 lat. Conclusions XI-2, p. 151; Conclusions XVII-1, vol.1, p. 222; Conclusions XII-2, p. 49; Conclusions XIII-2, p. 385; Ireland. Conclusions XIV-1, pp. 439–440; Addendum to Conclusions XV-1, pp. 32–33; Italy – 18 years. Conclusions XIII-3, p. 275; Conclusions XIV-1, pp. 478–479; Conclusions XV-1, p. 392; the Netherlands. Addendum to Conclusions XV-1, p. 116. Turkey. Conclusions XVII-1, vol.1, p. 497.
178. Case of Greece: Conclusions XIII-2, p. 201; Conclusions XIV-1, pp. 369–370; Conclusions XVII-1, vol. 1, p. 258; Case of Sweden: Conclusions XV-1, pp. 581–582.
179. Case of Austria: Conclusions XV-1, pp. 62–63; Conclusions XVII-1, vol.1, p. 50.
180. Case of Belgium: Conclusions XIII-2, p. 382–384; Conclusions XIII-4, p. 446.

migrant workers;[181] conditioned the right to bring children to the country on a period of residency of migrant workers;[182] health condition of family members of a migrant worker.[183]

The fact that many countries condition the right to a family reunion in a family where one of its members (mother or father) is employed in another Member State on the state of health of the children or a spouse remaining in the country of origin, gave the ground for the Committee to make a ruling stating the lack of conformity of the national regulations of these countries with the international standards.[184] The Committee takes the position that, with the exception of infectious diseases which can be dangerous to public health,[185] as included in the categories of exclusions of human rights allowed by the Committee, the existence of disease does not excuse the refusal of residency on the basis of a family reunion, for the family members of a migrant worker in a Member State where the said worker is employed.[186]

The Committee did not treat the requirements established by the Member States schematically. The requirements, when fulfilled, would allow for the right of a family reunion to be utilized. Taking the position that the health conditions of a family member are not dangerous to public health cannot form a basis for the refusal of the reunion of a family with a worker who emigrated for employment purposes,[187] and despite the fact that the residency of an ill person may lead to the necessity of granting him/her help from public funds,[188] the Committee declared that the refusal can be justified only if it can be proven that the intention behind the employment migration was to apply for free-of-charge benefits for the treatment of an ill family member from the national system of social security.[189]

A similar position was taken by the Committee in the case of residency requirements. The Committee claims that the requirement of one year of residency in a Member State for a migrant worker who wants to bring his family is well-grounded.[190]

181. Austria, Conclusions XVII-1, vol.1, p. 50.

182. Case of Greece: Conclusions XV-1, pp. 315–316: Conclusions XVII-1, vol.1, p. 258. The waiting period for utilizing the right to family reunion, which used to last 5 years, was limited to 2 years. In these two cases the Committee regarded this condition as restrictive. Case of the Netherlands: Addendum to Conclusions XV-1, p. 116; Case of Germany (Conclusions I, p. 69), who introduced the requirement of 3 years of residency in the new country where a migrant worker moved having earning purposes. (unclear)

183. Case of Turkey: Conclusions XV-1, pp. 614–615; Conclusions XVII-1, vol.2, p. 497.

184. Conclusions III, p. 95 (Austria); Conclusions V, p. 134 (France).

185. Listed by the World Health Organization (WHO) in International Health Regulation of 1969, which replaced International Sanitary Regulation No. 2 of 25 May 1951. Conclusions VIII, p. 214 (the Netherlands); Conclusions 2004, vol. 1, p. 116 (Cyprus).

186. Case of Greece (Conclusions XI-1, p. 162; Conclusions XII-1, p. 238), who deprived mentally ill family members of a migrant worker of the right to settle.

187. Conclusions I, p. 85 (Great Britain).

188. Conclusions II, p. 69 (Great Britain).

189. *Ibid.*

190. Conclusions III, p. 96 (Germany). The above requirement should be introduced into the binding provisions. It cannot be based on the practice of administrative bodies.

Prolonging the period of residency up to three years[191] or longer[192] was considered a violation of Article 19 § 6. Limitations on family reunions in the case of earning migrants in other Member States are accepted by the Committee on the condition that they do not release the authorities of a Member State from the obligation set by Article 19 § 6 'facilitating, as much as it is possible, the family reunion of a foreign worker who was allowed residency within a given territory'.[193]

The obligation imposed on Member States authorities is to facilitate the reunion of migrant workers with their families residing abroad, within the territory of other Member States. This obligation is interpreted by the Committee as a duty of removing all legal barriers for migrant worker's family members to settle in the state in which the worker is employed.[194] Member States are also obligated to undertake measures aimed at helping migrant workers' families who want to reunite. In particular, this help encompasses the action of supporting reuniting families in their search for a new dwelling.[195] The Committee claims that Member States should undertake the appropriate measures themselves to meet the housing needs of migrant workers and their families unless the interested parties clearly stated that they were able to take care of their lives themselves[196] or because of the serious legal obstacles involved making it impossible to provide them with such help.[197] Member States that are excused from the above obligation are those that have a small number of migrant workers and their family members.[198] The Committee does not accept the arguments of the Member States that refer to the term 'as far as possible' used in Article 19 § 6 claiming the range of application of this obligation was left for their unconstrained determination.[199] Practices that place conditions on the right to reunite with family members of migrant workers on residency requirements of the majority of family members in the particular state who are entitled to the said reunion[200] are regarded as violating Article 19 § 6. Likewise, limitations on these entitlements to some family members of a migrant worker allowing, for example, only a spouse and one child to settle[201] were regarded as violating Article 19 § 6 . The Committee accepted the necessary condition of executing the right to reunite families as being the availability of adequate financial measures on the side of a migrant worker to support the family and their accommodation.[202]

191. Case of Germany: Conclusions I, p. 69; Conclusions III, p. 96; Conclusions VI, p. 125; Conclusions XI-2, p. 151
192. Estonia – 5 years. Conclusions 2004, vol.1, p. 192.
193. Conclusions VIII, p. 211.
194. Conclusions II, p. 197 (Cyprus).
195. Conclusions I, p. 85 (Norway); Conclusions II, p. 70 (Great Britain); p. 197 (Cyprus); Conclusions III, p. 95 (Cyprus); Conclusions V, p. 133 (Austria); p. 134 (France).
196. Conclusions III, p.94; Conclusions IX-2, p. 98 (Austria); Conclusions XII-2, p. 225 (France); Conclusions XIII-1, p. 271 (Turkey).
197. Conclusions II, p. 69 (Norway).
198. *Ibid.* (Ireland).
199. Conclusions XIV-1, p. 314 (Germany).
200. Conclusions XIII-2, p. 384 (Germany).
201. Conclusions XII-2, p. 383 (Belgium); Conclusions XIV-1, p. 283 (France).
202. Conclusions X-2, p. 152 (Italy); Conclusions XII-2, p. 226 (Spain); Conclusions 2002, p. 210–211 (Slovenia)

The right to facilitate a family reunion can be utilized by migrant workers who were issued a 'residency permit' within the territory of a given state. Some authors specializing in social matters regulated within the Charter note that this condition is not identical to the condition formulated under Article 19 § 4 that deals with migrant workers 'legally residing' on the territory of a foreign Member State.[203] If one defines residency as residing with the intention of permanently staying in a Member State, then the right regulated by Article 19 § 6 cannot be exercised by either migrant workers employed on the basis of temporary work agreements or by their family members. This entitlement could have been utilized by migrant workers and their family members only after obtaining a permit of permanent residency within the territory of a given Member State where the migrant workers are employed. Obviously the referred to authors base their findings on British regulations, which make permanent residency dependent upon being able to remain within the country legally for a period of four years. Foreigners who have been granted the right of permanent residency are excused from the obligation of renewing their work permit.[204] Accordingly there are no legal grounds to conclude that Article 19 § 6 has a limited range of application, in comparison to Article 19 § 4. Member States are entitled to issue permits to foreigners who apply for legal residency within the territory of a particular state. As a rule, aside from the work permit, a permit allowing residency within the territory of a given state is also issued. The type of residency permit reflects the type of work agreement such as is specified at the given time or for an indefinite period of time. Usually before a foreigner obtains a permanent residency permit, he/she is given a temporary one. Obtaining such a permit allows a foreigner to settle in a certain state. The period of residency depends on the validity of the acquired permit. Article 19 § 6 gives no indication in terms of differentiating between temporary and permanent residence. This is why the Committee does not interpret the analysed provision of Article 19 § 6 as the standard granting the entitlements solely to foreigners permanently residing in a particular Member State.[205]

The entitlement regulated by Article 19 § 6 applies to workers emigrating for earning purposes who have a family residing in another state. This obligation cannot be applied to cases of lonely persons. The British authorities, as a rule, did not agree to the employment of foreigners who have a family member employed in house services. The exception was made for a childless husband employed by one employer. Great Britain presented the view that such an immigration policy allow for the accusation of violating Article 19 § 6, because the denial of facilitating the reunion can take place only when a migrant worker misled the authorities by concealing the fact he/she has left

203. D. Harris, J. Darcy, *op. cit.*, p. 226.

204. *Ibid.*, p. 227.

205. In the ruling made during the fourth supervisory cycle the Committee refers to permanent residency permits issued by the British authorities for persons having lived Great Britain for the period of over four years. Conclusions IV, p. 127. However it cannot be concluded on the basis of that (one what basis?) on the limited range of application of the said provision, because such permit was only given to persons who were granted the above status. Therefore it is possible to be residing in Great Britain without the right of permanent residency in this country, for example in the case of temporary residence for earning purposes and employment on the basis of a work agreement for the defined period of time.

the family (spouse and children) in the country of origin. Cases of misleading the authorities of a Member State in terms of a family situation of a migrant worker are not covered by the protection guaranteed by Article 19 § 6.[206] The Committee stated however that the denial of help to migrant workers and their families residing in other Member States cannot be excused because the condition introduced by the British authorities does not encompass all cases. In particular, it has no relevance when an unmarried foreigner employed in Great Britain as a house servant enters, during his period of employment, into marriage with another foreigner and sets up a family.[207] The Committee declared that Great Britain does not abide by the obligations formulated in Article 19 § 6.

Article 19 § 6 does not apply to citizens of states in the EU who are guaranteed the freedom of movement within the EU.

9.2.8. The Obligation of Equal Treatment of Citizens of other Member States in Legal Proceedings (Article 19 § 7)

The Member States' obligation to afford citizens of other Member States treatment that is no less favourable than that afforded their own nationals with respect to legal proceedings encompasses only matters listed in Article 19. They are as follows: court, administrative and appeal proceedings registered by employers concerning remunerations for work, conditions of work and employment, trade union rights, social security benefits, insurance premiums, residential taxes. Article 19 does not refer to criminal cases. The Committee declared that enforcement of equal treatment for citizen of other Member States in criminal and labour proceedings could not be regarded as a sufficient execution of the requirements determined by Article 19 § 7.[208]

Within the confines of the obligation formulated in Article 19 § 7, the authorities of the Member States in which migrant workers reside are obligated to grant them access to courts, administrative bodies and other bodies responsible for examining controversial matters regulated by Article 19 § 7 and to facilitate the use of the legal advice service delivered by professional lawyers under the same conditions as citizens of a certain Member State.[209] This refers to exemptions from court, administrative and legal service fees and charges as well as the option of taking advantage of free-of-charge legal assistance.[210] The only condition for utilizing the above entitlements is legal residency of a migrant worker within the territory of a Member State. Making permanent residency of a foreigner a condition to use the entitlements guaranteed under Article 19 § 7 was regarded by the Committee as violating international standards established on the basis of the Charter.[211] The necessary condition for classifying

206. Conclusions III, p. 97 (Great Britain).
207. Conclusions X-1, p. 152 (Great Britain).
208. Conclusions I, p. 217.
209. *Ibid.*, p. 86.
210. *Ibid.*
211. Conclusions VII, p. 108 (Sweden); Conclusions 2004, vol.2, p. 388 (Lithuania).

residency of a migrant worker on the territory of another Member State as 'lawful' is the lawful arrival of a migrant worker into the territory of a given Member State. In light of Article 19 § 7, a migrant worker who is a citizen of another Member State is still regarded as lawfully residing within the territory of a foreign Member State when he/she has lost the work and residency permit. This citizen is entitled to initiate court or administrative proceedings in order to regain his/her rights. It was also regarded as contradictory to international standards to make the option of free-of-charge legal assistance for foreigners conditional on the length of their residency within the territory of a particular Member State set at the limit of 12 months.[212]

The most evident example of unequal treatment of workers who are citizens of Member States and employed within the territory of other Member State is the obligation of depositing funds for covering the costs and fees of court proceedings *(cautio judicatum solvi)* introduced by some of the Member States, including Spain.[213] In Spain, this requirement applied solely to foreigners filing claims to court and administrative bodies. In the quoted case there was no issue of unequal treatment of migrant workers, as the Committee stated that the range of this obligation did not encompass the matters regulated by Article 19. For this reason the Committee made a ruling stating Spain abides by the standards established by the provision in question.[214] Judicial rulings of the Committee leave little doubt about the introduction of the obligation of depositing funds for covering the costs and fees of the court proceedings, imposed on citizens of other Member States as a violation of the Article 19 § 7 even though the provision applies only to an inconsiderable number of migrant workers.[215]

The subject of judicial decisions made by the Committee was the case of unequal treatment of foreigners who are citizens of other Member States whose authorities did not enter into reciprocal agreements regarding the access to legal assistance for citizens residing within the territory of other Member States.[216] The essence of the legal regulation of Article 19 § 7 is expressed in guaranteeing an equal position in court proceedings, administrative proceedings and other proceedings before the relevant bodies of Member States, not related to the Member States whose citizens file claims within the confines of the legal procedures taking place in another state that signed bilateral or multilateral international agreements. The analysed provision guarantees the legal protection of citizens of foreign states who are not protected in any other way.

Article 19 § 7 states the obligation to ensure that equal treatment encompasses the 'workers'. From the literature related to the topic,[217] the hypothesis emerges that the

212. Conclusions XV-1, p. 228 (Finland); Case of Portugal: Conclusions XIV-1, pp. 682–683; Conclusions XV-1, pp. 499–500.
213. Conclusions X, p. 153.
214. Conclusions XI-2, p. 152.
215. Case of Luxembourg: Conclusions XIV-1, p. 517; Addendum to Conclusions XV-1, pp. 73–74; Case of Belgium: Conclusions XIII-2, pp. 385–387; Conclusions XIII-4, p. 448; Conclusions XIV-1, pp. 682–683 (Portugal).
216. Conclusions 2002, pp. 252–253 (Sweden who does not guarantee such protection for citizens of Bulgaria).
217. D. Harris, J. Darcy, *op. cit.*, p. 231; L. Samuel, *op. cit.*, p. 430, footnote 1.

obligation of equal treatment of migrant workers imposed on the Member States entitles those workers who are citizens of other Member States to equal treatment in the proceedings initiated in matters regulated by Article 19 § 7, which, in turn, indicates a duty of a similar character – the duty of granting an equal position in legal proceeding as well as when the claims regarding matters regulated by Article 19 are registered by the family members of a migrant worker. One example would be a court case initiated by a family member of a migrant worker who demands – on the grounds of the right of a family reunion of migrant workers – that a particular Member State fulfil the obligation formulated by Article 19 § 6.

9.2.9. Protection against Deportation (Article 19 § 8)

Article 19 § 8 obligates Member States to protect migrant workers against deportation. The necessary condition for utilizing this right by migrant workers is the lawful residency of a migrant worker within the territory of a Member State. The Committee declares that a migrant worker who has valid documents allowing for residency and employment can be considered as legally residing within the territory of a foreign Member State.[218] The loss of employment causes the expiration of the work permit and justifies issuing a decision regarding deprivation of the right to residency, which, in turn, justifies deportation.[219] The loss of legal status of residency causes the loss of legal protection against deportation guaranteed by the Article 19 § 8.

The analysed provision includes three types of legal grounds for deportation of a migrant worker: threat of national security, violation of public policy or violation of morals. This list is of a limited nature; only these reasons justify deportation. The Committee claims that there are no legal grounds for a broad interpretation of this provision. Such an interpretation cannot be supported either by the grounds that justify a decision to refuse entry or those that justify limitations to and exemptions from applying all provisions in special situations. Article 19 § 8 is a special provision. It is applied only to cases of deportation of immigrating workers, whose residency on the territory of a Member State threatens national security and public policy, meaning state institutions and legal system or morals. The Committee ruled on the lack of conformity between national legal systems and Article 19 § 8 when it detected that Member States allow for deportations of migrant workers on a different basis than that described within this provision.[220] According to the Committee the following grounds do not justify deportation:

- Inability to self-support and usage of social service;[221]
- Drug usage;

218. Conclusions II, p. 197 (Cyprus).
219. *Ibid.*, p. 198.
220. Conclusions XVII-1, vol. 1, p. 224 (Germany); p. 260 (Greece); Conclusions XVII-1, vol.2, p. 402 (Poland); p. 468 (Spain).
221. Case of Cyprus: Conclusions III, p. 97; Conclusions IV, p. 128; Conclusions V, p. 137.

- Homelessness;
- Neglecting the duty of rearing children;
- Committing offence or crimes by children of a migrant worker;[222]
- Sentencing for deeds that do not threaten national security, public policy or morals;[223]
- Threat to public health.[224]

Deportation of a migrant worker does not provide the legal grounds for the deportation of his/her family members.[225] The Committee regarded the following as further justified grounds for deportation:

- The refusal of treatment by a person infected by infectious diseases;[226]
- The refusal of drug rehabilitation treatment by a drug addicted person;[227]
- Sentencing for offences or crimes against morals;[228]
- Engaging in political activity conflicting with the international relations of a given state;[229]
- Terrorist activity.[230]

Regardless, Article 19 § 8 regulates only material-legal guarantees of migrant workers' residency in a host country. The Committee notes the procedural guarantees of the above right. The deportation decision cannot be arbitrary.[231] The range of freedom for a body being in charge of such decisions cannot be too wide.[232] The deported worker should be entitled to appeal the decision to an independent appellate body, [233] such as a court. This requirement is not met when a worker is granted the right to appeal

222. Conclusions XV-1, pp. 51–52 (Germany); p. 61 (Luxembourg).
223. *Ibid.*, pp. 317–318 (Greece).
224. Case of Germany: Conclusions V, p. 138; Conclusions XIV-1, p. 341; Conclusions 2004, vol.1, p. 118 (Cyprus); Conclusions 2004, vol.1, p. 290 (Ireland).
225. Conclusions XII-1, vol. 1, p. 189 (Finland); Conclusions XVII-1, vol.2, p. 498 (Turkey); p. 538 (Great Britain).
226. Conclusions V, p. 138; Conclusions VI, p. 127.
227. Conclusions XIV-1, p. 342 (Germany).
228. Conclusions XV-1, p. 549 (Spain).
229. *Ibid.*
230. Case of Sweden: Conclusions V, p. 139; Conclusions VII, p. 109; Conclusions XI, p. 167; Conclusions XIII-2, p. 208; Conclusions XIII-4, p. 283; Conclusions XIV-1, pp. 752–753; Conclusions XV-1, p. 583.
231. Conclusions XIII-2, p. 206 (Ireland).
232. Conclusions XVII-2, vol.2, p. 498 (Turkey).
233. Greece does not provide the above entitlement, which implied the ruling stating the contradictory character of national legal regulations with the Article 19 § 8 of the Charter. (unclear) Conclusions XII-1, p. 242; Conclusions XIII-1, p. 211; Conclusions XIII-2, p. 206; Sweden grants the right of appeal from the decision upon deportation on the basis of accusation of partaking in terrorist action only when it is well- founded. Conclusions VII, p. 109; Conclusions XI-1, p. 167; Conclusions XIII-2, p. 208; Conclusions XIII-4, p. 283; Conclusions XIV-1, pp. 752–753; Conclusions XV-1, p. 583; Conclusions 2002, p. 254.

the deportation decision to a consultative body called up by a ministry of the interior.[234] The appeals procedure cannot be overruled by the possibility of calling to account a civil servant who made illegal decisions upon the deportation.[235] An independent body examining the appeal should be competent to perform a substantial control of the filed claim.[236]

9.2.10. Transferring of Remunerations and Savings (Article 19 § 9)

The authorities of Member States, within the binding regulations of the law, are obligated to allow migrant workers to transfer such a part of wages and savings, as are considered by the interested parties as adequate. Article 19 § 9 was formulated such that its literal interpretation would always place Member State authorities in a situation of abiding by this obligation and allowing migrant workers to use these entitlements. The essence of the problem is in the adequate benefit of this entitlement in national legal regulation that would allow migrant workers to transfer their wages and savings at a most desired level. The Member States introduce limitations in taking national currency abroad. The role of the Committee in this case is to evaluate the restrictions and bans set by the national provisions.[237] The Committee approves of the concept of restrictions and bans on taking national currency abroad. It takes the position that the authorities of the Member States have a right to undertake measures in order to protect their national currency. It opposes only introducing groundless bans and restrictions for migrant workers in terms of their own money disposal.[238]

Migrant workers are entitled to transfer a part of their remunerations and savings during the period of employment in a foreign country and after the termination thereof.[239] They have a right to transfer funds to their country of origin. Thus, the authorities of Member States are permitted to introduce a ban on transferring money by migrant workers to third countries. The Committee evaluated the case of Sweden where such restrictions were introduced, and declared it was in accordance with the standards established by Article 19 § 9 on the condition that the authorities of the Member State would allow for exceptions in cases of transferring funds to support family members of a migrant worker living in third countries.[240] While the fact that the bans or restrictions on transferring national currency abroad applies to a Member State's own citizens is taken into account, the Committee notes that abiding by the rule of equal treatment of foreigners and a Member State's own nationals does not guarantee a ruling stating the conformity of national provisions with the international standards.[241] In cases of restricting the transfer of funds abroad, foreigners employed in

234. Case of Great Britain: Conclusions VI, p. 128; Conclusions XIV-1, p. 825.
235. Case of Greece: Conclusions XII-1, p. 242; Conclusions XIII-1, p. 211; Conclusions XIII-2, p. 206.
236. Conclusions XIII-4, p. 284 (Great Britain).
237. Conclusions I, p. 86.
238. *Ibid.*
239. *Ibid.*, p. 87 (Norway).
240. Conclusions IX-1, p. 111; Conclusions X-1, p. 155.
241. Conclusions IV, p. 131 (Italy); Conclusions V, p. 140 (France).

a given Member State should be treated more favourably. They should be entitled to transfer their net remuneration as long as they have paid their tax and deducted amounts of 'necessary' expenses they should bear.[242] Limitations on transferring half of a worker's monthly wages were considered congruous with Article 19 § 9.[243] In the case of re-emigration, the Committee decided that it is justifiable for a state employing a migrant worker to make calculations in order to compare the amount of wages and amounts transferred abroad and to investigate whether all tax obligations had been met.[244] The Committee pays equal attention to the protection of the right of free disposal of money by a migrant worker and the protection of a Member State against possible attempts of tax evasions.

9.2.11. Protection of Self-Employed Persons on the Territory of a Member State (Article 19 § 10)

Member States that ratified Article 19 § 10 have been obligated to broaden the scope of protection determined by the provisions of Article 19 § 1–9, also ratified by the states, for citizens of other states who are self-employed on the territory of a particular Member State. These guarantees should encompass self-employed foreigners running businesses on the territory of a foreign Member State to the largest possible extent. This refers first of all to the obligations formulated by Article 19 § 4. There is an interesting relationship between Article 19 § 10 and the remaining provisions of Article 19 § 1-9, that can be applied to self-employed persons. The Committee's ruling on not abiding by any of the first nine paragraphs of Article 19 ratified by a certain state resulted in an automatic decision regarding a Member State not being able to meet the requirements of Article 19 § 10. One example is the rulings issued during the first supervisory cycle. The statement that a self-employed foreigner running a business on the territory of a Member State is unable to take advantage of legal protection guaranteed by the Article 19 § 6 was regarded by the Committee as not abiding by Article 19 § 10 .[245] During the following supervisory cycles the Committee developed the above mechanism and started making rulings that dictated that a Member State's failure to abiding to one of nine paragraphs of Article 19 § 10 in terms of the foreigner's treatment automatically resulted in a decision that the given Member State had not met the requirements of Article 19 § 10.[246]

The analysed provision of Article 19 § 10 introduces the obligation of abiding by all provisions ratified by a particular state as far as self-employed foreigners running a

242. Conclusions I, p. 87 (Great Britain).
243. *Ibid.*, pp. 218–219 (Ireland).
244. Conclusions XII-1, pp. 242–242; Conclusions XIII-1, p. 212.
245. Conclusions I, p. 88 (Norway).
246. Conclusions XVII-1, vol.1, p. 224 (Germany– par. 6 and 8); p. 261 (Greece – par. 6 and 8); Conclusions XVII-1, vol.2, p.403 (Poland– par. 8); p. 469 (Spain– par. 6 and 8); p. 499 (Turkey – par. 1, 4, 6 and 8); p. 539 (Great Britain – par. 6 and 8); Conclusions 2002, pp. 254–255 (Sweden – par. 7 and 8); p. 214 (Slovenia – par. 4, 6 and 8); Conclusions 2004, vol.1, p. 119 (Cyprus – par. 6 and 8); p. 291 (Ireland – par. 6 and 8); p. 194 (Estonia – par. 6); p. 388 (Lithuania – par. 7); p. 545 (Slovenia – par. 4 and 8); p. 591 (Sweden – par. 7 and 8).

business on the territory of that Member State are concerned.[247] In order to abide by the regulations of this provision it is necessary for the authorities of the Member States to legislate provisions prohibiting the discrimination of self-employed citizens of other Member States as well as to undertake measures aiming at guaranteeing the same scope of legal protection as experienced by migrant workers.[248] It should be recalled that migrant workers should be treated at least as favourably as citizens of a particular Member State. Therefore the rule encompassing migrant workers employed on the territory of a foreign Member State can also be applied to foreigners, citizens of other Member States who are self-employed and running businesses in other Member States.[249]

9.2.12. Promoting and Facilitating the Teaching of the National Language of the Receiving State to Migrant Workers and their Families (Article 19 § 11 RESC)

In order to facilitate and accelerate assimilation processes in the receiving countries, the authorities of these countries are obligated to promote and facilitate the teaching of the national language of the receiving state to migrant workers and their families. If two or more languages have an official status in a particular state, the authorities of this state are obligated to facilitate the teaching of one of them. The Committee obligates Member States to answer questions about measures undertaken in order to facilitate the teaching of the national language of the receiving state to migrant workers and their families residing on the territory of this state. In particular, the authorities of the Member States should deliver information on the number and type of educational units running courses on the official language in the receiving state, teachers and instructors of the official language in the receiving state employed by these institutions, possibilities of learning this language, the options of financing the language education, accessibility of these facilities for migrant workers and their families, as well as the number of persons participating in the language courses and tuitions.[250] The Committee remarks that the authorities of the Member States receiving migrant workers and members of their families should facilitate the teaching of the national language to immigrant children attending schools as well as to migrant workers and adult members of their families not encompassed by the schooling obligation. From the reports

247. The different opinion is presented by D. Harris, J. Darcy, *op. cit.*, p. 237. According to these authors the Member States are not obliged to abide by the regulations of the Article 19 § 7 of the Charter as far as self-employed foreigners running business on the territory of this Member State are concerned. They argue the above provisions should be applied only to taxes, insurance premiums and other public tributes that workers are obliged to pay. The quoted opinion does not stand in line with the judicial practice of the Committee. Compare with the case of France: Conclusions IX-2, p. 102; Conclusions XV-1, p. 288.
248. Conclusions III, p. 99; Conclusions IV, p. 131 (Norway).
249. Case of Germany: Conclusions I, p. 69; Conclusions III, p. 96; Conclusions VI, p. 125; Conclusions XI-2, p. 151.
250. Form for the reports ... *op. cit.*, p. 357.

presented during the two supervisory cycles[251] it can be concluded the official language in a country receiving migrant workers and members of their families is taught in primary and secondary schools. The Committee is of the opinion that this is insufficient to meet the requirements determined in the Article 19 § 11. The authorities of the Member States should undertake additional measures in order to teach the language of the receiving country to children of migrant workers who do not attend schools and to adults. The Committee interprets the provision in question as a standard obliging the authorities of the Member States to teach the language of the receiving country in workplace, higher education colleges, and private educational and pedagogical institutions. The costs of teaching should not be charged either to the migrant workers or to their employers.[252] The teaching of the language of the receiving country to adults is of great importance for the integration of migrant workers, their equal treatment on the labour market and in labour relations. The Committee is wary that the right of migrant workers who are citizens of other Member States to work in safe and hygienic conditions is jeopardized by the lack of knowledge of the language spoken in the country of employment. Those who do not know the language of the receiving country cannot properly react to different warnings in a workplace or to the requests of superiors managing the work process. In this respect the Committee demands from the authorities of the Member States information on measures undertaken in order to facilitate the teaching of the language of the country of residence to adults.[253] It warns the authorities of Member States that the refusal to answer these questions would force the Committee to rule the violation of the standards established in Article 19 § 11 RESC by the authorities of a certain Member State.[254] The Committee is interested in knowing the costs of teaching of the language of the given country.[255]

9.2.13. Promoting and Facilitating the Teaching of Migrant Workers' Mother Tongue to Children of Migrant Workers (Article 19 § 12 RESC).

The mother tongue is the language of the parents' state of origin. The authorities of a state receiving migrant workers and members of their families should promote and facilitate, as far as practicable, the familiarization of this language for the children of migrant workers. Questions addressed to the Member States by the Committee concerning the teaching of the language of origin of migrant workers' and their family members' are prepared according to the scheme approved for elaborating questions on

---

251. Conclusions 2002. During this supervisory cycle the authorities of four of the Member States delivered their reports: France, Italy, Slovenia and Sweden. Romania did not ratify the Article 19 § 11 and 12 RESC; Conclusions 2004. During another supervisory cycle the authorities of nine of the Member States delivered their reports: Cyprus, Estonia, France, Ireland, Italy, Lithuania (only Article 19 § 11 RESC), Norway, Slovenia and Sweden. Bulgaria and Romania did not ratify the Article 19 § 11 and 12 RESC.
252. Conclusions 2002, p. 56 (France).
253. *Ibid.*, p. 57; p. 215 (Slovenia).
254. Conclusions 2004, vol.1, p. 247 (France).
255. Conclusions 2004, vol. 1, p. 195 (Estonia); Conclusions 2004, vol.2, p. 546 (Slovenia).

the reports detailing the facilitation of language instruction to migrant workers and members of their families. The Committee expresses a conviction that migrant workers and members of their families are capable of learning some languages of their origin at school. France implemented into school programmes the teaching of the following languages: Arabic, Spanish, Portuguese, Turkish and Italian.[256] Migrant workers and members of their families, especially children, have the option of learning the language of their parents' origin within cultural institutions operating on the basis of bilateral agreements between a state of emigration and a state of immigration. However, this method of teaching of a foreign language is less common. The Committee stated that this option of learning a foreign language is guaranteed by the bilateral agreement between by the authorities of France and Italy.[257] The Committee requests that Member States deliver information on the following: the manner in which this obligation is enforced, in particular, in cases of persons not bound by the obligation of compulsory schooling;[258] the number of children and adults embraced by the programmes of teaching of the language of origin;[259] and practical possibilities of learning the official language of their state of origin as a foreign language at school.[260] During the last two supervisory cycles the Committee did not rule against any of the Member States violating Article 19 § 12 RESC. It obligated the authorities of some Member States to deliver additional information and postponed decisions in four cases, one in 2002 (France) and three in 2004 (Ireland, Slovenia, and Italy).

256. Conclusions 2002, p. 57.
257. *Ibid.*, p. 58.
258. *Ibid.*, pp. 215–216 (Slovenia); Conclusions 2004, vol.2, p. 546 (Slovenia).
259. Conclusions 2004, vol.1, p. 196 (Estonia).
260. *Ibid.*, p. 248 (France).

CHAPTER 10 RESTRICTIONS AND EXCLUSIONS IN ABIDING REGULATIONS OF THE EUROPEAN SOCIAL CHARTER

The legal issues surrounding limitations of and temporary exemptions from following the provisions of international treaties by the Member States raise the interests of lawyers specializing in international public law. Monographs dedicated to the detailed analysis of the content of social rights and the issues surrounding these limitations and temporary exemptions matter insofar as they relate to the warranty of enforcement of social rights protected by the Charter. Provisions regulating the admissibility of excluding and limiting the Charter regulations are listed in Part VI of the European Social Charter and in Part IV of the Revised European Social Charter. Exclusions and limitations are accepted in the case of war or other public emergency threatening the life of the nation (Article 30 ESC, Article F RESC). Exclusions and limitations of some provisions are possible in cases of the necessity to protect the rights and freedoms of others or the public interest, national security, public health, or morals (Article 31 § 1 ESC; Article G § 1 RESC). Stakeholders or the authorities of the Member States have a right to introduce exclusions and limitations with regard to some of the provisions (Article 2 § 1, 2, 3, 4, 5; Article 7 § 4, 6, 7; Article 10 § 1, 2, 3, 4) as far as the majority of interested workers are concerned (Article 33 § 1 ESC; Article I § 2 RESC). The authorities of the Member States determine the territorial range of the Charter's application. (Article 34 ESC; Article E RESC).

10.1. Temporary Derogations of the Charter in Case of War or National Security Threats

In cases of war or other public emergencies that threaten the life of the nation, the authorities of each Member State, party to the Charter, can take measures required by the exigencies of the situation, and are exempt from obligations undertaken by the ratification of the Charter. The necessary precondition for temporary derogation from abiding by Charter provisions is the occurrence of the conditions set in Article 30 § 1

ESC or Article F RESC, defined in terms of international public law. The Appendix to the Charter allows for the temporary derogations of the Charter by authorities of a Member State not in a state of war but prior to it (threatened by war). Public security threats are defined as an exceptional state of crisis embracing the whole of society that threatens public order.[1] The authorities of a Member State are empowered to make decisions about the derogations of the Charter in such cases. Once the decision is made it is subject to the control of the Council of Europe and its bodies. The authorities of the Member States enjoy the right to evaluate the situation and are granted significant latitude.[2] Any party that has availed itself of this right of exemption shall, within a reasonable period of time, inform the Secretary-General of the Council of Europe in detail about the measures taken. The notice should include the time when the provisions of the Charter ceased to operate and the period for which these provisions would be derogated on the territory of the particular Member State. Violation of this obligation formulated in Article 30 § 2 ESC and in Article F RESC does not imply the invalidity of the decision regarding the temporary derogation of the provisions of the Charter. The Secretary-General will inform the authorities of the Member States, party to the Charter, as well as the Director General of the International Labour Office about the decisions made.[3]

10.2. Derogations Necessary for the Protection of the Rights and Freedoms of others or for the Protection of Public Interest, National Security, Public Health, or Morals

Article 31 § 1 ESC and Article G § 1 RESC confirm the rule that the efficient enforcement of the rights established by Part I and II cannot be subject to any limitations that are not listed in these parts, with the exception of those determined by law legislated in Member States and essential for the protection of public interest, national security, public health, or morals. The Committee-declared derogations of the Charter should be well-founded, and should lead to the achievement of one of these aims.[4] The authorities of Member States refer to grounds on which the provisions of the Charter are not abided by or only partially followed in their reports. It was with regard to the right to strike colliding with the rights of other persons: patients in hospitals,[5] financial situation of employers,[6] limitations of the right to negotiate collective work agreements,

1. *See* the verdicts of the European Tribunal of Human Rights in the cases: *Lawless v. Ireland*, 3 Eur. Ct. H. R. (ser. A) 1961; *Ireland v. United Kingdom*, 25 Eur. Ct. H. R. (ser. A) 1978.
2. *See* the verdict of the European Tribunal of Human Rights in the case: *Branningan and Mc Bride v. United Kingdom*, 258 Eur.Ct.H.R. (Ser. A), 1993.
3. The history of the Council of Europe does not know a case of temporary derogation of the provisions of the Charter due to these reasons. Neither Turkish invasion of Cyprus of 1974 nor the threatening of public security in Northern Ireland initiated the analysed legal mechanism.
4. Conclusions XIV-1, p. 622 (Norway).
5. *Ibid.*, in case of limitations of the right to strike for the hospital personnel.
6. Conclusions XIV-1, p. 555 (the Netherlands).

introduction of the compulsory arbitration in cases of collective work disputes on the basis of protection of public interest.[7] National security considerations provided grounds to derogate the rights to associate of the governmental telecommunication centre in Great Britain.[8] Security reasons were used as the explanation for destroying housing resources by the Turkish authorities.[9] The Committee in the early stage of the supervisory cycle made a ruling that set a firm precedent for the following supervisory cycles, stating the reasons for derogations of the provisions of the Charter by the Member States listed in this document cannot be applied for any purpose other than that for which they have been prescribed. The limitations are necessary. They also should be proportionate to the aims they purport to further. In turn, these aims cannot be flagrantly disproportionate to the social rights guaranteed by the Charter. In the literature devoted to the social rights regulated by the Charter the terms deriving from the terminology of labour law are used *expressis veribis*, for example forbidding the authorities of the Member States to abuse power (*détornament de pouvoir*).[10] The rulings presented in the previous chapters of this book give evidence that the authorities of the Member States have groundlessly referred to the analysed provisions of the Charter (Article 31 § 1 ESC and Article G § 1 RESC) several times in order to limit the application of some provisions in particular situations. Derogations of the Charter are exceptionally permissible in a 'democratic society'. The Committee did not interpret this term. It was agreed by all Member States of the Council of Europe to meet the requirements in order to be considered democratic.[11] Membership in the Council of Europe gives each of the states the right to introduce derogations of the Charter in order to protect values listed in Article 31 § 1 ESC and Article G § 1 RESC.

10.3. Derogations of the Provisions Specified by the Charter to the Significant Majority of Workers

The Charter, which is listed among international sources of labour law and social security law, can be implemented into the internal legal system of Member States either by legal provisions legislated by the relevant state institutions (acts, decrees) or by collective work agreements or other normative acts negotiated by stakeholders. The Charter does not exclude other methods of incorporation of its provisions into the national legal system where the enforcement of these provisions is guaranteed. Some Member States have succeeded by using a combination of legislation and negotiated collective work agreements or employing other adequate measures (custom). Regardless of the legislative technique, the authorities of the Member States are responsible for adjusting national regulations to comply with the ratified provisions.

---

7. Conclusions XII, pp. 122–123 (the Netherlands); Conclusions XIV-1, p. 387 (Iceland); p. 623 (Norway).
8. Conclusions XI, p. 80.
9. Conclusions XIII-3, p. 466.
10. D. Harris, J. Darcy, *op. cit.*, p. 382.
11. *Ibid.*, s. 381; A. Bleckmann, *Interprétation et application en Droit interne de la Charte sociale européenne, notamment du Droit de grève*, Cahiers de Droit Europeen, 1967, p. 395.

Article 33 ESC and Article I RESC introduce some exceptions to this rule. They allow for the implementation of certain provisions (Article 2 § 1, 2, 3, 4; Article 7 § 4, 6, 7; Article 10 § 1, 2, 3, 4), while the Appendixes to the Charter broaden the range of this exemption onto Article 5 § 5 and Article 7 § 8, as far as the 'great majority of the workers' is concerned. The Committee declares that Member States that utilize these exceptions do not abuse their entitlements when provisions listed in Article 33 ESC and Article I RESC are complied with for 80 per cent of workers concerned.[12]

The provisions that allow the authorities of the Member States to introduce exceptions to the enforcement of the provisions cannot be abused, including the analysed provisions of Article 33 ESC and Article I RESC as well as the Appendixes to these Charters. Abuse of the latter takes place when 20 per cent of the workers' protected are located within one national or ethnic group.[13] In order to minimize abuse of the provision in question, it is necessary for the Charter to ensure that specified social rights are applied to the majority (at least 80 per cent) of workers concerned. This term stands for all categories of workers whose rights should be protected under the provision listed in Article 33 § 1 ESC and Article I § 2 RESC. It is of no significance to the Committee that the majority of workers on the national, occupational or regional scale are encompassed by the legal protection, if they are not, for example, young workers who should be legally protected under Article 7 § 4, 6, and 7.

10.4. Territorial Application of the Charter

The Charter is applied within the metropolitan territory of the Member States (Article 34 § 1 ESC and Article L § 1 RESC). Whether a territory is to be considered a metropolitan territory of a particular state is determined by the authorities of the Member State in a declaration addressed to the Secretary-General of the Council of Europe. The application of the Charter can be extended in whole or in part to a non-metropolitan territory or territories for whose international relations a particular Member State, party to the Charter, is responsible or for which it assumes international responsibility (Article 34 § 2 ESC and Article L § 2 RESC).[14] Member States with no metropolitan territories are not obligated to deliver reports on the lack of application of some parts or the whole Charter on such territories. According to Article 34 § 2 ESC and the Article L § 2 RESC declaration, the application of the Charter on non-metropolitan territory of a given Member State is considered as a necessary legal condition. Some Member States choose to deliver the declaration on not applying the Charter on the territory of non-metropolitan areas. [15]

12. Conclusions XIII-5, p. 47 (Finland); p. 158 (Portugal).
13. Conclusions VIII, p. 139 (Austria).
14. Making use of this provisions Great Britain extended the application of the Charter for the Isle of Man. The Netherlands introduced Article 1, 5 and 6 (with the exception of civil servants) and Article 16 of the Charter as well as Article 1 of the Additional Protocol and Article 1 of the Additional Protocol of 1988 on the Dutch Antilles and Aruba. France extended all provisions of the Additional Protocol of 1988 for all overseas districts.
15. Norway sent a declaration informing the Charter is not applied on the 'subsidiary territories'.

Changes to the metropolitan territories of the Member States imply automatic changes in the Charter's application. Incorporation of a state by a Member State such as in the case of the unification of Germany causes the obligations of the Charter to be applied to the new metropolitan territory.[16] The loss of a part of a territory by a Member State eventuates in cessation of *de facto* responsibility on behalf of the authorities of the said state for the Charter enforcement, if the territory that has divided itself off did not obtain international status.[17] New Member States, which gained independence, considered legal entities in terms of international public law, may decide independently upon the ratification of the Charter and the acceptance of the duties of applying its provisions in their metropolitan territories.[18] Territorial changes have a significant impact on the application or derogation of the Charter or its irrelevance.

The Charter does not allow for sending a declaration informing about derogation of the ratified provisions with regard to specified categories of workers. Some of the Member States (France, the Netherlands, Germany, Norway) delivered a declaration regarding the exemption from some provisions in cases of specified categories of workers.[19] The remaining Member States that were informed about these reservations did not respond. The Committee accepted the notified reservations and declarations as fact and made a ruling on the basis of a formal distinction between the notices delivered by the Member States authorities, stating that the case of violation of Article 6 § 4 by Germany in which civil servants were deprived of the right to participate in collective actions expressed in the declaration of not abiding by Article 6 § 4 was not regarded as a reservation.[20] From these cases it can be derived that in spite of the lack of a reservation clause in the Charter, the authorities of the Member States are capable, by formal notification, of limiting the Charter application (or at least some of its provisions) in cases of particular categories of workers.

16. Conclusions XII-2, p. 11; Conclusions XIII-2, p. 23.
17. Case of the northern part of Cyprus which, as a consequence of the Turkish invasion of 1974, tore off from Cyprus but is not a legal entity of international law.
18. Cases of the European states who came into being from the former republics of the Soviet Union and Yugoslavia.
19. The Netherlands and Germany ratified Article 6 § 4 of the Charter with the reservation that the right to strike cannot be utilized by the civil servants.
20. Conclusions IV, p. 49.

Part III The Supervision of Complying with the Laws of the European Social Charter

CHAPTER 11 SUPERVISORY BODIES

11.1. The European Committee of Social Rights

The Committee performs three basic functions: it establishes the European standards in terms of labour law, social security and social policy; examines the reports delivered by the authorities of Member States and declares compliance or non-compliance of the national regulations with the standards established under the Charter; and recognizes collective complaints registered by international workers and employers organizations as well as other non-governmental organizations against Member States. Originally the Committee operated under the name the Committee of Independent Experts. This name emphasized the independence of the Committee members from the authorities of the Member States. In 1998 the authorities of the Member States renamed the body 'The European Committee of Social Rights' in order to stress the role of the Committee as an objective body called up for the substantial supervision over the enforcement of human rights guaranteed by the Charter.

Article 25 § 1 ESC declares that the Committee consists of not more than seven members chosen from the list of independent experts 'of the highest integrity and of recognized competence in international social questions'. The Charter does not require the members of the Committee to be lawyers. With two exceptions,[1] the Committee consists of professors of labour law and social security law as well as former judges of the highest courts in the Member States.[2] The authorities of the Member States propose

1. Amongst the current members of the Committee, two are social policy specialists, one of them being the President the Social-Economic Council of Portugal.
2. Members of the Committee are: the former President of the national Norwegian labour court, the former judge of the Belgian Constitutional Tribunal (Cour d'arbitrage), the judge of the French State Council (Conseil d'Etat). About the qualifications of the first members of the Committee F.Sur writes in, La Charte sociale européenne: Dix années d'application 1965-1975, Annuaire européen, vol.12, M.Nijhoff, La Haye 1974, p. 91. In the past the members of the Committee had experience in the International Labour Organization. The members of the Committee were: the Belgian, L. Troclet (1972-1978), the former President of ILO, the British: W. James (1980-1982), the former President of the International Labour Conference, M. Morgan (1976-1980), the former representative of the government to the Administrative Council of ILO. Amongst the members of

candidates for Committee membership. The Committee has gained new competences that, since passage of the Additional Protocol to the European Social Charter in 1995 introducing the system of collective complaints, has included acting as an international quasi judicial body. Consequently, and in light of the increased number of Members States of the Council of Europe, the number of Committee members was increased to 9[3] and then to 15.[4] A comparison of the number of Member States (46) with the number of Committee members (15) indicates that only citizens of some Member States of the Council of Europe sit on the Committee. Unlike the judges of the European Tribunal of Human Rights who are equal in number to the number of Member States of the Council of Europe, the members of the Committee of Social Rights do not act as representatives of the Member States. They hold the seat 'on their own behalf'. While serving their mandate they are not allowed to perform any functions inconsistent with the requirements of independence, objectivity, or availability, connected with the above role (Article 3 of Amending Protocol ESC of 21 October 1991).[5] Taking into consideration the rule that members of the Committee do not represent the Member States, the Committee of Ministers attempts to gather representation of different geographical regions of Europe within the Committee. This tendency is manifest in the election proceedings. The Committee members are elected for a six year-long tenure. They can be re-elected. The tenure of the two members elected for the first time ends after four years. Members chosen to fill in for those who have left will stay for the remaining time of the tenure of the predecessor (Article 25 ESC). The Committee of Ministers regulates the election procedure that divides the Member States of the Council of Europe into five groups and determines the number of the future Committee members belonging to each group. The last Committee election took place in 2004 and the groups were divided as follows:[6]

- Group 1 (three seats on the Committee): Armenia, Austria, Czech Republic, Liechtenstein, Germany, Slovakia, Switzerland, and Hungary;
- Group 2 (two seats on the Committee): Azerbaijan, Belgium, Bulgaria, France, the Netherlands, Luxembourg, Moldova, Romania, and Turkey;
- Group 3 (three seats on the Committee): Denmark, Finland, Ireland, Iceland, Norway, Sweden, and Great Britain;

---

the Committee there were also outstanding scholars specializing in labour law: Sir Otto Kahn Freund, Great Britain (1966-1972) and Rudolf Strasser, Austria (1970-1973).

3. Decision of the Committee of Ministers made during the 509th sitting in March 1994, European Social Charter ... *op. cit.*, p. 189.
4. Decision of the Committee of Ministers made during the 751st sitting on 2-7 May 2001. *Ibid.*
5. Because of acceding the role of vice Commissary of Employment and Social Matters of the European Union, L. Samuel resigned from being the member of the European Committee of Social Rights in May 2005. Previously, to become a member of the Committee, L. Samuel gave up the role of the Secretary of State in the Labour Ministry of Cyprus. Her place was taken by Ms. E. Spatafora from Italy. In March 2006 Mr. G. Quinn stepped down from the Committee of Social Rights.
6. 4.3 decision of the Committee of Ministers made during the 881st sitting on14 April 2004, European Social Charter, ... *op. cit.*, pp. 190–191.

- Group 4 (three seats on the Committee): Albania, Andorra, Cyprus, Georgia, Greece, Spain, Malta, Portugal, Italy and San Marino;
- Group 5 (three seats on the Committee): Bosnia and Herzegovina, Croatia, Estonia, Lithuania, Latvia, the former republic of Yugoslavia Macedonia, Poland, the Russian Federation, Slovenia, Ukraine.

The Committee sits on plenary sessions as well as in two working groups, that take place on average 7–8 times during the calendar year. The sittings of the Committee are closed, and the Committee members are obligated to keep the debates confidential. The Committee is in charge of deciding upon the public session when it deals with collective complaints. The work of the Committee is managed and administrated by a board consisting of the chairman, the two vice-chairmen, the general reporter and the secretary executive. The rules of conduct for the Committee and its members are listed in the Statute of Conduct passed on 29 March 2004.[7] It specifies the procedure employed in the process of analysing the reports delivered by the authorities of the Member States. The Member States are obligated to deliver reports of two kinds, one under Article 21 about the ratified provisions and the other under Article 22 about the provisions that have not been ratified. The abovementioned provisions of the European Social Charter create legal grounds for delivering the reports by the Member States. According to the regulation of Article C of the Revised European Social Charter, the controlling mechanism determined in Article 21 and 22 ESC applies to the process of supervision over the enforcement of the ratified provisions of the Revised European Social Charter. As part of its supervision of the enforcement of the Charter by the Member States, the Committee, operating on the basis of Article 21, analyses the reports of the Member State authorities and makes a ruling declaring compliance or non-compliance with the national regulations and with the Charter. According to Article 22 the Committee familiarizes itself with the reasons why the authorities of the Member States did not ratify the provisions.

11.1.1. Reports Concerning the Ratified Provisions of the Charter (Article 21)

The authorities of the Member States are obligated to present to the Secretary-General of the Council of Europe reports on the enforcement of the provisions once every two years. The Secretary-General forwards these reports to the Committee, which performs a content-related examination. In the period of the first eight supervisory cycles, the Member States delivered the reports concerning the enforcement of all ratified provisions. In order to improve the supervisory process, the Committee of Ministers divided the Member States into two groups during the 336th session on 27 January 1984. The Member States of the first group were obligated to deliver reports in uneven years, beginning from the ninth supervisory cycle in 1985.[8] The Member States of the second

7. Rules of procedure in: European Social Charter ... *op. cit.*, pp. 193 and following.
8. Supervision of the application of the European Social Charter (in:) European Social Charter ... *op. cit.*, pp. 408 and following.

group were obligated to deliver reports in even years. A reservation that the reports dealt with only a part of the ratified provisions was issued in the annual deliverance of a report during the 13th supervisory cycle as a result of the increase in the number of Member States. During the 13th supervisory cycle that took place between 1994 and 1997, five types of supervisory cycles were distinguished.[9] Regardless of the above, the division of the Charter's provisions into the two categories was made: the first category encompasses the provisions listed in Article 20 § 1(b) ESC[10] and in Article A § 1(b) RESC[11] (*hard core provisions*); the remaining provisions were classified to the second category. The authorities of Member States were obligated to present the reports on the enforcement of the first category of Charter provisions in four-year cycles. In the following 14th supervisory cycle, only the provisions from the second category were examined. The frequency of these reports was set at the biannual level. A further division into two groups was made. The first group consisted of Articles 2, 3, 4, 9, 10 ESC and the Additional Protocol of 1988, while the second group included Articles 7, 8, 11, 14, 17, 18 ESC as well as Article 1 § 4 of the Additional Protocol of 1988. The chronological order of the analysis of the reports concerning the enforcement of the European Social Charter in the Member States performed by the Committee was as follows:

- 1999–2002 (XVII-2 supervisory cycle) – the provisions of the second group: Article 1 § 4, Articles 2, 3, 4, 9, 10, 15 and Articles 2 and 3 of the Additional Protocol of 1988;
- 2003–2004 (XVIII-1 supervisory cycle) – the provisions of the first group: Articles 1[12], 5, 6, 12, 13, 19;
- 2001–2004 (XVIII-2 supervisory cycle) – the provisions of the second group: Articles 7, 8, 11, 14, 17, 18 and 1 and 4 of the Additional Protocol of 1988;
- 2005–2006 (XIX-1 supervisory cycle) – the provisions of the first group: Articles 1[13], 5, 6, 12, 13, 19);
- 2003–2006 (XIX-2 supervisory cycle) – the provisions of the second group: Article 1 § 4, Articles 2, 3, 4, 9, 10, 15 and Articles 2 and 3 of the Additional Protocol.[14]

The chronological order of the analysis of the reports concerning the enforcement of the Revised European Social Charter in years 2002–2004 was as follows:

- 2002 – the provisions of the first group: Article 1 § 1, 2 and 3, Articles 5, 6, 7, 12, 13, 16, 19, 20;

9. *Ibid.*, pp. 439 and following.
10. Article 1, 5, 6, 12, 13, 16 and 19.
11. Article 1, 5, 6, 7, 12, 13, 16, 19 and 20.
12. With the exception of Article 1 § 4 ESC.
13. *Ibid.*
14. Reporting system (in:) European Social Charter ... *op. cit.*, p. 241.

- 2003 – the provisions of the second group: Article 1 § 4, Articles 2, 3, 4, 8, 11, 14, 17, 18, 21, 22, 24, 25, 26, 27, 28, 29;
- 2004 – the provisions of the first group: Articles 1, 5, 6, 7, 12, 16, 20.

The chronological order of the analysis of the reports concerning the enforcement of the Revised European Social Charter planned by the Committee for the period 2006–2011 is as follows:

- 2006 – the provisions of the first group: Articles 1, 5, 6, 7, 12, 13, 16, 19, 20;
- 2007 – the provisions of the second group: Article1 § 4, Articles 2, 3, 4, 9, 10, 15, 21, 22, 24, 26, 28, 29;
- 2008 – the provisions of the first group;
- 2009 – the provisions of the second group;
- 2010 – the provisions of the first group;
- 2011 – the provisions of the second group.[15]

The complicated system of supervision has been criticized by the authorities of the Member States.[16] The proposal presented by the German authorities intends to cancel the division of the provisions into the two groups and introduce the obligation of delivering the reports on the ratified provisions every four years. On the occasion of the tenth anniversary of the revised European Social Charter the Committee of Ministers at the 963rd meeting of the Ministers' Deputies on 3rd May 2006 adopted a new reporting system effective as from 31st October 2007. The new system is as follows:

- Member States shall present a report annually on a part of the provisions of the Charter (either the 1961 Charter or the 1996 Revised Charter), the provisions having been divided into four thematic groups: Group 1 - Employment, training and equal opportunities (art.1. 9, 10,15, 18, 20, 24, 25); Group 2 - Health, social security and social protection (art. 3, 11, 12,13, 14, 23, 30); Group 3 - Labour rights (art. 2, 4, 5, 6, 21, 22, 26, 28, 29); Group 4 - Children, families, migrants (art. 7, 8, 16, 17, 19, 27, 31);
- There will no longer be full reports for states having recently ratified the 1961 Social Charter and there will no longer be reports on all the non-hard core provisions for states having recently ratified the 1996 revised Social Charter.

Under the current system the dates of report delivery are either on 31 March or 30 June depending on the cycle. Under the new system established on 3rd May 2006 effective from 31st October 2007 the reports shall be presented on 31st October of each year. The European Committee of Social Rights is invited to publish its conclusions before the end of the following year. The Committee of Ministers regulates the

15. *Ibid.*, p. 245.
16. Governmental Committee XIII-3, p. 10.

form of the reports. A questionnaire used for the preparation of the reports on the enforcement of the provisions of the European Social Charter is 50 pages long.[17] A questionnaire concerning the Revised European Social Charter is 50 per cent longer.[18] The questionnaire was approved by the Committee of Ministers during the 689th session on 29 November 1999.[19] The authorities of the Member States comply with the obligation of delivering the reports.[20] Sometimes they deliver the report with a delay.[21] The reports are presented in one of the two official languages of the Council of Europe, English or French. The reports are usually exhaustive studies with the attached provisions written in the language of a state delivering the report. The authorities of the Member States can present copies or summaries of the reports to the International Labour Organization. Taking into account the differences in questionnaires used for the preparation of the reports for the Secretary-General of the Council of Europe and the International Labour Organization, the Committee of Social Rights expressed the opinion that delivering a copy of the report presented to the ILO cannot be regarded as automatically meeting the requirements regulated by the Charter.[22] As the Committee also supervises the practice of abiding by the provisions, it demands from the authorities of the Member States the quotation of the original statistical data. The above obligation is required particularly with regard to the enforcement of Article 2 § 1, 2, 3, 4, 5, Article 7 § 1, 2, 3, 4, art.10, Article 10, the standards ordering the fulfilment of the obligation to the great majority of the workers concerned. During the first three supervisory cycles the Committee rigorously demanded that this obligation be met. During the fourth supervisory cycle, the Committee decreased the requirements in order to reduce costs and declared that the authorities of the Member States can deliver their own statistical data from a different source.[23] The lack of delivery of the above

17. Form for the reports ... *op. cit.*, pp. 247–250.
18. *Ibid.*, pp. 307–383.
19. It was modified by the Committee of Ministers during the 737th session on 17 January 2001; *ibid.*, p. 247, footnote 1. In May 2005 the Committee of Social Rights proposed elaborating of a less complicated questionnaire. For more information on the functions of the questionnaire *see* J.F. Smyt, The implementation of the European Social Charter, Mélange Modinos, A. Pedone, Paris 1968, p. 295.
20. During the sixth supervisory cycle the authorities of Iceland did not deliver the report. Conclusions VI, s. xii
21. Ireland who ratified the Revised European Social Charter on 4 November 2000, entered into force on 1 January 2001 was obligated to deliver the report for the period from 1 January 2001 to 31 December 2004 until 30 June 2004. In May 2005 Ireland presented a part of the report. Italy who ratified the Revised European Social Charter on 5 July 1999 r. (entry into force on1 September1999) was obligated to deliver the report for the period from 1 January 2001 to 31 December 2002 until 30 June 2004. It did so a year later. Luxembourg, who ratified the Revised European Social Charter on 10 October1991 did not deliver the third report for the period of 1 January 2001– 31 December 2002. This report should have been delivered until 30 June 2004. The Committee of Social Right and the Governmental Committee systematically remind the authorities of the Member States about the obligation of presenting the reports within three to six months after the supervisory cycle is finished. *See* Conclusions XIV, p. 123; Governmental Conclusions XI-2, p. 9; Governmental Conclusions XIII, p. 116.
22. Conclusions III, p. xvii.
23. Conclusions IV, p. xvi.

data justifies the delay in ruling upon the compliance or non-compliance of the national regulations and practices with the international standards. The Committee has elaborated the practice of warning a Member State when it does not deliver the required information for the second time. When this occurs, the Committee includes in its notification of the postponed compliance ruling a warning that failure to fulfil this obligation for the third time will result in the negative ruling declaring non-compliance of the particular provisions by a given Member State.[24] The Amending Protocol to the European Social Charter passed on 21 October 1991 revises Article 24 ESC and authorizes the Committee to communicate directly with the Member States and to request the delivery of additional information and clarifications. It also allows for the organization of direct meetings with the representatives of the authorities of Member States when necessary. Either the Committee or the authorities of the interested states may initiate such a meeting (Article 24 § 3 ESC in relation to Article C RESC).

The rulings of the Committee are not of a binding character. They are well-prepared opinions of a group of international experts of labour and social security law as well as social policies that help the Committee of Ministers to take a position about a Member State not abiding by the human rights protected under the Charter.

11.1.2. Reports Concerning Provisions of the Charter that have not Been Ratified (Article 22)

The Committee of Ministers have a right to request the authorities of the Member States to deliver the reports concerning the relationship between the national regulations and the application thereof in practice and the provisions that have not been ratified. Until 1978 the Committee of Ministers never utilized this right. In 1978 it obligated the authorities of the Member States to deliver reports concerning Article 4 § 3, Article 7 § 1 and Article 8 § 1 and 2. In 1981 it demanded that the Member States deliver the reports concerning Article 2 § 4, Article7 § 4, Article 8 § 4 and Article 19. In 1993 it demanded the delivery of reports concerning Article 7 § 9 and Article 19 § 4. In 1995 it demanded the delivery of reports concerning Article 4 § 4. In 1997 it demanded the delivery of reports concerning Article 5. Finally, a decision was passed four to one by the Committee of Ministers during the 821st session on 11 December 2002, obligating the authorities of the Member States to deliver reports concerning the national legal regulations and the practical application of these provisions in relation to the unratified provisions of the Revised European Social Charter every five years.[25] The Committee of Ministers authorized the Committee of Social Rights to analyse the reports delivered on the basis of Article 22. The common practice of the Committee is to organize meetings with the representatives of the authorities in order to familiarize itself with the reasons why particular Member States did not ratify the provisions and to exchange

24. Conclusions V, p. xvi.
25. Implementation of Article 22 for states having ratified the Revised European Social Charter as from 2003 (in:) European Social Charter ... *op. cit.*, pp. 501–502.

thoughts and opinions on the possibilities of ratification of some of these provisions. On the basis of Article 22, the Committee analysed the reports and attended meetings with the authorities of the following Member States: Sweden[26] (2003), Romania[27], Slovenia[28] and Italy[29] (2004), Estonia[30] (2005). In 2005, the Committee planned its missions to Bulgaria[31], Ireland[32] and Cyprus[33] within the confines of the procedure regulated under Article 22. The procedure determined in Article 22 allows the members of the Committee to familiarize themselves with the system of labour law and social security law, as well as the social policies of the supervised state. On the other hand, the authorities of this state have the opportunity to acknowledge the judicial decisions of the Committee concerning provisions of the Revised European Social Charter that have not been ratified. The members of the Committee act as technical advisors. They examine the national regulations of labour and social security law as well as the application thereof in practice and are able to evaluate the chances that the Committee will make a ruling stating the conformity of the analysed provisions within the international standards. The opinions expressed by them are not binding on the Committee.

The copies of the report presented to the Committee by the Member States on the basis of Article 21 and Article 22 should be forwarded to the national organizations of workers and employers – the participants of the international organizations of stakeholders – who are invited, according to Article 27 § 2 ESC, to partake in the sittings of the Subcommittee of the Governmental Social Committee. The copies of the national reports are also sent to the relevant international non-governmental organizations that comprise the advisory bodies to the Council of Europe (Article 23 § 1). These bodies have the right to present their comments on the reports to the Secretary-General of the Council of Europe. The authorities of the Member States may inform the Secretary-General as to any response they may have tot these comments. Supervisory rights granted to the stakeholders under Article 23 create the fundamental element of the supervisory mechanism employed by the Committee to control the enforcement of the provisions of the Charter by the Member States. The reports, comments and responses are available once they are published.

11.2. The Governmental Committee

The Governmental Committee consists of the representatives of the authorities of the Member States. Each state has one representative on the Committee. They are civil servants of the respective ministries dealing with issues of labour and social policies. The authorities of those Member States that have signed but not ratified the Charter

26. Sweden did not ratify 15 provisions of RESC.
27. Romania did not ratify 33 provisions of RESC.
28. Slovenia did not ratify provisions of RESC.
29. Italy did not ratify provisions of RESC.
30. Estonia did not ratify 19 provisions of RESC.
31. Bulgaria did not ratify 37 provisions of RESC.
32. Ireland did not ratify 6 provisions of RESC.
33. Cyprus did not ratify 34 provisions of RESC.

have a right to delegate an observer to the Governmental Committee. The status of the observer is also enjoyed by no more than two international organizations of employers and two international organizations of workers (trade unions) invited to participate in the Committee sessions. Those international non-governmental organizations, that act as the consultative bodies to the Council of Europe may present, at the request of the Governmental Committee, opinions concerning the matters on the agenda of a particular session of the Committee.

The Governmental Committee is the political consultative body to the Committee of Ministers. Article 27 § 3 revised by the Amending Protocol to the European Social Charter passed on 21 October 1991 states that the Governmental Committee is obligated to prepare the decisions of the Committee of Ministers. Within the confines of this competence, the Governmental Committee is obligated to select the cases to be referred to in the recommendations issued by the Committee of Ministers addressed to the Member States that do not abide by the provisions of the Charter. In presenting the cases of non-compliance, the Governmental Committee chooses 'in a well-grounded way the basis of the examination concerning social and economic policies' situations which, according to its opinion, should be commented on in the recommendations addressed to the Member State according to Article 28 (Article 27 § 3). When selecting cases, the Governmental Committee should be guided by the evaluation and rulings made by the Committee of Social Rights. For a long period of time there were differences in terms of the application of the Charter between the Governmental Committee and the Committee of Independent Experts, renamed the Committee of Social Rights in 1998.[34] As early as the first supervisory cycle, the Committee of Independent Experts declared the lack of enforcement of a significant number of provisions in the case of the majority of the Member States that delivered the reports and postponed the decisions due to the missing information. This caused the Governmental Committee to react. The Governmental Committee accused the Committee of Independent Experts of too rigorous interpretations of the provisions of the Charter and produced its independent interpretation. This unclear division of the competences of the said Committees caused rivalry between them. From the time of the first to the 11th supervisory cycle, the reports of the Member States were evaluated differently by the two Committees, as the Governmental Committee claimed it had a right to make content-related evaluations of the reports previously evaluated by the Committee of Independent Experts. Like the Committee of Independent Experts, the Governmental Committee took into consideration political issues. According to the original version of Article 27 § 1 ESC, conclusions of the Committee of Independent Experts were forwarded for examination to the Subcommittee of the Governmental Social Committee of the Council of Europe. The Subcommittee delivered the report, including its own remarks, to the Committee of Ministers. The report of the Committee of Independent Experts was attached to this report (Article 27 § 3 ESC). Until the Amending Protocol to the European Social Charter of 21 October 1991 came into force, the Consultative Assembly of the Council

34. The details are presented in detail by D. Darcy, J. Harris, *op. cit.*, pp. 331 and following.

of Europe, renamed the Parliamentary Assembly in 1973, also partook in the supervisory process over the enforcement of the provisions of the Charter. It was entitled to pass the remarks regarding the report of the Committee of Independent Experts to the Committee of Ministers. The supervisory process over the enforcement of the international standards in terms of the protection of social rights by the Member States was complicated. The content-related evaluation made by the Committee of Independent Experts was given lesser importance because of the remarks made by the political bodies. The Amending Protocol to the European Social Charter of 21 October 1991 revised the content of Article 27 and 28. It excluded the Parliamentary Assembly from participation in the supervisory process and specified the competence of the Governmental Committee. It also changed the Committee into a body entitled solely to make decisions regarding cases of violation of provisions of the Charter by Member States, declared by the Committee of Independent Experts and presented to the Committee of Ministers. The Amending Protocol to the European Social Charter of 21 October 1991 regulated the mechanism of supervision over the enforcement of the provisions of the Charter. The Governmental Committee examines the negative rulings made by the Committee of Social Rights and relies on economic and social factors to decide which these cases should be presented to the Committee of Ministers. The Governmental Committee takes into account political factors as well. The high level of unemployment, which, according to the Committee of Social Rights is evidence of violating Article 1 § 1, can be justified by the Governmental Committee through measures aimed at economic reform. The Governmental Committee pays attention to whether the provisions belonging to the first or the second group of the provisions have been breached, what the position of the stakeholders was, and from what supervisory cycle the Committee of Social Rights makes such rulings on the non-compliance of a particular provision. Firstly, it is interested in the reaction of the authorities of a Member State to the negative ruling made by the Committee of Social Rights. The Governmental Committee has elaborated the practice of warning the Member State authorities that if they fail to adapt their national regulations and the applications thereof in practice to the international standards determined by the Charter, the next supervisory cycle will bring the matter before the Committee of Ministers with the request to pass the motion. The decision about the issuing of a warning is passed by a 2:3 qualified majority of votes of the Governmental Committee.[35] The practice of warning the authorities of the Member States was accepted by the European Tribunal of Human Rights.[36]

The reports of the authorities of the Member States on the relation between the national regulation, the application thereof, and the provisions not ratified by a particular Member State are also presented to the Governmental Committee (Article 27 § 1). The Governmental Committee presents its report to the Committee of Ministers. On the basis of this report, the Committee of Ministers is entitled to pass a resolution. The reports of the Governmental Committee are available to the public (Article 27

35. Governmental Conclusions XII-1, p. 14.
36. Sigurjonsson v. Iceland, 264 Eur. Ct. H.R. (ser. A) (1993).

§ 3 in a version revised by the Amending Protocol to the European Social Charter). The reports of the Governmental Committee concerning introduction of the provisions of the Charter in the Member States can provide the grounds for elaborate proposals suggesting undertaking research on social issues and the provisions of the Charter. The addressee of these proposals is the Committee of Ministers. The Governmental Committee operates as the consultative body to the Committee of Ministers in matters concerning the range and protection of social rights.

11.3. The Committee of Ministers

The Committee of Ministers adopts by a 2:3 qualified majority of votes of the representatives of the Member States that are party to the Charter[37] a resolution concerning the entire supervisory cycle as well as the individual recommendations addressed to particular Member States. The basis for the resolution passed by the Committee of Ministers is the report of the Governmental Committee (Article 28 § 1, a version revised by the Amending Protocol to the European Social Charter of 21 October 1991). The Charter does not specify any guidelines for the Governmental Committee in terms of adapting resolutions and recommendations. Article 28 § 2 states that the Committee of Ministers '*shall take such decisions as it deems appropriate'*. The alteration of the procedure eventuated in a situation when the Committee of Ministers from the 12th supervisory cycle in 1993 started passing resolutions and individual recommendations on the basis of the rulings of the Committee of Independent Experts (the Committee of Social Rights) concerning non-conformity between the national legal regulations, the application thereof and the international standards. The first two individual recommendations were general. They obligated the authorities of the Member States to inform about measures undertaken in relation to the negative ruling of the Committee of Independent Experts.[38] The Committee of Ministers in its third recommendation obligated the Norwegian authorities to change the regulation considered by the Committee of Independent Experts as contradicting Article 6 § 4 and Article 7 § 3.[39] During the 13th supervisory cycle, the Committee of Ministers adopted 22 individual recommendations sent to the authorities of 12 Member

37. Decision on voting in the Committee of Ministers Adopted by the Committee of Ministers in April 1993 at the 492nd meeting of the Ministers' Deputies (in:) European Social Charter, *op. cit.*, p. 225; Decision on the adoption of recommendations under the European Social Charter Adopted by the Committee of Ministers on 22 June 1995 at the 541st meeting of the Ministers' Deputies, *ibid.*, p. 227; Rules of Procedure for the adoption of recommendations under the European Social Charter. Adopted by the Committee of Ministers on 17 December 1998 at the 653rd meeting of the Ministers' Deputies, *ibid.*, p. 229.
38. Recommendations: No. R ChS (93)1 adopted on 7 September 1993 addressed to Greece (Article1 § 2, Article 13 § 1 and 4). Supervision of the Application of the European Social Charter (in:) European Social Charter, *op. cit.*, pp. 427-428; No.R ChS (93) 3 (Great Britain, Article 6 § 4, Article 8 § 1).
39. Recommendation No.R Chs (93) 3, *ibid.*, pp. 430–431.

States.[40] During the 14th supervisory cycle the Committee of Ministers adopted three individual recommendations.[41] During the two last supervisory cycles (15th and 16th) the Committee of Ministers adopted individual recommendations sent to the authorities of Ireland,[42] Malta,[43] Germany,[44] and Turkey.[45]

In 2005, in the course of supervising the enforcement of the provisions of the Revised European Social Charter, the Committee of Ministers passed a resolution addressed to the authorities of all Member States who had ratified this international treaty and prescribed taking into consideration observations made by the Committee of Social Rights published after the supervisory cycle had finished.[46] In 2003 the Committee addressed one individual recommendation to the Italian authorities.[47] The individual recommendations are not of binding character. Those Member States that have representatives within the Committee of Ministers act as judges in their own matters. Taking part in the resolution process is based upon substantial political reasons. The level of influence of the Committee of Ministers' resolution on the said authorities of the Member States is decided by the international pressure of the opinions of these Member States that are adapting to the international standards of human rights protection regulated by the Charter.

---

40. Austria (Article 5), Denmark (Article 5, 6 § 2 and 4); France (Article 1 § 2, Article 17); Greece Article 7 § 1,3, Article 18 § 2, Article19 § 1 and 8; Ireland (Article 1 § 2, Article 4 § 4, Article 6 § 4, Article 7 § 3, Article 19 § 8); Italy (Article 1 § 2, Article 3 § 2, Article 4 § 4 and 5, Article7 § 2, 4); Spain (Article 1 § 2); Malta (Article 5, 6 § 4); Germany (Article 6 § 4); Norway (Article 7 § 3); Portugal (Article 7 § 1); Sweden (Article 19 § 8); Turkey (Article 11 § 1, Article 16), *ibid.*, pp. 439 and following.
41. Austria (Article 5); Ireland (Article 5, 6 § 2); Turkey (Article 4 § 3), *ibid.*, pp. 469 and following.
42. ResChS (2001) 2, Article 6 § 4, *ibid.*, pp. 477-478; ResChS (2002)1, Article 7 § 3, *ibid.*, pp. 480–481; ResChS(2004)4, Article 5, 6 § 2, Article 19 § 8, *ibid.*, pp. 482–483;
43. RecChS (2001) 3, Article 6 § 2, *ibid.*, pp. 478–479.

CHAPTER 12 ADJUDICATING COLLECTIVE COMPLAINTS

12.1. Introduction

The Additional Protocol of 1995 to the European Social Charter introducing the collective complaint procedure gave the Committee of Social Rights the status of a quasi-judicial body.[1] The Committee was vested with the power to examine collective complaints lodged by selected international and national organizations against the authorities of those Member States that were violating the provisions of the European Social Charter or the Revised European Social Charter by failing to adapt their domestic labour and social insurance legislation to European standards. The Additional Protocol of 1995 was made available for signing on 9 November 1995. It came into force on 1 July 1998, upon ratification by eight European states.[2] The signatories of the Protocol could include only states that had ratified the European Social Charter of 1961. Six such states signed the Additional Protocol, undertaking to comply with its provisions.[3] Two other states, signatories of the Revised European Social Charter of 1996, declared that they would abide by the provisions of the Protocol.[4] Therefore, the examination procedure for collective complaints followed by the Committee of Social Rights, applies to 15 out of 46 Member States of the Council of Europe.

The provisions of the Additional Protocol of 1995 are based on the procedures applicable in proceedings of the ILO Committee on Freedom of Association.[5] This Committee has less power than the Committee of Social Rights of the Council

1. A. Świątkowski, *Quasi* judykacyjna funkcja ... (Quasi-Judicial Function ...) *op. cit.*, p. 46 and following; Idem, Funciones causijurisdiccionales ... *op. cit.*, p. 533 and following; Idem, European Social Charter: Protection of Human (Social) Rights by the Collective Complaints Procedure, Zeitsschrift für auslǒndisches und internatioales Arbeits-und Sozialrecht. vol. 6, 2006, p. 320 and following. R. Brillat, The Supervisory Machinery of the European Social Charter: recent Developments and Their Impact (in:) Social Rights in Europe, eds. G. de Búrca, B. de Witte, L. Ogertschnig, Oxford 2005, p.31 ff.
2. Cyprus, Finland, France, Greece, Norway, Portugal, Sweden and Italy.
3. Austria, Belgium, Croatia, Denmark, Netherlands, Slovakia.
4. Bulgaria and Slovenia.
5. The full name of the Committee is: the Freedom of Association Committee of the Governing Body of the ILO.

of Europe. The Committee on Freedom of Association deals only with complaints concerning the violation by the authorities of Member States of rights related to freedom of association. The Committee of Social Rights examines collective complaints lodged against the authorities of Member States of the Council of Europe concerning the violation of economic and social rights, including the freedom to organize in trade unions and in employers' organizations (Article 5), guaranteed under the Social Charters.

12.2. Entities Entitled to Initiate Collective Complaints Proceedings

Under the Additional Protocol of 1995 the following types of organizations are entitled to lodge collective complaints: international employers' organizations and trade unions invited by the Sub-committee of the Governmental Committee[6](Article 27 § 2 the European Social Charter). The cited provision provides for the invitation of no more than two international organizations of employers and no more than two international trade union organizations to be represented as observers in a consultative capacity at meetings of the Governmental Committee. Although the European Social Charter protects mainly the rights of employees,[7] one international trade union organization (the European Trade Union Confederation – ETUC) and two international employers' associations (the Union of the Confederation of Industry and Employers of Europe – UNICE and the International Organization of Employers – IOE) have been invited to participate in the proceedings of the Governmental Committee. These organizations are entitled to initiate proceedings in collective complaints (Article 1(a) Additional Protocol of 1995) UNDO with international non-governmental organizations (INGOs) having a consultative status with the Council of Europe and placed on a list established for this purpose by the Governmental Committee (Article 1(b) of the Protocol).[8] To be included on the list, an organization has to fulfil certain conditions stipulated in the decisions of the Committee of Ministers of the Council of Europe of 22 June 1995.[9]Any INGOs that

6. The former name of the Committee was the Governmental Social Committee.
7. Article 6 § 4 of the European Social Charter guarantees the employers the right to undertake collective actions, hence, it gives them the right to organize defensive lockouts. *See* European Social Charter, Committee of Independent Experts, Conclusions I, 1969-70, Council of Europe Press, Strasbourg 1995, pp. 38,40; Conclusions III, p. 38; Conclusions V, p. 48; Conclusions VI, p.39–40; Conclusions VIII, p. 95; Conclusions IX-2, pp. 47–49; Conclusions XV-1, vol. 1 (Belgium), p. 81, (Cyprus), p.123; Addendum to Conclusions XV-1 (Germany), p. 27. *See* The right to organize and to bargain collectively. Study drawn up based on case law of the European Social Charter, 2nd edition, Council of Europe Publishing, Strasbourg 2001, pp. 79-81; L. Samuel, Fundamental social rights. Case law of the European Social Charter, 2nd edition, Council of Europe Publishing, Strasbourg 2002, p. 167 and following.
8. Registry of 46 organizations placed on the list in Przewodnik po Europejskiej Karcie Społecznej, Wydawnictwo Prawnicze (Guide to the European Social Charter) LexisNexis, Warszawa 2001, pp. 59 and following.
9. Explanatory report to the 1995 Protocol (in:) European Social Charter. Collected texts, 4th edition, Council of Europe Publishing, Strasbourg 2003, p. 149 and following; Podstawowe dokumenty Rady Europy ... (Primary documents of the Council of Europe ...), *op. cit.*, p. 49.

has consultative status with the Council of Europe, is competent in matters governed by the European Social Charter, and has access to sources of information such that it is able to draw up and professionally (from a legal point of view) present its position on matters examined by the Committee of Social Rights of the Council of Europe, may apply for the right to lodge collective complaints.[10] The Secretary-General of the Council of Europe examines the applications for inclusion, and an application is considered accepted by the Governmental Committee unless it is rejected in a ballot by a simple majority of cast votes.[11] An INGO can be placed on the list for a period of four years after which the organization has the right to apply for renewal. The same procedure is applicable in cases of renewing applications.

National employers' representative organizations and trade unions have the right to act within the jurisdiction of a Member State of the Council of Europe, against a state, which they will be entitled to lodge a collective complaint (Article 1(c) of the Protocol). Only employers' and employees' organizations are entitled to apply to be placed on the list. Therefore, those employers who are not members of any employers' organization or association do not have the right to lodge any collective complaints. Trade unions enjoy the status of organizations and, hence, trade unions and associations of trade unions are entitled to apply for entry. Article 1(c) of the Additional Protocol of 1995 also entitles them to apply for entry to the list national organizations. The right of a national employers' organization or a trade union to apply for entry is not conditional on its membership in an international organization of similar character. Only 'represented' employers' organizations and trade unions are eligible for inclusion; however, none of the cited international documents specify any criteria for establishing whether an organization is or is not represented. Neither do they specify a body that would be entitled to make such a determination. The Committee of Ministers of the Council of Europe would rather leave this issue to the authorities of its Member States. Thus, an employers' organization or a trade union that, under the relevant domestic legislation, enjoys the status of a representative organization retains this status for the purpose of the Social Charter of the Council of Europe. Yet, in the absence of any criteria for assessing whether an organization is or is not a representative on a national level, the power to make decisions concerning the status of a national organization applying for entry to the list of organizations entitled to lodge collective complaints is vested in the Committee of Social Rights. Factors such as the number of members and the organization's actual role in national negotiations with stakeholders should be taken into account.[12]

10. R. Brillat, La Charte sociale européenne du Conseil de l'Europe – développemenets récents, Droit en Quart Monde 1996, No.12, p.3 ff. Several hundred of international non-governmental organizations have the right to express their opinions in the Council of Europe.
11. Three organizations that applied for the right to lodge collective complaints have not been included in the list by the Governmental Committee.
12. Explanatory report, *op. cit.*, p. 153. R. Birk (The Collective Complaint: A New Procedure in the European Social Charter [in:] Labour Law and Industrial Relations at the Turn of the Century. Liber Amicoum in Honour of Roger Blanpain, (eds) C. Engels, M. Weiss, Kluwer Law International, The Hague-London-Boston 1998, pp. 265–266 points out that the Additional Protocol has the status of

Representative national non-governmental organizations (NGOs) are entitled to carry out their statutory activities within the jurisdiction of the Member State of the Council of Europe, against which their complaint is made (Article 2 § 1 of the Protocol), if the state in question has previously issued a declaration in this respect. The Committee of Social Rights has been authorized to verify whether an NGO, other than the employers' organizations and trade unions, referred to in Article 1(c) of the Additional Protocol of 1995, entitled by the authorities of the Member States to lodge collective complaints, has the status of a representative organization, as construed under Article 2 § 1 of the Protocol. The authorities of the Member States have the right to authorize representative NGO*s* to initiate proceedings in accordance with the procedures laid down in the Additional Protocol of 1995. The authorization is valid for the period stated in the relevant authorizing document or for an unlimited period. An authorization to lodge collective complaints can be revoked by way of denouncement of the Protocol.[13] Finland is the only country among the states that ratified or signed the Additional Protocol, to authorize its representative NGOs to lodge collective complaints. None of the Finnish NGOs has ever exercised this power.

The Additional Protocol of 1995 makes a clear distinction between the organizations entitled to lodge collective complaints against their own state. Employers' organizations and trade unions that fall within one of the four categories of organizations entitled to lodge collective complaints have the right to make use of the powers vested in them in respect of every matter governed by the provisions of the European Social Charter. Other organizations that fall within any of the categories mentioned in the Additional Protocol are entitled to lodge collective complaints solely on those matters, which have been recognized by the Committee of Social Rights as those having particular competence (Article 3 of the Additional Protocol).

12.3. Examining the Admissibility of the Collective Complaint

The Committee of Social Rights plays a quasi-judicial role during the examination of the status of an organization lodging a collective complaint (a representative or non-representative); active or inactive in the areas regulated by the European Social Charter. Another important element of the quasi-judicial proceedings is the initial examination of a complaint and the determination as to its admissibility. Out of 25 collective complaints made to the Committee of Social Rights in the years 1998–2004, only one was lodged by an employers' organization,[14] 11 by

an international treaty which should apply identical criteria while assessing employers' organizations and trade unions. The report also postulates that the Committee of Social Rights should be vested with the power to assess all employers' organizations and trade unions – also those, which, pursuant to their domestic legislation, already enjoy the status of representative organizations. *See also* D. Harris, J. Darcy, The European Social Charter, 2nd edition, Transnational Publishers, Inc., Ardsley 2001, p. 358.

13. The notice period for denouncement is 12 months.
14. *Confederation of Swedish Enterprise v. Sweden*, Complaint No.12/2002. *See* European Social Charter. Collected texts, *op. cit.*, p. 500.

NGOs[15] and 13 by trade unions and trade union organizations.[16] During the 'pre-court' proceedings, the Committee of Social Rights examined the right of an international lawyers' association to lodge a collective complaint against the authorities of Portugal, who allow employers to employ children under 15 years of age, which constitutes a violation of Article 7 § 1 of the European Social Charter.[17] The Committee also had to decide whether a Quakers' organization had the right to lodge a collective complaint against Greece which violated the provision prohibiting forced labour (Article 1 § 2 of the European Social Charter) by introducing alternative forms of compulsory military service. To date, the Committee of Social Rights has decided that the INGOs that have made collective complaints meet the requirements laid down in the Additional Protocol of 1995. That is, they were established either to represent and defend economic and social rights expressed in the European Social Charter or to protect the rights of a particular social group, e.g. children or immigrants. The Committee decides whether a collective complaint should be afforded further examination or rejected during a plenary discussion. A report prepared by a member of the Committee selected by the President to be the spokesperson in a particular case serves as a basis for the discussion.

12.4. Grounds for Collective Complaints

A collective complaint can only be made in the event of an alleged unsatisfactory application of the European Social Charter by the authorities of a Member State (Article 1 of the Additional Protocol). Since Member States do not 'apply' the Charter and are only obliged to abide by the Charter's provisions, on the basis of which the Committee of Social Rights formulates European standards for social and economic rights, the phrase used in Article 1 of the Additional Protocol should be

15. *International Commission of Jurists v. Portugal*, Complaint No/. 1998; International Federation of Human Rights Leagues v. Greece, Complaint No/2000. *Quaker Council for European Affairs v. Greece*, Complaint No/. 2000; *Autisme-Europe v. France*, Complaint No.13/2002; *International Federation for Human Rights (IFHR) v. France*, Complaint No.14/2003; *European Roma Rights Centre v. Greece*, Complaint No.15/2003; *World Organization Against Torture (OMCT) v. Greece*, Complaint No.17/2003; *OMCT v. Ireland*, Complaint No. 18/2003; *OMCT v. Italy*, Complaint No. 19/2003; *OMCT v. Portugal*, Complaint No. 20/2003; *OMCT v. Belgium*, Complaint No.21/2003, European Social ... *op. cit.*, p.500 and following.
16. *European Federation of Employees in Public Services (EFEPS) v. France*, Complaint No.2/1999; *EFEPS v. Greece*, Complaint No.3/1999; *EFEPS v. Italy*, Complaint No.4/1999; *EFEPS v. Portugal*, Complaint No. 5/1999; *Syndicat national des professions du tourisme v. France*, Complaint No. 6/1999; *Confédération Française de l'Encadrement – (CFE) CGC v. France*, Complaint No.9/2000; *They ry and STTK ry v. Finland*, Complaint No.10/2000; *Council of Europe of Police Trade Unions v. Portugal*, Complaint No.11/2001; *CFE CGS v. France*, Complaint No. 16/2003; *Confédération Générale du Travaiul v. France*, Complaint No. 22/2003; *Syndicat Occitan de l'education v. France*, Complaint No.23/2003; *Syndicat Sud Travail Affaires Sociales v. France*, Complaint No.24/2004; *Centrale générale des services publics (CGSP) v. Belgium*, Complaint No. 25/2004, European Social ..., *op. cit.*, p. 500 and following.
17. *See* Complaint No1/1998: International Commission of Jurists against Portugal. Documents, Council of Europe. Publishing, Strasbourg 2000, p. 13 and following.

construed as stating that a collective complaint may be lodged, whenever the authorities of Member States fail to fulfil their obligations arising from the European Social Charter, which they have voluntarily accepted for implementation.[18] When lodging a collective complaint, a complaining party should identify particular provisions and indicate in what respect the state has not ensured a satisfactory application thereof (Article 4 of the Additional Protocol). When presenting its conclusions, the Committee of Social Rights has to assess whether or not the Member State concerned has ensured the satisfactory application of the provision, referred to in the complaint – Article 8(1) of the Additional Protocol. With regards to the supervision over the reports presented by the Member States, the Committee of Social Rights assesses whether the provisions of labour law and social security law and the common practice in this respect by Member States comply with the European standards set out in the Social Charters of the Council of Europe. Hence, a collective complaint can be made in the event of an alleged unsatisfactory application of the provisions of the European Social Charter and of the standards laid down by the Committee of Social Rights by a Member State.

The allegations made in a collective complaint should be general in nature. They ought to refer to a specific case of an unsatisfactory application by a Member State of a particular provision of the European Social Charter or non-compliance with a particular European standard laid down by the Committee on the basis of the Charter. The Committee of Ministers of the Council of Europe, in the above cited decision, ruled out the possibility of admitting complaints concerning individual cases where the state authorities or state administration violate a social or economic right included in the European Social Charter.[19] The analysis of the collective complaints examined by the Committee of Social Rights shows that they are concerned with an unsatisfactory application of the following provisions of the European Social Charter by Member States:

- Article 7 § 1 (ban of child labour);[20]
- Article 5 (the right to organize);[21]
- Article 6 (the right to bargain collectively);[22]
- Article 1 § 2 (non-discrimination with regards to the right to work and a prohibition of forced labour);[23]
- Article 10 (the right to vocational training);[24]
- Article 2 (the right to just conditions of work);[25]
- Article 2 § 4 (the right to a safe work environment);[26]
- Article 4 (the right to a fair remuneration);[27]

18. Cf. D. Harris, J. Darcy, *op. cit.*, p. 360.
19. Explanatory ... *op. cit.*, p. 155.
20. Complaint No.1/1998.
21. Complaint No.2/1999, No.3/1999, No.4/1999, No.5/1999, No.11/2001, No.12/2002.
22. Complaint No.2/1999, No.1999, No.4/1999, No. 5/1999, No. 9/2000, 11/2001, 16/2003.
23. Complaint No. 6/1999, No.7/2000, No. 8/2000.
24. Complaint No.6/1999.
25. Complaint No. 9/2000, No. 16/2003.
26. Complaint No. 10/2000.
27. Complaint No. 9/2000, No. 16/2003, No.17/2003, No. 18/2003, No. 19/2003, No. 20/2003.

- Article 27 (the right of workers with family responsibilities to equal opportunities and equal treatment);[28]
- Article 15 (the right of persons with disabilities to independence, social integration and participation in the life of the community);[29]
- Article 17 (the right of children and young persons to social, legal and economic protection).[30]

Collective complaints include allegations of violation of certain economic and social rights guaranteed in these provisions of the European Social Charter against authorities of some Member States of the Council of Europe. Collective complaints can be made on behalf of all citizens (not only employees or those having insurance) of a given Member State which, while introducing regulations with regards to a particular social group or to all social groups, does not abide by the provisions of the Social Charters and does not comply with the standards set out by the Charters. A case study of the complaints examined by the Committee of Social Rights shows that collective complaints can be made for the benefit of: children, young persons, families, disabled persons, persons deprived by the state of their right to organize and organizations deprived by the state of their right to bargain collectively. The expressions used in the Additional Protocol of 1995 suggest that a collective complaint can be made to protect the interests and rights of a particular community. As construed in the Additional Protocol, the admission of a complaint as a collective complaint does not exclude the possibility of identifying persons against whom the complaint has been made. The Committee of Social Rights admits the possibility of making a complaint on behalf of employees of a particular establishment, as in the case of employees of the British Governmental Communications Headquarters (GCHQ) – an organization responsible for intelligence, security and military communication systems – deprived of the right to organize in trade unions, guaranteed by Article 5 of the European Social Charter.[31] Another specific social group, for the benefit of which the Committee of Social Rights could admit a collective complaint, was a group of Norwegian workers employed in the oil drilling industry and nurses working on the drilling platforms, who were made to submit a collective dispute to be settled by an arbitration tribunal before they could decide to go on strike, which constituted a violation of Article 6 § 4 of the European Social Charter.[32]

12.5. Formal Requirements for Collective Complaint Proceedings

A collective complaint is addressed to the Secretary-General of the Council of Europe. The Additional Protocol requires the Secretary-General to acknowledge the receipt of the complaint, to notify the Member State concerned of the complaint and to

28. Complaint No.9/2000.
29. Complaint No.13/2002.
30. Complaint No. 13/202, No.14/2003.
31. Conclusions XI-1, p. 80. The right to organize ... *op. cit.*, p. 38.
32. Conclusions XII-1, p.130; Conclusions XIII-1, p. 38.

immediately forward the complaint to the Committee of Social Rights (Article 5). Formal requirements for making collective complaints have been laid down in the Rules of Procedure of the Committee of Social Rights.[33] A collective complaint should be made in writing, in one of the two official languages of the Council of Europe (English or French) and signed by a person authorized to represent the entities entitled to lodge collective complaints.

The fact that the case is pending before other authorities or that a judgment has already been passed (*res iudicata*) does not constitute any formal impediment to the examination of a complaint. There is no time limit, the lapse of which in the case of individual complaints results in the loss of rights to demand certain benefits. A collective complaint can be lodged even if not all available forms of legal action before domestic state authorities, against which the complaint is lodged, have been exhausted. The *ne bis in idem* principle (the prohibition on double jeopardy) does not apply either. The Committee of Ministers of the Council of Europe has clearly stated that a collective complaint may be declared admissible by the Committee of Social Rights, even if a similar case has already been submitted to another national or international body. Cases concerning the violation of the right to organize are dealt with by the ILO Committee on Freedom of Association and by the Committee of Social Rights of the Council of Europe. Making a complaint in one of these institutions does not preclude the possibility of referring to a legal opinion on domestic legislation concerning collective labour law and common practice in this respect to another institution authorized to assess the compliance of national collective labour law with the international standards laid down in the ILO Convention No. 87 of 17 June 1948 on freedom of association and protection of the right to organize (Article 2)[34] and Social Charters of the Council of Europe (Article 5). The examination of a collective complaint, subject to the provisions of the Additional Protocol of 1995, is also possible when the Committee of Social Rights has already presented its opinion on the subject in the course of its regular supervision over the reports submitted by the authorities of the Member States, concerning their compliance with the provisions of the Social Charters and with the European standards with regards to labour law and social insurance, based on the Charters. Other, less rigorous standards are set by ILO, a global organization, the members of which often vary considerably with regards to the level of economic, technological, social and cultural development. The standards established by the Council of Europe, with its Member States coming only from one continent, are definitely more stringent.

The Committee of Social Rights has two roles: it acts as a body setting the standards and supervising the compliance with these standards; and as a body authorized to examine collective complaints lodged against authorities of the Member States which do not comply with the standards concerning the protection of social and

---

33. Rules of Procedure of the European Committee of Social Rights. A legal basis for the Rules of Procedure is the provisions of Article 24 and 25 of the European Social Charter amended by the Amending Protocol of 1991. *See* European Social ... *op. cit.*, p. 189 and following.
34. Conventions and Recommendations ... vol. I *op. cit.*, pp. 353 and following.

economic rights. As a supervisory body, the Committee evaluates situations in Member States in legal terms and the evaluation is mainly based on reports submitted by the authorities of the states concerned. On occasion, stakeholders, especially trade unions, attach their own opinions to the reports. In the case of collective complaint proceedings, a different approach is followed. The legal environment and the common practice with regard to compliance with the provisions of the Social Charters of the Council of Europe and with the relevant European standards are assessed on the basis of a collective complaint. Proceedings initiated by an entity entitled to lodge collective complaints are contradictory in its nature. Every party has to present statements and evidence justifying the allegations raised in a collective complaint (the complainant) and in the response to the allegations (the authorities of the state against which the complaint is made). If a collective complaint is made by national employers' organizations, national trade unions, or national or international NGOs, the Committee of Social Rights has to notify – through the Secretary-General of the Council of Europe – the international employers' organizations and trade unions referred to in Article 27 § 2 of the European Social Charter of the proceedings and invite them to submit their observations on the subject and to consider the stand expressed by the organization acting in the collective complaint proceedings as *amicii curiae*.

The specific quasi-judicial role of the Committee of Social Rights results from a lack of any formal impediments to the examination of the case already examined or currently being examined by another organization or by the Committee itself. This opinion on the nature of the legal character of the role played by the Committee of Social Rights, as a body authorized to examine collective complaints is further justified by little formalization of the proceedings and the non-binding (for the parties) character of the Committee's conclusions.

12.6. Collective Complaint Proceedings

Unlike in the case of proceedings of the ILO Committee on Freedom of Association, the Committee of Social Rights may examine a collective complaint during a trial with the participation of the parties. The Committee makes the decision on the form of examination during a plenary session. The Committee decides to proceed with the participation of the parties before expressing the conclusions, whenever it believes that such procedure is 'necessary'. The trial enables the Committee to establish the facts that cannot be established on the basis of the procedural writs and documents.[35] Trials are held in the courtroom of the European Tribunal of Human Rights and are open to the public. The Parties and their representatives put forward their arguments and offer any additional explanations. Organizations acting as *amicii curiae* have the right to present arguments during the trial as well.

The proceedings of the Committee of Social Rights are concluded with a report stating the findings of the Committee and the rulings concerning the collective

35. Explanatory report ... *op. cit.*, p. 156.

complaint. The report of the Committee of Social Rights is presented to the Committee of Ministers of the Council of Europe and to the parties. On the basis of the findings and of the report of the Committee of Social Rights, the Committee of Ministers passes a resolution or a recommendation. A resolution stating the compliance of domestic labour and social insurance legislation with the Social Charters of the Council of Europe is passed by a simple majority vote of the Committee of Ministers. A recommendation stating unsatisfactory application of one of the two Social Charters of the Council of Europe requires a qualified majority of two-thirds of those voting. A report of the Committee of Social Rights accompanied by the resolution or recommendation of the Committee of Ministers is forwarded to the Parliamentary Assembly of the Council of Europe and to the parties engaged in the collective complaint.

The Committee of Ministers of the Council of Europe takes a stand on the basis of the information included in the report prepared by the Committee of Social Rights but is not bound by the conclusions of the report. In the case *International Commission of Jurists v. Portugal,*[36] the Committee of Ministers adopted a resolution approving the report of the Committee of Social Rights, that concluded that the authorities of Portugal unsatisfactorily applied Article 7 of the European Social Charter,[37] although, pursuant to Article 9 § 1 of the Additional Protocol of 1995, it should have adopted a recommendation stating the unsatisfactory application of the European Social Charter.[38]

The authorities of the Member State against which a collective complaint is lodged have the right to apply to the Committee of Ministers to consult the Governmental Committee of the Council of Europe before adopting a recommendation. An opinion of the Governmental Committee is required when the report of the Committee of Social Rights raises some 'new issues', or when the qualified majority of the Committee of Ministers wishes it so (Article 9 § 2 of the Additional Protocol). The 'new issues', that require the Committee of Ministers to consult the Governmental Committee, are legal issues that have not been dealt with thus far by the Committee of Social Rights while performing its supervisory role over the Member States' compliance with the provisions of the European Social Charter. The Governmental Committee, made up of the representatives of the Member States' authorities, is a political body. The Committee of Ministers is of identical nature. Including an additional political body in the proceedings counterbalances the assessment of findings made by the Committee of Social Rights that is independent of national authorities of the Member States. Although the recommendations of the Committee of Ministers are not biding upon the Member States, the authorities of the states against which proceedings have been initiated as a result of a collective complaint postulate that the Governmental Committee should participate in the proceedings to counterbalance the legal evaluation of the Committee of Social Rights with a political opinion.

---

36. Complaint No.1/1998.
37. There was a dissenting opinion of a Committee member to the report of the Committee of Social Rights, *op. cit.*, pp. 163–164.
38. D. Harris, J. Darcy, *op. cit.*, pp. 366–367.

CHAPTER 13 CONCLUSION

The Committee of Social Rights is not a judicial body. It does not deal with any individual complaints concerning instances of violation of the provisions of the European Social Charters by Member States of the Council of Europe. With regards to collective complaints, the Committee does not adjudicate. It gathers information and adopts a stance, whenever an entitled entity lodges a complaint against a Member State that ratified the Additional Protocol of 1995 and, thus, submitted its national labour and social insurance legislation and practice to the supervision and assessment of an independent international body. The procedure presented above for the examination of collective complaints shows that the Committee follows the path of international bodies of justice competent to examine complaints in matters governed by labour and social security legislation. Hence, the opinion is that the Committee of Social Rights plays a quasi-judicial role and therefore the role seems justified. This role is supplementary to the main function of the Committee, that serves mainly as an international body established to set European standards with regard to labour and social insurance legislation and to supervise the compliance of the Member States of the Council of Europe with the provisions of the European Social Charter of 1961, the Revised European Social Charter 1996, and the standards based on these Charters.

The Committee of Social Rights and its predecessor, the Committee of Independent Experts, is sometimes regarded as less influential than the European Committee of Social Rights and, presently, the European Tribunal of Social Rights– the bodies supervising the compliance of the Member States of the Council of Europe with the provisions of the European Human Rights Convention[1]. The Committee of Social Rights voices criticism in connection with the effective supervision over the compliance of the Member States of the Council of Europe with the standards concerning labour law, established on the basis of the European Social Charter and the

1. Ph. Alston, J. Crawford, The future of UN human rights treaty monitoring, Cambridge University Press, Cambridge, New York 2000; M.C.R. Craven, The International Covenant on Economic, Social and Cultural Rights. A Perspective on its Development, Clarendon Press, Oxford 2002; R. R. Churchill, U. Khaliq, The Collective Complaints System of the European Social Charter: An Effective Mechanism for Ensuring Compliance with Economic and Social Rights? European Journal of International Law, Oxford, 2004, vol. 15, Issue 3, p. 417.

Revised European Social Charter.[2] The Committee of Social Rights, as an independent, professional body, does not issue any binding adjudications. It presents its position on the technical aspects and is subject to the political control of the Governmental Committee and the Committee of Ministers of the Council of Europe. The above opinion concerning the quasi-judicial role of the Committee of Social Rights does not influence the number of collective complaints examined by this body of the Council of Europe. As of 30 June 2005, the Committee accepted 31 collective complaints for examination.[3] With an increase in the number of Member States deciding to ratify the Additional Protocol of 9 November 1995 to the European Social Charter providing for a system of collective complaints, methods applied by the Committee of Social Rights for supervision over the compliance of the Member States with the Charters will also change. The reports of Member States on compliance with international standards will be replaced with collective complaints lodged by stakeholders active in the national or international arena and by the international NGOs included in the list drawn up by the Council of Europe. The roles and the nature of the Committee will be changed as well. The Committee will be transformed from a supervisory body monitoring the compliance with the provisions of the Charters to a judicial body.

2. L. Betten, International Labour Law. Selected Issues, Kluwer, Deventer-Boston 1993, s. 416–417; T. Novitz, International and European Protection of the Right to Strike. A Comparative Study of Standards Set by the International Labour Organization, the Council of Europe and the European Union, Oxford Monographs on Labour Law, Oxford University Press, Oxford 2003, pp. 212 and following.
3. In 1998, the Committee examined one collective complaint; in 1999-5; in 2000-4; in 2001-1; in 2002 - 2; in 2003–10; in 2004–5. List of registered collective complaints (in:) European Social Charter ... *op. cit.,* p. 509 and following.

SUMMARY

The Charter is an international treaty that, in contrast to the directives released by the Council of Europe and the European Parliament of the European Union,[1] does not directly make conclusions about the internal affairs of Member States.[2] Some courts in Member States cite chosen provisions of the Charter directly.

This is made all the more obvious in cases where there is no domestic labour legislations.[3] On the other hand, Dutch courts ruled Article 1 § 2, Article 6 § 1 and 2, Article 12, Article 13 § 4, Article 18 § 1–3 may not be cited by the national courts as a basis for judicial decisions.[4] Those who analyse the European Social Charter have great difficulty in making conclusions about the level of influence the supervisory institutions of the Council of Europe have on Member States.[5] They attempt to show examples of such jurisdictional influence of the Committee and how it is appropriated to law and practice by some Member States.[6] One way of analysing the level of influence of the Charter on international social rights protection is to look at the decisions handed down by the judiciary in matters concerning labour law and social security, to see how provisions are cited and how they are applied. It is important to

1. S. Prechal, Directives in European Community Law. A Study of Directives and Their Enforcement in National Courts, Clarendon Press, Oxford 1995, *passim*; N. Półtorak, Odpowiedzialność odszkodowawcza państwa w prawie Wspólnot Europejskich (Limited Liability of countries in the European Community), Zakamycze, Kraków 2002, pp. 138 and following.
2. O.Kahn-Freund, *op. cit.*, p.193.
3. Supreme Court in the Netherlands (Hoge Raad) in 30.05.1986, NJ 1986/688. Citing G. Gori, *op. cit.*
4. *Ibid.*
5. D. Harris, J. Darcy, *op. cit.*, p. 402.
6. France appropriated its deportation provisions to the standards of Article 12 § 4(d) of the Charter. The Netherlands altered its provision concerning the length of time of giving notice to comply the domestic laws with the standards of Article 4 § 4 of the Charter. In an attempt to comply with the provisions set by Article 8 § 2 of the Charter, Great Britain introduced compulsory maternity leave of two weeks. Portugal appropriated its collective labour law provisions to that Article 5 and 6 § 2 of the Charter. Malta ensured the right to family benefits to all citizens of Member States of the Council of Europe. Poland ensured its migrant workers reunification with their families. Compare with D. Harris, J. Darcy, *op. cit.*, pp.402-403, footnotes 8 and 11; G. Gori, Domestic Enforcement of the European Social Charter: The Way Forward (w:) Social Rights in Europe, Eds. de Búrca, B. de Witte, L. Ogertschnig, Oxford University Press, Oxford 2005, p.69 ff.

note, however, that domestic courts tend to cite the Charter in an attempt to strengthen their own arguments when handing down a decision that is based on domestic legal regulations. Such cases have existed in Belgium,[7] Sweden,[8] Norway,[9] Italy,[10] Romania,[11] and Germany.[12]

The High Court of Poland cited the provisions of the Charter on four occasions. Three of those concerned the definition of 'decent' remuneration (Article 4).[13] The other concerned the specific legal protection that should be ensured to women before and after giving birth and the application of the provision with regards to the ban of discrimination that may be based on sex (Article 8 § 1).[14] It did not, however, use any of the abovementioned provisions in drawing content related conclusions.

The rulings handed down by the European Tribunal of Human Rights are much more clearly understood. When handing down the decisions concerning freedom of association (Article 5),[15] the right to benefit from social welfare (Article 14)[16] or vocational guidance, the right to choose the place and type of work (Article 1 § 2),[17] and particular protection of workers' representatives (Article 28 RESC),[18] the European Court of Justice cited the rulings of the Committee of Social Rights and made its decisions accordingly. The cited rulings prove that the international standards of social rights protection are approved by international and domestic jurisdictions and that these standards are adhered to by the authorities of Member States that are party to the Charter.

7. Decision handed down by the Constitutional Tribunal (Cour d'Arbitrage) from 15 May 1996 (Article 1 of the Charter). Citing G. Gori, *op. cit.*
8. Decision of the Highest Administrative Court in matter No. 4642/ 1989 (Article 13 of the Charter), *ibid.*
9. Decision from 11 September 2001 *A v, Norwegian People's Aid* (Article 5 of the Charter), *ibid.*
10. Decision 163/1983; 86/1994; 46/2000 (Article 8 of the Charter), *ibid.*
11. Decision of the Constitutional Tribunal No.24/2003, 25/2003,108/2003,351/2003 (Article 1,21,29 as well as Article E of the Charter), *ibid.*
12. BAGE 46, 350 (Article 31 ESC, Article G RESC), *ibid.*
13. Verdicts from: 5 November 1998 r., I PKN 419/98, OSNAPiUS (Polish Court Report of Cases) 1999, No 24, pos. 783; 26 November 2002, I PKN 632/2001, OSNP 2004, No 10, pos. 172; decisions from 12 January 2004, I PZ 109/2003, OSNP 2004, No 24, pos. 405.
14. Verdict from 3 December 1999, II UKN 233/99, OSNAPiUS 2001, No 7, pos. 235. In this case the High Court also cited point 1 of Part 1 of the Charter.
15. *Sigurdur A. Sigurjónsson v. Iceland*, ECHR (1993) Ser. A, No.254, p.35.
16. *Kuoa Poirrez v. France*, decided on 30 September 2003. Citing G.Gori, *op. cit.*
17. *Sidabras and Džiautas v. Lithuania*, decided on 27.7.2004, *ibid.*
18. *Sanchez Navajas v. Spain*, decision Nr 57442/00, *ibid.*

SELECTED BIBLIOGRAPHY

Akandji-Kombe, J.F., 'L'application de la Charte sociale européenne: la mise en œuvre de la procédure de réclamations collectives' (2000) 9/10 *Droit Social* 888

'Le bilan de la relance du mécanisme de contrôle – le regard extérieur' [10 November 2000] *Journée d'étude à l'IHEE, L'Europe des Libertés* 9 (Strasbourg, 2000)

'La procédure de réclamation collective dans la Charte sociale européenne – Chronique des décisions du comité européen des droits sociaux' 48 *Revue trimestrielle des droits de l'homme* 1035 (Bruylant, Bruxelles 2000)

'Les rapports entre la Charte sociale européenne et les droits internes et internationaux Charte sociale et droit communautaire', in Akandji-Kombé, Jean-François et Leclerc, Stéphane (eds), *La Charte Sociale Européenne* (Bruylant, Bruxelles 2000), pp. 149–178

'La France devant le Comité européen des droits sociaux' (November 2001) 11 *Droit Social* 977 (2000)

'Actualité de la Charte sociale européenne – Chronique des décisions du Comité européen des droits sociaux sur les réclamations collectives' (1 January 2003 – July 2001 – July 2002) 53 *Revue trimestrielle des droits de l'homme* 113 (Bruylant, Bruxelles, 2000)

Belorgey, J.M., 'Préface', in Jean-François Akandji-Kombé et Stéphane Leclerc (eds), *La Charte Sociale Européenne* (Bruylant Bruxelles 2001), p. XIII

'De quelques problèmes liés à la prohibition et à l'élimination des discriminations – Essai de clarification des concepts et éléments de droit comparé' (July – August 2002) 7/8 *Droit Social* 683

'La gestion des conflits du travail en Europe: le choc des cultures' (December 2002) 12 *Droit Social* 1125

'Qui droit social?' (March 2004) 338 *La Revue Administrative* 156

Berchtold, K. 'Council of Europe activities in the field of economic, social and cultural rights', in Kehl-Strassburg-Arlington, N.P. Engel Verlag (eds), *Die Durchsetzung wirtschaftlicher und sozialer Grundrechte: Einerechtsvergleichende Bestandsaufnahme* (Matscher, Franz, 1991), p. 335

Bercusson, B., 'Implementation of social rights in Europe. The role of social dialogue and collective agreements' (1992) Anno XX, N° 1 *Affari sociali internazionali* 133

'Social rights in the European constitution' *Communication à la Conférence Social Rights in Europe, 18–19 juin 2004* (Florence, 2004)

Bernstein, A., 'Le développement et la portée des droits économiques et sociaux' (July – September 1982) Vol. 7, N° 3 *Travail et Société*

'La Carta Social de Europa' in R. Caldera (ed), *Estudios sobre Derecho Laboral Homenaje* (Sucre, Caracas, 1977), Tome II, p. 1381

'The System of Supervision of the European Social Charter', in Betten, Harris and Jaspers (eds), *The Future of European Social Policy* (Kluwer Law, 1989), p. 41

Betten, L., 'Prospects for a Social Policy of the European Community and its impact on the functioning of the European Social Charter', in Betten, Harris and Jaspers (eds), *The Future of European Social Policy* (Kluwer Law, 1989), p. 101

Betten, L. and Jaspers T. 'Implementation of the European Social Charter in the Netherlands', in Jaspers & Betten (eds), *25 years – European Social Charter* (Kluwer, 1988)

Betten, L. and Grief, N. *EU Law and Human Rights* (European Law series, Longman, London and New York, 1988)

Biagmi, M. and Salomone, R., 'Social Europe and Labour Law: the Role of the European Social Charter, The Council of Europe and the Social Challenges of the XXIst Century' (Kluwer, 2001) 39 *Bulletin of Comparative Labour Relations* 71

Billum, S. 'The European Social Charter – a unique instrument for the strengthening of social rights', report submitted during the 5th Round Table with European Ombudsmen, Limassol (Cyprus), 8 – 10 May 1996, *Proceedings of the 5th Round Table with European Ombudsmen* (Council of Europe Publishing, 1996), p. 147

Birk, R., 'The Collective Complaint – A new Procedure in the European Social Charter' in *Labour Law and Industrial Relations at the Turn of the Century* (Kluwer, 1998), p. 261

'The European Social Charter and the European Union' International Conference Brussels, 9 May 2000, *The Council of Europe and the Social Challenges of the XXIst Century* (Kluwer, 2001), p. 41

Blanpain, R., 'Equal Treatment and the Prohibition of Discrimination in Employment and Occupation. Implementation in the European Union and Belgium' in *The Council of Europe and the Social Challenges of the XXIst Century* (Kluwer, 2001), p. 121

Bleckmann, A. 'Interprétation et application en droit interne de la Charte sociale européenne, notamment du droit de grève' (1967) 4 *Cahiers de droit européen* 388

Bonnechere, M., 'Les rapports entre la Charte sociale européenne et les droitsinternes et internationaux – Charte sociale et droits nationaux', in Akandji-Komb and Leclerc (eds), *La Charte Sociale Européenne* (Bruylant, Bruxelles, 2001), p. 105

Brillat, R., 'A New Protocol to the European Social Charter Providing for Collective Complaints' [January 1996] *European Human Rights Law Review* 52

'La Charte sociale européenne du Conseil de l'Europe, développements récents' (October 1996) 12 *Droit en Quart Monde* 2

(1997) 'Les nouvelles voies ouvertes par la Charte sociale européenne révisée et les nouveaux moyens de contrôle' (Pierrelaye, France, December 1997) 9–10 *Revue Quart Monde – dossiers et documents n °6, Extrême pauvreté et droits de l'homme en Europe* – Actes de la session 'Justice et quart monde' 93

'La protection des enfants dans la Charte sociale européenne', *Studi in onore di Giovanni Maria Ubertazzi* (Milano) Anno XLVI Gennaio-Aprile 1999 Jus Rivista Di Scienze Giuridiche 89

'Le système de contrôle de l'application de la Charte sociale', Communication lors de la Première Rencontre européenne de Caen: *La Charte sociale européenne* (Caen, 17 mars 2000)

'Les perspectives d'évolution du mécanisme de contrôle – perspectives internes: propositions pour une nouvelle relance de la Charte sociale européenne' (November 2000) Journée d'étude à l'IHEE Strasbourg sur le mécanisme de contrôle de l'application de la Charte sociale européenne, *L'Europe des Libertés*, numéro spécial, p. 13

'Opening address of the International Conference', Brussels, 9 May 2000, *The Council of Europe and the Social Challenges of the XXIst Century* (Kluwer, 2001), p. XIII

'Economie générale de la Charte sociale européenne – Le système de contrôle de l'application de la Charte sociale' in Akandji-Kombé and Leclerc (eds), *La Charte Sociale Européenne* (Bruylant, Bruxelles, 2001), p. 45

'L'activité pré-conventionnelle et para-conventionnelle du Conseil de l'Europe dans le domaine des droits sociaux' in Flauss (ed), *Droits sociaux et droit européen – bilan et prospective de la protection normative* (Bruylant, 2002), p. 127

Les droits sociaux ou la démolition de quelques poncifs – Actes du colloque (Presses Universitaires de Strasbourg, 2003), p. 83

'Toward the unified protection of social rights in Europe (substantive and procedural issues)' in *European Social Charter: Towards common application of the Revised Charter* (C.H.Beck, Warszawa, 2005), s. 13–21

'The Supervisory Machinery of the European Social Charter: Recent Developments and their Impact' in *Social Rights in Europe* (Oxford, 2005)

de Broek, G., 'Droit à la sécurité et à l'hygiène dans le travail droit à la protection de la santé' *La Charte sociale européenne Dix annеés d'application* (Institut d'études européennes, Université libre de Bruxelles, 1978)

de Búrca, G., de Witte B and Ogertschnig L., *Social Rights in Europe* (Oxford University Press, Oxford, 2005)

Burrows, N., 'Implementation of the European Social Charter in the United Kingdom' in Jaspers & Betten (ed), *25 years – European Social Charter* (Kluwer, 1988)

Cholewinski, R., 'The protection of the right of economic migrants to family reunion in Europe' (July 1994) Vol. 43, pt. 3 *International and comparative law quarterly* 568

Clapham, A., 'Is there any competition between the two social charters?' (1992) Anno XX, n° 1 *Affari sociali internazional* 189

Colucci, M., 'The European Social Charter and the Right to Information and Consultation of Workers. Its Implementation in the European Union and in Italy', International Conference Brussels, 9 May 2000, *The Council of Europe and the Social Challenges of the XXIst Century* (Kluwer, 2000), p. 87

European Social Charter – Collected texts (Second edition, Council of Europe Publishing, 2005)

Cullen, H., 'The collective complaints mechanism under the European Social Charter' [2000] *European Law Review*, Human Rights Survey, p. 18

Harris D., and Darcy J., *The European Social Charter* (Second Edition, The Procedural Aspects of International Law Book Series, Volume 25, Transnational Publishers Inc., Arsdley, New York, 2001)

Darcy J., 'Forced labour in Greece' (April 2002) Vol. 27, No 2 *European Law Review* 218

Dehaene, J.L., 'Fundamental Social Rights, the European Union and the Convention' *The Council of Europe and the Social Challenges of the XXIst Century* (Kluwer, 2001) p. 49

Drzemczewski, K., 'The work of the Council of Europe's Directorate of Human Rights – the European Social Charter' (1990) 11 *Human Rights Law Journal* 110

'The European Social Charter and Polish Legislation and Practice', in Drzewicki, Krause and Rosas (eds), *Social Rights as Human Rights – A European Challenge* (Institute for Human Rights, Abo Akademi University, 1994), p. 211

Drzewicki, Krause and Rosas, 'The right to work and rights in work', in Eide, Krausse and Rosas (eds), *Economic, social and cultural rights* (Martinus Nijhoff Publishers, 1995) p. 169

Engels C., 'The European Social Charter: Freedom of Association and Free Collective Bargaining. European and Belgian Implementation' in *The Council of Europe and the Social Challenges of the XXIst Century* (Kluwer, 2001), p. 169

Evans, M., 'The European Social Charter' (Bridge, Lasok, Perrot, Plender, London, 1973).

Evju, S., 'The European Social Charter' *The Council of Europe and the Social Challenges of the XXIst Century* (Kluwer, 2001) p. 19

Fabricius, F., *The Future of European Social Policy* (Kluwer Law and Taxation Publishers, 1989), p. 97

'Strike and Lock-out in the Order of the European Social Charter and Human Rights of All' in *Human Rights and European Politics – The Legal-Political Status of Workers in the European Community Questions internationals* (Presses de la Fondation Nationale des Sciences Politiques BERG, Oxford/Providence, 1992), p. 81

Fonteneau, G., (1996): 'Pan-European instruments (Council of Europe) – the European Social Charter', *Labour and social rights in the standardised systems of the International Labour Organisation, the Council of Europe, the European Union* (ACV, 1996), p. 18

'Collective bargaining – Council of Europe' in *Labour and Social Rights in the Standardised Systems* (ACV, 1996), p. 32

'European Trade Unionism and the European Social Charter', International Conference Brussels, 9 May 2000, *The Council of Europe and the Social Challenges of the XXIst Century* (Kluwer, 2001) p. 243

'la Charte sociale de 1961 et sa révision en 1996', *La dimension sociale dans la mondialisation de l'économie* (Bruylant Bruxelles, 2001) 23 Revue de la Faculté de Droit Université Libre de Bruxelles 33

Fuchs, K., 'The European Social Charter : Its Role in Present-Day Europe and its Reform', in Drzewicki, Krause & Rosas (eds), *Social Rights as Human Rights, A European Challenge* (Institute for Human Rights, Abo Akademi University, 1994), p. 151

Giugni, G., 'La Carta sociale eurcpea' (September–October 1991) Anno II, n° 5 *Acque & Terre* 52

Gommers, P., 'Prospects for a European Social Policy' (Kluwer Law and Taxation Publishers, 1989) [April 1989] *The Future of European Social Policy* 161

Gori, G., 'Domestic Enforcement of the European Social Charter: the Way Forward' in *Social Rights in Europe* (Oxford, 2005)

Grevisse, S., 'Le renouveau de la Charte sociale européenne' (September–October 2000) 9/10 *Droit social* 884

'Economie générale de la Charte sociale européenne – La Charte sociale: rapport introductif' in Akandji-Kombé and Leclerc (eds), *La Charte Sociale Européenne* (Bruylant, Bruxelles, 2001), p. 3

Harris, D., 'The European Social Charter' (July 1964) Vol. 13, n° 3 *The International and Comparative Law Quarterly* 1076

The European Social Charter (The University Press of Virginia, Charlottesville, 1984)

'The system of Supervision of the European Social Charter – Problems and Options for the Future' in Betten, Harris and Jaspers (eds), *The Future of European Social Policy* (Kluwer, 1989), p. 11

'A fresh Impetus for the European Social Charter' (July 1992) 41 *The International and Comparative Law Quarterly,* p. 659

Law and Practice of the European Convention of Human Rights and the European Social Charter (Council of Europe, 1996), p. 377

'The European Social Charter and social rights in the European Union', in Betten and Mac Devit (eds), *The Protection of Fundamental Social Rights in the European Union* (Kluwer Law International, 1996), p. 107

Harris D. and Darcy J., *European Social Charter*, Second Edition, The Procedural Aspects of International Law Monograph Series, Volume 25 (Transnational Publishers Inc., Arsdley, New York, 2001)

Hendriks, A., 'Revised European Social Charter' (September 1996) vol. 15, n° 3 *Netherlands Quarterly of Human Rights* 341

'Towards a New System of Supervision for the European Social Charter' (June 1991) 46 *For the Rule of Law: The Review* 42

Hohnerlein, E.M., 'Implementation of the European Social Charter in the Federal Republic of Germany' in Jaspers and Betten (eds), *25 years – European Social Charter* (Kluwer, 1988)

Imbert, P.H., 'Rights of the Poor, Poor Rights? - Reflections on Economic, Social and Cultural Rights' (December 1995) 55 *For the Rule of Law, The Review* 85

Jacobs, A., 'The Right to Work and the Freedom of Work' (Kluwer, 2001) 39 *The Council of Europe and the Social Challenges of the XXIst Century,*_Bulletin of Comparative Labour Relations 59

Jaconsen, P., 'Implementation of the European Social Charter in Denmark', in Jaspers and Betten (eds), *25 years – European Social Charter* (Kluwer, 1988)

Jaeger, M., 'Current legal developments – The additional Protocol to the European Social Charter providing for a system of collective complaints' (Kluwer Law International, 1997) 10 *Leiden Journal of International Law* 69

Jaspers, T. and Betten, L., 'Implementation of the European Social Charter in the Netherlands' in Jaspers and Betten (eds), *25 years – European Social Charter* (Kluwer, 1988)

'Desirability of European Legislation in particular Areas of Social Policy' in Betten, Harris, & Jaspers (eds), *The Future of European Social Policy* (Kluwer, 1989), p. 53

Kahn-Freund, O., 'Labour relations and international standards – some reflections on the European Social Charter' in van der Meersch (ed.), *Mélanges* (Bruxelles, Paris, 1972), p. 131

'The European Social Charter' in Jacobs (ed.), *European Law and the Individual* (Amsterdam, New-York, Oxford, 1976)

The Right of Strike – Its Scope and Limitations (Strasbourg, 1974)

Kallstrom, K., 'Implementation of the European Social Charter in Sweden' in Jaspers and Betten (eds), *25 years – European Social Charter* (Kluwer, 1988)

Kojanec, G., 'Droit au travail – Droit de la famille à une protection sociale, juridique et économique – Droit de la mère et de l'enfant à une protection sociale et économique' in *La Charte sociale européenne, Dix années d'application* (Université libre de Bruxelles, 1978)

Koncar, P., 'Equality between women and men in the revised European Social Charter' in Beck (ed), *European Social Charter: Towards common application of the Revised Charter* (Warszawa, 2005), s. 23

Kranidiotis, J., 'The European Social Charter, 1961 – 1976' (uniquement en grec, Athens, 1976) 28 *Greek Review of Social Research*

Kulakowski, J., 'En marge de la Charte sociale européenne' (1961) 34e année, n° 5 *Labor* 222

Lapeyre, J., 'Pan-European instruments (Council of Europe)' (European Trade Union Confederation, 1997) *Social rights in Europe – vade mecum*, p. 16

Larralde, J.M., 'Les rapports entre la Charte sociale européenne et les droits internes et internationaux – Charte sociale et Convention européenne des droits de l'Homme' in Akandji-Kombé and Leclerc (eds), *La Charte Sociale Européenne* (Bruylant, Bruxelles, 2001), ∝p. 123

Laroque, P. (1976): 'Droit à la sécurité sociale – Droit à l'exercice d'une activité lucrative – Droits des travailleurs migrants et de leurs familles à la protection et à l'assistance', *La Charte sociale européenne, dix années d'application* (Université libre de Bruxelles)

de LARY de Latour, H., 'La Charte sociale européenne' (March 1979) 3 *Droit social* 100

Leclerc, S., 'Economie générale de la Charte sociale européenne – Les restrictions et limitations à l'application de la Charte sociale', in Akandji-Kombé and Leclerc (eds), *La Charte Sociale Européenne* (Bruylant Bruxelles, 2001), p. 67

Levy-Puech D., 'L'égalité entre les femmes et les hommes en matière d'emploi : Charte sociale européenne (révisée) et autres normes du Conseil de l'Europe' (Collections de l'Université Robert Schuman, Presses Universitaires de Strasbourg, 2003) Nouvelle série n° 6 *Le droit social – Le droit comparé – Etudes dédiées à la mémoire de Pierre Ortscheidt* 207

Lyon-Caen G. and Lyon-Caen, A., 'Charte sociale européenne : son mécanisme – son contenu - application de la Charte' in *Droit Social International et Européen* (Dalloz, Paris 8e édition, 1993) p. 146

Maryan-Green N.A., 'Droits sociaux et normes régionales' (Etude du rapport existant entre les droits sociaux énoncés dans le Pacte international relatif aux droits économiques, sociaux et culturels et les divers instruments régionaux, dont la 'Charte sociale européenne', January–March 1969) 1 *Journal du Droit international* 58

Matey, M., 'The European Social Charter: The Rights of Children and Young Persons to Protection' (The Council of Europe and the Social Challenges of the XXIst Century, Kluwer, 2001) 39 Bulletin of Comparative Labour Relations 157

Mayer-Fabian G., 'Social assistance and social services in the case-law of the European Social Charter' in Council of Europe: Proceedings of the joint meeting on human rights and social workers, Doc DH-ED 87(13) (Strasbourg, 1987), p. 25

Miehsler, H., 'The European Social Charter and the Civil Servants Right to Strike: The German Case' in *Jus Humanitatis, Festschritt zum 90 geburtstag von Alfred Verdross* (Hrs. H. Miehlser n.a., Berlin, 1980), p. 474

Mikkola, M., 'The European Social Charter and the CEE-Countries' (The Council of Europe and the Social Challenges of the XXIst Century, Kluwer, 2001) 39 *Bulletin of Comparative Labour Relations* 33

'Children of residential homes – a million army, still missing the basic rights' (December 2002) 10. Jahrgang, Nr 12 *Europäisches Arbeits- und Sozialrecht* 253

'European Social Charter and Health', in Roscam-Abbing and Bopp (eds), *Health, ethics and human rights – the Council of Europe meeting the challenge* (the Hague/Strasbourg, Council of Europe, 2004), p. 27

'Social security in Europe – a Human Right and a Basic Right', in Beck (ed.), *European Social Charter – Towards common application of the Revised* (Warsawa, 2005), s. 119

Mohr, M., 'The Turin Protocol of 22 October 1991: A Major Contribution to Revitalizing the European Social Charter' (1992) Vol. 3, n° 2 *European Journal of International Law* 362

O'Higgins, P., 'The European Social Charter' in *Human rights for the 1990s – legal, political and ethical issues* (Mansell, 1991), p. 121

Pancracio, J.P., 'Les rapports entre la Charte sociale européenne et les droits internes et internationaux – Charte sociale et droit international public', in Akandji-Kombé and Leclerc (eds), *La Charte Sociale Européenne* (Bruylant Bruxelles, 2001)
Pellonpaa, M., 'Economic, Social and Cultural Rights', in Macdonald, Matscher and Petzold (eds), *The European System for the Protection of Human Rights* (Martinus Nijhoff Publishers, 1993), p. 855
Pettiti, C., 'Le droit de ne pas s'affilier à un syndicat en droit européen, Cour européenne des Droits de l'Homme, 20 avril 1993' (December 1993) 12 *Droit social* 999
'La Charte sociale européenne révisée' (January 1997) 8e année, n° 29 *Revue trimestrielle des droits de l'homme* 3
'La Charte sociale du XXIe siècle' (October 1997) 8e année, n° 32 *Revue trimestrielle des droits de l'homme* 791
Prouvez, N., 'The European Social Charter, an instrument for the protection of human rights in the 21st century ?' (December 1997) 58–59 *The Review – International Commission of Jurists* 30
Pugsley, D., (1969): 'The European Social Charter' (The Hague, 1969) 39 *Yearbook of the A.A.A.* 97
Quinn, G., *The European Social Charter and EU Anti-discrimination Law in the Field of Disability : Two Gravitational Fields with One Common Purpose, Social Rights in Europe* (Oxford. 2005)
Ramm, T.H., *Europäische Sozialcharta* (Handwörterbuch des öffentlichen Dienstes. Das Personalwesen, Berlin, 1976)
Droit syndical et droit de négociation collective (Assemblée parlementaire du Conseil de l'Europe, Strasbourg, 1977)
Renucci, J.F., 'Les droits économiques et sociaux dans la Charte sociale européenne' in *Droit européen des droits de l'homme* (2e édition, LGDJ, 2001), p. 290
'La Charte sociale européenne' in *Droit européen des droits de l'homme* (2e édition, LGDJ, 2001), p. 580
Rey, J., 'Le Conseil de l'Europe et la sécurité sociale' (June 1999) 94 *Echanges – santé-social* 98
de Richemont, J., 'La Charte sociale européenne' in *Le Droit européen* (1963), p. 333
Robertson, A.H., *Human Rights in Europe* (University Press, Manchester, 1962), p. 140
Rodriguez-Pinero, M., 'Antecendentes, genesis y significado de la Carta sociale Europea' (Instituto de Estudios Politicos, Madrid, 1962) 53 *Separata de la Revista de Political Sociale*
Rosas A. and Scheinin M., 'Implementation mechanisms and remedies – Reporting under the European system', in Eide, Krausse and Rosas (eds), *Economic, social and cultural rights* (Martinus Nijhoff Publishers, 1995), p. 363
Roucounase, E., 'La réforme des institutions de protection des droits de l'Homme du Conseil de l'Europe' in *La réforme des institutions de protection des droits de l'homme du Conseil de l'Europe* (1993), p. 227

Russo, C., 'La justiciabilité des droits économiques et sociaux' in *Collected Courses of the Academy of European Law* (Volume III, Book 2, Kluwer Academic Publishers, 1994), p. 213

Samuel L., *Fundamental social rights – case law of the European Social Charter* (Council of Europe Publishing, 1997)

Droits sociaux fondamentaux – jurisprudence de la Charte sociale européenne (Editions du Conseil de l'Europe, 1997)

Sanetra W., 'Standards for Social Rights protection in the Revised European Social Charter as compared with the Polish labour and social security law', in Beck (ed.), *Eueropean Social Charter. Towards common application of the Revised Charter* (Warszawa, 2005), s. 143

Scheinin, M., 'Existing forms of institutionalized practices in the international monotoring of economic and social rights', in Eide, Krause and Rosas (eds), *Economic, social and cultural rights* (Martinus Nijhoff Publishers, 1995), p. 53

'The right to social security' in Eide, Krause and Rosas (eds), *Economic, social and cultural rights* (Martinus Nijhoff Publishers, 1995), p. 159

Scheinin M. and Rosas A., 'Implementation mechanisms and remedies – Reporting under the European system' in Eide, Krause and Rosas (eds), *Economic, social and cultural rights* (Martinus Nijhoff Publishers, 1995), p. 363

Schoetter, P., (): 'La Charte sociale européenne: considérations critiques' (La Charte sociale européenne, Bruxelles, 1966) Numéro spécial, n° 1 *Revue de l'Institut de Sociologie* p. 109

Schokkenbroek, J.G.C., 'The results of the Ministerial Conference on the European Social Charter' (April 1992) Vol. 13, n° 4 *Human Rights Law Journal* 177

'Towards a New System of Supervision for the European Social Charter' (June 1991) 46 *For the Rule of Law – The Review* 42

Sciotti, C., 'L'applicabilité de la Charte sociale européenne dans l'ordre juridique des Etats contractants' in Flauss (ed.), *Droits sociaux et droit européen – Bilan et prospective de la protection normative* (Bruylant, 2002), p. 175

Smyth J.F., 'The Implementation of the European Social Charter' in A. Pedone (ed.) *Mélanges Modinos* (Paris, 1968) p. 290

Sperduti, G., 'Le raccord entre la Charte sociale européenne et la Convention européenne des droits de l'homme' in *Cahiers de droit européen* (1979)

Spyropoulos, G., 'Encadrement social de la mondialisation de l'économie : bilan et perspectives d'avenir de l'action normative au niveau international dans le domaine du travail' (June 1995) 6 *Droit social* 551

Strasser, R., 'European Social Charter' in *Encyclopedia of International Public Law*, Instalment 8, (Bernhardt, Amsterdam, 1985)

Sudre, F., 'Le protocole additionnel à la Charte Sociale Européenne prévoyant un système de réclamations collectives' (A. Pedone, Paris, 1996) 3 *Revue Générale de Droit International Public* 715

'Les droits sociaux et la Convention européenne des droits de l'homme' (September 2000) Vol. 12 N° 1-2 *Revue Universelle des Droits de l'Homme (RUDH)* 28

Sur Fadil, H., 'La Charte sociale européenne. Dix années d'application 1965-1975' (Martinus Nijhoff, La Haye, 1974) 12 *Annuaire européen*

Swiatkowski, A-M., 'Legal Aspects of the Social Policy in the European Union and Poland in the Years 2000-2005' in *Social Policy* (2002), p. 14

'Scope *ratione personae* of Article 5 of the European Social Charter (the right to organize) and its application in Poland (w:) Facing the European Union – challenges for Polish law' (2002-2003) Vol. XXXV-XXXVI *Archivum Juridicum Cracoviense* 83

'Control administrativo del derecho del trabajo (deste la perspectiva de la Carta Social Europea)' in *Revista de Derecho Laboral y Seguridad Social* (Buenos Aires, fasc.16, August 2004), p.1120

'Funciones causijurisdiccionales del Comité de Derechos Sociales del Consejo Europeo' in *Revista de Derecho Laboral y Seguridad Social* (Buenos Aires, No. 7, April 2005), s. 533

'Protection of employee rights in the case of restructuring of their employer and in other cases' in Beck (ed.), *European Social Charter. Towards common application of the Revised Charter* (Warszawa, 2005), s. 45

'Prospects of social welfare in Poland seen from the European perspective', in 'The Future of Social Security System : Poland Comapred to Europe' [December 2005] *Social Policy* 39

'European fundamental social rights and the legal, social and economic position of young workers and adolescents in European industrial relations during the period of globalisation' (2005) vol.13, No. 2 *Tilburg Foreign Law Review*

'Problems of Surveillance and Control of Labour Standards (lesson from the European Social Charter)' (2006) 58 *Bulletin of Comparative Labour Relations* 91

European Social Charter: the right to strike' (2005) Vol. 47, No.6 Managerial Law

'Balance of Economic Weapons During Collective Labour Dispute' in *Liber Amicorum Reinhold Falbeck,* (Lund, 2005), p. 601

'European Social Charter: Protection of Human (Social) Rights by the Collective Complaint Procedure', Zeitschrift für auslǒndisches und internationales Arbeits- und Sozialrecht, (2006) Vol.4 284

Tapiola, K., 'The European Social Charter and the International Labour Organization' in *The Council of Europe and the Social Challenges of the XXIst Century* (Kluwer 2001) p. 53

Tennfjord, F., 'The European Social Charter – an instrument of social collaboration in Europe' (Nijhoff, La Haye, 1961) 9 *Annuaire européen* 71

'The Charter of the 19 rights' (May-June 1965) n° 153, 14th year *World Veteran*

Thayer, C., 'The European Social Charter and European health policies' (March 1995) Vol. 6, n° 1 *Journal international de bioéthique* 16

Treu, T., 'Implementation of the European Social Charter in Italy', in Jaspers and Betten (eds), *25 years – European Social Charter* (Kluwer, 1988)

Troclet, L.E., 'La Charte sociale européene' in *Eléments de droit social européen*, (Université libre, Institut de Sociologie, Bruxelles, Edition préliminaire, 1963), p. 95

'La Charte sociale européenne' (April-May 1977) 18e année, 205/206 *L'Europe en formation* 15
Valticos, N., 'La Charte sociale européenne. Sa structure, son contenu, le contrôle de son application' (September-October 1963) n° 9, 26e Année *Droit social* 466
'Mise en parallèle des actions et mécanismes de contrôle au niveau du Conseil de l'Europe et de l'Organisation internationale du Travail' in *La Charte sociale européenne. Dix années d'application* (Université libre de Bruxelles, 1978)
Vandamme, F., 'La justiciabilité des droits sociaux dans la Communauté européenne – Comparaison avec la Charte sociale européenne' (1992) Anno XX, no 1 *Affari sociali internazionali* 118
'The revision of the European Social Charter' (1994) Vol. 133, n° 5-6 *International Labour Review* 635
'Les droits protégés par la Charte sociale, contenu et portée' in Akandji-Kombé and Leclerc (eds), *La Charte Sociale Européenne*, (Bruylant Bruxelles, 2001), p.11
Verdier, J.M., 'Les droits économiques et sociaux: relance au Conseil de l'Europe ?' (April 1992) 4 *Droit social* 415
Villars C., 'L'influence de normes de L'OIT sur l'harmonisation de la sécurite sociale au sein de Conseil de l'Europe' (Geneva BIT) [1979] *Revue internationale du travail* s. 367
Vogel-Polsky, E., (1966): 'L'Article 6 de la Charte sociale européenne' (La Charte sociale européenne Numéro spécial, Bruxelles, 1966) 1 *la Revue de l'Institut de Sociologie* 83
'Droit des travailleuses à la protection' in *La Charte sociale européenne. Dix années d'application* (Université libre de Bruxelles, 1978)
Wasescha, L., (1980): 'Le système de contrôle de l'application de la Charte Sociale européenne' (Sa genèse, sa mise en pratique, ses résultats et propositions d'amendement, Librairie Droz S.A., Genève, 1980)
Wiebringhaus, H., 'La Charte sociale européenne' (1963) 9e Année *Annuaire français de Droi international* 709
'Première mise en œuvre du système de contrôle instauré par la Charte sociale européenne' (1968) 14e Année *Annuaire français de Droit International* 784
'Le Champ d'application 'ratione personae' de la Charte sociale européenne' in *Libro-Homenaje al Profesor Luis Sela Sampil Oviedo* (1970), p. 525
'Les effets de la Charte sociale européenne en droit interne' in *In Memoriam Sir Otto Kahn Freund* (Collection internationale d'études, München, 1980), p. 755
'La Charte sociale européenne. Des travaux préparatoires aux premiers résultats pratiques' (March 1977) Année 19, n° 3 *Revue belge de sécurité sociale* 196
'Article 7: Droits des enfants et des adolescents à la protection' in *La Charte sociale européenne. Dix années d'application* (Université Libre de Bruxelles, Bruxelles, 1978)
'Rapport introductif sur la Charte sociale européenne' in *La Charte sociale européenne. Dix années d'application* (Editions de l'Université de Bruxelles, Bruxelles, 1978)

'La Charte sociale européenne: Vingt ans après la conclusion du Traité' (Editions du CNRS, 1982) 28 *Annuaire Français De Droit International* 934

Wiebringhaus, H. (1989) : 'Le «droit à la sécurité sociale/ et la Charte sociale européenne' in *Le droit social à l'aube du XXIe siècle* (1989), p. 355

Worrell, J., 'The System of Supervision of the European Social Charter' in *The Future of European Social Policy* (Kluwer Law and Taxation Publishers, 1989), p. 49

Zacher, H.F., 'Le droit syndical et le droit aux actions collectives d'après l'Article 5 et l'Article 6 paragraphe 4 de la Charte sociale européenne' in *Assemblée parlementaire du Conseil de l'Europe* (Strasbourg, 1977)

Zardi, A., 'Les procédures de conciliation et d'arbitrage dans le cadre de l'Article 6, paragraphe 3, de la Charte Sociale Européenne' (1984) 1 *Affari sociali internazionali* 432

List of publications in this series

STUDIES IN EMPLOYMENT AND SOCIAL POLICY

1. W. Beck, L. van der Maesen and A. Walker (eds.): *The Social Quality of Europe*. 1997. ISBN: 90411 0456 9
2. F. Pennings: *Introduction to European Social Law*. 2001. ISBN: 90411 1628 1
3. R. Blanpain, M. Colucci, C. Engels, F. Hendrickx, L. Salas and J. Wouters: *Institutional Changes and European Social Policies after the Treaty of Amsterdam*. 1998. ISBN: 90411 1018 6
4. Vai Jo Lo: *Law and Industrial Relations: China and Japan after World War II*. 1998: ISBN: 90 411 1075 5
5. A. Den Exter and H. Hermans (eds.): *The Right to Health Care in Several European Countries*. 1998. ISBN: 90 411 1087 9
6. M. Biagi (ed.): *Job Creation and Labour Law from Protection towards Pro-action*. 2000. ISBN: 90 411 1432 7
7. W. Beck, L.J.G. van der Maesen, F. Thomése and A. Walker (eds.): *Social Quality: a Vision for Europe*. 2000. ISBN: 90 411 1523 4
8. J. Murray: *Transnational Labour Regulation: The ILO and EC Compared*. 2001. ISBN: 90 411 1583 8
9. R. Blanpain and C. Engels (eds.): *The ILO and Social Challenges of the 21st century*. 2001. ISBN: 90 411 1572 2
10. M. Biagi (ed.): *Towards a European Model of Industrial Relations?* 2001. ISBN: 90 411 1653 2
11. J. Clasen (ed.): *What Future for Social Security? Debates and Reforms in National and Cross-National Perspective*. 2001. ISBN: 90 411 1671 0
12. A. Numhauser Hennings (ed.): *Legal Perspectives on Equal Treatment and Non Discrimination*. 2001. ISBN: 90 411 1665 6
13. R. Blanpain (ed.): *Labour Law, Human Rights and Social Justice*. 2001. ISBN: 90 411 1697 4
14. M-C. Kuo, HF. Zacher and H-S Chan (eds.): *Reform and Perspectives on Social Insurance: Lessons from the East and West*. 2002. ISBN: 90 411 1819 5
15. P. Foubert: *The Legal Protection of the Pregnant Worker in the European Community*. 2002. ISBN: 90 411 1842 x
16. M. Biagi (ed.): *Quality of Work and Employee Involvement in Europe*. 2002. ISBN: 90 411 1885 3
17. F. Pennings: *Dutch Social Security Law in an International Context*. 2002. ISBN: 90 411 1887 x
18. T. Carney and G. Ramia: *From Rights to Management: Contract, New Public Management and Employment Services*. 2002. ISBN: 90 411 1889 6
19. R. Blanpain and M. Colucci: *European Labour and Social Security Law, Glossary*. 2002. ISBN: 90 411 1905 1

20. I.U. Zeytinoğlu (ed.): *Flexible Work Arrangements. Conceptualizations and International Experiences*. 2002. ISBN: 90 411 1947 7
21. J. Berghman, A. Nagelkerke, K. Boos, R. Doeschot and G. Vonk (eds.): *Social Security in Transition*. 2002. ISBN: 90 411 1969 8
22. R. Blanpain: *The Legal Status of Sportsmen and Sportswomen under International, European and Belgian National and Regional Law*. 2003. ISBN: 90 411 1980 9
23. R. Blanpain and M. Weiss (eds.): *Changing Industrial Relations & Modernisation of Labour Law, Liber Amicorum in Honour of Professor Marco Biagi*. 2003. ISBN: 90 411 2008 4
24. J. Malmberg (ed.), B. Fitzpatrick, M. Gotthardt, S. Laulom, A. Lo Faro, T. van Peijpe, A. Swiatkowski: *Effective Enforcement of EC Labour Law*. 2003. ISBN: 90 411 2160 9
25. M. De Vos (ed.): *A Decade Beyond Maastricht: The European Social Dialogue Revisited*. 2003. ISBN: 90 411 2163 3
26. M. Seweryński (ed.): *Collective Agreements and Individual Contracts of Employment*. 2003. ISBN: 90 411 2190 0
27. R. Blanpain, M. Van Gestel: *Use and Monitoring of E-Mail, Intranet and Internet Facilities at Work. Law and Practice*. 2004. ISBN: 90 411 22 66 4
28. A.C. Neal (ed.): *The Changing Face of European Labour Law and Social Policy*. 2004. ISBN: 90 411 2312 1
29. E. Sol and M. Westerveld (eds.): *Contractualism in Employment Services: A New Form of Welfare State Governance*. 2005. ISBN 90 411 2405 5
30. F. Pennings (ed.): *Between Soft and Hard Law – The Impact of International Social Security Standardson National Social Security Law*. 2006. ISBN 90 411 2491 8
31. L. Dickens and A.C. Neal (eds.): *The Changing Institutional Face of British Employment Relations*. 2006. ISBN 90 411 2541 8
32. G. Sebardt: *Redundancy and the Swedish Model in an International Context since 2006*. 2006. ISBN 978 90 411 2503 3
33. A.M. Świątkowski: *Charter of Social Rights of the Council of Europe*. 2007. ISBN: 978 90 411 2 608 5